D1258416

PRENTICE-HALL, INC.

Englewood Cliffs, New Jersey 07632

Withdrawn

JAMES T. CAREY

University of Illinois at Chicago Circle

AN INTRODUCTION TO CRIMINOLOGY

Library of Congress Cataloging in Publication Data

Carey, James T (Date)
  Introduction to criminology.

    Includes bibliographical references and index.
    1. Crime and criminals.   I. Title.
HV6025.C32   364   77-13941
ISBN 0-13-481143-7

PRENTICE-HALL SOCIOLOGY SERIES
Neil J. Smelser, *editor*

90086

© *1978 by* PRENTICE-HALL, INC., *Englewood Cliffs, N.J. 07632*

All rights reserved. No part of this book
may be reproduced in any form or
by any means without permission in writing
from the publisher.

PRINTED IN THE UNITED STATES OF AMERICA
10 9 8 7 6 5 4 3 2 1

PRENTICE-HALL INTERNATIONAL, INC., *London*
PRENTICE-HALL OF AUSTRALIA PTY. LIMITED, *Sydney*
PRENTICE-HALL OF CANADA, LTD., *Toronto*
PRENTICE-HALL OF INDIA PRIVATE LIMITED, *New Delhi*
PRENTICE-HALL OF JAPAN, INC., *Tokyo*
PRENTICE-HALL OF SOUTHEAST ASIA PTE. LTD., *Singapore*
WHITEHALL BOOKS LIMITED, *Wellington, New Zealand*

For

BENEDICT, SIMON, RACHEL, AND NOAH

What is criminology?

A common sense answer is that it is simply the study of crime. This usually translates into two questions: who are the criminals and what are their motivations? Some criminologists argue that the field should include the study of law-making, law breaking and reactions to the breaking of laws. Others suggest a broader definition: criminology should not be confined to the study of crime in the legal sense alone but should also include the study of various kinds of control systems and anti-social behavior in general. It should be addressed to the emergence of the criminal law, various theories of criminality, and present issues in the political context of crime.

As the policy implications of various positions have become more explicit, this latter topic—the political context—has become more important. For example, a view of crime as biologically determined has implications for the sterilization and segregation of the criminally inclined, while a view of crime as reflecting the definitions of those who are powerful

enough to have their views encoded into the criminal law suggests more fundamental solutions related to who gets what and why.

Criminology, as it is presently organized, is not a mature science with a set of distinctive models. Instead it is an heterogeneous amalgam of several different disciplines adapted to the investigation of crime and criminality. The various parts of what constitute criminology need to be understood by beginning students as parts of a whole that is yet to be fully developed. The synthesis that emerges in the future will not reject what has gone before but will, in all likelihood, place that past in a new interpretive framework.

The goals of this text are modest: to cover what is known in an intelligible way, in an interesting fashion, and point toward a possible synthesis.

Some of the assumptions that have influenced the organization of the text should be made explicit.

The first assumption made is that the synthesis which is developing will come mainly from the field of sociology and law. These two disciplines have had the most continuous and sustained interest in the problems of crime. Any developing synthesis must recognize that why people behave as they do and why certain behavior is defined as criminal are two distinct problems. This latter concern is most effectively addressed by studying the relationship between law and society, a focus, which, until quite recently, criminologists have neglected. Hence more attention is devoted in this text to historical studies of law as a response to the social problems than in the traditional introductions to criminology.

A second assumption is that the large scale structures characteristic of advanced industrial societies must be humanized. In the criminal justice area this suggests a scaling down of the size and authority of police, courts and prisons and a narrowing of the scope of the criminal law. Most critics in criminology would agree that any move in this direction would be desirable though they are divided on the rationales invoked for reducing discretion. Legal scholars have been the primary advocates of limiting the criminal law. What is the least law a complex society requires to function?

The book is divided into three main sections. The first discusses the contributions of the historians of law and sociologists in explaining crime and criminality. The second traces the establishment of the law enforcement and corrections organization. And the third section deals with research done on the behavior systems of the criminally defined. A concluding chapter summarizes the present state of the field and possible future directions.

Sections two and three contain case studies of particular organizational problems in criminal justice agencies or brief life histories of those involved in specific patterns of criminality. The case studies in section two consist of critical incidents in the day-to-day operations of police, courts and corrections as described by insiders, highlighting in a concise fashion, the organizational imperatives under which these agencies and their personnel operate. In section three interviews with knowledgeable informants about particular behavior patterns defined as criminal are presented.

The aim in both sections is to provide the student with concrete materials that speak to the theories discussed in section one, and reveal the gaps that exist in our knowledge of crime both as a label affixed on those who are "troublesome" and as objectively observable behavior.

James T. Carey
*University of Chicago
at Chicago Circle*

1

introduction

A public official in Snowmass, Colo. recently was convicted for stealing $218,000—almost a quarter of a million dollars—in tax payers' money, and a judge decided he should be placed on probation for five years, without spending a day in jail.

But in another Colorado court case the same day, a young man in Greeley was sentenced to at least five years in prison for stealing $500 worth of auto parts. . . .[1]

This particular scene is newsworthy because it is so exceptional; rarely do we see the issue of unequal treatment before the law so starkly portrayed. But in fact this situation is quite common across the United States, and underscores one of the dilemmas of criminology.

There are two major responses to situations such as the one described above. One is the response of the sentencing judge—the individual with more financial resources cannot really be a criminal and justice would not be served by giving him a harsh penalty. Loss of reputation and public embarrassment are punishment enough. This viewpoint argues that the discretion we allow the judge in sentencing permits or encourages individualized justice; or to put it another way, the person with fewer resources can be more aggressively rehabilitated. If the sentencing judge were accused of a miscarriage of justice, he might reply that poverty is

[1] *Denver Post,* March 24, 1974, p. 1.

to blame, and that the criminal justice system should not bear the brunt of social inequality in the United States. Also, more resources are needed by the low-income defendant in the ill-matched struggle between him and the criminal justice system to make justice truly available to all.

The second major response would view this illustration as a dramatic example of the inherent injustice of a system that has institutionalized inequality and a criminal law that embodies this very inequality. Few middle-income people who violate laws are processed up to the stage of sentencing, much less sent to jail. Covert social processes eliminate or reduce the impact of the criminal justice system upon certain social groups. Thus fewer middle-class crimes come to official attention. When they do, they are handled differently than the same crimes committed by lower-class persons.

What does all this mean? Two major views hypothesize about law and society. The first is the *consensus* outlook, which sees the law developing out of public opinion and as a reflection of the popular will. The second is the *conflict* approach. It sees laws as originating in a political context where influential interest groups pass laws that are beneficial to them. These two positions address a major question being discussed in criminology today: what role, if any, do interest groups play in law making and law enforcement? We can gain a more thorough understanding of these two approaches by looking at how each deals with a specific problem in contemporary American society: should the use of marijuana be legalized?

THE CONSENSUS APPROACH

The consensus approach has been strongly influenced by anthropological and sociological studies of primitive law. As Fuller states:

> . . . in a primitive society where there is almost complete agreement on moral values the public opinion enforced mores for all practical purposes comprise the unwritten criminal code of the tribe. What is immoral is by hypothesis criminal.[2]

This perspective seems appropriate when looking at small homogeneous communities where the legal system actually embodies a set of widely shared values. It has less relevance when looking at a large-scale industrial society like our own. However even in diverse societies there is widespread consensus about the community's reaction to certain offensive

---

[2] Lon Fuller, "Morals and the Criminal Law," *Journal of Criminal Law, Criminology and Police Science,* 32 (March–April 1942), 624–30, 627.

personal and property assaults, and this consensus is encoded into the law. The consensus position on marijuana is that legislation prohibiting its use actually reflects the opinion of an overwhelming proportion of the population.

Very few studies on marijuana usage have been conducted with the *explicit* purpose of demonstrating that there is widespread support for marijuana legislation. Some surveys indicate that public opinion supports the present marijuana laws, or at least opposes any change.

The difficulty with polling public opinion (which is the major method employed by the consensus approach) is that opinions are personal and subject to change. Polls cannot reveal whether the expressed opinions represent a solid, carefully worked out position, or an ephemeral view which will likely evaporate. Further the usual demographic categories in which polls are reported—age, sex, class, level of education, and the like—do not coincide with organized groups nor do they indicate the respondent's relationship to these groups.[3] (It would be possible to overcome these limitations by finding out the extent to which opinion regarding marijuana regulation were held intensely and also the character of a respondent's affiliations.)

What do the polls reveal about marijuana attitudes? They suggest that a large number of adults are concerned about teen-agers' use of it. In fact, a majority perceived marijuana as a problem in the public schools.[4] The perception of the problem varied by section of the country: the west was most concerned, followed by the east, the south, and lastly the midwest. Perception of this problem also varied by size of the community: respondents in communities over 500,000 were more likely to view marijuana use in the public schools as problematic than those in communities under 25,000. When asked to list the biggest problems with which the public schools must deal, 11.6 percent of those queried named "dope/drugs" in a sample of parents (both those with children in public and parochial schools and those with no children in school), teachers, and junior and senior high school students.[5]

An overwhelming proportion of adults feels that marijuana should not be legalized.[6] There is strong college student sentiment, on the other hand, for legalization. The intensity of the feelings against marijuana is suggested by the response to a question on what the jail term should be, if any, for those using marijuana. Fifteen percent of the adults thought

[3] Herbert Blumer, "Public Opinion and Public Opinion Polling," *American Sociological Review*, 13 (October 1948), 542–49.
[4] Gallup Poll, *Gallup Opinion Index*, 59 (Princeton, N.J., May 1970), 15–16; 65 percent of adults perceived marijuana as a problem in the public schools.
[5] Ibid., pp. 15–16.
[6] Gallup Poll, *Gallup Opinion Index*, 93 (Princeton, N.J., March 1973), 25; 78 percent of those queried felt that marijuana should not be legalized.

there should be no penalties and 74 percent thought there should be a jail term ranging from less than a year (23 percent) to life imprisonment (1 percent).[7]

In sum, the polls, taking into account the deficiencies mentioned earlier, suggest that there is widespread concern among adults regarding the harmful effects of marijuana and a resistance to having it legalized. The marijuana regulations as presently constructed seem to reflect their feelings. However, with increased usage of marijuana by young people, an opposite opinion is developing. In this emerging view marijuana is seen as harmless, and there is a substantial opinion favoring its legalization. Marijuana legislation as it now exists does not reflect this public's opinion.

THE CONFLICT APPROACH

Typically a social problem has a career of its own. Individuals or groups begin with a picture of a problematic situation and work to get their view of the scene more widely recognized—some try to prevent recognition of a problem and others try to advance a particular condition as a problem. Mobilization of action then leads to public participation and an official plan, in some cases legislation. This phase is a product of bargaining where diverse interests and views are brought together. The last part of the process is the implementation phase in which the official policy or law is put into practice.[8]

This process led to the passage of the Marijuana Tax Act of 1937.[9] Lindesmith notes that the campaigns conducted against marijuana use prior to 1937 were generally spearheaded by temperance advocates.[10] Marijuana was opposed for the same reasons that alcohol and tobacco were: that it was physically debilitating, led to insanity, and enslaved the user. Some of the themes of reformers of the period were utilized by the Federal Bureau of Narcotics when they decided to press for legislation to curb marijuana usage. Becker notes that three themes were stressed in the educational campaigns mounted by the FBN:[11] that mari-

---

7 Gallup Poll, *Gallup Opinion Index*, 59 (Princeton, N.J., May 1970), 11.

8 A recent statement of this formulation can be found in Herbert Blumer, "Social Problems As Collective Behavior," *Social Problems,* 18 (Winter 1971), 298–306.

9 See Howard S. Becker, *Outsiders* (New York: Free Press, 1963), pp. 121–46.

10 Alfred R. Lindesmith, *The Addict and The Law* (New York: Vantage Books, 1967), pp. 228–29.

11 Becker, *Outsiders,* pp. 135–36.

juana use leads to loss of self-control, that ecstasy should not be pursued for its own sake, and that laws to suppress use would prevent the "enslavement" of users and protect them from giving in to their weaknesses. Articles stressing the menacing character of marijuana were widely circulated in the press. The end result was sufficient public arousal about marijuana as a problem to permit the Treasury Department (of which the Federal Bureau of Narcotics was a part) to request special legislation.

Gusfield, in his analysis of the temperance movement, tried to show that the symbolic value of prohibition legislation was that it conferred status on the rural, white, Protestant and denied it to the urban, Catholic immigrant.[12] The legislation tended to honor the values or practices of one group at the expense of another. Some observers have applied Gusfield's notions to marijuana usage in this country, viewing the legislation as supporting or reaffirming traditional American values relative to earned pleasure, leisure, and self-restraint. Kaplan calls this the "life style argument:"

> In a large portion of our population, then, marijuana is associated with a life style focusing on immediate experience, present rather than delayed gratification, non-competitiveness and lessened interest in the acquisition of wealth. And even if one is not prepared to use even stronger terms, such as irresponsibility, laziness, and a lack of patriotism, there is no doubt that the life style, like the use of the drug itself, involves a disregard for many of the conventions that the older society regards as dear. It is hardly surprising, then, that many people will wish strongly that the criminalization of marijuana be retained if only as a reminder to marijuana users—and indeed to many who do not use marijuana but who are like users in other ways—that this life style and these values are less worthy.[13]

An unpublished study by Schofield as well as studies of police and legislators have noted that the "hang loose ethic" conflicts with traditional American values and evokes a repressive response in some groups in our society.[14] These groups view the new ethic as challenging tradi-

---

[12] Joseph R. Gusfield, *Symbolic Crusade* (Urbana: University of Illinois Press, 1963).

[13] John Kaplan, *Marijuana: The New Prohibition* (New York: World Publishing, 1970), pp. 4–5.

[14] See Glen W. Schofield, "Marijuana: Its Relationship to Aggressive Behavior," 1968; Richard H. Blum and Jeanne Wahl, "Police Views on Drug Use," in Richard Blum et al., *Utopiates* (New York: Atherton Press, 1964); Richard H. Blum and Mary Lou Funkhouser, "Legislators on Social Scientists and a Social Issue: A Report and Commentary on Some Discussions with Lawmakers About Drug Abuse" (Palo Alto, Calif. Stanford University Institute for Study of Human Problems, 1965).

tional life styles and are convinced that it is in their interest to use marijuana legislation to symbolize the legitimacy of older ways.

The conflict approach is more helpful than the consensus approach in understanding the marijuana issue, and other issues in which there is a considerable amount of community ambivalence. Widespread opposition to marijuana's legalization suggests that the law corresponds to some strong attitudes about loss of self-control, the inappropriateness of seeking ecstasy for its own sake, and so on. To that extent the prohibitions against its use can be considered an expression of public opinion. There is no doubt, however, that this consensus is breaking down. The shortcoming of the consensus approach is that it does not suggest a course of action when the law ceases to reflect the views of a large number, though still a minority, of citizens. Nor does it suggest how the sentiments of a majority of adult Americans might be expressed in ways other than criminal law.

The conflict approach is more promising in understanding marijuana as a social problem. It not only takes public sentiment into account, but it also tries to demonstrate how public opinion can be shaped or even created where it doesn't exist in order to support particular positions. A preexisting public opinion is not passively transformed into legislation. Interested parties initiate the process and have a vital stake in the outcome. This approach also identifies the critical elites who must be persuaded if any rational control policy is to be worked out. The inadequacy of the conflict approach is that it has not developed beyond a case by case indictment of self-serving interest groups to a systematic analysis of conflicting claims and the order in which they are likely to be resolved.[15] A more systematic analysis would combine elements of the conflict and consensus models and rescue the criminologist from the role of ironic commentator.

TOWARD AN INTEGRATED VIEW

If we had chosen to illustrate the conflict and consensus approaches with murder, rape, or incest laws, the consensus approach might have better explained how deeply held sentiments are crystallized into laws and continually affirmed in their implementation. The argument in criminology circles about the superiority of one or the other approach does not suggest how they might be reconciled. But a growing body of

[15] Edwin M. Lemert, *Human Deviance, Social Problems and Social Control* (Englewood Cliffs, N.J.: Prentice-Hall, 1972).

research addresses the question of which perspective is most appropriate in particular situations.

An important distinction to make at the outset is whether we are discussing the creation or the operation of a criminal law. The conflict approach seems more appropriate to explain the creation of criminal law, and the consensus perspective the operation of the law. There is some evidence to suggest also that law created in a situation of group conflict may become an object of consensus—for example, laws relating to racial discrimination in the United States. More recently we have seen efforts to decriminalize specific behaviors, such as abortion and sexual activity between consenting adults. This type of decriminalization evokes as much conflict as does new legislation, but once policy has changed a new consensus develops around it. The conditions under which this consensus develops have not been systematically studied to date.

Another consideration is how dangerous the behavior is perceived to be. There is more consensus on the undesirability of violent personal assault than there is on the necessity of regulating business activities. Thus, a consensus approach seems more appropriate when looking at deeply held values; a conflict approach is more helpful in exploring values which are less deeply held or about which there is considerable disagreement.

The statement that law comes into existence as a result of the activities of various more or less organized interest groups is not particularly controversial. We can generalize that the success of an enterprising interest group is related to the amount of resources it can command on the one hand and the support (or lack of it) of the community on the other. Conflict theorists have generally assumed that the powerful business interests regularly prevail in contests. But it would be more accurate to say that the locus of power shifts depending on the issues involved. In one instance it might be organized economic interests, in another it might be powerful politicians, in another it might be a prestigious and highly respected elite separate from economic or political interests. Success in the conflict is also related to community reaction. We can distinguish three kinds of community reaction: active support, indifference, or outright opposition. A consensus orientation would be most appropriate in looking at the first two reactions but a conflict approach would be better for the third.

We should also specify what is meant by success. In reality there are often no clear-cut winners or losers in a conflict. Instead accommodations are worked out on the basis of "give a little, get a little." Organized groups with roughly similar resources compromise, make deals, and pressure each other so that no one set of interests predominates.

A final consideration is the kind of stratification system under investigation. The historical material in chapter 2 suggests that in societies characterized by extensive, overt class conflict, an interest group approach to law seems more reasonable. Societies with high social integration, widespread commitment to constitutional principles, and high participation in civic affairs are better examined by the consensus approach.

What the foregoing discussion suggests is that the conflict and consensus models are not competitive. The student of criminal law should ask which model is appropriate to specific situations. The adequacy of various models of criminalization or criminal behavior can also be measured against the criteria of social utility. Any consideration of the adequacy of various theories must include questions about their implications for public policy. The objection might be made that it is unfair to evaluate scholarly work in terms of criteria that were not important to the author; thus we must not fault those who were not advancing theoretical explanations and who were not concerned with the social utility of their work. We must simply try to obtain a more comprehensive and integrated view of crime and criminality.

We start with the proposition that a defensible theory must be able to account for both crime and criminals. The argument that has developed in criminology recently is whether crime is an ascribed status imposed on the relatively powerless (hence the central task is the study of criminalization), or whether criminal behavior is intrinsically different from law abiding behavior (so that the central concern is the study of criminal behavior patterns). The dispute arose in the wake of empirical studies of law violations that suggested that criminal behavior was pervasive throughout all social classes. Yet only a small fraction of a large group of violators receives official attention. This led to the question, "Why was this particular offender and not another singled out and identified as criminal?"[16] It is argued that the most important aspect of crime is not specific behaviors that all would agree were criminal, but the ability of one group to affix the status "criminal" on an individual *independent* of his behavior:

> Students and criminologists are beginning to see that crime is a function of who is doing the defining, how people who are able to do the defining are able to make definitions stick on a legislative level and are able to carry out these definitions on an administrative level.[17]

Scholarly attention to other than lower-class crime was first initiated by Edwin Sutherland who began his research on white-collar and cor-

[16] Austin Turk, *Criminality and Legal Order* (Chicago: Rand McNally, 1969), p. 17.
[17] Jerome Skolnick, *The Politics of Protest* (New York: Simon & Schuster, 1969), pp. 115–16.

porate crime in the late 1920s. He focused on law violations among middle- and upper-class people, and seriously questioned explanations based on studies of low-income criminal behavior.

A landmark study published by Wallerstein and Wyle in 1947 asked a sample of the general population which of 49 offenses they had committed as adults.[18] *Ninety one percent* of the subjects admitted that they had committed one or more offenses for which they could have received a jail or prison sentence. This suggested that criminal activity was quite common; no theory that ignored the widespread character of law violation could qualify as an adequate explanation of criminality.

Other studies have since corroborated the original findings.[19] Two schools of thought have developed. Some theorists suggest that if criminality is pervasive throughout the social structure then the criminologist's attention must be directed to the function of enforcement as an explanation for the designation "criminal." Other criminologists have taken the position, with some supporting data, that when a "law abiding group" is contrasted with a "convicted group," the latter's hidden delinquencies are more serious and more numerous. Hence, however inadequate and biased our enforcement machinery may be, it does manage to select the most serious offenders and incarcerate them.

The major preoccupation in American criminology has been to explain why some people commit crimes. This has tended to deemphasize the study of how the criminal law has become institutionalized as a response to social problems. Concern with the relationship between law and society developed in the United States partly because of the focus on the "law in action" versus the "law on the books" among influential legal scholars. Chapter 2 traces this development against the background of the emergence of the criminal law in complex societies and the criminological reactions to this phenomenon.

[18] James S. Wallerstein and Clement Wyle, "Our Law-Abiding Lawbreakers," *Probation*, 25 (April 1947), 107–12.
[19] See Eugene Doleschal, "Hidden Crime," *Crime and Delinquency Literature*, 2 (1970), 546, 572.

2

criminal law and criminology

The Austrian jurist Eugene Ehrlich (1862–1922) first made the distinction between "positive law" and "living law."[1] It was his contention that positive law, that which is enacted, could not be effective if it were at odds with the cultural patterns of a people (living law). It was Ehrlich who influenced Roscoe Pound (1870–1964), a professor of law at Harvard, to take up his own study of legal institutions.[2] He called for a study of "law in action" as distinct from law on the books. He was a pioneer in the practice of using evidence from the social sciences in court cases. But his major contribution was the study of law as a social system having inherent strains, contradictions, and limitations. Law reflects society but is more than a social product. It acts as a force in its own right. The law adjusts and reconciles conflicting interests. It serves the larger purposes of society by performing this task. Oliver Wendell Holmes, a colleague of Pound's at Harvard, explored how judges make law rather than simply apply it.[3] He was unsympathetic to a purely logical system of legal rules.

The work of the sociological jurisprudence school and the legal realists who followed moved the study of law away from the narrow preoccupa-

[1] Eugene Ehrlich (Walter L. Mohl, trans.), *Fundamental Principles of the Sociology of Law* (Cambridge, Mass.: Harvard University Press, 1936).
[2] Roscoe Pound, "Sociology of Law," in Georges Gurvitch and Herbert Moore (eds.), *Twentieth Century Sociology* (New York: Philosophical Library, 1945).
[3] Oliver Wendell Holmes, *The Common Law* (Boston: Little, Brown, 1881).

tions with case law to a broader consideration of comparative legal systems. This has encouraged the joint efforts of legal scholars, lawyers, and social scientists. The effect on criminology has been to shift attention from the study of criminal behavior to the study of legal institutions themselves and the way in which law develops as a response to social problems. This chapter briefly summarizes the research conducted on criminal law, and tries to link criminology's growth and concerns with changes in social structures and relationships.

CRIMINAL LAW AND CIVIL LAW

Legal scholars distinguish three types of law regulating human behavior: contract law, tort law, and criminal law.[4] *Contract law* provides criteria for arriving at agreements and for settling breaches of agreement. A contract involves at least two parties who enter into agreement; if subsequent conduct is contrary to the agreement, the offended party may initiate legal action against the offending party. Transactions involving rental or sale of property, borrowing money, or buying insurance are examples of contracts. Almost every purchase of food, clothing, furniture, and the like comes under the scope of contract law.

Tort law provides redress for someone suffering injury at the hands of another. The offended party may sue the wrongdoer for damages. Tort law specifies the circumstances under which such actions may be taken to court as well as the appropriate court and the procedures to be followed. The person offended, if the judgment is in his favor, is awarded a sum of money for compensation. The use of this type of law has grown enormously in modern society.

Criminal law applies to an infinite number of individuals—not just two parties as in contract law. According to Sutherland and Cressey it involves *politicality*—promulgated by political authority; *specificity*—refers to strict definitions of specific acts; *uniformity,* that is it applies to all to which rules refer and *penal sanction.*[5] A legal reactor may take action under criminal law with or without the request of another person. Violation of criminal law involves a crime against the state. There is some overlap between tort law and criminal law. For example, a rape victim can recover damages in a civil court (under tort law) while the state proceeds separately with its case in the criminal courts (under criminal law).

[4] Noel T. Dowling, Edwin W. Patterson, and Richard R. Powell, *Materials for Legal Method* (Chicago: Foundation Press, 1946).
[5] Edwin H. Sutherland and Donald R. Cressey, *Criminology,* 9th Ed. (Philadelphia: J. P. Lippincott, 1974), pp. 4–8.

It seems clear that not all law is punitive. The bulk of western law has to do not with criminal offenses but with civil disputes (contracts and torts) arising in everyday social and business life. Criminal law is only a small part of the total law in modern industrial societies.

Criminal law makes a distinction between acts that are evil in themselves (mala in se: murder) and those that are prohibited or not evil in themselves (malum prohibitum: traffic regulation). The criminal codes of the eighteenth century dealt mainly with behavior that was evil in itself. Since the eighteenth century, however, criminal law has been used more and more for the purposes of regulating those acts not evil in themselves. The criminal codes have been continually expanded so that in the United States some state penal codes run to thousands of sections and attempt to regulate almost every conceivable kind of behavior. This has made a detailed analysis of particular codes a monumental undertaking. But all communities have a conception of social harm which identifies and prohibits certain acts. Murder, incest, and rape, for example, are universally regarded as dangerous and sanctionable. There is, however, wide variability among societies in the way these wrongs are handled.

The consensus and conflict views of the functions of the law also interpret the origins of criminal law. The differences between consensus and conflict interpretations revolve around three major issues: the relationship of inequality to the emergence of criminal law, the emergence of the state as guarantor of the criminal law, and the relationship between custom and criminal law.

THE CONSENSUS APPROACH

As human communities grow certain privileges and rights are acquired by one part of the population because of its intelligence, hard work, or ability to discern what is necessary for the tribe or community to survive. This is the beginning of a system of inequality which stratifies the population into higher and lower categories.[6] Kingsley Davis has argued that systems of stratification arise in response to two specific group needs: the need to instill in the abler members the motivation to occupy important and difficult positions which require greater than average ability, and the need to provide these able individuals with a set of rewards that will motivate them to perform the duties attached to these

[6] Gerhard E. Lenski, *Power and Privilege: A Theory of Social Stratification* (New York: McGraw-Hill, 1966), Ch. 1

difficult positions.[7] The subjection of one group to the domination of another comes about usually as the result of a division of labor with the accumulation of agricultural surpluses. It becomes the task of the dominant group to deal with disputes that threaten the community's survival; this group typically strengthens the dispute-settling mechanisms of the tribe. Its motivations, whether aggrandizing or benevolent, are unimportant. The consequences for the community in the long run are beneficial.

The state develops necessarily out of this situation. It usually evolves out of a settled agricultural context and a fairly stable class system. The state embodies the consensus of the people which is slowly forming and appears basically to deal with the conflicts which arise between opposing sub-groups. It strives to restore the peace which has been broken. If the violence begins to deteriorate into anarchy some organized and centralized force commanding the allegiance of the local population is required to heal and protect those whose lives are threatened. It was the feudal lords, with the breakdown of feudalism, unable to protect themselves from depredations of professional highwaymen who demanded protection. The king responded and a criminal law was the result. The state's role is to reconcile opposing values and to formalize the law-making and law-applying process. It stands above the conflicting sub-groups; it is value-neutral. The state comes into existence when informal mechanisms prove inadequate. Cantor describes the way the state developed through the monarchy in pre-Norman England.[8] The king was considered the greatest of chieftains or lords but his sway was not universal. At the urging of churchmen (whose model of a king was the Roman emperor), the Anglo Saxon chieftain took more and more people under his personal protection. All lords had a variety of people and places dear to them within the scope of their personal protection—families, retainers, soldiers, drinking halls, and fortresses. The king was persuaded to take churchmen under his protection also. This meant he had a much wider area for which he was responsible:

> . . . he had drawn a line of obligation for himself that might easily include monasteries a hundred miles away from his big drinking hall. The king having once fundamentally altered the scope of the mundbyrd [personal protection] by bringing the church within it, it was natural that he should go on expanding it so that by the eleventh century the circle of his protective responsibilities was slowly expanded to include, in theory, just about everyone in the

[7] Talcott Parsons and Kingsley Davis, *Human Society* (New York: Macmillan, 1949).
[8] Norman F. Cantor, *The English: A History of Politics and Society to 1760* (New York: Simon & Schuster, 1967).

whole realm except for the no-man's land in the wild frontier region.[9]

The legislation that followed this was designed to enforce the special protections that the king provided. The state at this juncture codifies the law, creates new laws appropriate to changed conditions, and guarantees the criminal law.

There is continuity, in the consensus view, between custom and criminal law. Criminal law reflects and reinforces local custom. The state codifies the custom, sharpens its punitive character, and gives customary procedure legal force. The state's authority is accepted as legitimate. The major function of criminal law is an integrative one. Legal norms are an expression of those societal values which transcend the immediate interests of individuals or groups.

THE CONFLICT APPROACH

Unlike the consensus approach, which distrusts human nature, the conflict approach is deeply suspicious of restraining institutions. Its account of the emergence of human inequality emphasizes force, fraud, and inheritance. Also called into question is the necessity of systems of human inequality. Primitive communities recognize particular gifts relating to leadership or contact with the supernatural, yet this does not necessarily involve domination. Authority is exercised without domination—it is under the control of its subjects. It is only when institutionalized power is joined to authority that domination occurs and the process is initiated by which the state is born.

A system of stratification generally precedes the emergence of the state in the conflict account as in the consensus perspective. The class that has achieved dominance at the expense of dissatisfied subjects now seeks to extend its control over a wider territory. The emerging state promises preservation of internal order and protection against attacks from outsiders. Nadel, in discussing the Nupe, addresses himself to the question of what the individual received from the state:

> What did the tax-paying, law-abiding citizen receive in return for allegiance to king and nobility? Was extortion, bribery, brutal force, the only aspect under which the state revealed itself to the populace? The people were to receive, theoretically, on the whole, one thing: security—protection against external and internal enemies,

[9] Ibid., p. 57.

and general security for carrying out the daily work, holding markets, using the roads. We have seen what protection and security meant in reality. At their best, they represented something very unequal and very unstable.[10]

The state is not viewed as an external power standing above all society and creating laws in the interest of all. It is an integral part of the unending social struggle between antagonistic interests that comprise society. The machinery of the state becomes the prize for which these antagonistic interests struggle. The criminal law that emerges after the creation of the state is designed to protect the interests of those who control the machinery of the state.

According to the conflict approaches, the relation between custom and law is one of contradiction, not continuity. Diamond maintains that a legal order and criminal law was necessary only when the state broke down communal solidarity and divided kindred groups into conflicting factions. The criminal law had its origins in the pathology of social relations created by the state. "Law and order is the historical illusion; law versus order is the historical reality."[11]

These two views represent contrasting interpretations of criminal law. They agree on the historical fact that stratification precedes the emergence of the state, but disagree on the inevitability of inequality. They agree on the origin of the state, but disagree when it comes to defining its purpose. They agree on the importance of custom, but disagree on the amount of continuity between custom and law.

A close examination of historical and comparative materials suggests that both approaches have something to contribute to our understanding of the emergence of the criminal law. The conflict approach more accurately depicts politically organized society as the setting within which various struggles take place. The focus on society as a social system of its own whose needs must be met if the values of its constituents are to be realized ignores or underestimates the role of conflicting interests in social change. Both approaches have something to say about the nature of the state and law. In some periods they are clearly employed by the ruling classes for their own benefits; in other epochs they seem to function more as the instruments of the total society acting basically to promote the common good. The means by which privileges and rights are acquired, the basis of social stratification, also vary by how necessary they are to a group's survival. The emphasis on force, fraud and inheritance

---

[10] Siegfried F. Nadel, "Nupe State and Community," *Africa*, 8 (1935), 257–303.
[11] Stanley Diamond, "The Rule of Law Versus the Order of Custom," *Social Research*, 38 (Spring 1971), 42–72.

seems most appropriate when discussing the distribution of a society's surplus, less relevant in determining the necessities of life where hard work and delegation by others seem to be decisive.

The emergence and development of the criminal law is a complex subject. It is helpful to make some rather elementary distinctions which will organize the available materials and permit some generalizations. The remainder of this chapter, following Seagle's classification, divides the topic of criminal law by kind of society: primitive, archaic, and modern.[12]

PRIMITIVE SOCIETY

In societies without political organization all social relationships are regulated by custom. This is characteristic of a society of *hunters and herdsmen*. Some observers have identified this kind of social arrangement as "pre-legal." It precedes the written word and custom itself is thought of as part of the forces of nature.[13] Law as we know it does not exist. Customary procedures enfold the individual and describe simply the way things are. There is no highly developed conception of the individual. According to Durkheim, primitive man is the slave of custom and ancestral mores.[14] The low level of technology makes starvation an ever present threat; mutual support and solidarity are necessary for community survival. The disputes that arise in primitive societies are generally resolved informally and the aim is in effect a reconciliation between conflicting parties. Sanctions are mainly restitutive in the form of damages paid to the injured party. Minor personal injuries may be atoned for by gifts.

Murder was the first wrong to be recognized in primitive society. It was the greatest disturbance of the peace but it was treated as a private wrong. The relatives of the deceased, his kin group, had recourse to procedures that would heal the breach caused by the killing. Apart from pecuniary payment they could be satisfied by an expiatory encounter, or a regulated fight. Sometimes the vengeance of the injured parties developed into a blood feud. The killing of one clan member leads to the killing of someone equivalent in the murderer's clan—usually not the

[12] William Seagle, *The Quest for Law* (New York: Knopf, 1941), "Introduction."

[13] Henry Maine, *Ancient Law* (London: J. M. Dent, 1972) originally published in 1861; p. 5.

[14] Emile Durkheim (George Simpson, trans.), *The Division of Labor in Society* (New York: Free Press, 1964).

murderer himself. The retaliation and counter-retaliation between clans could get out of hand however and threaten the whole community's survival. It was the blood feud (war among clans) that required some kind of regulation. Cantor's description of Anglo-Saxon society prior to the Norman invasion makes much of the blood feud:

> Everyday life was so conditioned by mayhem that the blood feud was continually in operation. Furthermore the blood feud had a tendency to be self perpetuating; revenge once taken by an aggrieved kin upon a slayer would call forth a new blood feud by the family of the man upon whom the revenge had been taken, and such feuds could involve hundreds of people and could persist in the most brutal fashion for several decades.[15]

The early English clans that Cantor depicts could be spending most of their time engaged in various blood feuds to the point where they had no time to do anything else. It became clear to the more foresighted that a less costly alternative had to be worked out. But the blood feud in so far as we can tell never led to the complete extermination of clans. It was more controlled than that. The blood feud apart from the Anglo-Saxons was a rare event because violence is almost entirely absent among food gatherers. It is a modern fiction that primitive man lived in a state of uninterrupted warfare.

The wrongs done by an individual in primitive society involved all of his kin. The dominating principle of customary procedure in primitive communities is the unity of the kindred group. Hence no outside force, like a territorial group, could lodge and process complaints; this was a prerogative of relatives alone. Forgiveness was a matter to be settled or granted or arranged with indemnity between disputing clans. The wrongs committed in primitive societies were almost entirely personal— even those which appeared to be violations of property rights. Among hunters, food gatherers, and nomadic horsemen private property in land is almost entirely unknown. They are interested in the yield of the land not the land itself. Key implements for survival (like fishing canoes) are collectively owned, not the possession of any one member. Personal objects in primitive society are not owned in the modern sense; they are extensions of one's self. Thus a man's spear is an extension of his hand and is destroyed upon his death, not traded or sold. He who steals the spear commits a personal injury to its owner. It is understandable that law or customary procedure relating to the ownership of private property—so important in later developments—would be scant in primitive societies. So too the development of a body of civil procedures is meager

[15] Cantor, op. cit., pp. 33–34.

since there is little room for the development of civic obligations in primitive economic life.

ARCHAIC SOCIETY

Diamond asserts that archaic societies, where law and customs exist side by side, are critical in understanding the evolution of law.[16] In archaic societies, people derive their livelihood from agriculture and perhaps handicrafts and commerce. In the history of the west, the primary example of archaic society is the first feudal age before the middle of the eleventh century.[17] Local social worlds based on the appropriation of land began to appear, but private property as we know it did not exist. Though the feudal lord owned the land it was not viewed as commodity that could be exchanged or sold. Landowners were required to treat their serfs with care, and the status of the serf was relatively favorable.[18] On the continent, free land was available to the east for tilling and one could always move on if the landowner became too oppressive.[19] The ethic that knit the society together was one of shared responsibility. This found institutional expression in vassalage, feudal land tenure, and the feudal system for the distribution of goods and services. Trade was almost completely absent so that no one lived by buying and selling. The customary law of the times bore no similarity to that which developed after the fifteenth century.

The major difference between primitive and archaic social organization is best highlighted in historical situations where there has been an evolution from one form to the other. Cantor provides us with a detailed history of the development of English society from a primitive pattern to an archaic one. It can be most clearly seen in the agricultural triangle of the English midlands where a society based on farming was possible. As the kindred groups grew larger their inadequacies in dealing with problems became more apparent. Cantor takes the position that the lordship developed naturally out of the kin system:

> In the kinship bond a man followed a leader in his own family, perhaps his father, or brother or uncle. . . . In the community which

[16] Diamond, op. cit. "The Rule of Law."

[17] Mark Bloch, *Feudal Society,* vol. 1 (Chicago: University of Chicago Press, 1964).

[18] See Mark C. Kennedy, "Beyond Incrimination: Some Neglected Facets of the Theory of Punishment," *Catalyst,* 5 (Summer 1970), 1–38.

[19] George Rusche and Otto Kirchheimer, *Punishment and Social Structure* (New York: Columbia University Press, 1939).

can no longer organize itself effectively along blood lines, either because the kin are too numerous, large and disorganized to limit the effects of the blood feud or because the kin have already been decimated by incessant violence, the lord replaces the headman of the family or several disintegrating families.[20]

The lord is a kind of father-substitute and functions pretty much like the older chieftains. When one of the more powerful lords is chosen by a group of his peers to become monarch the state is born. The process as it developed in early English society took several centuries. In its beginnings the monarchy was weak and untried and its centralizing thrust resisted by local units. It developed at the expense of kin groups.

Sometimes, as in England, the evolution of the state is speeded up through invasion. The Norman conquerors subjected the Anglo Saxons to their domination and sharpened the inequality that already existed. The inequality was maintained by coercion. The Norman conquerors undermined the kinship bond, and the laws promulgated were designed to isolate individuals so they could be more easily dealt with. Seagle suggests that the isolation of the individual is the basic condition for the growth of law.[21] The situation of conquest most sharply depicts the opposition of custom and law. The legislation that emerges does not reinforce custom; it is distinct because of its *unprecedented* character. Diamond's study of the Dahomean protostate shows that laws relating to the need for labor, mustering an army, levying of taxes and tribute, the maintenance of an army and the extent and location of the numbers of population being subject had little or no analogues in tribal custom.[22] Crimes are manufactured or invented for other purposes. In Dahomey a certain category of women in the King's court were distributed in the local villages. Those males who made the mistake of having intercourse with them were accused of rape. Their punishment was conscription. The purpose of the legislation, in short, was conscription.

The success of the newly developing state's encroachment on old allegiances is its ability to gain a monopoly on the use of force and violence. This can be most clearly seen in the act of homicide. It came to be regarded as an offense against the state and only the state had the authority to punish it. By making homicide along with theft of the King's property a capital offense the monarch discouraged violent opposition to the imposition of his civil order.

As the King's authority becomes more widely extended the legitimacy of local arbitrators is also undermined. According to Seagle the first courts didn't evolve from arbitrators but destroyed them:

[20] Cantor, op. cit., p. 46.
[21] Seagle, op. cit., p. 64.
[22] Diamond, op. cit.

It was the court really that launched the 'state' for it was in the court that the sentiment of etatism, with all its devotions and loyalties, was first nurtured. The court was responsible for the etatistic myth because it was only through its officials that the common man was brought into contact with authority. The only 'social service' . . . performed by the governing class was the administration of justice—that is the holding of a court. The waging of war and the collection of taxes, the only other functions of early government, were more difficult to disguise as civil sacraments.[23]

The famous legal historian John Austin in looking at the English system of common law argued that the role of judges was innovative.[24] Though they claimed to be only *applying* law that was part of customary procedure or that which was implicit in custom they were *actually* making new law. The curious anomaly is that the judges denied their rule creating role even as they were creating new rules. Maine in tracing the evolution of law from status to contract calls this stage the one of "legal fictions."[25] Reforms are introduced under the cover of fictions. The problem was to fit changes that seemed necessary into established law so that they did not clash with those parts of the system that weren't altered and to reassure the population that nothing was being changed. Judicial decisions were legitimized by the appeal to local values. As a body of decisions accumulated the custom was what the judges said it was and not what the people involved held. Common law courts came to be the primary source of new rules of law. They remain as others have pointed out, the most important source of law to this day throughout the common law world.

Preservation of the peace was the primary concern of archaic societies. Rusche and Kirchheimer give some feel for how wrongs were reconciled in the first feudal age:

If, in the heat of the moment or in a state of intoxication, someone committed an offense against decency, accepted morality, or religion or severely injured or killed his neighbor—violation of property rights did not count for much in this society of landowners—a solemn gathering of free-men would have to be held to pronounce judgment and make the culprit pay *Wergeld* or do penance so that the vengeance of the injured parties should not develop into blood feud and anarchy. . . . The chief deterrent to crime was fear of the private vengeance of the injured party. Crime was looked on as an act of war. In the absence of a strong central power the public peace was endangered by the smallest quarrel between neighbors,

---

23 Seagle, op. cit., p. 65.
24 John Austin, *Lectures on Jurisprudence* (London: J. Murray, 1890).
25 Henry Maine, *Ancient Law* (London: J. H. Dent, 1972) originally published in 1861.

as these quarrels automatically involved relatives and servants. The preservation of peace was, therefore the primary preoccupation of criminal law. As a result of its method of private arbitration, it performed this task almost entirely by the imposition of fines.[26]

Though the authors describe this form of dispute settlement as "criminal law," technically it was not. The dispute-settling procedure was not promulgated by a political authority nor was the sanction backed up by the coercive apparatus of any state. In the first feudal age any "law" having politicality and penal sanction would have been scorned as an attempt by outsiders to violate the bonds of kinship and companionage. But as feudal estates expanded the bonds of fealty were weakened and petty violence increased in frequency and savagery. The breakdown of feudal institutions became apparent when they could no longer control reprisals and counterreprisals. This occurred in the second feudal age and was aggravated by repopulation and the makings of an economic revolution that was taking shape. As feudal institutions waned, the state consolidated its political power. During this transitional period, class conflict became more pronounced which, in turn, led to the creation of new criminal laws.

As Seagle has noted, "the criminal law springs into life in every great period of class conflict."[27] Archaic law in its later phases rests on force and violence. It becomes particularly harsh in its final development. Persons are treated as property and debtors allowed to be sold into slavery.

> Archaic law emphasized institutions of pledge and suretyship which because kinship solidarity was disintegrating and mutual suspicion and distrust were rife, required debtors either to post forfeits or to find guarantors to ensure the discharge of legal obligations.[28]

At this point, the upper strata push hard for centralization and consolidation of political authority. A new set of social goals pursued by a new and unanticipated power in society becomes embodied in the criminal law. An ever increasing degree of control over the system of composition occurs; self-help is eliminated and a disaffiliated individual is created whose bearings no longer depend on kinship or custom. Crime and the laws which served it are covariants of the evolving state.[29] The laws that were enacted against treason, theft, and homicide in this period all assumed an emergency character. The luxuriant growth of the criminal law was ad hoc. In thirteenth-century England there was only a small number

[26] George Rusche and Otto Kirchheimer, *Punishment and Social Structure* (New York: Columbia University Press, 1939) p. 9.
[27] Seagle, *The Quest for Law*, p. 232.
[28] Ibid., p. 68.
[29] Diamond, "The Rule of Law."

of crimes which entailed the loss of life or limb and the confiscation of goods—that is, felonies. By 1780 there were over 200 capital offenses punishable by common law or statute.[30]

Early criminal law reveals itself to be an instrument of domination. Legislation is enacted openly directed against the lower classes. The most important consideration, however, in the growth of criminal law, according to Rusche and Kirchheimer is fiscal: the administration of criminal law proved to be highly remunerative for those who administered it. A sharp rise in population occurred during the middle ages which combined with the exhaustion of the soil forced those who made their living on the land into the towns seeking employment. Their numbers increased and since they possessed no property they could not realistically be fined.

This led to the evolution of corporal punishment. Lower class wrongdoers unable to pay the fines levied against them were severely beaten, tortured or mutilated. The penal system thus came to be restricted to a minority of the population. Kennedy has suggested that the structure of formal law at this stage is an alliance of capital and the state.[31] As a result two kinds of citizenship and responsibility are created: the laboring forces of the early industrial society are bound by the criminal law and punishments associated with it, the owners of labor are bound by a civil law which regulates their competition between each other.

Internal trade came into its own after 1250. With it came the institutionalization of private property, citizen-entrepreneurship and the market system. Petty merchants who were objects of scorn in the second feudal age began to develop institutions of private property and a labor force freed of feudal ties. The institutions regulating conflict under the old feudal system were in a state of collapse. The philosophy of the emerging merchant group was the pursuit of gain. They grew with every decline of feudal institutions. The ethic of individual responsibility replaced the ethic of shared responsibility. Crimes came to be conceived in terms of individual transgressions for which individuals should bear responsibility. Thus "political considerations" like an individual's ties to a wider group were removed from "legal" considerations that were handled by courts:

> It was made a purely legal question by pretending that the only interest before the court was that of the litigants—in other words by pretending that the supporters of the litigants—their clans, families, friends were not involved. . . .[32]

It is the class character of the criminal law emerging that leads to Kennedy's conclusion: criminal law and penal sanctions are subdued war-

[30] Seagle, *The Quest for Law.*
[31] Kennedy, "Beyond Incrimination."
[32] Seagle, *The Quest for Law,* p. 67.

fare waged by one powerful segment of civil society against an individuated segment of citizens—it is a thinly disguised system of state vengeance.[33] Further the warfare can be conducted without fear of reprisal. The essential characteristic of a criminal act is that it can't be compromised by the individuals involved. The criminal law proscribed far more behaviors as crime than had ever existed in the second feudal age.

THE GROWTH OF CAPITALIST
SOCIETY AND MODERN LAW

There are many differences between archaic and modern criminal law. The most obvious difference is that modern society is law-ridden whereas archaic society had only a few laws. The emphasis on which crimes are most serious also shifts. Theft is a much more serious crime in capitalist society because private property is the basic institution. Seagle summarized the difference between archaic and modern criminal law:

> The archaic penal code has Ten Commandments. The mature penal code may have ten thousand commandments. But far more important than the quantitative aspect is a shift in the category of major crimes. It has sometimes been said that homicide is the very "centrum" of the criminal law, which developed primarily in relation to the need for its suppression. But . . . archaic penal law pays precisely the least attention to those offenses which in mature civilizations are treated as the most vicious crimes—namely, ordinary murder and theft. Nothing is more symptomatic of the spirit of the archaic criminal law. It may be said perhaps without paradox that the failure to treat violence against private persons and property as crimes against the state may have corresponded to a truer public conception of crime as an act which directly affects the whole community.[34]

He goes on to say that theft is the great crime in capitalist society and that the criminal law must suppress with great severity all forceful means of amassing capital precisely because as an end it commands such universal respect. With the consolidation of political power the older forms of justice became criminal as the state specifically forbade them thus obtaining a monopoly over the processing of acts of violence. To pursue commercial activity with a sufficient amount of vigor the merchants needed the cooperation of the crown. It became increasingly clear to the

[33] Kennedy, "Beyond Incrimination."
[34] Seagle, *The Quest for Law*, p. 229.

monarchs of the period that their destiny was linked to that of the merchants. The tradesmen gained wealth and power by loaning money, using land as collateral, to feudal lords to finance local wars. The end result was the landed wealth of Europe fell into their hands. Land became a commodity for buying and selling as private property in the interests of profit.

> The creation of a law effective in combating offenses against property was one of the chief preoccupations of the rising urban bourgeoisie. Wherever they had the monopoly of legislation and jurisdiction they pursued this demand with the greatest energy. . . . They even attempted to restrict the right of private settlement resulting from feuds. . . . In France, too, it was the bourgeoisie who always tried to obtain from the Crown an intensification of the repressive system. . . . The bourgeoisie demand for increased efficiency in the administration of law were largely promoted by the growing centralization of the administration in the hands of a bureaucracy trained in Roman law.[35]

In the later middle ages punishment became more harsh and severe. Capital punishment for relatively minor offenses increased dramatically as did various kinds of mutilation. The mutilations generally marked the offender for life and assured that he would remain part of the "criminal class." As a labor surplus built up in the towns the value set on human life decreased. Rusche and Kirchheimer saw crime and punishment as a way of regulating the pool of labor:

> The hard struggle for existence molded the penal system in such a way as to make it one of the means of preventing too great an increase in population . . . the system acted as a kind of artificial earthquake or famine in destroying those whom the upper classes considered unfit for society.[36]

There were no prisons in which to incarcerate apprehended criminals until much later so justice, such as it was, was quickly executed. The conception of maintaining criminals at public expense in prison was inconceivable to the men of that time.

The cruelty of criminal law seemed to increase as the gulf between those in the highest and lowest strata became greater. Seagle states:

> The greater the subordination of classes and the greater the inequality of classes, the more vigorous and cruel does criminal prosecution become. The greater and more miserable the proletariat and the greater the gulfs of social opportunity, the stronger the cry of

[35] Rusche and Kirchheimer, *Punishment and Social Structure,* pp. 15–16.
[36] Rusche and Kirchheimer, *Punishment and Social Structure,* p. 20.

the possessing classes for more and more criminal law, and the more bloody and arbitrary does it become.[37]

Criminal law becomes more humane only when the opposing classes have something approaching equal strength. The rising living standards of the lower classes had an effect on criminal policy. Prosperity and steady employment gradually softened the spirit of violence which earlier had revealed itself on the slightest provocation.

By the eighteenth century, pressure began to build to limit the discretion of judges and to standardize penalties for particular offenses. It was at this point that the first criminal law reformers of the modern era appeared. Beccaria, an Italian aristocrat, first published his *Essay on Crimes and Punishment* in 1764.[38] The reforms he proposed in the criminal codes were all supportive of the rising bourgeoisie. Bentham went further in trying to relate seriousness of offense to degree of punishment. At the same time Romilly was leading the struggle for the practical reform of the English criminal law.

Classical Theory

The classicists, led by Beccaria, Bentham, and Romilly, all proceeded on a common set of assumptions.[39] Briefly these are:

Since all men are by nature self-seeking, they are liable to commit crime.

There is a consensus in society on the desirability of protecting private property and personal welfare.

In order to prevent a "war of all against all," man freely enters into contracts with the state to preserve the peace within the terms of this consensus.

Punishments must be proportional to the interests violated by the crime.

There should be as little law as possible. Its implementation should be delineated by due process.

The individual is responsible for his actions and is equal in the eyes of the law.

Men are possessed of free will. They are calculating animals and base their action on pleasure and pain. Men will be discouraged from criminal

---

[37] Seagle, *The Quest for Law,* p. 232.

[38] Cesare Beccaria, *An Essay on Crime and Punishments* (London: Alman, 1767).

[39] See Jeremy Bentham, *An Introduction to the Principles of Morals and Legislation* (London: Pickering, 1823); and Coleman Phillipson, *Three Criminal Law Reformers: Beccaria, Bentham, Romilly* (London: J. M. Dent and Sons, 1923).

activity if threatened with punishments that outweigh any gain resulting from their actions. But as Seagle points out:

> . . . this calculus will work only if every crime and its punishment are stated in advance in a complete and systematic criminal code. The criminal presumably is to consult the book before embarking upon a particular act of crime.[40]

The impact of the suggested reforms was decisive. Their recommendations coincided with the state's need to express its complete monopoly of force and prosecution. The first of the revised codes was published in Austria by Joseph II in 1787. Perhaps the most famous, though, was the French Penal Code of 1810. One significant feature of the new codes was the provision of imprisonment. It emerged during the period of the Enlightenment as the primary penalty, and reflected the basic values of the triumphant bourgeoisie system—every penalty must have its fixed price. When a criminal paid his "debt" to society he repurchased his freedom. Every day had a labor value and the criminal paid with a specified number of days.

> Since the penalty of the classic penal codes is a price, it must be fixed in a free and open market, which in this case is the public judicial forum where the accused and the prosecutor enter into the bargaining process. The revolutionary reform had as its objective the restoration of the judicial duel, which now achieved unparalleled development.[41]

For Beccaria laws were the conditions whereby free and independent men united to form society. The basis of punishment lies in the necessity to restrain men from encroaching on the freedom of one another defined and established by the terms of a social contract. The primary purpose of punishment for Beccaria was to insure the continued existence of society. He classified crimes in terms of their seriousness—high treason or acts of an individual against the state were most serious, followed by crimes that injure the security of property and individuals, and crimes disruptive of the public peace (e.g. riots and inciting disorders). Beccaria thought punishment should be prompt and inevitable. He maintained that it was not cruelty or severity that was effective but rather the certainty of punishment and the denial of the expected advantage produced by the crime.

These classical ideals have been incorporated into the criminal law of most modern states. But their inherent contradiction has been the emphasis on equality and the inviolability of private property. Seagle states:

[40] Seagle, *The Quest for Law*, p. 241.
[41] Ibid., p. 343.

. . . in reality these [ideals] mean all too often the costly luxury of litigation, the delivery of the individual to the tender mercies of the judicial duel, the hegemony of judges, who despite Acts of Settlement and guarantees of tenure, cannot free themselves from the limitations of their class and race and all the multitudinous prejudices of life. The employment of legal equality remains empty and illusory in the presence of economic inequality. At best the rule of law has neve ensured more than the minimum of decency in the social struggle.[42]

The classical emphasis on uniform penalties applied to specific acts rather than to the suspect or special circumstances surrounding his act. This was difficult to apply, and later codes were modified to take into account mental incompetence and to distinguish between the first offender and the repeater. This *neoclassic* position was an attempt to link the individual actor with the social world. He was no longer the isolated, atomistic, calculating man of pure classicism. The neoclassicists held to the notion of free will but conceded that some structures might inhibit its exercise. The neoclassical position has become the major model of human behavior held by agencies of social control in all advanced industrial societies. Court and penal practices to this day are dominated by a neoclassical model of human behavior.

Positivism

The neoclassical position allowed technical experts to testify as to an offender's responsibility. From this small beginning a major reform movement developed. Its rallying cry was that the criminal is defective and the concept of moral guilt is irrelevant. The idea of a science of society (introduced by Darwin's *The Origin of the Species* in 1859) intoxicated the intelligentsia of western Europe.[43] Scientific method, so productive in exploring nature's secrets, could now be expanded into the human realm. The unity of scientific method was one of the fundamental assumptions of positivism and of the new reformers. The only task required was to develop instrumentation so that behavior could be quantified. But notions such as free-will had to be abandoned and the criteria of "social dangerousness" substituted. The shift entailed a closer investigation of the attributes of the offender to determine how dangerous he was.

Cesare Lombroso, often referred to as the "father of criminology," introduced biological positivism to criminologists.[44] He was a medical

[42] Ibid., p. 227.
[43] Charles Darwin, *Origin of the Species* (London: J. Murray, 1859).
[44] Cesare Lombroso, *L'Uomo Delinquent* (Torino, Italy: Bocca, 1896–97).

doctor who based his generalizations on research with military personnel and inmates of Italian military prisons. His focus shifted attention from the social to the individual. It represented a departure from the approach earlier developed by the Belgian statistician Quetelet (1796–1874) who pointed out that crime was not something purely individual but a mass phenomena.[45] Quetelet's approach was supplemented by Guerry of France, a lawyer, who studied the variation in crime rates by geographical areas.[46] Both Quetelet and Guerry's work anticipated the approach and methods of the ecologists discussed in chapter three. But their promising approach was eclipsed for several generations because of the enthusiastic reception given to Lombroso's work. Lombroso contended that the person likely to commit crimes can be recognized by a series of physical indicators. These "stigmata" are overly small or large head, asymmetry of face, ears of unusual size, receding chin, flattened nose, scanty beard, and low sensitivity to pain. Lombroso held that these physical characteristics do not of themselves cause crime but help to identify the personality predisposed to it. If the circumstances of life are particularly favorable for the "born criminal" he may be able to get through without committing any serious crime. Lombroso originally thought that the "born criminal" constituted almost 100 percent of the criminal population. Twenty years later (1897) he estimated that about 40 percent of the criminal population were born criminal and the remainder could be accounted for by a variety of other factors. He ended up with what we would call today "a multiple factor approach." His focus, however, on the criminal rather than the crime, led to a host of studies on criminal traits and an emphasis on individualization.

The other two criminologists associated with Lombroso—the three are usually called founders of "The Italian School"—were Enrico Ferri, a professor of criminal law, and Raffaele Garofalo, who spent part of his career as a magistrate.[47] Though Ferri was a socialist he accepted Lombroso's biological determinism. The biological school dominated continental criminology up to the early part of the twentieth century when Charles Goring, a British physician, took issue with the conception of criminals as a distinct physical type.[48] His research showed no statistically significant physical differences between criminals and noncriminals.

[45] For a discussion of Quetelet's contributions see Herman Mannheim, *Comparative Criminology* (Boston: Houghton Mifflin, 1965), Ch. 5.

[46] Andre M. Guerry, *Essai Statisque, Morale de la France* (Paris, 1833).

[47] Enrico Ferri (J. I. Kelly and John Lisle, trans.), *Criminal Sociology* (Boston: Little, Brown, 1917); Raffaele Garofalo (Robert Wyness, trans.), *Criminology* (Boston: Little, Brown, 1914).

[48] Charles Goring, *The English Convict: A Statistical Study* (London: His Majesty's Stationary Office, 1913).

Others have pointed out that the Italian positivists never had a clear picture of the savage that the criminal was supposed to resemble. In addition, people with pronounced physical "criminal" characteristics may be treated differently and come to think of themselves in a certain way—a kind of self-fulfilling prophecy. Most important, from a scientific point of view biological variation can't begin to account for the variation in cross-cultural crime rates and does not address the question of how and why law arises in the first place.

Taylor, Walton, and Young suggest that the appeal of biological positivism cannot be understood apart from the relationship between expert, bureaucrat, and politician.[49] The assumptions about consensus, determinism and the key role of the scientific expert all tend to support the status quo or at least not raise any serious questions about it. Vold has expressed consternation about the ease with which positivistic theory has fit into totalitarian patterns.[50] Both Ferri and Garofalo managed to adapt themselves to the Mussolini regime in Italy.

It would be a mistake to overestimate the importance positivism has had on criminal law or its operation. Criminal law and its administration still rest on classical assumptions. Positivism implied the abolition of the jury system and its replacement by a team of experts; the judiciary in this view would also be severely limited. This has not happened nor is it likely to happen in the near future. The chief contribution of the positive school in criminal law has been in its theories for treatment. The suggestion that juveniles and adults be treated differently has led to the creation of a separate juvenile justice system. The classical notions of criminal responsibility have been abandoned in dealing with juveniles. The execution of sentence in the Juvenile Court, and in the adult criminal courts as well, has increasingly been left to psychiatrists, criminologists, and social workers. Positivism searched for alternatives to incarceration—wider use of fines, probation, and parole. It also introduced the indeterminate sentence fixing the minimum and maximum of permissible periods of confinement. (The extent to which the indeterminate sentence represents a humanitarian development will be discussed later.) The logic of the positivist position also suggests that the judiciary's role be recast, but positivist reformers are content to separate the determination of guilt from the imposition of sentences. The first is to be entrusted to a qualified judge, the second to a "social physician." This seems to retain the guarantees of procedure built up since the eighteenth century while pro-

[49] Ian Taylor, Paul Walton, and Jock Young, *The New Criminology: For a Social Theory of Deviance* (New York: Harper Torchbooks, 1973).
[50] George Vold, *Theoretical Criminology* (New York: Oxford University Press, 1958).

viding some kind of rehabilitation which would protect society's security. The implications of the rehabilitation movement in criminology and corrections will be discussed more fully in chapter 9.

SUMMARY

Criminal law arises out of a specific social situation and is designed to address the needs of particular interest groups. It can only be understood in terms of the social relationships prevailing at any given period. Whether these interest groups reflect some kind of consensus or simply the views of a powerful and strategically placed minority is problematic. Table 2-1 summarizes the differences between primitive, archaic and modern society and patterns of criminal law.

TABLE 2-1   Criminal Law in Three Different Societies

	Primitive	*Archaic*	*Modern*
Kind of Community	Nomadic: hunters, herdsmen, food gatherers. Subsistence economy, low level of technology, small population, simple division of labor.	Settled agricultural community, some surplus, development of agricultural technology. Larger population, increased division of labor.	Politically organized nation-state, surplus economy, high level of technology based on market system. Large population; complex division of labor.
Kind of Law	"Prelegal," no written law, custom is king.	Custom and written law coexist.	Rational, formal codified law; rich development of specialized law.
Source of Authority	The clan.	Chief and council of elders (heads of kin groups).	State judiciary.
Crimes Emphasized	Torts (offenses against persons), acts "evil in themselves" (mala in se)	Torts and crimes against the community. Concern with factual evidence, distinction between criminal and civil.	Treason, theft, homicide. Acts not evil in themselves (mala prohibita)
Dispute-settling Machinery	Informal resolution, use of ad hoc, occasional arbitrators. Purpose: reconciliation.	Private arbitration using officially recognized, permanent arbitrators. Purpose: reconciliation.	Criminal courts. Purpose: rule enforcement.
Sanctions	Damages paid to injured party.	Fines.	Fines, imprisonment.

Some scholars of the criminal law argue that its character is related less to social and economic arrangements than to deep-seated destructive human impulses. Fuller takes the position that the criminal law bears the same relation to the impulse of revenge that the institution of marriage bears to sexual impulse.[51] It regularizes and controls a deep instinct of human nature which, if not given legitimate expression, would seek disruptive outlets. Yet the revenge impulse is related to only a fraction of the crimes included in criminal codes. What is the revenge motive in crimes against public order or public morality (like drunkenness) which constitute most of the recorded crimes in the United States? Of the persons arrested by the police in 1967, 40 percent were arrested for drunkenness or disorderly conduct or vagrancy.[52]

A growing body of research suggests differential consensus relating to the support for criminal laws.[53] Laws proscribing murder, rape, robbery, burglary, child molesting, personal assault, and auto theft all receive strong support. Statutory rape, homosexual behavior, marijuana use, and exhibitionism receive less enthusiastic support. Crimes relating to the regulation of business and professional activities evoke an apathetic response. On the other hand public response to price rigging and fraudulent advertising is strong but the laws relating to them are relatively mild.

Chambliss makes the point that law doesn't always reflect the imposition of one value system on another.[54] But legislation, he concludes, invariably does *not* conflict with the interests of the well-born and highly placed. Even in instances where this observation doesn't seem to apply, as in anti-trust legislation, the law serves the purpose of dampening the demand for more sweeping social changes.

However, criminal law and how it emerges has only recently become the concern of criminolgy. The major preoccupation of criminology after it made its entrance on the American scene was criminal or more generally antisocial behavior. The first American criminologists were overwhelmingly concerned with socialization—how individuals become members of groups—following the social psychological leads provided by George Herbert Mead, Charles Cooley, John Dewey and William I. Thomas. What they accomplished however became part of the legacy of crimi-

---

[51] Lon L. Fuller, *The Morality of Law* (New Haven, Conn.: Yale University Press, 1964).
[52] In 1965 one of every three arrests was for public drunkenness. See Federal Bureau of Investigation, *Uniform Crime Reports* (Washington, D.C.: Government Printing Office, 1965), p. 117.
[53] Don L. Gibbons, "Crime and Punishment: A Study in Social Attitudes," *Social Forces*, 47 (June 1969), 391–97.
[54] William J. Chambliss, "A Sociological Analysis of the Law of Vagrancy," *Social Problems*, 11 (Summer 1964), 67–77.

nology. These early contributions can be more adequately analyzed by raising a series of questions against which the various explanations of crime can be measured. This permits us to make some judgments about the strengths and weaknesses of each explanation. It is to these critical questions that we now turn.

Part One

QUESTIONS A THEORY MUST ANSWER

The following questions concerning theories on criminal behavior are answered differently by the consensus and conflict perspectives:

1. *What are the structural origins of criminal behavior?* Consensus theories locate the source in the nature of man himself. Aggressive or acquisitive impulses account for criminality and all societies try to check these impulses. Some consensus criminologists go further and say that crime is a constant in societies—all societies need and produce crime. Another way of putting it is that crime is functional for the society—it establishes boundaries that cannot be violated and generates cohesion and solidarity among the upright. Some consensus adherents do not specify the wider origins of criminal behavior but suggest that there is a set of supporting values in society that is linked to criminal behavior. Criminal values, then, reflect the values of society as a whole, but in a somewhat distorted way.

Conflict theorists are more explicit in discussing the wider origins of criminal behavior. Generally, conflict interpretations are more distrustful of the restraining institutions than they are of man's nature. The restraining institutions support a system of inequality, and generate the aggressive and acquisitive impulses that consensus theorists mistake for part of man's nature. But in the conflict account the impulse of mutual aid is at least as important as acquisitiveness. Conflict theorists would agree that crime is functional to our present society but not that all societies need crime. The character of criminal behavior is linked to a society's political and economic development. Crime varies from society to society. Instances of personal and property assault are higher in capitalist societies because they reinforce a system of inequality. Crime is, in fact, functional to the capitalist political and economic system: it enables those who rule to create "false consciousness" among the ruled by making them think their own interests are identical to those of the ruling class; it creates employment for those who benefit from crime; it diverts the attentions of the lower class from the exploitation they experience toward other members of their own class rather than toward the economic system.

These two views of the wider origins of criminal behavior reflect different traditions in western social thought. An integrated view would assert that man has both aggressive and mutual aid impulses. Social and economic arrangements decisively affect how and to what extent these impulses are expressed. It is the task of the student of crime to specify more precisely the conditions that affect the expression of these impulses. An important first step would be to rephrase the question posed. This involves transforming categorical concepts (*either* a given social system encourages the expression of aggression *or* it doesn't) into variable concepts (to what degree?). The question at this point on the extent to which crime functions to sustain social solidarity is left open. An integrated approach, while giving primary consideration to the wider structural origins of criminal behavior, would also consider intermediate areas like subcultural location and distribution of opportunities. Men and women may be endowed with social and antisocial impulses as well as a variety of other attributes that contribute to the social order. Consensus theorists assume that these unequal endowments lead directly to systems of inequality; some are more intelligent, more discerning, and stronger, and they inevitably assume dominant roles. Conflict theorists deny that natural inequalities are the ultimate source of inequality. An integrated view would see that natural endowments lead to dominant positions in the community but that they are not the primary source of inequality. Inequality is institutionalized when those who are dominant pass their positions on to their children and deny access to others.

2. *Where in the social structure does the impulse arise to label particular behavior as criminal?* Some theorists do not address this question at all. They do not view the emergence of legal norms as problematic or something to be explained. Consensus theorists are generally less concerned with this question, but argue that the impulse is a widely shared one related to group survival. Behaviors that threaten group survival—such as murder—are condemned. Uncontrolled personal vendettas can annihilate key members of a community; thus, regulation is essential. The criminal law that results is a reflection of the general will.

Conflict theorists feel that those who have acquired privileges and rights want to retain them. The criminal law that results is directed at those who question these rights and privileges or somehow pose problems for the powerful. There can be no general will expressed in a situation of oppression and class conflict. If there is a society at all it is only an amalgam of subgroups with varying views and differential power to enforce those views. The crimes most often used to illustrate this approach are those that threaten private property.

An integrated approach would focus on the extent of consensus relating to different types of crime. There seems to be a higher consensus relating to homicide, forcible rape, and incest as contrasted with fraudulent advertising. A consensus perspective would probably show considerable unanimity across cultures and political systems about "serious" crimes; an interest group view would more accurately portray the forces at work in health and public safety legislation.

3. *Which parts of the social structure supply a disproportionate amount of crime?* To consensus theorists, the question of distribution is the central task of criminology. Criminal behavior must be mapped before it can be explained. Once we know which parts of the social structure supply a disproportionate amount of crime or delinquency, we can search systematically for reasons for the variation. Since official statistics show a higher incidence of law violation among low-income people, the explanations focus on lower-class crime.

Conflict theorists are critical of official statistics. Some contend that they reveal nothing more than activities of control agents, hardly anything at all about "real" criminal behavior. The fact that low-income persons are more often processed is not in dispute, but the significance of this fact is. Criminal activity is concentrated in the lower class because only acts which grow out of lower-class living patterns are defined as criminal. Low-income persons are more likely to be arrested and labeled criminal because the middle class controls the state apparatus and protects itself from such labeling. The conflict accounts rely on studies of hidden crime and delinquency to show that the official rates are misleading. In addition they add other "social harms" to their definition of crime that are absent or insufficiently emphasized in capitalist codes: namely war crimes and corporate criminality. They feel that the powerful are more likely to engage in serious crime that harms the general community.

An integrated view would look at the kind of crime that was the subject of concern. It would seriously study hidden crime and delinquency, and view official statistics with skepticism. To challenge the myth of low-income criminality an integrated veiw would be concerned with the crimes of the powerful. Studies of theft patterns in working-class neighborhoods would be contrasted with similar theft patterns among middle- and upper-middle-class persons. Recent reports of adolescent violations using self-report techniques have been refreshing in their questioning of traditional assumptions about delinquency (i.e. that it is mainly urban, working-class, and concentrated among boys), yet somewhat misleading in suggesting that delinquency is patternless. An integrated view would expect variation by social class, sex, age, and place of residence.

4. *What causes crime, or to what is criminal behavior a response?* A consensus perspective asserts that criminality is preceded by "strain." Motiva-

tion for a violation is crucial. Strain is brought about by the discrepancy between widely shared societal goals and the limited means for achieving them. Those who systematically participate in criminal behavior have been inadequately socialized to generally shared values. Consensus research done on this question has focused on criminal behavior that is systematic and patterned rather than casual and episodic. It identifies parts of the social structure where adjustment problems exist, and describes how they become shared and finally develop into distinctive adaption patterns.

The conflict orientation argues that the cause of crime is a system of inequality which values certain kinds of aggressive behavior. The crime that results is a reaction to the life conditions of one's social class: acquisitive behavior of the powerful on the one hand, or the high risk property crimes of the powerless on the other. Conflict accounts, though concerned with patterned criminality, would also be concerned with less organized violation. Their question is not why do persons violate the law, but given such widespread impulses to violate in a society such as ours is there so much conformity? The organization of the response is related to extent of class consciousness.

An integrated view would see criminal behavior as a result of inadequate socialization quite remote from any political or prepolitical response. (But the proposition that all crime is political is valid if we mean that it is a definition of human conduct created by authorized agents in a politically organized society.) An integrated approach would utilize the high aspiration/limited opportunity explanation to explain the crimes of the middle and upper-middle class rather than the lower class. It would direct the researcher's attention to casual and episodic violations to challenge traditional assumptions about criminals being "a breed apart."

5. *What are the policy implications of each model?* Some theorists make this explicit, others do not. Consensus theorists imply that the family, the local community, the school, or the marketplace should be the focus of the attack on crime. Broad proposals relate to the explanatory schemes employed; thus if inadequate socialization is a cause of crime, a program to strengthen family life and the schools might be instituted. If a local community is disorganized, then efforts should be made to reorganize it. If employment opportunities are limited, then they should be expanded.

Conflict theorists are likely to attack the master institutions of the society rather than intermediate or "caretaking" institutions. Their analyses generally point to the isolation of individuals under certain stages of capitalist development and the destruction or enfeeblement of nonstate institutions. Such analyses imply that nonstate associations be strengthened and more spontaneous and informal social control be sought.

An integrated approach would look to the master institutions for change in the long run, but in the short run it would favor policies that restored local controls and citizen participation. Proposals that increase the authority of experts at the expense of citizens or clients would be greeted with considerable skepticism. The problem at this stage for an integrated perspective is that it is not easy at first glance to make policy implications explicit. Some authors disavow any kind of social utility to their schemes; they claim to be scientific, objective, and essentially value-free. But these explanations have *in fact* been used as rationales for public policies. The student of crime must therefore carefully examine the policy implications of a given theory. But we must be careful that our analysis is not a mask to cover our own political biases. Thus to gain an accurate assessment of an author's policy implications we look at three things:

1. the social history of the period within which the theories emerged; this helps to situate each thinker within a specific context;

2. biographical or other influences on the theorist including the intellectual tradition within which he was functioning (to the extent this information is available);

3. the social and political context within which the ideas were made public and how they were used or could be used.

Table 1-1 on facing page summarizes the differences between the three perspectives.

We will discuss four major criminological theories in this book: the ecological, the cultural-transmission, the anomie, and the interaction-conflict. Each emerged within an historically specific situation. Most developed in the American context although they were made possible by combined efforts of an international community of scholars. Radzinowicz, the British criminologist, characterized the United States as a "vast laboratory" where a number of original contributions have been made.[1] The United States has assumed leadership in criminology according to Radzinowicz because it perceived crime as a national problem, and its investigation has been given much support.

[1] Leon Radzinowicz, *In Search of Criminology* (Cambridge, Mass. Harvard University Press, 1962).

TABLE 1-1 Conflict, Consensus, and Integrated Models
of Crime and Criminality

	Conflict	*Consensus*	*Integrated*
1. What are the wider origins of criminal behavior?	Oppressive and restraining social institutions that suppress mutual aid impulses.	The nature of man; restraining institutions necessarily arise to check aggressive impulses.	Man's nature contains aggressive and mutual aid impulses; social and economic institutions affect their expression.
2. Where in the social structure does the impulse arise to label behavior as criminal?	Powerful elites; illustrative crimes: those related to property, its possession and control.	The general will; illustrative crime: murder.	Depends on kind of crime; if considered serious (e.g., murder), the general will; if not considered serious (e.g., tax evasion), powerful elites.
3. Which parts of the social structure supply a disproportionate amount of crime?	Powerful elites as in war crimes or corporate crime.	Lower class as in high risk personal property offenses.	Crime is pervasive throughout social structure; varies by social class. Cost of the crimes of powerful is higher than that of powerless.
4. What causes crime, or to what is criminal behavior a response?	System of inequality. Crime is a reaction to the life conditions of one's social class—e.g., the acquisitive behavior of powerfuls or desperate crimes of powerless.	Strain, social disorganization, inadequate socialization —e.g., personal property offenses of lower class.	Some crime caused by systems of inequality, others by strain, social disorganization or inadequate socialization.
5. What are the policy implications of each model?	Reorganize the master institutions to eliminate the illegal possession of rights, privileges.	Strengthen family, reorganize local community, expand employment opportunities.	In the long run, reorganize master institutions; in the short run, narrow scope of control agencies, restore citizen participation.

3

ecological and cultural transmission theories

LOMBROSIAN POSITIVISM CHALLENGED

The Lombrosian theory of a physical "criminal type" dominated criminological thinking through the early twentieth century. But a number of factors gradually diverted attention from this individualistic approach to one that focused on social factors as the cause of crime. Let us briefly examine how this change in thinking came about.

The Social Climate

The economic and social changes that took place after World War I brought a new group of people to prominence in all the major cities of the United States. They were salaried professionals, sometimes called a "new middle class." They were concerned with efficiency and reshaping the urban environment to make it more hospitable to their professional interests. Their definition of what was problematic was formed by their positions in governmental, civic, welfare, and crime control organizations. The problems that concerned them related to population movements, the dislocations they engendered, and the social disorder they created. Proposals for action were designed to guide urban growth along desirable lines which would eliminate the unpredictability of population shifts, and address the problems of housing, health, employment and crime among the new urban masses. Proposals for action however needed to be based upon information that had been impartially collected; academic experts were required to provide the data upon which decisions would be made. As Karl put it:

> The early years of the twentieth century saw a transition taking place—from the older emphasis on sin and corruption to be investigated by vigilantes armed with public virtue to a new emphasis, now upon "efficiency" and "economy" to be investigated by experts armed with technical training and science. . . .[1]

Hence, research relating to crime and delinquency was sponsored by state and city governments, welfare organizations, and criminal justice agencies, as well as by foundations preoccupied with problems that lent themselves to administrative solutions.

The social changes that were occurring between the end of World War I and the Depression—the depopulation of farms and small towns, the concentration of heterogeneous groups in large urban centers—were not accomplished without considerable strain and tension. The major problem was defined as a conflict between the authentic values of small town America and the new urban values that were threatening them. The response of those who ascribed to the older values was to reaffirm cultural beliefs and to eliminate alien influences.

Because the "older" Americans, or their representatives, were strategically placed in Congress, they were able to force their particular views on the nation as a whole and to visit violence upon those who would not conform. The response was a nativist one: hostility toward particular minority groups (especially radical and recent immigrants), fanatical patriotism, and a conviction that internal enemies (who seriously threatened national security) must be eliminated. The passage of the Prohibition amendment (designed to change the alien ways of urban immigrants), the Red Scare of 1920, immigration restriction, the growth of the Ku Klux Klan, and the ban on teaching evolution in the public schools all were part of the same nativist reaction. All showed deep-seated hostility toward the city whose cosmopolitanism seemed to confront the fundamental values of small town America.

In spite of Prohibition, however, there continued to be a widespread demand for alcohol. Because of this demand and ambivalence about enforcement efforts, an illicit distribution system sprang up.[2] Organized

---

[1] Barry Karl, *Executive Reorganization and the New Deal: The Genesis of Administrative Management, 1900–1939* (New York: Oxford University Press), p. 51.
[2] John Landesco, *Organized Crime in Chicago* (Chicago: University of Chicago Press, 1929).

bootlegging of liquor modeled itself after capitalist business enterprise. The violence and the bloodshed associated with bootlegging were linked to efforts by rival gangs to obtain monopolies. In Chicago alone there were over 1,000 murders in the three-year-period from 1923 to 1926. Using the illicit distribution of beer and liquor as his base, mobster Al Capone was able to expand into areas of gambling and vice. By 1927 the gross income of his operation was estimated at $60,000,000 a year.[3] But these developments were not due to Prohibition alone:

> Organized vice and gambling had long been the curse of American cities; and gangsterism, racketeering and organized blackmail developed almost in direct proportion to the speed of the automobile and the ease with which criminals could purchase weapons of whole-slaughter like the Thompson submachine gun. The fact remains, nonetheless, that bootlegging was the chief livelihood and sole source of income of the gangs.[4]

Influential community opinion was aroused when organized crime began to move toward racketeering. Business leaders became seriously disturbed and crusades to clean up the city were initiated. It was this situation that gave rise to studies of gang life, organized crime, and juvenile delinquency. The growth of the city led to the growth of crime and delinquency as well as to social problems of all kinds. Urban conditions were identified as crime producing and criminology was thought of as an urban science.

Geographical Factors: The Growth of the Cities

Early observers of the city had noted that official crime and delinquency seemed to be located in specific areas. In 1912 Breckenridge and Abbott published a study showing the geographical distribution of cases of juvenile delinquency in the city of Chicago. They relied upon statistics gathered by the Juvenile Court for the years 1899–1909.[5] The locale of gangs was a semicircular area around the central business district. Thrasher characterized this area as "interstitial."[6] It had a number of distinctive features that loosened the influence of traditional rules on newcomers, especially younger people. Interstitial areas were identified as "criminogenic;" here, conventional and criminal values were inter-

[3] Fred D. Pasley, *Al Capone: The Biography of a Self Made Man* (New York: I. Wahburn, 1930).
[4] Arthur S. Link, *American Epoch: A History of the United States Since the 1890's* (New York: Knopf, 1958), p. 345.
[5] Sophonisba Breckenridge and Edith Abbott, *The Delinquent Child and the Home* (New York: Russell Sage Foundation, 1912).
[6] Frederick Thrasher, *The Gang* (Chicago: University of Chicago Press, 1927).

twined and anticrime norms were neutralized. Boys growing up in these communities could model themselves after those attractive and highly visible adults who made their living illegally. The family's authority in this situation was undermined and its ability to supervise the transition from boyhood to adulthood was compromised. The results for Thrasher were clearly identifiable: juvenile gangs, adult criminal groupings, and an alliance between them and the city-wide political structure.

Burgess first suggested that the growth of the city follows a concentric pattern; he reported great differences in the various neighborhoods of Chicago immediately after World War I.[7] In an attempt to make sense of these differences he had his students gather available statistics on each community. In 1925 he proposed that the growth of cities could best be understood in terms of gradual expansion outward from the initial settlement. He identified five zones:

1. The main business district is where the most intensive land use occurs and where the administrative functions for the commercial, financial, and management aspects of the city are located.

2. The zone of wholesale light manufacturing immediately adjoins the central business district. He called this the "zone of transition." Land is often held by real estate speculators in the anticipation that Zone 1 will expand and force the land value in Zone 2 to rise. This concept has created a permanent blighted area around the central business district.

3. Zone 3 is that of working men's homes. This is a lower-income residential district. Immigrant groups that have improved their status move from Zone 2 into this section.

4. This is a residential zone. It has higher rental costs than Zone 3 and a higher proportion of home ownership.

5. Farther out is the commuters' zone, Zone 5, which lies at the outer edge of the city. This zone is inhabited by stable middle-class families whose breadwinners usually work in the central section of the city.

Later studies have questioned the applicability of this pattern.[8] Suffice to say that the pattern holds when there is a rapid influx of heterogenous residents, when growth is unregulated, and when there are no peculiarities of topography such as hills, gorges, and so forth.

[7] Ernest W. Burgess, "The Growth of the City," in Robert E. Park and Ernest W. Burgess (eds.), *The City* (Chicago: University of Chicago Press, 1925).
[8] See Walter Firey, *Land Use in Central Boston* (Cambridge, Mass.: Harvard University Press, 1947); Warner E. Gettys, "Human Ecology and Social Theory," *Social Forces* 18 (May 1940), 469–76; August B. Hollingshead, "A Re-Examination of Ecological Theory," *Sociology and Social Research* 31 (January–February 1947), 194–204.

Shaw, one of Burgess' earlier students, systematically plotted the geographical distribution of known juvenile delinquents. He found that delinquents were not spread evenly over the city; in some communities no boys were arrested or convicted. In other communities the rate was as high as 20 percent in a given year.[9] Young noted that in some communities over 80 percent of the boys of juvenile court age had appeared before the Court at one time or another, though not of course all in the same year.[10] These areas of high concentration of official delinquents were nearest the center of the city, the zone of transition, and tended to decrease as the distance from the center of the city increased. Shaw found too that the distribution rates for various forms of delinquency were similar—areas with high rates of truancy, for example, also had high rates of more serious offenses. These areas also had high rates of adult crime.

It is important to point out (in the light of later criticism of use of official statistics in this kind of measurement) that Shaw was aware that middle-class status provided a child with immunity. The crucial difference between the low-income and middle-class areas was the availability of institutional resources to address the problems of youth. In high delinquency areas the institutional structure was weak or almost absent. It was this institutional incapacity that Shaw's Chicago Area Project (see page 59–60), a delinquency prevention program, was designed to remedy.[11]

The Immigrant Population

Another factor that focused attention on the social aspects of criminology was the rapid growth in the population of the cities. Between 1910 and 1930, Chicago gained over one million new residents. An overwhelming number of these newcomers had never lived in an urban environment before. The institutional wherewithal to absorb the in-migrants simply did not exist. Bruce states that:

> . . . the growth of Chicago has been too rapid for the proper coordination and formulation of its governmental structure.[12]

[9] Clifford Shaw, Harvey Zorbaugh, and Leonard Cottrell, *Delinquency in Urban Areas* (Chicago: University of Chicago Press, 1929).

[10] Pauline V. Young, "Urbanization as a Factor in Juvenile Delinquency," *Publications of the American Sociological Society*, 24 (1930), 162–66; Pauline V. Young, *The Pilgrims of Russia-Town* (Chicago: University of Chicago Press, 1932).

[11] Anthony Sorrentino, "The Chicago Area Project After 25 Years," *Federal Probation* (June 1959), pp. 40–45; Solomon Kobrin, "The Chicago Area Project: A Twenty-Five Year Assessment," *Annals of the American Academy of Political and Social Science*, 322 (March 1959), 20–29.

[12] Andrew Bruce, "Introduction," in John Landesco, *Organized Crime in Chicago* (Chicago: University of Chicago Press, 1929), pp. 3–4.

He goes on to say that two-thirds of the population of the city were born on foreign shores or were the children of newly arrived immigrants. The places of their first settlement were described by Park as "frontiers."

> The thing that gives the frontier, so conceived, its peculiar character and significance is the fact that the invading people in their efforts to accommodate themselves to the conditions of life in a new country invariably discard or lose their inherited and traditional ways of life and as a result new peoples and new cultures arise. It follows that a frontier is not merely a mark where peoples meet but a zone of transition where they intermingle.[13]

Thrasher referred to the frontier as an "interstitial" area which underscored the breaks or fissures in the institutional web which in turn led to the breakdown of social control.[14] The authority arrangements in the immigrant groups were undermined in ways that the new settlers did not anticipate. The taken-for-granted objectivity of the newcomers' social reality was called into question by contact with American society. Not only was the host society's reality more powerful and more pervasive, but it viewed immigrant definitions of reality as ignorant, contemptible, or sometimes evil.

In the new setting the old supports that maintained the authority system of the group were absent. There were no links between the family and secondary groups which could give external support to the system and hold it together. The immigrants' children were exposed to American values through school and mass media, and became interpreters of these values to their parents. Thus, the immigrants experienced the conflict between two cultures, where at least two sets of opposing rules existed on how to act. This situation intensified the parent-youth tension in immigrant families. As Gordon and others have noted, Americanization programs contributed to the disruption of the immigrants' social order inasmuch as they demanded the abandonment of old institutions, organizations, and ethnic identity.[15] The demand that the newcomers deny their roots widened the gap between parents and children.

The most influential perspective for interpreting this situation in the early decades of the twentieth century was the *social pathological* one. It was an evolutionary view that saw society as a social organism. Anything that hampered the natural workings of this social organism could be designated as pathological. This early approach was derived from social philosophy and did not represent any distinctive sociological contribution. The notion of what constituted the normal functioning of so-

[13] Robert E. Park, *Race and Culture* (New York: Free Press, 1959), p. 118.
[14] Frederick Thrasher, *The Gang.*
[15] Milton Gordon, *Assimilation in American Life* (New York: Oxford University Press, 1964).

ciety was very much related to what existed at the time. This gave the perspective a decided conservative bias. The outlook was congenial to a system whose major concerns related to socialization failures, and whose assumptions about the superiority of American institutions and values were not questioned. The shortcomings of the social pathology perspective soon became apparent. Its explanatory power was limited in predicting what would happen when a previously functioning system with a history and tradition of its own came into contact with the American culture of the times. It also offered no remedies for the conflicts that occurred when two different cultures met. The limited biographical information that exists on the early ecologists show them to be products of the middle border states and very concerned about explaining social change. Their individual backgrounds were decisive in shaping their perspective on social disorganization.

INDIVIDUAL BACKGROUND

Those people who were part of the ecological school were a diverse group and cannot be characterized briefly. Rather than look at all of them it makes more sense to confine our inquiry to Shaw and McKay.[16] Both identified themselves as criminologists and unlike the other ecologists wrote almost exclusively on crime and delinquency. Both came from rural backgrounds and came to Chicago in the 1920's to take graduate work at the University of Chicago. Shaw was born in 1895 in Luray, Indiana, a small farming community thirty miles southeast of Muncie. He was the fifth of ten children. Shaw's father was a farmer and worked occasionally as a harness-maker and shoemaker. His family was Republican, Scottish-Irish and Methodist. He studied for the Methodist ministry at Adrian College in Michigan but was not ordained. He reported that the experience prompted him to leave the Church and he came to feel that "religion [was] a barrier to the progress of humanity."[17] Shaw lived in a settlement house in an Eastern European neighborhood while taking graduate courses at the University of Chicago. He took a part time job as a parole officer for the Illinois State Training School for Boys at St. Charles, Illinois in 1921. He abandoned his graduate studies in 1924 to take a position as probation officer for the Cook County Juvenile Court. He never completed the PhD requirements but taught criminology at George Willimans College and the Central YMCA College in Chi-

---

[16] Biographical information on Shaw and McKay is drawn from Jon Snodgrass, *The American Criminological Tradition,* PhD dissertation (Philadelphia: University of Pennsylvania, 1972), Ch. 4.
[17] Ibid., p. 131.

cago throughout his professional career. He was appointed Director of the newly formed sociology department at the Institute for Juvenile Research in 1926 where he remained until his death in 1957.

Henry McKay was born on a farm near Orient, South Dakota in 1899 of Scottish Presbyterian parents. He was fifth in a family of seven children. He worked on his father's farm and went on to receive a BA from Dakota Wesleyan University. He arrived in Chicago in 1923 and met Shaw there as a fellow graduate student. The following year he left to continue his studies at the University of Illinois and returned in 1927 to take a research assistantship under Shaw at the Institute for Juvenile Research. There he remained until his retirement.

Both scholars have reported that their investigations were shaped by the intellectual orientations they absorbed in their graduate training. The delinquency statistics they compiled so carefully were supplemented by cases and life history materials drawn from the local communities. High crime rates or those associated with mental illness, unemployment, infant mortality and the like were interpreted as indices of an underlying state of social disorganization.

SOCIAL DISORGANIZATION THEORY

Sociologists needed new conceptual tools to explore the changes that were occurring in American cities and American society. The term social disorganization was used to describe the disruptive impact of life in a strange new environment. It was defined as the decrease of the influence of existing rules of behavior on individual members of the group. As Wirth has noted, referring to a community as "disorganized" implies some criteria by which an organized society may be identified.[18] The degree to which the members of a community lose their common understandings is the measure of that community's state of disorganization. This does not mean that all deviations from norms are evidence of social disorganization. There can be quite a range of individual differentiation without generating disorganization. Personal disorganization and social disorganization are separate phenomena and do not bear any necessary relationship to one another.

> In other words, social organization is not coextensive with individual morality nor does social disorganization correspond to individual demoralization.[19]

[18] Louis Wirth, "Ideological Aspects of Social Disorganization," *American Sociological Review*, 5 (August 1940), 472–82.
[19] William I. Thomas and Florian Znaniecki, *The Polish Peasant in Europe and America* (New York: Knopf, 1927), p. 1129.

Because these two phenomena are distinct it is not valid to use individual pathology like crime and delinquency as an indicator of social disorganization. This distinction enabled Thomas and Znaniecki to isolate several possibilities in looking at a society, a community, or a group:

1. Social disorganization can exist without personal disorganization. The "creative man" is one who appears during a period of disruption and realizes his interest by violating traditional rules and incorporating into his own life plan elements of schemes which are competing with traditional ones.

2. Personal disorganization can exist without social disorganization. Personal demoralization can occur in the happy village. An individual may fail to realize his life goals precisely because of his conformity and lack of flexibility. This personality type was labeled the "philistine."

3. Personal disorganization may result from social disorganization. This is the response of "bohemian" personality.

The relationship between individual and social disorganization has caused much confusion among later social disorganization authors. Cooley and later writers of disorganization texts rejected the distinctions made by Thomas and Znaniecki and expanded their conception of disorganization to cover all of society, not just the Polish peasantry, or a larger group of immigrants whose group life was disrupted upon impact with the city.[20]

For Thomas and Znaniecki social disorganization was a temporary state followed by reorganization. There was no such thing as a permanently disorganized state, community, or group. It was the lack of conceptual rigor on the part of the later textbook writers of disorganization, the "social pathologists," and their eagerness to enlarge the notion of disorganization as a symbol of what was happening to small town ways in the first decades of the twentieth century that led to the later criticism of the disorganization theory as a whole.

Disorganization, according to Thomas, can occur as a result of excessively rapid change, like an increase in the volume and density of population. It might also be caused by its opposite, a sudden decline in population. Or rapid changes in technology or material culture might generate a temporary state of disorganization. Sudden booms, depressions, crises, and natural disasters may cause a state of disorganization.

Thomas and Znaniecki see social disorganization as a continuum ranging from organization to disorganization to reorgnization. Disorganization is but one phase of a three-stage process; it is not viewed as a con-

[20] Charles Horton Cooley, *Social Organization: A Study of the Larger Minds* (New York: Scribners, 1909).

dition but as part of a process. In the *Polish Peasant,* social disorganization was discussed under two general categories: family disorganization and community disorganization. Family disorganization was limited to the economic field alone and referred to the

> decay of the institution of economic family solidarity . . . actual common ownership of property and common use of income.[21]

Family disorganization occurs when there is a complete shift from "we" to "I." This shift can be identified by looking at the attitudes of the individuals who constitute the family system though opportunities to manifest such attitudes might be quite limited.

A community is organized when social opinion concerns itself

> . . . with all matters, outside happenings or individual acts which possess a public interest, when its attitudes toward these matters are consistent and able to reach approximate unanimity and when any common action considered necessary to solve situations defined by social opinion is carried on in harmonious cooperation.[22]

The indicator of community disorganization is the absence of public opinion. This leads to a decline in the sense of community solidarity and its supporting institutions.

Park attempted to specify the various stages of organization and reorganization. He suggested that there were four processes within this cycle, beginning with a change in spatial and food relationships in a community. Every change in man's sustenance relationships brings about changes in population, social organization, and cultural life. This stage he characterized as "competition," a kind of disguised social conflict which generates a new division of labor. The second stage of the cycle was identified as "conflict." Populations representing different life schemes are thrust into contact with one another. Now the conflict goes on at the political level rather than the economic one. The adjustments made to situations created by competition and conflict were characterized by Park as "accommodation." The last stage in the process of reorganization is "assimilation," the development of a new consensus, the formation of a new web of custom and mutual expectation. The process begins all over again with a new change in technology.

Park's cycle suggested an interpretation of the fluctuation of crime rates. Patterns of criminal behavior were insignificant in preindustrial communities. They appear at the conflict stage of the cycle, endure sometimes through the accommodation stage, and become insignificant again at the assimilation stage. Whatever reservations one may have

[21] Thomas and Znaniecki, *The Polish Peasant,* p. 1138.
[22] Ibid., p. 1171.

about the cycle, it did provide a framework for the criminologists of the time to understand why crime rates seemed to increase dramatically among urban newcomers.

EVALUATION OF SOCIAL DISORGANIZATION THEORY

A number of criticisms of the Chicago ecological studies have dampened the enthusiasm of criminologists for social disorganization theory. Some of the criticisms were well founded and pointed to conceptual inadequacies. However others were based upon a misunderstanding of what social disorganization actually meant and how it was utilized. The criticisms can be reduced to three major objections: (1) the concept is too vague and subjective to be useful, (2) there is a bias in favor of homogeneity and against heterogeneity, and (3) disorganization has been equated with its consequences—i.e., disorganization has been measured by its predicted outcomes (social problems).

Social Disorganization is a Subjective Notion

Nowhere in the Chicago writings is the notion of social disorganization explicitly defined. Therefore, it is up to the individual researcher to piece together a definition from various monographs of the 1920s. This process involves the judgment of the researcher; personal bias is introduced and the possibility of total objectivity eliminated.

Mowrer has pointed out that to characterize an institution, community, group, or nation as disorganized suggests that certain conditions are bad for social welfare and should be eliminated by the group.[23] The previous state which has been disrupted is considered normative and the decline deviant. The concept contains an evaluative component which considerably reduces its usefulness. This poses a methodological problem for the investigator: who will decide what is normal and what is deviant? Some have equated "normal" with that which is statistically more frequent; hence any deviation from that statistical norm could be described as disorganization. Some have labelled the group under examination as normative; hence if they see themselves as unable to realize their values, whereas they once could, they are in the process of disorganization. And lastly, when a group, community, or institution has not readjusted to changes in material culture, then it can be characterized

---

[23] Ernest Mowrer, "Methodological Problems in Social Disorganization," *American Sociological Review*, 6 (December 1941), 839–52.

as disorganized.[24] The concept, in short, means different things to different people: there is no consensus on what the components of disorganization are nor how to resolve the methodological problems posed by its use.

Homogeneity and Heterogeneity

According to Matza, the Chicago conception of pathology suppressed the facts of diversity. The existence of variant worlds with considerable vitality, autonomy, and integrity of their own was denied in theory, if not in practice.[25] The most serious criticism made against Shaw's depiction of delinquency areas is that it masked his pronounced status quo orientation, and institutionalized a stereotype of the delinquent or criminal which later theorists have not been able to escape. This criticism maintains that the delinquency area, later translated into a delinquent subculture, is a more sophisticated version of earlier theories of physical, psychological, or racial inferiority.

The ecologists would probably respond that the identification of the local environment with a particular set of crime-producing social conditions was a considerable advance over previous explanations related to the criminal propensities of the people who occupied the area. Delinquency areas revealed a uniform behavior pattern no matter who actually lived there. The task of the criminologist then was to specify more precisely what these criminogenic conditions were.

However it must be noted that although Shaw and McKay were aware of the fact that there were variations in police and court policies, they did not systematically explore the extent of unrecorded delinquency in more advantaged areas. If they had, they might well have expanded their ideas about local cultures to include more than that behavior narrowly prohibited by law, and discovered more dramatically the overlap between the delinquency area and the larger community.

This was an insight contributed later by the functionalists who pointed out that delinquency areas are not so much in conflict with the larger culture but an essential component of it. This notion has highlighted the symbiotic link between the well-to-do and the poor who meet for their mutual exploitation in what one author has called "functional tracts of depravity." This point is discussed more fully in another section of this book.

The ecologists were committed to a philosophy of cultural pluralism

[24] William F. Ogburn, *Social Change with Respect to Culture and Original Nature* (New York: Viking, 1922).
[25] David Matza, *Becoming Deviant* (Englewood Cliffs, N.J.: Prentice-Hall, 1969).

unusual for the period in which they wrote—a policy of social change which incorporated newcomers more vigorously into the political and social life of the community. They also recognized the connection between the problems they were discussing and the city itself and some of the influential elements in it. Their recommendations were addressed to decision makers who may have had the means to effect changes. In retrospect, since few of the recommendations were accepted, it would appear that the ecologists overestimated the concern of these influential citizens or the extent to which they, themselves, were part of the problems the sociologists were examining.

It is clear, however, that the ecologists were aware that the homogeneity represented by the larger society was not something to celebrate. They did not believe that the host's culture was morally superior to that of the newcomers', and their works are studded with appreciations of the heterogeneity they found.

In summary, the conception of social disorganization was not a masked judgment on ways of life considered inferior. Since the phenomenon of social disorganization was conceived of as part of a three-stage process—organization, disorganization, and reorganization—the total theory heralded the emergence of newer, more complex, and more cohesive forms of organization:

> Normally the processes of disorganization and organization may be thought of as in reciprocal relationship to each other, and as cooperating in a moving equilibrium of social order toward an end vaguely or definitely regarded as progressive. So far as disorganization points to reorganization and makes for more efficient adjustment, disorganization must be conceived not as pathological, but as normal.[26]

Disorganization and Its Consequences

The tendency to equate disorganization with its consequences is related to the difficulty in keeping personal and social organization separate. The Chicago group accepted the distinction between these two features, yet failed to state explicitly the relationship between them. This distinction was difficult to maintain in field research. The incidence of delinquency, suicide, and other forms of individual failure were taken as indicators of social disorganization. The Chicagoans were plagued with the constant tendency to equate disorganization with its causes or consequences. If social disorganization is the independent variable, then

[26] Ernest W. Burgess, "The Growth of the City," in Park and Burgess (eds.), *The City*, p. 54.

it should be possible to measure it apart from its predicted consequences.

Although this problem did not receive explicit attention, we can identify a number of instances that attest to the fact that it was perceived. Burgess indicates that he saw this dilemma in his discussion on the growth of the city:

> If the phenomena of expansion and metabolism indicate that a moderate degree of disorganization may and does facilitate social organization, they indicate as well that rapid urban expansion is accompanied by excessive increases in crime, disorder, vice, insanity and suicide—rough indexes of social disorganization. But what are the indexes of the causes rather than the effects of the disordered metabolism of the city? The excess of the actual over the natural increase of population has already been suggested as a criterion.[27]

Another corollary of disorganization is the variable of political stability as measured by political scientists. In his earlier discussion of party politics and publicity, Park implies that political stability is one index of organization in a community.

It seems clear that once the components of disorganization are specified—low income, heterogeneity, high population turnover—that the task of developing indicators for it is considerably simplified. The indices of disorganization culled from the Chicagoans as well as those that have been mentioned more recently suggest that it is possible to measure the kinds of industrialization and differentiation that have been equated with disorganization.

1. WHAT ARE THE WIDER ORIGINS OF CRIMINAL BEHAVIOR? The ecologists believed that weak social organization led to crime and delinquency. This can be seen in certain slum communities where social organization is weak. In these unstructured and unstable conditions, the ability of the community to withstand the emergence of a delinquent subculture may be quite limited.

The ecologists also believed that human nature required a set of constraining institutions. When control institutions are not operating effectively or are disrupted, impulses would be given free play. The theory suggests that there are variations in morality: some people are freed from moral sensitivities when social control breaks down.

The ecological theory assumes a value consensus; it does not believe that a set of warring subcultures makes up the urban community. The capacity of a society such as ours to generate alternative structures and subcultures is limited because the tendency of industrial societies is to absorb subgroups; if egalitarian traditions exist they undermine the conditions that are necessary for separate subcultures to arise and flourish.

[27] Ibid., p. 57.

There is a value consensus, however general, as to the importance of health, long life, lawful conduct, economic sufficiency, family stability, and so on, even though these values may be given a variety of expressions.

What does it mean to say that institutions are weak? It means simply that they are not able to prevent high rates of unemployment, infant mortality, and delinquency from arising and persisting. For the Chicago group the primary causes of social disorganization are those structural and cultural conditions which allow these "problems" to develop. Economic segregration is the ultimate causal variable because it causes communities to differ in respect to the social characteristics of their populations.[28] Those areas of the city that house the lowest income groups attract immigrants and rural migrants and have a high population turnover.[29] These three structural variables—low economic status, heterogeneity, and mobility—lead to the outstanding cultural cause of disorganization: diversity with respect to conventional values.[30] Thus both structural and cultural factors militate against new values being built up. This means that the community can't be an effective agent of social control.

Even though delinquent traditions may have persisted for several generations, the ecologists thought of the situation as a temporary one. Neighborhoods where crime and delinquency flourished were like frontier towns where vigilante justice prevailed. Given time, the law abiding citizens (who always constituted the overwhelming majority in the delinquency areas) would eventually stabilize it.

The ecologists' conception of the wider origins of criminal behavior implied some links between delinquency and the larger society but these relationships were not spelled out. They suggested that there was a reciprocal relationship between organized crime and politics, but they did not explore the positive functions that the delinquency areas served for the city as a whole. The idea that the city, and particularly some of the influential law abiding groups within it, "needed" the delinquency areas would have been quite foreign to them.

2. WHERE IN THE SOCIAL STRUCTURE DOES THE IMPULSE ARISE TO LABEL CERTAIN BEHAVIORS AS CRIMINAL? The ecologists have no real answer to this question. They assume that there is a value consensus in the society, and that it is reflected in the laws relating to criminal behavior. The de-

---

[28] Ruth Kornhauser, "Theoretical Issues in the Sociological Study of Juvenile Delinquency" (Berkeley, Center for the Study of Law and Society, University of California, 1963).

[29] Ibid.

[30] Clifford Shaw, *The Jackroller: A Delinquent Boy's Own Story* (Chicago: University of Chicago Press, 1930), p. 40.

linquencies they focused on were common law crimes relating to personal and property assault, not the more ambiguous kinds of behavior later defined as delinquency, such as truancy, incorrigibility, curfew violation, and the like.

3. HOW WELL DOES THE SOCIAL DISORGANIZATION THEORY EXPLAIN THE DISTRIBUTION OF CRIME AND DELINQUENCY? The ecologists suggested that where social control is weak, crime and delinquency can be expected to result. Their explanation of the geographic distribution of delinquency laid the foundation for later interpretations of crime and delinquency that related it to the disparity between the values to which people aspire and the availability of facilities for acquiring these values in conventional ways. This theory, however, did not suggest ways of accounting for crime and delinquency that were not associated with lower-class areas.

4. WHAT CAUSES CRIME, OR TO WHAT IS CRIMINAL BEHAVIOR A RESPONSE? The ecologists' description of areas where there were things to steal, people to buy stolen goods, and places to hide without adult supervision suggested how particular communities facilitated delinquency. In local communities or neighborhoods where adults were making their own livings illegally (and had high status as a result) crime and delinquency were *attractive*. The ecologists' depiction of such communities, the tolerance of conventional adults to it, and the prevalence of political ties which protected it also suggested an environment that was *morally supportive* of delinquent behavior. And finally the ecologists' description of a large number of youth groups competing for limited space and resources suggested the *coercive* effect of the neighborhood upon gang formation. The ecologists systematically focused on both the communities' constraints against delinquency and the pressures toward it, and the interpretation of legitimate and illegitimate institutions at the neighborhood level.

The transition from spontaneous play group to gang was portrayed as a matter of survival, of participating in the struggle for life of adolescents under the peculiar conditions of the slum. The various life histories collected by Shaw and Thrasher show how these groups became increasingly engaged in illegal activities to support themselves, and the body of learning and attitudes that developed to enhance it. Once established the criminal pattern became stabilized and passed its traditions on to younger boys growing up in the same area.

5. WHAT ARE THE POLICY IMPLICATIONS OF THE ECOLOGICAL APPROACH? Since the local community's failure to function effectively as an agency of social control is the immediate cause of delinquency, it must be the locus of any prevention program. This was Shaw's rationale for creation of the Chicago Area Project. Three high delinquency areas were selected

as delinquency prevention targets in 1932. A field worker from Shaw's staff entered the area to form community councils of local residents who tried to stimulate organization for civic betterment. The staff worker's role was a catalytic one and was not designed to stifle or supplant local leadership. Shaw was convinced that any effective program of neighborhood organization would have to be developed by indigenous leaders, not be imposed from the outside. The kinds of activities the local community councils sponsored were not as important as the fact that they were addressing their own problems. In fact the content of the programs —recreation and social—were similar to those of conventional agencies. The difference was in the methods used to foster local neighborhood activities. The aim of the project was to mobilize adults in neighborhoods to promote law abiding sentiments. The issues selected for attention tended to be internal problems of the community, those amenable to solution by local residents. The Chicago Area Project expanded from the original three locations to more than a dozen and has aroused considerable national interest because of its emphasis on citizen participation. How effective the program has been in preventing delinquency is difficult to assess, but it has demonstrated that low-income residents can organize and administer welfare programs.

The Chicago Area Project has tended to avoid activities with distinctively "political" aims. But Saul Alinsky, one of Shaw's staff workers, has extended some of the Chicago Area Project notions in political directions.[31] Alinsky was concerned not just with crime and delinquency but with broader problems of unemployment, inadequate housing, and institutional effectiveness. Citizens were organized for political action to improve their own welfare and Alinsky consistently worked for the development of a nationwide federation of people's organizations that could exercise enormous political influence.

SUMMARY

Although they have been criticized for environmental determinism, the ecologists did not maintain that the physical characteristics of an area could completely account for the behavior of its residents. Their master conception—social disorganization—powerfully organized and interpreted the data they collected. They provided a model for the collection of enormous amounts of data long before the era of the computer.

[31] Saul D. Alinsky, *Reveille for Radicals* (Chicago: University of Chicago Press, 1946).

Their perspective was sufficiently complex to look separately at the influence of social structure and culture in the generation of criminality and can still be utilized fruitfully today. The ecologists, because of their secure academic base and close ties with local decision makers who partly sponsored their work, were able to produce an impressive body of literature which commanded wide attention. The major weaknesses of their approach were the uncritical acceptance of official rates of delinquency, the lack of attention to law making and enforcement as aspects of social conflict, and the lack of appreciation of the functional connection between the larger society and the delinquency areas.

Those who immediately followed the ecologists, however, were more interested in their portrait of criminal traditions and less in their structural explanations. This interest led to the work of Edwin Sutherland who initiated what has been characterized as the "cultural transmission" school of criminal traditions.

CULTURAL TRANSMISSION THEORY

Cultural transmission theory focuses on the development of delinquent and criminal traditions in specific settings and tries to account for the communication of these patterns.

Shaw and McKay noted that weak social organization in the slum community permits the development of a delinquent system whose values compete with the conventional ones of the larger community. The delinquent system in later analyses hardens into a robust and persistent oppositional "delinquent subculture" (in the work of Albert Cohen) or a hardy but nonreactive subsystem of a more widespread lower-class culture (in the work of Walter Miller). Let us first examine the work of Edwin Sutherland who laid the groundwork for these later theories.

The Work of Edwin H. Sutherland

Edwin Sutherland was the foremost American criminologist from the early 1920s until his death in 1950. He had close ties to the Chicago ecologists and maintained contacts with them throughout his life. But he differed from them in important ways, most notably in the primary role as ascribed to conflicting values in generating criminal behavior. For the ecologists, crime was a product of common values incapable of realization because of deficiencies in social structure. Sutherland's work can best be understood as a response to the shortcomings of the ecological approach: he attempted to identify the mechanisms relating social structure to criminal behavior.

Sutherland: Social Context and Individual Background. The combination of social and technological trends that required sociological expertise after World War I decisively affected the way the ecologists responded and gave a distinctive policy orientation to their work. The policy orientation is not as salient in the work of Edwin Sutherland. He functioned for most of his academic career as an individual scholar unrelated to any larger research enterprises without a distinctive urban "laboratory," and with fewer links to policy makers than did his colleagues at Chicago. But he was responsive to the same social realities that the ecologists were: the massive population changes that were transforming the character of city life, contact between immigrant and host cultures and the impact of urban industrialism on the rurally bred. These concerns are evident in his first criminology text published in 1924 and in his summary of research on the criminality of immigrants that he produced for the President's Committee on Recent Social Trends in 1933.[32] His participation in the work of that committee demonstrated his sympathy with the role of criminologist as policy scientist—his summary was designed to provide a factual basis for federal legislation.

Sutherland was born in Gibbon, Nebraska in 1883. His father was a Protestant minister and communicated to his son a sense of the moral importance of meeting one's obligations and carrying out life's duties. His early background encouraged a strong identification with the plight of the small farmers and businessmen who were the focus of his father's ministry. Sutherland completed his undergraduate work at Grand Island Nebraska College in 1903 and three years later enrolled as a graduate student at the University of Chicago, drawn there by the work of Charles Henderson, a sociologist-minister concerned with social reform.[33] The strong influence of the social gospel movement in the pre-World War I Sociology Department at the University of Chicago was quite congenial with Sutherland's outlook. His work with the Juvenile Protective Association gave him first hand contact with the life of newcomers to the city where his faith in piece-meal reforms was somewhat shaken. He professed to yearning for some kind of dramatic social reorganization such as socialism which would better the economic situation of the newcomers. Sutherland took as his dissertation topic the practical problem of unemployment and a research appointment with the Chicago Com-

---

[32] Edwin Sutherland, *Criminology* (Philadelphia: J. B. Lippincott Co., 1924). Edwin Sutherland and Charles E. Gehlke, "Crime and Punishment" in President's Committee on Recent Social Trends, *Recent Social Trends* (New York and London: McGraw-Hill, 1933).

[33] Karl Schuessler, "Introduction," in Karl Schuessler (ed.), *Edwin H. Sutherland On Analyzing Crime* (Chicago: University of Chicago Press, 1973), p. xi.

mission on Unemployment was arranged for him. The dissertation that resulted focussed on the relationship of public employment agencies to the problems of unemployment. He received his Ph.D. in 1913 with the conviction that sociology's primary justification was in its ability to solve practical problems. He regularly reviewed publications on employment problems for the *American Journal of Sociology* from the time he began his work at Chicago until well after his intellectual interests shifted to criminology. He reported that Thomas and Znaniecki's *Polish Peasant in Europe and America,* in which the notion of social disorganization was first introduced, had a profound impact on him. Schuessler points out that the theory of criminal behavior Sutherland later developed "may be regarded as an adaption of interactional sociology as expounded by W. I. Thomas."[34] Sutherland was affiliated with five different academic institutions but they were all within a restricted geographical area in the midwest and his lifelong contacts were with scholars located there. American criminology, as Geis has observed, has been decisively influenced by a small group of "populist criminologists" (of whom Sutherland was a part) who were located at Big Ten land grant universities.[35]

Sutherland's theory held that social disorganization, later restated as "differential social disorganization," was the cause of criminality. Sutherland's conception of social organization referred simply to the ratio of favorable to unfavorable definitions of crime. That is, those subgroups that approve of criminal behavior will have higher violation rates than those subgroups that look unfavorably on crime. Social organization in this conception is a patterned set of values that relates to a subgroup's idea of what is important. One element of this patterned set of values has to do with the definition of what is lawful. If a subgroup condones certain kinds of delinquent behavior, then the children socialized into that culture will automatically try to realize those values. Hence it is not unmet needs that cause crime and delinquency—as Thrasher believed— nor the opportunity to commit illegal acts, nor the absence of social control, but the acting out of subcultural values.

The main outlines of Sutherland's contributions are found in the various editions of his *Introduction to Criminology,* but probably the most important is the 1939 edition wherein he makes his systematic presentation of the "theory of differential association."[36] Another volume, *The Professional Thief,* underscored his interest in patterns of criminality.[37]

---

[34] Ibid., p. xi.

[35] Gilbert Geis, "Avocational Crime," in Daniel Glaser (ed.), *Handbook of Criminology* (Chicago: Rand McNally, 1974).

[36] Edwin Sutherland, *Principles of Criminology,* 3rd ed. (Philadelphia: Lippincott, 1939).

[37] Edwin Sutherland, *The Professional Thief* (Chicago: University of Chicago Press, 1937).

This book was published under Sutherland's name but written by "Chic Conwell," a knowledgeable and articulate professional thief who describes his occupation much as anyone else would a conventional occupation. The professional thief's account was the beginning of an entire body of literature on illicit occupations.

Sutherland's book on white-collar crime initiated serious study of middle-class criminal behavior.[38] He began to study the violations of law by businessmen at about the same time that he was researching professional theft.[39] It was his conviction that an explanation of professional theft should also be applicable to white-collar crime. He felt that criminology could not emerge as a full-fledged scientific discipline until it moved away from "multiple factor" approaches.[40]

The multiple factor investigations being conducted during the period when Sutherland was writing suggested long lists of factors related to crime or delinquency. One combination of factors might account for criminal behavior in one individual and a completely different set of factors be responsible in another individual. Although this multiple factor approach constituted a creative break with earlier and obviously inadequate single theory explanations of crime, it was clearly not an explanatory scheme. Sutherland's conception of differential association stated that persons engage in criminal behavior because they perceive more favorable than unfavorable definitions of law violation. These definitions are picked up in the same way as other cultural prescriptions. One boy learns to become delinquent by the same process that another learns to become a boy scout.

Sutherland reported that his theory of differential association was an elaboration of the notion that "the conflict of cultures is the fundamental principle in the explanation of crime."[41] He started out with seven propositions or working hypotheses and these were eventually expanded to nine. His theory was built on the observation that groups differ in respect to the importance they attach to the respect for law and that an individual will be drawn toward or away from crime depending on the values of his intimate associates. The nine propositions are as follows:

1. Criminal behavior is learned; or stated another way, criminal behavior is not inherited. The person who is not trained in criminal behavior does not invent it any more than a person who has not been trained in mechanics makes mechanical objects.

---

[38] Edwin Sutherland, *White Collar Crime* (New York: Dryden Press, 1949).
[39] Edwin H. Sutherland, "Crime of Corporations," in Schuessler (ed.), *Edwin H. Sutherland.*
[40] William Healy, *The Individual Delinquent* (Boston: Little, Brown, 1915).
[41] Schuessler (ed.), *Edwin H. Sutherland,* p. xiv.

2. Criminal behavior is learned in interaction with others in a process of communication, both verbal and nonverbal (gestures).

3. The principal learning of criminal behavior occurs within intimate personal groups. Impersonal agencies of communication, such as movies, newspapers, etc., play a relatively minor part in the genesis of criminal behavior.

4. The learning of criminal behavior includes:
   a. the techniques of committing the crime—sometimes complicated, sometimes simple—and
   b. the specific direction of motives, drives, rationalizations, and attitudes.

5. The specific direction of motives and drives is learned from favorable or unfavorable definitions of the legal codes. An individual may be surrounded by persons whose definitions are favorable to the violation of legal codes. In American society these definitions are almost always mixed with consequences that produce culture conflict with respect to the legal codes.

6. A person becomes delinquent because of an excess of definitions favorable to law violation over definitions unfavorable to violation of law.

7. Differential association may vary in frequency, duration, priority, and intensity. Priority means it developed early; intensity has to do with the prestige of the source.

8. The process of learning criminal behavior by association with criminal and anticriminal patterns involves all of the mechanisms required in any other learning; this learning is not restricted to imitation.

9. Although criminal behavior is an expression of general needs and values, it is not explained by those general needs and values since noncriminal behavior is an expression of the same needs and values.[42]

The controversy following the initial publication of his theory led Sutherland to reformulate and clarify what he was doing. It seemed to him that the theory could account for crime in a wide variety of apparently disparate situations. He felt that continued research on factors that interfere with the operation of the hypothesis might result in valid generalizations regarding the importance of personality factors or opportunities. In short, the formulation should give direction to criminological research. But Sutherland was convinced that his theory could explain

[42] Edwin H. Sutherland, *Principles of Criminology*, 4th ed. (Philadelphia: Lippincott, 1947), pp. 5–9.

a broad range of criminal behavior. For instance he thought that participation in embezzlement was one of the illegal practices learned as one became indoctrinated into the subcultural ways of American business:

> As part of the process of learning practical business, a young man with idealism and thoughtfulness for others is inducted into white collar crime. In many cases he is ordered by the manager to do things which he regards as unethical or illegal, while in other cases he learns from those who have the same rank as his own how they make a success. He learns specific techniques of violating the law, together with definitions of situations in which those techniques may be used. Also he develops a general ideology.[43]

Sutherland did not deal systematically with opportunities to commit crime. If opportunities to violate were present as well as definitions favorable to violation, criminal behavior would inevitably follow. Opportunity was not an independent variable; it was either present or it was not. If there were no opportunity, there would be no crime. The example he gives is that low-income blacks do not embezzle because they are not often in the positions where they can violate this kind of trust. Nor does General Motors violate the Pure Food and Drug Act because they are not engaged in the production of food or drugs. In later explanations of criminal behavior, opportunity as a variable is more systematically incorporated. The question then is not whether opportunity is present, but what kinds of opportunities are available, to what degree they are organized, and who has access to them.

In Sutherland's view the various subcultures that make up the United States are all equally adequate; all cultures have the resources and wherewithal to socialize their own members successfully. Subcultures are powerful and ever present. They have the capacity to articulate distinctive subcultural values and to generate commitment to them. There is no such thing as the imperfectly socialized individual. The individual raised in a subculture that condones delinquency will automatically commit delinquent acts in those situations where it is defined as appropriate. All criminal and delinquent behavior is *valued* behavior. Individuals cannot bear to commit delinquent or criminal acts unless they have been defined as proper by the groups of which they are a part. They act as cultural agents or, one might be tempted to say, cultural automatons. Sutherland's later views considerably expanded on his notion of differential social organization. The major cause of theft in his later work is not conformity to values condoning it, but structural-cultural weaknesses that lead to the breakdown of social control.

What is crime for Sutherland? It is those acts, as defined by criminal

[43] Edwin Sutherland, *White Collar Crime*, p. 240.

law, that threaten the values and interests of powerful groups. Law is the instrument of force imposed by the powerful on the powerless. The machinery of the criminal law is a device for labeling and punishing those acts that threaten the values and interests of powerful people.

> . . . crime can be seen to involve four elements: a value which is appreciated by a group or part of a group which is politically powerful; isolation of or normative conflict in another part of this group so that its members do not appreciate the value or appreciate it less highly and consequently tend to endanger it; political declaration that behavior endangering the value is henceforth to be a crime; and pugnacious resort to coercion decently applied by those who appreciate the value to those who disregard the value. When a crime is committed, all these relationships are involved. Crime is this set of relationships when viewed from the point of view of a social system rather than that of the individual.[44]

Sutherland goes on to say that criminal laws prohibiting vagrancy, cattle rustling, automobile theft, and discrimination against blacks and women illustrate this conflict view of crime. There are no overall values that knit the society together, values that all of its members internalize. Values of appropriate conduct come from smaller intimate groups that make up the various subcultures. There may be overall agreement on some laws in a society (prohibiting murder, for example), but the meaning of these laws and the situations to which they are applied varies by particular subculture.

Evaluation of Differential Association Theory

Sutherland's contention of universality is somewhat ambitious. His theory seems more appropriate to those who live in lower-class areas with delinquent traditions. The theory is less applicable to upper-income crime like embezzlement. Donald Cressey, a student and later a collaborator of Sutherland's, tried to account for decisions to violate financial trust using differential association theory to develop his hypotheses. He found that it was not applicable. Some of the embezzlers he interviewed reported that they knew the behavior to be illegal and wrong. They were not acting on definitions favorable to that kind of law violation. Others said they knew of no one in their business or profession who was carrying on practices similar to theirs. Cressey also found that not everyone who had experienced grave financial difficulty and who was in a position to do so did not in fact embezzle funds. He concludes by emphasizing the psychological isolation of the person who selects embezzlement as a solution and

[44] Edwin H. Sutherland and Donald Cressey, *Criminology*, 8th ed. (Philadelphia: Lippincott, 1970), pp. 11–12.

suggests three conditions to be essential in the violation of a financial trust:

> 1) When the person conceives of himself as having a financial problem that is nonshareable . . . 2) When the person becomes aware that his nonshareable problem can be secretly resolved by violation of his financial trust . . . 3) When the person is able to apply to his own conduct rationalizations that enable him to adjust his conception of himself as a trusted person to his conception of himself as a user of the entrusted funds or property.[45]

Another criticism is that Sutherland's theory assumes that some special skills must be learned to commit a crime. This is true for some kinds of theft where the craft element is high (e.g., safecracking) but ignores the more frequent kinds of crime that require little sophistication. The more serious crimes like murder and serious assault need little in the way of special skills.

A third problem is the difficulty in operationalizing the concept. What precisely does it mean to say that an individual has an "excess of criminal over anticriminal patterns?" Research shows that persons often cannot name those from whom they have learned particular behavior patterns much less count the number of criminal over law abiding ones. Cressey has argued that the difficulty in finding empirical indicators does not undermine the validity of the theory in general. He suggests that it may not be able to account for individual criminality but it can account for group crime. But its validity here is questionable also because high crime rate areas are explained by "criminal traditions" existing in certain areas. And how do we know that there are criminal traditions? Because there are high crime rates. The theory, in short, is measuring the independent variable (criminal traditions) by its predicted outcome (high crime rate), a methodologically invalid procedure. If criminal traditions is the independent variable then it should be measurable apart from its consequences. The fact that many sociologists report that differential association seems to be supported in their research can also be interpreted as a weakness. It suggests that the theory is so general that it can explain almost anything. What seems to be supported is the "bad companion" notion—those who associate with delinquent peers are likely to become delinquent themselves. They are mechanically pushed into criminal behavior because of imitation.

Glaser has suggested some modifications in the theory of differential association indicating that human behavior, including criminal behavior, is not simply a mechanical response. Rather it develops in a groping, ad-

---

[45] Donald Cressey, *Other People's Money: The Social Psychology of Embezzlement* (New York: Free Press, 1953), pp. 16–20.

vancing, backtracking, and sounding out way. His modification would restore the individual's role-taking and choice-making abilities. The crucial fact is not *association* in Glaser's revision but *identification:*

> The theory of differential identification, in essence, is that a person pursues criminal behavior to the extent that he identifies with real or imaginary persons from whose perspectives his criminal behavior seems acceptable. Such a theory focuses attention on the interaction in which choice of models occurs, including the individual's interaction with himself in rationalizing his conduct.[46]

Sutherland's theory of differential association, despite its problems, has fared better than his conception of values as cause of crime. Some research has attempted to show that delinquents have different values than nondelinquents but it has proven enormously difficult to get the delinquents to admit their values. Instead values have been inferred from their behavior; verbal statements about what is desirable have been held suspect. If we can safely conclude that delinquents do have different values, then the next step in verifying Sutherland's scheme would be to show that the groups from which they come have cultural values condoning crime. The limited amount of research done in this area casts doubt on the notion that there is extensive value variation related to law. We could go a step further and suggest that even if we demonstrated that delinquents came from groups that condoned delinquency, we would still be faced with the question of whether or not it was a distinctive subculture. Persons may share similar orientations because of their position in the social structure without sharing a distinctive subculture. A more modest restatement of the position on value conflict might assert that variant values (not necessarily subcultural) may under certain circumstances lead to conflict and crime. But it seems more reasonable to suggest that it is not conflicting values that generate criminality but a conflict of interests on the part of two groups who prize and covet the same thing.

The extent to which Sutherland's theory fits the empirical world is one crucial aspect in evaluating it. The others relate to how well it answers the questions posed earlier:

1. WHAT ARE THE WIDER ORIGINS OF CRIMINAL BEHAVIOR? Sutherland does not answer this question very well. His theory of human nature corresponds in part to the conflict theorists' assumption that man is basically good; his nature is so in harmony with society that he never breaks socially inculcated rules. But Sutherland parts company with the conflict theorists in their identification of restraining institutions as the

---

[46] Daniel Glaser, "Criminality Theories and Behaviorial Images, *American Journal of Sociology,* 61 (March 1956), 433–44.

cause of crime. He believed that crime was caused by values that condoned crime. These values eventually became enshrined in criminal traditions passed on from one generation to another. He does not say how or for what reason these values condoning crime appear in the first place. In short, he does not account for the genesis of criminal traditions. The most he says is that conflicting subgroups (in disagreement over what constitutes right conduct) emerge because of "social differentiation." He does not specify what is meant by social differentiation, only that it is a consequence of industrialization. Nor does he adequately define culture and social structure. Sutherland was impressed with the array of heterogenous subgroups that constituted modern society and tried unsuccessfully to incorporate that reality in his theory. Since we all belong to many subgroups we are at a loss to specify which are more important in developing violating definition without some idea of how these subgroups are linked. Marx, for instance, whose conception of social structure was well developed, could assert that classes and economic organizations determined the linkages between a person's subgroups—hence they would have priority in determining behavior. Sutherland was unable to do this with his theory.

2. Where in the social structure does the impulse arise to label certain behaviors as criminal? In Sutherland's view the impulse comes from the powerful and strategically placed who somehow are made to feel threatened and use state and criminal law to protect themselves.

> A certain group of people feel that one of their values—life, property, beauty of landscape, theological doctrine—is endangered by the behavior of others. If the group is politically influential, the value important, the danger serious, the members of the group secure the enactment of a law and thus win the cooperation of the State in the effort to protect their value. The law is a device of one party in conflict with another party, at least in modern times.[47]

What role do interest groups play in making and enforcing the law? Sutherland would say that they play a crucial role. Law making cannot be understood apart from the contending groups that attempt to get their views enshrined into the law. His article on the diffusion of sexual psychopath laws illustrates this conviction.[48]

Sutherland's emphasis on criminal behavior as normal in specific cultural contexts suggests that the basic problem is one of social and political organizations that determine what may or may not be permitted. Later Vold noted that crime in this sense becomes political behavior and

---

[47] Schuessler, *Edwin H. Sutherland*, p. 103.
[48] Edwin H. Sutherland, "The Diffusion of Sexual Psychopath Laws," *American Journal of Sociology*, 56 (September 1950), 142–48.

the criminal is therefore a member of a minority group without sufficient public support to dominate and control the police power of the state.

3. How well does the differential association theory explain the distribution of crime and delinquency? Since Sutherland's notions of social structure were not well developed he does not satisfactorily answer this question. He simply notes that the rate will be higher in those subgroups that have strong criminalistic traditions. Thus the high rates among blacks, working-class persons, and young males are attributable to the criminalistic traditions existing in these groups. Sutherland did not take issue with official rates that revealed a high incidence of personal and property assault among low-income persons. But he was aware that there was widespread law violation throughout the social structure.

Among the middle or upper-middle class, violations are more likely to be in the form of misrepresentation of financial statements, manipulation in the stock exchange, commercial bribery, bribery of public officials, and embezzlement. He also thought that these violations were more socially injurious than the crimes committed by lower-class persons. The upper-middle class is able not only to influence legislation relative to its own kind of criminality—defining it as less serious—but also to influence the way the law is implemented. Lower-class criminals are handled by police, prosecutors, and judges with penal sanctions in the form of fines, imprisonment, and death. Upper-class crimes either result in no official action or damage suits, or are handled by inspectors, administrative boards, or commissions with sanctions in the form of warnings, orders to cease and desist, occasionally the loss of a license, and, only in extreme cases, fines and prison sentences. White-collar criminals are segregated administratively from other criminals and as a consequence are not regarded as "real" criminals by themselves, the general public, and the criminologists.

4. What causes crime, or to what is criminal behavior a response? Criminal behavior is a response to values that condone it. All persons who are socialized into these values are potential violators. For Sutherland values are embodied in traditions that govern the lives of people who share them. It is possible for these traditions to provide a set of techniques appropriate to particular violative patterns. There may not be colleges devoted to the recruitment and training of criminals but there are analogous learning structures which graduate "students." Sutherland does not require a situation of "strain" prior to criminal behavior to account for it. Violators are not at odds with their subgroups; the varied subgroups that make up the total society all have adequate mechanisms for assuring that its members will successfully internalize its particular values. Each subculture is as efficient as any other in socializing its members.

5. WHAT ARE THE POLICY IMPLICATIONS OF SUTHERLAND'S WORK? Sutherland's early work for the President's Committee on Recent Social Trends called into question erroneous beliefs about the criminality of immigrants, and by implication called into question restrictive immigration policies.[49] He put himself on record again and again in favor of the Chicago Area Project, a community organization approach to the prevention of delinquency.[50] His lifelong battle against biological and psychogenic explanations of criminal behavior placed him firmly on the side of those who resisted programs to identify predelinquents and segregate the criminally inclined. His comparative work on the declining prison population of England suggested more imaginative penal policies as alternatives to incarceration.[51] At a more modest community level, he even recommended improvements in criminal statistics to the Chicago Police Department; in an article published in 1934 he reported that some of the modifications he suggested were incorporated into the reorganization of the department.[52] But perhaps his most provocative recommendation was in connection with his studies of white-collar crime. He was impressed by the way the legal processing of various crimes operated to the distinct advantage of the privileged. His remedy was not, however, to deal with white-collar criminality in a more punitive manner; rather,

> I do not say that it is improper to deal with businessmen in this manner but that until we extend the same courtesy in our system of criminal justice to persons of the lower socio-economic classes, we cannot expect them to have much respect for the law.[53]

The Work of Walter B. Miller

Miller began his research on gang delinquency in Boston during the 1950s using a settlement house as his base of operations. He interviewed a number of lower-class gang members and their families and conducted extensive observations of street corner groups. He reports that the delinquency research conducted during this period was motivated by a desire to reduce gang violence which was receiving extensive news coverage. The end of the Korean War shifted national attention from international problems to domestic violence but the bitterness generated by World War II, the Cold War and the Korean War lingered.[54] The second

[49] Sutherland and Gehlke, "Crime and Punishment."
[50] Schuessler, *Edwin H. Sutherland*, pp. 131–40.
[51] Ibid., pp. 200–226.
[52] Ibid., pp. 257–69.
[53] Ibid., p. 169.
[54] For a summary of the climate of the 1950's see David Apter (ed.) *Ideology and Discontent* (New York: The Free Press, 1964). How this situation affected sociological concerns is discussed in C. Wright Mill's *Sociological Imagination* (New York: Oxford University Press, 1959) and Alvin Gouldner,

world war brought social scientists in great numbers to Washington and strengthened their role in national policy making circles. One result has been that outside research support has become an essential feature of an academic career in the social sciences. The role of policy scientist that the Chicago ecologists experimented with on the municipal level was projected to the national scene. But in some ways the social climate of the 1950's was quite similar to the 1920's. There was a powerful nativist reaction to the changes taking place. This was evident in the resurgence of the Ku Klux Klan, the growth of right wing movements, and more restrictive legislation related to immigration. There was a deep desire for a return to normalcy. But in the 1920's the concern was related to foreign ideologies and their possible contaminating influence on authentic American values. In the 1950's the preoccupation was with internal enemies. The internal enemies were those intellectuals who left the universities for government service during the 1940's. The nativist resurgence symbolized by the Joseph McCarthy movement identified these scholars as traitors responsible for the growing influence of the Soviet Union in world affairs.

The impact of this climate on social scientists was detailed by Lazarsfeld and Thielens in their mid 1950's study *The Academic Mind.*[55] The political attack on the academic community led to greater acts of caution and withdrawal on the part of social scientists. This led to care in joining political organizations, expressing political opinions but most important in choosing research topics. The research characteristic of the period was decidedly non-controversial. It related to the maintaining and strengthening of large scale organizational structures. Though Federally sponsored research continued to expand during this period, the kind of research supported was politically conventional, neutral or harmless. It helped remove academics from a too close and continuous scrutiny or harassment by officialdom under the banner of a "value-free" science.

Children and youth were considered a legitimate research interest in the face of a growing child population and the appearance of a teen-age market separate from the adult one. Morris and Hawkins point out that the term "teen-ager" was unknown before 1946.[56] There were more children in school also; in the 1900's only 11% of the school age population was in high school, in 1930: 51% and by 1960 over 90%.[57] Concomitant

"Anti-Minotaur: The Myth of a Value-Free Sociology," *Social Problems* 9 (1962), pp. 199–213.
[55] Paul F. Lazarsfeld and Wagner Thielens, Jr., *The Academic Mind: Social Scientists in a Time of Crisis* (Glencoe, Ill.: The Free Press, 1958).
[56] Norval Morris and Gordon Hawkins, *The Honest Politician's Guide to Crime Control* (Chicago: University of Chicago Press, 1969), pp. 149–150.
[57] James Coleman, *The Adolescent Society* (Glencoe, Ill.: The Free Press, 1961).

with the growth of the youth population and their increased attendance in school was the expansion in the number of professionals working with youth. These professionals constituted a national audience for research on "youth problems," "adolescent adjustment," and "juvenile delinquency." It was in this context that Miller's work was done.

There is less biographical information available on Miller than on Shaw, McKay or Sutherland.[58] He is part of that second generation of American criminologists that came to prominence after World War II. He was born in 1920 about the same time that Shaw was beginning his career in Chicago. He differed from the earlier criminologists in social origins—he was urban born (Philadelphia) and not from a ministerial or strongly religious family. He entered military service at the age of 22 and served for four years during World War II and after. He entered the anthropology department at the University of Chicago soon after and completed his master's degree there in 1950. He worked there under the supervision of the anthropologist Sol Tax who pioneered in the development of "applied anthropology." His research during those years was with the Fox Indian Applied Anthropology project. The experience there partially accounts for his concern about how anthropology could aid in solving social problems. He held appointments later in Harvard's School of Public Health, Graduate School of Education and Center for Criminal Justice as well as in Boston University's school of social work and the Center for Urban Studies sponsored jointly by Harvard and the Massachusetts Institute of Technology. He completed his anthropology PhD in Harvard's Department of Social Relations in 1954. His dissertation was on the Indians of the Great Lake region, a far cry from urban delinquency. His credentials as a criminologist were established under a National Institute of Mental Health grant to study delinquency in Boston. His influence has been considerable despite his limited publication in criminology. This is related to his role as consultant to the President's Committee on Juvenile Delinquency and Youth Crime during the Kennedy-Johnson years and his persuasive restatement of the cultural transmission approach.

Miller does not refer to Sutherland in his writings and there is no information on whether or not he was influenced by Sutherland. But his formulation of the problem of inner-city delinquency showed that a cultural transmission interpretation could not be dismissed as irrelevant to present day problems. Miller has nowhere discussed his own intellectual orientations in detail nor the circumstances that accounted for his shift from anthropology to criminology. All that we know is that he considers

[58] *Biography Index,* 12th ed., Volume 2, 1973, p. 1709.

himself to be an anthropologist and is most comfortable using theories and methods developed from that discipline.

Miller's theory asserts that the prime motivation of delinquent activity on the part of street corner groups is an attempt to realize the values of the lower-class community itself.[59] The pattern of activity is not primarily defiant and reactive but comes out of the lower-class culture, "a long established, distinctly patterned tradition with an integrity of its own."

Conformity to the norms of lower-class culture automatically violates middle-class norms but there is no element of malice or resentment directed against middle-class standards. The behavior would exist if there were no middle-class norms proscribing it. For Miller, as for Sutherland, all behavior is valued. Miller uses the term "focal concern" rather than value because it is more readily derivable from direct field observation and doesn't suggest that there is any "official" ideal. Anthropologists, however, characteristically distinguish between all behavior and behavior which is valued or preferred. As Kluckhohn has put it:

> A value is not just a preference but is a preference which is felt
> . . . to be justified . . . (it is) not just the desired. The desirable
> is what it is felt or thought proper to want.[60]

This focus enables the investigator to distinguish those behaviors that are expressions of values as opposed to those that are adaptations to a particular situation. Miller ignores this distinction in his scheme; he implies that we must assume that all behavior is an expression of values. For Miller, as for Sutherland, delinquency is conforming behavior.

The major focal concerns that Miller observed listed in order of priority were:

1. concern with trouble versus law abiding behavior;

2. toughness and masculinity versus weakness and effeminacy;

3. smartness or achievement by mental agility, as opposed to gullibility or achievement through routine;

4. excitement and thrill as opposed to boredom and safety;

5. fate, fortune, or luck as opposed to their opposites;

6. autonomy and freedom contrasted with dependency and constraint.

[59] Walter B. Miller, "Lower Class Culture as a Generating Milieu of Gang Delinquency," *Journal of Social Issues,* vol. 14, no. 3 (1958), pp. 5–19.
[60] Clyde Kluckhohn, "Values and Value-Orientations in the Theory of Action," in Talcott Parsons and Edward Shils (eds.), *Toward a General Theory of Action* (Cambridge, Mass.: Harvard University Press, 1951), pp. 395–96.

The lower-class culture he describes is a result of the shaking down process of immigration, internal migration, and vertical mobility. It represents the common adaptation of unsuccessful immigrants and blacks. Sociological descriptions see lower-class culture in terms of its deficiencies by middle-class standards, or in terms of what lower-class street boys are *against* rather than what they are *for*. But the stable lower-class culture that Miller sees emerging is not reactive to middle-class norms—even though street corner boys spend 10 years in middle-class schools, these values remain external to them. Miller describes three groups: a law abiding street corner group, an aspiring but conflicted group, and a successfully aspiring upwardly mobile group. It is from the group that aspires to achieve but is blocked in its pursuits that delinquency comes. The first group includes boys who have accepted their situation and are adapting to it. The third group is moving up and out.

The key to Miller's explanation of delinquency is the female-based household. Households consisting of a mother, offspring from several males who move in and out of the household episodically, plus a grandmother and possibly several aunts make up the unit. Miller suggests that the female-based household is a natural adaptation to the instability of male employment. It is functionally related to the demands of the lower-class occupational style in which unskilled laborers have the appropriate outlook to tolerate the menial jobs offered—it is a culture that is extremely resistant to change. Miller is uninterested in changing this household pattern; in several articles directed to school personnel and social workers he has argued for acceptance and toleration of this distinctive family arrangement.

But at the same time that the female-based household provides recruits for the lower-level tasks that must be performed in our society, it also generates delinquency. The intense mother-son tie in lower-class culture creates problems of sex role identification for the boy. He views his mother as "sacred" and accepts her definition of men as "no good." His anxiety about masculinity propels him to the adolescent street corner group for the socialization that his family cannot provide.

There he picks up more fully the focal concerns that may eventually make him a delinquent. His need to belong to the street corner group and to maintain status in it leads to the demonstration of the valued qualities of lower-class culture: toughness, smartness, and the like. It is not clear from Miller's work just how lower-class themes get translated into delinquent prescriptions nor how the stable lower-class boy is able to remain law abiding. The implication is that lower-class focal concerns become sufficiently intensified or distorted only among those boys who are most acutely suffering the problem of masculine identification.

Evaluation of Miller's Theory

The most serious problem with Miller's theory is its lack of clarity. His focal concerns include elements of culture, social organization, and personality system. Miller's selection of the delinquent act as the unit of analysis also contributes to the confusion. As Cloward and Ohlin have observed:

> The problem with a definition that focuses exclusively upon delinquent acts is that it encompasses many street-corner groups whose core members generally disapprove of, at best tolerate, the delinquencies of other members. In such groups, delinquent acts are not a requirement of or a desideratum for membership. By Miller's definition, a social or athletic group which becomes involved in a delinquent episode is no less delinquent than are groups which are organized specifically for theft, street warfare, or other illegal activities. Failure to recognize the relationship between a delinquent act and the social and cultural structure of the group in which it occurs thus leads to serious problems of definition.[61]

Miller's central contention, that lower-class culture is a generating milieu of gang delinquency, seems invalid. Rather it would seem to be a generating milieu for conformity. The extensive research conducted on socialization by social class indicates that lower-class persons overwhelmingly become conformists.[62] They favor conventional goals for their children and use authoritarian methods (sometimes unsuccessfully) to help them realize them. They also support achievement values though not as overwhelmingly as their middle-class counterparts. This seems more related to structural barriers in realizing achievement values than to an alternate set of values that discourages conventional achievement.

Finally, Miller's theory suggests that there should be wide disagreement among different strata youth in their evaluations of conventional images. Yet the opposite seems to be true. Studies using Miller's focal concern design reveal that delinquents, lower-class youths, and middle-class youths all accept and evaluate conventional images more highly than delinquent ones. There are minimal class differences in the proportion endorsing delinquent perspectives, and all prefer conventional values over other ones. In short there seems to be no lower-class culture.[63]

---

[61] Richard Cloward and Lloyd E. Ohlin, *Delinquency and Opportunity* (New York: Free Press, 1960), p. 70.

[62] See Richard S. Crutchfield, "Conformity and Character," in Don E. Dulany, Jr. et al. (eds.), *Contributions to Modern Psychology* (New York: Oxford University Press, 1963); and Melvin L. Kohn, *Class and Conformity* (Homewood, Ill.: Dorsey Press, 1969).

[63] Robert A. Gordon et al., "Values and Gang Delinquency," *American Journal of Sociology*, 69 (September 1963), 109–28; Travis Hirschi, *Causes of De-*

90086

Miller's responses to questions of the wider origins of crime, its causes, and implications for prevention are determined by his conception of an autonomous lower-class culture:

1. WHAT ARE THE WIDER ORIGINS OF CRIMINAL BEHAVIOR? There are no wider origins of criminal behavior in Miller's account. Rather, separate cultures pose socialization problems for its participants. But he does note the links this lower-class culture has with the occupational structure of the larger society. These links account for its persistence. American society requires a pool of unskilled laborers who will perform the dirty work of society, and it is among these groups that delinquency flourishes. Apart from this observation Miller goes no further. Miller's theory suffers from the same deficiency as Sutherland's—there is no clear-cut conception of social structure and how it differs from culture.

2. WHERE IN THE SOCIAL STRUCTURE DOES THE IMPULSE ARISE TO LABEL CERTAIN BEHAVIORS CRIMINAL? Miller does not ignore this question, but it does not figure importantly in his explanation. He states:

> . . . it should be again noted that the statutes, usually prepared by middle class and upper class individuals who sit in legislative assembly, tend to endorse and perpetuate middle class norms.[64]

He does not see the criminal law as generating any antagonisms between the middle and lower classes. This seems strange in light of the fact that the lower-class group he is depicting, using female-based head of household as an indicator, turns out to be quite sizeable. He estimates that it constitutes 15 percent of the child-bearing units in the United States, or about 25 million people. The percentages range from 25 percent to 40 percent for the slum areas of large cities.

Miller's explanation of middle-class delinquency is that it represents the acceptance by middle-class youth of lower-class focal concerns. These concerns are diffused upward through the middle-class mainly through the mass media. But the behavior system is basically lower-class. This enables Miller to include those who act and think in accordance with lower-class culture as part of the lower class. The size of the lower-class population, on the basis of Miller's subjective definition of class, expands considerably to include between 40 percent and 60 percent of the population of the United States![65]

Although the lower and middle classes place different values on such

linquency (Berkeley: University of California Press, 1969); Paul Lerman, "Individual Values, Peer Values and Subcultural Delinquency," *American Sociological Review*, 32 (April 1968), 219–35.

[64] William C. Kvaraceus and Walter B. Miller, *Delinquent Behavior: Culture and the Individual* (Washington, D.C.: National Education Association, 1959), p. 119.

[65] Ibid., p. 63.

minor offenses as truancy, the use of profanity, loitering, and the serial mating pattern, in the final analysis there is no major conflict between the classes on fundamental values:

> Rape, murder, theft and assault fall in the more serious category. Such a violation . . . whether committed by an adult as a "crime" or by a juvenile as a "delinquency" tends to disturb citizens and officials profoundly. Killing a noncriminal member of one's own social group or committing forcible sexual assault on a woman of forbidden status is defined as a serious violation in all societies.[66]

3. How well does Miller explain the distribution of crime and delinquency? Miller's law violations occur with greatest frequency and seriousness among lower-class street corner groups. The delinquent group is differentiated from the street corner group in that its members engage in delinquent acts more frequently. He implies that for some reason the delinquent group is composed of boys who are "aspiring upward but conflicted" because of the lack of opportunity or cultural equipment. Miller is somewhat inconsistent on this point. He does not locate the delinquent activity among the "stable lower-class boys" who are primarily law abiding, but among those who are suffering some discontent. The reader is led to expect that the delinquent activity would be more characteristic of stable lower-class boys who would be the primary culture carriers. They would be the ones, neither frustrated nor conflicted, who would be enacting lower-class focal concerns most fully.

Miller accepts official rates of delinquency as accurate indicators of the real situation. He does not systematically take into account the biases of law enforcement. In response to those who point out that middle-class children may commit as many and as serious delinquencies as the lower class, Miller says:

> (Some) argue that the "hidden delinquency" . . . resulting in the middle class creates a situation in which a disproportionate amount of adolescent crime is unfairly attributed to lower class groups. However, the possibility of a far greater proportion of "hidden delinquency" to adjudicated delinquency in the lower classes should not be overlooked. A great deal of "customary" behavior in lower class communities (e.g., hanging out, gambling . . .) automatically violates legal norms. Yet only an extremely small proportion of these behaviors eventuate in legal actions.[67]

4. What causes crime, or to what is criminal behavior a response? For Miller, the problem that lower-class boys face is how to develop an appropriate masculine identity. Those who experience this problem most

---

[66] Ibid., p. 117.
[67] Ibid., p. 120.

acutely will act out lower-class themes related to toughness, excitement, and so forth to obtain status and a sense of belonging in a street corner group; but these acts automatically bring them into conflict with middle-class norms. The wider lower-class context is basically supportive of delinquency; some street corner groups condone delinquent acts more than others but why this is so is unclear in Miller's analysis. Nor does Miller account for shifts in the content or amount of delinquency. All he permits himself to say is:

> There is, however, wide variation in the forms and frequencies of illegal activity—among different gangs, at different age levels, in different communities, at different periods. Like tastes in popular music, preferred forms of crime are strongly influenced by fashion.[68]

5. WHAT ARE THE POLICY IMPLICATIONS OF MILLER'S WORK? The main agency impinging upon the lower-class family is the school, by virtue of nationwide compulsory attendance laws. Less significantly, social agencies also become involved with lower-class clients. Miller's injunction to both institutions is simple; develop an affirmative view of lower-class culture. He reminds school personnel that lower-class culture is by and large law abiding, and that their task should be to train and prepare youngsters for a law abiding lower-class life. He feels that this makes more sense than assuming that all lower-class children can or want to enter the middle class, or that all lower-class boys are inherently delinquent. Once teachers and other educators become acquainted with the adaptive style of lower-class life they can be encouraged to develop more realistic educational goals.[69]

The most mischievous implication of Miller's work is the assumption that lower-class culture is self-perpetuating. The notion of a self-perpetuating lower-class culture was utilized several years later to explain the failure of the various programs to eliminate poverty. Several additional features were added to the stereotype of the lower class that was incorporated into national policy: not only did the lower class have different focal concerns, but also fragile identity, weak character, and disorganized world views. This led to profound apathy on the part of lower-class youth so that even if opportunities were made available to them, they could not take advantage of them. In short, the failure of

[68] Walter B. Miller, "American Youth Gangs: Past and Present," in Abraham S. Blumberg (ed.), *Current Perspectives on Criminal Behavior* (New York: Knopf), p. 217.
[69] William C. Kvaraceus and Walter B. Miller, *Delinquent Behavior, Culture and the Individual* (Washington, D.C.: National Education Association, 1959); and William C. Kvaraceus and William E. Ulrich, *Delinquent Behavior, Principles and Practices* (Washington, D.C.: National Education Association, 1959), ch. 6.

lower-class youth to achieve in the world of work is not due to structural features like the absence of stable employment for males but rather to the internal deficiencies of lower-class life itself.

SUMMARY

The cultural transmission school includes other distinguished criminologists, but only Sutherland and Miller were selected for detailed treatment as representative of this larger group,[70] and such a selection is always somewhat tentative.

The scheme followed here is based upon the affinity of specific ideas and their chronological development. There is no doubt that with the decline of the Chicago group in the late 1930s that the cultural transmission approach dominated the field for a quarter of a century.

The first questions about its adequacy were raised by Merton in 1938 but not systematically pursued until after World War II. The new emerging approach pointed to a whole body of social theory previously neglected by criminologists as relevant to a comprehensive explanation of crime, delinquency, and deviance. This development is analyzed in chapter 4.

[70] A more extended discussion of cultural transmission approaches would include the work of Thorsten Sellin and Donald Cressey. See Thorsten Sellin, *Culture, Conflict and Crime* (New York: Social Science Research Council, 1938), and Donald Cressey, "Culture Conflict, Differential Association and Normative Conflict," in Marvin E. Wolfgang (ed.), *Crime and Culture: Essays in Honor of Thorsten Sellin* (New York: John Wiley, 1968).

4

anomie theories

The famous French sociologist Durkheim is credited with introducing the term anomie into the sociological literature in his book *The Division of Labor in Society* in 1893.[1] Parsons's analysis of Durkheim's contributions appeared in 1937 and began to introduce him to a wider reading public.[2] Because Parsons and his student Robert K. Merton were both located at Harvard University, the American anomie theorists have often been called "The East Coast School of Deviance."

By anomie Durkheim meant a state of normlessness or lack of regulation. Its opposite is overregulation or overintegration into the society. The explanatory power of the concept was demonstrated in Durkheim's book on Suicide, which suggested that anomie could explain a broader range of deviant behavior.[3] It is helpful to understand how Durkheim originally employed the notion of anomie and how this was changed after its introduction to the American scene.

[1] Emile Durkheim (George Simpson, trans.), *The Division of Labor in Society* (New York: Free Press, 1964).
[2] Talcott Parsons, *The Structure of Social Action* (New York: Free Press, 1937).
[3] Emile Durkheim (John A. Spaulding and George Simpson, trans.), *Suicide* (New York: Free Press, 1951).

THE THEORIES OF DURKHEIM AND MERTON

Durkheim, like many other European social scientists, was concerned with the transformation of a folk society to a modern one and the attendant problems caused by this shift. In the process of such a transition, a number of intermediate groups operating between the individual and the state (local government, the church, the extended family) disappear or are eliminated and, thus, human life loses its meaning. Anomie refers to the disordered relationship between the individual and the social order. Durkheim illustrates anomie using the world of business and finance. He noted that in a business crash, many people find that their personal expectations are suddenly and radically altered. Similarly, in a boom, persons who gain great windfalls can also become disoriented because their previous expectations become upset by strange new possibilities. In both instances the important element is the discontinuity between experiences and expectations, not the element of deprivation and gratification. People who find themselves in such situations are without regulation or rules. Society plays a regulatory role in the lives of people, which is necessary for their well-being. This regulation includes the distribution and control of an individual's gratification.

As Durkheim later discussed anomie, it was characterized as an absence of rules. In short, it was one type of social disorganization. The immigrants that Thomas and Znaniecki studied were faced with an absence of guides to their behavior in a new situation. Normlessness was one manifestation of the underlying process of disorganization. On the other hand, the immigrants could also be faced with a plentitude of rules that were unclear, inconsistent, or in conflict. Thomas and Znaniecki included culture conflict in their concept—at least two opposing sets of rules on how to act.

In 1938, Merton's influential article on anomie applied the term more broadly to deviant behavior.[4] This paper "is possibly the most frequently quoted single paper in modern sociology."[5] Merton later reported what he was trying to do in that landmark article:

> . . . I found myself focusing on the theoretical problem of the master sources of anomie and systematically conceptualized types

[4] Robert K. Merton, "Social Structure and Anomie," *American Sociological Review*, 3 (October 1938), 672–82.
[5] Albert K. Cohen, "Sociology of the Deviant Act: Anomie Theory and Beyond," *American Sociological Review*, 30 (February 1965), 5–14.

of response to anomie, . . . for, by this time, it was bound to become evident that the notion of anomie had broad implications that
went far beyond the special phenomenon of suicide, just as it was
evident that the concept was not an ad hoc idea, unconnected with
ways of thinking about social and cultural structure.[6]

Merton, like Durkheim, took the social system as his point of departure
and asked the general question: how is malintegration in society related
to deviance? In Merton's formulation, anomie does not stress the discontinuity between the life experiences of an individual, but between the
lack of fit between values and norms which confuse the individual. The
value he uses as an illustration is economic success in American society,
and he tries to relate this to the institutionalized and approved ways of
achieving it (getting an education, speculation on the stock market, etc.).
When there is a disjunction between cultural goals and the means specified for achieving them, specific and predictable adaptions can be expected to develop.[7] His paradigm focuses on the acceptance (plus signs)
or rejection (minus signs) of cultural goals and the means for achieving
them, and specifies typical adaptions by differentially located groups
within the population.

Modes of Adaption	Cultural Goals	Institutionalized Means
Conformity	+	+
Innovation	+	−
Ritualism	−	+
Retreatism	−	−
Rebellion	±	±

The first adaption, *conformity*, does not lead to deviance. It is basically
a middle-class response: to achieve monetary success in American society
one conforms and uses legitimate means. The experience of middle-class
people suggests that the fortunes of men bear directly on their merits and
efforts. The virtuous and industrious apprentice can be expected to
succeed while the wicked and idle will fail.

Innovation is the adaption that occurs, however, when the opportunities
to achieve monetary success are restricted. Persons who adopt this response accept the value of economic success but invent illicit means to
get to it. They take the shortcut (the long way around being closed off to
them). The pressure, Merton thought, to take the shortcut was greater in

[6] Robert K. Merton, "Anomie, Anomia and Social Interaction: Contexts of
Deviant Behavior," in Marshall B. Clinard (ed.) *Anomie and Deviant Behavior* (New York: Free Press, 1964), p. 215.
[7] Robert K. Merton, *Social Theory and Social Structure* (New York: Free
Press, 1957), pp. 131–60.

the lower strata, but he thought his scheme could also be applied to white-collar crime:

> On the top economic levels, the pressure toward innovation not infrequently erases the distinction between business-like strivings this side of the mores and sharp practices beyond the mores.[8]

Merton defines *ritualism* as a lower-middle-class response. The person holds onto the approved means but has basically given up on realizing the goal of monetary success for himself. ". . . Though one draws in one's horizons, one continues to abide almost compulsively by institutional norms."[9] Like conformity, this adaption does not seem to be a deviant response unless overcompliance with the rules is considered deviant. But according to Merton, the timidity, rigidity, and preoccupation with rules characteristic of low-level functionaries in large-scale organizations represents a departure from the cultural injunction whereby all are required to strive.

Retreatism is essentially an escapist response. Persons who choose this adaption reject both the cultural goals and the institutionalized means of achieving them. The examples he gives—drunkards, autists, drug addicts, vagrants, and the like—characterize this adaption as lower-class, occurring among those who, though they may have internalized the success goal, lack the opportunities or motivation to achieve legitimately, and so withdraw from the race.

Rebellion also represents a rejection of the goals of success and institutionalized means of attaining them. It differs from retreatism in that the condemnation is not secretly desired. The response is a revolutionary one. The example that Merton used—economic success—has been criticized as being too narrow. He tried to indicate later that other goals highly prized in a society could also be substituted and the same kind of adaptions would appear. Thus in a 1957 presidential address to the American Sociological Society he demonstrated how deviance develops among scientists because of their emphasis on originality.[10] Since originality is in short supply and the opportunities for realizing it are limited, deviance results. Thus devices such as reporting only data that support one's hypothesis, secrecy, stealing ideas, and fabricating data are employed by those who ascribe an unlimited value to originality. His comments about economic success could as well be said about scientific success:

> It is only when a system of cultural values extols, virtually above all else, certain *common* success-goals for the population at large while

[8] Ibid., p. 144.
[9] Ibid., p. 150.
[10] Robert K. Merton, "Priorities in Scientific Discovery: A Chapter in the Sociology of Science," *American Sociological Review*, 22 (December 1957), 635–59.

the social structure rigorously restricts or completely closes access to approved modes of reaching these goals *for a considerable part of the same population,* that deviant behavior ensues on a large scale.[11]

In summary, the approach proposed by Merton emphasized the values we hold in common. The value he selected for illustrative purposes was the one of economic success. It is a commonly shared value in the United States, and in an egalitarian society all are enjoined to realize it. The fact that the goal cannot be realized by a large proportion of the population increases the pressure to deviate. He concedes that this goal might not be internalized by the same proportion of persons in each social class. But his scheme only requires that a relatively large proportion in each strata be oriented in this direction. The disjunction between values and the approved means for reaching them constituted for Merton an indication of the malintegration of the social system.

Differences between Durkheim and Merton

Durkheim felt that in the course of a society's development it is possible for a state of anomie to emerge. This is considered an abnormal state, and a temporary one. Large-scale societies can exhibit a great deal of solidarity. The cement that binds them comes from their occupations and interest groups. Solidarity is achieved when these new bonds are finally substituted for the ancient regime, the church, or the medieval guild as a source of moral sentiment and internalized social control.

Anomie in Merton's definition is no longer a temporary phenomenon; it is a permanent feature of all modern industrial societies. For Durkheim, anomie was endemic in industrial societies but it developed only under the conditions of economic crises or burgeoning industrialism. For Merton, and even more clearly for Cloward and Ohlin later, there is something in the nature of industrial society that makes the emphasis on achievement characteristic.

> The industrial society, in short, emphasizes *common* or universal success goals as a way of ensuring its survival. If large masses of young people can be motivated to reach out for great social rewards, many of them will make the appropriate investment in learning and preparation, and a rough correlation between talent and ultimate position in the occupational hierarchy will presumably result.[12]

[11] Merton, *Social Theory,* p. 146.
[12] Richard A. Cloward and Lloyd E. Ohlin, *Delinquency and Opportunity* (New York: Free Press, 1960), p. 82.

The pressures leading to deviance can be explained in the normal functioning of the social order. By holding this goal of economic success constant, Merton has accepted it as a normal state of affairs. Thus according to Horton:

> The politically and essentially conservative content of his definition is apparent when it is compared to Durkheim. Anomie, defined as a disjunction between the success goal and legitimate opportunities to achieve success, may very well be a socially structured discontent in American society, yet Merton's anomie differs from that of Durkheim's in one crucial respect—in its identification with the very groups and values which Durkheim sees as the prime source of anomie in industrial societies. For Durkheim anomie was endemic in such societies not only because of inequality in the conditions of competition, but more importantly, because self interested striving (the status and success goals) had been raised to social ends. The institutionalization of self interest meant the legitimation of anarchy and amorality. Morality requires, according to Durkheim's views, social goals obeyed out of disinterest and altruism not self interest and egoism. To maximize opportunities for achieving success would in no way end anomie. Durkheim questioned the very values which Merton holds constant.[13]

Horton goes on to say that Merton's usage of the term would be an example of anomie for Durkheim. To define the concept in terms of the success goal, or to try and make it value-free, suggests that the sociologists are themselves pursuing the self-interest of the middle class. The situation where sociologists unwittingly identified with the values of the dominant groups and reified them as the values of the total social system was historically specific. Sociology in its earlier days represented a critique of existing social arrangements but the social trends and political developments of the 1950's discussed in Chapter 3 generated pressures for a more compliant and applied sociology as part of a national welfare policy.

However, the major contribution of Merton to criminological theory was not in the challenge he posed to existing social values but in his provocative formulation of the problem. Cloward and Ohlin claim that his system is a distinct advance over Durkheim's in consistency, completeness, and power to generate further hypotheses. Cohen has summarized most clearly what he thought were important contributions:

> The starting point, let it be noted, is not a definition of deviant behavior, but the specification of two dimensions along which be-

---

[13] John Horton, "The Dehumanization of Anomie and Alienation: A Problem in the Ideology of Sociology," *British Journal of Sociology*, 15 (December 1964), 294–95.

havior may vary. The classification of all points that can be located along these two dimensions defines the full scope of a sociological field which comprehends both conformity and deviant behavior. Furthermore, the varieties of deviant behavior are not described in terms of their unique and incommensurable concrete characteristics but are derived from the logic of the classification itself and stated in terms of the same conceptual scheme. Also, the scheme is a way of classifying actions, not personalities. The widespread use of this scheme testified to the felt need for such a scheme; the near monopoly it enjoyed testifies to the paucity of original thinking in this field.[14]

Acceptance and application of anomie theory did not follow immediately after Merton's restatement of it in 1938. His essay produced little immediate reaction. It only began to resonate in sociological circles after World War II. The first major application of anomie theory was sketched by Albert K. Cohen in his book *Delinquent Boys*.[15] It suggested how the theory could be applied at the national level. But it required a national climate that would be accepting of this new version of applied criminology.

THE WORK OF ALBERT K. COHEN

The political and social climate of the 1950s was characterized by a growing interest in an expanding youth population, and the emergence of a national audience of professionals working with young people. "Youth problems" were defined as a national problem by government and foundation policy makers, and an increased level of funding was available for research on juvenile delinquency. This initiative was part of a broader expansion of the federal government into health and welfare concerns previously ignored or dealt with by private or local groups. The central political fact was the appearance of what has been called "The Welfare State." The World War II experience had convinced government and industry of the utility of social science. The Welfare State's growth was accelerated by World War II but according to Gouldner it developed as a response to the earlier economic crisis of the 1930's.[16] That crisis

[14] Albert K. Cohen, "The Study of Social Disorganization and Deviant Behavior," in Robert K. Merton, Leonard Boorm, and Leonard S. Cottrell, Jr. (eds.), *Sociology Today: Problems and Prospects* (New York: Harper & Row, 1959), p. 464.
[15] Albert K. Cohen, *Delinquent Boys: The Culture of the Gang* (New York: Free Press, 1955).
[16] Alvin Gouldner, *The Coming Crisis of Western Sociology* (New York: Basic Books, 1970), p. 144.

called into question government's inactive role in the economy and created a demand for deliberate planning and governmental intervention to stabilize the economy as well as to address other social problems. The conviction grew that social problems (mental illness, crime, delinquency) could be solved by experts and advisors drawn from the social sciences. It is in this post–World War II period that the role of criminologist or sociologist as policy scientist comes into its own. During this period, according to Gouldner:

> Above all, what one sees is a vast growth in the demand for applied social science: the policy oriented use of social science by governments, both for welfare and warfare purposes, and by industry, though on a considerably smaller scale, for purposes of industrial management.[17]

The mass demand for social science talent during World War II swelled the ranks of the professionals. The impact on universities was a mass demand for higher education and an enormous postwar expansion. It was in this context that Cohen opted for an academic career.

Albert Cohen was born in Boston, Massachusetts, in 1918 and received an undergraduate degree from Harvard in 1939, just prior to the outbreak of European hostilities. He went to Indiana University to study sociology and received his master's degree there in 1942 as a student of Sutherland. The following year he entered military service and served in the European theater until his discharge in 1946. Soon after he began his doctoral studies at Harvard where he received his Ph.D. in 1951. His first academic position was at the University of Indiana where he remained until 1965. He coedited a series of Sutherland's papers in 1956 and saw his own work to some extent as an extension of Sutherland's efforts. His early work can be interpreted as an attempt to synthesize cultural transmission and anomie theory. His book on delinquent boys is not original research but a lengthy essay on working-class delinquency. It was not subsidized by federal or foundation monies but did suggest, however tentatively, the utility of social sciences in developing national policies for including working-class males more systematically in the economy.

It was in this social and professional climate that Cohen began to formulate his theories. He suggested that the crucial question a sociologist must ask is not how do people become the kind of individuals who commit criminal acts, which was Sutherland's concern; but rather, what is it about the structure of social systems that determines the kinds of criminal acts that occur in these systems, and the way in which such acts are distributed within these systems. The latter question is the central one posed by the anomie theorists who are concerned with the etiology of

[17] Ibid., p. 245.

crime and delinquency and its differential occurrence throughout the social structure.

Sutherland saw society as a set of warring subcultures with no center. Cohen's society is a class society where the major conflict is between the middle and working classes. He attempts to specify in more detail what it is about the situation of the working class that creates problems for boys who are socialized into it, and why it generates a delinquency subculture.[18]

American society, according to Cohen, places a high value on ambition, on getting ahead, on achievement. Academic achievement and the acquisition of skills that have long-range economic payoff are applauded. Middle-class families socialize their children to exercise self-control, to postpone gratifications, and to plan for the future. An extensive support system ensures that the middle-class child's intellectual, technical, and social skills will be rewarded later in an impersonal competitive order. The values related to ambition are routinely propagated through the public school system and are the basis upon which a child is judged. In Cohen's terminology all children are subject to the "middle class measuring rod."

The working-class child quickly learns that he is disadvantaged in the struggle for status. His working-class socialization did not emphasize order, punctuality, and time consciousness. It tended to be relatively easy going and spontaneous with little anxiety about achievement. The ethic of reciprocity rather than individual responsibility was stressed; responsibility was simply helping family and friends in distress. None of this is designed to insure mobility or success in school or in later life. The working-class boy, discovering that he is handicapped in the struggle for status measured by middle-class values, becomes anxious about the fact that he and his family seem to have lost in the struggle. He has a problem of adjustment and is in search of a solution. His solution is not an individual one since he shares the problem with others who come from the same class background. He is in effective interaction with other boys who have similar problems. Together they reject the school, the church, the settlement house—all representatives of the middle-class system. The delinquent gang emerges from this situation and is a collective protest against a status system that places lower-class youth at the bottom of the heap. It constitutes a primitive political reaction but one that is essentially self-defeating because the gang represents only a narrow range of interests, is highly visible to police, and lacks sophisticated skill in avoiding unequal tests of strength. According to Cohen, the pattern of the gang's activity is mainly determined by its flouting of middle-class values: gang boys play truant because good boys don't; they defy the

[18] Cohen, *Delinquent Boys*, ch. 4.

rules that stigmatize them as inferior. In terms of Merton's adaptions discussed earlier the working-class gang represents a *rebellious* adaption.

For Cohen delinquency is a cultural pattern with some distinctive features: *a strong sense of solidarity* with the gang, usually with hostility to the world outside. In-group solidarity is developed to a high degree; the gang is free of adult interference or control. The strong sense of solidarity makes gang members unusually sensitive to the gang reputation and alert to possible insults. *Acts are committed which do not bring financial gain.* Delinquent activity of the gang is purposeless and nonutilitarian. Acts are committed with an eye to immediate pleasure; there is little interest in long-term gain or cost. Cohen refers to this as "short run hedonism." Finally, there is a strong element of *malice and negativism* in the gang's delinquencies. Since the gang pattern is reactive, middle-class targets are selected for acts of vandalism with special pleasure in the aimless, violent destruction of property.

These features constitute a specific cultural pattern. In this context the behavior is typical and expected. The pattern is more likely to be found among boys than girls, among the lower socioeconomic strata than among the middle and upper class. Cohen relies upon official statistics to locate his delinquent subculture. In response to the criticism of official record keeping—that it reflects the bias of police and courts—Cohen retorts that no matter how inadequate official rates may be, they do reflect the actual situation, i.e., that working-class boys commit more serious and more frequent delinquencies than do their middle- and upper-middle-class counterparts.

Delinquent subcultures emerge among those whose status, power, and security of income are relatively low but whose level of aspiration is high, so that one cares about being at the bottom. Cohen sees the working class as a cultural setting where distinctive outlooks are shaped, but he denies that it positively encourages or condones stealing, vandalism, habitual truancy, and the general negativism characteristic of delinquent subcultures. He utilizes Whyte's distinction between the "corner boy" and the "college boy" response which is part of working-class culture.[19] He notes that there is a stable corner-boy pattern in working-class areas. Cohen does not discuss why a boy would be likely to choose a delinquent response over the more conventional corner-boy response. His analysis suggests, however, that the delinquent response is more likely to be chosen where status anxiety is strongest, where opportunities to share and express anxiety with others is greater, and where family supervision is less effective.

Cohen asserts that working-class culture is not able to protect its chil-

---

[19] William F. Whyte, *Street Corner Society* (Chicago: University of Chicago Press, 1943).

dren against negative evaluations because it is not sufficiently insulated from middle-class values. These values are proclaimed through the media and the school. But, more fundamentally, the "democratic status universe" characteristic of American society is accepted by the working class. Everyone is expected to strive and everyone is measured against the same standard.

Complex industrial societies with a commitment to moral universalism encourage the incorporation of subgroups and discourage the development of alternative values. The requirements of a democratic society for total participation and total assent generate pressures for the restriction of certain kinds of social differentiation which prevents the appearance of integral and distinctive basic value orientations.

In Cohen's view, the United States had become more stratified along economic lines during the 1950s than it had been during the 1920s. The desire for incorporation into the larger society by the older ethnic immigrants was an attempt to reduce social inequalities, but the effort also produced its own problems. The older ethnic subcultures lost their capacity to serve as a creative source of alternative values. The Chicago ecologists could observe the emergence of revitalization movements among the immigrants that insulated them, at least in part, from the larger society and made the assimilation process less harsh. But by the 1950s, if we accept the implication of Cohen's position, the only basis for the development of divergent values was a class one and this possibility was doomed because of the dominance of middle-class institutions.

Evaluation of Cohen's Theory

Rabow has challenged the proposition that working-class boys accept middle-class success goals.[20] Short and Strodtbeck found little evidence that members of delinquent gangs reject either middle-class values or those who administer the middle-class measuring rod.[21] By postulating a reactive subculture Cohen must account for delinquent behavior by imputing malice to the delinquents. This imputation of subjective dispositions has also been questioned.[22] By stressing malice and negativism, Cohen has missed some of the positive nature of delinquent activities. As one observer has noted, much that is labeled delinquent is not reactive or defiant but simply done for kicks—e.g., skipping school, rolling drunks,

[20] Jerome Rabow, "Delinquent Boys Revisited: A Critique of Albert K. Cohen's *Delinquent Boys,*" *Criminologica,* 4 (May 1966), 22–28.
[21] James F. Short, Jr., and Fred L. Strodtbeck, *Group Process and Gang Delinquency* (Chicago: University of Chicago Press, 1965).
[22] John I. Kitsuse and David C. Dietrich, *"Delinquent Boys: A Critique,"* *American Sociological Review* 24 (April 1959), 208–15.

snatching purses, being chased by the police, and staying out all night long.[23]

Wilensky has raised the question of whether theft—the most common type of offense for working-class boys—can be explained as purposeless or negativistic especially if it is done for gain.[24] Cohen's later clarification suggested that the nonutilitarian delinquent subculture he described is age-related.[25] It was basically a problem of early adolescence in urban working-class areas. But this nonutilitarian subculture gives way to a utilitarian pattern after age 17. That pattern, he states, is characterized by more systematic and pecuniary crime where the negativistic elements are almost completely absent.

Finally, DeFleur has shown that parts of Cohen's theory are not applicable cross-culturally.[26] Her study of delinquency in Argentina showed that short-run hedonism rather than status deprivation was a major motive for delinquency. She related this to the rigid class structure of Argentine society where there was a strong emphasis on remaining in one's station rather than striving for status.

Cohen's theory as reformulated and with the limitations suggested above fits well with the facts of working-class delinquency. How well does it measure up in terms of what it says about origins of delinquent behavior, policy implications, and so on?

1. *What are the wider origins of criminal behavior?* Cohen does not link delinquency to bad or evil conditions that most people might deplore, but rather to a quality the society as a whole cherishes and esteems: namely, ambition. He clearly points out the negative impact a widely shared value like ambition has across those social positions where the possibilities of achievement are limited. What Cohen suggests is that delinquency is one of the prices we pay for holding on to this value. Any attempt to eliminate it may involve a complete change in our existing social order. He implies that social disapproval of delinquency is not so strong or so widespread that we are willing to alter societal values relating to individual achievement. The situation creates status anxiety for working-class boys that is relieved somewhat by joining a gang. Cohen's perspective is an excellent example of what has been called in the delinquent literature a "strain model." It specifies the structural and

[23] Gwynn Nettler, *Explaining Crime* (New York: McGraw-Hill, 1974), p. 165.
[24] Harold Wilensky and Charles Lebeaux, *Industrial Society and Social Welfare* (New York: Russell Sage Foundation, 1958), ch. 9.
[25] Albert K. Cohen and James F. Short, Jr., "Research in Delinquent Subcultures," *Journal of Social Issues,* 14 (1958), 20–38.
[26] Lois B. DeFleur, "Delinquent Gangs in Cross-Cultural Perspective: The Case of Cordoba," *Journal of Research in Crime and Delinquency,* 3 (January 1967), 132–41.

cultural sources of the motivation to delinquency. Our achievement values create ambitious, hard-working achievers in the middle class and, at the same time, resentful, defiant, delinquent boys in the working class. In short, Cohen does not systematically analyze the wider structural origins of criminal behavior. His emphasis is on intermediate explanations relating to subcultural location.

2. *Where in the social structure does the impulse arise to label certain behaviors as criminal?* Cohen doesn't deal with this question at all. The society and its set of laws are a given. He accepts Parson's view of society as a relatively persistent, stable structure of elements that is relatively well integrated. Society is accepted as an equilibrium held together by certain patterned and recurrent processes. He also assumes that the social structure is based upon a consensus of values among its members. In this stance he completely rejects Sutherland's coercion theory of society. Also absent in Cohen's formulation is the suggestion that sociologists or criminologists should explore how laws are made and enforced. He does not focus on the critical role of defining agencies in the creation of rates.

3. *Which parts of the social structure supply a disproportionate amount of crime?* Cohen's acceptance of official statistics as a rough but accurate indicator of the real situation leads him to focus on working-class delinquency as more important than middle-class delinquency. His description of the behavior that is typical and expected among those working-class boys who choose this response captures some elements of resentment in their outlook. But in the initial formulation he did not account for other patterns of delinquency where the elements of financial gain played a more positive role. His later clarification depicts the malicious, negativistic, and hedonistic pattern as the "parent culture" in the sense that it is adopted at a fairly early age and is followed by more differentiated delinquent patterns where these early features are obscured or replaced.

Cohen's formulation did, however, permit him to go beyond Sutherland in locating more precisely where delinquency was likely to occur in the social structure. It even permitted him to say something about middle-class delinquency that related it to the occupational determinants of middle-class life.

He sees the development of a delinquent subculture among lower-class boys as the solution to status anxiety; the development of a similar pattern among middle-class boys is a way of coping with anxiety about the achievement of a male identity. The smaller nuclear family associated with the middle class, with the home located far from relatives and from work, makes the mother the dominant value disseminator and the dominant object of identification. Boys raised in this setting typically experience sex-role anxiety which can be relieved by engaging in "masculine protest." Middle-class delinquency provides reassurance of one's masculinity. Cohen does not discuss why, given his analysis, there isn't more middle-class delinquency. He implies that the anxiety may not reach the intensity sufficient to produce a delinquent solution, or that the boy's opportunities to share and express this anxiety with others may be quite limited.

4. *What causes delinquency?* Pressures to engage in delinquency result from the discrepancy between the generally accepted values of achievement and the inability to realize them. In this sense the culture is "malintegrated." However it can be made more integrated by a reallocation of priorities that would allow for working-class boys to "make it."

In an article published several years after *Delinquent Boys,* Cohen noted that the delinquency pattern sketched in that book was the common variety of delinquency out of which other patterns grew.[27] One of the sprouts is a subculture of adolescent theft, another is a conflict pattern, and the third is a heroin-using pattern. The theft and conflict patterns are both adolescent phenomena. Whether or not a boy's delinquency evolves into one pattern or the other depends upon the neighborhood in which he lives. If criminal and conventional values are integrated locally, the boy gravitates toward a theft pattern; if not, he chooses the conflict pattern. The heroin-using pattern, he suggests, emerges out of either of the former or both of them.

5. *What are the policy implications of Cohen's theory?* Apart from the family, which provides working-class socialization, the key institution for Cohen is the school. He points out that "it is the school in which working class children are most likely to be found wanting."[28] The major function of the school is to promote, motivate, and reward ambition and conformity. He also states that the boy reacts to the teacher. He can't easily shrug off the teacher's indifference and contempt.

One recommendation he cautiously makes is that steps should be taken to enable working-class males to compete more effectively for status, or that the norms of the middle-class world relating to ambition should be changed. He seemed keenly aware of the difficulties in changing middle-class values. In his view the societal situation is a given and something to which one adjusts. He seems pessimistic about any kind of intervention. One must always be wary of the unanticipated consequences of social action. There isn't much that anyone can do to make the system work better. Even though it may be malintegrated, there are built-in order-maintaining mechanisms that bring it back into equilibrium when it gets

[27] Cohen and Short, "Research in Delinquent Subcultures."
[28] Cohen, *Delinquent Boys,* p. 112.

out of kilter. Any attempt to interfere with these mechanisms might create further problems.

THE WORK OF CLOWARD AND OHLIN

The National Institute of Mental Health's mandate after it was created in 1946 was stated broadly enough to encompass any kind of problem that might bear on the nation's emotional health. Almost every conceivable kind of project was funded if somehow its relationship to mental illness was spelled out. One area NIMH staked out was the crime and delinquency one. They funded a project in the mid-1950s on New York's Lower East Side designed to address the kind of delinquency associated with educational and economic inequality. The project researchers were Cloward and Ohlin, who were attempting to translate some of their notions into an action project that involved expanding educational and economic opportunities as well as community organization. The project was called *Mobilization for Youth.* Presumably the solutions that were worked out in the slums of New York City could facilitate planned and deliberate change that could be implemented nationally in relation to poverty-linked delinquency. The project was being watched also by Ford Foundation officials concerned with the inactivity of the Eisenhower administration in the face of deteriorating urban areas. As part of this concern they funded a number of projects designed to restore the "grey areas" surrounding the downtown districts of a number of American cities. The term "grey area" referred to the zone of deteriorating real estate lying between the downtown and the suburb. Today we would refer to the same area as the "inner city." The school system in these areas was generally impoverished, careers were not available to young people, and the public and private agencies that served these areas were not responsive to the needs of the local citizens. The Ford Foundation projects were mainly concerned with this urban condition, but in the course of their evolution these projects came to focus primarily on the problems of youth. Cloward and Ohlin's conception of delinquency as a response to educational and economic inequality, suggested a broad program of intervention for dealing with the problems of poverty. These ideas became the common property of the specialists at the Ford Foundation and their governmental counterparts at NIMH both were determined to develop new initiatives, with sociological assistance, as soon as possible. Cloward and Ohlin's book *Delinquency and Opportunity,* published in 1960, was a statement of the new position and they acknowledge the support the Ford Foundation provided in developing their ideas.

Richard Cloward was born in Rochester, New York, in 1926. He received his bachelor's degree from the University of Rochester in 1949, his master's in social work in 1950 from Columbia and his Ph.D. in sociology from Columbia in 1958. His mentor at Columbia was Robert K. Merton and he states that his work on opportunity theory is an attempt to extend and somewhat modify Merton's notions. His teaching career has all been at Columbia's School of Social Work.

Lloyd Ohlin was born in Belmont, Massachusetts, in 1918. He was awarded a B.A. from Brown University in 1940 and his M.A. at Indiana University in 1942. He had contact with Sutherland there and was a fellow graduate student of Cohen's. His educational career was interrupted by a three-year period with the armed forces during World War II. When he returned he resumed his doctoral studies at the University of Chicago where he received his degree in 1954. During his graduate career he was a research criminologist for the parole and pardon board of the State of Illinois. After he completed his studies he was appointed director of the Center for Education and Research in Corrections at the University of Chicago. He joined the Columbia University School of Social Work faculty in 1945 and began his collaborative work with Richard Cloward.

Cloward and Ohlin saw delinquency as a response to educational and economic inequality. The development of their position in their book on *Delinquency and Opportunity* represented a conscious attempt to joint the cultural transmission views of Sutherland with the structural views of Robert K. Merton.

Ohlin was presented with an unparalleled opportunity to influence national policy on delinquency when he was appointed special assistant to the secretary in the Department of Health, Education and Welfare soon after the Kennedy administration took office. His position there was a logical outcome of his previous consultant relationships with NIMH and the Ford Foundation. His career illustrates the new kind of academically based policy maker that was one result of the growth of the Welfare State; a career that tied more closely together the overlapping worlds of university, foundation, and government.

For Merton the more serious the anomie the greater the amount of deviance. Strain is the important element. But Cloward in a paper written in 1959 noted that opportunity also is a prerequisite.[29] There are differentials in access to the goals of success which predispose someone to be deviant, but if illegitimate opportunities are not available, then illicit behavior does not result. The individual is also situated with regard to his

---

[29] Richard A. Cloward, "Illegitimate Means, Anomie and Deviant Behavior," *American Sociological Review*, 24 (April 1959), 164–76.

access to illegitimate means. Merton assumes that illegitimate means are freely available.

Cloward and Ohlin focus their concern not just on delinquency but on that delinquent activity that occurs in a subcultural context. They are interested in those forms of delinquent activity that result from the performance of social roles specifically provided for, supported, and required by the delinquent subculture. Access to these illegitimate roles is not freely available to all, but varies by type of community. In some communities there is a learning environment, and opportunity to practice new roles—differential association.

Cloward and Ohlin go on to say that the form of delinquency adopted is conditioned by the presence or absence of appropriate illegitimate means. The local milieu affects the delinquent's choice of a solution to his problems of adjustment. The degree to which deviant and conventional value systems are integrated in slum communities affects the relative accessibility of illegal means. Neighborhoods with a high degree of integration provide a training ground for the acquisition of criminal values and skills. It is in this kind of neighborhood—a *stable slum* area—that Cloward and Ohlin located their criminal adaption. Delinquency in this area was essentially a preparation for an adult criminal career.

The delinquent subculture was modeled after older criminal gangs engaged in thefts, extortion, and similar activities for illegal income and status. The opposite situation occurred when there was no integration between conventional and deviant values because of the rapid turnover of diverse populations. This neighborhood—an *unstable slum*—was the locale of Cloward and Ohlin's "conflict" adaption. Models for delinquent behavior come from other adolescents and tend to take the form of a conflict gang engaging in violence and vandalism. According to Cloward and Ohlin this is the least serious of the delinquent adaptions and the easiest to change. There is a narrow age range concentrated in adolescence when this pattern flourishes; it disappears after the boys enter the work force and/or marry. Not so the criminal adaption which integrates various age levels, in which criminal learning and performance are age graded, and in which powerful links are forged with the political order.

Also located in the unstable slum area is a "retreatist" adaption—members using drugs, specifically heroin. These boys or young men are characterized as "double failures" by Cloward and Ohlin. They have failed at gaining access to legitimate or illegitimate means. For Cloward and Ohlin retreatism has a somewhat different definition than Merton gave it. For Merton retreatism refers to those who have internalized some constraint in using illicit means. For Cloward and Ohlin retreatism is a response of those who are failures in both conventional and illegitimate worlds. The retreatist subculture is integrated with the criminal subculture as consumers are to distributors, and it is also highly resistant to change.

Their theory focuses more specifically on economic and educational success goals of slum boys. With some supporting evidence they state that these success goals are appreciated throughout the society and diffused among all strata. This assertion has been challenged by some critics who ask for further documentation. Closely connected with this criticism is the assumption that law violation is higher among the lower class.

Evaluation of Cloward and Ohlin's Theory

Some of the same criticisms leveled against Cohen's scheme on aspiration levels of working-class boys also apply to Cloward and Ohlin. The goal Cohen discusses is "status," for Cloward and Ohlin it is "success." The discrepancy between goals and opportunities for realizing them does not lead to delinquency directly in either theory. For Cohen the intervening mechanism is social-psychological, i.e., status frustration; for Cloward and Ohlin it is differential illegitimate opportunity. Both formulations have been criticized for the assumption that deviant behavior is more prevalent in the lower class, for the assumption of value consensus which underlies both theories, and for confusion on what disjunction between opportunity and aspiration means.

Cloward and Ohlin rely on official statistics as a rough but accurate indicator of law violation. Those rates reveal a higher incidence of delinquency and crime among the lower class. But studies of hidden delinquency indicate that law breaking is widespread and that official figures do not reflect this.[30] The whole theory is called into question if the assumption of more lower-class criminality is rejected. If lack of fit between opportunity and possibility of realizing aspirations is put forward as an explanation of lower-class motivation to delinquency, what accounts for middle-class deviation? More information on patterns of deviant and delinquent behavior by social class is needed to resolve the question. What seems to be valid is that low-income criminality is more visible and defined as more serious (unsophisticated personal and property assault)—hence more likely to be reported and recorded.

---

[30] Ivan Nye and James F. Short, "Extent of Unrecorded Juvenile Delinquency, Tentative Conclusions," *Journal of Criminal Law, Criminology and Police Science,* 49 (November–December 1958), 296–302; Maynard L. Erickson and LaMar T. Empey, "Court Records, Undetected Delinquency and Decision-Making," *Journal of Criminal Law, Criminology and Police Science,* 54 (December 1963), 456–69; Martin Gold, "Undetected Delinquent Behavior," *Journal of Research in Crime and Delinquency,* 3 (January 1966), 27–46.

Middle-class delinquency as revealed by unofficial rather than official reports seems "less serious." In short, the criticism on amount of lower-class criminality should not lead us at this juncture to reject Cloward and Ohlin's explanation out of hand.

Anomie theorists assume that there is a dominant set of values in American society that helps integrate it. These core values, even though highly abstract, are the direct cause of deviant behavior. Lemert has pointed to the difficulty in identifying a set of values that could be considered universal.[31] To the extent that there is agreement the values become meaningless—all men search for status, success, and so forth. He asserts that the distinction between values and means can't be maintained. Values become ends or means only in the context of a particular act in progress. There are no values that constitute ends all the time or means all the time. To apply this scheme Lemert suggests that the investigators determine what are "really" ends. Thus, in the United States the pursuit of money as a goal without respect to approved means can be called excessive emphasis on goals, but he insists that it is equally logical to say that money is the means toward more ultimate goals like happiness, and that excessive concentration on money is at the expense of ends.

He does not deny that there are traditional values that exist in the society as part of the folkways, mores, and the law, but even though they may be internalized, they do not account for much behavior. These values are more important in primitive societies where the link between values and behavior is more direct. Day-to-day behavior in complex societies can be accounted for by more salient up-close groups. Such groups are the determinants of our action. They expect us to do certain things or make claims upon us. They have more weight than abstract values in evoking our actions.

Douglas goes even further than Lemert in his critique.[32] People, he says, do not act on the basis of abstract views. Rather they construct meanings about what they do in the course of their interaction with others. These meanings are not generally stated—they are understood; they are background meanings, understood by the circle within which the meaning is constructed.

The discrepancy between opportunity and aspiration as a cause of deviation seems particularly fruitful if it is used more generally than in a lower-class context. It doesn't seem to fit lower-class deviation because

31 Edwin M. Lemert, "Social Structure, Social Control and Deviation," in Marshall Clinard (ed.), *Anomie and Deviant Behavior* (New York: Free Press, 1964).
32 Jack D. Douglas, "Deviance and Order in a Pluralistic Society," in John C. McKinney and Edward A. Tiryahian (eds.), *Theoretical Sociology: Perspectives and Developments* (New York: Appleton-Century-Crofts, 1970).

there is some indication that aspiration levels are not inordinately high there, the reverse of what Merton argued. But it seems quite appropriate in looking at pressures in other parts of the social structure. Thio has pointed out that wherever the aspiration-opportunity gap is great it generates deviation.[33] A wide array of studies done on interdisciplinary research in science, professional careers, an orthodox Jewish community, a military prison, the army, a governmental bureaucracy, and a Soviet firm supports this conclusion.

Cloward and Ohlin's theory has some empirical validity which is crucial in any assessment of a scientific explanation. But important also is how well it responds to the questions posed earlier.

1. *What are the wider origins of criminal or delinquent behavior?* It seems clear that Cloward and Ohlin, like Cohen before them, do not look to the master institutions of the society as causal. Their problematic orientation, much more explicit than Cohen's, implies that the society is basically sound and not in need of any radical reformation—rather, as Gouldner has phrased it, a "fine tuning." Their theory is framed to reply to current tensions—lack of economic opportunities among the lowest strata—within the framework of the existing institutions of middle-class society. Their theory, like Cohen's, does not devote much attention to the wider structural sources of criminal behavior. The questions they put to various explanations in a chapter entitled "Questions a Theory Must Answer" disavow any attempt to deal with wider causes. They recognize the legitimacy of questions relating to the social functions of deviant behavior but decline to discuss them systematically. They agree that crime and delinquency might serve important societal purposes but mention them only in passing. Their criminal subculture requires a community where criminal and conventional values are integrated and stable ties made with local political organizations. They did not go so far as to say like Durkheim that society "needs" its criminals, however. Instead their strategy of intervention suggested resocialization for those who had learned criminal ways, and reduction of opportunities for contact with delinquent role models. Their plan assumed that there was a consensus on the importance of preventing delinquency, hence all parties could be persuaded to support a nonpartisan program of reform. If there is a conflict of interest over delinquency reduction, then their plan for amelioration can be seriously challenged.

Their contention that the origin of delinquent behavior is subcultural can be evaluated on its own merits. By characterizing their adaptions as subcultures Cloward and Ohlin assert that the culture is able to recruit boys experiencing blocked aspirations, nurture their sense of injustice,

[33] Alex Thio, "Class Bias in the Sociology of Deviance," *American Sociologist* 8 (February 1973), 1–12.

neutralize larger societal proscriptions against illicit behavior, and provide a set of justifications for specific delinquent activity. Matza has raised the question of whether adolescent boys have the resources to manage such an undertaking.[34] Even if they were quite inventive they spend most of their time surrounded by adults who resist the values the subculture embodies. At any rate the persistence of the pattern is mainly related to the subcultural support it receives. These supports are not likely to be weakened unless functional alternatives to the delinquent adaptions are generated. The extent to which the group can attract new recruits and integrate itself with other groups in the immediate social environment will determine whether or not it persists. Another aspect of the persistence of delinquent patterns relates to the stability provided by links with conventional or quasi-conventional groups in the community.

Cloward and Ohlin's discussion of patterns of change in delinquent subculture directs our attention to the stages in the assimilation of ethnics characterized by differences in access to legitimate and illegitimate opportunity systems. These bring with them different forms of delinquent adaption. The first stage is one of acute personal and social disruption with the emergence of violent gangs. This is followed by an alliance with political elements to stabilize the area. As political power increases so too does access to legitimate opportunities. During this second stage the integrated slum comes into being. Alliances develop between racketeers and police and politicians. The delinquent subculture then takes the form of apprenticeship to organized crime. Out-migration speeds up at this stage. Slum organization enters the third stage when only the "failures" of the old ethnic group remain. Progressive deterioration follows. A new ethnic group enters and the cycle starts all over again. Retreatism is the response of the old inhabitants and a conflict adaption on the part of the new. Retreatism occurs when criminal opportunities lessen.

Cloward and Ohlin's discussion in terms of variations in access to legitimate and illegitimate opportunities historically represents a decided advance over previous contributions. Unlike Miller they are able to account for an increase in the amount of delinquency and change in its content without positing new, variant, and instant subcultures or the infusion of new value conflicts into the system. The superiority of their analysis is indicated by their approximately accurate prediction of what the future of delinquent adaptions would be.

2. *Where in the social structure does the impulse arise to label certain behaviors as criminal?* Anomie theorists operate with functional assumptions. They assume that a set of shared values knits the larger society together and that the cause of deviance is the fact that a large number of

---

[34] David Matza, *Delinquency and Drift* (New York: John Wiley, 1964).

individuals at the lower reaches of the social system accept these same values but are unable to realize them because of lack of legitimate opportunities to do so. This then generates a sense of injustice, which in turn leads to the use of illicit means to achieve, or to withdrawal. The values are ones about which there is consensus. The criminal law reflects this consensus. Parsons, Merton's mentor, viewed society's law systems as integrative, not disruptive, and certainly not as the view of one dominant class imposed by coercion upon another.[35]

Merton, Cloward, and Ohlin did not give much attention to the law, either historically or comparatively, although it seems clear that they did not view it as the result of any special interest activity. Their particular view of society, which stressed its consensual character, did not sensitize them to the role that interest groups play in the political arena, nor did it alert them to criminal and juvenile justice agencies as interest groups. The role of defining agencies in the creation of rates was not considered problematic.

3. *How well do Cloward and Ohlin explain the distribution of crime and delinquency in the community?* For them this was the first question to ask prior to any search for explanations. But they did not systematically take into account the bias of official statistics; hence their crime and delinquency is concentrated among urban, low-income, adolescent boys. Their focus is on norm violation studied statistically by the use of rates. They are concerned with the etiology of crime and delinquency and its differential occurrence within and between societies. There is no inherent reason why this perspective cannot map the widespread crime and delinquency that exists throughout the social structure but there is some question as to how appropriate their strain or discontinuity model would be in accounting for crime among the affluent.

Their scheme pinpoints where in the social structure strain is experienced as well as what conditions must be present before the strain can evolve into a shared solution. Their attempt to wed two different kinds of explanation—the cultural transmission approach and the structural—must be judged a qualified success. They point to the intermediate structural situations that are conducive to crime, and locate specific adaptions within particular neighborhoods. The blending of social structure with local milieu, whatever reservations one may have about the political thrust of the theory, must be considered an advance over previous formulations. The theory is inadequate insofar as it assumes discontinuity and then a leap to some delinquent solution. Cohen notes that this obscures the sense in which human behavior is constructed, and it is not

[35] Talcott Parsons, *The Social System* (New York: Free Press, 1951), ch. 7.

an automatic response to some stimulus. He suggests that this short-coming would be overcome by integrating George Herbert Mead's role theory with the anomie perspective.[36]

4. *What causes delinquency, or to what is it a response?* Basically, delinquent behavior is a response to strain. For the types of strain depicted—restricted opportunities for gaining societal ends, a feeling of stress, and limited access to modes of relief—this approach answers the question very well. It does not explain at all situations in which there is no apparent discontinuity or the kind of strain they posit.

Merton suggested that his scheme had relevance to white-collar crime but he did not systematically show how. No one has yet extended the theory to account for conforming as well as violative behavior though all would agree that compliant behavior is as problematic as deviance. Cohen has tried to go beyond anomie theory in suggesting that there are types of strain of which the disjunction between goals is only one.[37] People reacting to varied types of strain may get together and evolve a collective solution to their adjustment problems. Cohen also suggested that a theory should explain differential participation in a deviant sub-system. Thus description of a theft subculture would include not only older boys who are making it illegally in the absence of conventional opportunities but also the people who buy stolen goods. The delinquent gang, he suggests, should be considered part of a larger structure of action through which each by his deviance serves the interests of the other.[38]

5. *What are the policy implications of the Cloward and Ohlin approach?* More has been written on the social utility of their scheme than on any of the others discussed, and more effort has been expended to implement their recommendations. Hence more attention is devoted here to an analysis of their policy implications. Ohlin was asked specifically to help develop the federal attack on delinquency.[39] He and others worked out the idea of a special executive committee to be charged with drawing together the federal program. The creation of the President's Committee on Juvenile Delinquency and Youth Crime, established in May 1961 by executive order, was the result. Its chairman was the Attorney General and its members were the Secretary of Labor, the Secretary of Health, Education, and Welfare, and their designees. The committee was designed to function as a cabinet pressure group for a national and coherent

[36] Cohen, "Sociology of the Deviant Act."
[37] Ibid.
[38] Ibid.
[39] Peter Marris and Martin Rein, *The Dilemmas of Social Reform* (New York: Atherton, 1967).

policy on juvenile delinquency. At the same time, supplementary legislation to provide grants for research training and technical assistance for delinquency prevention and control was passed by the Congress.

The initial impetus was in the area of delinquency prevention but as more projects were funded a broader range of interests were addressed: migration, the cultural handicaps of slum children, adult illiteracy, and legal aid to the poor. It was, in short, the forerunner to the federal war on poverty; in fact, its congressional critics accused it of smuggling in a program to eliminate poverty under the noncontroversial slogan of "delinquency prevention." As the concepts of the program broadened so too did the various community organizations involved: schools, employment agencies, development authorities, welfare departments, city and county governments, churches, and a wide variety of voluntary associations.

Marris and Rein pay tribute to the early achievement of the program:

> To have drawn so many interests together was itself a triumph of diplomacy and disinterested idealism. To have concerted a strategy with so universal a range was all the more impressive. The principles of action became on the whole only sharper and less compromising as their scope grew more ambitious.[40]

There were two major assumptions underlying the programs that were funded to deal with the problem of delinquency. The first was that poverty was the major issue and related to poverty was the breakdown in the distribution of opportunities. Second, this breakdown was linked to a failure of institutional structures.

To address the problem of poverty meant an expansion of opportunity first and foremost. But implied in the view about poverty as cause is the notion of a self-perpetuating lower-class culture which was discussed earlier. It is not clear what reaction there was to this assumption by Ohlin and his colleagues, nor the extent to which it was their contribution.

Anomie theory does not imply anything about poverty cycles but, as formulated by Cloward and Ohlin, the anomie theory had a lot to say about differential opportunities. It seems likely that the assumptions underlying the action programs that were funded came from several different sources with the anomie perspective being the most influential. At any rate the causes of the self-perpetuating lower-class culture were perceived as circular:

> The children of the poor and ill-educated start school at a disadvantage and soon fall behind. Their parents can give them little help or encouragement; school becomes a humiliating experience, where they cannot meet the teacher's demands, and finally lose her

[40] Ibid., p. 31.

interest. They take the first opportunity to drop out. Without skills or confidence in themselves, they remain marginally employable. Some work off their frustrations in crime and violence, most will always be poor. Robbed of the self-respect that comes from earning a decent livelihood, the young men cannot sustain the responsibilities of marriage, and so they bequeath to their children the same burden of ignorance, broken homes and apathy by which they were themselves crippled.[41]

This has meant that a strategy for alleviating poverty could intervene at a number of points—the schools, the local community, the workplace, or the struggling family. For the President's Committee on Juvenile Delinquency, it meant dealing with the problems of low-income youth within the same framework of interrelated causes.

Also implied in the funded programs was a critique of institutional practices. It is not clear exactly how this particular set of assumptions was incorporated or who was responsible for it, but the notion is one congenial to sociologists since the days of Max Weber. Weber pointed out that while bureaucratic organizations are more rational, they also impose upon their officials greater pressures to conform.[42] Preoccupation with organizational loyalty then takes precedence over its ultimate goal—organizational survival becomes more important than service.

The institutions that formerly played an enabling role in assimilation of urban newcomers no longer play this role. It was the assumption about the failure of institutions requiring some basic restructuring that made the delinquency prevention effort different from a conventional social work solution. If one assumed that the poverty cycle was the major cause of delinquency, then an extension of social welfare would be all that was required. But the poverty cycle was joined with the assumption about bureaucratic self-serving. Both were responsible for the crisis in the inner city. Institutional practices were criticized on a number of grounds: first, agencies did not recognize the interdependence of all aspects of all poverty, i.e., that each agency in the low-income community carved out its own service area and carried forward its activities without reference to the others. Second, current practice was not innovative; agencies failed on this score not because of lack of resources but because of lack of flexibility or adaptability. Since all bureaucratic structures tend to regress, it is only by demanding innovativeness that the grip of self-justifying routine can be broken. The staff who recommended program funding developed some criteria for accepting or rejecting proposals. Money was not to be granted to do the same thing in the same way. Community

[41] Ibid., pp. 38–39.
[42] Max Rheinstein, *Max Weber on Law in Economy and Society* (Cambridge, Mass.: Harvard University Press, 1954), pp. xxii–xxiv.

programs had to indicate in what sense their programs were innovative and how they proposed to deal with the interdependence of the varied aspects of poverty. In addition, since all structures are inherently liable to rigidification, no new ones would be created as they would be subject to the same morbid life cycle. Instead a plan for revivifying the old structures was worked out. Old leadership under the plan was not to be replaced but new initiative drawn forth.

The committees that were set up in the various communities to receive monies were required to be self-liquidating. Since they were not designed to replace the conventional structures, the membership consisted of institutional members. The idea was that if second-level leadership (an "insurgent" group) could be drawn from the older bureaucracies and encouraged to work together, several things might occur. First, with the ideas brought from this community committee, the older institutions could be stimulated to be more coherent and responsive and, second, the morale and sense of purpose among the insurgents would generate the outlines of a new public service profession cutting across the traditional school, welfare, employment, and police bureaucracies.

Marris and Rein detail the difficulties the President's Committee on Juvenile Delinquency had in trying to implement their goals, and they call into question this entire sophisticated strategy of change. From the point of view of Cloward and Ohlin's notions about opportunity structure, the key question was the extent to which work opportunities were actually opened up by the program. Marris and Rein state:

> Such sporadic statistical data as we have been able to collate suggests that, while the project could claim many individual successes, and may well have increased somewhat the range of opportunities, they did so at great cost, and without benefit to perhaps two-thirds of those who sought their help.[43]

They go on to say that the strategy might have worked out but for the fact that the projects could not control the number of jobs that would be available. The program, if coordinated with a national employment program that was committed to the expansion of public service, might have succeeded. The projects could only achieve their aim, according to Marris and Rein, "within the framework of a national redistribution of resources which deliberately redressed the balance of opportunities between rich and poor communities."[44] They then suggested that more fundamentally the assumptions underlying the program may have been at fault in the meager success attained.

It may be that opportunities cannot be expanded without threatening

[43] Marris and Rein, *The Dilemmas of Social Reform*, p. 89.
[44] Ibid., p. 91.

someone and so the solution is not to appeal to institutions to reform themselves because present practice is an expression of the middle-class interests which support them. A better strategy might be to assert the conflicting interests of the lower strata with enough moral and political sanction to compel concessions and create a new order of priorities.

> Bureaucracy, as the instrument of power, can be taken to reflect the interest of the dominant classes. The apparent irrelevance of social services, judged by the needs of the poor, could have a harsher explanation than the devotion to ritual of organization men. It may suit the needs of the middle classes, whose well-being would be threatened by more generous and effective services to the poor. Those who pay for, control and staff the bureaucracies may well be reluctant to tax themselves more heavily so that slum schools may compete with the suburbs for the best teachers and their pupils for college places or the skilled jobs already decimated by automation.[45]

The experience of collaboration between criminologists and policy makers in programs of delinquency prevention and the elimination of poverty has raised some deeply unsettling questions about American society.

Herbert Gans has suggested looking at the poverty in the United States from a perspective other than the consensus one espoused by the anomie theorists. Instead of assuming that there is no conflict of interest between the poor and community and organizational leaders, he takes the position that there is. He believes that poverty is "functional" to the middle class economically, politically and culturally, and sets out to document his claim:

> The existence of poverty makes sure that 'dirty work' is done. Every economy has such work: physically dirty or dangerous, temporary, dead-end and underpaid, undignified and menial jobs. . . . The poor subsidize, directly or indirectly, many activities that benefit the affluent. . . . Examples of this kind of subsidization abound even today; for example, domestics subsidize the upper middle and upper classes, making life easier for their employers and freeing affluent women for a variety of professional, cultural, civic, or social activities. . . .
>
> Poverty creates jobs for a number of occupations and professions which serve the poor, or shield the rest of the population from them. . . .[46]

Gans goes on to say that apart from their economic significance, they also function as "symbolic constituencies and opponents" for a different

[45] Ibid., p. 45.
[46] Herbert J. Gans, "The Positive Functions of Poverty," *American Journal of Sociology* 78 (2) (September, 1972), 275–89.

political grouping. Conservatives need "welfare chiselers" to justify their demands for tax relief and an economy based on an ideology of laissez-faire needs a deprived population that is supposedly unwilling to work—in short, a negative reference group for the nonpoor.

From a criminological standpoint the suggestion by Gans is that we need the poor to uphold the legitimacy of dominant norms. The un-organized poor can be identified and punished as alleged or real deviants. The implication of this analysis is clear. If, as others have noted, the en-forcement bureaucracy selects those who can be processed without causing any trouble for the organization thereby, and more importantly providing proof of the significance and quality of the legal order, then liberal reform efforts like the poverty program seemed doomed to fail.

SUMMARY

The post World War II period was a propitious time for the evolution of criminological theory. The war experience had solidified public accep-tance of the social sciences and a close working relationship was forged between social scientists and policy makers.

In the crime and delinquency area the relationship culminated in the effort to develop a national policy for the elimination of delinquency and the poverty associated with it. But the relationship was short-lived, partly because its lack of success, and the growing disenchantment of social scientists with American policy, most importantly abroad but also at home. It was during the 1960s that a small group of sociologists inter-ested in social problems began questioning the pieties of society gen-erally.

Their effort led eventually to a full-scale critique of American society and a new development in criminology. The image of society that the critics presented was at odds with the consensus view of the anomie theorists. Society is perceived by the new criminologists as sprawling, highly diverse, amorphous, and deeply conflicted. The critical area of concern becomes, for them, not criminal behavior but how behavior be-comes defined as criminal and how control institutions generally operate. A discussion of their approach follows in Chapter 5.

5

interactionist

and

conflict

approaches

The anomie theorists introduced the term "deviance" to describe the kind of rule breaking they were interested in studying. The term was an effort to get away from the biases of reformers who were concerned about traditional social problems such as crime, suicide, drug use, prostitution. By renaming the social problems area, presumably rule breaking could be studied in a "value-free" way. It represented for the deviance specialists a break with the view that "evil causes evil" and more simplistic notions about eliminating or reducing crime and delinquency.

As noted in Chapter 4, they ignored questions about how crime rates are generated and what they represent. "It is this topic that is the central concern of the interactionist (or labeling) and conflict schools. Rather than focusing on the causes of criminal behavior, as do the anomie theorists, they look at the process of criminalization itself, or how the label "criminal" is constructed. They contend that the label is the end product of a series of interactions between interest groups and individuals whose life styles or values make them "vulnerable" to official processing. The ascendance of this critical view of crime causation was the result of the work of a small group of scholars working from what may be described as a "conflict tradition" in sociology and criminology."

HISTORICAL BACKGROUND

Edwin Lemert in a very influential book published in 1951 first raised the question of the social reactions to "improper" behavior which have the effect of generating deviant commitment and possibly a criminal career.[1] His insight pointed to a phenomenon that we have experienced at one time or another: the self-fulfilling prophecy. The same observation was made by other social investigators prior to Lamert, most notably by Marx.

In his discussion of English criminal statistics over 100 years ago Marx foreshadowed what later came to be called the "labeling approach":

> The apparent decrease in crime, however, since 1854 is to be exclusively attributed to some technical changes in British Jurisdiction; to the juvenile offender's act in the first instance and, in the second instance, to the operation of the Criminal Justice Act of 1855, which authorizes Police Magistrates to pass sentences for short periods with the consent of prisoners. Violations of the law are generally the offspring of the economical agencies beyond the control of the legislator, but, as the working of the Juvenile Offender's Act testified, it depends to some degree on official society to stamp certain violations of its rules as crimes or transgressions only. This difference of nomenclature so far from being indifferent, decided on the fate of thousands of men, and the moral tone of society. Law itself may not only punish crime but improvise it.[2]

The American criminologist Frank Tannenbaum, writing in 1938, called the phenomenon "the dramatization of evil."[3] By loudly announcing the violator's infraction both he and the community accept the judgment as a fixed description. Thereafter he is expected to live up to his reputation.

But neither Marx nor Tannenbaum incorporated this observation systematically into their investigations of crime. Based upon this insight, Lemert proposed three different areas for investigation which emphasized societal reactions to behavior: (1) the structure and process of social control and control agencies; (2) the social-psychological impact of reactions to erstwhile and unpatterned deviations; and (3) historical and comparative themes.

[1] Edwin M. Lemert, *Social Pathology* (New York: McGraw Hill, 1951).
[2] Karl Marx, "Population, Crime and Pauperism," *New York Daily Tribune,* September 16, 1859.
[3] Frank Tannenbaum, *Crime and the Community* (New York: Columbia University Press, 1939).

It was in his early work on social pathology that Lemert introduced the notions of primary and secondary deviation. Primary deviation arises in a variety of contexts and its causes are varied. Lemert maintains that these deviations are not significant until they are organized subjectively and transformed into active roles and become the criteria for assigning status.

> The deviant individuals must react symbolically to their own behavior aberrations and fix them in their sociopsychological patterns. The deviations remain primary deviations or symptomatic and situational as long as they are rationalized or otherwise dealt with as functions of a socially acceptable role . . . When a person begins to employ his deviant behavior or a role based upon it as a means of defense, attack, or adjustment to the overt and covert problems created by the consequent societal reaction to him, his deviation is secondary.[4]

He traces the passage from initial deviation, a penalty associated with it, further primary deviation, followed by stronger penalties and rejections, further deviation, community stigmatization, and ultimate acceptance of deviant social status by the original actor. Lemert states then that

> In effect, the original causes of the deviation recede and give way to the central importance of the disapproving, degradational and labeling reactions of society.[5]

In Lemert's imagery, and that of many labelists who have followed him, initial deviance is usually unwitting or impulsive, not well thought out or conscious. Lemert's scheme was sufficiently comprehensive to include the initial process of rule making. The study of how rules are made inevitably directs attention to social conflict and the interests underlying the process by which laws are made and enforced. He was keenly aware of the crucial role played by interest groups in law creation. His concern was shared to some extent by Sutherland though there is little indication that Sutherland exerted any influence on Lemert or vice versa.

Sutherland's major contribution to the interest group tradition in criminology was his study of sexual psychopath laws and their diffusion.[6] Sutherland noted that the pressures to enact legislation dealing with sexual offenders typically goes through three stages.

The process begins when a few serious sex crimes are committed in

---

[4] Lemert, *Social Pathology*, pp. 75–76.
[5] Edwin M. Lemert, *Human Deviance, Social Problems and Social Control* (Englewood Cliffs, N. J.: Prentice Hall, 1967), p. 17.
[6] Edwin H. Sutherland, "The Sexual Psychopath Laws," *Journal of Criminal Law and Criminology 56* (January–February 1950), 543–54.

rapid succession creating widespread fear and tension. The news media are critical at this stage because they capture and hold public attention further adding to the tension. The second stage is agitated community activity linked to the fear, usually involving calls for more effective legislation and increased police activity. The third phase, prior to the enactment of a law, is the creation of a committee to determine what should be done. Sutherland pointed out that the psychiatrists enter the picture at this phase and exercise decisive influence. Their view is that sexual offenders should be treated as patients. The sexual psychopath laws usually specify that court diagnoses shall be made by psychiatrists. In short, psychiatrists have an economic interest in an extension of the procedure. Sutherland questions the underlying assumptions of the sexual psychopath laws: that danger to women and children from sexual offenders is very great and the situation is worsening, most sex crimes are committed by "degenerates" who persist in sexual assaults throughout their lives, that they give warning by first committing minor offenses, that any psychiatrist can diagnose them at an early age, and that those defined as sexual psychopaths should be confined until a psychiatrist states they are cured. The psychiatrists in this situation function as an interest group committed to enlarging their authority and practice at the expense of a relatively small and harmless part of the population.

The position represented by Sutherland in his 1950 articles and by Lemert in his discussion of social pathology published one year later did not attract much attention among criminologists impressed by anomie explanations of crime. It represented a point of view that stressed social conflict in a period when most students of crime were more concerned with problems of order and social cohesion. It was only in the 1960s that the critical focus of Sutherland's and Lemert's perspective was "rediscovered" by a wider audience.

Howard S. Becker: Social Context and Individual Background. Becker reports that he wrote the original statement on labeling in 1954.[7] His interest at that time was not in challenging any kind of orthodoxy about crime causation. Rather he was trying to extend some insights developed in the study of educational and work organizations to the social control area. His work was published in 1963 and struck strong responsive chords among younger sociologists and criminologists. It became a focus for dissent in the 1960's. A burst of critical studies followed. Their concern was less with the theoretical inadequacies of anomie theory than with accounting for the increasing social conflict in the 1960s. The labeling

[7] Julius Debro, "Dialogue with Howard S. Becker," *Issues in Criminology* 5(2) (Summer, 1970), 159–79.

perspective was partly a response to the postwar acceleration of social change as well as to the growth of large scale bureaucratic organizations and their increasing oppressive involvement in the lives of individuals.

The easy identification of criminologists with government policy was shaken in the 1960s by the civil rights and antiwar movements. The civil rights movement showed how law and public policy could be utilized to discriminate against blacks. Obviously the laws that justified these patterns were not a crystallization of the general will but the result of interest-group pressure. The question as Skolnick put it became:

> How is it that these laws, which were based upon both irrational assumptions and phony evidence, how is it that the political structure allowed these laws to be passed?[8]

The civil rights movement had its roots primarily in the agricultural communities of the South and later spread to the ghettos of the North. Its demands for justice exerted a powerful appeal on idealistic college students who identified with the struggle and became participants in it. The civil rights movement formed the training ground, inspiration, and stimulus to the antiwar movement composed of disaffected college students. The struggle both for black liberation and for disengagement in Vietnam had its supporters among social scientists, especially among those just beginning their professional careers who were not that far removed from their students in age or social condition. The impact of the student movements in the 1960s was to politicize university campuses and to challenge their insulation and remoteness from practical life. The student critique of American institutions focused specifically on the university as an impersonal and dehumanizing bureaucracy. The flowering of the labelists at this particular historical moment is not understandable apart from this context. Their talent for demystifying the labeling process and laying bare the self-serving interests of control agencies has given a kind of exposé quality to their work, as Lemert notes. It is not surprising that much of the style, theme, and findings of the labelists have made their way into the protest literature. The appearance of Becker's book *The Outsiders* in 1963 became a platform—one might be tempted to say, manifesto—of the new approach.[9] This is somewhat incongruous since Becker was a generation removed from those who so enthusiastically embraced his perspective.

Becker was born in Chicago in 1928, a contemporary of Miller, Cohen, Cloward and Ohlin, though their intellectual or professional careers never

[8] Gene E. Carte, "Dialogue with Jerome Skolnick," *Issues in Criminology* 4(2) (Fall 1969), 109–22.

[9] Howard S. Becker, *Outsiders: Studies in the Sociology of Deviance* (New York: Free Press, 1963).

intersected. Becker attended the University of Chicago where he received his undergraduate degree in 1946. He completed his master's degree in sociology in 1949. His master's thesis was on dance musicians and he reports that he played piano at local clubs all during his university career. His life style and work could be considered the embodiment of the "cool" sociologist. He completed his Ph.D. in 1951 with a dissertation on the career of the public school teacher. He reports that his labeling views developed out of a study of occupations and professions rather than as a reaction to a wider political context. His interests were ones that were "internal" to sociology rather than external. He indicates that I. L. Horowitz' article on political deviance made him more explicitly aware of the political character of deviance.[10] Yet the so-called "Chicago style" gave him an orientation that cultivated the role of sociologist as critic: an irreverence for authority and established institutions. Becker noted that there could be careers other than occupational. In a highly differentiated society persons have many careers, for example: workers, family members, association members. It was a short step from this observation to looking at deviant careers. While still a graduate student Becker became a research sociologist at the Institute for Juvenile Research and completed a study of marijuana use among jazz musicians that emphasized sequential involvement. He states quite modestly that his involvement in the field of careers has been quite minimal. He considers himself basically a sociologist whose primary interests are in educational organizations, social psychology, and qualitative methodology.

THE INTERACTIONIST APPROACH: LABELING

Proponents of this approach agree that it does not yet constitute a full-blown theory with a set of identifiable propositions. Whether it ever will is debatable. Instead the interactionist approach, or labeling perspective as it is also called, consists of a number of ideas designed to sensitize us to specific features of deviance and crime. Becker has pointed out that social groups create deviance, and crime and deviant behavior is that which is so labeled. The social audience is the critical factor of deviance definition. This central idea has led some criminologists to speak of the "social reaction school" rather than the labeling approach as a more accurate description. This orientation represents a sharp break with older conceptions of deviance, which assumed that there was something in-

[10] Irving L. Horowitz and Martin Liebowitz, "Social Deviance and Political Marginality: Toward a Redefinition of the Relation Between Sociology and Politics," *Social Problems* 15 (Winter 1963), 280–96.

herent in criminals or deviants that distinguished them from non-deviants. In this newer conception the criminal is one to whom the label has been successfully applied. Crime then is not a quality that lies in the behavior but in the interaction between those who perform certain acts and those who respond to them. As Becker has put it:

> The conventional style of studying deviance has focused on the deviant himself and has asked its questions mainly about him. Who is he? Is he likely to keep being that way? The new approach sees it as always and everywhere a process of interaction between at least two kinds of people: those who commit (or are said to have committed) a deviant act and the rest of society, perhaps divided into several groups itself. The two groups are seen in complementary relationship. One cannot exist without the other. . . .[11]

Becker has indicated that he prefers "interactionist" rather than labeling as a more accurate term for the perspective. The formulation introduces a political dimension to crime definition. It becomes rule violation in the context of two groups in contention: one that feels threatened and has the power and organization to do something about it, and the other, which is unable to resist. This interpretation points the investigator in the direction of the immediate origins of social reaction rather than the wider context within which it occurs. Most of the research done from the labeling stance has focused on immediate social reactions and the impact on the actor, not on the creation of labels in the first instance.

The deviance-defining process described by the labelists makes questions about the cause of crime or deviance inappropriate. Since crime is not a static entity but a dynamic process the question posed by anomie theorists (what causes crime?) is not asked. The question on crime causation would be rephrased by the labelist as: what is the cause of the label "criminal" being affixed? Their response would be: the extent to which the "crime" is known, or known about. There can be no labels affixed until the alleged violation is known to others. The critical questions posed in this perspective are: (1) who labels whom, and (2) what consequences does the application of the label have for the labeled and the labelers? The labelers are usually in a position to benefit by the application of a label, but to do so they must have a negative label to apply and the power to do so. To be effective that power must be accepted by others, both those who are being labeled and critical third parties. Labelers are control agents like police, judges, and guards who have a mandate to deal with "problem" populations. Self-labeling is also possible but the perspective has focused more on public stigmatization.

[11] Howard S. Becker (ed.), *The Other Side: Perspectives on Deviance* (New York: Free Press, 1964), p. 3.

The sympathy of the labelists (those who adhere to the labeling perspective) as opposed to the labelers (those who label others) is generally on the side of the powerless who are the victims of the process. There is a strong identification with the criminal or deviant. Labelists, as Gouldner has noted, not only study the deviant's social world, they speak on his behalf and affirm the authenticity of his life style.[12] Some sociologists have characterized this approach as "underdog sociology" and refer to its exponents as "the cool school."

Becker has characterized the major orientation of the underdog sociologists:

> (They have) . . . a disposition to assume that normals are less moral than typically portrayed and a disposition to assume that deviants are considerably more moral than is commonly thought—the sociologists of deviance assume that the underdog is always right and those in authority always wrong.[13]

Taking the perspective of the victimized is defended on the grounds that conventional sociology narrowly reflects the viewpoint of established authority. Hence labelists are generally likely to argue for tolerance of lifestyles different from those of the dominant middle class, and to argue that deviant subcultures should be "appreciated" rather than "corrected." In their view, the major obstacles to appreciation of diversity are powerful interest groups who have a stake in enforcing deviant labels. This insight has generated some limited research into social structure to answer Becker's question: "Who rules and why?"

Consequences of Labeling

The impact on the labeled person is generally negative. If we are talking about someone defined as a delinquent, the end product would be a boy declared a ward of the juvenile court and adjudged to be delinquent by peers, school, family, and finally by himself. The process creates expectations that the person will persist in violating, thus leading to a self-fulfilling prophecy. The delinquent's life chances are also affected, his opportunities are restricted. This may lead to further elaboration of the delinquent role as an attack on or defense against the labelers. This phenomenon is called "secondary deviation." In short the major consequence of labeling for the labeled is to speed him along on a delinquent or criminal career.

---

[12] Alvin W. Gouldner, "The Sociologist as Partisan, Sociology and the Welfare State," *American Sociologist*, 3 (1968), 103–16.
[13] Becker, *The Other Side*, p. 5.

Not much has been done to date to explore the impact of labeling on the labelers. Erikson's landmark study of witchcraft in Puritan New England showed that labeling had positive consequences for the community or groups that applied the label. The deviant act in early New England "creates a sense of mutuality among the people in the community by supplying a focus for group feeling."[14] Erikson goes on to say:

> Deviant forms of behavior, by marking the outer edges of group life, give the inner structure its special character, and thus supply the framework within which the people of the group develop an orderly sense of their own cultural identity.[15]

Evaluation of the Labeling Perspective

Fisher designed a study to test the labelist hypothesis that the public label is antecedent to the negative evaluation.[16] He compared the school records and evaluations of high school students publicly known as delinquents and those not. He found that negative evaluations were slightly more evident in the records of the experimental group. However, there were no significant differences between the academic performance of the experimental group prior to and following labeling and the control group over the same period of time. Fisher concluded that Becker's formulations as stated were too vague and that more specific hypotheses were needed.

The evidence on impact of the label on those labeled has been mixed. Labelists assert that it produces negative consequences. Chambliss has attempted to show that imprisonment produces a mixed reaction: it provokes more deviance in those who are powerless (like public drunks and drug addicts) but discourages further deviance on the part of the powerful.[17] Schwartz and Skolnick's study of legal stigma addressed the question of the impact a negative label has on a person's life chances.[18] They tested the responses of potential employers to an individual's past prosecution for crime. They discovered pronounced class differences in terms of deprivation. Unskilled workers whose records indicated that they were acquitted of a crime were more negatively evaluated by prospective em-

---

[14] Kai T. Erikson, *Wayward Puritans: A Study in the Sociology of Deviance* (New York: John Wiley, 1966).

[15] Ibid., p. 13.

[16] Sethard Fisher, "Stigma and Deviant Careers in School," *Social Problems,* 20 (Summer 1972), 78–83.

[17] William J. Chambliss, "Types of Deviance and the Effectiveness of Legal Sanction," *Wisconsin Law Review* (Summer 1967), pp. 703–23.

[18] Richard D. Schwartz and Jerome H. Skolnick, "Two Studies of Legal Stigma," in Becker (ed.), *The Other Side*, pp. 103–17.

ployers than those never accused; those who had been convicted experienced even greater negative response than those acquitted. On the other hand, malpractice actions, even when they resulted in a judgment against the doctor, were not usually followed by negative consequences; in some cases it seemed to have a positive effect on the professional position of the defendant.

Other studies have shown that school children who are viewed as educationally backward become educationally backward, and that children viewed as educationally capable become so.[19] The labelists assert that the self is a social construct and the way we come to see ourselves is in part a response to the way others see us. Whether or not we accept the label is another question. This hypothesis seems more appropriate when discussing those whose identities have not yet been formed or who, for some reason, are peculiarly vulnerable to being labeled. It seems more accurate to say that adults involved in rule breaking generally know what they are doing, take the larger group's disapproval into account, and are aware of the potential negative consequences; but they do not necessarily accept any public label as a part of their own identity. In short, people are not passive objects whose behavior is ultimately determined by other labelers.

Thio has pointed to another shortcoming of the labeling perspective: its conservative bias.[20] Thio asserts that by focusing on officially labeled deviance or crime the labelists accept status quo definitions of what constitutes deviance. There is no place in their scheme for looking at the deviance of the powerful. Since the ruling class and their control agents do not define themselves as deviant neither do the labelists.

The hypothesis on the consequences of labeling for the labelers has hardly been addressed at all. But the studies of Erikson and Currie are convincing in their suggestion that periodic recruitment into deviant careers helps strengthen the social order.[21]

Our assessment of the labeling perspective can be rounded out by noting how well it responds to other questions relating to comprehensiveness and utility.

1. *What are the wider origins of criminal behavior?* To date the label-

---

[19] Robert Rosenthal, *Pygmalion in the Classroom: Teacher Expectations and Pupil's Intellectual Development* (New York: Holt, Rinehart & Winston, 1968); Jack D. Foster, Simon Dinitz, and Walter C. Reckless, "Perception of Stigma Following Police Intervention for Delinquent Behavior," *Social Problems*, 20 (Fall 1972), 202–9.

[20] Alex Thio, "Class Bias in the Sociology of Deviance," *American Sociologist*, 8 (February 1973), 1–12.

[21] Erikson, *Wayward Puritans*; Elliot P. Currie, "Crimes without Criminals: Witchcraft and its Control in Renaissance Europe," *Law and Sociology Review*, 3 (August 1968), 7–32.

ists have tended to focus their attention on microlevel problems to the exclusion of broader structural questions. The emphasis has been on control institutions and their activities on the one hand or the social-psychological impact of reactions to deviance on the other. This neglect might be remedied by historical research into "deviance production" under different social conditions. The research of Erikson on deviance among the Puritans of New England and Currie's study of witchcraft in Renaissance Europe moves in this direction. Both take the position that deviation and its public disavowal perform the important function of deepening social solidarity and identity. Cohen notes that control agents help define the limits of toleration, and censure does instruct group members on what the limits are.[22] In this view the social control apparatus performs the important societal function of "boundary maintenance" and crime is seen as an essential and "normal" part of any society.

Chambliss has criticized Erikson's boundary maintenance conclusion in the interpretation of his data suggesting that the "crime waves" generated by the Puritans were not precipitated by crises of morality but by power struggles between those who ruled and those who were ruled.[23] Currie's interpretations of witchcraft pointed to its integrative functions but he was more aware of the vested interests of the control agencies involved.[24] His research more clearly supports the interest group tradition and the assumptions made by labelists than does Erikson's work.

Whether one assumes that crime is necessary for social cohesion or that it is one outcome of the unchecked growth of control bureaucracies has profound implications for action. The former assumption suggests that crime cannot be eliminated since it performs an important social function; the latter assumption allows some room for tinkering with control structures. The analysis of bureaucratic structures in this latter view is compatible with the diagnosis made by the President's Committee on Juvenile Delinquency discussed in the last chapter. There is no implication, however, that these structures, even though they may reflect powerful interests in the society, cannot be reorganized. They do not "need" a class of criminals or deviants to keep them operating. The position taken by Schur is that research on control agencies has attracted public attention to their deficiencies and led to greater caution in the use of negative labels and more concern with due process. Whether or not this is true it does not assume that deviance and crime are functional.

---

[22] Albert K. Cohen, *Deviance and Control* (Englewood Cliffs, N.J.: Prentice-Hall, 1966).
[23] William J. Chambliss, "Functional and Conflict Theories of Crime," *MSS Modular Publications*, N.Y. Module 17 (1974), pp. 1–23.
[24] Currie, "Crimes without Criminals."

2. *Where in the social structure does the impulse arise to label certain behaviors as criminal?* The impulse usually arises from an organization or interest group with something to gain by a new definition. Becker's study of the marijuana tax act is illustrative of how labelists would usually answer this question. In looking at the Federal Bureau of Narcotic's role in producing the marijuana legislation, Becker utilized the same interest-group approach pioneered by Sutherland in his study of sexual psychopathic laws. His analysis indicated that the FBN furnished most of the enterprise in the passage of the federal Marijuana Tax Act of 1937. He characterized the bureau as a "moral entrepreneur" and concluded that whenever rules are created or applied we should be alert to the possible presence of an energetic individual or group who has something to gain from the new arrangements. His account of the passage of the act showed how the bureau tried to enlist the support of other interest groups in order to develop a favorable climate of opinion. Finally he suggested that the end product—a new law—was shaped by complex political bargaining. Other studies conducted by labelists have come to similar conclusions.[25]

The very powerful emphasis on stigmatization and the tendency of bureaucracies to operate in predictable fashion in a society of secondary contacts (i.e., their lack of due process considerations, tendencies to stereotype, and unwillingness to be responsive to their clients or victims) implies that it is much more difficult to change an official audience reaction once it has been made than to prevent it in the first instance. In short, the procedure creates a class of criminals or deviants who, in the process of being "isolated," "treated," "corrected," or "punished," forge a set of very sturdy expectations on how both the definers and defined should behave. The process gives life, persistence, and vitality to the subcultural solutions of those defined as "outsiders" that would not otherwise exist.

3. *Which parts of the social structure supply a disproportionate amount of crime and delinquency?* There is no question that those who are officially processed are relatively powerless, that is, they are lower class. "Primary deviation," however, is more pervasive but is usually ignored by the labelists because the central concern is how social reaction necessarily amplifies the original deviation. Lemert dismisses primary deviation as "polygenetic, arising out of a variety of social, cultural, psy-

---

[25] See Troy Duster, *The Legislation of Morality: Law Drugs and Moral Judgment* (New York: Free Press, 1970); Joseph R. Gusfield, *Symbolic Crusade: Status Politics and the American Temperance Movement* (Urbana: University of Illinois Press, 1963); and Pamela A. Roby, "Politics and the Criminal Law: Revision of the New York State Penal Law on Prostitution," *Social Problems*, 17 (Summer 1969), 83–109.

chological and physiological factors." He seems to imply that no adequate
explanation of primary deviation is possible, or even desirable, since the
deviation becomes significant only when it has been transformed into a
social role that the deviant actor plays, that is, secondary deviation.

The social reaction approach began as an attack on what society considered to be cruder structural approaches, which lost sight of the social
control apparatus as an independent variable in the creation of crime. In
emphasizing the fact that the criminal or deviant is "just like the rest of
us," the labelists shifted concern from criminality as a static entity to one
that is the outcome of dynamic processes of social interaction. Hence
rates have not been a basic concern in this perspective. The labelists seem
impressed with the massive amounts of rule breaking that go on in society
all the time. They point out that only a fraction of this behavior is defined
as criminal or deviant. Behavior becomes criminal only when some official
audience labels it as such. The labelists are not attempting to build a
theory of rule breaking in general. They consider it a legitimate task to
narrow their concern to definitional processes in the creation of crime.
Note that there is little attention given to the "crimes" of the powerful in
labeling explanations because they rarely come to official attention.

4. *What causes crime?* Operating on the assumption that there would
be no crime without labels, some labelists would argue that those who
affix the labels "cause" crime. This extreme relativism suggests that almost
any meaning can be assigned to any human activity. The impression one
gets is that if the reactors are sufficiently powerful and determined, the
person who, let us say, spits on the street, can end up in the electric chair.
This approach loses sight of the objective aspects of criminal or deviant
behavior. Societal reaction varies with objective differences in the behavior. As Durkheim noted:

> Robbery and simple bad taste injure the same altruistic senti-
> ments, the respect for that which is another's. However, this same
> sentiment is less grievously offended by bad taste than by robbery;
> and since, in addition, the average consciousness has not sufficient
> intensity to react keenly to the bad taste, it is treated with greater
> tolerance. This is why the person guilty of bad taste is merely to
> blame, whereas the thief is punished.[26]

But Lemert himself has taken issue with the extreme relativism
evidenced in some of the labeling studies. He reminds us that human
interaction always occurs within limits—biological, psychological, ecological, technological, and organizational.[27] The meanings assigned to the

[26] Emile Durkheim (George Simpson, trans.), *The Division of Labor in Society*
(New York: Free Press, 1964), p. 68.
[27] Lemert, *Human Deviance*, 2nd edition, 1972, ch. 1.

interaction consequently are not completely random or variable. Schur in his defense of the labeling approach has taken the position that although it is less concerned with rates of deviation, the labeling perspective is not incompatible with approaches that focus on rates.[28] The labeling view at this stage constitutes a powerful critique of explanations that ignore societal reactions but does not represent a well developed theory.

Becker has suggested that we look more closely at conforming rather than deviant motivation as one way of answering the question of crime causation. He states that much nonconformity is unintended and that deviant impulses are widespread in our society. He proposes asking another question—not why do deviants have deviant motivation but why don't conventional people act on the deviant impulses we all have.[29] He suggests that they do not because they become progressively involved in conventional institutions and that to act on deviant impulses would be too costly—it would endanger interests that are not connected with the deviant act but would be adversely affected by it. One example he uses is narcotics: the conventional person is discouraged from indulging his curiosity or looking for immediate pleasure because his job, family, and reputation would be endangered.

Sociologists have characteristically looked at the various positions within an organization and a person's mobility from one to another over a period of time. Becker, following the approach of Hughes, noted that individuals are involved in a variety of careers. Hence any full account of deviance or crime must include the progressive involvement of the actor.

> . . . we need a model which takes into account the fact that patterns of behavior *develop* in orderly sequence. In accounting for an individual's use of marihuana, . . . we must deal with a sequence of steps, or changes in the individual's behavior and perspectives, in order to understand the phenomenon. Each step requires explanation, and what may operate as a cause at one step in the sequence may be of negligible importance at another step. We need, for example, one kind of explanation of how a person comes to be in a situation where marihuana is easily available to him, and another kind of explanation of why, given the fact of its availability, he is willing to experiment with it in the first place. And we need still another explanation of why, having experimented with it, he continues to use it.[30]

There is a place in Becker's scheme for an explanation of initial deviance in terms of motivation and opportunity. Yet in fact the labeling approach has

---

[28] Edwin M. Schur, *Labeling Deviant Behavior: Its Sociological Implications* (New York: Harper & Row, 1971).
[29] Becker, *Outsiders*, pp. 26–27.
[30] Ibid., p. 23.

done a better job in explaining secondary rather than primary deviation.

Rule breakers who are discovered and subjected to the disapproving, degradational, and labeling reactions of society become fundamentally different from rule breakers who are not caught and processed. The primary cause of commitment to a criminal or deviant career is societal reaction. The institutions of social control speed the rule breaker along to a deviant career. Since little attention is paid to situations where societal reaction deters rather than amplifies initial rule violations the implication is that the social response inevitably contributes to the evolution of sub-cultural solutions. It seems clear that there are numerous instances in which this secondary deviation leading to further commitment actually occurs, but the stress on the crucial significance of label application has obscured other situations in which the label is successfully rejected or leads to some other outcome.

5. *What are the policy implications of the labeling approach?* Labelists believe it is the control bureaucracies that are the problem. They operate with their own self-generated momentum as moral entrepreneurs inter-fering in the private lives of powerless individuals and groups. It is from the labelists that the most cogent arguments for removing "victimless crimes" from the criminal code have come.[31]

The major attack on oppressive organizations has been to suggest that more detailed and effective due process procedures are required to pro-tect individual citizens who are caught in the net of control organizations. Schur, one of the major labeling exponents, has proposed "radical non-intervention" as a strategy.[32] Generally this means that, apart from procedural safeguards, the scope of the jurisdiction of control agencies should be considerably narrowed. Implied in this strategy is the belief that the involvement of official agencies is almost inevitably complicating. His example was in the area of delinquency but can be expanded to cover a wide variety of rule infractions. Not only does official action confound the problem but it also actively prevents or discourages any informal solutions. For Schur, cutting down the size and authority of control agencies would have another advantage: it would encourage the de-velopment of local custom and informal social control. Whether this would actually occur or not is debatable. The strategy suggested by Schur may only be a short-range emergency solution preliminary to a more humane reorganization of social control institutions.

---

[31] Edwin M. Schur, *Crimes Without Victims: Deviant Behavior and Public Policy—Abortion, Homosexuality and Drug Addiction* (Englewood Cliffs, N.J.: Prentice-Hall, 1965).

[32] Edwin M. Schur, *Radical Non-Intervention: Rethinking the Delinquency Problem* (Englewood Cliffs, N.J.: Prentice-Hall, 1973).

The most searching criticism of the political stance of the labeling school has come from Alvin Gouldner.[33] He admits that by studying the world from the perspective of the underdog we elevate into public view certain underprivileged aspects of reality, and this has the effect of calling into question managerial conceptions of reality. But at the same time Gouldner is also troubled by the portrait of the underdog presented by the labelists. The underdog is a "man on his back"—the classic victim. He is sly but not defiant, tricky but not courageous, sneering but not accusing, "making out" without making a scene. Gouldner accuses the labelists of being attracted to the underdog because of his exotic quaintness; hence underdogs are "collected" much like specimens for viewing in the hip sociologist's urban museum.

Gouldner thinks it significant that the labelists, by and large, have not been concerned with political deviance. The political deviant does not fit the labelist's view of the underdog as a passive nonentity, responsible neither for his suffering nor its alleviation. Gouldner notes that the critical cutting edge of the labeling perspective has not seriously affected federal funding of underdog research. He concludes that the labelists are really identified with one of the conflicting elites in the national welfare establishment. The labelists view the underdog increasingly from the vantage point of benevolent, college-bred, upper strata decision makers—the American administrative class. What seems to be a rejection, Gouldner claims, by the superior turns out to be only a rejection of the middle-level superiors—those who run the caretaking institutions, not the master institutions—which ultimately produce underdog suffering. The labeling critique focuses on the lower middle class who staff the caretaking institutions. It is this group that is being criticized—their remedial efforts are ineffectual, their custodial efforts brutal, and their rule enforcement techniques self-interested.

THE CONFLICT SCHOOL: A RETURN TO STRUCTURE

Just about the time that younger criminologists were beginning to question the adequacy of anomie theory, Ralf Dahrendorf, a German sociologist, published his influential book *Class and Class Conflict in Industrial Society*.[34] Dahrendorf was not concerned with the problems of

---

[33] Gouldner, "The Sociologist as Partisan."
[34] Ralf Dahrendorf, *Class and Class Conflict in Industrial Society* (Stanford, Calif.: Stanford University Press, 1959).

crime but with introducing his readers to Marx. He represents an important figure in contemporary criminology though he does not explicitly discuss the implications of inequality for criminalization. Austin Turk researched some of Dahrendorf's implications for a theory of criminalization in an attempt to correct some of the shortcomings of the labeling approach. Dahrendorf's work, however, unintentionally accomplished the extraordinary feat of reorienting the field of criminology from the narrow preoccupations of technicians to the critical understanding of society and broader social theory. Its reception by those concerned with crime and delinquency in effect ended criminology's intellectual isolation from the rest of social science. It is for this reason that some of the themes discussed by Dahrendorf are presented here as background despite the fact that he was not concerned with crime.

Dahrendorf's critique of Marx recognized the importance of accounting for social change through class conflict. Conflict groups and their clashes do make for social change according to Dahrendorf. But he faults Marx for maintaining that all changes can be explained in terms of class conflicts and that change always occurs in a revolutionary fashion. Dahrendorf holds that social change sometimes begins in one sphere, like the industrial order, and spreads to others; but sometimes the change remains confined to that one sphere and doesn't result in complete system change. Too, Dahrendorf rejected Marx's notion of the manifest antagonism between classes—conflict varies by type and intensity from an unrecognized or latent antagonism of differing interests to acute and violent conflict. Perhaps his most fundamental criticism of Marx is that private property is no longer the basis of social class in what he calls "post-Capitalist" society characterized by the separation of ownership and control. Control over the means of production as a basis for class formation is replaced by the exercise of, or exclusion from, authority. Thus the centrality of industrial conflict emphasized by Marx gives way to conflict arising out of authority-subject relations in a variety of situations. Authority is the probability that a command within a given specific context will be obeyed by a given group of persons. Those who issue commands are said to dominate. Those excluded from authority are in subjection—their duty is to obey authoritative commands. We are all enmeshed in a variety of associations (Dahrendorf calls them "imperatively coordinated associations") in which two and only two aggregates of position may be distinguished: domination and subjection. Individuals may belong to one aggregate in one association and the other in another one.

Dahrendorf suggests that his sociology of conflict approach supersedes

Marx and is more comprehensive in explaining conflicts in advanced industrial societies. Whether or not he is correct—more recent conflict criminologists take issue with him on this point—he did rehabilitate the notion of conflict for criminologists. He pointed to the large and distinguished group of thinkers in the history of the West who utilized a coercion view of society and criticized the American fascination with consensus, order, and stability. Dahrendorf maintains that every society is based on the coercion of some of its members by others, that within all societies dissent and conflict are the normal state of affairs.

The Work of Austin Turk

Austin Turk begins his discussion of criminality by asserting that the key factor in criminalization or the assignment of criminal status to individuals is the ability of some people to announce and enforce legal norms.[35] He accepts Dahrendorf's picture of society—a tenuous approximation of an order, a temporary resolution of conflicting notions about right and wrong and incompatible desires. He suggests that criminal status is ascribed to persons not because of what they *do*, rather it is ascribed because of what people *are*. Not only should the criminologist be concerned about the criminal status, but also the status of "suspect" and "accused" because the latter are variants of criminality associated with the degree, kind, and officialness of deprivation. Turk proposes to sketch a theory of interaction that tells us under what conditions the conflicts between those who are dominant and those who are subject— more specifically the legal authorities and "norm resisters"—lead to criminalization. There can be a great deal of conflict which does not lead to criminalization.

He suggests looking at subjects along the two dimensions of organization and sophistication to anticipate conflict between them and authorities. He hypothesizes that conflict is more probable the less sophistication there is among subjects (this enables them to avoid head-on collisions with authorities) and the higher their organization. The illustration of a group with low sophistication but high degree of organization is the delinquent gang. It is by this very fact in a highly conflicted relationship with authorities and has a high potentiality for being criminalized. His scheme is best illustrated by the following fourfold table which pinpoints the likelihood of conflict based on organization and sophistication:

[35] Austin Turk, *Criminality and Legal Order* (Chicago: Rand McNally, 1969).

Probability of Conflict between
Legal Authorities and Norm Resisters

		Sophistication	
		High	*Low*
Organization	*High*	Less probable; example: syndicate criminals	Most probable; example: delinquent gang
	Low	Least probable; example: professional con men	Probable; example: skid row habitues

These variables can be used to characterize authorities as well as subjects, but for his purposes organization is a constant for enforcers (i.e., always high). The critical variable in looking at authorities is their degree of sophistication—the less sophistication the more conflict. He goes on to develop a complex typology which systematizes what we know about probabilities of normative legal conflict occurring. Modern society for Turk, as it was for Sutherland, is composed of a variety of subcultures. Differences in social position imply differences in cultures—ideas about right and wrong as well as attitudes related to what is desirable.

Culture conflict is endemic and in a situation where one group is disadvantaged, the likelihood of their criminalization is high; it is not inevitable, however. It depends on the interaction between those who are dominant and those who are subject. The enforcers must move in such a way that their authority is not called into question. They must be careful not to initiate too much or too little coercion; otherwise the authority relationship that maintains stability becomes open to critical assessment.

A more frequent error in "conflict moves" made by superordinates in modern society is to permit the authority relationship to deteriorate to its power core alone. This leads to questioning, resistance, and eventual change. The moves made by subordinates can also affect the outcome. Norm resisters can increase the probability of criminalization by increasing the visibility of the offensive attribute or behavior, by further violation which forces authoritative action, thus alarming the public and increasing the power differences in favor of the superordinate group. Thus the conflict moves of subordinate groups may increase the possibilities of criminalization.

The tenuous character of the stability that comes through in Turk's depiction of modern society raises the question of why men accept authority at all. Turk rejects Weber's notion that people accept authority because they believe the order is in some sense legitimate, that is, their acceptance is not based on their belief in its "rightness" or "fairness." He also rejects the structural-functional notion that people accept authority because they have "internalized norms." This idea, he states, in an extreme form assumes a portable replica of the social order built into each properly socialized member. Hence all crime and deviance is attributed to "undersocialization." Turk says that people accept authority rather than having it forced on them (i.e., there is a kind of consensus-coercion balance) but the basis of their acceptance is not clear. His conclusion is that both authorities and subjects learn and continually relearn to interact with one another as performers of dominating and submitting roles. Those who are dominated come to accept it because they are conditioned to think of it as a fact of life. Authorities are there and they must be reckoned with.

But it takes some time to resign oneself to this fact. The law abiding, in Turk's view, or more precisely those who accept society's norms most fully, are older white men and women. Those who resist norms of domination come from various cultures that are in conflict with superordinates. These cultural norms are almost endless, as they were for Sutherland, but Turk focuses on the cultures of age, sex, and race/ethnicity as most resistant. It is no surprise to the beginning criminologist that young male members of racial minorities are most likely to be criminalized in the United States.

Both Dahrendorf's and Turk's analyses have received wide acceptance among American sociologists and criminologists because they showed promise in dealing with the hard realities of conflict without completely subscribing to a Marxist analysis. In their post-Capitalist society men do not act in accord with their class position but in accord with their position in a pluralistic society where a range of authority-subject relationships determine individual action. These authority-subject relationships seem so diffuse for Turk that in his discussion of those most likely to be criminalized he completely excludes social class. Though Turk sees his work as an extension of Dahrendorf's ideas on social conflict, some critics have interpreted his elaboration as a retrenchment. Taylor, Walton, and Young claim that for Dahrendorf conflict and protest against systems of stratification are necessary and lead to ongoing readjustment, but for Turk stability is the necessity.[36] Thus he attempts to stabilize the ongoing social conflict and permanently adjust the subordinate to the powerful. Taylor et al. dismiss both Dahrendorf and Turk as consensus rather than conflict theorists who by dealing with conflict and its functions have merely expanded the catalogue of integrationist questions; i.e., they have developed further assumptions about consensus, not denied it.

[36] Ian Taylor, Paul Walton, and Jock Young, *The New Criminology: For a Social Theory of Deviance* (New York: Harper Torchbook, 1974), pp. 240–52.

The Work of Willem Bonger: Marxist Criminology

Willem Bonger was born in 1876 and educated at the University of Amsterdam. He is best known for his book *Criminality and Economic Conditions*, which was translated into English in 1916.[37] He is somewhat analogous to Durkheim in being considered the "father of conflict criminology" as Durkheim is considered the "father of consensus criminology," though with less justification. Bonger basically shares Durkheim's perspective with some qualifications. He sees society divided into a ruling class and a ruled class with law being constituted according to the will of the former. The division into two classes is not a result of variable innate capacities but of the system of production. The system is held together by force. But he agrees with Durkheim in regarding the criminal law and its enforcement as a genuine reflection of some universal social and moral sentiments. He, like Durkheim, was mainly concerned with explaining criminal behavior rather than law creation. In his account capitalism gives unbridled reign to "egoism" which takes over individuals and leads to criminality. The capitalist environment generates egoistic influences rather than altruistic ones, hence all are crime prone. The reason the bourgeoisie are less likely than the proletariat to become criminals is their egoistic actions are legitimized. They aren't required to steal because they have surer and more lucrative means of gaining wealth. Those bourgeoisie who do commit crime do so because they have an opportunity to gain an illegal advantage and they have an underdeveloped moral sense. Bonger ascribes an independent force to egoism much like Durkheim would. In this he differed from Marx, who held that social arrangements are primarily causal and egoism is a reflection of them. Taylor and his colleagues suggest that Bonger was not able to escape the predominant orientations of European criminology so deeply affected by Durkheim. They conclude that his work represents a purely formal attempt to claim a Marxist pedigree and then rely mainly on Durkheim.[38]

At any rate the openness of American criminologists to conflict approaches after Dahrendorf's work led to the "rediscovery" of Bonger in 1969, when an abridged edition of *Criminality and Economic Conditions* with a new introduction by Turk was published.[39] Turk's introduction is

---

[37] Willem Bonger, *Criminality and Economic Conditions* (Boston: Little, Brown, 1916).

[38] Taylor, Walton, and Young, *The New Criminology*, 222–34.

[39] Willem Bonger, *Criminality and Economic Conditions,* abridged with an introduction by Austin T. Turk (Bloomington: University of Indiana Press, 1969).

an attempt to establish the significance of Bonger for an American audience and to reconstruct the conflict tradition. Turk criticizes Bonger's posited relationship between egoism-altruism and crime as untenable but points out that his notions on the inequitable distribution of opportunities are valid. Freedom to compete in a capitalist society is not equally available because the system is fundamentally unjust. Hence it's impossible to extend equal opportunity to all within capitalist structures. It was in the context of renewed appreciation of what Bonger represented that Richard Quinney's work comes into focus.

The Work of Richard Quinney

By 1970 the disillusionment with the Vietnam war had spread to most sectors of American society. The feelings of helplessness and powerlessness on university campuses had deepened. In May 1970 widespread protests were mounted on campuses all over the country in response to President Nixon's decision to extend the war into Cambodia. On May 4, 1970, four protesting students were killed by Ohio National Guardsmen at Kent State University; a little over one week later two black students were killed by the Mississippi Highway Patrol at Jackson State College. The ugly reality of the war was brought dramatically to the campus. A sign on one campus read: "This is Vietnam and we are the Cong." It was this series of events combined with growing domestic governmental repression that shaped Richard Quinney's thinking. He was most troubled about the research and programs sponsored by the U.S. Department of Justice through the Law Enforcement Assistance Administration. He noted that about 65,000 students in 1970 received Justice Department funds for their studies while $20 million was being made available to colleges and universities for law enforcement education programs.[40] The Law Enforcement Assistance Administration received its legislative mandate in the 1968 Safe Streets Act passed in the wake of the unrest triggered by the assassination of Martin Luther King, Jr. Quinney was concerned that this agency would be the instrument for establishing domestic order precisely the way the military had so unsuccessfully tried to establish international order in Indochina.

> . . . LEAA has become the fastest growing agency of government, its budget increasing twenty-five fold from $63 million in fiscal year 1969 to the latest authorization of $1.75 *billion* for fiscal year 1973. The majority of LEAA's money goes to the purchase of weapons

[40] Richard Quinney, *Critique of Legal Order, Crime Control in a Capitalist Society* (Boston: Little, Brown, 1974).

and electronic hardware for police departments around the country.[41]

At any rate the heady enthusiasm of the mid-1960s seems to have vanished. Increasingly questions were raised about the autonomy of the social sciences in relation to the federal government. The labelist reaction seemed to be a declaration of independence but obscured the actuality of scientific collaboration with the national government. Gouldner has pointed out that once the state becomes committed to intervening in social problems, it acquires a vested interest in "advertising" the social problems it wants to solve. These problems were previously addressed by regional or local bodies and it is at their expense that the federal government's mandate to intervene is created. This accounts.for their sponsorship of a kind of "critical" research.

> This creates a situation in which the new and higher levels have an interest not only in exposing the existence of a social problem but also in unmasking the inadequacy of the older arrangements for dealing with it and in undermining the local elites formerly in charge of these arrangements, and whom the higher levels now wish to displace or to bring under their own control. There is, consequently, a tendency of the new and higher governmental levels to foster what are, in effect, *"evaluation"* researches, studies that analyze the effectiveness and, most especially, expose the *ineffectiveness* of the elites and of the traditional procedures on the lower, local levels. The upper apparatus of the Welfare State, then, needs social research that will "unmask" their competitors; it needs a kind of limitedly "critical" research.[42]

If we accept Gouldner's interpretation it is not surprising that some sociologists and criminologists would find this limited critical role unsatisfactory. Instead they have proposed a more thorough critique of social arrangements that focuses on the underlying causes for the transfer of control functions from local civil society to the nation-state. It is in this context that Quinney's views take on meaning.

Richard Quinney was born in rural Wisconsin in 1934 and went to nearby Carroll College for his bachelor's degree. He received an M.S. in sociology from Northwestern in 1957 and his Ph.D. in sociology from the University of Wisconsin in 1962. His dissertation was on prescription violations among pharmacists which is discussed in Chapter 15 on occupational crime. He reports that he didn't get interested in criminology until his last year at Wisconsin when he began to do some reading on the sociology of law. His first position was at the University of Kentucky

---

41 Ibid., pp. 87–88.
42 Alvin Gouldner, *The Coming Crisis of Western Sociology* (New York: Basic Books, 1970), pp. 349–50.

where he taught for three years after which he went to New York University. It was not the internal problems of criminology that influenced him, he states, but injustices occurring in the real world. The kind of training that he received in liberal social theory, especially Durkheim, did not prepare him to address these injustices. He gravitated to a transitional position, somewhat like the labelists, in calling into question managerial conceptions of reality. He contended in his first criminology text that social reality was a "construction" and there were many such realities each with its own legitimacy.[43] He indicated that he found this position quite unsatisfactory because it did not provide him with a powerful enough critique of present social arrangements. His later work was an attempt to modify his approach. As with Sutherland and the earlier midwestern criminologists, the most powerful influence on Quinney was populism:

> What is more important to me [than liberal social theory] is a kind of sensibility that was inherent in the Midwest rather than academic institutions. It is a sensibility that is populist, concern for the rights of the people and a questioning of authority . . . I think we're beginning to see a certain style in the Midwest which is comparable to European Marxism. The liberal social theorists, though, have put down for twenty-five years any kind of populism as action or as thought. I think part of the radical movement now is typically American though much of the rhetoric is European. But there are ideas that are basically American and I'm thinking from my own experience, Midwestern also. Even in Republican country there was still the basic idea of questioning authority, of an attempt to obtain basic human rights, but also the pursual of a decent life that was more than economic.[44]

Quinney proposed to explain crime and criminality by a close look at the various institutional orders existing in America and their conflicting interests. He saw American society then as characterized by diversity, conflict, coercion, and change. Modern criminal law was the result of the operation of diverse interests and was created by the interests of specific groups in the society. These groups were linked to major institutional concerns (political, economic, religious, kinship, educational, and public). Quinney noted that these segments of society differed in the extent to which their interests were organized but the interest structure was characterized by the unequal distribution of power. But some groups

[43] Richard Quinney, *The Social Reality of Crime* (Boston: Little, Brown, 1970).
[44] Eileen Goldwyn, "Dialogue with Richard Quinney," *Issues in Criminology* 6(2) (Summer 1971), 41–54; 48–49.

had the wherewithal to translate their interests into public policy. He claimed that to build a more adequate criminology the pluralist notion that law represents the compromise of diverse interests in society must be rejected; rather law supports some interests at the expense of others.

Among the newer conflict criminologists the dominant orientation in sociology and political science (called pluralism or democratic pluralism) is sharply criticized. The pluralist imagery suggests that society is composed of a number of interest groups, each with sufficient power to strike a bargain in its own interest. The weakest interest group need only have enough power to force some kind of exchange with more powerful groups. This idea assumes that there will be some kind of parity, if not equality, of power between conflicting interest groups. But C. Wright Mills earlier had pointed out that this is not the situation in the United States.[45] Not only is there no parity of power among different interest groups, but a majority of citizens don't belong to any organization large enough to be politically significant. Even if they do, the leadership within these organizations frustrates their expression. The pluralist model also assumes that the state, when necessary, acts as an impartial referee in various disputes: since it expresses the public interest it transcends various narrow private interests and is best suited to contain conflict. In short, there is no even-handed playing off of varied interests in a dynamic and even-handed way. The model simply does not fit American society.

Quinney acknowledged that he was attempting to extend the analysis of Dahrendorf and Turk on the relationship of conflict to criminality. His position evolved from the critical one presented in his 1970 work to an explicit Marxist position in his more recent work.[46] In his earlier analysis he saw the state not as the impartial arbiter of conflicting interests but as the *prize* sought after by powerful contending groups. Yet curiously, the pluralism he so vigorously criticizes in his 1970 book influenced the suggestions he made there on alleviating the condition whereby private interests function as a government separate from the public one. He suggested that even though the state was captive to powerful private interests, it could still defend "the public interest" if only to satisfy some kind of public relations imperative. The second recommendation that Quinney made was to build a movement united in the defense of the individual safeguards enshrined in Anglo-Saxon law.

By 1974 his optimism about the benign intervention of the state to secure individual liberties had vanished. He suggests in his book *Critique of Legal Order* that the escalation of legal repression in the early 1970s has convinced him that it is a logical extension of an innately oppressive

---

[45] C. Wright Mills, *The Power Elite* (New York: Oxford University Press, 1957), ch. 7.
[46] Quinney, *Critique of Legal Order*.

system. The sharp individual-society separation that Quinney emphasized in his 1970 work is also absent in his critique of crime control in a capitalist society. It is replaced by the notion that the ethic of individualism, the ethic of competitive self-interest, emerged at the same time the state did. Individualism, which makes much of the conflict between the individual and the state, turns out in the last analysis to be an ideology that underlies capitalism. It provides a set of justifications for a particular economic system. This becomes clear when looking at precapitalist communities where individual and societal interests are identical. The emergence of the state dispossessed the family, destroyed larger kin organization, atomized religion, and replaced the ethic of shared responsibility with the fiction of individual responsibility.[47]

Quinney directs criminologists to conduct research that is mainly critical history, showing how the modern state and its control apparatus emerged and how it functions today to buttress the capitalist system.[48] He includes in his *Critique of Legal Order* an analysis of those who make criminal policy. He does not urge criminologists, as do the labelers, to conduct further investigations of underdogs; rather his emphasis is on "overdog research." He closely examines the composition of specially appointed legislative bodies, crime control bureaucracies, and advisory groups (The President's Crime Commission, the Violence Commission, the Riot Commission, the Senate Subcommittee on Criminal Laws and Procedures, the Law Enforcement Assistance Administration and the Committee for Economic Development). He concludes that the class composition of these six groups is remarkably similar and that they all share a basic set of interests. The six groups also have overlapping memberships and they function to promote and protect the continuation of the national corporate economy through a domestic "war on crime." He follows this analysis with a more detailed examination of the Law Enforcement Assistance Administration (LEAA) and its operation. He tries to show that the federal government began to increase its role in crime control in 1965, and by 1974 was well on its way to a comprehensive national crime control program under the guise of decentralization. According to Quinney, the federal crime-in-the-streets war expanded to suppress any action that threatened the status quo. He stresses the similarity between military operations and domestic crime control with examples of the technology grants made by LEAA. He sees the increasing correctionalization of American life as the reflection of some kind of fundamental crisis in capitalism.

[47] Mark C. Kennedy, "Beyond Incrimination: Some Neglected Facets of the Theory of Punishment," *Catalyst*, 5 (Summer 1970), 1–38.
[48] Richard Quinney (ed.), *Criminal Justice in America: A Critical Understanding* (Boston: Little, Brown, 1974).

Other Conflict Approaches

The critical studies of social structure going on in the United States have not gone so far as to constitute a "school" similar to that of the ecologists. Rather, the work is primarily that of individual scholars who are deeply disturbed over the crisis of American institutional life and are searching for ways to explain it. The return to Marx is an attempt to locate the problems of the age in economic class relations. The most serious effort to work out a Marxist criminology is taking place in Great Britain around the National Deviancy Conference.[49] This group consists of a handful of sociologists and individuals involved in social action in the United Kingdom.

They suggest a formulation that utilizes Marx's assumptions about the nature of man, not his observations about crime, since they were not fully spelled out. Marx wrote little on crime, and according to the British deviancy group, the most telling feature of his discussion of crime was its atypicality when compared to the rest of his work—he adopted a form of simple economic determinism in looking at crime that he avoided in the rest of his work. Marx was at one with his contemporaries in seeing crime as concentrated in the "dangerous classes."[50] These classes were criminal because they were unproductive and unorganized workers. Marx thought them to be parasitical—they didn't contribute to the production of goods and commodities. Marx sees criminal activity therefore as an expression of a false and prepolitical form of individualistic consciousness. The criminologist searching Marx's work for a discussion of crime control in a capitalist society will find little. Nor will he find any picture of a crime-free society in which the forced division of labor has been abolished. Instead we are provided with a caricature:

> Insofar as attention is paid by Marx to the question of causation and motivation, the picture is not so much of criminals rationally engaging in a redistribution of wealth in an individualistic fashion, but is rather a caricature of what Gouldner (1968) has called "man on his back," that is, a man demoralized and brutalized by the day-to-day experience of employment (and unemployment) under industrial capitalism, but a man still able to grasp at the necessities of life through theft and graft. Though the criminal life might be a necessary response to the closing-off of life-chances under capital-

---

[49] Taylor, Walton, and Young, *The New Criminology*.
[50] See Paul Q. Hirst, "Marx and Engels on Crime, Law and Morality," *Economy and Society,* 1 (February 1972), 28–56.

ism, it is depicted eventually as the response of the demoralized, and little attention is paid to the varieties of ways in which a man might choose his options, the ways in which he might attempt to create a viable and moral existence in all but impossible conditions.[51]

The promise of a Marxist theory of crime and deviance, according to the British group, is its comprehensiveness and its potential explanatory power. By directing us to historical studies it begins to explain the ways particular sets of social relationships and means of production in various periods have given rise to attempts by the powerful to order society in specific ways. Studies of law and crime can show the complex interaction between developments in institutional and social structures and the consciousness of men living within those structures.

A Marxist orientation, they contend, asks more searching questions about who makes the rules and why. It assumes, too, a degree of consciousness on the part of men bound with their location in a structure of production, exchange, and domination which of itself would influence the ways in which men defined as criminal would try to live with their outsider status. This approach, the British group believes, would rescue criminology from the crude structural outlook posed by anomie theorists and the uncritical relativism and subjectivism of the labelists. Their Marxist theory is not value free, since no science in the service of human betterment can be. It is from this vantage point that Taylor and his colleagues survey the history of criminology and evaluate previous contributions. Their structural approach, they maintain, involves the recognition of intermediate structural questions that have traditionally been the domain of criminology (ecological areas, subcultural location, and opportunity systems) but would place these against the overall social context of inequalities of power, wealth, and authority in industrial society.

In short, they propose a *political economy of crime*. This political economy of crime would be wedded to a *social psychology of crime* which proposes to answer the question of why men choose certain paths as well as why social audiences react. Since the treatment of social reaction against the criminal is implicit sociologies of the state, it calls for an explicit *political economy of social reaction.*

This programmatic statement—not yet a body of literature—raises questions that the older criminologies ignored like: Under what conditions is moral and social consensus possible in advanced industrial societies? Can authority be exercised without coercion or must it always involve the domination of man by man? How can the power to criminalize be abolished? They end their book with a call to create a new society:

[51] Taylor, Walton, and Young, *The New Criminology,* p. 218.

For us, as for Marx and for other new criminologists, deviance is normal—in the sense that men are now consciously involved (in the prisons that are contemporary societies and in the real prisons) in asserting their human diversity. The task is not merely to "penetrate" these problems, not merely to question the stereotypes, or to act as carriers of "alternative phenomenological realities." The task is to create a society in which the facts of human diversity, whether personal, organic or social, are not subject to the power to criminalize.[52]

Evaluation of Conflict Theory

If we raise the question of how adequately conflict theory fits with the facts of crime, it is fair to say that it has made a substantial contribution to the role that interest groups play in the creation and maintenance of law. It seems less relevant when focusing on trivial kinds of rule violation and does not adequately explain socialist criminality. Conflict theory has suggested some of the issues around which groups are likely to organize their values and some probable outcomes of struggles. But specification of the social conditions under which conflict is likely to occur and the dynamics involved in the criminalization process are still sketchy. What is required, according to Lemert, is a model of group interaction which focuses on ". . . interests, values and the order in which they are likely to be sacrificed or satisfied in the light of group commitments, availability and cost of means."[53]

Akers has raised the objection that conflict approaches are less appropriate when looking at common infractions that are universally proscribed.[54] The studies done from a conflict perspective suggest the validity of this criticism. To date little attention has been paid to relatively harmless rule breaking such as traffic violations. However, there is no inherent reason why this could not be done. The laws relating to traffic violations and their implementation are the result of the same kind of interest-group pressure (though perhaps not that of "the ruling class") as any other law. The implementation of traffic laws is probably more even-handed than that related to theft, yet we could legitimately expect class variations as the conflict theorist hypothesizes.

The questions raised on the character of socialist criminality are somewhat diversionary at this stage but still legitimate to pose. Bonger maintained that crime would decrease as a society moved from laissez-faire

---

[52] Ibid., p. 282.

[53] Lemert, *Human Deviance*, 2nd edition, 1972, p. 20.

[54] Ronald L. Akers, *Deviant Behavior: A Social Learning Approach* (Belmont, Calif.: Wadsworth, 1973), p. 20.

capitalism to monopoly capitalism to socialism. But even under socialism there would be crimes committed by "pathological" individuals. Turk has criticized Bonger for expecting socialist man to be utterly selfless.[55] There would still be more than enough venality to keep control agents busy, because men require not only material goods but status which inherently involves invidious distinctions. Status needs seem insatiable and there is no reason for believing that socialist society would be more effective in addressing them according to Turk. The discussion is somewhat polemical to date and the information unavailable to move beyond the present argument. What is required are detailed studies of crime under varying social, political, and economic conditions. A more detailed assessment of the conflict approach can be made by looking at its response to the questions raised earlier.

1. *What are the wider origins of criminal behavior?* More than any of the other schemes discussed so far the conflict school underlines the centrality of larger social structures in generating law, crime, and social control. Spitzer has argued that the main task of a Marxist theory is the development of a general theory of deviance production which can be understood in relationship to the development of a class society. This includes all the aspects of the process

> . . . through which populations are structurally generated, as well as shaped, channeled into, and manipulated within social categories defined as deviant. This process includes the development of and changes in: (1) deviant definitions, (2) problem populations, and (3) control systems.[56]

Thus if we are concerned with how a group becomes problematic we must look at the structural characteristics—the economic and political dimensions—of the society in which these definitions about who is troublesome emerge. If American society is our focus Spitzer notes that we would observe that certain correlates of capitalist development like "proletarianization" and "nuclearization" of the family weakened traditional methods of assimilating newcomers. Coincident with this development was the emergence of "scientific and meritocratic ideologies" that justified "differential handling." Finally other trends relating to the attraction of unskilled labor and population concentrations heightened concern over the "threat" that these groups were perceived to pose. The form and content of crime definition can thus be related to both structural and ideological change.

---

[55] Austin Turk, "Introduction," in Willem Bonger, *Criminality and Economic Conditions*, abridged edition (Bloomington: University of Indiana Press, 1969).
[56] Stephen Spitzer, "Toward a Marxian Theory of Deviance," *Social Problems*, 22 (June 1975), 638–51; 640.

There is a discoverable and dialectical relationship between the dominant institutions and those who must relate to them. Taylor, Walton, and Young quote Marx in saying that crime is functional in sustaining capitalist social relationships. But they point out that crime is not universally "necessary" or "normal" as Durkheim maintained. Crime—or at least the kind of crime characteristic of capitalist societies—would disappear once the system that generated it was abolished.

2. *Where in the social structure does the impulse arise to label certain behaviors as criminal?* The foregoing makes clear that the initiative always comes from powerful elites who are trying to advance or maintain their own interests. These elites are not always the same group but shift with the type of economy and character of the society. A theory of change therefore is essential.

The conflict criminologists would maintain that their perspective is best equipped to deal with change, not only in outsider subcultures but in the master institutions themselves. The historical and comparative dimension they bring to their work is a powerful aid in specifying the structural and cultural conditions that must be present for subcultures to appear in particular historical epochs and how they change. Taylor, Walton, and Young hold that the content, direction, and persistence of criminal or deviant action must be related to shifts in the structure of opportunity for types of criminality and whether they vary coterminously with, or independently of, shifts in social reaction. They suggest that an adequate model in the evolution of deviant action should include the following:

a. The wider origins of the initial infraction. These should be sought in structural, cultural, and social-psychological conflicts existing in the larger society.

b. Immediate origins of the violation. This should provide a depiction of the situated background of the deviant action and the general problems pertaining to that type of deviance.

c. The actual act itself should be set against the background of (a) and (b) above in an attempt to examine the nature of the action.

d. The immediate origins of social reaction. What form does it take? Is it variable in severity and degree? Is it formal or informal? Is it widespread or specific?

e. The outcome of social reaction on the deviant's further action or commitment. Is the context of social reaction internalized or resisted by the actor? Does amplification occur, or does social reaction deter? Does social reaction circumscribe deviant choices or change the range of choices?

f. The character of the delinquent action, its content, persistence and change must be constantly assessed in the light of (a) to (e).[57]

3. *How well does the conflict perspective explain the distribution of crime and delinquency in the social structure?* The conflict theorists have not addressed themselves, with the exception of Taylor and his colleagues, to the question of the distribution of crime and delinquency. The rates themselves are suspect and are the end result of a complex series of interactions whereby powerful and strategically located authorities assign criminal status to disadvantaged groups in the general population independently of their behavior. The rates therefore tell us nothing about what is going on "out there." They are only indicators of a deeply conflicted situation and can best be used as an index of control activities. Thus Turk looks at the statistics on a variety of offenses to get some notion of who the target group is, what norms seem to be at stake, and how important they are to the enforcers.

The British deviancy group rejects the assumptions behind the effort to compute rates. Taylor, Walton, and Young are skeptical of the premises underlying the question of distribution. They state that unless it can be demonstrated that infractions really are a departure from a compact that an individual has, so to speak, made with the community and which he accepts, then the statistics are meaningless. Self-report studies indicate that crime is ubiquitous, and Taylor, Walton, and Young imply, almost patternless. They suggest that something more than counting deviant heads is necessary:

> What is ignored is the problem of what is really (objectively) going on in those heads (and the way what is going on there is a reflection of the oppression of state and the law, the facts of social inequality, and the structures of outside society in general).[58]

It is only in a society where there is a genuine consensus, where individual, social, and industrial interests are identical, where forced division of labor has been abolished and there is no political, economic, or socially induced need to criminalize deviance that the question of variable rates of infraction makes sense.

4. *What causes crime?* Basically, the conflict criminologists see the relationship between the powerful and the powerless as a situation of strain for the disadvantaged. This gives a political character to a resistant response, which is adjudged to be delinquent by those in authority. The

[57] Taylor, Walton, and Young, *The New Criminology*, p. 271ff.
[58] Ibid., p. 21.

strain in this account is caused by the distinctive form of stratification based on an individual's possession or lack of income, and position, in a system of industrial production. It is oppressive to those coerced to accept it. Their crime then can be viewed as a struggle or reaction against accepted, taken-for-granted, power-invested, common-sense rules. At the same time the stratification system engenders "criminal" responses among the powerless, it also encourages the greed and self-serving activity on the part of the powerful—in short, white-collar crime. In Marx's view, the system of domination and control that flourishes under capitalism is itself criminogenic. But even within this context some of the conflict criminologists, most notably Taylor, Walton, and Young, have stressed the diversity and creativity exercised by those who are reacting to strain. Sometimes the response is a problem-solving one, sometimes the activity is instrumental, sometimes expressive, and can be individual or collective. Their view of man's nature is one that underlines the exercise of choice even in extremely constricted situations. Response to the strain generated by capitalism can be predicted in a general way, but for the individual, the response is never automatic. Men are seen as purposive creatures and innovators of action.

Either explicitly or implicitly, the conflict theorists give less emphasis to secondary deviation—that caused by social reaction and labeling—than do the labelists. It is not excluded as an explanation for the development of criminal subcultures, especially for those who inadvertently violate some rule and are almost willy-nilly caught up in society's control apparatus. But the naive rule breaker is seen to be in a decided minority. Some conflict criminologists think the emphasis given the naive rule breaker in the labeling perspective underestimates man's intelligence and rationality and depicts him as a passive nonentity upon whom social forces play. For a conflict criminologist like Turk, the diversity that exists in advanced societies is created by the increasing division of labor. This orders the population into various social positions around which subcultures spring up, much as they did for Sutherland. This is a precondition for the emergence of subcultural solutions.

The conflict criminologists who follow Marx's analysis more closely maintain that a subcultural solution can only evolve when persons in a particular strata are insulated from the communications of superordinate groups. Another requirement for the development of a subcultural solution is ready communication within the class—members must not be socially isolated from one another. A social structure for Marxist criminologists is a structure of opportunities, a structure of communication, and a structure of relationships with patterned links between the units. The conflict criminologists would have no difficulty in accepting the perspective of the cultural transmission school. They would only point out that it has to be placed within a framework that accounts for the causes of conflict between groups and a more detailed working out of the manner in which values are involved in the process of conflict.

5. *What are the policy implications of the conflict approach?* Just as there is no one conflict approach, so there is no one set of policy implications. Dahrendorf, and to some extent, Turk, subscribe to pluralist conceptions of the state. As Lefcourt has said of the pluralists:

> They depict a society in which widely varied groups compete with each other, in which decision making rests on give and take among various groups. Groups compromise, make deals, and pressure each other; public officials and law-makers respond to these various group pressures so that no one political, economic, social, religious, regional, or racial group will dominate. This creates the "natural" system of checks and balances which maintains a democracy. People become part of the decision making process as soon as they organize: as big labor checks big business, Catholics check Protestants, farmers check urbanites, students check school administrators.[59]

Taylor, Walton, and Young point out that for Dahrendorf's "permanent readjustment" to occur both authorities and subjects would have to acquiesce to any compromise or agreement. But this assumes a rough equality of the two groups, which does not exist. The situation of domination, instead of being condemned by Dahrendorf, is accepted as inevitable as long as it is continually readjusted. The implications of Turk's analysis are also disturbing. His book *Criminality and the Legal Order* seems to be directed to those in authority. Once they understand the varied interactions of the authority-subject game they can make more "sophisticated" and "realistic" conflict moves.

The policy implications of Quinney's approach are more explicitly stated. He suggests that criminologists proceed further in the process of demystification of the legal order in America and its accompanying ideology. He suggests that criminologists break with a reform tradition that does not change the fundamental character of the society. Their work should anticipate a social order based on equality, participatory democracy, and decentralized control. A much more thorough proposal for dealing with bureaucracies is made by Quinney than by the labelists: since bureaucracy can't be humanized it should be eliminated. The job as Quinney sees it is one of reconstruction. Since the capitalist state shattered custom and isolated persons from one another, the task is to

[59] Robert Lefcourt (ed.), *Law Against the People* (New York: Random House, 1971), p. 32.

return to custom for the patterning of our daily lives. One example he cites to show the possibility of community custom is the popular tribunal in Cuba.

> Neighborhoods in Cuba now have their own courts, staffed by personnel elected democratically from within the community. Little emphasis is placed on sanctions of any kind. Instead, violators continue to be educated in the community. Custom plays an educative role in the community, rather than a punitive one. What is important is maintaining peace and understanding in the community rather than enforcement of the legal system.[60]

Apart from the demystification of the assumptions underlying criminal law—especially related to the ethic of individual responsibility—there are other things that Taylor, Walton, and Young point to. They suggest the "direct action criminologists" in Scandinavia as models, who not only described the defenses of the weak but helped them organize, much like labor organizers. This led to the formation of a prisoner union—a trade union of Scandinavian inmates—which was able to coordinate a prison strike across three national boundaries and several prison walls.[61]

SUMMARY

The Gouldner critique of the labelists noted earlier is part of a continuing debate and has struck responsive chords among many of those who were or are part of this school. They are concerned by what seems to begin as an attack on official or unofficial power holders in society ends up in ambiguity. But they see nothing inherently incompatible with further investigations of structural, cultural, and social conflicts in the larger society as a supplement to what has already been done on the social-psychological level. Some maintain that the labeling approach is best viewed as a corrective to earlier views of crime and criminality. Schur avers that one of its main strengths is its power to challenge conventional thinking, in particular the deterministic assumptions about the causes of crime.[62] He reminds us that all social reality is construct and any theory which does not take subjective distinctions and meanings into account is not valid. It is this "subjectivism" which has evoked the most criticism because of its extreme relativism. But Goode has pointed out that different acts command varying probabilities of exciting moral out-

---

[60] Quinney, *Critique of Legal Order,* p. 191.
[61] Taylor, Walton, and Young, *The New Criminology,* p. 281.
[62] Schur, *Labeling Deviant Behavior.*

rage among segments of the community and the probabilities can be determined.[63] This rescues us from complete relativity. If we keep in mind the foregoing qualifications, then we can recognize the potential power of the labelist or interactionist perspective.

This chapter has tried to demonstrate that there is a link between those criminologists and sociologists whose common concern recently has been the increasing size and authority of control bureaucracies in modern western society. Hence, a wide variety of things have been included under the category "conflict criminologists" even though they might not so classify themselves. The emergence of Marxist criminology is partly a response to correctionalizing trends and partly an attempt to deepen and build on the insights of the social reaction theorists as well as earlier criminologists. It holds promise of synthesizing what we know about crime and criminality and pointing us in new research directions.

This recent development holds great promise for liberating criminology from eclecticism, superficial reformism, and correctionalism. Whether or not this occurs depends on the scholarship produced by the new criminologists. If the emphasis on the centrality of industrial conflict produces powerful, complex, and sophisticated paradigms for the explanation of crime and criminality this may be sufficient to persuade those criminologists who deplore "ideological approaches" to crime and delinquency.

This concludes the section on theories of crime and criminality. The beginning student should now have some overall notion of what criminology is all about, what arguments have dominated the field, and what directions research is taking.

The next section of the book is devoted to the emergence and development of the social control establishment and how it operates. The cases that follow each section are designed to give some feel for what the criminal justice system is, as well as the problems it poses for society and the individuals who are processed by it. It is in the case study section that the relevance of the theories discussed so far will be weighed.

[63] Erich Goode, "On Behalf of Labeling Theory," *Social Problems* 22(5) (June 1975), 570–83.

Part Two

CRIME
CONTROL
AND
CRIMINALIZATION

The following chapters on the administration of the criminal law present and interpret most of the research done on police, courts, and corrections. These three agencies are generally referred to as "the criminal justice system." It is somewhat misleading, however, to refer to this complex as a system. The term "criminal justice system" has received wide currency and general legitimation since 1967, when the President's Commission on Law Enforcement and the Administration of Justice in its task force report on science and technology proposed to use systems analysis to improve the operation of police, courts, and corrections. The problem with the simulated model they developed was that it relied on official accounts of how the real complex operated, and ignored the way in which day-to-day operations were carried out. In the day-to-day activity of all organizations official rules are sometimes carried out, sometimes ignored, or sometimes subverted for a variety of reasons. The "system" we are referring to in this section includes both official and informal definitions as well as the cooperative and conflicted relationships within and between the various components that exist.

There is a substantial literature on the police written by policemen. This literature is valuable for the insights it provides on present or past police doctrine and what they see to be their problems. But it is almost valueless for developing a scholarly understanding of the police. Recently scholars from more traditional disciplines (sociology, political science, law, and history) have turned their attention to the police, and an impressive and richly documented literature is beginning to emerge. Legal scholars concerned with the issue of due process have explored ways in which this ideal is difficult to realize at the police level. Political scientists have focused on how the political culture of a community affects police organization and styles of operation. Sociologists have looked at the police much as they would any other occupation, noting recruiting patterns, training, and types of colleague and client relationships. The police have staked out a mandate that professes to be efficient, nonpolitical, and professional enforcement of the law. The problems in carrying out this mandate create unusual problems for them, especially in their dealings with the public.

Full enforcement of the law is an impossible goal. It would require that, at least, every other person be a policeman. Societies, or, more accurately, segments of them, generally decide on a set of priorities, and punish wrongdoers accordingly. Any attempt to punish all wrongdoers would create a situation of savage repression. Yet the sieve which sorts out those to be processed does not operate in an impartial way. The research reported in the previous section indicates that our enforcement apparatus selects those most vulnerable to successful labeling. As Blumberg, among others, has noted, the selection of candidates for the adjudication process is not some version of a roulette game where everyone has an equal chance to be included.[1] It disproportionally draws from the lower classes. Persons are arrested who can offer the fewest rewards for nonenforcement of the laws and who can be processed without causing any undue strain for the police organization. Middle-class persons and those engaged in professional crime have the resources to discourage enforcement of the law against them and create much difficulty in being processed. As noted earlier, 40 percent of those arrested in 1967 were arrested for drunkenness, disorderly conduct, or vagrancy.[2] Along with shoplifting, armed robbery, and homicide, these largely make up the crime statistics. They are all highly visible crimes committed by socially marginal strata.

The case following the police section is designed to sensitize students to one of the major issues in policing today: police mistreatment of citizens. The theories discussed in Part One on criminality provide little by way of identifying the structural determinants of this behavior. We must look to explanations that focus on the imperatives of the work organization and work setting.

The criminal courts have been less thoroughly studied than the police by social scientists or historians. This is the domain of the lawyer or legal scholar. There is a certain kind of research on the criminal courts—the crime survey—that has received public acceptance but it is not very helpful in understanding the court as an organization with unique problems. The criminologist can determine from these surveys something about the character of the court's clients (sex, race, and previous convictions). They can also

[1] Abraham S. Blumberg, "Criminal Justice in America," in Jack D. Douglas (ed.), *Crime and Justice in American Society* (Indianapolis: Bobbs-Merrill, 1971), p. 46.
[2] President's Commission on Law Enforcement and Administration of Justice, *The Challenge of Crime in a Free Society* (Washington, D.C.: Government Printing Office, 1967), p. 233.

analyze convictions by type of crime and develop rough indexes of the court's productivity and "efficiency." But the sociological perspective focuses on the criminal court's organizational context and the implications this has for the work performed. The court is a bureaucracy and operates much like other bureaucracies. The term "bureaucracy" is not used in a derogatory sense but in a technical sense. Max Weber has pointed out the technical superiority of bureaucratic organization over any other form.[3] It is the most rational way to deal with a complex task involving a large number of people. The task is broken down into its component parts, a specialized staff is hired to perform various facets of the task, authority is centralized and impersonal, and the staff member performs in conformity with set policies and work routines. A well-ordered bureaucracy operates with clearly defined rules and the element of caprice or arbitrariness is absent. Yet in the criminal court's efforts to maximize its resources and minimize strain with the critical public, the rights of the accused are denied. The point of this chapter is to indicate how a system that propels almost everyone caught up in it, whether innocent or guilty, toward a guilty plea can be unscrambled and made to operate more humanely. The case tries to demonstrate the difficulties inherent in the use of plea bargaining to address the problem of intolerably large caseloads.

The chapter on the criminal courts is followed by a discussion of corrections. Corrections is not a unitary phenomenon. In the United States the correctional system is an amalgam of facilities, theories, techniques, and programs. A survey of American corrections conducted as a substudy for the President's Commission on Law Enforcement and the Administration of Justice in 1967 reported that this system handles nearly 1.3 million offenders on an average day; it has 2.5 million admissions in the course of a year; and its annual operating budget is over a billion dollars, less than half of what is spent on policing.[4] The fact that corrections is relatively smaller than the police should not obscure the importance of the correctional system, especially in the United States where there is a more pronounced tendency to incarcerate. Norwegian criminologist Christie estimated the imprisoned population of a number of advanced industrial nations and found that there were proportionally more prisoners in the United States (200 per 100,000 population compared to Norway's 44 per 100,000 population).[5] Compared with the other two components of the criminal justice system, corrections is the most reactive—it must accept those who are sentenced. Both the police and the courts are more proactive—they can decide which clients they will accept and which they will reject. The correctional apparatus is constrained by statutes and policies that limit its discretion and initiative. In this they are unlike the police who can generate their own customers. The amount of

---

[3] Max Rheinstein (ed.), *Max Weber on Law in Economy and Society* (Cambridge, Mass.: Harvard University Press, 1954), pp. xxxii–xxxiv.

[4] President's Commission on Law Enforcement and Administration of Justice, *Task Force Report: Corrections* (Washington, D.C.: Government Printing Office, 1967).

[5] Nils Christie quoted in Leslie Wilkins, *Social Deviance, Social Policy, Action and Research* (Englewood Cliffs, N.J.: Prentice-Hall, 1965), p. 83.

initiative that can be exercised by the correctional component is limited but not entirely absent. Indeterminate sentences and the discretion to parole an offender immediately back to the community increase the initiative available to the correctional bureaucracy. Of the three parts of the criminal justice system, corrections is the most remote from the local community both physically and psychologically.

The isolation of corrections obscures its enormous political significance. The central function of the prison is not the segregation of those who are "dangerous" but deterrence in the broadest sense. The existence of prisons creates a significant risk factor in the commission of crime. The focus of the punishment apparatus is the mass of people on the outside, not primarily those who are inside. As many critics of the prison system point out, it does not seem to deter crime; that is, the threat of punishment is not important in the decision to commit or not to commit a crime. But it is important in determining the kind of crime committed. The threat of punishment has great impact on how individuals choose to break the law. It is a potent force for regulating criminal activity in ways which are less threatening to the social order. It is this regulatory function which makes its role in the criminal justice system so critical.

The symbol of the old penology—which continues today to coexist with the new—was the fortress prison. The symbol of the new penology is the quasi-medical facility. Its watchword is rehabilitation. The transformation of the offender from a sinner to a patient and the problems this has created are discussed. A more recent development, still largely in the discussion stage, is the substitution of a due process model for the medical one that is dominant in the treatment of inmates. The case included in this section highlights one of the main problems for corrections: the unintended consequences of the ideology of rehabilitation.

The three organizational case studies in Part Two are each followed by a brief analysis of their plausibility, typicality, and the extent to which they confirm, modify, or challenge existing explanations. The analyses are designed to provoke further discussion, not substitute for it. The "Questions for Further Discussion" are best used in a group setting.

6

the police

The emergence of the professional police organization is a fairly late development. Prior to the nineteenth century, policing in Britain was done primarily by officers of the courts. The beginnings of the modern police system are discernible with the growth of town watchmen and constables. With the growth of commerce and a variety of products to steal came demands for a more effective kind of policing. The first American police department was set up in Boston in 1822.[1] In 1829 the London municipal police organization was established, followed by the creation of the New York force in 1844, and the Chicago force in 1851.

The Metropolitan Police of London is the prototype of modern police organization.[2] The bureaucratized police force had several distinct advantages over private police or the army from the point of view of those whose property they defended. First, the army wasn't equipped to meet the enduring needs of safety; it was difficult for it to act continuously in small dispersed units in civilian society. Second, the newly formed police force relieved the merchants from performing police functions themselves and thus antagonizing the local population. They patrolled designated beats regularly and operated under strict rules. They quickly

[1] Roger Lane, *Policing the City: Boston, 1822–1885* (Cambridge, Mass.: Harvard University Press, 1967).
[2] J. L. Lyman, "The Metropolitan Police Act of 1829," *Journal of Criminal Law, Criminology and Police Science,* 55 (1964), 141–54.

demonstrated that their fluid organization, which enabled rapid concentration, could overcome numbers.

The oldest American police department established in Boston was organized as a night watch to keep peace in the streets. Beginning in 1834, men drafted from the citizenry were required to take their turns in seeing "that all disturbances and disorders in the night shall be prevented and suppressed." Interestingly, apprehending robbers or burglars was not among the duties of the night watchman. As Wilson put it:

> . . . indeed it was not even among the duties of the government. A victim was obliged to find the guilty party himself. Once a suspect was found, the citizen could, for a fee, hire a constable who, acting on a warrant, would take the suspect into custody. Even after detectives—that is, men charged with law enforcement rather than the maintenance of order—were added to the force in the nineteenth century, they continued to serve essentially private interests. The chief concern of the victim was restitution, and to that end, the detectives would seek to recover loot in exchange for a percentage of the take. Detectives functioned then as personal-injury lawyers operate today, on a contingency basis, hoping to get a large part, perhaps half, of the proceeds.[3]

Wilson maintains that the emergence of a municipal police force out of its watchmen antecedents was not so much the result of mounting crime rates as of growing levels of civil disorder. The Boston police department seems to have been created to deal with riots as was the Philadelphia department.[4] A series of civil disorders beginning in the early 1820s and continuing through the 1830s vividly underlined the inability of the watchmen organization to maintain or restore civil order. Evidence presented by Lane suggests that much of the rioting was a reaction to the changing ethnic composition of Boston's population. The pattern in Philadelphia was similar. Though Wilson says the constabulary was created to deal with riots among youthful gangs, the rioting was semiofficial. It was not the work of irrational mobs. It occurred because of the existence of competing volunteer fire companies called to fires set by gangs to find out who could get there fastest.

> To a degree, the riots were under semiofficial auspices, thus magnifying the embarrassment the politicians faced. It seems that volunteer fire companies were originated to handle conflagrations. The young toughs who sat about waiting for fires to happen found this boring, and worse, unrewarding, whereupon some hit upon the idea of starting a fire and racing other companies to the scene to

[3] James Q. Wilson, "What Makes a Better Policeman?" *Atlantic Monthly*, 223 (March 1969), 129–35.
[4] Lane, *Policing the City*.

see who could put the blaze out more quickly, and just as important, who could pick up the most loot from the building. Though this competitive zeal may have been a commendable aid to training, it led to frequent collisions between companies speeding to the same fire, with the encounter often leading to a riot. It is only a slight exaggeration to say that the Philadelphia policemen were created in part to control the Philadelphia firemen.[5]

THE FUNCTION OF THE POLICE

Until the twentieth century the major function of the police organization was order maintenance; only a minor part of its work consisted of law enforcement (the catching of criminals). These two functions are relatively independent of one another and to some extent in conflict with each other. When operating as "law officers," police have an eye on the future disposition of a case in the courts. When operating as "peace officers," their primary aim is to maintain order or keep things quiet. These two aspects of the police mandate have always been part of the police role. Yet not too much is known about the peace-keeping role, though by all accounts it constitutes the bulk of day-to-day police activity. It is dealt with only casually in police texts and police training, the assumption being that it involves personal wisdom, integrity, and altruism that come only from experience. Much more systematic attention has been given to law enforcement. According to the research division of the International Association for the Chiefs of Police, "the percentage of the police effort devoted to traditional criminal law matters probably does not exceed ten percent."[6] In a study of 801 incoming telephone calls to a metropolitan police department Cumming et al. noted that only 20 percent were related to crime or violence.[7]

Order maintenance rarely leads to an arrest. It involves police intervention in altercations between citizens as in domestic squabbles. The parties to the dispute are generally known to one another, if laws are broken they are usually misdemeanors and require that one of the parties swear out a formal complaint. The discretion of the patrolman gives him a wide range of options: he can simply do nothing when he confronts a trouble situation. He can overlook, ignore, or dismiss many enforceable breaches. This

[5] Wilson, "What Makes a Better Policeman?" pp. 131–32.
[6] Quoted in Richard A. Myren and Lynn D. Swanson, *Police Contacts with Juveniles*, 2nd rev. draft (Washington, D.C. Children's Bureau, Department of Health, Education and Welfare, June 1961), pp. 1–4.
[7] Elaine Cumming, Ian Cumming, and Laura Edell, "Policeman as Philosopher, Guide and Friend," *Social Problems,* 12 (Winter 1965), 276–86.

is most likely to happen, LaFave contends, when the crime has very low visibility and the lack of enforcement is unlikely to be detected or challenged.[8] The police can also mediate arguments, disperse offenders, or issue warnings. None of these options involve arrest, although arrest is the ultimate resource.

Organizationally the police are responsible to the executive branch of government, but their day-to-day law enforcement functions are under the control of the judiciary. Police activities relating to law enforcement come under judicial review and recently have been the source of continuing conflict between the police and the appellate courts. Those police activities that do not eventuate in arrests or prosecution are not under supervision of the judiciary. The assumption is that the executive branch controls these nonprosecution activities, but to what extent it controls is debatable, because the police have one organizational feature that makes them unique: discretion increases as you move down the hierarchy. Because of the character of patrol activity it is extremely difficult to supervise. Patrolmen are given more instructions on what *not* to do than firm guidelines for maintaining order.

It is only recently that the peace-keeping function of police has come under systematic investigation, notably in the work of James Q. Wilson and Egon Bittner. Wilson has suggested that there are various organizational and community contexts that affect the use of police discretion in the vast majority of citizen-police contacts (His contribution is discussed in more detail below.) Bittner has tried to clarify the structural determinants of peace keeping in typical situations that police perceive as demand conditions for action without arrest.[9] He notes that there is considerable skill involved, that the police themselves have standards of skilled performance, and that peace keeping is only tangentially related to the officer's personality. There are five situations he identifies as calling for a peace-keeping response: (1) the activity of supervising licensed services or premises and the regulation of traffic; (2) control of behavior where public response on the best course of action is conflicted, as in the case of juveniles; (3) public demand for police intervention that involves no criminal or legal aspects, as in family disputes; (4) controlling crowds in the incipient stages of disorder; and (5) situations involving those who may not be thought fully accountable for their actions and thus produce special problems that necessitate continuous attention and use of special procedures, as in the case of the mentally ill. The activities called for in these situations are not addressed by judicial proscriptions on unlawful

[8] Wayne LaFave, Arrest, *The Decision to Take a Suspect into Custody* (Boston: Little, Brown, 1965).
[9] Egon Bittner, "The Police on Skid Row: A Study of Peace Keeping," *American Sociological Review*, 32 (October 1967), 699–715.

arrest, unlawful search and seizure, and inadmissible confessions and admissions. The implication is that some aspects of peace keeping are illegal. The police are expected to react to conflicting demands. On the one hand they are enjoined to observe due process and on the other to control crime. Skolnick summarizes the police dilemma:

> The police in democratic society are required to maintain order and to do so under the rule of law. As functionaries charged with maintaining order, they are part of the bureaucracy. The ideology of democratic bureaucracy emphasizes the initiative rather than disciplined adherence to rules and regulations. By contrast the rule of law emphasizes the rights of individual citizens and constraints upon the initiative of legal officials. The tension between the operational consequences of ideas of order, efficiency, and initiative on the one hand, and legality, on the other constitutes the principle problem of police as a democratic legal organization.[10]

Historical evidence is sketchy, but in the United States there was strong community acceptance of the police function under public auspices and few challenges to it until the mid-twentieth century. Public support for policing, however, remains strong. The relatively crude data examined by Clark in 1965 showed a basic congruence between public and police views on desired police operations both in Britain and America. Whatever criticisms may be made, no one has suggested that the police function no longer be performed or that some parts of policing should be returned to private enterprise.

The early police organizations had all the characteristics of a craft. Learning was by apprenticeship, there was little specialization, minimum deference to hierarchy and few employees in staff positions. Many police organizations today still display these characteristics. Wilson characterized this pattern as a "watchman style" in contrast to the "legalistic" and "service" styles.[11] Police are recruited locally; they are given the minimum in initial training and no in-service education. Characteristically in this style there are no rewards for higher education. Since the major activity of the police is maintaining order their discretion is great. The individual policeman can decide by and large which laws to enforce by arrest, which behavior he will respond to informally or not at all. His authority is personal not bureaucratic. Patrolmen are encouraged to follow the path of least resistance in carrying out routine assignments. They withdraw from as many adversary relations with the public as they

[10] Jerome Skolnick, *Justice Without Trial* (New York: John Wiley, 1966), p. 6.
[11] James Q. Wilson, *Varieties of Police Behavior* (Cambridge, Mass.: Harvard University Press, 1968).

can. In this earlier pattern the police also performed many functions that today would be considered inappropriate. They administered services to those who, because of alcohol or circumstance, were likely to become sources of public disorder. Lane notes that the Boston police in 1856 provided lodgings for over 9,000 persons.[12] This number jumped to 17,000 in 1860. The Boston police chief was also charged with public health responsibilities. The police offered a wide range of other services— providing coal for the needy, running soup kitchens and informal employment agencies. The emphasis on keeping the peace and the proportion of police activity devoted to service administration provided many pleasant contacts with the community. Today this watchman style is more likely to be found in smaller, more homogeneous communities rather than large municipalities. A good part of the policeman's task in smaller communities still consists of service administration, though police themselves tend to view these activities as "unprofessional."

Unlike police of today, early police did not feel stigmatized because of their occupation nor did they sense that they were in a pariah status. Police isolation and conflict with local communities began when police were charged with enforcing liquor laws. Under these laws they could initiate prosecutions on their own authority rather than citizen complaint. Coincident with this development was the curtailment of the service function and the bureaucratization of the detectives (those charged with law enforcement). Wilson states that there is no intrinsic reason that the bureaucratization of detectives and the enforcement of unpopular liquor laws should overshadow the order maintenance function. But two other events, Prohibition and the Depression, gave emphasis to the law enforcement function. Prohibition, Wilson observes, required police everywhere to choose between being corrupt and making a nuisance of themselves. The Depression focused attention on the daring exploits of a handful of bank robbers. The two seemed to be related—police corruption and rising crime rates. The implications seemed clear-cut: the police were not attending to their law enforcement functions.

The study of crime and the police role in preventing it has been the subject of many local investigations and three major national commission reports. The Wickersham Commission was created by President Hoover as a consequence of the dissatisfaction generated by police enforcement of unpopular liquor laws and the dramatic increase in violent crime during the 1920s concomitant with the growth of the bootlegging industry. The increasing annoyance with law enforcement was reflected in the recommendations of that commission. The recommendations emphasized

[12] Lane, *Policing the City,* ch. 6.

that law enforcement, rather than order maintenance, was of central importance and suggested the police be removed from politics to reduce corruption. They also suggested that police be put on civil service, that more modern equipment be added, that better men be hired and given better training. That report set the police on a course from which they have not swerved in more than 40 years. Its rallying cry was "police professionalism." Most municipal police departments have been removed from narrow political control since, police jobs are mainly civil service, and an enormous expansion of their technological resources has taken place. The direction the police took was in response to a particular set of problems but has created some more of its own as a consequence.

The professional model that has developed has emphasized the technical aspects of police work and has reduced the discretion available to patrolmen. Authority resides in well-defined offices as in other bureaucracies. The pattern of the departments that have chosen a professional response is to recruit nationally and to emphasize formal education. Efficiency as measured by crime rates is stressed. Wilson has characterized this police style as "legalistic." In such a department, many traffic tickets are issued, many juvenile offenders are detained and arrested, illicit enterprises are acted against vigorously, and misdemeanor arrests are often made even when public order has not been breached. There is a single standard of behavior to which all citizens are expected to conform. Hence there is no recognition of different standards to be invoked when dealing with juveniles, blacks, drunks, and the like. The legalistic departments produce more arrests and citations than do their watchmen style counterparts, especially arrests that are police rather than citizen invoked. Impersonality, good appearance, a single standard, and courtesy are emphasized. Wilson suggests that this style may develop when a "reform chief" tries to get hold of his department. Formal hierarchal authority is strengthened at the expense of informal clique authority. There is much filling out of forms and the police are constantly reminded that they are being evaluated in terms of their energy in imposing rules and efficiency in completing reports about incidents. Specialized staff is expanded in this style. Wilson concludes that though the legalistic departments are more even-handed in their treatment of citizens, the increased frequency of contact makes for more citizen hostility. Where this style is successfully created it seems to depend on the existence of a city manager who stands as a buffer between the legalistic departments, political pressure and the existence of a supportive group of upper strata business executives.

The first systematic study of the police as an occupational group was conducted after World War II. Westley's examination of a midwestern police department focused on how the police department's adversary relationship with the local community gave rise to a collective emphasis on secrecy in an attempt to gain respect from the public.[13] Westley noted that the police are in a service occupation but of an unusual kind—they must discipline those whom they serve. To do their job and survive in what they perceive to be a hostile environment, they must shield their operations, especially those aspects that would lead to community criticism. This, he suggests, gives rise to a collective emphasis on secrecy, an attempt to coerce respect from the public, and a belief that almost any means are legitimate in completing an important arrest. Feelings of being on the spot generated a strong sense of solidarity. It was an unwritten law in this midwestern department that police must never inform on each other. Westley asked a series of questions to explore how strong the solidarity was. He reported that three-quarters of the policemen he interviewed would not report a partner's illegality and if required to testify against a coworker would perjure themselves. Westley notes that there are strong sanctions supporting secrecy. An informer would not get the full support of his partners in dangerous situations and would be cut off from the police grapevine. In short, Westley's study showed that the police had constructed a subculture to insulate themselves from the community. The subculture permitted them to control themselves—they were able to define their own norms and to defend, reward, and promote policemen who adhered to them.

Another element of police work that contributes to the present problems of police is that the emphasis on professionalism has led to a stress on crime statistics. The statistics demonstrated police concern with scientific data and indicated their capacity to control crime. Thus in the police view—and the view of substantial and powerful segments of the American public—efficient law enforcement is an attainable goal. Efficiency is measured in terms of the fluctuations of the crime rate. Manning points out that police inability to cope with the causes of crime has led them into symptomatic concerns like preoccupations with rates of crime, not its causes.[14] The community assumes falsely that the police can prevent crime. Wilson notes that most crime is not prevented and most criminals not caught even in the best-run, best-manned departments.[15] Most crimes occur in secret. But whether a department is regarded as "backward" or "modern," neither seems able to bring about a substantial re-

[13] William Westley, *The Police: A Sociological Study of Law, Custom and Morality* (unpublished Ph.D. dissertation, University of Chicago, 1951).
[14] Peter K. Manning, "The Police: Mandate Strategies and Appearances," in Richard Quinney (ed.), *Criminal Justice in America: A Critical Understanding* (Boston: Little, Brown, 1974), pp. 170–200.
[15] Wilson, "What Makes a Better Policeman?"

duction of the crime rate. Police are burdened with unrealizable goals and Wilson concludes that their response is like that of all organizations judged by unattainable standards—they lie. Because of the demands placed on them the police are put in the position of *appearing* to prevent crime, thus satisfying the community's concern for safety.

A more comprehensive description of the police subculture and the working personality of the police was given by Skolnick in his 1966 study of a West Coast police department.[16] Skolnick maintains that the policeman's role contains two principal variables—danger and authority—which he interprets under pressure to appear efficient. The element of danger makes him especially alert to signs indicating a potential for violence. This leads to suspicion. Wilson, in his later study of eight police departments, goes further in saying that the element of danger also carries over into order maintaining functions.[17] The apprehension communicated to citizens thus may increase the possibilities of danger. Too, he suggests, the tendency to act suspicious is not simply because of the dangers inherent in police work but because of police doubts about the "legitimacy" of the victim:

> . . . the police have seen it all before and have come to distrust victim accounts . . . of what happened. Instead of offering sympathy and immediately taking the victim's side, the police may seem cool, suspicious, or disinterested because they have learned that "victims" often turn out not to have been victimized at all—the "stolen" TV never existed or was lost, loaned to a boyfriend or hidden because the payments were overdue; the "assault" was in fact a fight which the "victim" started but was unable to finish.[18]

This element of suspicion isolates the police officer from that group he regards as dangerous and also from conventional citizens. The police, according to Skolnick, develop a perceptual shorthand for identifying certain kinds of people as "symbolic assailants." Their occupational assumptions about the everyday world showed how important the potential danger and suspicion are.[19] Their ten assumptions are:

1. people cannot be trusted; they are dangerous;

2. experience is better than abstract rules;

3. you must make people respect you;

4. everyone hates a cop;

[16] Skolnick, *Justice Without Trial.*
[17] Wilson, *Varieties of Police Behavior*, pp. 19–20.
[18] Ibid., p. 25.
[19] Manning, "The Police," p. 175.

5. the legal system is trustworthy—police make the best decisions about guilt or innocence;

6. people who are not controlled will break the law;

7. police must appear respectable and be efficient;

8. police can most accurately identify crime and criminals;

9. the major jobs of police are to prevent crime and enforce the law;

10. stronger punishment will deter criminals from repeating their errors.

According to Manning, these assumptions apply primarily to the American noncollege-educated patrolman. They are less applicable to administrators of urban police departments and to members of minority groups within them. They don't apply to nonurban, state, and federal police. The municipal police, who are the central focus of this chapter, constitute the largest proportion of police in the United States. The President's Commission on Law Enforcement and the Administration of Justice in 1967 noted that some 420,000 people work for approximately 40,000 separate agencies and spend more than $2.5 billion per year.[20] An extensive sheriff system exists in the United States as well as a number of national police organizations. The most famous is the Federal Bureau of Investigation but other federal departments have agents for enforcement of laws pertaining to currency, narcotics, internal revenue, customs, immigration, and the post office. There are also state police organizations and a network of private police. Private police are selected, financed, and controlled privately. They include detectives employed for the protection of banks, department stores, and other business-industrial concerns. Other special police include inspectors and examiners appointed by public authorities such as food inspectors, inspectors of weights and measures, bank examiners, and the like. But it is the urban police who have the day-to-day contact with citizens and whose assumptions about the world and their job have public consequences.

Under the banner of professionalism, according to Manning, the police are able to defend their mandate—to build self-esteem, organizational autonomy, and occupational solidarity. This sense of professionalism helps the police to insulate themselves from community criticism but it leaves unanswered the question of what an ideal relationship with the

[20] President's Commission on Law Enforcement and the Administration of Justice, *The Challenge of Crime in a Free Society Task Force Report: The Police* (Washington, D.C.: Government Printing Office, 1967), pp. 7–9.

community would be. Antagonism to the police varies by community and seems greatest in those cities where there is a large lower-strata population and considerable heterogeneity. If the community is small, middle-class, and homogeneous there seems to be little antagonism to the police function. Wilson identified a third police style that seemed more characteristic of these communities: the "service style."[21] In these communities the police take seriously all requests for either law enforcement or order maintenance but are less likely to respond by making arrests. The police intervene frequently but not formally. According to Wilson the police can act as if their task were to estimate the market for police services and to produce a product that meets the demand. The police in this setting are as highly professionalized as their legalistic counterparts but "closer" to the community and more concerned about the services they can provide. Wilson seems to think this style combines the best features of the other two without any of their negative consequences. However, he does not see its workability in large heterogeneous communities with a substantial lower-class population. Despite the fact that particular patrol styles can be identified, the fact of the matter is that patrol discretion is extremely difficult to control from the top. These styles only emerge when the administrator's orders are binding on patrolmen. This in turn is dependent on the capacity of the administrator to create loyalty to his internal policies.

POLICE PROBLEMS

Police officers, because of their "impossible" mandate and the conflicting demands of the public, pursue contradictory and unattainable ends. Manning points out that the police respond to this situation by giving the appearance of attaining the goals of law enforcement and peace keeping.[22] Technology and official statistics are the major strategies by which this is accomplished. But Manning also observes that they are driven to secrecy as a means of controlling public response to their operations, driven to collaboration with criminal elements to foster the appearance of a smoothly run, law-abiding community, and compelled to participate in a symbiotic relationship with the criminal justice system that minimizes public knowledge of its flaws. Tension between police and community has centered around two major issues: excessive use of force or denial of the right of due process, and police corruption.

21 Wilson, *Varieties of Police Behavior*, ch. 7.
22 Manning, "The Police."

Citizen Mistreatment

One explanation of citizen mistreatment by the police is related to personality factors. It is hypothesized that persons with strong authoritarian impulses are drawn to police work. Several studies have tried to demonstrate that police officers value obedience and self-control over individual spontaneity, tolerance, and lenience.[23] Other investigators reject personality explanations in favor of occupational determinants of police behavior. They suggest that there is a "cop personality" but this is more related to the police subculture than it is to social background factors or the personal makeup of individual officers.[24]

Whether this "cop personality" is related to social background, personality selection, or socialization into the occupational subculture is unclear. What does seem evident is that the character of some police work betrays negative feelings about the public in general, cynicism about people's motives, and strong feelings of isolation from the community. One major problem perceived by the police is the lack of community cooperation. They feel their task is complicated by a hostile or apathetic public. Tifft has demonstrated that the reaction of police to the public is more complex than simple hostility.[25] Police reaction varies by the kind of task performed (patrol, traffic, detective) and by the type of citizen encounter. Traffic officers were more likely to perceive the general public as friendly and cooperative than all other units studied. Tifft queried his police officers on the significant elements in their task environment that most affected how their job was performed. There was a wide variation among units in identifying citizen attitudes as salient, from 18 percent in traffic to 48 percent in general assignment. Concern with danger, however, was frequently mentioned by policemen in all units, except those whose work did not involve serious crime or conflict situations. The courts were viewed as the most significant element by those who had major responsibility for case development or court testimony. The reaction to the courts was in terms of the constraints they placed on police behavior. To do their job, police feel they must sometimes break the law. Over the past 20 years, the police have been under a great deal of pressure to conform to the rule of law. The officially prescribed norms for the criminal process as laid down by the Supreme Court have emphasized that due process be

[23] Milton Roheach, Martin S. Miller, and John Snyder, "The Value Gap Between Police and Policed," *Journal of Social Issues*, 27 (1971), 155–72.
[24] Larry Tifft, "The 'Cop Personality' Reconsidered," *Journal of Police Science and Administration*, 2 (1974), 266–78.
[25] Ibid., pp. 275–77.

scrupulously observed. The procedure for arresting citizens on suspicion of having committed a crime has been specified. Police authority to search people on the basis of suspicion and the conditions for acceptable confessions have also been spelled out. The thrust is to "judicialize" each stage of the criminal process. Packer notes that this enhances the capacity of the accused to challenge the operation of the process. Packer has described the shift in the Supreme Court from what he calls a "crime control" model to a "due process" model:

> The Crime Control model sees the efficient, expeditious and reliable screening and disposition of persons suspected of crime as the central value to be served by the criminal process. The Due Process model sees that function as limited by the subordinate to the maintenance of the dignity and autonomy of the individual. The Crime Control model is administrative and managerial; the Due Process model is adversary and judicial. The Crime Control model may be analogized to an assembly line, the Due Process model to an obstacle course.[26]

Thus the rules of due process have been expanded and strengthened through the right to counsel, the right to remain silent, the limitations of confession. They are predicated on the existence of an adversary system. These rules of due process introduce an element of contingency or uncertainty in police work. It is to be expected that police would try to rework these rules for organizationally prescribed ends so as to reduce the uncertainty and chances of work failure.

Criticism from influential sections of the white liberal community between 1940 and 1965 focused on "police brutality," especially toward black citizens. The police were accused of using questionable enforcement procedures to carry out their mandate. Dissatisfaction continued when, during the 1960s, police abused young white dissidents and members of ethnic working-class communities. The crux of the problem, according to Chevigny, is that the police operate with the conviction that their authority is not validated by the local community, and are extremely sensitive to challenges posed to it in citizen encounters.[27] Banton reports that both British and Scottish police, unlike their American counterparts, don't need to establish their authority in citizen encounters.[28] The fact that American police face greater danger and deal with a more heterogeneous population probably aggravates the problem of public accep-

---

[26] Herbert L. Packer, "The Courts, the Police and the Rest of Us," *Journal of Criminal Law, Criminology and Police Science,* 57 (September 1966), 238–43.
[27] Paul Chevigny, *Police Power* (New York: Pantheon Books, 1969).
[28] Michael Banton, *The Policeman in the Community* (London: Lavistach, 1964), pp. 227–40.

tance. In encounters where police perceive challenges to their authority, they demand submission and if it is not given they respond antagonistically.[29]

Hostile citizen-police encounters are most likely to occur when departmental policy encourages aggressive field interrogations. If the police have "probable cause" to believe that a crime has been committed and that a suspect is the perpetrator, the suspect can be interrogated on the street. Recently some states have passed "stop and frisk" legislation which has expanded police discretion even more—when a policeman reasonably believes that he is in danger, he has the authority now to stop and frisk anyone for a possible weapon. The President's Commission on Law Enforcement and the Administration of Justice reported in 1967 that "stop and frisk" authority was being primarily used against residents of urban slums. The practice has been seriously criticized by those who have been exposed to it as victims. A police manual on how to frisk states that the suspect is told to stand facing the wall with his hands raised. Then:

> The officer must feel with sensitive fingers every portion of the prisoner's body. A thorough search must be made of the prisoner's arms and armpits, waistline and back, the groin and area about the testicles, the entire surface of the legs down to the feet.[30]

The 1967 Task Force Report on the Police indicated that field interrogation was being abused because it was being used to control minor crimes like vagrancy and loitering. Reiss looked at police mistreatment of citizens by observing police-citizen encounters in Boston, Washington, D.C., and Chicago.[31] He included the following practices in his definition of brutality: the use of profane and abusive language; commands to move on or get home; stopping or questioning people on the street or searching them and their cars; threats to use force if not obeyed; prodding with a night stick or approaching citizens with a drawn pistol; actual use of physical force or violence itself. These are ways the police have traditionally behaved in dealing with the lower class. It was only as police came in contact with middle-class citizens that the elements of politeness and courtesy were introduced. Sutherland reported that the man who had been police chief in Milwaukee at the turn of the century explained how police practice shifted:

[29] John H. McNamara, "Uncertainties in Police Work," in David J. Bordua (ed.), *The Police: Six Sociological Essays* (New York: John Wiley, 1967).
[30] Quoted in Abraham S. Blumberg, "Criminal Justice in America," in Jack D. Douglas (ed.), *Crime and Justice in American Society* (Indianapolis: Bobbs-Merrill, 1971), p. 59.
[31] Albert J. Reiss, Jr., "Police Brutality—Answers to Key Questions," *Trans-Action,* 5 (July–August 1968), 10–19.

"This emphasis on courtesy began when policemen began to come in contact with those who drove automobiles." Automobile drivers forty years ago [approximately 1910] were almost all persons of considerable wealth and social importance. They did not appreciate the sarcasm and rudeness of the patrolmen of that day and complained bitterly about it to the chief of police, who then trained the patrolmen to be polite. This had gone unnoticed when policemen came in contact principally with poorer people.[32]

Reiss reported that the police used "excessive force" on 519 of every 1,000 citizens involved. The comparable rate for blacks was surprisingly low: 2.8 per 1,000. The application of force seemed to operate without respect to the race of the offender. In fact, Reiss reports that police are more likely to use force against a member of their *own* race. Force was more likely to be used in settings that the police controlled. About one-third of them took place at the police station—the administrator's domain—where control can be most easily exercised. According to Reiss open defiance of authority or resisting arrest most often precipitated use of police force. Sometimes a simple refusal to acquiesce prompted violence. The conclusion supports some of the early observations about police concern with establishing their authority. The violence was likely to occur when there was some question about who was in charge.

Police Corruption

Because the police are charged with the supervision of certain licensed services and premises, they must make judgments on their worthiness. Bittner points out that police concentrate on the moral aspects of establishments rather than their technical adequacy because certain types of businesses lend themselves to exploitation for undesirable and illegal purposes.[33] Since this can't be fully controlled, it is to be expected that police would at least favor licensees who are cooperative. Their job is transformed then from one of scrutinizing credentials to the creation of a network of connections that conveys influence, pressure, and information. The networks acquire additional value for solving crimes and maintaining order:

> Bartenders, shopkeepers, and hotel clerks become, for patrolmen, a resource that must be continuously serviced by visits and exchanges of favors. While it is apparent that this condition lends itself to cor-

[32] Karl Schuessler (ed.), *Edwin H. Sutherland On Analyzing Crime* (Chicago: University of Chicago Press, 1973), p. 168.
[33] Bittner, "The Police on Skid Row," Schuessler, *Edwin H. Sutherland On Analyzing Crime,* p. 703.

rupt exploitation by individual officers, even the most flawlessly honest policeman must participate in this network of exchanges if he is to function adequately. Thus, engaging in such exchanges becomes an occupational task that demands attention and time.[34]

It is this situation that can create a relationship between police and professional criminals. Chambliss maintains that it is virtually impossible for a law enforcement system to operate effectively and efficiently without developing policies and practices that are mutually advantageous to professional criminals and the legal system.[35] For example, the police need information from those who buy and sell stolen goods in order to recover stolen property. By professional criminals Chambliss is referring to those who make their living on organized crime—those who systematically violate gambling, prostitution, and sex laws about which there is some community ambivalence. Community ambivalence creates a dilemma for the police. Some powerful people insist that all laws be rigorously enforced; others demand that some not be enforced, at least against them. The police follow the line of least resistance, they adopt a "tolerance policy" toward the vices and selectively enforce pertinent laws only when it is to their advantage to do so. They control the location where the vices are most visible and thus minimize complaints. Their corruption then can be viewed as a natural consequence of societal demands for illegal services. In short, they control crime by encouraging the existence and persistence of behavior they are supposed to suppress. They end up regulating illegal activities. Chambliss notes one curious outcome of this relationship: the police are both controlling and controlled by the organizations that provide the vices. However, this overstates the strength of the relationship between the police and criminal elements. Manning points out that collaboration is relatively infrequent for entire departments—it is more likely to be present in those units that patrol the areas of segregated vice.[36] Where collaboration with organized crime is pervasive in a department it is supported by an informal social system that is at odds with legal statutes.

The acceptance of small bribes and favors that flow naturally from the licensing function sometimes sets a pattern which is difficult for the individual policeman to resist. Stoddard examined the character of the police code in one department which supported some police corruption.[37] He reported that the practices of mooching, chiseling, favoritism, and prej-

[34] Manning, "The Police," p. 173.
[35] William J. Chambliss, "Vice, Corruption, Bureaucracy and Power," *Wisconsin Law Review*, 4 (1971), 1150–73.
[36] Manning, "The Police," p. 190.
[37] Ellwyn R. Stoddard, "The Informal 'Code' of Police Deviancy: A Group Approach to 'Blue Coat-Crime,'" *Journal of Criminal Law, Criminology and Police Science*, 59 (June 1968), 201–13.

udice were accepted as a fact of life by this department and the local community. *Mooching* involved receiving free items as a consequence of being underpaid or for future acts of favoritism which might be received by the donor. *Chiseling* was the term used for police demands for free admission to entertainment. *Favoritism* referred to the practice of using license tabs, window stickers, or courtesy cards to gain immunity from traffic arrest or citation. *Prejudice* entailed showing less than impartial attention to those who have no political clout.

Informal norms also supported more serious kinds of illegality such as shopping, bribery, shakedowns, and perjury. *Shopping* and *shakedown* referred to the appropriation of items for personal use while attributing this form of corruption to criminal activity when investigating a break-in or burglary. Shakedown differed from shopping by the greater cost of the items appropriated. *Bribery* involved the payment of cash or gifts to avoid prosecution. It differed from mooching in the higher value of the gift and in the mutual understanding regarding services to be performed upon acceptance of the gift. *Perjury* entailed lying to provide alibis for fellow officers apprehended for illegal activity. Stoddard also queried his informant on *extortion*—the demand for advertisements in police magazines, the forced purchase of tickets to police functions, or "street courts" where minor traffic tickets were settled by cash payments without receipt. (Extortion practices did not receive support from the police code in this department.) Stoddard also discussed premeditated theft by police which included the use of tools, keys, extensive preparation, and the like. He noted that this activity was not supported by the informal police system in the department he studied. Occasionally stories of "burglars in blue" come to public attention and are usually given much publicity, but there is reason to believe that such activity is infrequent; the individual policeman involved is usually considered "deviant" by his coworkers.

Proposals for Reform

The response of upper levels of police administration to problems of excessive use of force is to professionalize further. Their contention is that this will address the problem of police mistreatment of citizens and corruption. Many big city departments have now instituted psychological tests to screen out sadists, have introduced human relations training to soften racial prejudices, have required college degrees and have increased salaries to instill a professional sense and discourage corruption, and have initiated internal review boards to discipline violators of professional norms. Though the President's Commission on Law Enforcement and the Administration of Justice expressed more concern than police administrators over police secrecy and collaboration with criminal systems, their solution is substantially similar: better trained men. Others have proposed to deal with police-minority antagonism by increasing the minority representation on local police forces and decreasing the use of white police in ghettos. Other reformists have tried to address the accountability issue more directly by suggesting that police live in the communities they patrol.

Wilson thinks that the goals of maintaining order and reducing the opportunities for crime are reasonable ones.[38] He proposes that both objectives would be served by increasing the capacity of the patrolman to make reliable judgments about the character, motives, intentions, and likely future actions of those he must police. This ability is improved by increasing the patrolman's familiarity with the neighborhood, even to the extent of having him live there. Wilson suggests that present measures of performance, stressing the "good pinch" (leading to conviction), are irrelevant to realizing a peace-keeping function. Other measures should be developed to measure the performance of peace keeping. Those who excel in it should rise in pay and rank without giving up their function. He suggests what an organization based on peace keeping rather than law enforcement would look like. There would be a family disturbance squad, a drunk and derelict squad, and a juvenile squad. Law enforcement matters would be addressed by a "felony squad." This would define and legitimate the peace-keeping function and at the same time improve police morale by removing some of the contradictions inherent in their work.

Manning's recommendations are to modify and update the criminal law and develop specific ways for the police to become more accountable.[39] This would be assisted, he thinks, by three interrelated organizational changes: a reorganization of police departments along functional lines aimed at peace keeping rather than law enforcement, allocation of rewards for keeping the peace rather than enforcing the law, and a decentralization of police functions to reflect community control without the diffusion of responsibility and accountability to a central headquarters. His proposals are substantially the same as Wilson's.

Some scholars who have conducted searching and radical critiques of criminal justice have proposed less sweeping reforms of the police. Chambliss notes with consternation that the police are immune from the surveillance of those institutions which elsewhere in American law are the primary means of keeping governmental operations legitimate. He feels that ultimately the economic, political, and social structures must be altered if we are to successfully alter police behavior. But in the mean-

[38] Wilson, *Varieties of Police Behavior*, ch. 9.
[39] Manning, "The Police."

time some progress can be made by improving the recruitment and socialization of police officers, formulating rules for the control of their discretion in the direction of a due process model, and changing the distribution of rewards in the bureaucracy to favor those whose practices conform to this model.[40]

Both Chambliss and Blumberg believe that the radical isolation of the individual (especially the low-income individual) in advanced capitalist countries is compensated for somewhat by the elaborate procedures to safeguard individual rights. Blumberg is aware that equality before the law is illusory in the presence of economic inequality and proposes to remedy that by making more legal and financial resources available for those vulnerable to police mistreatment.[41] He also proposes to narrow the police function and remove those tasks relating to alcoholics, gamblers, and addicts. Also traffic control and aiding the injured, lost, and helpless would be reassigned as civil occupations. Inevitably the mistakes and abuses that are part of a broad and ambiguous mandate would be remedied by this reorganization. The problem of secrecy would be somewhat mitigated by extensive use of civilian personnel.

Perhaps the most extensive reform of police structures has come from Waskow whose concern is the reestablishment of democratic civilian control over the police organization.[42] He finds the increasing insularity of the police and their gradually expanding power over the lives of citizens ominous. The hope of liberals from 1950 until the mid-1960s was that civilian review boards would make police more accountable to the communities they serve. But where review boards have been instituted they have triggered intense opposition from the police without mobilizing any real political base for themselves. Nor have they been able to go beyond particular instances of brutality or harassment to the deeper questions of what the police are, or what priorities they should follow in law enforcement. The unworkability of civilian review boards has led to their demise in all the major cities where they have been established.

Waskow suggests the sense in which they could work using the experience of the Watts Community Review Board. The board was not based on a quasi-judicial civilian review model, but on the notion that countervailing power was necessary to confront the police—in effect a "trade union" of those policed. The Watts board assumed that the police were an independent political force, not a neutral peace-keeping body. The board was linked to a political constituency which could press grievances against the police and compel more even-handed treatment. This griev-

[40] Chambliss, "Vice, Corruption, Bureaucracy and Power."
[41] Blumberg, "Criminal Justice in America," pp. 75–76.
[42] Arthur I. Waskow, "Toward Community Control of the Police," *Trans-Action*, 7 (December 1969), 4–6.

ance-processing formula does not challenge the basic assumptions of present-day policing and from Waskow's view this is its deficiency. The advantages, however, are obvious: The Watts experiment and the Crusade-for-Justice experience in Denver suggest that it can work; no major reorganization of the police is required; it can be undertaken without the agreement of those in power and it can defend a scattered population.

But Waskow favors a more radical decentralization that involves neighborhood control of the police function. His solution would require governmental consent and would involve breaking up present municipal police organizations into neighborhood federations with control of each force in the hands of local citizens. Local control means communities can determine their own priorities in law enforcement or they may decide to devote all of their energies to peace keeping. They would have the authority to determine their own particular patrol style; police would be chosen locally and required to live in the area. In response to the criticism that this would "Balkanize" the metropolitan area with different and conflicting patterns of control and police styles, Waskow responds that municipalities are already a patchwork of different and conflicting police jurisdictions. The key difference between the present set of arrangements and the one he envisages is that the differential patterns would be determined by the community, not the police.

One major consequence that would issue from this reorganization is that the career subculture of police would probably be broken. Local people could be recruited for peace-keeping activities for not more than three years from a broad cross section of the population. They would wear nonmilitary uniforms, remain unarmed, and be quite unlike traditional police. This radical deprofessionalization of the police does not seem a realistic possibility for large numbers of municipalities because of police and city government resistance, but it does suggest more serious consideration of how control bureaucracies can be made more responsive to their clients.

ROYAL CITY POLICE DEPARTMENT: THE ISSUE OF EXCESSIVE USE OF FORCE

The following case is drawn from a large heterogenous metropolitan area with a police department that defies easy classification. Police in the upper-income areas function with a service style, those in the low-income areas operate much like an army of occupation. The case materials were drawn from two commission reports on the Royal City Police Department (one sponsored by the American Civil Liberties Union, the other by the

Royal City Bar Association), interviews with policemen, and newspaper accounts.

The department has been subject to a variety of investigations during the past 10 years. The American Civil Liberties Union found significant disparities between its own investigation of abusive police conduct and the results of internal investigations of police misconduct. A survey conducted by the International Association of Chiefs of Police several years ago pointed up the shortcomings of the disciplinary system used by the police. The local bar association in their report concluded that "it is clearly evident that there is a lack of confidence in the handling of complaints concerning verbal abuse and the excessive use of force." No serious proposal has ever been made for a civilian review board because of lack of success elsewhere and intense police opposition. The Internal Investigation Division (IID) was created to process complaints about police misconduct as a response to newspaper exposure of a police-operated theft ring. During the first year of its operation it sustained only 3.4 percent of the complaints it received.

The next major revision of the investigation unit occurred as a result of a public outcry related to the alleged police mistreatment of a black dentist. He was picked up while parked in his car in dazed condition at the edge of a low-income area. He was charged with being drunk and disorderly and confined to the municipal jail to sleep it off. He refused to plead guilty to the charge claiming that the arresting officers verbally and physically abused him and endangered his life because they responded to his confused state as intoxication when in reality he was a diabetic suffering from insulin deficiency. The arresting officers contended that the man was "acting suspiciously," did not inform them of his condition, and resisted arrest (for which he was not charged). They denied verbally or physically abusing him. The dentist was acquitted of the drunkenness charge.

The incident caused great consternation in the black community. It fed fears that the department was racist and that blacks, no matter what their social position or community ties, were all vulnerable to being brutalized. A local black state representative opened a series of public hearings on the misuse of police power and informally urged the dentist to lodge an official complaint against the arresting officers. The dentist filed a complaint with IID and asked the U.S. Attorney to bring charges against the police officers for violation of the Federal Civil Rights Law. The U.S. Attorney explored the facts surrounding the incident and formally charged the two officers with violation of the dentist's civil rights. While the federal attorney was moving ahead, the IID began processing the complaint it received. The police investigators exercised their option to interview the dentist (in some cases the complainant is not interviewed) but did not ask him to testify. On the basis of the information the dentist supplied, the department moved swiftly for a hearing to dampen demands for more sweeping changes in the accountability procedures. The accused policemen were interviewed prior to the hearing and were present, without counsel, at the hearing. The hearing board consisted of five command level officers and a representative from the superintendent's office. No civilians were present during the proceedings. The IID found that the complaint was *not sustained*—that is, there was insufficient evidence to come to any other conclusion. The other possible dispositions utilized by the police department were: *exoneration,* which means that the events actually occurred but the officer's action was in the line of duty; *unfounded,* which means that the accusations were false or not factual; and *sustained,* which means that the accusations were supported by sufficient evidence to justify disciplinary action. The decision created a furor among black community leaders and the local newspapers. The superintendent promised to review the division's findings and make his own independent assessment of the complaint. Informed observers concluded that the superintendent would await the outcome of the federal charges against the officers before deciding what he should do.

The accused officers were charged in federal court within six months and chose to be tried by a jury. They were represented by an attorney from Royal City and the case was prepared by the IID. (Its mandate was not only to investigate complaints against police but to help in the defense of those police alleged to have violated a citizen's civil rights.) The defense attorney emphasized the lack of corroboration of the dentist's story, the ambiguous character of his behavior, and the lack of any evidence of physical mistreatment. The jury brought in a verdict of acquittal. One of the federal attorneys reported to the newspapers that he thought the government had a good case but juries are notoriously reluctant to convict policemen because it undermines public confidence in the department. The attorney speculated that had the police officers elected for a bench trial the results would have been different. Two days after the acquittal the superintendent reported that he had examined IID's handling of the complaint and upheld their decision. A spokesman for the police department told newsmen that the dentist was being exploited by segments of the community who wanted to tie the hands of the police in their fight on crime.

Several months after the case was closed the superintendent announced in a news conference that he was accepting the local bar association's proposal for an expanded procedure of police accountability. The new unit, he stated, would investigate only citizen complaints of excessive use of force by the police but not corruption. It would monitor all shooting incidents resulting in a wounding or death in which a department member was involved as well as all injuries. The old investigative division (IID) was to continue, but its charge was narrowed to corruption and aiding officers charged with crimes. In response to questions the superintendent stated that he thought police brutality and corruption were the most serious forms of police misconduct because they destroyed confidence in the police. He rejected one journalist's suggestion that the new disciplinary unit be an independent investigative agency staffed by civilians. The superintendent thought that civilian review of police operations was as inappropriate as civilian monitoring of the medical profession. Civilians, he argued, lack sufficient technical information required in performing law enforcement duties so that their reviews are not helpful or generally informed. The superintendent rejected a separate investigative agency as inefficient and "organizationally unsound." He reported that the new investigative unit would be headed by three civilians, all lawyers—one black, one white, and one Latino—and staffed by twenty full-time investigators, seven of whom would be civilians.

DISCUSSION

The problems the Royal City Police Department had in adapting the universal standards of the law to the requirements of citizens and public officials are not atypical of large urban departments. The major question civil libertarians raise about this kind of operation is its lack of even-handedness in different neighborhoods, though they would agree that the police in a low-income community should adapt to the local situation. Their response usually is to coerce respect but while this may solve short-range problems it creates more long-range ones. Reiss has pointed out the necessity of some kind of trust that citizens must extend to the police that would encourage minimally cooperative arrangements. The relationship between police and citizen must not be allowed to deteriorate to its power core:

> It is the willingness of the public to live up to an obligation to mobilize the police for violations of the law, whether against themselves, others, or the public order, that is a major element in maintaining a civil society. It mirrors their acceptance of responsibility for and to the whole society. A police force that works mainly by responding to citizen requests for police service is more consistent with a civil society than is one that relies mainly on police initiative.[43]

[43] Albert J. Reiss, *The Police and the Public* (New Haven, Conn.: Yale University Press, 1971).

This case focuses on the excessive use of force, though it could just as well have concentrated on corruption which has been a continuing police problem both in Royal City and elsewhere. Because of the secrecy code that operates within the police organization it was not possible to uncover the operating policies for policing low-income and surrounding areas. It does seem plausible that the officers' rule of thumb procedures in this instance were not exceptional. The citizens' report (prepared by the local black state representative) contended that physical abuse for low-income black suspects was 50.6 per 1,000 citizens, about twice as frequent as Riess's study indicated. The data were not available on white mistreatment in Royal City or on whether excessive use of force was more likely to be intraracial—that is, black officers against black suspects. The encounter between the two officers and the black dentist is atypical and was selected for discussion because there was considerably more information available on it than on more typical encounters. The organizational imperatives that were operating in the Royal City Police Department seem similar if not identical to reports of other police departments in the literature. The case presented basically confirms the generalizations made by Skolnick, Riess, Wilson, and others.

The "professionalism" so highly prized by the Royal City superintendent of police tended to underemphasize the variety of other services the police perform which are not considered professional. One hypothesis suggested is that the extent to which these services are increased and law enforcement activities decreased, low-income community acceptance of the police will be greater.

QUESTIONS FOR FURTHER DISCUSSION

1. What does this case reveal about the problems of the police?
2. The two officers were represented by a city attorney in their trial. What impact does this official involvement have on the outcome of the case, on other officers, and on the community at large?
3. How would you evaluate the superintendent's performance from the initial furor to the final decision to create a new disciplinary unit on the basis of the limited information given?
4. The superintendent argued that the police profession is analogous to the medical profession in that it is the best judge of what constitutes professional performance. How valid is his argument?

5. How would a conflict and consensus perspective interpret this series of events and what further information would each look for in this case?

6. What hypotheses are suggested in this case that would be worth exploring further?

SUMMARY

A broader historical and comparative perspective suggests that some of the routine functions the police perform, like peace-keeping, are necessary in any community, but whether that function should be lodged with them as presently constituted is an open question. There is nothing eternal and inevitable about any form of police organization and our conception of what is possible should go beyond present patterns and practices. It is important to remind ourselves that the police constitute a powerful interest group in all advanced industrial nations and we should look critically at their recommendations for safeguarding "the public interest." The critical implications that flow from Wilson's work, though he might disavow them, indicate that police control is not a natural consequence of criminal behavior taking place "out there." This image of police work underestimates police initiative and the extent to which they can control the working conditions. To repeat—they are not simply reactive to citizen criminality. Their organization and activity greatly reflect the distribution of power in the community. The *watchman* and *service* style suggest a homogenous community which is highly integrated where there are strong feelings of legitimacy by the citizens. There is a stratification system but it is not perceived as unjust—the upper levels are open to all who would strive. The police in this context may genuinely operate to promote the common good and may be viewed as "philosophers and friends." Communities may be studied as if they were organizational units as Etzioni has done.[44] The highly integrated community then would look much like a university or church where the involvement of members is high and conforming behavior is based on the internalization of norms and identification with authority. The sanctions police use in this situation are mainly symbolic rather than physical or material: lawbreakers are persuaded to comply with norms the whole community shares or are shamed into compliance.

The *legalistic* style may point to two other systems of power distribu-

[44] Amitai Etzioni, *A Comparative Analysis of Complex Organizations* (New York: The Free Press, 1961), pp. 3–21.

tion: one in which sharp class differences are accommodated and the other in which it is not. Wilson's description of the city, in which his legalistic style predominated, revealed a strong commercial class supporting a municipal government that insulated police from citizen grievances. The situation was somewhat conflicted and there were clearly identifiable social classes but they had achieved an accommodation with each other because the economic situation was favorable. This kind of community would be analogous to Etzioni's "utilitarian" organization where material sanctions to insure conformity are dominant. The upper strata in this kind of community decisively control material resources and rewards through the allocation of salaries, wages, services, and commodities. The kind of compliance we would expect of citizens in this community would be calculative; they are able to calculate the risks of offending but they share no enthusiasm for the values of local elites. The police in this context push professionalism strongly and assume, somewhat incorrectly, that their position is legitimated by all segments of the community. The image projected of the police in this context is "faithful bureaucrat."

The third situation is a heterogenous community characterized by extensive and overt class conflict. Here the police operate with a legalistic mandate but are perceived by those whom they presumably serve as a hostile army of occupation. The community is analogous to Etzioni's *coercive* organization (prison or concentration camp). There is a great gulf between elites and subordinates in this kind of community and little social cohesion. Because legitimation is not forthcoming from citizens the police attempt to coerce acceptance of their role. The orientation of subordinate community members in this situation is extremely alienated. Citizens react adversely to police exercising legitimate power. The image of the police projected in this context is one of "authoritarian enforcer."

Wilson has implied that the crime rates in his three styles varied. The police can inflate or deflate their rates at will. Rates were not important or used to evaluate police in the watchman and service style, hence they tended to be lower than crime rates in legalistic departments. In short, the extent of criminalization varied somewhat independently of the actual violations. In sum, the classification employed here using Wilson's suggestive observations, combined with Etzioni's analysis of organizational compliance and deviation, suggest that we should expect the impulse to criminalize would be low in highly integrated communities (index: rates of common crime like assault, theft, drunkenness, vice, traffic, and disorderly conduct) and high in "coercive" communities.

Though the discussion in this chapter has stressed the isolation of the police from the community, it is important to note that they are not isolated from the rest of the criminal justice system. Their own emphasis on law enforcement and making arrests that will hold up in court, and the concern with "batting averages" indicates that a major imperative is to push the case on to the next stage—the criminal court—whether or not the accused is guilty. Despite the strained relationships between the police and the criminal courts they are symbiotically linked to one another in the criminal justice system. The relationship is largely sustained by denial of the right of due process. By working in collusion with the criminal courts in its objective of "bargain justice," the police are allowed to maintain their rate of good pinches. How the criminal courts have come to play this role and how they operate on a day-to-day basis is the subject of Chapter 7.

7

the
criminal
court

After a suspect has been arrested and interrogated, the police decide whether he should be moved along to the next stage. He goes before a magistrate, ideally an impartial referee, for a preliminary hearing. The magistrate decides whether there is enough evidence to charge the suspect with a felony. The procedure is not a trial but a screening device to select those cases that warrant further proceedings. Though the present arrangement casts the magistrate in the role of neutral umpire it did not start out that way. This part of the criminal proceeding was created by English statute in the sixteenth century.[1] At that time preliminary inquiries into felonies followed an inquisitorial rather than a judicial method. The magistrate served as detective and arresting officer; he conducted the preliminary examination, committed prisoners for trial, and appeared at the trial as the principal witness. The development of the preliminary examination in the English system gradually provided safeguards for the accused.

The British Police Act of 1829 which established the London police force also differentiated between the functions of magistrate and police officer. The magistrate or lower court judge was no longer responsible for the arrest of offenders and could no longer use the preliminary examination to establish his case. Earlier the accused was examined without any

[1] Sir Henry S. Holdworth, *A History of English Law,* vol. 3 (Boston: Little, Brown, 1934).

important limitations: he had no right to counsel, no right to cross-examine witnesses, nor could he get copies of the evidence against him. The legislation of 1829 and legislation following it introduced several features to protect the accused. There was no compulsory preliminary examination; rather the accused was invited to make a statement. The information gathered was no longer for the court alone but the testimony was open, accusatory, and confrontative. The accused was also entitled to copies of testimony given in open court and the right to inspect all depositions taken against him.

NORM ENFORCEMENT VERSUS DISPUTE SETTLEMENT

The court's analogue to the police peace-keeping role is its *dispute-settling function*. This can be most clearly seen in the court's operations in simpler societies. When all else fails, litigants come before a judge who resolves the dispute between them. The aim of the procedure is to reconcile the conflicting parties. Before the emergence of state-appointed judges, arbitrators accepted by the contending parties helped resolve private wrongs. But the system of private vengeance and restitution gave way to the state's interest in suppressing individual violence. Violence is conceived as an offense against the state, not simply an offense against an individual or family or clan. The role of the original victim or complainant is taken over by the state-appointed prosecutor who decides on the basis of the evidence how seriously the accused has offended community codes. The evolution in all modern societies has gone in the direction of state monopoly of prosecution. One crucial ingredient of the criminal offense is that it can't be compromised legally by the parties.

The monopoly secured by the state in criminal proceedings undermined the earlier system of private criminal justice where the victim's role was dominant. The victim's role under the new arrangement is almost nonexistent. Schafer points out, "In contrast to the understanding of crime as a violation of the victim's interest, the emergence of the state developed another interpretation: the disturbance of the society."[2] The consequence was that the victim was habitually ignored. The state exacted the entire payment and offered no remedy to the unfortunate victim. The victim's participation in criminal proceedings was limited to an evaluation of wrongs he suffered in order that the seriousness of the offense might be weighed. But he could not take the law into his own

[2] Stephen Schafer, *The Victim and His Criminal* (New York: Random House, 1968), p. 29.

hands, exact revenge or payment, or affect the outcome of the proceedings. The dispute the court was to settle became one between the accused and the state rather than between the accused and the victim. The emphasis shifted from a compromise of differences between contending parties to norm enforcement. There has been a tendency recently to reintroduce the idea of restitution and to introduce practices that recover more fully the court's dispute-settling function, but ironically this has led to a new set of abuses that require remedy. This development will be discussed in more detail below.

PHILOSOPHIES OF PUNISHMENT
AS DETERMINANTS OF COURT ACTION

Society's need for social order was justified by the criminal law reformers discussed in Chapter 2, and led to the emphasis on rule enforcement in the courts. Bentham, for instance, held that the basic objective of the criminal law was to deter potential criminals by example. This doctrine, called *general deterrence*, proposes that offenders who are guilty should be held up as examples, thus deterring other potential criminals. This was based on Bentham's psychological theory related to pleasure and pain. Every man presumably calculates the pleasure and pain to be derived from a specific act. Hence punishment should be slightly more painful than the pleasure derived from the criminal act itself, thus instructing the weak in the virtue of living a law-abiding life. The acceptance of the doctrine of general deterrence in the criminal law thrust the courts into the role of norm enforcers rather than dispute settlers. As part of the rule-enforcing task, court functionaries must determine the specific facts of a case. This alerts them to whether or not the accused is guilty and whether the evidence is sufficient for a conviction. They ask questions related to the specific case, such as whether there is reason to believe that illegal behavior occurred, whether the accused's conduct (by intent, reckless action, or inaction) brought about harmful consequences, and whether "criminal intent" was present.

Criminal intent, or *mens rea*, has had a complex history in Western thought. In the Middle Ages, before distinctions between sin and crime were developed, *mens rea* referred to consciousness of guilt. A person could not be judged guilty of a crime unless he was morally blameworthy. If the offender was to blame, it was expected that he should be made to suffer for his transgression. Ideally there should be some connection between the harm done to the community and the degree of punishment. The implication was that the social order would be maintained if there were a balance between severity of the offense and the degree of punishment. But from the later Middle Ages to the middle of the eighteenth century there was little relationship between offense and punishment. Extremely severe penalties were meted out for relatively trivial crimes. Some commentators have ascribed this pattern to the cruelty of an epoch now vanished. Rusche and Kirchheimer among others, however, have tried to link the severity of punitive reaction to the heterogeneity of a society and class antagonisms.[3] Thus severe penalties are more characteristic of heterogeneous and conflicted societies (especially during periods of rapid social change) than homogeneous ones. The idea of retribution implied *special* deterrence: an effort to prevent this specific wrongdoer from further offending. Once the group's sense of justice or revenge was satisfied by the sinner's doing penance he was restored to the community. Retribution as a goal of punishment has, until recently, been criticized as outmoded, appropriate only to an earlier stage of human development, and out of phase with current scientific and humanitarian thought. The reappearance of the retribution philosophy as one of the aims of the criminal law has provoked a spirited discussion as to whether or not there is or should be a moral basis for the law, and the extent to which blameworthy conduct should be publicly denounced.

Retribution carried out by the state is the political counterpart of individual revenge. Those who have defended it as one of the fundamental aims of the criminal law have suggested that without it many acts now penalized would become objects of private revenge, and that this unregulated private vengeance would inevitably degenerate into a war of reprisal and counterreprisal. The early eighteenth- and nineteenth-century rationalists, appalled by arbitrary and capricious sentences, questioned whether retribution was a worthy aim of punishment and suggested the idea of general deterrence discussed above—inflicting pain upon those convicted so that others might be discouraged from crime. Criminals could be treated or sacrificed in this view as a means of realizing society's values. The impact of the criminal law reformers was remarkable. Their analyses pointed to a way out of the chaos and brutality characteristic of the penal practices of the time, a chaos and brutality ill suited to a society that had consolidated the gains of the Industrial Revolution.

The criminal codes that followed accepted the assumptions of the deterrence approach—i.e., to be effective every crime and its punishment must be stated in advance so that citizens could calculate the cost of offending. Since that time the deterrence doctrine has become the pri-

---

[3] George Rusche and Otto Kirchheimer, *Punishment and Social Structure* (New York: Columbia University Press, 1939).

mary and essential postulate of almost all modern criminal law systems. On the surface deterrence as a justification for punishment seems to have carried the day, but retribution never completely disappeared. In practice the appeal of deterrence was its impact on specific offenders rather than the general community. The question was not usually "How can we make an example of this person?" but more likely, "What should we do to insure that this specific person will not repeat his offense?" The philosophy of general deterrence with its broad concern for the regulation of criminal conduct was little concerned with the guilty mind of the offender. For deterrence to work, criminal intent was irrelevant. If the goal is to instill fear in the potentially dangerous, then it matters little whether or not the suspect is even legally guilty. Punishing the innocent may serve the purposes of deterrence as well or better than punishing the guilty. The more the philosophy of general deterrence took hold in British jurisprudence the more it came into conflict with *mens rea*. A compromise eventuated: consciousness of guilt was abandoned in favor of two different notions—one that the act be voluntary, and the other the so-called general defenses. Those acts which are involuntary, not caused by criminal intent, are not liable to penalty. The general defenses that affect the accused's consciousness of guilt are insanity, immaturity, mistake of fact, necessity and coercion, intoxication, and mistake of law. All of the defenses point to circumstances in which an ordinary person could not have had the capacity to control his actions. These specifications have reinterpreted *mens rea* so that it can be utilized for special deterrence. The accused's perceptions of wrongdoing correspond to what the judge might have perceived had he been in the accused's situation and possessed his physical characteristics.

Historically the philosophy of deterrence, both general and special, was added to the aims of retribution as a guide to punishment. A third aim added more recently is that of *rehabilitation*. The attack on deterrence came from those who claimed that punishment in fact did not deter potential violators. Rising crime rates in all advanced industrial nations seemed to give substance to the criticism. It was argued that since all those convicted of crime must one day return to civilized society, the major goal of criminal sanctions should be reform or rehabilitation. Allen described the rehabilitative approach as follows:

> The rehabilitative ideal is itself a complex of ideas which, perhaps, defies exact definition. The essential points, however, can be identified. It is assumed, first that human behavior is the product of antecedent causes. These causes can be identified as part of the physical universe, and it is the obligation of the scientist to discover and to describe them with all possible exactitude. Knowledge of the antecedents of human behavior makes possible an approach to the sci-

entific control of human behavior. Finally, and of primary significance for the purposes at hand, it is assumed that measures should be designed to effect changes in the behavior of the convicted person in the interests of his own happiness, health and satisfactions and in the interest of social defense.[4]

This doctrine tends to undermine the notion of *mens rea* because it emphasizes the determinism of human behavior. There are no right and wrong choices nor does the notion of criminal intent have any validity. Crime in the rehabilitation view is an index for a more intimate knowledge of the criminal's personality; hence the question of the crime which he has committed (or whether he has committed any at all) is forced into the background. The logic of the rehabilitation approach conflicts basically with earlier justification of criminal sanctions. In practice, however, treatment justifications are used in conjunction with retributive ones. Thus society's desire for revenge can be satisfied at the same time that the socially dangerous offender is confined and "rehabilitated." In short, punishment and rehabilitation can be indistinguishable. Some critics have maintained that the ideology of rehabilitation, though it has led to more humane kinds of corrections (wider use of probation, parole, and fines) can be more punitive than a system whose sanctions are carefully measured by law. Under the rehabilitation rhetoric the reality may be longer sentences. Gerber and McAnary also point out that the approach

> . . . is an invitation to personal tyranny and denial of human rights. Once a prisoner is placed in the hands of the doctor to be cured before he is released, there is no one who can predict how long the cure will take, nor control the autonomy of the doctor's judgment.[5]

All the rationales for criminal sanctions assume the central role of the court's norm-enforcing function. If the criminal code is to be enforced it must be ascertained whether in fact a crime was committed and how responsible the accused was in its commission. If a tribunal's main purpose is dispute settlement via reconciliation of conflicting interests, then it does not try to determine which one of the litigants has breached the norm (or even what the norm is); rather, it tries to reach a compromise solution that will enable parties to live together after the dispute. Neither party in this arrangement should be so strongly aggrieved as to make future relationships impossible. The tribunal operates more as an arbitration mechanism. In this context we can see that no elaborate justification for what should be done to the party who "loses" is required. Is it valid to

---

[4] Francis Allen, *The Borderland of Criminal Justice* (Chicago: University of Chicago Press, 1964), p. 26.
[5] Rudolph J. Gerber and Patrick D. McAnary," The Philosophy of Punishment," *St. Louis University Law Journal*, 11 (Summer 1967), 502–35.

look at the dispute-settling function of the criminal court at all in the light of its overwhelming emphasis on norm enforcement today? Mileski has observed that conflict resolution takes time and requires attention to individuals on a case-by-case basis.[6] This is best accomplished in an informal, nonbureaucratic setting. Modern courts with heavy case loads are ill-equipped to do this. Hence any trend toward individualized treatment of offenders is thwarted by the formalization of the processing organization.

THE ROLE OF THE PROSECUTING ATTORNEY

The story of the transformation of the criminal courts in the United States is the growing power of the public prosecutor. There is no equivalent to the public prosecutor in civil law, where the key figure is the judge. Civil law is made by the judge; criminal law is made by the prosecutor. The powers of the American prosecutor can be described in relation to each step in the criminal process:

1. The prosecutor may refuse to issue a warrant, thus terminating the efforts of the arresting officer. As Chambliss and Seidman point out, he stands astride the criminal process controlling the gates that lead to a court trial. He alone decides whether or not to enforce the law. His discretion is almost unlimited and unreviewable.

2. He may participate actively in the preliminary hearings and in coroner's inquests. His power in the examining magistrate's court is greater than that of the judge. If the magistrate refuses to hold the accused, the prosecutor may take the case directly to the grand jury. If he doesn't participate actively in the hearings before the magistrate the case may be lost. The grand jury in its present form is very much a creature of the prosecutor. When it was established in England in the twelfth century it consisted of a group of reputable citizens who made a decision on whether or not there was probable cause that an accused committed the crime charged by the prosecutor. The proceeding is inquisitorial—that is, there is no defense. The grand jury considers only the evidence presented by the prosecutor. A number of legal scholars and criminologists have called for the abolition of grand juries because they are anachronistic, expensive, time consuming, and overly responsive to the control and domination of the prosecutor. Grand juries were abolished in France in 1808 and in England in 1933.

[6] Maureen Mileski, "Courtroom Encounters: An Observation Study of a Lower Criminal Court," *Law and Society Review,* 5 (May 1971), 473–538.

3. If the case goes to trial the prosecutor represents the state.

4. In the course of the trial his participation may even extend to matters over which the judge is supposed to have exclusive jurisdiction. Many judges rely on the prosecutor for instructions to the jury and for recommendations on bail.

5. The prosecutor's power extends beyond the verdict. He is frequently consulted by the judge in fixing sentences, suspending them, or granting probation.[7]

Evolution of the Prosecutor's Authority

In the United States the office of the public prosecutor was grafted to the traditional system of private litigation. It assimilated the functions of the private prosecutor. The cost of prosecution was initially borne by the private prosecutor but later he obtained the right to recover, after conviction, the cost of prosecution. Private prosecution meant that enforcement of the criminal law was like civil law: a matter of litigation between parties with the state acting as arbiter between private interests.

A thorough study by William E. Nelson of trial court records in colonial Massachusetts traces the evolution of the criminal court from about 1760 to 1810, when the main outlines of the modern American criminal court were completed.[8] The main function of the prerevolutionary court was the identification and punishment of sinners. But by 1810 the law's function had changed to the protection of property. The fears that led to the founding of the Boston police department (discussed in Chapter 6) also led to legislation designed to address political and economic disorders. In the 1780s there were a number of reported attacks on authority and property which had the effect of strengthening ". . . the fear which society's well-to-do had of the designs of the lower classes upon their wealth and standing. The simultaneous increase in the incidence of theft appears to have contributed to both a strengthening and modification of the fear."[9]

The prerevolutionary colonists were deeply suspicious of all governmental institutions and their potential for interfering with individual liberty. But the court was held in high esteem because the judiciary was

---

[7] William J. Chambliss and Robert B. Seidman, *Law, Order and Power* (Reading, Mass.: Addison-Wesley, 1971), ch. 19.
[8] William E. Nelson, "Emerging Notions of Modern Criminal Law in the Revolutionary Era: An Historical Perspective," *New York University Law Review*, 42 (May 1967), 450–82. Reprinted in Richard Quinney (ed.), *Criminal Justice in America* (Boston: Little, Brown, 1974), pp. 100–126.
[9] Ibid., p. 112.

viewed as being independent of the crown. Any abuses judges were prone to could be remedied by the jury system which was widely used. It introduced popular safeguards on arbitrary use of judicial authority. The power of the state was neutralized under this arrangement because it was basically uninterested in the outcome of most criminal cases. "Although prosecutions were formally instituted by a governmental agency . . . many criminal trials were in reality contests between subjects rather than contest between government and subject."[10]

In theft cases the government was not the interested party because it couldn't control the imposition of damages or receive them. The damages were paid to a complaining individual. Nor was government interested in cases against God or religion. In this prerevolutionary situation the government couldn't affect the outcome of most cases. The important issues were almost always decided by a jury of the accused's neighbors who were opposed to any further strengthening of the government's authority.

The situation changed radically after the Revolution when the government became interested in the outcome of many criminal cases. The government was especially interested in cases involving challenges to political authority such as treason or rioting and those contributing to economic instability such as counterfeiting. The struggle was on to enlist the judiciary in the service of the state. By 1810, according to Nelson, government as a representative of the propertied elements of society became the truly interested party in theft cases and treble damages paid to the victim were no longer used as a penalty.

> The true magnitude of [the state's] interest as compared with the interest of private individuals, is perhaps best illustrated by the practice developed by 1810 of the state's paying private individuals the expenses they incurred in assisting the prosecution of cases. A social expectation had developed that, without a promise of recompense, no one but the government would have any interest in participating in the criminal process.[11]

These developments enormously increased the scope and authority of the public prosecutor at the expense of judge and jury. The postrevolution situation in the United States was one where juries were viewed as representing the interests of popular government rather than the interests of the judiciary. The jury had the most authority in the courts, and the public prosecutor had the least. The jury could determine issues of law and of fact. Juries could ignore the instructions of the judge and reject

---

[10] Ibid., p. 114.
[11] Ibid., p. 119.

the expertise he presumably represented. Chambliss and Seidman summarize the changes in the nineteenth century which led to the reversal of the position of judge and jury. The jury's authority was increasingly narrowed as the judiciary reclaimed for itself the right to lay down the law. The situation today is one of almost complete judicial control over juries: the judge can direct a verdict of acquittal, he can set aside a verdict after conviction, he can influence the jury through terms of the charge, and he can declare specific issues to be issues of law, not of fact. The jury system as it was initially conceived was to determine the guilt or innocence of those accused of crimes. It was constituted of people like the defendant himself ("a jury of his peers") rather than people like the judge. The early system functioned well since jurors generally knew the defendant and may have had personal knowledge of the case. Later this personal knowledge became grounds for disqualification as juries became impersonal triers of fact. The change partly reflected the shift from a folk society to an urban one.

This development has raised some serious questions about the role of the jury, such as whether the integrative function performed in a simpler society is suited to modern conditions, and what constitutes a jury of one's peers in a large heterogenous and conflicted society. Some legal scholars have suggested that because the juries are largely composed of retired persons or middle-class women (others are reluctant or unable to serve), the jury system should be abolished. The question has not been seriously debated because in practice jury trials are so rare. Only one or two percent of all persons accused of crime are tried by a jury.

Citizen participation in the criminal justice process has, therefore, dramatically declined. Citizens today are likely to play the role of complainant or defendant. This lack of satisfying direct citizen participation partially accounts for the dissatisfaction with the judicial process. Mayhew and Riess have shown that, on the average, participants are more negative in their views than nonparticipants.[12] More than a third of those who had experience in criminal trials as witness or juror reported some dissatisfaction with the proceedings. Two-thirds of the witnesses reacted negatively to some aspect of the proceedings; 20 percent reacted to the conduct of court officials; and another 25 percent objected to the adversary form of proceeding, particularly the cross-examination. Their reactions paralleled those of the distinguished legal scholar Jerome Frank, who criticized the adversary system because it fails, by and large, to bring out the facts of cases at issue.[13] It insures that some facts will not

---

[12] Leon H. Mayhew and Albert J. Reiss, Jr., *In Search of Justice* (Ann Arbor: University of Michigan, Detroit Area Study, 1967).
[13] Jerome Frank, *Courts on Trial* (Princeton, N.J.: Princeton University Press, 1949), pp. 81–85, 94–96.

be developed for consideration because the courtroom atmosphere bewilders witnesses, cross-examination is used to discredit honest witnesses, the lawyers coach their witnesses before a trial, the use of surprise as a tactic and the financial weaknesses of the parties often prevent proper investigation of the facts.

The task of the prosecutor in relation to the jury is to assemble the case and argue it in such a way that a guilty verdict is forthcoming. The prosecutor's many functions are handled by specialized units in large prosecutorial offices: criminal investigators look into the case, much as the police do; the magistrate decides who should be brought to trial and who not; the solicitor prepares cases for trial; and the advocate tries cases and argues appeals. The Wickersham Commission in 1931 was the first official national body to discuss the role of the prosecutor and make recommendations for improving the office.[14] These recommendations were reiterated by the President's Commission on Law Enforcement and the Administration of Justice in 1967.[15] The nub of the problem according to the earlier commission was that local elections of prosecutors led to widespread abuses. The appeal of the locally elected prosecutor seems to be that he is responsive to local community opinion. With the decline of the jury system and increasing use of judges selected by appointment rather than election, it may be that the prosecutor is viewed as the only check against arbitrary judicial authority. As the earlier Wickersham Commission report on prosecution put it: "We have been jealous of the power of the trial judge, but careless of the continued growth of the power of the prosecuting attorney."[16]

The profile of the prosecutor then as now shows that he attains his low-paying post early in his career, holds it for a short period, and soon finds a way to attract public attention so as to be selected for higher office. Candidates for local prosecutor are put forward by political parties and expected to be responsive to the concerns of the party. Assistants are more often selected because of their political connections than because of educational background, experience, or competence. The Wickersham Commission complained that organization in the prosecutor's office was inefficient and because of the elective system there was a lack of continuity in administration. The preoccupation with local problems because of the decentralization of prosecution meant that local prosecutors were ill equipped to deal with problems that transcended local concerns. The

[14] National Commission on Law Observance and Enforcement, *Report on Prosecution*, 4 (Washington, D.C.: Government Printing Office, 1931).
[15] President's Commission on Law Enforcement and the Administration of Justice, *The Challenge of Crime in a Free Society Task Force Report: The Courts* (Washington, D.C.: Government Printing Office, 1967).
[16] *Report on Prosecution*, p. 11.

later commission lamented the low salaries paid to prosecutors and suggested increasing them so as to draw more talented attorneys to prosecution. Recommendations for the reform of the prosecutorial function have usually proposed that it be centralized under a state prosecutor and that the disadvantages of the elective system be seriously addressed.

THE CRIMINAL COURT AS A BUREAUCRACY

The increasing formalization of the criminal justice process came about as a result of urban growth. This formalization is not peculiar to the criminal court but has affected all governmental activities. The process has proceeded apace in all modern states whatever their political philosophy. As Rheinstein has pointed out, if the machinery of the modern bureaucratic state were to cease functioning sheer physical existence would become impossible for all except immediate suppliers of food.[17] The appeal of bureaucratization has been its efficiency in dealing with large numbers of people and tasks. The President's Commission on Law Enforcement and the Administration of Justice estimated that there were over four million cases brought to court in 1962 dealing only with petty crimes.[18] Blumberg estimated that some 300,000 persons a year appear before felony courts and another five million persons appear who are charged with lesser offenses.[19]

Increased formalization has been actively encouraged in the criminal justice system by lawyers, scholars, and the judiciary because of its promise of equal justice for all. Bureaucracy's interest in universal recruitment from among those best qualified by objective measure produces a trend toward social equalization. Because of its emphasis on impersonalism and formalism, decisions can be rendered without hatred or passion; hence all persons can be handled equally according to some universal criteria. Ideally this eliminates capriciousness and increases predictability in the work of the court.

If the system worked well, presumably defendants would feel that they had been fairly treated. But the system in operation tends to aggravate the sense of injustice not only of those who are being processed, but of jurors and witnesses as well. Casper has shown that convicted offenders perceive prosecutors as central figures who dominate defense lawyers and

[17] Max Rheinstein (ed.), *Max Weber on Law in Economy and Society* (Cambridge, Mass.: Harvard University Press, 1954), p. xxxiv.
[18] President's Commission, *The Challenge of Crime*.
[19] Abraham S. Blumberg, *Criminal Justice* (Chicago: Quadrangle Books, 1967).

judges.[20] Defendants feel that judges abdicate their authority in favor of the prosecutor whose grounds for judgment are not explicit. Bureaucratic administration designed to achieve justice by its universalistic application of standards is undermined by the ambiguous discretionary power of court personnel. The discretion available within the court framework, especially the prosecutor's, opens the door to unequal treatment. Schrag has summarized the growing body of evidence indicating that poor and minorities accused of violating the law are more likely to be sanctioned more severely and to be denied their rights and the full opportunity to defend their interests.[21] The safeguards of due process are fragile and can be reworked for organizational ends.

Mileski reported that the pressures of heavy case loads led to the reduction in time taken to apprise defendants of their rights.[22] Some judges did not inform the accused of their rights at all; some made an announcement to the audience in the courtroom before the work of the court actually began; others called defendants in groups before them to satisfy the legal requirement. Judges were likely to inform defendants of their rights individually only when the case was a serious one and an appeal was a possibility.

The shortage of court personnel—judges, prosecutors, defense counsel, probation staff clerks, and attendants—and the large number of cases have led to an overriding preoccupation with "moving the cases," or clearing the docket. One way to do this is to discourage jury trials which are slow, cumbersome, and expensive. As a consequence, the practice of letting defendants elect a trial by judge without jury has grown to monumental proportions. One argument court personnel use to persuade a defendant to waive a jury trial is that juries tend to mete out harsher treatment than judges. But the empirical evidence doesn't bear this out. If anything, juries tend to be less conviction-minded than judges in criminal cases. The Chicago jury project found that the maximum divergence between juries and judges was in statutory rape and drunken driving cases with judges much more likely to convict.[23]

Jury trials, according to Chambliss and Seidman, despite their rarity or possibly because of it, are models of the due process system; the proceedings are public, the accused's right to counsel is recognized as well as his

---

[20] Jonathan D. Caspar, *American Criminal Justice: The Defendant's Perspective* (Englewood Cliffs, N.J.: Prentice-Hall, 1972).
[21] Clarance Schrag, *Crime and Justice American Style, Crime and Delinquency Issues,* A Monograph Series, Rockville, Md., Center for Studies on Crime and Delinquency, N.I.M. Publication No. HSM-72-9052, 1971.
[22] Mileski, "Courtroom Encounters."
[23] Harry Kalven, Jr., and Hans Zeisel, *The American Jury* (Boston: Little, Brown, 1966).

right to remain silent and cross-examine the state's witnesses.[24] In brief, the adversary system works according to the norms laid down for its conduct. The law in action matches the law on the books by and large in jury trials.

Though the court may be organized like a bureaucracy it is one quite different from the usual industrial or military organization. Newman has observed that the overall role structure of the court is more like an affiliation of semiautonomous professionals, closer to a medical clinic or a university faculty.[25] The judge is at the top of the court pyramid and is charged with the task of administering the court's activities, yet his direction must take into account the autonomy of the prosecutor (over whose activities he has little control) and the relative autonomy of the probation staff (over whom he has some control). Both the prosecution and probation staff view themselves as professionals and their major identification is with their own fields rather than with the court organization. The situation is further complicated by the fact that each court is an island of relative autonomy within its jurisdictional authority. Proposals for reform have addressed themselves by and large to the centralization of prosecution, usually under a state-appointed prosecutor, and unification of all the courts in a state under one judicial executive. There are several assumptions underlying these suggestions: that the work of the courts could be made more "efficient" and rational by furthering the bureaucratization process, and that disparity between the ideal and the practical can be eliminated by removing the anachronistic or feudal elements which impede efficiency.

THE ROLE OF THE JUDGE

The limited research done on the judiciary has focused mainly on the upper levels—the Supreme Court and the appellate structure. Schmidhaurer's collective portrait of Supreme Court justices shows that they come from families of high social status, that they were educated in prestigious colleges and law schools, and that they were recruited from the ranks of lawyers who were primarily politicians.[26] Judges in intermediate level appellate courts are usually selected by the governor and approved by the state legislature. A typical career pattern for the inter-

---

[24] Chambliss and Seidman, *Law, Order and Power,* p. 416.
[25] Donald J. Newman, "Role and Role Process in the Criminal Court," in Daniel Glaser (ed.), *Handbook of Crime* (Chicago: Rand McNally, 1974).
[26] John A. Schmidhauser, "The Justices of the Supreme Court: A Collective Portrait," *Midwest Journal of Political Science,* 3 (1959), 2-37, 40–49.

mediate appellate court judge is graduation from a second-level law school, development of a "dignified" law practice, followed by the kind of service to the local political party that leads to selection as a judicial candidate. Candidates for the lower-level courts generally run for office on a partisan basis. A good deal of their time after election to the lower bench is spent attending social events which bring high visibility for the inevitable reelection campaign. Performance on the lower bench that demonstrates loyalty, astuteness, efficiency, and some imagination is rewarded by an appointment to the intermediate appellate court. The President's Commission on Law Enforcement and the Administration of Justice compared the various alternatives for selecting judges—appointment, partisan election, and nonpartisan election—and concluded that a merit selection plan would best remedy the defects in present selection methods. Qualified candidates would be nominated by a nonpartisan commission appointed by the executive and approved by the voters.

Blumberg's profile of lower-level criminal court judges shows that they have usually attended a part-time, low-status law school whose primary emphasis is on preparing students to take the state bar examination.[27] This is followed by a long apprenticeship in party activities that assures early acceptance of clubhouse norms and expectancies as to future conduct on the bench. None of this prepares the potential judge for the kind of decision-making, administering, and overseeing functions required in the court. Inevitably judges permit themselves to be socialized into their new role by civil service functionaries more familiar with the operation of the court.

Personal attributes do seem to condition judicial decision making. Nagel examined the background characteristics of over 300 state and federal supreme court judges and the decisions they made.[28] He found that decisions for and against the defense in criminal cases was significantly related to membership in various groups. There was a greater tendency to decide for the defense among judges who were Democrats, those who were not members of the ABA, those who had served as prosecutors, and those who were Catholics. But personal attributes of the judges and the values they bring to their tasks are of less importance in the lower courts than they are in the appellate courts. The assembly-line character of the work of the criminal courts does not permit much value expression on the part of the judge. The cases coming before the lower courts are perceived by all court personnel as "clear" cases—that is, the facts are not at issue. "Trouble cases," where the rule is not clear, call for

[27] Blumberg, *Criminal Justice.*
[28] Stuart S. Nagel, "Judicial Backgrounds and Criminal Cases," *The Journal of Criminal Law, Criminology and Police Science,* 53 (September 1962), 333–39.

creative application of the law or the fashioning of new rules. These cases are more likely to occur at the appellate level where the work of the court is more leisurely. It is in the resolution of "trouble cases" that the personal values of the judge can come to the fore. But at the lower levels it is mainly situational and organizational pressures that determine the activity of the judge.

Bail Decisions

The pressures operating on the criminal court judge can be observed in examining bail decisions. After a suspect has been arrested he can be released on his own assurance that he will return for the disposition, he can be released on bail, or he can be detained. The bail system requires that a bond be posted to assure the suspect's later court appearance; in practice it has often been used as a form of punishment. Bail in excess of what the suspect can reasonably be expected to raise is posted, thus assuring that he will be detained "to protect the community" or "to teach him a lesson." This practice is at odds with the Eighth Amendment guarantee against excessive bail and the Supreme Court's judgment that the only legitimate function of bail is to guarantee the appearance of the defendant in court. What constitutes "reasonable" bail is determined by the magistrate. If the accused can't raise bail himself he may secure the services of a professional bail bondsman who lends him the money. Regardless of whether he is later found innocent or guilty, he must still pay the bondsman. The system seriously discriminates against those who can't buy freedom.

Proposals for reform have generally suggested that the transition time from arrest to disposition be shortened so as to reduce the need for bail or preventive detention. No serious efforts have been initiated to guarantee defendants a speedy trial. The 1967 President's Commission on Law Enforcement and the Administration of Justice lamented the fact that in Britain the period from arrest to final appeal is often as short as four months, while in the United States it may be nearly two years. Other reforms proposed that in the absence of speedy trials, courts should make wider use of releasing defendants on their own recognizance. This is one alternative favored by the President's commission. The workability of this alternative was demonstrated in the Manhattan Bail Project begun in 1961 in New York City.[29] In this project "community ties" were substi-

[29] Charles E. Ares, Anne Rankin, and Herbert Sturz, "The Manhattan Bail Project: An Interim Report on the Use of Pre-Trial Parole," *New York University Law Review*, 38 (January 1963), 67–92. Other projects to secure pre-trial release of low-income defendants are summarized in Dorothy C. Tompkins,

tuted for money as a means of assessing the individual's probable appearance at trial. From 1961 to 1962 the project recommended 363 persons for release, the court agreed in 215 of the cases. Only 3 of the 215 (less than 2 percent) failed to appear in court. This was in striking contrast to bail jumping, which was over 7 percent.

The project suggested that fact-finding procedures could be introduced that would immediately furnish verified information about the defendant's community ties upon which a decision could be made. This information was supplied by the project during its one-year experiment but the fact-finding function was taken over by the probation department following the experiment. Suffet's study of bail setting in the New York City County Criminal Court concluded that the judge's concern about releasing defendants who would not subsequently show up could be addressed by diffusing the responsibility between the prosecutor and the probation department.[30] Excessively high bail is set in the absence of information on the suspect's community ties, just to be on the safe side.

His study also provides some insight into the relationships between judge, prosecutor, and defense attorney as well as the prestige structure of the court. The patterns of interaction in bail setting must necessarily be brief because of the heavy schedule. The modal pattern is for the judge to fix bail without discussing the matter with either of the attorneys (49 percent of the cases). The judge makes the first bail suggestion and meets with no objection from either side. In only 18 percent of the cases is there disagreement of any kind (such as the attorneys countering the judge's suggestion or vice versa). Suffet shows that the prosecutor's objections are more seriously taken by the judge than the defense attorney's. The judge almost invariably follows the countersuggestion of the prosecutor. Their roles in the work of the court are reciprocally supportive. Both must cooperate to move cases along, hence disagreements must be kept to a minimum.

In short, what appears on the surface to be the exclusive decision-making domain of the judge turns out on closer scrutiny to be heavily influenced by the prosecutor. In addition, bail decisions are not made dispassionately with regard to the individual merits of a case but according to explicit rules of thumb relating to seriousness of offense, and a cautious concern for the key publics who may criticize the decision.

Bail in the United States, a Bibliography (Berkeley, Calif.: Institute of Government Studies, 1964). See also Ronald Goldfarb, *Ransom: A Critique of the American Bail System* (New York: Harper & Row, 1965); and Caleb Foote, "The Bail System and Equal Justice," *Federal Probation*, 23 (September 1959), 43–48.

[30] Frederic Suffet, "Bail Setting: A Study of Courtroom Interaction," *Crime and Delinquency*, 12 (October 1966), 318–31.

Despite organizational constraints, the values or personality needs of the judge can find expression in the court as long as they do not seriously interfere with the attainment of the court's objectives. Blumberg has identified a number of judicial behavior patterns produced partly by the demands of the court organization and individual idiosyncracies.[31] The key patterns relate to accomplishing the work of the court, dispatching the cases that come before it, and dealing with external publics. Blumberg suggests that there are several types of judges. The *scholar* keeps his hand in everything, works long hours, and tries to be creative in addressing the problem of caseload. The *hack* handles cases much as a supermarket checker handles groceries. Together these two judicial types clear the docket each day and keep the court machinery humming. The external problems of the court are addressed by the "hatchet man" and the "contract man." The *hatchet man's* function is a public relations one; he takes those cases that may embarrass the municipal administration and affirms the legitimacy of the court by stage-managing an impression of swift justice impartially administered. The *contract man* is assigned the task of translating bargains struck by the local political machine into judicial reality. This may involve trivial favors or a major fix. He may also be the liaison man with the police, representing their interests in the court operation. Blumberg also mentions the *political adventurer* (who uses the bench as a steppingstone), the *pensioner* (rewarded with a judicial post as a result of a lifetime of party service), and the *tyrant* (defeated in his aspirations for higher office). These do not contribute directly to the functioning of the court and may even disrupt its operations. Blumberg implies that if the essential work of the court is being carried out it can afford the luxury of judges who do not contribute.

Sentencing Decisions

Another area of decision making which seems to allow for the full expression of the judge's values is in *sentencing*. Penal codes are the result of piecemeal development and are "wildly contradictory."[32] This invites uncontrolled discretion. Defenders of present practices explain widely disparate sentences, even within the same jurisdiction, as individualized justice being meted out by different judges. Critics have emphasized the lawless or ruleless character of sentencing practices as well as the fact that sentences are rarely reviewable. Their proposals for reform would make the sentencing activity less of an administrative process

[31] Blumberg, *Criminal Justice*, ch. 6.
[32] President's Commission, *The Challenge of Crime*, pp. 25–26.

than it is now and more of an adversary one. Others have advocated narrowing the judge's discretion in sentencing. The American Friends Service Committee observed that a nondiscretionary system would probably make life more tolerable for the disadvantaged, though it might disturb those who benefit from a discretionary system:

> To prove this point we refer the reader to the area of property inheritance tax or business law or any area, for that matter, in which the affairs of the more powerful and rich segments are being regulated. In these areas the specificity of the law is extreme. Little margin is left for discretion. Two companies in a contract dispute or relatives contesting the division of property in a will would not tolerate a judge making a discretionary decision based on his conception of the "best interests of society and of all parties involved," even if these motives were those actually operating in a discretionary system. . . . In general, in any area of law where the persons being regulated have resources, there is practically no discretion operating.[33]

All observers of the sentencing process agree that there are no standards that instruct the judge which elements to take into account and how much weight should be given to each. The President's Commission recommended the development of sentencing councils that would enable judges to discuss recommended sentences. It was hoped that this would develop more cogent rationales for sentencing and eliminate arbitrariness. They also suggested appellate review of sentences as a way of curbing judicial capriciousness.

The emphasis on judicial discretion, however, can obscure the patterned character of the sentencing process. The organizational constraints on judicial behavior in bail setting and plea bargaining (discussed below) also operate to a lesser extent in the judge's sentencing behavior. The large number of persons brought before the court for minor infractions leads to an almost completely automatic sentence for certain types of offenders. The rules of thumb on what is an appropriate sentence for specific offenses and offenders are accepted by judge, prosecutor, police, and critical publics of the court in the interest of efficiently processing large numbers of people. The judge's role in the sentencing process has actually diminished recently:

> The history of penal policy . . . is in no small measure one of erosion of judicial power and the evolution of a highly complex process of administrative punishment fixing that directly involves

[33] American Friends Service Committee, *Struggle for Justice* (New York: Hill & Wang, 1971), p. 135.

prosecutors, parole boards and the disciplinary committees. . . . From this functional perspective, judges are doing less and less of the real decision-making, their role being merely one step in a process in which law enforcement, prosecutors, probation officers, parole boards, parole agents or correctional staff may play major roles.[34]

Even in more serious cases where sentencing is not automatic the pressure is on the judge to act quickly. This leads to his heavy reliance on specialists who supply him with presentence reports. Smith and Blumberg conclude that it is possible to diffuse the anxieties and responsibilities of decision making in the criminal court:

> As any other bureaucracy, in the lower level court, the span and scope of decision making is limited. Because there is perhaps even greater anxiety generated in the criminal court due to the nature of the decisions made, the Central Sessions judges make an even more active effort to diffuse responsibility and authority than is usual in bureaucracy. They simply are reluctant to carry the entire burden, and unlike the appellate courts, there are ample intermediaries and interstitial people, and groups who can be invoked, to share in the responsibilities which are ultimately only that of the judge.[35]

PLEA BARGAINING

Perhaps the most serious criticism of the operation of the criminal court relates to the practice of trying to achieve justice by negotiation or compromise. The accused agrees to plead guilty to an offense less serious than the one originally charged. The purpose of plea bargaining is to reduce the volume of cases by quickly processing the accused and doing away with the necessity for a court trial. The criticism is aimed at the secret character of the negotiations, the lack of guidelines on how they should operate, and the absence of any judicial review on the propriety of the bargain struck.

Raymond Moley quoted from a newspaper humorist on the practice:

> "Did you take the $1,000 from Sam?" inquired the judge.
> The defendant pondered a moment and answered, "If I say I did what will you give me?"

[34] Caleb Foote, "A Program for Prison Reform," unpublished manuscript, (June 1972), pp. 17–18.
[35] Alexander B. Smith and Abraham S. Blumberg, "The Problem of Objectivity in Judicial Decision-Making," *Social Forces,* 46 (1967), 96–105.

The judge mentioned a series of years that mounted into two figures. The defendant was non-commital.

"Are you going to plead or not?" inquired the ass't district att'y.

"What kind of pleas have you?" asked the defendant.

The ass't district att'y rubbed his hands briskly and beamed at the customer.

"We have some very nice pleas today. What would you say to the first degree robbery?"

"How much?" shopped the defendant.

"Oh, twenty years," assured the ass't district att'y.

"Too much," objected the defendant. "I can't give that much."

"First degree suits you so well. You're just the type."

"No-o! What else have you?"

"Well, we have some nice second degree robberies."

"How much are those?"

"Fifteen years. . . ."

(Defendant indicates that the penalty is too high, the DA moves down to third degree robbery for ten years.)

"It's getting terrible, these sentences," he declared. "It's getting so you can't look at a crime for less than five or ten years now. . . . Have you any petty larcenies? I'll take a nice petty larceny if you have one."

At this point, according to the commentator, the judge stopped the colloquy and said, "This is not bargain day here. You go on trial for a first degree robbery."[36]

Moley goes on to say that this account is not a serious exaggeration:

Sophisticated defendants call arraignment time, "bargain day," and assistant district attorneys often approach the defendant much in the spirit of a market place.[37]

The practice seems to have sprung up initially to provide for individualized treatment in the face of harsh mandated sentences. Judges are compelled by statute to give mandatory sentences for some offenses even though they may feel the penalty is too harsh. This led to their cooperation with the prosecutor in the interest of providing a less severe disposition.

Plea bargaining was an effort at humanizing the criminal justice system by recovering the dispute-settling function of the court. In many cases coming before the criminal court the state does not have any serious interest in imposing sanctions. The President's Commission pointed out that thoughtful prosecutors are reluctant to seek penalties on domestic

[36] Raymond Moley, *Politics and Criminal Prosecution* (New York: Minton, Balch, 1929), pp. 173–74.
[37] Ibid., p. 174.

disturbances, assault, and petty thefts (in which victim and offender are in a family or social relationship); statutory rape, when both parties are young; first offense car theft (joy riding); checks drawn on insufficient funds; shoplifting by first offenders; and criminal acts that involve offenders suffering from emotional disorders. If the prosecutor is reluctant to seek penalties against these offenders it is unlikely that their cases would ever come before the court. They are screened out beforehand. But if the prosecutor does bring charges the judge can fulfill this conflict resolution function much the same way the police perform their peace-keeping tasks: he can dismiss the case, he can try to mediate arguments between intimates or neighbors, he can refer them to another agency, or he can warn them. None of these options involves affixing any penalty. The major reasons these options are not used more frequently is that cases that lend themselves to conflict resolution are usually handled by the police or prosecutor. The court's resources to recommend or supervise treatment are limited and the judge is reluctant to press for a resolution that the prosecutor doesn't recommend because he is so dependent upon him.

Moley saw some promise in the negotiation between the accused and the court. He saw the informality as a desirable move away from the court's norm-enforcement functions; the compromising he saw as a development in the direction of individualizing treatment. If it could work effectively, and about this there was serious question, the criminal court of the future would presumably function somewhat like an administrative tribunal. But whatever the initial hopes, justice by compromise has tended to subvert the ideals of due process in practice.

Blumberg's 1967 observational study of a felony court in a metropolitan area was the first major sociological inquiry into the criminal court as a bureaucracy.[38] He described in detail the pressures operating on court personnel to reduce the number of defendants who elect jury trials. The success of their efforts is revealed by the high proportion of those accused (over 90 percent) who plead guilty to a lesser charge. Most of the remaining 10 percent waive jury trials in favor of a judicial hearing. As in an industrial bureaucracy there are pressures on the prosecuting attorney to meet production quotas. He is evaluated on the number of convictions he can produce. Each case is treated as a unit of production. A plea of guilty that is accepted or negotiated is part of a district attorney's "batting average." The total output of cases must be maximized to deal with the overwhelming volume facing the court. Superior efficiency is the goal; the criterion is the number of convictions or pleas produced.

[38] Blumberg, *Criminal Justice.*

But the prosecutor is not alone in the production of guilty pleas. He is aided by the judge (who, to a lesser extent, is being evaluated in the same terms), the probation officers, psychiatrists, public defenders, and defense lawyers ("courthouse regulars"). The courthouse community is a system of cooperation which includes all the professional participants but excludes the defendant. The negotiated plea is a shortcut that uses questionable procedures in order to meet production norms. The questionable procedures that Blumberg mentions include the use of multiple count indictments ("throwing the book at him"), the promise of leniency for cooperation, and the threat of short-term detention if the defendant decides to go to trial. It is the rare defendant who is not persuaded that a guilty plea is preferable. In the process defendants plead guilty to crimes they did not commit.

In response to the ritualistic query from the judge, the defendant, defense counsel, and prosecutor all deny that a prior bargain has been made. The formal ceremony where the guilty plea is accepted is designed to assure everyone that it was not reached as a result of improper coercion, trickery, or the promise of lenient treatment. Consequently, the guilty plea is beyond review. All the participants in the criminal justice system, excluding the defendant, seem to be convinced of the pragmatic value of the practice. When a defendant pleads guilty the police are assured that their suspicions were justified, the prosecutors are satisfied that another case has been expeditiously handled, the judges are assured that their conduct is beyond appeal, and correctional authorities are satisfied that rehabilitation can occur because a wrong has been admitted.

The President's Commission identified the practice of negotiating pleas as one of two major issues related to the criminal court. The other was the prosecutor's decision to charge. The commission was less critical of the guilty plea system than Blumberg and pointed out that the court system would break down if most defendants went to trial. Also they asserted that if facts were not in dispute, going to trial (which is designed to establish the facts) was wasteful. They did note, however, that the practice of negotiating pleas caused a sense of bewilderment and injustice among defendants. Their recommendations would further protect the accused by including his counsel in the bargaining sessions, by making the practice available to everyone, by making explicit the procedures and standards by which the plea reduction is carried out, and by listing factors deemed relevant. Under their restructured system the judge would no longer be an accomplice to invisible and unreviewable proceedings but an independent examiner of the propriety of the plea.

THE ROLE OF THE DEFENSE LAWYER

Of all the roles played in the criminal court process the defense lawyer's seems to be most deeply compromised by the guilty plea system. In a "trial by combat" theory of justice the defense lawyer is the defendant's advocate and the prosecutor's adversary. The guilty plea system makes him part of the prosecutor's team. Blumberg asked his defendant respondents which agent mediator was most influential in the accused's plea and who first proposed it.[39] The defense counsel was perceived as most influential in persuading the defendant to plead guilty in a majority of the cases (56.7 percent); others listed the district attorney (16 percent) or a relative (16.6 percent) as most influential. Blumberg also found that the defense counsel usually suggested the guilty plea strategy in the first place (56.2 percent of the cases). He further asked his respondents at which stage counsel suggested that they plead guilty. The surprising discovery was that legal aid lawyers and those assigned by the court (public defenders) usually made the suggestion at their first contact with the accused. Privately retained lawyers were more likely to make the suggestion at the second meeting, perhaps giving lip service to their role as advocates. It is this situation that led Blumberg to characterize the defense counsel in the criminal court as a "double agent." He performs an extremely valuable service for the court organization and the accused:

> He ties the entire criminal justice system together—and makes it more palatable for the defendant. He assumes different roles at different stages in his client's case, using them alternately and sometimes in combination. The real professional is a consummate actor who at the preliminary stages of criminal case will make every conceivable legal motion and use every conceivable legal opportunity to demolish the prosecutor's case. Beyond the preliminary stages, his options become much more limited and his role changes to that of negotiator or fixer—the man of influence with access to the seats of power, the possessor of secret knowledge, the path smoother who at the same time must begin to "cool out" his client in case of defeat.[40]

A more detailed picture of how deeply implicated the defense lawyer is in carrying forward the work of the court is provided by Sudnow in his

[39] Ibid., pp. 92–93.
[40] Abraham S. Blumberg, "Criminal Justice in America," in Jack D. Douglas (ed.), *Crime and Justice in American Society* (Indianapolis: Bobbs-Merrill, 1971), p. 67.

investigation of a public defender's office.[41] He examined more closely how a plea typically is reduced by the public defender. The practice is patterned and requires the collaboration of the prosecutor and the judge. Since it is too time consuming to persuade defendants to plead guilty to the original offense the practice of reducing charges to make the guilty plea more palatable has grown up. The character of the public defender's task, wherein he repeatedly encounters the same offenses, leads to a working perspective that includes the notion of a "normal crime." A normal crime is one that regularly is committed in a particular manner by certain kinds of persons in predictable settings with predictable victims. For any series of offenses, like rape, burglary, assault, and child molestation, the public defender can provide a proverbial characterization. Knowledge of the properties of offense types and the offenders who commit them is the mark of any given attorney's competence.

A major task of socialization in the public defender's office is to teach the new attorney to recognize these attributes. This knowledge or occupational lore is necessary to decide what modifications should be made in the original charge. Over the course of the interaction between public defender and district attorney a set of unstated recipes for reducing original charges to lesser ones is developed. The reduction recipes are constructed so that they will be attractive to the defendant (sufficient reduction so that it is perceived by the defendant as a "break"), but will not let him off too easily. The conception of a normal crime and its permissible reduction is built around typical problems that repeatedly call for a solution. Though Sudnow did not examine this area it seems likely that both the prosecutor and the judge share the working perspective of the public defender on what constitutes a normal crime or normal case.

PROPOSALS FOR COURT REFORM

The major problem facing criminal courts is the volume of cases they must process. As we saw, this has led to the questionable practice of plea bargaining. Proposals to remedy that situation would make the process more visible, would clearly define acceptable reductions, and would review all bargains. Another recommendation that would weaken the practice would be to limit the kinds of behavior controlled by criminal sanction. The President's Commission has observed that offenses for which

[41] David Sudnow, "Normal Crimes: Sociological Features of a Penal Code in a Public Defender's Office," *Social Problems,* 2 (Winter 1965), 255–76.

there are no complaining witnesses clog the courts and are costly to process; the laws relating to them are often ineffective.[42] Offenses related to drunkenness, gambling, bad checks, nonsupport, disorderly conduct, vagrancy, and some types of sexual behavior should not, they suggest, be part of the criminal code. If they were removed from court dockets, case congestion would cease to be a problem, and the pressure to negotiate guilty pleas would decline.

Blumberg has suggested an independent ombudsman system that would scrupulously examine each guilty plea to see that minimum standards of justice had been met.[43] The reduction in the number of cases coming before the courts would also indirectly affect another of the court's problems: the large number of persons detained in lieu of granting bail. Fewer cases being processed should lead to fewer defendants being detained. But others have proposed more positive steps to reduce the number of defendants detained. Various reform groups concerned with preventive detention have questioned the injustice of the practice since it operates only against those who have limited economic resources. They have proposed the abolition of the bail system and wider use of release in the defendant's own recognizance.

The organizational reforms suggested are addressed to upgrading the qualifications of court personnel, centralizing the court system and the prosecutorial function, and narrowing the discretion of all court officers. One facet of the suggested reorganization is inevitably the improvement of court administration. Organizational reforms usually include suggestions for further protection of the accused like giving defendants access to presentencing reports and providing machinery for the review of sentences.

There are no suggested court reforms that are analogous to making the police more accountable to the local community (discussed in Chapter 6). The closest any of the critics have come is to suggest the provision of broader social services for those who would no longer be serviced by the courts. But one conclusion that emerges from a historical and contemporary review of lower criminal court operation is that its dispute settlement function has all but vanished for most citizens in a complex society characterized by highly formal processes and secondary contacts. If maintaining peace and understanding in a community is a goal, then this may be best served by the creation of neighborhood tribunals staffed by locally elected personnel. Their task would be dealing with relatively minor offenses which are now the province of the criminal court.

---

[42] President's Commission, *The Challenge of Crime*, pp. 129–57.
[43] Blumberg, "Criminal Justice in America," p. 77.

GRESHAM CRIMINAL COURT:
THE ISSUE OF PRODUCTIVITY

The Gresham Criminal Court is located in a city of some 400,000, which, in terms of Wilson's classification of communities, is conducive to a legalistic style in law enforcement. There is an influential business stratum and an accommodation forged among the different classes. The criminal court is one part of the judicial system in the city administered by a chief judge who is appointed by the mayor (though other judges are elected for four-year terms). The city has been controlled by the same political party for the last 15 years so nomination by the party is tantamount to election. The chief judge of the municipal court has been on the bench for 30 years and considers himself somewhat of an innovator. After the President's Commission made its report on the criminal courts in 1967, the chief judge sought out ways that he could implement some of the recommendations. He asked a management consultant firm that specialized in governmental and industrial reorganization to make some recommendations on streamlining the criminal court. They provided a confidential report to the chief judge after three months of observing court proceedings and interviewing court personnel. For some reason the chief judge did not release their recommendations and refused to discuss them with court personnel. There was some evidence that he was displeased with their suggestions. He briefly described them as "young punks, time and motion study experts who cost a fortune" to his administrative assistant. He next asked his in-house research unit to read the commission report carefully, to study the court operation, and to come up with recommendations for change.

The task was given to a young staff member who had a law degree but whose previous background was in marketing research. He interpreted his mandate to come up with recommendations that would (1) reduce the court's case load, (2) computerize court records, and (3) regularize the plea-reduction practices. He early concluded that suggestions on computerizing court records were beyond his competence so his final report to the chief judge recommended that computer experts be hired to do this.

He prepared an interview guide to use with court personnel to get at their suggestions for speeding up the work of the court and remedying its problems. He thought it important to interview the judges (four in all), the prosecutor's staff, the public defenders, and a handful of defendants.

He ignored court clerks, private lawyers who occasionally represented defendants, bailiffs, and the probation staff because their role in the court he thought minimal. He rounded out these interviews with courtroom observations and some assessment of the time each judge spent on the bench as well as the proportion of cases heard.

He recommended that one of the judges be transferred out because of his low productivity. He further recommended that the remaining three judges work out a plan to make plea reduction more visible and uniform, and to reduce the disparity in sentencing practices. The chief judge discussed these recommendations with the four judges and they vehemently rejected them. They contended that the researcher's lack of legal expertise led him to misunderstand the significance of variability in judicial productivity. They argued that the low-productivity judge actually spent a great deal of time in getting at the facts in each case and individualizing justice. They rejected suggestions on uniformity in plea bargaining procedures and sentencing practices as an invasion of judicial prerogatives.

The recommendations made on reducing the case load were acceptable to the judges but resisted strenuously by the prosecutor's staff. The researcher found the prosecutorial staff very difficult to study. They were suspicious of what they anticipated was going to be a negative "evaluation." They were reluctant to give him access to their files, missed appointment dates he made with them, and let him observe only a handful of discussions with defendants on plea reduction. They rejected recommendations that the public prosecutor use his discretion to ignore minor violations of the law in favor of informal settlements. They reported that only a fraction of the cases that were brought to their attention were acted upon. The prosecutor's staff claimed to focus on just the serious violations and argued that their relationship with the police department would be seriously compromised if they reduced the number of cases any further. The researcher specifically focused on reducing the number of drunkenness charges and sexual misdemeanors between consenting adults. The prosecutor's rejoinder was that influential local public opinion was in favor of enforcing these laws and until other provisions were made for handling drunks or the city council liberalized the municipal code relating to proscribed sexual activity, he would continue to enforce it. The prosecutor's staff refused to comment on the recommendations relating to judicial productivity and sentencing uniformity.

The public defenders were less antagonistic than the prosecutors but not much more helpful. They denied the researcher access to discussions with defendants on plea reduction and protested interviews with defendants, especially when questions relating to plea bargaining were to be raised. The researcher interviewed 20 defendants processed by the court to get their reactions to the proceedings, and to discover who first suggested plea bargaining. The public defenders agreed with the recommendations of making the pleas available to all and informing defendants about the procedure beforehand. They felt that judicial control of the process would be beneficial. They tended to share the perspective of the prosecutor on reducing the number of cases; that is, they tended to resist it. One public defender expressed the concern that the suggested reductions would cut the public defender staff in half. They had no reactions to the proposal for increased judicial productivity; on sentencing uniformity they asked only that the recommendation of the public defender be given the same weight as the prosecutor's recommendation.

The chief judge met with each group in sequence over several weeks but without the presence of the research staff. One month after the meetings were concluded the chief judge wrote the research unit director thanking him for his efforts and informing him that he was taking the recommendations "under advisement" until his own plans for computerizing court records were completed. The staff member responsible for the report concluded that it would be quietly filed and forgotten. He toyed with the idea of sending a copy to a local newspaper critical of the city administration but decided against it on the remote possibility that the chief judge actually agreed with the reorganization but was waiting for a more propitious time to implement it.

DISCUSSION

The account of the Greshman Criminal Court seems plausible but there are important bits of information missing because the case is reconstructed from the vantage point of the staff member charged to come up with recommendations for court improvement. He did not have access to all relevant information. For instance, he was unable to account for the suspicions of court personnel about his research. They were not amenable to interviews so we don't know what their interpretation of events was. We do know that the criminal court was part of a larger municipal court that included the juvenile court, probate court, and domestic relations court among others, and did not function autonomously from the larger court structure. Judges were regularly rotated to other courts, the average stay being about four years. Yet it was only the criminal court that the chief judge wanted to reorganize. There is no indication why. A lengthy interview with the chief judge might have clarified his own motivations in suggesting change as well as what he ultimately planned to do with the report. Court personnel were sufficiently sensitive to the fact that their court was singled out for study. This may have partly accounted for their resistance to any kind of "evaluation" of their work.

We can't tell how typical Gresham Criminal Court is. It's smaller than the one Blumberg studied but the same dynamics seemed to operate. Blumberg's analysis underlined the linkages his court had with both the police and critical community groups. We don't get any clear sense of the relationship the Gresham Criminal Court had with the police. The prosecutor mentions the importance of keeping their cooperation but the specific kind of pressures or demands they placed on the court are not discussed. The Gresham Criminal Court also operated in a larger social and political environment (as did Blumberg's court) that set limits on what it could do. This is only briefly hinted at in the prosecutor's reaction to the nonenforcement of the law recommendation.

By and large the case study tends to confirm the generalizations made by Blumberg and others with one minor qualification. One of the Gresham Court judges seemed genuinely less self-serving than Blumberg's judges. He seemed to have a strong sense of fairness and resisted the assembly line pressures by spending a great deal of time with each defendant. Though the range of dispositions was limited, he consistently chose the less severe one. His role in the court surprisingly was defended by the other judges. They seemed convinced that ideally this is what judges should do, though the day-to-day pressures militate against it. One of the topics covered in the defendant interviews was their own perception of the "fairness" of the proceedings. The judge operated with the assumption that those who participate in the proceedings must not have their own sense of injustice aggravated.

The role this judge played seemed to be a legitimatizing one—keeping the court close to the community and emphasizing its fairness and concern about those it processed. This suggests that in communities where there are sharp but accommodated class differences, the criminal court must spend part of its energies in symbolically reaffirming this accommodation and working for the court's acceptance among the low income stratum it characteristically processes.

QUESTIONS FOR FURTHER DISCUSSION

1. What does this case reveal about the problems of the criminal court?

2. What combination of circumstances would make it more likely

that the recommendations would have been accepted by all the factions involved?

3. Why did the judge, prosecutor, and public defender take different positions on judicial performance, productivity, reduction of caseload, and plea bargaining?

4. How decisive do you think the procedure for introducing the research project and the procedures for informing court personnel of the final report were in their rejection of the recommendations?

5. How would a conflict and consensus perspective interpret this series of events and what further information would each look for in this case?

6. What hypotheses are suggested in this case that would be worth exploring further?

SUMMARY

We have seen in this chapter that the court organization does not passively process the mass of defendants sent by the police. It plays a more proactive role in the criminalization process. The prosecutor decides which cases will be processed and which rejected. Because of the enormous authority wielded by the prosecutor, the activities of the police can be decisively shaped. If the district attorney decides not to prosecute certain kinds of offenses the police will cease making arrests for those violations. The potential for conflict between these two units in the criminal justice system is great but their need for collaboration is greater. The police and the criminal court must jointly work out a set of understandings that enable each to perform its task with a minimum amount of strain and the least intrusion from a hostile and ill-informed public. This isolation of the lower courts from the community suggests that more thoughtful consideration should be given to making the court organization more responsive to those it was established to serve. The official public most importantly linked to the court is the police, but another critical official public is corrections. Its role in defending the corrections mandate in the face of increasing public criticism is the subject of Chapter 8.

corrections

The modern prison is a recent phenomenon. Some commentators give credit to America for this ingenious development. It was in the United States during the nineteenth century that the main outlines of the present-day prison were sketched. Only a fairly advanced economy can afford the luxury of facilities that house thousands of prisoners for long periods of time. But there were historical antecedents to today's prisons—the term "penitentiary" comes from the place where the Church confined sinners. But the usual punishment for serious offenders was death or banishment. For less serious offenders, England set up a House of Correction. It was a method of exploiting labor and training new labor reserves, and was the immediate predecessor to the modern penal institution. It was originally established to control the wandering unemployed. The growing population of beggars, freed from the land and from feudal ties, seemed to threaten the safety and the moral sensibilities of the bourgeoisie. Since beggars were unwilling to work they had to be coerced to meet the demands of developing capitalism. The House of Correction addressed an economic need while at the same time it controlled vagabondage. Its appeal even extended to those who had a humanitarian concern for the outcast. Rusche and Kirchheimer observe:

> The essence of the House of Correction was that it combined the principles of the poorhouse, workhouse and penal institution. Its

main aim was to make the labor power of unwilling people socially useful. By being forced to work within the institution the prisoners would form industrious habits and would receive vocational training at the same time. When released, it was hoped, they would voluntarily swell the labor market. . . . The institution of houses of correction . . . was not the result of brotherly love or of an official sense of obligation to the distressed. It was part of the development of capitalism. . . . Houses of correction were primarily manufactories, turning out commodities at a particularly low cost because of their cheap labor. It is probable, then, that they were generally paying concerns. That was clearly the intention of their founders.[1]

The conditions of the labor market were favorable to the lower class. This was a period of labor shortage and their labor could be withheld. The House of Correction was a coercive measure to prevent withholding of labor in the absence of any economic pressures on the working class. With overpopulation and the development of a surplus of labor the need for houses of correction vanished. The poor were compelled to work out of sheer poverty.

PRISON AND THE "DANGEROUS CLASSES"

The class character of punishment is apparent throughout the evolution of the penal institution. To the casual observer the most puzzling aspect of the prisons is their humanitarian justifications. In the United States the prison was the result of reform movements aimed at improving the offender. The offender was always a member of "the dangerous classes"— those who threaten existing social arrangements. In the United States, as Sarbin points out, the concept of dangerous classes developed during the period of rapid social and technological changes following the Civil War.[2] All newcomers threatened the old agrarian system. The effort was made to assimilate the newcomer and speed his adaptation to the existing social order. If there were any trouble, the prison stood ready to help. Irwin suggests that the reformers who pioneered the modern penal institution were persuaded that incarceration was for the offender's own good.[3] They were opposed to cruel punishment, but were animated by a

[1] George Rusche and Otto Kirchheimer, *Punishment and Social Structure* (New York: Columbia University Press, 1939), p. 50.
[2] Theodore Sarbin, *The Myth of the Criminal Type* (Middletown, Conn.: Wesleyan University Press, 1969).
[3] John Irwin, "Adaption to Being Corrected," in Daniel Glaser (ed.), *Handbook of Criminology* (Chicago: Rand McNally, 1974).

mixture of hatred, fear, and revulsion of those who didn't share their values, life styles, or Christian ethics. The revulsion was disguised by a humanitarian concern for the health and well being of the dangerous classes. Imprisonment was a suitable response for the complicated and contradictory feelings of the reformers.

Sarbin traces the origin of the word "danger" to relative position in a social structure. It referred to the relationship between roles on a power dimension. Those who benefited from a particular set of social relationships viewed those below them in the power pyramid as "dangerous." The dangerous group in the latter nineteenth century was the lowest stratum of the population—those who were unwilling or unable to adapt to the factory system. Sarbin points out that the concepts of danger and criminality were in fact virtually identical. The interchangeability of the two concepts led, he hypothesized, to the "myth of the criminal type."[4] It is a myth, he contends, because everyone violates some ordinance, civil regulation, or penal code in the business of meeting life's contingencies, but the label of criminal is applied to only a fraction of the potential candidates. Social science, both then and now, has willingly or unwillingly perpetuated the myth of the criminal type. The pervasiveness of the myth is illustrated by Banfield's depiction of the urban lower-class slum dweller. His life style lacks discipline:

> . . . the lower class individual lives from moment to moment. . . . Impulse governs his behavior . . . he is therefore radically improvident; whatever he cannot use immediately he considers valueless. His bodily needs (especially for sex) and his taste for "action" take precedence over anything else—and certainly over any work routine.[5]

The prescriptives implied in this portrait are obvious. The lower-class person should be placed in a structured environment where he can learn good work habits and respect for authority. It was around the themes of obedience, labor, and separation (from the community, from each other) that officials organized the American prison in the nineteenth century. Rothman indicates that the orderly prison was paralleled by the growth of the factory intent on bringing an unprecedented discipline to laborer's lives.[6] Both organizations were among the first to try to transfer people from casual routines to rigid ones. It is no surprise then that the aim in prison administration became to help the inmate submit willingly to the

---

[4] Sarbin, *The Myth of the Criminal Type.*
[5] Edward S. Banfield, *The Unheavenly City Revisited* (Boston: Little, Brown, 1974), p. 61.
[6] David Rothman, *The Discovery of the Asylum: Social Order and Disorder in the New Republic* (Boston: Little, Brown, 1971).

fate of the lower classes. A necessary condition for reentry into society is unconditional submission to authority:

> If the prisoners resign themselves to a quiet, regular and industrious life punishment will become more tolerable for them. Once this routine becomes a habit, the first step toward improvement has been taken.[7]

Some criminologists have contended that early prisons and dungeons were the forerunners of the modern penal institution. But these earlier prisons were established for the long-term confinement of upper-class offenders—a handful of royal personages or influential heretics. Some were even permitted the personal ministrations of their household retinue. But for lower-class offenders, though they might be confined for long periods of time, prison was basically a detention facility until trial; the modern equivalent is the county jail. After conviction the offender might be put to death, mutilated in some way, or sent to a distant colony that was plagued by labor shortages.

In the colonial period the less serious offenses, like violation of the Sabbath and fornication, were dealt with by fines, flogging, or some kind of public ridicule. The less serious offender was not a member of any particular social stratum. He could be found anywhere since all men were sinners. The offender was basically a sinner and after being appropriately punished he was restored to the community. The more serious offender was more likely to be a pauper or a stranger or somehow defective. He was not thought of as a sinner but as less than human—someone to be excluded permanently from the community. Hence, his fate was most often the gallows.

By 1870 there was no doubt in anyone's mind, least of all the emergent professionals in corrections, that criminal types and immigrants were the same thing. Brace noted in 1872 that:

> An immense proportion of our ignorant and criminal class are foreign born; and of the dangerous classes here, a very large part, though native born, are of foreign parentage.[8]

Their criminality or criminal predispositions are nurtured by a long history of strife. The characteristics of these potential criminals are made more vivid some 35 years after this by Brown commenting on the increasing crime rate in America:

> In the poorer quarters of our great cities may be found huddled together the Italian bandit and the bloodthirsty Spaniard, the bad

[7] Rusche and Kirchheimer, *Punishment and Social Structure*, p. 107.
[8] Charles Loring Brace, *The Dangerous Classes of New York and Twenty Years Work Among Them* (New York: Wynkoop and Hallenbeck, 1872), p. 35.

man from Sicily, the Hungarian, Croatian and the Pole, the China-man and the Negro, the Cockney Englishman, the Russian and the Jew with all the centuries of hereditary hate back of them.[9]

For all these criminally disposed persons the prison could be beneficial. The most serious problem they posed, as noted by the American Friends Service Committee, was their lack of adherence to prevailing cultural norms: cleanliness, industry, saving, and accumulation. Their crimes (theft, killing, pickpocketing, prostitution, robbery) when compared with middle-class crimes (fraud, bribery, commercial deception, embezzlement) were relatively insignificant. Yet their significance was not in their cost but in their challenge to the legitimacy of Anglo-Saxon cultural values. In short, their criminality could have revolutionary consequences. Hence it was dealt with more severely. The person being corrected was coercively indoctrinated into the host culture's values. The American Friends Service Committee then suggests a disturbing analogy to the prison's attempt to induce cultural conformity in the nineteenth century: the policy of compulsory assimilation carried out by the American Indian Bureau on American Indians from 1849 onward.[10] The program to regulate the lives of the Indians bore an uncanny resemblance to the correctional program being initiated across the land.

THE FUNCTION OF CORRECTIONS

The function of corrections has never been clouded by the dilemma facing the police or the courts: peace keeping versus dispute settlement versus law enforcement. Correction's role has always been law or norm enforcement. Their task, as correctional officials saw it, was to discipline and control the population sent to them in hopes of sending them back to the free community able to adjust to authority. The major issue of contention has long been whether the experience should be punitive or rehabilitative. All agreed that whatever rehabilitation took place had to be in a situation where the prisoner was confined against his will. The arguments revolved around the use of corporal punishment. But as time passed the necessity for harsh physical treatment had largely vanished in the face of more sophisticated and effective control measures, hence, arguments about corporal punishment were irrelevant.

[9] John E. Brown, "The Increase of Crime in the United States," *The Independent* (1907), pp. 832–33.
[10] American Friends Service Committee, *Struggle for Justice* (New York: Hill & Wang, 1971), p. 44.

An early debate in American corrections was related to the merits of congregate prison versus solitary confinement. The argument prompted a tremendous amount of interest among the general public and much argumentative literature. The high level of interest in prisons in the nineteenth century was based on the conviction that the fundamentals of proper social organization could best be established in the prison.[11] It was a belief related to the insecurity of the new republic. If crime were symptomatic of the breakdown in traditional community practices then penitentiaries could point the way to reconstruction. There were even some enthusiasts who advocated that everyone serve some time in prison for the good of their soul: "Could we all be put on prison fare for the space of two or three generations, the world would ultimately be better for it."[12]

In 1790 the Walnut Street jail was the first facility to be designated for postconviction purposes. It looked much like a family dwelling—an ordinary large frame house. The prisoners lived together in large rooms, took their meals in a dining room, and moved about freely. The casual and undisciplined regime, however, was not conducive to security. To make escape more difficult, the inmates were required to wear uniforms. Everyone who was aware of the Walnut Street jail was dissatisfied with its operation. The results of its work program were meager. According to Rothman there wasn't enough incentive on the part of prisoners or enough close supervision on the part of jail officials to make convict labor profitable.[13] The experiment proved too costly. The original hope that convict labor would make the jail self-supporting was unrealized. By 1820 the critics were so numerous that some kind of change in the treatment of the convicted was inevitable.

The Quakers were an influential interest group concerned about the welfare of prisoners; they commissioned a new prison that they thought would remedy the defects of the Walnut Street jail. It was constructed in Philadelphia and designed to isolate prisoners from one another in solitary confinement. Eastern State Penitentiary, as it was called, was opened in 1829. It was intended to serve as a place for meditation and reflection in solitude. The experience ideally would lead to repentance. The difficulties in managing the system as well as in meeting its cost discouraged any imitations and the plan was never given a fair trial. The extent to which it aided reformation is not known but it had its share of influential critics. Dickens, on a journey to the United States in the latter part of the nineteenth century, visited this model prison:

[11] Rothman, *The Discovery of the Asylum.*
[12] James P. Finley, quoted in Ibid. pp. 84–85.
[13] Rothman, *The Discovery of the Asylum.*

In the outskirts stands a great prison, called the Eastern Penitentiary; conducted on a plan peculiar to the state of Pennsylvania.
The system here is rigid, strict, and hopeless *solitary confinement*.
I believe it, in its effects to be cruel and wrong. In its intentions, I
am well convinced that it is kind, humane, and meant for reformation; but I am persuaded that those who devised this system of
Prison Discipline, and those benevolent gentlemen who carry it into
execution, do not know what they are doing. . . . I hold this slow
and daily tampering with the mysteries of the brain, to be im-
measurably worse than any torture of the body; and because its
ghastly signs are not so palpable to the eye . . . it extorts few cries
that human ears can hear; therefore I the more denounce it, as a
secret punishment which slumbering humanity is not roused up to
stay.[14]

About the same time that Eastern State Penitentiary was founded an
alternate plan was developed in Auburn, New York. Inmates were
housed in single cells but fed and employed in common. They were
forbidden to speak to one another and marched in silent lockstep from
cell to workplace to dining hall. The congregate work program was
profitable and the economy of the operation was appealing to legislators.
The plan was widely copied in the United States and Europe. Each year
brought a host of international visitors to inspect the now famous American penological experiments as represented by the Philadelphia and New
York plans. The advocates of the two plans clashed frequently on their
respective merits. In retrospect there was never any doubt about the
outcome. The Auburn plan won out because it was more economical. Its
success was evident in the emergence of fortress prisons with congregate
work plans after 1820. The prisons were characterized as fortresses because they looked like medieval castles and were located far from urban
areas. Since custody was the major consideration the structures were
built of stone, steel, and concrete. As the President's Commission noted:
"They are noteworthy for their endurance. Sixty-one prisons opened be
fore 1900 are still in use."[15] The location and architecture of the fortress
prison limited the kinds of activity that could take place. Its remoteness
worked against any kind of community reintegration of the offender and
made the recruitment of professionals difficult.

The fortress prisons, called by correctional professionals "maximum
security institutions," looked very much like quasi-military establishments
and a high proportion of the top administration were former military
officers. For economy's sake the institutions were built to handle large

[14] American Friends, *Struggle for Justice*, pp. 18–19.
[15] President's Commission on Law Enforcement and the Administration of
Justice, *The Challenge of Crime in a Free Society Task Force Report: Corrections* (Washington, D.C.: Government Printing Office, 1967), p. 4.

numbers of prisoners. A population of 2,000 was not uncommon and by 1965, 4 of the 21 maximum security institutions in the United States had over 4,000 inmates.[16]

The size of the facility lent itself to the mass handling of inmates and a high degree of impersonality. Official policy discouraged fraternization, and special forms of etiquette emerged to maintain the social distance between staff and inmates. For instance, the custodial staff was required to address prisoners by their first name, last name, or nickname while inmates addressed officials by their title.

Cressey ascribes the rigid discipline in the traditional prison to the administrators' fear of escapes.[17] The fear is not an irrational one. Every top prison official can relate in detail, either from personal experience or that of fellow professionals, what can happen if one or more inmates escape. It can be what Ohlin calls a "crisis precipitating event" which unleashes an immense flood of criticism against the prison administration.[18] In this intense climate of criticism and public awareness the escape may be magnified sufficiently to initiate a searching public investigation. If the administration is able to ride out the investigation and keep its crucial publics mobilized in opposition to any change, then well and good. But the risk to one's professional career in this situation is very high. Given this context it should come as no surprise that tight security should be highly valued by prison administrators.

THE EMERGENCE OF CORRECTIONAL PROFESSIONALS

The American Social Science Association—from which the National Prison Association (later the American Correctional Association) evolved—consisted of clergymen, well-to-do reformers, professionals, legislators, newspaper editors, and philanthropists concerned about social problems.[19] Their constituency was a national one, though very much concentrated in the northeast. They saw their role as shaper of national policy; their proposals for action, whether addressed to the problems of

16 Ibid., p. 4.
17 Edwin Sutherland and Donald R. Cressey, *Criminology,* 8th ed. (Philadelphia: Lippincott, 1970), p. 512.
18 Lloyd Ohlin, "Organizational Reform in Correctional Agencies," in Daniel Glaser (ed.), *Handbook of Criminology* (Chicago: Rand McNally, 1974).
19 Harry Elmer Barnes and Negley K. Teeters, *New Horizons in Criminology,* 3rd ed. (Englewood Cliffs, N.J.: Prentice-Hall, 1959) give a detailed account of the reform movement that led to the American Prison Association on pp. 322–47; for a history of the American Social Science Movement, see Luther L. Bernard and Jesse Bernard, *Origins of American Sociology: The Social Science Movement in the United States* (New York: Russell & Russell, 1965).

the mentally ill, pauperism, or prisons, commanded a respectful hearing. It was in this circle that prison officials moved. However marginal they may have felt themselves to be professionally, their contact with this larger audience gave them an influence far beyond what their numbers would suggest.

It was in the American Social Science Association that the first proposals for replacing the fortress prison were aired; the view gradually emerged that the prison should be used not for punishment but for rehabilitation of offenders. In addition, the impact of the fledgling social sciences can be credited for shifting the preoccupation from crime to the criminal and his personality. The developing set of ideas about crime and its corrections appealed both to the humanitarians (since it promised more humane treatment for offenders) and to those concerned with economy (since it seemed to be cheaper). During this period, ideas relating to individualized treatment, diagnosis, classification, probation, and parole were elaborated. Rusche and Kirchheimer state:

> It was in this social atmosphere that the literature of modern prison reform arose. Its insistence on treating crime as a psychological-medical problem, that is to say, on the social necessity of healing the prisoner if possible or of isolating him if no cure could be achieved, spread to every section of the population.[20]

Much of the enthusiasm by which these notions were greeted by the American Social Science Association was due the promise they held for helping prison professionals: the prison gates were soon flung open to the clinicians—social workers, educators, and religionists—and a new cluster of professions was born.[21]

The new penology argued for the indeterminate sentence—no specified penalty for a particular offense, but a wide range of possible penalties from no incarceration to life imprisonment. The length of imprisonment would be determined by prison officials and other experts on the basis of satisfactory proof of reformation. The plan also involved a "mark system" by which one could earn privileges within the institution and eventually parole by the accumulation of marks. The new picture of the criminal was not the pariah who should be banished, nor the penitent who must be guided into the right path, nor the prisoner who must pay for his crimes by a carefully measured period of punishment, but a *patient* who must be treated.[22] His offense is evidence of a disease, not of willfulness or malice. This view was given official legitimation by the newly formed

---

[20] Rusche and Kirchheimer, *Punishment and Social Structure*, p. 151.
[21] David Fogel, *We are the Living Proof: The Justice Model for Corrections* (Cincinnati: Anderson Co., 1975), pp. 51–62.
[22] Ibid., pp. 62–64.

American Prison Association at its first meeting in Cincinnati in 1870; it became the professionally dominant view of crime and its correction from then until the present time. (Recent challenges to this disease model of corrections will be discussed in more detail below.) The declaration of principles endorsed by the 1870 convention was evidence that the social movement linked to the new view of the offender had carried the day.

The first concrete manifestation of the new principles was the establishment of the Elmira Reformatory in New York in 1876. It had solitary confinement at night but congregate work and eating areas. Its chief distinction was that its prisoners were subject to indeterminate sentences and assigned to three groups according to progress and deportment. The Elmira model set the pattern for most correctional facilities through 1900. To underline the kind of reformation that was expected, the newer institutions provided libraries, recreations, schools, vocational programs, and expanded probation and parole programs.

The dramatic results expected of the new plan did not materialize and enthusiasm for the reformatory idea declined after a brief 25 years. Fogel notes that after 1900 the prison population began to spiral upward and the newer facilities followed a more retrogressive pattern.[23] Yet the most important innovation represented by the Elmira reformatory—the indeterminate sentence—remained. The rehabilitation ideal was embraced by prison administrators because of its effectiveness as a control device. Under a rehabilitation system "dangerous persons" could be held indefinitely. The goals of rehabilitation superficially seemed to be at odds with a punitive philosophy but in practice fitted in quite conveniently. Prisoners could be classified into a limited number of types with prescriptive treatments for each without calling into question the motives of prison officials in so classifying. The continued evaluation of offenders to determine "parole readiness" in practice reminded inmates that unless they conformed they could be confined indefinitely. The system rewarded compliance with regulations by sentence reductions. The expectation of the reformers that the absolute authority of the traditional warden would be undermined by the introduction of treatment personnel also proved illusory. Traditionalists within the prison welcomed the development because it had the opposite effect—it increased their power. The history of treatment in American prisons is vivid testimony to the resources of the correctional bureaucracy to absorb new functions and a host of new professionals to authoritarian ends.

The period from after World War I through the early 1930s witnessed an upsurge in nativism and fear of foreign ideologies in American life.

[23] Ibid., ch. 3.

This was reflected in corrections by increased severity in sentencing, a reappearance of the revenge rationale in incarceration, and an increase in the absolute number of persons incarcerated. Rubin characterized this period as one of the most dismal in American correctional law.[24] Increased severity was viewed as a solution to increased crime and an antidote to judicial softness. The 100-year-old American experience with corrections seemed to be circular: punishment and suppression, followed by halting attempts to rehabilitate, followed by a new cycle of punishment and suppression. The difference between 1830 and 1930 was that for the imaginative prison administrator a new rhetoric of healing could be used to justify almost any practice.

In sum, the prison as we know it today did not appear out of the blue nor is it a product of random or aimless growth. The key to understanding the prison today is the role correctional professionals have played as an interest group. Characteristically they and their allies have tried to achieve specific goals generally related to the expansion of prison facilities. Like other interest groups they have worked to extend their sphere of influence, fight off enemies (especially those calling for abolition or serious reform of the prison), develop relationships with friendly legislators, and mobilize a loyal constituency. In short, behind the rhetoric of reformation and public protection we can discern the realities of a professional group on the ascent.

PRISONS AND THE ECONOMY

The movement from a philosophy of punishment to reformation and back again did not fluctuate independent of economic conditions. In most interpretations of the history of corrections this point is not made forcefully enough, if at all. By 1870 the correctional professional appeared on the scene and established a somewhat shaky accommodation with political interest groups like the judiciary, other criminal justice agencies, and community welfare groups. It is within the state legislatures that the correctional professionals and their allies made their fight. The conflicts revolved around facilities and number of jobs. The economic considerations are apparent in debates about site selection for a new prison. The usual correctional history emphasizes the random character of site selection and absence of any clear-cut pattern of growth. A closer look at the arguments about site selection, however, reveals that the overriding con-

[24] Sol Rubin, *The Law of Criminal Corrections* (St. Paul, Minn.: West Publishing Co., 1963).

sideration was public employment for a handful of needy, most often rural, constituents. The fascination with the political trade-offs that eventuated in the final selection sometimes obscures this fact.

The second aspect of correctional history that links it to economic history is the chronicle of prison labor. Prison labor is usually given short shrift in standard accounts of prison history. The original plans for both the Auburn and Pennsylvania facilities envisioned convict labor that would at least reimburse the state for the costs of the facilities, and possibly show a profit. Economic considerations coincided with humanitarian ones: the reformers took the position that work was rehabilitative so no objections to the various work methods were forthcoming. As Rothman observed, the contracts made with private manufacturers served the goals of reform and economy simultaneously.[25] The private contractors reimbursed the prisons for convict labor. And for a while the arrangement proved profitable; the Auburn prison netted over $25,000 in profits from 1828 to 1833.[26] The contract system emerged in a period of full employment where there was need of new labor reserves. It declined in the latter part of the nineteenth century largely because of the opposition of the labor movement. Worker organizations had become stronger with the disappearance of the frontier. An important factor in the demise of contract labor was the growing opposition of prison management to the arrangement:

> From their debates on the subject as reported in the proceedings of the early prison congresses, it appears the objections of prison management to contract labor were threefold: the contractors tended to usurp too much authority, sometimes virtually taking over the prison and relegating the warden to a subordinate role. The immense profits from contract labor, much of it siphoned off by the contractor-middlemen, could just as well be garnered in toto by the prison.[27]

The piece-price system gradually replaced the contract system. Under this arrangement the contractor paid the state a stipulated sum for finished products rather than for each prison worker. The advantage from the point of view of prison management was that the prisoners were not farmed out for parts of each day. This led to "prison industries" in the 1930s which replaced all previous arrangements. An agreement was made with the leadership of the labor movement that secured their cooperation with the new plan. Under prison industry the state becomes an entrepreneur, purchases raw materials, manufactures products, and sells them

[25] Rothman, *The Discovery of the Asylum.*
[26] Jessica Mitford, *Kind and Usual Punishment, The Prison Business* (New York: Vintage Books, 1974), p. 213.
[27] Ibid., p. 213.

to a restricted market. The market usually includes colleges, mental hospitals, and other state agencies. While this system does not completely support corrections (especially the construction of new facilities) it is enormously profitable, principally because of the low wages (the average in 1970 was 26 cents an hour) paid to convict labor. But even in the few periods of low profitability, prison labor could be justified for its deterrence potential. Rusche and Kirchheimer have observed that when the price of free labor was high, prison officials tried to make convict labor as productive as possible. But when there was a labor surplus and the price of free labor dropped so did concern about convict productivity.[28] In that situation prison labor is used as a form of punishment to deter other lower-class persons from committing crimes. Prison labor, in short, becomes a new method of torture supplanting the older discredited ones.

THE SOCIOLOGY OF PRISON LIFE

The Inmate Subculture

The toehold that the helping professions managed to secure in a number of prisons by 1930 provided the opportunity for the entry of research sociologists.[29] The ecologists discussed in Chapter 3 were the first ones on the scene. Some of the key figures of the Chicago group had pioneered in the construction of parole prediction scales in the 1920s and, in the process, gained the confidence of some prison administrators and parole boards. The first serious sociological study of prison life was done by Clemmer in the 1930s.[30] He looked at the prison as if it were a community and tried to trace the same social processes that existed on the outside—competition, conflict, accommodation, and assimilation. The new prisoner was analogous to the new immigrant and the process of his acculturation could be mapped in the same way. There is an initial period of early unsettledness, a time of transitional grouping for redefinition, a time of provisional acquiescence to prison values, and a period of preparation for return to the free community. Clemmer called the process "prisonization." The process seems also to affect the inmate's perception of justice. Glaser and Stratton found that 60 percent of an inmate sample thought their sentence fair; by the middle of their stay only 36 percent were so convinced; at the end of their stay 70 percent thought their

---

[28] Rusche and Kirchheimer, *Punishment and Social Structure*, pp. 84–113.
[29] Morris Janowitz, "Professionalization of Sociology," *American Journal of Sociology*, 78 (July 1972), 105–35.
[30] Donald Clemmer, *The Prison Community* (Boston: Christopher, 1940).

sentence fair. This suggests the changing character of normative commitments that parallel stages of incarceration.[31]

Another aspect of early prison research was emphasis on the sources and substance of the prison society to which the inmate must come to terms. Sykes argued that the boundaries of prison life are set by adaptation to what he called the "pains of imprisonment."[32] This situation gives rise to individual and collective modes of adaptation. The circumstances of prison life lead to the creation of an inmate subculture. He identified these circumstances as:

Deprivation of liberty: The inmate is cut off from family, relatives, and friends, and contained by a set of detailed rules, sanctions, rewards, and punishments. Not only is he deprived of his liberty but he is set apart from "decent" people and made continually aware of his rejection by them.

Deprivation of goods and services: None of the amenities available to those in the free community are accessible. There is a scarcity of materials that on the outside are taken as sure indicators of a man's worth.

Deprivation of heterosexual relationships: The deprivation is physiological and psychological. A society composed exclusively of men tends to generate masculinity anxieties in its members regardless of whether they are coerced, bribed, or seduced into homosexual liaisons. The status of an inmate's maleness is called into question. His self-conception is changed by the lack of women who, by their polarity, give much of the male world its meaning.

Deprivation of autonomy: The endless series of rules and regulations have the effect of reducing the prisoner to helpless dependency. In more traditional institutions the staff refuses to give explanations of the rules since they feel this tends to weaken their position.

Deprivation of security: The individual is thrown into prolonged contact with others who have a long history of violent aggressive behavior. The inmate is acutely aware that sooner or later he will be "tested," that someone will push him to see how far he can go, and that he must be prepared to fight for the safety of his person and his possessions.

This situation of deprivation generates a distinctive set of values or an "inmate code." It has been summarized as follows:

[31] Daniel Glaser and John R. Stratton, "Measuring Inmate Change," in Donald R. Cressey (ed.), *The Prison: Studies in Institutional Organization and Change* (New York: Holt, Rinehart & Winston, 1961); see also Stanton Wheeler, "Socialization in Correctional Communities," *American Sociological Review,* 26 (October 1961), 697–712; and Peter S. Garabedian, "Social Roles and the Processes of Socialization in the Prison Community," *Social Problems,* 11 (Fall 1963), 140–52.
[32] Gresham Sykes, *Society of Captives: A Study of a Maximum Security Prison* (Princeton, N.J.: Princeton University Press, 1958).

1. Don't interfere with inmate interests; serve the least possible time and enjoy the greatest possible number of pleasures and privileges. This means that a fellow captive should never be betrayed to institutional authorities; in brief, the injunction states: "be loyal to your class."

2. Don't lose your head, play it cool, do your own time. A value is placed on curbing effect—discouraging feuds and grudges—unless the inmate has been subjected to legitimate provocation.

3. Don't exploit inmates; don't break your word, don't steal from cons, don't sell favors, don't be a racketeer, don't welsh on debts.

4. Don't weaken, whine, or cop out. The inmate should be able to take it and maintain his integrity in the face of privation. The injunction, in brief, is: "be tough, be a man."

5. Don't be a sucker; don't be taken in by the values of hard work and duly constituted authority. The path to success lies in forming a "connection," being sharp, capitalizing on the hypocrisy of the law abiding. This entails learning to use power. With the destruction of other indicators of worth like knowledge or material success inmates tend to regard the possession of power as the highest personal value.[33]

The values of the inmate subculture might be functional for survival within an institution but may be less so on the outside. To the extent that the inmate internalizes them it might jeoparidize his chances for success on the outside.

There were also individual modes of adaptation in Sykes's prison or a set of scripts or roles that could be played.[34] The "merchants" and "gorillas" adapted to the deprivation of goods and services by running a store, i.e., selling or trading goods in short supply or by coercing goods from fellow prisoners. "Wolves," "punks," and "fags" were adaptations to the deprivation of heterosexual relationships. The system also generated the roles of "rats" (squealers) and "center men" who tried to lessen their own deprivations by passing on information—a highly valuable service in a totalitarian setting. "Ball busters" and "real men" were roles generated by the deprivation of autonomy. The deprivation of security creates the roles of "tough" and "hipster."

Sykes suggested that these roles could be related to the functioning of the prison system. Some of them are alienative—disruptive of the equilibrium of the prison community. Those who try to ease their pain of im-

---

[33] Gresham M. Sykes and Sheldon L. Messinger, "The Inmate Social System," in Richard A. Cloward et al. (eds.), *Theoretical Studies in the Social Organization of the Prison* (New York: Social Science Research Council, 1960).
[34] Sykes, *Society of Captives*, 95–99.

prisonment at the expense of others choose alienative roles. Some of the roles are cohesive—they lessen the extent of inmate conflict and significantly lessen the pains of imprisonment for all. Stability is based on these cohesive elements, and official attempts to tighten up control undermines them. Prison riots then are not the result of too little control. Sykes sees custodial attempts to increase control as creating a situation where individualistic and alienative role players displace the cohesively oriented prisoners as the foci of power and authority within the group, thus increasing conflict and resentment.

Those scholars who followed Sykes in prison research also emphasized the significance of status degradation in the formation of an inmate subculture. In some of these accounts the subculture is portrayed as collectively unified and mutually supporting, almost monolithic, brought together by a rejection of officials and quest for support. This view does not do justice to the factions that exist within the prison or to the fragile character of the inmate subculture. Schrag first questioned the extent to which the inmate system is unrelated to the larger community outside the prison.[35] He gathered evidence on preprison experience and related these to inmate type and allocation of leadership in prison. Inmate leadership was fragmented and not mutually supportive. He found that the inmates chosen for leadership roles were selected on the basis of characteristics and experiences that they brought into the prison with them. In short, there were external sources to the prison society not completely accounted for by adaptation to deprivation.

Irwin and Cressey developed this point further.[36] They observed that in the course of incarceration not all inmates come into association with the same set of norms and values in the same way. That which is called an inmate subculture is more precisely characterized as a "convict subculture." It arises within the institution and is dominated by those who have largely grown up in institutions. They are the ones who seek power, influence, and sources of information. Their reference groups are within the institution and the convict seeks status through means available there. But Irwin and Cressey also identify the "thief subculture." Within this pattern the prison is viewed as a temporary problem in a broader criminal context. As they put it:

> An inmate oriented to the thief subculture is simply not interested in gaining high status in the prison. He wants to get out.[37] The in-

[35] Clarence A. Schrag, "Leadership Among Prison Inmates," *American Sociological Review*, 19 (1954), pp. 37–42; and Clarence A. Schrag, "A Preliminary Criminal Typology," *Pacific Sociological Review*, 4 (1961), 11–16.
[36] John Irwin and Donald R. Cressey, "Thieves, Convicts and the Inmate Subculture," *Social Problems*, 10 (1962), 142–55.
[37] Ibid., p. 151.

mate code described above is basically part of the criminal code existing outside the prison which the thief subculture member brings with him. The largest group Irwin and Cressey identify within the prison, however, are those prisoners oriented to legitimate subcultures. They are variously called "straights," "square Johns," or "do rights." They either reject the thief and convict subcultures or for some reason are isolated from them. Irwin and Cressey conclude that there is differential participation in prison activity on the basis of subculture membership. The total system represents an adjustment or accommodation of these three patterns within the official administrative system of deprivation and control. Thus prison society is both generated and imported. This perspective has generated a series of further investigations along the same lines.[38]

The Role of the Prison Guard

Sykes's emphasis on the prison as a system of power permits him to ask questions about it that do not come up in Clemmer's analysis. Sykes can ask why the prison is there in the first instance rather than accepting it as a given. This enables him to discuss what he calls "the defects of total power." For Sykes also there is more to the prison system than the inmate subculture. A key feature of the system is staff relationships and how they are intertwined with the inmate network.

Sykes briefly sketched the role of the guard in his prison settings, one of the few scholarly observations of this occupation.[39] The guard role is a unique one. Since he is caught in an in-between position, neither part of top management nor the prisoner group, he is most often compared to the foreman in industry. But Cressey points out that there is no exact counterpart in the business and industrial world to the prison guard.[40] The closest analogy is overseer of a crew of slaves. Sykes's guards were not sadistic though they did have a rather low opinion of their charges. But because the guard is evaluated in terms of how well he "handles" those under him, he needs their cooperation. It is this dimension of the guard's

[38] John Irwin, *The Felon* (Englewood Cliffs, N.J.: Prentice-Hall, 1970); Stanton Wheeler, "Socialization in Correctional Institutions," in David H. Goslin (ed.), *Handbook of Socialization Theory and Research* (Chicago: Rand McNally, 1971); Ester Heffernan, *Making It in Prison: The Square, the Cool and the Life* (New York: Wiley Interscience, 1972).
[39] Gresham M. Sykes, "The Corruption of Authority and Rehabilitation," *Social Forces*, 34 (March 1956), 257–72.
[40] Donald R. Cressey, "Contradictory Directives in Complex Organizations: The Case of the Prison," *Administrative Science Quarterly*, 4 (June 1959), 1–19.

task that leads to "the corruption of authority and rehabilitation."[41] The guard can't continually report prisoners or call for help. He is under pressure to run a smooth cell block. This means ignoring minor offenses and not being put in the position of discovering minor infractions of the rules. This patterned overlooking of minor violations tends to make guards liable to prisoner manipulation. Inmates can blackmail the guard with the threat of a "snitch kite" to the prison administration documenting in detail past employee infractions.

Women in Prison

If there is meager literature on the prison guard there is even a more disturbing absence of literature on women in prison. Fogel has summarized what little there is available.[42] Women are prosecuted less frequently but if they are convicted they are treated more severely since they are now in the category of "fallen women." The female prison population has remained between 3.4 percent and 5 percent of the total prison population for the last quarter of a century. Housing is usually of the cottage type. The sexism that prevails outside the prison is also reflected within it—women are not usually paid the same wages as men for the same work. The vocational programs consist of domestic science and cosmetology courses. Women seem to be the forgotten group in corrections. Not one reference was made to women by the 1967 President's Commission on Law Enforcement and the Administration of Justice. Nor does the new concern with community reintegration of offenders seem to apply to women. Fogel points out that at a time when male prisoners are moving to the community, a second round of "better" prisons for women is being built.

The pains of imprisonment identified by Sykes are also features of women's prisons but the adaptations to the deprivations takes a different form. Two major sociological inquiries into women's prisons (with similar results) have been reported.[43] Ward and Kassebaum suggest that removal of husband, home, and family, all sources of great emotional support for most women, generates a high degree of homosexual involvement organized around a make-believe family. The cottage type of housing may actually contribute to this accommodation. They identify the role of

41 Sykes, "The Corruption of Authority."
42 Fogel, *We Are the Living Proof*, pp. 48–50.
43 David A. Ward and Gene C. Kassebaum, *Women's Prison* (Chicago: Aldine, 1965); Rose Giallombardo, *Society of Women* (New York: John Wiley, 1966); see also Kathryn W. Burkhart, *Women in Prison* (Garden City, N.Y.: Doubleday, 1973).

"butches" and "femmes" analogous to male and female on the outside. Giallombardo discovered a very complex structure of social roles in the woman's prison she studied. The roles were mainly a response to the deprivation of heterosexual relationships and deprivation of security. The differences between male and female inmate systems seem to reflect the differential socialization of men and women. Thus there is the absence of aggressive violent roles like the "gorilla" and "tough" in women's prisons, the lack of authoritarian and dominating roles, the lack of adaptations related to protecting one's femininity, and the formation of a variety of roles related to the functioning of a family group (like husband, wife, father, mother, son, daughter, and sometimes nephews and nieces).

IMPLICATIONS OF PRISON STUDIES

The solid scholarship represented by studies of inmate subculture has been one major source of efforts to change the conditions of confinement and reduce the deprivation involved. Other studies of correctional effectiveness, which will be discussed below, have led to growing disenchantment with any kind of incarceration and a vigorous movement toward community-based corrections. The attempts to alter the conditions of deprivation have been more often tried in juvenile than adult corrections, and the adult experiments have generally followed models tried in youth institutions.

The two most important patterns are the *clinical treatment model* and the *therapeutic community*. Ohlin has compared the differences between these two newer models and the protective custody pattern along a number of dimensions.[44] Each pattern is based on a particular view of crime causation and a corresponding remedy. Thus in the protective custody model, criminality is caused by deficient character training and the loss of respect for authority. Its correction requires teaching respect for authority and cultivating the virtues of obedience and proper conduct. The clinical treatment model names emotional deprivation and psychological conflicts as the causes of crime; thus individual counseling with professional clinicians leading to personal insight is the desirable remedy. For the therapeutic community the loss of respect for self and others as well as failures in interpersonal socialization leads to crime. Its remedy is group therapy sessions with other inmates and staff. The ratio of treatment staff to inmates is high in the two newer models, and staff recruitment is on the basis of professional, clinical, and/or group therapy skills. Because of

[44] Ohlin, "Organizational Reform."

the amount of staff time devoted to inmate treatment, the newer patterns imply smaller institutions.

The differences between the protective custody and individual clinical patterns seem to be in what group makes the decisions. In the more traditional institution it is nontreatment staff; in the clinical plan it is the treatment staff. But in both institutions decision-making authority is centralized and the criteria on which decisions to release are based are unclear. The subcultural norms and roles seem to be similar in both institutions. This has led some critics to suggest that the individual clinical treatment system is merely an exercise in label switching which does not change the fundamental conditions of deprivation. The therapeutic community pattern moves more in the direction of shared decision making between staff and inmates, though the decisions of the therapy group are subject to staff approval. Discussion of violations takes place in the group therapy sessions and group advice on release is heeded by staff. There is a high visibility of the criteria on which decisions are based. And the subculture that arises in this setting seems quite different than what is found in a traditional institution. The subculture is open to the staff and the role model is the active participant in group discussions.

Ohlin has summarized the limited amount of literature available on the transformation of a correctional institution from a traditional arrangement to a more open one. He suggests that a primary goal in correctional research should be to identify the major barriers to change and the most appropriate means for introducing innovations. A study done by Studt et al. underlined the difficulties in bringing about a change in correctional administration.[45] She and her colleagues attempted to employ a reintegration model in a single housing unit of a large prison. Inmates were involved in the operation of the unit and by and large managed their own affairs. The inmates seemed to respond quite well, were drawn into closer relations with the staff, and learned to cooperate more with one another in solving their problems. But the program failed, according to Studt, because of the opposition of other housing units, decisions issued from the central office, resistance of some inmates who were already being given favored treatment, and conflict among the experiment's employees. The experiment pointed up the problem of implementing a new approach when both staff and inmates were unable to accept the philosophy of reintegration or to carry out its implications.

The limited evaluations done on experiments in therapeutic communities suggest that the group process itself shapes the culture and social system of the entire program; it keeps inmates for a shorter period of time

45 Elliot Studt, Sheldon L. Messinger, and Thomas P. Wilson, *C-Unit: Search for Community in Prison* (New York: Russell Sage Foundation, 1968).

and thus in the final analysis is less costly. The dilemma for those who are convinced of the negative impact of prison is that no matter how benign the newer experiments are, they still require that inmates be incarcerated involuntarily.

> There is an easy test that can be applied to any purported abolition of punishment or imprisonment. Is the proposed alternative program voluntary? Can the subject take it or leave it? If the answer to any of these questions is 'no,' then the wolf is still under the sheepskin.[46]

The inevitable questions to be raised at this point are: how successful is incarceration, and what is the impact of the prison as a deterrent to potential violators? To date the larger question of the prison as a deterrent to potential violators has not been systematically addressed. The prison as a means of incapacitation works very well. It is almost 100 percent successful in protecting the community from inmate predation. The usual index of success or effectiveness is recidivism—the extent to which an ex-prisoner repeats the same offense or another one and is returned to prison during a specified time after release. The most detailed analysis of recidivism was conducted by Glaser. He concluded that "in the first two to five years after their release, only about a third of all the men released from an entire prison system are returned to prison."[47] Morris and Hawkins note that this two-thirds "success" rate also holds for English prisons but probably masks a good deal of "spontaneous remission." A similar conclusion is voiced by Martinson, who has speculated that age, first offender status, or type of offense are more important in determining future recidivism than the fact of incarceration or type of treatment provided.

David Greenberg, in an attempt to clear up popular confusion and conflicting estimates of how many released prisoners repeat, analyzed the success and failure of 50,000 parolees released in 1969.[48] He reports that at the end of the first year, 20 percent of those released were back in prison. But of that total only 5 percent were sent back with a new major conviction; the other 15 percent were sent back as technical violators—that is, they had violated the conditions of their parole. The new offenses that occasioned the 5 percent return to prison were for various forms of

[46] American Friends, *Struggle for Justice*, pp. 23–24.

[47] Daniel Glaser quoted in Norval Morris and Gordon Hawkins, *The Honest Politician's Guide to Crime Control* (Chicago: University of Chicago Press, 1970), p. 117.

[48] David Greenberg, "How Dangerous is the Ex-Convict?" (Committee for the Study of Incarceration, 1972) cited in Mitford, *Kind and Usual Punishment,* pp. 244–45.

theft and violations of alcohol and narcotics laws. Only 2 percent were returned because of a violent or "potentially violent" crime. What components of the system have been designed specifically to discourage criminality?

The Treatment Philosophy in Practice

The three key components of the new treatment philosophy, according to Irwin, are individualization, indeterminacy, and discretionary power.[49]

INDIVIDUALIZATION. Ideally each inmate has a program individually tailored to his needs. Thus if he is without a high school education, one is provided. If he is without vocational skills, he is enrolled in a vocational program. If he is diagnosed as having emotional problems, then some kind of clinical program may be recommended. The extent of individualization is limited by the resources of the institution. The first step in individualized treatment is *classification.* The inmate is typed according to his background characteristics as age, sex, and offense. At initial classification a panel of institutional staff, after interviewing the prisoner, testing him, and looking at his record decides on the type of individualized treatment he will have and assigns him to particular programs. The classification committee makes its decisions partly on the basis of what kind of personality the inmate has so as to insure that he will benefit from any program recommended. The personality typologies employed are numerous but the major types of offender are:

1. *The prosocial offender.* This prisoner is characterized as "normal." He looks most like the "square john" type described by Irwin and Cressey. He has no identification with criminal subcultures. He is most frequently convicted of crimes of violence or naively executed property offenses like forgery. This kind of offender doesn't need any kind of rehabilitative treatment at all.

2. *The antisocial offender.* This is the inmate who identifies with a delinquent subculture. From the treatment standpoint he needs an environment with clear and consistent demands so that his value system can be changed to a more law-abiding one.

3. *The pseudosocial manipulator.* This offender is without conventional standards; he is guilt free, self-satisfied, power oriented, nontrusting, emotionally insulated, and cynical. He looks most like a member of Irwin and Cressey's "convict subculture." The prospects for his treatment are dim.

[49] Irwin, "Adaption to Being Corrected."

4. *The asocial offender.* Unlike the antisocial offender the asocial offender is unable to identify with others at all. He is an isolate and requires elementary training in human relations.[50]

Using this classification system we can note that only the antisocial and asocial offenders would benefit at all from any treatment. But all inmates at the initial classification are assigned to a program in the hope of some kind of rehabilitation.

The next step after assignment is *evaluation.* The classification committee tries to keep abreast of the inmate's progress and, if necessary, reclassifies him. Information on the inmate, including his pre- and post-institutional history, is inserted in the inmate's file which constitutes the official perception of each inmate. All new information added is in terms of the initial classification.

How does the system operate in practice? Irwin concludes from his own research and personal history that the tests, interviews, and evaluations are applied in a cursory fashion, and assignments made on the basis of administrative convenience.[51] The total impact is to amplify the sense of injustice that inmates feel. The inmate is encouraged to participate in programs that he feels are "phony" and ineffective. The most ineffective from the inmate's point of view are the therapeutic programs. Most inmates have had contact with group counseling and are contemptuous of it. The limited amount of studies done on group counseling using recidivism as an index suggests that its relationship to recidivism is "slight, inconsistent and of questionable reliability."[52]

Irwin reports that the record of educational and vocational programs is not so dismal, possibly because their goals are more clear-cut and modest than "behavioral change."[53] But there aren't enough openings for those prisoners who want to learn a trade and they don't equip a man for a job outside. Adams is hopeful on the future of correctional effectiveness research but after an examination of 231 of the "more rigorous" evaluations of correctional treatment Martinson has concluded, perhaps more arcurately, that there is very little evidence that any mode of correctional treatment has a decisive effect on recidivism.[54]

INDETERMINACY. Irwin's observations while a prisoner in California in the 1950s was that convicts initially accepted the promise of rehabilitation and a deterministic view of themselves but now reject the model. It has

[50] President's Commission, *The Challenge of Crime,* pp. 20–21.
[51] Irwin, "Adaption to Being Corrected."
[52] Walter C. Bailey, "Correctional Outcome: An Evaluation of One Hundred Reports," *Journal of Criminal Law, Criminology and Police Science,* 57 (June 1966), 153–60.
[53] Irwin, "Adaption to Being Corrected."
[54] Robert Martinson, *The Treatment Evaluation Survey* (New York: Office of Crime Control Planning of the State of New York, 1971).

led to an increase in suffering because of the indeterminacy of sentence and the coercion employed to force inmates into therapeutic programs. It seems also to have led to longer sentences and an increased number of persons who are sentenced.

The one encouraging development in Irwin's otherwise bleak picture of rehabilitation is what he calls the increase in "gleaning."[55] The growing number of educational and vocational programs has led to a new style of inmate adaptation. The convict can follow a carefully devised plan to "better himself." The adaptation is voluntary and self-determined. Irwin cites some evidence that the number of gleaners in the California system is increasing. He doesn't speculate on the relationship of this style to recidivism but one could hypothesize that the gleaner's chances would be better on the outside than those of his resentful and estranged inmate counterparts.

DISCRETIONARY POWER. The discretionary power granted to the parole board under the indeterminate system further enhances the prisoner's sense of injustice. There is endless speculation on how board members make their decisions to grant or not to grant parole. The one that seems to have the most currency among inmates is that an outward display of participation in treatment programs is the most important factor. The criteria on which the board makes its decision are not made explicit by the board itself nor are their decisions reviewable. It has been suggested to those who still favor the indeterminate sentence that the parole board's discretion be made more narrow, that the criteria on which decisions are made be spelled out, and that board decisions be routinely reviewed.

The decision to grant a prisoner parole is not a decision to discharge him. He is still a convict though now functioning in the free community. If his behavior is questionable his parole can be revoked and his full sentence reinstated. Parole, originally called "aftercare," was a feature of the Elmira Reformatory. The stated purpose of parole is to aid in offender reintegration. If the decisions about parole release are made wisely in the institution, presumably the chances for reintegration will be good. The organization of the parole service charges the parole officer with the frequently incompatible roles of helping and surveillance. The parole officer might help the parolee in finding a job or a place to live while at the same time making sure that he abides by a host of regulations designed to insure "public protection." The parolee may not leave the county, change his residence, buy or drive a car, sign contracts, or get married without the permission of his parole agent. To secure parole, the inmate must sign a contract to abide by these regulations. A violation of any one of them can lead to his return to prison. The rules are so strict

[55] Irwin, "Adaption to Being Corrected."

that the parole officer characteristically doesn't enforce them.[56] In fact the parolee is almost always violating them. This means that at any time the agent can revoke parole. The history of parole that links it with ideas of grace and clemency makes arbitrariness and unpredictability an essential part of it. Its operation in practice further aggravates the parolee's sense of injustice. Suggestions for reform of the parole system predictably have argued for removing the notions of clemency, granting it to all inmates as a right, narrowing the discretion of parole officers to revoke parole, and insuring due process considerations at revocation hearings.

THE CHANGING ROLE OF THE PRISONER

The gains made by reformers to change the conditions of deprivation have been slight. Whether this has been due to a lack of political power to make the necessary changes or a faulty diagnosis of the situation is unclear. One thing, however, is clear: reform strategies to change conditions of confinement prior to the 1960s rarely involved the convicts themselves. Sporadic attempts have been made by prisoners to better their conditions. Fox has catalogued at least 400 prison disturbances or riots from 1855 to 1955 in American prisons.[57] Such protests have not been too well documented. Most of what we learn from them is through the eyes of prison officials. In this respect they are very much like slave revolts.

But the resources of prison officialdom to suppress information or interpret prisoner dissatisfaction was shaken in the 1960s. The impact of the social ferment during that period spilled over into the prison as a new and more sophisticated type of prisoner came to the fore. The black militants, civil dissenters, and college-age drug users who entered correctional institutions were able to establish solidarity with the older inmate population. A wave of strikes and riots swept American prisons with a remarkable unanimity in demands for change: decent food and medical care, educational and trade training opportunities, minimum wages, right to due process in disciplinary hearings, law libraries, and an end to mail censorship. The grievances of a group of prisoners at San Quentin touched directly on the uncontrolled discretion available to officials: the prisoners proposed the abolition of the indeterminate sentence law, removal of sentence-setting power from the state parole board, and the

[56] Ibid.
[57] Vernon Fox, *Violence Behind Bars* (New York: Vintage Press, 1956).

introduction of due process into parole violation hearings.[58] The strikers' demands captured nationwide attention and precipitated intense criticism of prison conditions. The public spotlight has led to a series of fact-finding committees where advocates of change have had significant impact. The crisis—for this is how some correctional authorities have defined it—has crystallized dissatisfaction among interest groups that are concerned about corrections. The discontent has been mobilized, the public issues defined, and a series of coalitions criticizing and defending the prison have emerged. The groups involved are anticipating a long-term struggle before the present crisis is resolved. The outcome of the attempt to change the prison with the support of inmates, ex-prisoner organizations, and their allies in a growing prison reform movement may be no more successful than previous attempts to make the correctional bureaucracy more accountable. The difference between present and past efforts is the degree of militancy and political sophistication of the inmate group pressing for change.

A major strategy has been to attempt to change the prison through the courts. Traditionally U.S. courts have maintained a "hands off" policy in relation to prisoner grievances. They have claimed separation of powers, lack of judicial expertise, and fear of undermining prison discipline. The first breakthrough occurred in the early 1960s when the Black Muslims won a court decision affirming their right to practice their religion "within reasonable restrictions" behind bars. They were assisted by lawyers mobilized by the civil rights movement and the OEO war on poverty. Central to the new litigation was the revival of the Federal Civil Rights Act of 1871 originally passed to enable blacks to bypass state courts to enforce their newly won constitutional rights. In 1964 the Supreme Court confirmed that the Civil Rights Act entitled prisoners to sue officials in federal courts.

The decisions rendered between 1964 and 1972 prohibit prison authorities from interfering with prisoner efforts to obtain judicial relief or from discriminating against prisoners on the basis of race, religion, or sex. They also outlawed the worst conditions and forms of prison punishment, required that prison officials provide some procedural safeguards when they discipline a prisoner, and protected some forms of political expression by prisoners. We now have the beginnings of a correctional case law.[59] The courts are in disagreement over whether prisoners have any legal standing to challenge racial discrimination in prison hiring practices.

[58] "A Convict Report on Major Grievances," cited in Mitford, *Kind and Usual Punishment*, pp. 257–58.
[59] Brian Glick, "Change Through the Courts," in Erick O. Wright (ed.), *The Politics of Punishment* (New York: Harper & Row, 1973).

Though corporal punishment has been prohibited, along with exceptionally degrading conditions of solitary confinement, the courts have not specified minimum standards nor have they said that prolonged isolation is unconstitutional. Forced labor is not yet outlawed; medical care must be provided but there are no minimum standards prescribed. There is no recognition of the right of prisoners to refuse potentially harmful medical treatment. Though several decisions require that officials meet the constitutional standards of due process before punishing a prisoner, no appeal outside the prison is guaranteed. The political rights guaranteed relate to possession of revolutionary literature but not to letting others read it. No court has upheld the right to assemble freely and organize for political purposes. Officials are free to disband prisoners' organizations, stop them from distributing literature within the prison, and transfer organizers out.

The decisions have encountered considerable resistance on the part of prison officials. Officials characteristically ask for a Supreme Court review as they do with decisions requiring fair disciplinary proceedings. District courts, fearing that their rulings might be overturned by the Supreme Court, have not exercised their power to enforce their orders pending appeal, so the condemned practices continue. Glick reports that even after a decision is in force the order finds only for the parties named in the lawsuit.[60] No suit can cover more than one state's prison system. The process must be repeated over and over again. To date the attempt to change conditions through the court has not basically affected the lives of most prisoners, but the occasional victories have affected prisoner morale favorably and have addressed the sense of inmate powerlessness.

However minimal the gains through the judicial process, the fact is that the prison organization has been opened up. The opening tends to work against institutional arbitrariness. The presence of a lawyer or the possibility of a legal action discourages illegal, unfair, or inhumane practices. As one lawyer put it:

> Once you put a prison administrator on the stand and you make him answer "Why," you've made a step forward. It may be the first time he's ever had to explain an action he's taken.[61]

The transformation of the prisoner from patient to plaintiff has yet to reduce the *stigmatizing* effect of conviction and incarceration. Studies of

[60] Ibid.
[61] Quoted in Mitford, *Kind and Usual Punishment*, p. 291.

the impact of prison on prisoners have generally neglected its effect on prisoner life chances after release. The imposition of criminal status has a profoundly disabling impact on one's chances for success in the free community. Some observers have questioned how far we have advanced from the period when outlaws were branded or maimed so that stigmatization would be permanent. The consequences of a criminal conviction are the loss of one's civil rights (right to vote, hold public office, serve as juror, and testify in court). Ex-convicts are prohibited from participating in activities regulated by the government and barred from obtaining numerous professional, occupational, and business licenses. Equal employment legislation does not apply to the ex-convict. It is possible to have citizen rights restored but the usual procedure—executive clemency—is erratic and irrational. If one of the goals of punishment is reintegration, then the imposition of stigma seems to be dysfunctional.

PRISON REFORM

Most advocates of prison reform do not go so far as to propose the immediate abolition of prisons. They tend to assume the necessity of restraining some persons against their will if they represent an immediate and obvious danger to public welfare—a persistent assaulter, for example. They also generally accept the notion that some basic rules are required in organized society and that these rules need to be enforced. Most reformers would probably agree with the American Friends Service Committee that punishment is a necessary evil and should only be used as society's "last resort" when all other educational or control efforts fail.[62]

Mitford notes that we must distinguish between two kinds of reform proposals: those that strengthen the correctional bureaucracy, and those that challenge the basic premises of the prison.[63] In the former proposals more money is called for to hire more prison personnel, researchers, and experts, and to increase utilization of scientific knowledge in handling prisoners. No defense of the fortress prison is put forward. Rather the suggestions are for smaller community-based treatment institutions. If experience with rehabilitative institutions is any guide, community-based corrections should lead to placing a larger proportion of the population under some form of correction.

[62] American Friends, *Struggle for Justice.*
[63] Mitford, *Kind and Usual Punishment,* p. 319.

Proposals that challenge the prison's basic premises

> are aimed at reducing the discretionary power of authorities all up
> and down the line, at reducing prison populations, and at restoring
> to prisoners those constitutional rights that will enable them to
> organize and fight injustice within the system.[64]

One of the most provocative proposals of this type has been put forward
by David Fogel, a criminologist and former commissioner of corrections
in Minnesota.[65] He identifies his approach as "neo-classical" and his plan
for changing prison conditions as "the justice model"; it was developed
basically out of a consumer perspective and represents a sharp break with
the prevailing rehabilitative outlook. The prisoner is regarded as responsible, volitional, and aspiring—not as one who is sick. Fogel begins with
the observation that justice stops at the prison gate. Both guards and
inmates are victims of an arbitrary, whimsical, uncoordinated, unplanned, and unaccountable system. The correctional bureaucracy is like
a rogue elephant on the rampage. The overriding consideration must be
to bring the system to heel. Since the prison is basically lawless it is
unrealistic to expect its inmates to become lawful.

Fogel sees the condition of lawlessness in prison as a product of the
indeterminate sentence and the enormous power it confers on prison
officials and parole boards. His strategy calls for the eventual abolition of
the indeterminate sentence and the substitution of "flat time" subject to
judicial review. His suggestions closely follow those made by Richard
McGee, former California director of corrections.[66] One advantage of
the Fogel proposal is that it is cast in a form attuned to the realities of
state politics. It has been embodied in a series of legislative proposals in
Illinois. The first stage, however, does not require legislation or new
appropriations. It can be accomplished by executive action. It involves
restructuring the prison so that it would abandon any pretense of treatment. Its only responsibility would be for executing the sentence—the
legal cost of violating the law—not rehabilitating the offender. The penal
sanction involves only a temporary deprivation of liberty. The academic,
vocational, and clinical programs would be dismantled and all offered on
a contractual basis. A voucher system would be provided for the delivery
of services and the prisoner's release date would not be contingent on his
use of educational, vocational, or therapeutic services as it is now.

Some immediate short-range goals to operationalize justice in the
prison are realizable. Harshness can be mitigated, peaceful conflict-
resolution machinery set up, and a safer staff work-environment created.

---

[64] Ibid., p. 312.
[65] Fogel, *We Are the Living Proof*, pp. 179–271.
[66] Richard A. McGee, "A New Look at Sentencing," Part II, *Federal Probation* (September 1974), pp. 7–8.

The world of the offender and those who guard him is a microworld where the emphasis is on day-to-day relationships and realities. It is possible to address the deep sense of injustice offenders experience by developing conflict-resolution mechanisms that would make the day-to-day milieu safer, make life more tolerable, and create a new route to status enhancement. Another strategy would be the development of inmate staff governance groups and a prison legal aid system whose services would be available both to inmates and guards. Protection against arbitrary action would be afforded on major disciplinary decisions. Since large-scale organizations are enormously resourceful in subverting any planned change, the whole process would be overseen by an ombudsman. He would see that prisoners are accorded all the rights of free citizens consistent with mass living and the execution of a sentence restricting freedom of movement. Correctional ombudsmen now exist in nine states. Characteristically they are created by state legislatures to handle complaints against the correctional agency. Acting either on his own or on receiving a complaint alleging governmental abuse, an ombudsman investigates and intervenes on behalf of the complainant.[67]

At the intermediate level, the return to flat-time sentencing would involve new legislation, as would the abolition of parole and the creation of a narrow and reviewable system of fixed good-time rules. Some kind of legislation might be necessary to dismantle the fortress prison or transform it into an institution for no more than 300 persons as well as to insure that prison labor would be reimbursed at prevailing wage rates. Fogel does not suggest any long-range solutions, since debates about long-range goals can only slow the momentum for immediate change. Like the American Friends he feels that "the octopus must be mastered one step at a time."[68]

The issue of what a long-range strategy would involve divides liberals and radicals. Many liberal reformers see the fundamental task of reform as convincing those in power of the soundness of particular change. A more radical view sees prisons as intimately bound up with the class and power structure of society as a whole; this suggests that piecemeal changes are of no avail. Yet Wright, an advocate of radical change, contends that modifications in concrete prison conditions are achievable and desirable.[69] They can be accomplished, he suggests, without fundamental social change. He sees legislative resistance to further appropriations as an opportunity for change. The climate is more open to alternatives to incarceration and officials can be squeezed to let volunteers, a force for

[67] Lance Tibbles, "Ombudsmen for American Prisons," *North Dakota Law Review*, 48 (1972), 386.

[68] American Friends, *Struggle for Justice*, p. 16.

[69] Erick D. Wright (ed.) *The Politics of Punishment*.

change, into the prison. The struggle to change prison conditions may lead to unexpected beneficial consequences. He notes that California in 1970 decided to reduce the number of inmates in California prisons from a high of around 29,000 to just over 20,000 in 1972 because of the pressure generated by prisoners within the system. Curiously, the reduction of numbers was never an explicit demand of the strikes and revolts.[70]

EL TORO CORRECTION FACILITY: PUNISHMENT AS TREATMENT

Ronald Johnson is a black male who was convicted of burglary five years ago and given a 5- to 10-year sentence. He was confined in a medium security institution whose staff prides itself on the facility's treatment orientation. When Ronald first arrived at the *El Toro* Correctional Facility he was housed in the diagnostic center for one month. There he was interviewed a number of times by a social worker and given a variety of psychological tests. The results of the interviews and tests went into his institutional folder or "jacket." The combination of interest and aptitude tests as well as the interview led his social worker to recommend that he be enrolled in an educational program that would permit him to finish high school, and in a vocational program in auto mechanics since he had a history of auto theft as a juvenile and "a preoccupation with cars." Ronald resisted this suggestion, claimed not to be interested in cars, and pleaded to go into the institution's program on barbering. Since there were no openings immediately available he was assigned to a program in carpentry. Ronald's rejection of the social worker's suggestion was duly noted in his jacket as evidence of "a lack of cooperation."

During his first year in the institution the phrase "lack of cooperation" appeared again and again in his jacket: two of his high school teachers indicated that this was a problem with him as did his carpentry instructor, a guard in his cell block, and a group counselor. He was required to attend weekly group counseling sessions. He was also assigned to work in the prison laundry. The comments of his work supervisor were consistently favorable. One of the inmates who befriended him during his first year in the institution warned him that he was developing a reputation for being too independent and that would count against him in future parole hearings. The warning went unheeded at the time since Ronald would not be considered seriously for parole until he had served 20 months, one-third of the minimum term. The parole board was re-

[70] Ibid., ch. 15.

quired by law to review each inmate every year but no serious effort was made to determine eligibility for parole until one-third of the minimum sentence had been served.

Ronald picked up the rich lore that developed at *El Toro* on the parole process and how it operated. He concluded at the end of his first year that the picture he was presenting of himself did not correspond to the staff perception of what a "healthy," "adjusted," or "cured" inmate looked like and he began a systematic campaign to change it. He regularly attended church services and for a time sat in on an Alcoholics Anonymous group though he was not an alcoholic. He accepted the inmate view that one must participate in treatment if only in a token way since this is what the parole board looks for. He even risked his reputation as a stand-up guy by claiming in his group counseling sessions that the reason he got into burglary was because of the lack of maternal affection. He discovered much later that this "confession" was also recorded in his jacket.

The parole board visited *El Toro* every three months and Johnson concluded that his case would come before them in their first visit after he had served 20 months. The board was composed of nine members, all from law enforcement and corrections backgrounds. Ronald developed a profile on each member in anticipation of his hearing and added bits and pieces that he gleaned from other inmates who had previously come before them. He knew, for instance, that one of the former law enforcement officers was very negative about blacks who were concerned about black identity. This evidence could be gathered from the institutional folder where the kind of literature the inmate received and the kind of identification revealed in group counseling sessions were recorded. Another parole board member thought regular church attendance and bible study groups very rehabilitative. A third member often queried inmates on how remorseful they felt and seemed hostile to inmates who were interested in the law. A fourth member seemed thoroughly convinced that all crimes were alcohol related. The usual procedure of the parole board was to split up into teams of three to expedite hearings at each institution, so Ronald could not be sure which three members would decide his case.

One month prior to the scheduled hearing Ronald was interviewed by a correctional counselor who was assigned to present his case to the parole board. He noted that Ronald's record looked good—he had never been charged with a disciplinary infraction—but that the parole board looked for more subtle indicators of readiness for parole. The counselor had Ronald's jacket before him during the interview but did not reveal what was in it. Ronald noted later that he seemed to spend an inordinate amount of time asking Ronald about his early family background. The counselor refused to comment on Ronald's chances and reminded him that the job of correctional counselor in this situation was to present a summary of his institutional experience, not to make a recommendation. At one point early in the interview the counselor asked Ronald why he refused to go into the auto mechanics program and why he was so emotionally negative about the occupation of auto repairman.

Ronald rehearsed answers to hypothetical questions board members might ask after his meeting with the correctional counselor. All were designed to show that he sincerely wanted to improve himself, had availed himself of every opportunity during his stay at *El Toro*, was not a "militant," and had learned the bitter lesson on the costs of crime.

Ronald was ushered into a small conference room on the day of his hearing and greeted heartily by one of the parole board threesome. All had folders before them and occasionally flipped through them. One of the board members did not look up at all and seemed to be reading something else. He remained silent during the seven minutes that the board spent with Ronald. The first question put to him by the member who greeted him was, "Do you still maintain that you were treated unfairly at your trial?" The question was surprising since Ronald did not deny his guilt but early in his prison stay had complained often that he was harshly treated by the sentencing judge. He replied that he originally thought so but after talking to others who had been through the same process he changed his mind. The second question was asked by another parole board member whom Ronald had difficulty identifying. Later he decided that the parole board member was the most recently appointed one, a social worker with most of his experience in prison settings. He asked if Ronald planned to live with his mother when he was paroled. Ronald replied that he would do so until he had saved enough money to get his own apartment. The board member then asked, "How do you propose to deal with your feelings about her in the meantime?" Ronald replied that he had come to terms with his feelings about her and did not experience any resentment or anticipate any problems in reestablishing contact with her. The first board member interrupted the topic of Ronald's mother to ask why he dropped out of Alcoholics Anonymous. Ronald replied that he was not an alcoholic and found little in common with the inmates who were. The board member thanked him and asked Ronald to excuse himself.

The parole board remained in *El Toro* for the rest of the week hearing cases and did not report their own decisions until after they left the institution. The following week Ronald was called to his correctional counselor's office and handed a memo from the parole board. It stated: "In the case of Ronald Johnson: Parole denied." The decision stunned him and the counselor tried to console him by saying his chances next year would be better. In response to the question, "Why did they turn me down?" the counselor replied, "They obviously didn't think you were rehabilitated."

But the counselor's speculations on why parole was denied were as likely to be valid as Ronald's since the board gave no reason for their decision nor did they suggest anything else Ronald might do to rehabilitate himself in the coming year.

DISCUSSION

The report of the encounter with the parole board was provided by Ronald. He was interviewed while on parole and a member of an ex-inmate group. He was paroled on his third appearance before the board. The account was presented to a discussion group of ex-inmates who vouched for its believability. If anything they seemed to think that Ronald's encounter was relatively benign. Some reported more unpleasant experiences: *less* than seven minutes for review, more antagonistic questioning, or, worst of all, friendly supportive questions and discussion of plans for parole followed by parole denial. Since parole board hearings are closed to the public and no record is kept of reasons for decisions we can't be sure how typical the experience is. One thing is certain: the broad discretionary power available to parole boards, the lack of guidelines on how decisions should be made, and the absence of any review procedure makes the elusive goal of rehabilitation difficult, if not impossible, to realize.

The description of *El Toro* Correctional Facility corresponds to profiles of other treatment-oriented facilities in the literature. Not enough information is provided to note how they differ. Some of the more recent research on institutions suggests that the staff is almost as cynical of "treatment" as the inmates. This did not seem to be characteristic of the *El Toro* staff, however, who seemed genuinely convinced that treatment was the answer.

Criticisms of rehabilitation have been focused on the board discretion available to institutional personnel and parole boards in assessing a prisoner's readiness for release. They conclude that the arbitrariness that is an essential part of the process deepens the inmate's sense of injustice and powerlessness and may in fact decrease his chances for "making it on the outside." This contention could be put into hypothetical form and tested. It should be possible to design an experiment that would eliminate the indeterminate sentence for a group of those convicted, and make their early release determined by a narrow and reviewable system of fixed good-time rules. One important part of the design would be the provision of opportunities for self-improvement, but whether or not an inmate used them would not be made a condition of freedom. This experimental group would be compared with a matched group of inmates subjected to a more traditional kind of treatment. The hypothesis is that what might be called the "due process group" would have a clearer sense of being addressed fairly and a lesser sense of their own lack of power than the control group. Whether or not they would do better in the free community might be answered in a follow-up study.

QUESTIONS FOR FURTHER DISCUSSION

1. What does this case reveal about the problems of corrections generally?

2. What factors did the parole board seem to react to in Ronald's case and was their reaction justified?

3. What impact did the board's decision seem to have on Ronald and his correctional counselor?

4. In what way could the operation of the parole board be modified so as to reduce its arbitrary character?

5. How would a conflict and consensus perspective interpret this series of events and what further information would each look for in the case?

6. What hypotheses are suggested in this case that would be worth exploring further?

SUMMARY

This chapter has touched on five main themes: the function of the prison in maintaining a system of inequality in the larger society, the prison as product of community attitudes and interest-group initiative, the role that the rehabilitation ideal played in this development, sociological contributions to the disenchantment with the prison, and the politicization of the convict group.

Attempts to control or manage inmates over the last 100 years have met with varying degrees of success. The more things seemed to change the more they remained the same or, as Rothman suggests, possibly became worse. The difficulty in controlling or molding any group of human beings, no matter how structured the environment or how determined the controllers, is that the response by the controlled can't be accurately predicted. However unequal the contending parties in prison are, the patterns staff and inmates work out are the result of negotiations and the accomodation of conflicting interests. The behavior patterns of the criminally defined are one such joint production of control agencies and those who are criminalized. The interaction has produced a number of fairly durable and stable "criminal behavior patterns" that have held a strong fascination for criminologists. Since criminal justice agencies have characteristically focused on low-income crime they have had a more powerful impact on the creation and maintenance of some criminal behavior patterns than others. For instance, the role of control agents in the development of robbery or burglary patterns is more salient than their contribution to political or corporate criminal behavior patterns. A typology of deviant behavior can be constructed on the basis of the likelihood of its criminalization. This suggests a continuum from high-risk crimes like homicide to low-risk violations such as occupational crime. Likelihood of criminalization, however, is only one of the dimensions that must be considered in developing a comprehensive and adequate typology of criminal behavior. Part three suggests such a typology which includes the role of defining agencies, the extent of group support for their behavior, and the strength of the social and legal reaction.

Part Three

PATTERNS OF CRIMINALITY: the interaction between enforcement and behavior

Our earlier analysis of the emergence of criminal law and the day-to-day operations of law enforcement agencies suggests that one crucial area for criminologists to explore is how and under what conditions criminal status is applied. It is important to know what groups are likely candidates for criminalization as well as what norms are considered more important by enforcement authorities. Our discussion in Part Two on the administration of the law suggested that the process of application is problematic, especially in situations where there is a disagreement between different levels of enforcement on how important enforcement in particular instances is. The literature is underdeveloped, however, and no body of generalizations except of the most abstract character—e.g., when organization is high and sophistication of law enforcement is low, attempts to criminalize will be greater—is available. There is, however, a more substantial literature on the behavior patterns of those defined as criminal developed on the basis of legal, psychological, or social classifications. Most of the typologies, however, do not take into account the variable administration of the law that is critical in the definition of who is the criminal as well as the continuation of adult criminal roles.

The earliest classifications of criminals were the physical typologies developed by Lombroso, Garofalo, and Ferri.[1] Though present-day criminology

[1] See Hermann Mannheim (ed.), *Pioneers in Criminology* (London: Stevens and Sons, 1970), chs. 9, 12, and 13; and Stephen Schafer, *Theories in Criminology* (New York: Random House, 1969), chs. 6 and 7.

rejects these physical typologies, the literature for the past one hundred years is replete with a variety of constitutional classifications attesting to its continuing attraction for students of crime. Lineal descendants of the Italian positivist school are the Americans Kretschmer[2] and Sheldon[3] who tried to link criminality with body type. The most prominent recent biological explanation of criminality tries to relate it to genetics in the XYY chromosome theory.

The normal complement of chromosomes for the female is XX and for the male XY but geneticists have noted that occasionally there may be additional chromosomes. Brown in 1962 reported that the rate of delinquency among his male patients was higher among those with chromosome abnormalities than among normals.[4] The follow-up studies of Price et al. associated the extra Y chromosome in males with increased psychopathy.[5] The hypothesis is that the extra Y chromosome causes those who have it to be uncontrollably aggressive. Most of the research has been done on institutionalized populations that have a higher proportion of XYY males than the general population. The results to date are inconclusive. There has been no attempt to identify the mechanisms whereby the XYY chromosome is translated into behavior. Those who make the claim that there is a basis in genetics for aggressive criminality have yet to prove their case. Since the prison population contains only a fraction of those who commit crime it must be demonstrated that XYY males in the general population have a higher incidence of aggressive criminality due to heredity. It is more likely that what is transmitted is a general tendency that may lead to aggression rather than a direct relationship between biological structure and criminal behavior.[6]

Eysenck has attempted to construct a typology that goes beyond the simple genetic or physical theories.[7] Eysenck's criminal is high on extroversion, but not all extroverts are criminal. What makes the criminal distinctive is that there is a deficiency in his conditioning. Consequently he does not feel as much distress as would a "normal" person when doing something forbidden. Eysenck also notes that persons are variable in their susceptibility to being conditioned. Introverted persons are more susceptible. Social factors are taken into account in Eysenck's scheme and he attempts to formulate more precisely how genetic influences manifest themselves in behavior. The major

[2] Ernest Kretschmer, *Physique and Character* (London: Kegan Paul, 1937).

[3] William H. Sheldon, *Varieties of Delinquent Youth: An Introduction to Constitutional Psychiatry* (New York: Harper & Row, 1949).

[4] See Saleem A. Shah and Loren H. Roth, "Biological and Psychophysiological Factors in Criminality," in Daniel Glaser (ed.), *Handbook of Criminology* (Chicago: Rand McNally, 1974), 134–39, for a review of evidence on chromosomal abnormalities and aggression.

[5] William Price et al., "Behavior Disorders and Patterns Among XYY Males Identified at a Maximum Security Hospital," *British Medical Journal*, 1 (1967), 533–36.

[6] Richard G. Fox, "The XYY Offender: A Modern Myth?" *Journal of Criminal Law, Criminology and Police Science*, 62 (March 1971), 59–73; Theodore Sarbin and Jeffery E. Miller, "Demonism Revisited: The XYY Chromosomal Anomaly," *Issues in Criminology*, 5 (Summer 1970), 195–207.

[7] Hans J. Eysenck, *Crime and Personality* (London: Granada Press, 1970).

problem from a sociological viewpoint is that he takes societal reaction for granted and does not see it as problematic.

The most obvious typology relating to crime is a legal one that distinguishes between types of offense. Curiously, these attempts have yielded little of sociological value. The attempt to distinguish between felonies and misdemeanors tells us something about how seriously the law views certain violations but doesn't tell us much about the persons involved in particular acts, their motivations, or the social milieu within which the behavior takes place. Nor does a simple legal classification recognize the widespread phenomenon of "plea copping"—the reduction to a less serious charge so that the original charge is obscured.

There are a host of social classifications based on offender background data—e.g., age, sex, race, and social class. The data are drawn from a convicted population and raise some serious questions about any attempts to develop typologies of criminals based on background information. These social classifications have reinforced popular stereotypes. For example, the popular stereotype of the robber depicts him as young, urban, lower class, and probably a member of a minority group. If this picture were constructed from a prison population it would be accurate since what Clinard and Quinney call the "conventional criminal" (those convicted of larceny, burglary, and robbery) constitute about 50 percent of the prison population and they are disproportionately drawn from urban lower-class minority groups. The criminologist's perception of the robber is more detailed—the robber starts out as a predatory gang delinquent, goes through a process of increasing differential involvement with older professionals from whom he learns his crime skills, and ultimately retires into a noncriminal occupation—but basically corresponds to the popular stereotype. The problem with the stereotype is that it is based on what one observer has called "police failures."[8] Only a fraction of robberies known to the the police, mainly through citizen complaints, result in arrest. Further, not all robberies are reported. In a study by Ennis on victimization he noted that only 65 percent of those who had been robbed reported the offense to the police; 35 percent of those victimized by robbery did not make an official complaint.[9] Thus, in any given community only 65 out of 100 robberies would be reported to the police and of that 65 the police would clear about 20 or one-fifth of the robberies committed. Unless we assume that the 20 arrested account for all 100 robberies committed—a highly dubious assumption—then the question of what the rest of the robber sample looks like is crucial to our understanding of this crime. The uncritical acceptance of the robber stereotype violates a fundamental law of social science research methodology—that generalizations can only be made about

[8] Dennis Chapman, *Sociology and the Stereotype of the Criminal* (London: Taristook, 1978), ch. 2.
[9] Phillip H. Ennis, *Criminal Victimization in the United States: A Report of a National Survey* (Field Surveys, II, President's Commission on Law Enforcement and the Administration of Justice, Washington, D.C.: Government Printing Office, 1967).

particular behaviors if they are based on a random sample of *all the people* who engage in that behavior.

Does this mean that the enormous mass of material collected by criminologists on patterns of criminality should be thrown out? By no means. It does mean, however, that it should be interpreted within a framework that sees the pattern as the end product of the interaction between the enforcement apparatus and its clients. It is possible to recognize the central role of defining agencies without at the same time denying that there are actual "behavior systems" that function more or less autonomously from them. A useful classification should include a legal dimension since it is the offense description which indicates the problem a particular pattern creates for society or its designated enforcers. The offense description and the penalties associated with it tell us something about what may happen once a crime has occurred and an arrest has been made. A useful classification should also include the extent to which group support is available for the behavior under consideration.

This interest in group support led Sutherland to a study of career crime in an attempt to escape the limitations of simple legal classifications.[10] Career crime, like professional theft, includes a set of codes, traditions, and social relationships that constitute a group way of life, not simply an aggregation of individual acts. The behavior of theft is not unique to any particular individual within this behavior system but common to all members of the group. Finally there is a feeling of identification by those who participate in it.

The career approach to the study of crime has been criticized for excluding serious offenses like murder or kidnapping, which do not readily lend themselves to a career analysis. The Winslows have suggested developing a typology based on a common-sense view of seriousness.[11] This may correspond to legal definitions of seriousness but in some cases does not. They construct a continuum, based on public opinion rankings of various offenses, from most serious to least serious. Most serious are those who commit predations against persons or property (murderers, forcible rapists, armed robbers). Least serious are public-order offenses like drunkenness, gambling, or truancy by juveniles. Our stress on conflict and consensus approaches to the study of crime suggests that a useful classification of criminal behavior patterns should take into account the seriousness with which they are viewed as well as the extent to which they are part of an organized behavior system.

Glaser, a criminologist with practical experience in the area of corrections, has proposed a typology based on the seriousness of the threat particular offenses pose to the larger society.[12] His analysis, developed for policy

[10] Edwin H. Sutherland, "The Professional Thief," *Journal of Criminal Law and Criminology,* 28 (July–August 1937), 161–63.

[11] Robert W. Winslow and Virginia Winslow, *Deviant Reality: Alternate World Views* (Boston: Allyn & Bacon, 1974), ch. 1.

[12] Daniel Glaser, *Adult Crime and Social Policy* (Englewood Cliffs, N.J.: Prentice-Hall, 1972), ch. 2.

guidance purposes, describes the offense and the extent of career commitment. He states that it is necessary to distinguish between predatory (and if predatory whether it is against persons or property) and nonpredatory behavior. Nonpredatory crime is less serious and requires different intervention strategies and policies than do the more serious offenses. He develops 10 policy-revelant typifications of adult crime careers:

1. adolescent recapitulators who continue the patterns of delinquency begun in adolescence;

2. subcultural assaulters;

3. addiction-supporting predators who commit property crimes to procure funds for mind-altering drugs;

4. vocational predators like professional confidence men;

5. organized illegal sellers, those involved in organized crime;

6. avocational predators, those who engage in property crime as a part-time activity;

7. crisis-vacillation predators like embezzlers;

8. quasi-insane assaulters like forcible rapists operating without a supporting subculture of violence;

9. addicted performers like those arrested for drunkenness;

10. private illegal consumers, or those who engage in purchasing illegal services or consuming illegal drugs.

The advantage of the Glaser typology is that it provides the criminologist with a policy framework for assessing the rationality of our criminal laws and a set of strategies for reducing the amount of criminal behavior.

The stress on behavior systems of the criminally defined allows for a more complex analysis of the varied roles available in a given system and how people are recruited and trained to play them. One of the most comprehensive attempts to develop a criminal typology based on role careers is that outlined by Gibbons.[13] He includes both definitional and background dimensions in his typology. The definitional elements include the nature of the offense behavior, the interactional setting within which it takes place, the self-concept of the offender, stages in the role career of the offender, and attitudes toward society and agencies of social control. In looking at background dimensions he includes social class, family background, peer group associations, and contact with defining agencies. On the basis of his typology he sets up a number of adult and juvenile types that encompass the range of violative behavior. The advantage of the Gibbons typology is that it provides the criminologist with a synthesis of all the important dimen-

---

[13] Don C. Gibbons, *Society Crime and Criminal Careers,* 3rd ed. (Englewood Cliffs, N.J.: Prentice-Hall, 1977), ch. 10.

sions previously identified within the framework of a career analysis. His property offender categories include professional thieves, professional "heavy" criminals, semiprofessional property criminals, "one-time losers," automobile thieves, naive check forgers, and amateur shoplifters. He has a separate category for crime committed by respectable citizens. His crimes against persons include murder and assault. Another broad category includes patterns of sexual deviation, organized crime, drug addiction, and alcoholism.

Clinard and Quinney have developed a typology along somewhat similar lines.[14] Their typology gives a more central role to defining agencies. One of the dimensions they employ is the formulation and administration of the criminal law. Their typology shows how persons with certain characteristics and behaviors develop patterns that have a certain probability of becoming defined as criminal and receiving a particular reaction from society. The five dimensions on which they construct their typology are:

1. the legal aspects of selected offenses;

2. criminal career of the offender;

3. group support of criminal behavior;

4. correspondence between criminal and legitimate behavior;

5. societal reaction and legal processing.

The dimensions constitute a set of questions about each of the criminal patterns they identify (nine in all): what specifically are the laws related to this behavior, to what extent is there a career and a criminal self-conception, how much group support is there for it, what is the relationship between the criminal and legitimate patterns, and finally how strong is the social and legal reaction?

This brief summary of various classification systems implies that the number of possible criminal typologies is well nigh infinite, especially if attempts are made to combine them or develop a variety of subclassifications within them. No one typology is completely satisfactory nor are any likely to completely win the day among criminologists since they are developed to serve different purposes. The development of a set of scientific generalizations in criminology requires some kind of typology that identifies a range of behavior systems that can be usefully studied. Common sense dictates that the types developed correspond to the actual behavior "out there," that they not be so abstract as to include everything or so concrete that generalizations are impossible.

The behavior systems selected for analysis in Part Three closely parallel the Clinard and Quinney typology with one significant addition. There is some attempt to discuss the behavior in terms of how seriously it is viewed utilizing public opinion data. Thus in our typology the most serious criminal behavior

[14] Marshall B. Clinard and Richard Quinney, *Criminal Behavior Systems: A Typology,* 2nd ed. (New York: Holt, Rinehart & Winston, 1973).

is violent personal crime (like murder and forcible rape) and the least serious, occupational crime. But it is not entirely clear from available data how other criminal behavior is ranked. There seems to be a high public tolerance for organized crime as well as for certain kinds of corporate crime, but how do they compare with each other? Inevitably the biases of the author must come into play. Consequently political crime, such as crimes by government against citizens, and corporate crime are rated more seriously in this analysis than public order offenses, like drunkenness, because they involve enormous power differentials between the criminal and his victim.

The following chapters analyze seven behavior systems of the criminally defined:

1. Violent personal criminal behavior, which includes murder and forcible rape.

2. Conventional-professional crime, which includes armed robbery, professional theft, burglary, and larceny whether done as a full-time or part-time vocation.

3. Political criminal behavior, including crimes against the government (such as treason, sedition, sabotage, violation of military draft regulations, and civil rights violations), as well as crime by agents of the government (including violations of international law as in war crime, and the violation of constitutional guarantees and civil rights legislation).

4. Corporate criminal behavior, including violations against restraint of trade, false advertising, misuse of trademarks, manufacture of unsafe foods and drugs.

5. Organized criminal behavior, including provision of illegal services such as gambling and loan sharking as part of a hierarchical structure.

6. Public order criminal behavior, which includes violations of the laws against prostitution, homosexuality, drunkenness, and drug use.

7. Occupational criminal behavior involving violations committed in the course of one's occupational activity, including offenses of employees against employers.

For each of the major offense categories the legal dimensions are presented as well as how widespread the offense is. Further, the characteristics of offenders are summarized to indicate the age, sex, and social class characteristics for specific crimes insofar as they are known. Finally there is a discussion of how much group support for the offense exists. This includes the extent of correspondence between legitimate and criminal behavior, the extent to which it is a career, the self-concept of the offender, and social-legal reaction to it.

Seven brief life histories are included in Part Three to give concrete illustrations of the typologies as well as to discuss their relevance to the theories presented in Part One. The life histories provide inside accounts of some of the criminality discussed, and underline the importance of developing explanations for behavior patterns that are not too remote from the common sense of the participants in them.

violent
personal crime

The pattern of violent personal crime includes criminal homicide. Homicide can be differentiated into first and second degree murder and manslaughter. Those distinctions rest on whether there was premeditation or malice aforethought. Some homicides are considered by criminal law to be justified or excusable, hence are excluded from our discussion. If a police officer shoots and kills a fleeing suspect as part of his job, this is generally defined as justifiable. Excusable homicide is that which occurs accidentally as an outcome of behavior not defined as illegal—such as the death of a patient due to medication. Aggravated assault is also considered a violent personal crime along with forcible rape (unlawful sexual intercourse with a woman against her will). This is usually distinguished from statutory rape (sexual intercourse with a female under a specific age). Statutory rape is usually not associated with violence and is not included under this category.

Homicide on the one hand and statutory rape on the other are at two ends of the continuum in terms of how accurately their incidence is reflected in official crime rates. Homicide is fairly accurately reported and does not suffer as much from the underreporting or class-linked processing that cast doubts on crime rates generally. Statutory rape, on the other hand, is underreported by all professional estimates because of the stigma that attaches to the victim.

264

There is considerable justification for including a discussion of homicide, aggravated assault, and rape in the same chapter. Each offense could logically be dealt with separately and at much greater length, but when treated separately, the similarities between them are obscured. Studies of aggravated assault and forcible rape situate them in the same context. Not only is there a disproportionately high incidence of murders, assaults, and rapes in particular neighborhoods, but those who commit murder have had a history of violent assault; they were assaulters before they became murderers. The same can be said of those who commit forcible rape. Both aggravated assault and forcible rape can lead to homicide. In short, the three patterns are fundamentally similar and the offenses may even be committed by the same persons.

EXTENT OF VIOLENT PERSONAL CRIME

Since 1930 the Federal Bureau of Investigation has collected information on local, county, and statewide crimes for the purpose of developing nationwide uniform crime statistics. The statistics are published in the Uniform Crime Reports issued annually. Data for 1974 indicated that conventional property offenses (burglary, larceny, robbery, auto theft) far outnumbered personal crimes such as murder, forcible rape, and aggravated assault.[1] The rate per 100,000 of the population is more than 10 times greater with property crimes reported to the police than with personal crime (see Table 9-1).

Homicide

Since the statistics on homicide are more accurate, it has been possible to make international comparisons. In a study published in 1969, the

TABLE 9-1   Incidence of Violent Personal Crime, 1975

	Number of occurrences	*Rate per 100,000 inhabitants*
Murder	20,510	9.6
Forcible rape	56,090	26.3
Aggravated assault	484,710	227.4

Source: Federal Bureau of Investigation, *Uniform Crime Reports* (1976), p. 11

[1] Federal Bureau of Investigation, *Uniform Crime Reports* (Washington, D.C.: Government Printing Office, 1976) p. 11.

National Commission on the Causes and Prevention of Violence reported the U.S. rate per 100,000 was 6.0, much higher than that of most European countries (England-Wales: 0.7, Finland; 2.3), but lower than most Latin American and African countries.[2] In the United States there has been a dramatic increase in the rate from 1960 to 1974 but the 1967 President's Commission on Law Enforcement and the Administration of Justice suggested that there has actually been a long-run decline from what it was in the 1930s. One of the studies included in the commission report was on criminal victimization.[3] A random sample of 10,000 households was chosen and persons queried on whether they or any member of the household was victimized within the past year. This provided a comparison of the extent to which crimes known to the police reflect the actual incidence of crime. The Uniform Crime Report (UCR) rate per 100,000 of the population for willful homicide was higher than the National Opinion Research Center (NORC) survey, but lower for forcible rape and aggravated assault. The extent of assault is about twice that of official figures.

Because of its dramatic character and the attention devoted to sensational killings in media accounts, homicide evokes a profound public reaction. Despite the fact that the offense is rare there is considerable fear of murder as well as fascination with it. There is a widespread public belief that the murder rate is increasing. The Uniform Crime Report substantiates this belief—there was a 21.5 percent increase in the murder rate between 1970 and 1975.[4] Whether or not this reflects a long-term upward trend is debatable. We do know as far as official figures go that the percentage increase in the aggravated assault and rape rates was greater during the same period (38 and 40.6 respectively).[5]

The public also believes that murder varies by type of community, with large urban centers and, more specifically, low-income areas within them being the most dangerous. This perception also seems to fit with the reported facts: though the overall rate in 1975 was 9.6 per 100,000 inhabitants it was higher in large urban areas.[6] There was also a variation by urban area with Montgomery, Alabama, having the highest rate (23). But public fascination with murder usually focuses on the most atypical kind: either that which is premeditated (as in most mystery novels) or that which is "insane or senseless." The garden variety murder is neither

[2] National Commission on the Causes and Prevention of Violence, *Violent Crime: Homicide, Assault, Rape, Robbery* (New York: George Braziller, 1969).

[3] Phillip Ennis, *Criminal Victimization in the United States: A Report of a National Survey* (Field Surveys II, PCLAJ, Washington, D.C.: Government Printing Office, 1967).

[4] *Uniform Crime Reports*, p. 11.

[5] Ibid., p. 11.

[6] The metropolitan murder rate was 10.6 per 100,000; the rural rate was 8.1; *Uniform Crime Reports*, p. 11.

TABLE 9-2   Types of Interpersonal Relationships Between Murderers and Victims

Relationship	Percent
Family member (husband, wife, parent, child, sibling)	25
Friend, lover	9
Acquaintance (business relationship, neighbor, sexual rival, spouse's lover)	28
Strangers	17
Unknown	21

Source: *Crimes of Violence,* Staff report to the National Commission on the Causes and Prevention of Violence, Vol. 2 (1969), p. 217.

premeditated nor senseless. It is the end result of a fight between intimates, sometimes called "murder in the heat of passion." It constitutes 91 percent of reported cases of homicides. The senseless or random kind of killing accounts for about 3 to 4 percent of homicides. Premeditated murders, the major theme of detective fiction or that associated with organized crime ("contract killing"), accounts for only 5 percent of reported homicides. In short, homicide is an interpersonal crime. Table 9-2 summarizes the types of interpersonal relationships between murderers and their victims.

The high proportion of "unknowns" points up the inadequacies of police statistics. The 17 percent where the murderer and victim were strangers included police killings and the majority of interracial killings. Blacks and whites overwhelmingly kill those they know; murder is characteristically intraracial. Only 10 percent of homicides were interracial: whites killing blacks and vice versa.

Studies conducted on homicide in the U.S. indicate that murderers were generally younger than their victims. The majority of offenders were between ages 20 and 30, the victims were on the average five years older. The offense was more common among working-class groups. Both offenders and victims are likely to be black. In Wolfgang's Philadelphia study, 73 percent of the victims and 75 percent of the offenders are black.[7] Usually the parties are known to each other and the homicide is the outcome of an altercation. The offense is overwhelmingly committed by males. Wolfgang found that 82 percent of the offenders were male as were 76 percent of the victims. The most common time for the homicide to occur is on the weekend between 8 P.M. in the evening and 2 A.M. in the morning. It fits into a pattern of weekday labor and weekend leisure pursuits. The areas in which the homicides take place are predominantly black, characterized by dense population, overcrowding, and physical deterioration. The characteristics of homicide and aggravated assault are

[7] Marvin E. Wolfgang, *Patterns in Criminal Homicide* (Philadelphia: University of Pennsylvania Press, 1958).

similar in all respects and suggest that they represent basically similar behavior. Wolfgang classified 26 percent of the Philadelphia murders he studied as "victim precipitated," i.e., the victim seemed to be asking to be killed. The victim in these circumstances starts the fight, or acts in a very aggressive, provocative way, sometimes daring his antagonist to kill him, even to the point of handing him the murder weapon.

Rape

Forcible rape refers to a man's sexual intercourse with a woman without her consent. It can also include instances where informed consent cannot be given, as in child molestation, and offenses where offender and victim are males, as in homosexual rape. (Both child molestation and homosexual rape are important topics but are excluded from the category of violent personal crime for the purposes of this discussion.)

There were 56,090 forcible rape cases reported to the police in 1975. Because of the shame connected with the crime, victims are reluctant to report it. Some studies estimate that about 20 percent of all forcible rapes are reported.[8] Le Grand's study suggests that the nonreported incidence is much higher; only 2 of the 30 rape victims in her inquiry reported the crime, about 7 percent.[9] The President's Commission estimated that the actual incidence of forcible rape is more than three-and-a-half times the official figures.[10] If we accept this conservative estimate, the rate per 100,000 jumps to 78, still much less than the official incidence of aggravated assault. If we project the rate from Le Grand's study, the incidence would be higher than officially reported assaults. In short, forcible rape may be the most frequent serious personal offense.

If we can generalize from official figures, rape follows the same temporal pattern as homicide, occurring mostly on the weekends. It differs from the typical homicide in that it is not impulsive. Amir's study showed that 71 percent of the rapes he studied involved planning and were not situational.[11] Rape is generally less of an interpersonal crime (that is, where the participants know each other) than homicide, but still more so than popular myths about the rapist-stranger suggest; Amir's figures showed that 50 percent of the victims were known by the

[8] The President's Commission on Law Enforcement and the Administration of Justice, *The Challenge of Crime in a Free Society* (New York: Avon Books, 1968), p. 97.

[9] Camille E. LeGrand, "Rape and Rape Laws: Sexism in Society and Law," *California Law Review*, 61 (May 1973), 919–41.

[10] President's Commission, *The Challenge of Crime*, p. 97.

[11] Menachim Amir, *Patterns in Forcible Rape* (Chicago: University of Chicago Press, 1971).

offender. The victim who is not known to the rapist is likely to be retarded, older, sleeping, or under the influence of alcohol or drugs. If the victim is known to the offender she generally has a reputation for being a "loose woman," or is vulnerable because of her age. Amir noted that the high-risk group is from ages 10 to 14. Like homicide, rape is mostly an intraracial occurrence. Only 5 percent of the rapes Amir studied were interracial—mostly black offender and white victim. Of the violent personal crimes it seems to be the one that has shown the greatest increase; officially reported rapes increased by 62 percent from 1968 to 1973.[12] This figure may not reflect any real increase, only the increased willingness of victims to report the offense.

Forcible rape is generally committed by young unmarried males, aged 15 to 25, who come from the lower class. Gebhard et al. suggest that forcible rape is related to more aggressive patterns of the lower class in sexual matters.[13] Areas with high rates of forcible rape also have high rates of crime against the person. The same areas that generate homicides and aggravated assaults also generate forcible rape.

Amir's figures on rapes in Philadelphia indicate that black men are 12 times as likely as white men to be rape offenders; black women are also 12 times as likely as white women to be rape victims. The chronically unemployed supply a disproportionate amount of rapists. The place in which rapes commonly occur is one which is relatively isolated: restrooms, laundromats, and empty streets. If the rape is intraracial, the offenders are generally older than the victims, if the rapist is black and the victim white, the victim is usually ten years older. Group rapes account for an unusually large percentage (43) in Amir's study; the rapists are adolescents, aged 10 to 19. Amir classified 19 percent of the rapes he studied as "victim precipitated," that is, the victims were acting in such a way as to be "asking for it." Amir's conclusion has been challenged by some female authors as biased:

> The concept of victim precipitation hinges primarily on male definitions of expressed or implied consent to engage in sexual relations, and is shaped by traditional restrictive stereotypes of women. Thus, hitchhiking and walking alone at night in a rough neighborhood may be considered behavior encouraging a sexual attack. This view of what a *man* can assume to be a sexual invitation is unreasonable. . . . When the female hitchhiker first sets out to get a ride, she normally is not expecting—or hoping for—a sexual encounter. A woman should not be made to feel guilty for acts that do not involve express sexual invitation, nor should she be denied the

[12] *Uniform Crime Reports,* 1974, pp. 7, 12, 14, 16, 20, 23, 27.
[13] Paul H. Gebhard et al., *Sex Offenders: An Analysis of Types* (New York, Harper & Row, 1965).

right to change her mind. In its failure to accord any consideration to the woman victim's intentions, victim precipitation becomes nothing more than a male view of the circumstances leading up to the incident.[14]

GROUP SUPPORT FOR VIOLENT PERSONAL CRIME

Though violent personal behavior may constitute a pattern in particular neighborhoods of large cities and among the males who live there, it is not career oriented. Killing or maiming is seldom done for profit or as part of one's livelihood. The persons who engage in violence do not see themselves as criminal nor are they involved with groups who sanction violent behavior. Some social scientists, however, have contended that although little or no explicit support is given to violence, it is tolerated. The National Commission on the Causes and Prevention of Violence noted that in this setting:

> . . . proving masculinity may require frequent rehearsal of the toughness, exploitation of women, and the quick aggressive responses that are characteristics of the lower class adult male. Those who engage in subcultural violence are often not burdened by conscious guilt, because their victims are likely to belong to the same subculture or to a group they believe has exploited them. Thus, when victims see their assaulters as agents of the same kind of aggression they themselves represent, violent retaliation is readily legitimized.[15]

They suggest that the higher rates of violent behavior among lower strata groups can be explained in terms of a higher tolerance for expression of violence, and norms directing that it be employed in specific situations.

The fact that forcible rape is considered the most serious crime after murder suggests that there is no group support for it. Yet it seems clear that there are widespread beliefs about the nature of women and their sexuality that secretly encourages males to assault females. These beliefs seem characteristic of a highly competitive society in which women are considered inferior to men and there is a sharp segregation of the sexes. This context encourages males to use women to prove their masculinity. The winner is the one who "makes out" with the largest number of women. The object of the masculinity game is to score no matter how much the woman is humiliated, hurt, or frightened. These attitudes are

[14] LeGrand, "Rape and Rape Laws," pp. 929–30.
[15] National Commission on the Causes and Prevention of Violence, *To Establish Justice, To Insure Domestic Tranquility* (Washington, D.C.: Government Printing Office, 1969).

most evident in one-sex peer groups like the army, male boarding schools, and overwhelmingly male occupations. There the pressures to play the game are strongest and men are discouraged from showing any signs that might be considered "feminine." The hints on how to play are not written down as they would be in a course of formal instruction but involve injunctions to press one's advantage until the unwilling female submits. The lore includes the belief that women want to be overpowered and that there is no such thing as rape "because a girl with her dress up can run faster than a guy with his pants down."

SOCIETAL REACTION AND LEGAL PROCESSING

Social reaction to violent personal offenses are mixed. Legitimate violence—committed in the course of war—is expected and tolerated. Violent personal crime by lower-class persons, however, elicits strong public reactions. This is reflected in the harsh punishments meted out to those who are convicted of homicide or aggravated assault.

This is in sharp contrast to the legal processing of rapists. The belief about the willing victim has generally meant that the rape victim is presumed guilty. The rapist's attorney is permitted to question the victim on past sexual conduct in an effort to show that she was sexually active or promiscuous. Juries tend to be sympathetic to the rapist and willing to believe that no one could actually be raped unless they wanted to be. When rapists are convicted the victim is usually a "respectable" married woman unknown to the offender and likely to have struggled to such an extent that she can show visible bruises. The reaction to the offender under those circumstances tends to be quite harsh. Some feminist authors have contended that this reveals the assumptions behind the laws against rape: basically the laws are designed to protect the male's "property." The rapist is actually committing the crime of vandalism or theft against a father or husband to whom the victim belongs. If the woman "belongs" to no one—that is, does not have the protection of father or husband—then she is considered fair game by predatory males.

HOW BEST DETER VIOLENT CRIME?

Violent personal assault is all but universally condemned. It is considered to be socially threatening and is not explicitly condoned by any significant segments of society. Packer has cogently summarized the social reaction to murder, assault, and forcible rape:

> These . . . offenses are supremely threatening for differing reasons, but in each case one's physical security is placed at the mercy of a person intent on violating that security. Nothing makes either the victim or the community feel more helpless than an occasion on which someone has used force to work his will on another. Violent injury or the threat of it is the brute negation of the minimum that all of us—from the most self-sufficient to the most dependent—expect from life in organized society.[16]

Public sentiment is strongly in favor of incapacitating persistent assaulters for the length of time that is required to insure that their predations will cease. Criminologists on the whole share this sentiment, though the reasons given and the length of incarceration favored varies.

The major issue surrounding how to deal best with homicide and personal assault is the effectiveness of the *death penalty*. Law enforcement and prosecutorial groups tend to be strongly supportive of capital punishment; criminologists, social scientists, and legal scholars tend generally to be opposed.[17] The opponents of the death penalty point to several kinds of evidence to suggest that it does not deter. If we compare the homicide rates in states that have the death penalty to those that do not we can note that the homicide rates seem to be two or three times higher in states that retain the death penalty.[18] This is not convincing proof, however, since the states that retain capital punishment (mostly southern) are much different in their population and cultural characteristics than those states that have abolished it. If we look only at states with common population and cultural characteristics, however, the homicide rate is still somewhat higher in those states that retain the death penalty. Another kind of evidence comes from the comparison of homicide rates before and after abolishing capital punishment. There seem to be no significant differences in homicide rates before and after. There is also some evidence from states that have restored the death penalty after initially banning it; in those states there has been no significant decrease in the homicide rate. Others have looked at the number of homicides before and after highly publicized executions. Again the fluctuation in rates was not significant. These scattered investigations have convinced criminologists that the death penalty does not deter the potential murderer, probably because he is not the rational, calculating person that the law assumes. However, it may be quite effective in deterring the small fraction of homicides that are the result of premeditation.

[16] Herbert L. Packer, *The Limits of the Criminal Sanction* (Stanford, Calif.: Stanford University Press, 1968), p. 298.
[17] See the arguments for and against capital punishment in James A. McCafferty (ed.), *Capital Punishment* (Chicago: Aldine-Atherton, 1972).
[18] William C. Bailey, "Murder and the Death Penalty," *Journal of Criminal Law and Criminology*, 65 (September 1974), 416–23.

The argument in favor of capital punishment has little empirical evidence to support it. Its primary utility, argue its proponents, is that its existence and the possibility of its use elicit cooperation from otherwise antagonistic defendants. Other recurrent themes in advocating capital punishment are: justice demands that the murderer pay for his crime; it is more economical than imprisonment; it is necessary in order to prevent the public from lynching criminals; and it is the only certain penalty since those sentenced to life imprisonment often are pardoned.[19]

A second issue on deterring violent crime relates to *firearms control*. The debate surrounding this issue is almost as bitter as the death penalty argument but the sides are somewhat different. Criminologists, social scientists, and law enforcement personnel tend to favor firearms control of some sort; associations of hunters and sportsmen are strongly opposed. The evidence seems to support the advocates of firearms control; that is, if there were fewer death-dealing weapons in the community, there would be fewer deaths. The proportion of murder by firearms varies by the proportion who own firearms. It is highest in regions where a higher percentage of the population own guns; conversely, the proportion of murder by firearms is lowest in those regions where the smallest proportion of the total population own firearms.[20] Overall, firearms accounted for 68.5 percent of the homicides in 1975.[21]

EXPLANATIONS OF VIOLENT PERSONAL BEHAVIOR

Studies done from a psychological vantage point rely on the personal characteristics of individuals. There is frequent reference to the "violence-prone personality."[22] However, some sociologists have suggested that boys who were physically punished expressed aggression as adults more directly than those who were punished psychologically.[23]

Criminologists, no matter what their basic policy convictions, agree that violence that becomes defined as criminal is distributed unevenly throughout the society—that is, there is more of it in the lower class. But they disagree on what this means. Quinney has noted that legitimized violence used in military operations, policing riots, and controlling subversives is widespread throughout the society:

[19]McCafferty, *Capital Punishment.*
[20] *Uniform Crime Reports*, p. 18.
[21] Ibid.
[22] Esther Penchef (ed.), *Four Horsemen: Pollution, Poverty, Famine and Violence* (San Francisco: Canfield Press, 1971).
[23] Martin Gold, "Suicide, Homicide and the Socialization of Aggression," *American Journal of Sociology*, 64 (May 1958), 651–61.

> Violence, wherever it originates and however it is promoted in our society, becomes culturally diffused throughout the society as a cultural theme that affects the lives of us all.[24]

The violence theme, in short, is generally shared but mediated by social class membership. The need to be tough or express toughness may be expressed physically by those who lack control over resources and power that would enable them to demonstrate their masculine toughness in ways available to the more privileged: nonphysical competitiveness, ambition, ruthlessness, and authoritarianism. Valentine points to evidence that achievement of relative wealth or power within disadvantaged communities tends to exempt a man from the more direct requirements of physical toughness.[25] The options provided by the larger social structure are significantly different for those in the lowest stratum and the middle class. The illegal options available to the middle class do not require the use of violence. Filling out income tax forms fraudulently or deciding to deceive consumers on food or drugs characteristically does not take place in the streets or require direct confrontation with the victim. When there is direct confrontation, violence is much more likely to be the outcome. As Wright has put it:

> This does not mean that the poor are necessarily more violent than the rest of society. Rather, it means that the nature of the illegal options open to them tends to make violence more common in their crime.[26]

Glaser speaks of the violent personal offender as a "subcultural assaulter" but says that the violence is associated with educational and economic deprivation.[27] His policy recommendation for reducing the incidence of violent personal crime is to upgrade the education of the educationally deprived and reduce the extent of their insecurity in employment and status.

Henry and Short tried to look at suicide and homicide in a unified framework rather than assuming them to be unrelated.[28] They start with Durkheim's observations about the two: "While family life has a mod-

[24] Richard Quinney, *The Social Reality of Crime* (Boston: Little, Brown, 1970), p. 232.
[25] Charles A. Valentine, *Culture and Poverty: Critique and Counter Proposals* (Chicago: University of Chicago Press, 1968), p. 136.
[26] Erik O. Wright (ed.), *The Politics of Punishment* (New York: Harper & Row, 1973), p. 10.
[27] Daniel Glaser, *Adult Crime and Social Policy* (Englewood Cliffs, N.J.: Prentice-Hall, 1972), ch. 3.
[28] Andrew F. Henry and James F. Short, Jr., *Suicide and Homicide* (New York: Free Press, 1954).

erating effect upon suicide it rather stimulates murder."[29] Both suicide and homicide are viewed as differentiated aggressive reactions to frustration generated by differential changes in status positions. Changes in status position inevitably accompany business expansion and contraction. Ultimately, then, suicide and homicide are generated by economic forces. What Henry and Short call "the strength of relational system" (degree to which individuals are involved in relations with others), if low, leads to suicide, and if high may lead to homicide. But they note that there is a negative relation between status and homicide. If your socioeconomic level is high you are unlikely to seek expression through homicide, no matter how deeply involved you are with others. It is the situation of low status and strong relational bonds that leads to homicide. They also add another variable: strength of external restraint or social control. The higher the restraint the lower the number of suicides (just as Durkheim hypothesized) but the higher the number of homicides. They suggest that when external restraints are weak, aggression generated by frustration will be directed against the self and when external restraints are strong or social control oppressive, aggression will be directed outwardly. If their theory is correct homicide rates should be higher in the married than the unmarried category—among those who were involved in intimate primary associations and among those who have many restraints that limit their freedom. Data collected since the mid-1950s when they wrote their book indicate that it is generally the unmarried, young, low-income male who is disproportionately involved in homicides. In brief, their theory has been partially borne out (locating the murderer in the lowest stratum), but is not valid in predicting higher rates among marrieds. The introduction of the variable external restraint, however, links both suicide and homicide to social organization, and makes the Henry-Short formulation compatible with ecological and opportunity structure approaches.

But by far the most influential contemporary explanation among criminologists interested in the determinants of violence is the cultural one. The argument holds that the rate of violence can be understood as part of a specific cultural configuration. It is accepted as normative among particular subgroups. A more diffuse employment of the same notion has also been used to explain violence in the United States as a whole.[30] Sociologists, however, have been more interested in interpreting the rates of violence within particular subgroups. The scheme that has received the most currency recently in order to explain offenses is Wolfgang and

[29] Emile Durkheim (John H. Spaulding and George Simpson, trans.), *Suicide* (New York: Free Press, 1951).
[30] Hugh D. Graham and Ted. R. Gurr (eds.), *Violence in America: Historical and Comparative Perspectives* (New York: Praeger, 1969).

Ferracuti's "subculture of violence" thesis.[31] The socially disorganized area identified by the ecologists earlier is the locale for the violent behavior. It is inhabited by young males who are preoccupied with ways of protecting and enhancing their masculinity. They seem to be acting out injunctions relating to toughness provided by a separate lower-class structure. However, Wolfgang and Ferracuti do not go as far as Walter Miller in creating a separate lower-class culture. Rather their subculture is linked to the dominant one through a general set of shared values, but is in conflict with it on the issue of the appropriate use of violence. In certain situations violence is expected. As Wolfgang has pointed out:

> . . . the significance of a jostle, a slightly derogatory remark, or the appearance of a weapon in the hands of an adversary are stimuli differentially perceived and interpreted by Negroes and whites, males and females. Social expectations of response in particular types of social interaction result in differential "definitions of the situation." A male is usually expected to defend the name and honor of his mother, the virtue of womanhood . . . and to accept no derogation about his race (even from a member of his own race), his age, or his masculinity. Quick resort to physical combat as a measure of daring, courage, or defense of status appears to be a cultural expression, especially for lower socioeconomic males of both races. When such a culture norm response is elicited from an individual engaged in social interplay with others who harbor the same response mechanisms, physical assaults, altercations and violent domestic quarrels that result in homicide are likely to be common.[32]

The studies of Wolfgang on homicide and Amir's parallel study on forcible rape are attempts to examine closely specific types of offenses and explain them preliminary to a more general theoretical formulation. Both Wolfgang and Amir conclude that the subculture of violence thesis fits their data. Wolfgang feels that the subculture of young black males explains the higher incidence of homicide among them. Wolfgang sees homicide in the same category as other types of aggressive behavior such as rape and aggravated assault. A study by Pittman and Handy in 1964 on patterns of criminal aggravated assault clearly demonstrates the similarities between assault and homicide.[33] Their assaulters looked very much like Wolfgang's murderers.

[31] Marvin E. Wolfgang and Franco Ferracuti, *The Subculture of Violence* (London: Social Science Paperbacks, Tavistock Publications, 1967).
[32] Marvin E. Wolfgang, *Patterns in Criminal Homicide* (Philadelphia: University of Pennsylvania Press, 1958), pp. 188–89.
[33] David J. Pittman and William Handy, "Patterns in Criminal Aggravated Assault," in Bruce J. Cohen (ed.), *Crime in America* (Itasca, Ill.: F. E. Peacock, 1970).

Pokorny tried to compare homicide, aggravated assault, suicide, and attempted suicide as part of a general violence pattern.[34] He concludes that suicide and homicide are the opposite of each other both in the characteristics of offenders and the locale of the offense. Little systematic attention has been paid to the relationship between homicide and other forms of violence such as childbeating and fatal automobile accidents. Porterfield has suggested that there is some validity in linking traffic fatalities with homicide.[35] His research convinced him that aggressive hazardous driving is likely to be characteristic of persons similar to those who have suicidal or homicidal tendencies, and vice versa.

The subculture of violence theory has also been extended to explain rapists. Psychogenic explanations of the rapist depict him as abnormal because of unpleasant childhood experiences that do not permit him to relate to women in a normal way. As a consequence he becomes sexually inadequate and can only become aroused by women who put up a fight against his advances. The subcultural theory does not assume the abnormality of the rapist; rather he is normal and behaving according to a particular set of subcultural prescriptions. The lower-class black pattern that Amir describes emphasizes the importance of searching for kicks through aggressive behavior and sexual exploitation. It is within this context that the masculinity game discussed earlier is most ferociously played out—masculinity is proved by brief and transitory sexual encounters with women. As Amir put it:

> The Negro male's aggressive sexuality seems . . . due to the strong need to overcome problems of masculinity and of sexual identity. This is so because of the Negro family structure (mother-based family) and the need to overcome general social disadvantages, by substituting sexual aggressive masculinity for failures as a man in the economic and social status spheres.[36]

A variation of the *frustration-aggression* theory has been applied to rape by Chappell et al.[37] He compared the rates of two cities, one that was sexually restrictive (Boston) and another that was permissive (Los Angeles). He tried to account for the fact that there was a higher incidence of rape in the more permissive setting, quite the opposite to what

[34] Alex D. Pokorny et al., "Suicide, Suicide Attempts and Weather," *American Journal of Psychiatry*, 120 (1963), 377–81.

[35] Austin L. Porterfield, "Indices of Suicide and Homicide by States and Cities: Some Southern, Non-Southern Contrasts with Implications for Research," *American Sociological Review*, 14 (August 1949), 481–90.

[36] Menachem Amir, *Patterns in Forcible Rape* (Chicago: University of Chicago Press, 1971), p. 330.

[37] Duncan Chappell et al., "Forcible Rape: A Comparative Study of Offenses Known to the Police in Boston and Los Angeles," in James M. Henslen (ed.), *Studies in the Sociology of Sex* (New York: Appleton-Century-Crofts, 1971), pp. 169–90.

the casual observer would be led to expect. He explains this by *relative frustration*, that is, the male who is rejected by a woman in a permissive society feels much deeper frustration than the male in a restricted society who does not take the rejection so personally and identifies with others who are in the same boat as he. The formulation is suggestive but still lacks any rigorous testing.

Bloch and Geis analyzed cross-cultural studies of rape and postulated a kind of opportunity theory explanation. Their four salient factors were:

> (1) severe formal restrictions on nonmarital sexual relations of females, (2) moderately strong sexual inhibitions on the part of the female, (3) economic or other barriers to marriage that prolong the bachelorhood of some males into their late twenties, and (4) the absence of physical segregation of the sexes.[38]

If their theory is valid we can expect that forcible rape rates would be high among unmarried men who are in close contact with females who are restricted or inhibited from having sexual intercourse.

Evaluation of Theories of Personal Violence

Not all of the explanations have been put to the test. The subculture-of-violence explanation seems to make sense out of a number of disparate pieces of information but it has been challenged on its validity and applicability. Ball-Rokeach in 1973 put the subculture-of-violence thesis to the test on a national probability sample of American males and a group of incarcerated felons (both those convicted of violent crimes and those not).[39] We should expect according to the subculture-of-violence position that persons who vary in participation in violent behavior should also vary in attitudes toward violence and values related to violent behavior. The national sample was asked about its participation in interpersonal violence both as assaultist and victim, and asked to rank a set of values in terms of their importance as guiding principles in the lives of the respondents. Ball-Rokeach went on to identify a subset of values that represented a "machismo" life style based on Wolfgang's descriptions. Differences between those who subscribed to these values and those who didn't did not differentiate between those with high and low violence participation. In a second version of the "machismo" theory she examined the

[38] Herbert A. Bloch and Gilbert Geis, *Man, Crime and Society*, 2nd ed. (New York: Random House, 1970), p. 253.
[39] Sandra J. Ball-Rokeach, "Values and Violence: A Test of the Subculture of Violence Thesis," *American Sociological Review*, 38 (December 1973), 736–49.

argument that some men are more violent because of a stronger commitment to the overall American male value system. She asked whether men who were more concerned with economic and personal success and hedonistic pursuits (traditional "male" values) were more violent. Again her findings were negative. In summary she states:

> Significant value differences found between groups with different participation in violence are few in number, small in magnitude and not consistent with either version of the "machismo" subculture of violence. All these findings suggest that values play little or no role as determinants of interpersonal violence.[40]

Her study of the incarcerated population was equally negative. She suggests that the subculture-of-violence thesis is at best incomplete and at worst invalid. She concludes that violence may be more plausibly linked to such situational, ecological, or demographic factors as access to weapons, exposure to alcohol, population density, or level of intergroup conflict.

The external restraint theory as applied to murder and rape shows some promise but not enough has been done to test its validity. Conflict theorists would translate the notion of "external restraint" into social oppression inevitably linked to a system of inequality. The fact that powerless persons occasionally are provoked into violence by this situation should surprise no one. But aggression is not the only response to this kind of frustration. A more comprehensive view of possible human responses would note aggression as one response and identify the more immediate conditions which must be present for it to occur. A more adequate theory of external restraint would also identify the range of other possible responses to situations of strain or deprivation. This elaboration would undoubtedly anchor this theory more firmly in the area of social movements.

GEORGE: A MURDERER

The extent to which any of these explanations applies in specific instances remains to be seen. The following interview was conducted with a black male convicted of killing a man in 1961. He was 31 at the time of the interview, had served 12 years of his sentence, and had been out of prison for 18 months. At the time of the interview he was employed assisting ex-convicts readjust to life in the open community. He completed his high school education while in prison and went on to receive a college diploma within the institution. He was

[40] Ibid., p. 749.

recommended by an attorney working with the ex-convict organization because of his ability to articulate some rather complicated observations about crime and prison life.

QUESTION: To begin, maybe you could tell me a little about your contact with the criminal justice system.

GEORGE: When I was sixteen I got involved in a burglary with several others. We broke into a factory where radio and television equipment were stored.

QUESTION: Were you discovered at the time?

GEORGE: No, we were apprehended later. Once they gathered certain pieces of material, interviewed neighborhood people, and found where we stored the stuff they picked us up.

QUESTION: What was the outcome?

GEORGE: I was given seven months with the Youth Commission and incarcerated in a facility about 50 miles from here.

QUESTION: The sentence seems a little severe for a first offense, doesn't it?

GEORGE: Yes, it was, but there had been a rash of break-ins in the area and the police seemed to think we were involved. But they weren't able to tie us into anything else.

QUESTION: Were you in school at the time of the burglary?

GEORGE: No. I lost my incentive to complete school. I didn't see where an education would fit into my pattern of behavior. As I perceived the situation at the time I think even with an education I would have had a number of hassles in terms of getting a job. For that reason I just lost all interest, more or less. Education wasn't the order of the day.

QUESTION: What was your family situation at the time you were sent to the Youth Commission?

GEORGE: I was living with my mother and two younger brothers. My father left the picture when I was about four years old. My mother was on public aid. When I was released from the Youth Commission I looked around for a job because public aid reduced our grant because I was in this difficulty.

QUESTION: Were you able to find a job?

GEORGE: I wasn't qualified to do very much. What skills or training did I have? It took me about nine or ten months to land a decent job. Most employers wouldn't even grant you an interview.

QUESTION: What kind of job was it?

GEORGE: I was a stock boy in a small department store.

QUESTION: How long did you stay on the job?

GEORGE: I stayed there three years until I was laid off. The situation was bad, almost like day labor. It got to be pretty unstable, sometimes they'd call and ask me not to come in for a week or so. Finally they just let me go.

QUESTION: Was it about this time that you got into the difficulty that led to your being sent to prison?

GEORGE: Yes. I was having a tough time generating any revenue. I took to hanging out with three other guys who were into stealing auto parts and selling them. But it wasn't much of a living. It was part-time night work and we'd sleep during the day. On the weekends we'd go out to a tavern and have a little fun. There were about three places we usually hung out at because there always seemed to be some action there. The place I liked best was called the "Kit Kat Club." The dice girl who worked there and I had a thing going. I'd wait until the tavern closed and then we'd go back to her place.

QUESTION: What were the circumstances that led to the fight in the tavern?

GEORGE: Well it was over Tina [the dice girl]. It was late Friday night, no, I guess Saturday morning just about the time they were getting ready to close. We all were drinking pretty heavily and one of my partners started getting pretty nasty. He couldn't hold his liquor. He got into an argument with Tina and claimed she was cheating him on the dice game. He started calling her names and looked like he was going to hit her. I moved in to calm him down and he jumped me. I figured I could handle him; this wasn't the first fight we got into and he was pretty loaded. But all of a sudden he pulls out a gun and starts shooting at me. He hit me three times, but I grabbed the gun and turned it on him.

QUESTION: How many times did you shoot him?

GEORGE: Just the once. Everybody cut out of there right away and I'm lying on the floor bleeding. One of my other partners pulled me out of there and took me to the hospital. I was sure I was going to die too.

QUESTION: How did you know the man you shot was dead?

GEORGE: I didn't for sure, but the guy who took me to the hospital said he was.

QUESTION: Were you carrying a weapon at the time?

GEORGE: No, I owned a gun, we all did, but I usually didn't take it with me when we were going out to have some fun.

QUESTION: Did the police enter the picture at any point?

GEORGE: Yes, at the apprehension. I was apprehended when I was in the hospital with three bullet holes in me.

QUESTION: Where were you shot?

GEORGE: Once in the abdomen, once around the heart, and once by my kidneys.

QUESTION: Any permanent damage that you suffer with today?

GEORGE: No, I guess that was just one of my fortunate moments. With that many holes in me and bleeding profusely for more than two hours, I came out of it. I don't really believe in miracles but that's the only term I can use that would describe my situation at that time. I definitely thought I wouldn't pull through. I knew I had lost more than enough blood for any man to die. I was going to die whether I went or stayed. I chose to go and die in the process.

QUESTION: Was anyone else in the tavern wounded?

GEORGE: No, I was the only one.

QUESTION: What was involved in your apprehension in the hospital?

GEORGE: Well, you know whenever someone is shot the hospitals usually notify the police so you didn't have to be an Einstein to know that I had three bullet holes in me, I had recently gotten shot, and there was an incident nearby where another person had been shot. They did have witnesses in this establishment. They brought them to the hospital. They made a positive identification so far as I was concerned.

QUESTION: What happened after you left the hospital, after those four weeks?

GEORGE: I went to the County Jail and went through all these court procedures.

QUESTION: What were you charged with?

GEORGE: I was charged with murder and I was indicted. I was convicted and sentenced for second-degree murder.

QUESTION: What was the length of time from the point you left the hospital until the trial started?

GEORGE: About eight or nine months. I was confined in the County Jail all that time.

QUESTION: When the actual trial started who did they bring in as witnesses?

GEORGE: People that were in the tavern at the time, about ten. Their stories varied. Everything was trumped up—it was a kind of kangaroo hearing. They claimed I started the fight. Tina just disappeared. I didn't know what happened to her. Charges were trumped up that weren't true in order to get a conviction. Everything was just a farce. They must have brought in at least 10 or 12 witnesses that either had been in the establishment or near it, whether they actually saw what happened or not that didn't matter a whole lot. They brought these witnesses in primarily on hearsay. It was a sordid phase of the whole incident—the court procedures. They were such a farce.

QUESTION: Was there much publicity about the crime?

GEORGE: Enough for a conviction. The press was making a big thing of it. It was a very serious crime. Anytime a life is taken it's a serious crime, although at the time it didn't mean that much to me because I didn't have an appreciation for life. Since that time I have acquired that appreciation. I say to you here and now it was a big thing.

QUESTION: How long did the trial itself last?

GEORGE: We started out in the morning and came to a halt in the early part of the afternoon. I decided to plead guilty to the crime and save some humiliation because that's what it was all about, I was being humiliated.

QUESTION: Was there any attempt to bargain with you by the prosecution?

GEORGE: Bargaining goes on thoughout the country in all your judiciary systems, you know. There's always plea bargaining.

QUESTION: So the idea was to settle for a lesser charge and save the state some money?

GEORGE: Originally it was stated like that and when the prosecuting attorney saw that he had an open and shut case then bargaining became rather difficult, you know. He said they had enough to give me the death penalty. If I didn't plead guilty that's what I would have got. They weren't trying to prove that the killing was premeditated—that's first-degree—but only that it involved malice—second-degree murder. I figured like this, you get apprehended. Once you're apprehended on a serious crime you go through a number of hassles, frustrating moments. Once you go into court you've got to go through that again. And whether or not you're remorseful, going though it over and over again you can more or less see exactly what the end result is going to be long before you get there. And I figured I'd be saving myself a lot of time, humiliation, and pain as well as some concerned people who were in the courtroom by just saying, "Hey listen, do whatever you will, do it and let it be over." I was just physically drained and psychologically whipped. I didn't feel like going through it over and over again.

QUESTION: Once you decided to plead guilty then the trial was over—like one day?

GEORGE: Right, and sentencing occurred the same day.

QUESTION: Then at the end of one day you were transferred from the County Jail to the state penitentiary?

GEORGE: No, we waited about two months before we were transferred.

QUESTION: Was that two months dead time?

GEORGE: It counted eventually. We had to wait on a shipment. They have weekly shipments, monthly shipments. They have x number scheduled to be shipped in one week and x number another week.

QUESTION: What kind of reputation did the institution you went to have?

GEORGE: Any institution in this state is considered a hard place to serve time. Period. First of all because the structuring, the programming, everything that goes on in an institution isn't set up or geared to attain that ultimate objective, that is, rehabilitation. That's a lot of hogwash, to be more specific, it's bullshit, it doesn't occur.

QUESTION: So you were sentenced to 99 years. That meant you were eligible for parole, when?

GEORGE: At that time I was eligible for parole after serving 33⅓ years. The laws were changed that enable the inmate to appear before the parole and pardon board having served 11 years, 3 months regardless of the sentence. After 11 years and 3 months you become eligible for parole.

QUESTION: What sort of things do they take into consideration in determining whether you will be paroled?

GEORGE: Crime, institutional record, your behavior during incarceration, and your criminal past.

QUESTION: Would you say that the institutional record weighed pretty heavily in determining whether or not you were granted parole?

GEORGE: In my case it did. It may help to have institutional personnel on your side but it depends on the case. If you're Speck [Richard Speck convicted of brutally killing eight nurses in 1965] it matters little who you've got on your side.

QUESTION: While incarcerated were you treated any special way by inmates because of your crime, or did it seem not to make any difference?

GEORGE: Not at first, but after you're there for a year, two or three years, then you branch off into cliques. You find yourself running with old-timers. By old-timers I mean someone who has to do 10, 15, 20 years before he gets out. This is an ideal relationship—you've got a lot in common as you perceive it. It's related to the type of crime but only because of the long sentences involved.

QUESTION: Apart from the length of sentence would you say there was anything in common among those who were in for homicides? Would they tend to be a certain type of person?

GEORGE: The person that commits a murder is a . . . it's a one-time type of thing, more or less. And 85 to 90 percent of those people who serve a long sentence for murder seldom go back. It's a once-in-a-lifetime type of deal. I wouldn't say it's because of the amount of time given as opposed to the type of person who commits a murder. Some murders are committed in the process of another crime, some murders are committed in passion and things like that. There are a number of people in institutions who are not criminal but are made criminal coming out of the institution thinking with this concept of a criminal primarily because of his associates. He learns to speak the language. He acquires those things that he needs in order to exist. And the language is one of the most vital things. In that sense people are made criminals.

QUESTION: You're also saying that the person who is in for murder is a pretty good parole risk?

GEORGE: I'd say he is one of the better risks because it's not a real pattern. It's seldom a premediated type of thing, even when a man goes out to rob a store, it's not a premediated thing. The purpose of the gun is to frighten off his opposition, whatever that opposition may be. If in the process of fighting him off you have to use the gun then it becomes a different story. But initially he'd be as afraid to use the gun as someone is to see the gun. The fear, I believe, would balance out more or less.

QUESTION: So it's really accident or passion as you see it?

GEORGE: Yes, more or less. You could start shooting out of fear and frustrations and things like that.

QUESTION: Some criminologists have speculated that there is a violent-prone person. What would your reaction be to that?

GEORGE: There are those violent-prone type of persons, I'd concur up to a point. Then, too, I'd say that people are forced to be violent in some instances. It becomes a force issue when we lock up our frustrations and disappointments. We don't know at what point we're going to explode. And what we're going to do should we explode. If it occurs, then hostility could be coming out that occurred five or ten years ago. You become a very violent person. You don't have to be a criminal to become a very violent person. You can be Joe Blow, average daily citizen.

QUESTION: Would you characterize yourself as a violent person at that time, say when you were 19?

GEORGE: No, not at all. I didn't consider myself a violent person with that background. I was just misdirected, making a living in the ghetto in the slum area, trying to exist by any means at my disposal.

QUESTION: Some sociologists have speculated that there are violent-prone areas or neighborhoods, or cultures, not necessarily personalities. Would you agree?

GEORGE: 100 percent. The cause is the area itself.

QUESTION: What is it about the area—more tolerance for personal assault or opportunity to do it or what?

GEORGE: Well, I don't know whether you'd say it like that or could put it like that really. So I wouldn't say it like that.

QUESTION: In the violence-prone neighborhood the boys somehow get status, prestige, or their reputation is built on being the best kind of fighter, the best kind of assaulter—is that part of it?

GEORGE: I think that's part of it in any society, in any neighborhood in any area. We all seek recognition whether we be man, woman, or child. There's a need for a certain amount of recognition, a personal need. We don't all go about getting this recognition in the same way. Different methods are employed. The type of recognition I need very well may differ greatly from the type of recognition you need. It's like a stroke, I stroke you the right way or say the things you want to hear or treat you the right way or that I'm stroking you giving you a certain amount of respect or recognition in that sense. Some of us are in greater need, go to greater lengths to get this recognition.

QUESTION: You mentioned earlier about economic causes. Would you also relate that to violence?

GEORGE: Yes, you can't get around it. If the economic situation is better the violence subsides, because the frustration level subsides.

QUESTION: Would you have been considered less a man in the tavern incident if you had just backed off or backed down when your friend pulled a gun?

GEORGE: No, it would have been out of context for me to look at him and say, well, I'm afraid of him because he's bigger and walk out—that's out of context, if you're already into a fight.

QUESTION: You couldn't really do that?

GEORGE: No, well, I don't say you can't do anything, let's just say it's not a rule. If you're going to get into a fight you follow it through. You can't look at someone and say, "Wow, he looks like he's tough. I don't think I'm going to mess with him." That just doesn't go along with the game.

QUESTION: In other words you don't get into it in the first place if you're going to do that?

GEORGE: Right.

QUESTION: In the violence-prone area is there a strong concern among the boys, young men about being called a coward or a punk or a . . .

GEORGE: It depends on who's doing the calling. Those are terms that are commonly used in certain areas, certain cliques, certain communities. So if I'm associated with you, with others in a similar area, or the same area and tend to refer to you periodically as a punk, then you wouldn't get so uptight that you'd want to go home or go someplace and get a gun and come back and shoot me merely because I decided to call you a punk. That's an accepted term in certain areas. As I said it depends on who's saying it. If you're Joe Blow from the northside and I'm on the southside and you're white and I'm black and you come over there and call me a punk then it becomes a different situation.

QUESTION: Did the same kind of thing carry on over into the institution, would you say?

GEORGE: Yes, it's been my experience in talking to people that they have a lopsided concept regarding incarceration and offenders, ex-offenders. But people tend to forget that being incarcerated in an institution and your movement and behavior is limited, nevertheless that fact remains that it is a society. There are rules in this society. They might not be the same rules as in the open society. They're going to be modified to a great extent in a closed society, in order to exist. But those are similar rules, more or less. I'm accustomed to going out on a Friday night in the streets in the open society. I'm accustomed to dropping in certain clubs, dropping by a certain lady's house, associating with certain associates. OK? In a closed society Friday comes you can't do that association in a physical sense but you can do it in a vicarious sense. You tend to more thinking, wondering, participating vicariously during the weekend, Friday, Saturday, Sunday, than we'd normally do from Monday to Friday.

QUESTION: Would the violence route be a way to go in the institution? Knocking people around as a way of making it?

GEORGE: That does go on. You've got men that do time conservatively and you've got men that are very aggressive in doing time. They are radicals, extremely radical in terms of doing time. Not political radicals just radical in terms of behavior. But some are institutionalized and some are not institutionalized. There are those who accept what is as opposed to changing it and if you do any changing you do it gradually and reluctantly. In short, don't rock the boat. And radicalism you turn the damn boat over, tear it up, and build a new one. We characterize and classify people in institutions just as we do in this society. Lower class, middle class, upper middle class, it's just the same. A white-collar job in the institution is the same as having a white-collar job out here. You get white-collar jobs in there. The only difference is we don't wear the white collar. There are job classifications inside.

QUESTION: What did you do inside?

GEORGE: I guess you'd say I had one of the white-collar jobs. I was . . . I did a lot of clerical work. That was a good job inside the institution.

QUESTION: Is it mostly the older guys who do that, I mean, those serving long terms?

GEORGE: No, you couldn't restrict it to those doing extremely long sentences, as opposed to doing short sentences. I guess it's the frame of mind a person is in, the pattern he sets for himself, the image he projects.

QUESTION: You started talking about rehabilitation in prison earlier. Would you say any more about that?

GEORGE: The only rehabilitation that takes place is within. It has to be within. You know the officials of an institution, the concerned people can assist in bringing about this change but in the final analysis it's left up to the person. You provide certain assistance, certain services that will enable him to make these changes. No one person in an institution, or staff personnel, can bring about this change without the man or woman's consent. You can lock him up, throw away the key, treat him as cruel as you possibly can, and if he's determined not to change, then you're not going to change him. He can suppress his hostility and might come out and kill five people as opposed to robbing a store this time. That's all the frustration and hostility within him. It's all buried more or less. It wasn't dealt with in his initial incarceration, it was made worse. Essentially what you're doing is letting out a person who is far worse than previously. But we all jump on this rehabilitation bandwagon.

DISCUSSION

Studies reveal that homicides do not occur randomly throughout urban communities but occur predominantly in low-income black areas. The areas are also characterized by dense populations, overcrowding, and physical deterioration. The tavern where George's offense took place was located in just such a section. Each homicide is unique but the studies cited above indicate a number of common characteristics that were also part of this particular situation. The offender and victim were lower-strata black males; offenders were generally between 20–30; George was 19. Most homicides occur on weekends between 8 P.M. and 3 A.M.; George's crime occurred early on a Saturday morning between 12:30 and 12:45 A.M. Wolfgang noted that alcohol was present in 64 percent of homicide occurrences. It was also part of George's offense. He and his associates were drinking while waiting for the tavern to close. Too, as in other homicides, George had a prior juvenile record and reported that he was involved with other crimes at the time of his conviction for murder. This particular offense is also similar to the general pattern in that the offender and victim did know each other and the homicide was the result of an altercation. George's recall of the episode was somewhat hazy, perhaps because it happened so long ago. But it is possible that the crime may have been victim-precipitated. He states that the man who was killed induced his own death through initial menacing actions or by striking the first blow, and then by drawing his gun and firing it.

The explanations for high homicide rates are primarily middle-range generalizations rather than comprehensive ones. In the conflict perspective, which aspires to a more comprehensive explanation, there is a promise of placing these middle-range explanations into a broader structural context. The inequalities of power, wealth, and authority generate disorganized areas with high homicide rates. But in the conflict account these areas are not something that occurs fortuitously in the struggle for space and sustenance as the ecologists would have it. The struggle for space is not independent of the struggle for power, prestige, and material well-being in the society at large. Disorganized areas are the end result of the clash of real social interests, not the natural outgrowth of unplanned competition. A conflict approach challenges the ecologist's view of the city as an impersonal sieve which selects out peoples, populations, and functions and locates them in specific areas. It challenges Darwinian notions about the selection of the naturally superior in more favorable locations and social positions and the inferior in disorganized areas.

At the middle range of explanation three perspectives compete for acceptance, each of which may be valid, each of which could be incorporated into a broader conflict view. These three are the subculture of violence, the lack of external restraint, and the absence of legitimate opportunities. These latter two explanations may actually be combined. In the subculture-of-violence explanation, group traditions are the cause of high rates of homicide in those neighborhoods where proviolence values hold sway. The explanation does not purport to explain the genesis of these values but they can be viewed as the end product of intergroup conflict, or of rapid social change. The external restraint explanation argues that it is not proviolence values that cause high homicide rates but the inadequacy of social control. Social organization is inadequate in generating commitment to antiviolence values which all cultures share. Opportunity theory situates the impact of larger social structures in particular milieus where certain learning structures—differential association—exist that socialize young men into a reactive defiant pattern. This is Cloward and Ohlin's disorganized slum where there is an absence of legitimate or illegitimate opportunities, and fighting gangs abound. Opportunities for recognition of any kind are in short supply so some young men seek it by their assaultive behavior.

Which of the explanations seem most appropriate to George's situation? He recognized the existence of violence-prone people but was not prepared to put this forward as an explanation of homicide. He felt that there were violent-prone people in and out of prisons and that this characteristic was not related to murder. He did not define himself as a violent person nor did he view his activity as a way of gaining status among peers who valued assaultive behavior. He saw his activity as a way of making out, he didn't want the killing to occur and saw it as the outcome of a situation he couldn't control.

The area in which the homicide occurred was a disorganized slum much like the one Shaw and others have described. When asked about violent-prone areas George replied emphatically that they existed and that they generated violence. His common-sense explanation underlined the fact that the economic situation was the fundamental causal variable. In low-income areas opportunities are restricted and the frustration quotient is high. This facilitates violence.

There are two explanations compatible with George's account—one on the absence of external restraint in the community where the murder occurred, and one related to opportunity structures. No detailed account is given of what kind of social organization existed but the area is un-structured and unstable, that is, institutional fabric of the community was meager, disconnected, and a high turnover of population, all contributing to disorganization. The community's wherewithal to socialize its young people was quite limited. But the opportunity-structure explanation seems most congruent with George's account. George underlined the frustration of young men who could not find jobs. This led to aggression. At one point he states that violence is related to the economic situation: ". . . you can't get around it. If the economic situation is better the vio-lence subsides, because the frustration level subsides." This observation directly contradicts Henry and Short's data which showed black homicide rates *decreasing* during periods of business contraction.

The subculture-of-violence thesis seems inappropriate in this instance though it was developed precisely to explain this kind of homicide. George resisted the idea that there were group traditions of violence which give prestige to the assaultive person. He states that everyone needs recognition and that people get it in different ways. The questions about a warrior code among young black males and the fear of being called a coward drew blank responses from George. He bristled at several points in the interview when the subculture-of-violence thesis was put to him. It was as if the interviewer were asking, "Why are young black males so violent?" He responded as if the subculture-of-violence explana-tion was a racial theory reborn in modern anthropological language. His response was that violence was a normal reaction for all men under specific conditions whatever their subculture. The policy implications of the subculture-of-violence theory are substantially the same as Miller's lower-class culture explanation. The violence then in this formulation is not related to structural features such as the absence of stable employ-ment for males, but to the internal deficiences of the culture.

QUESTIONS FOR FURTHER DISCUSSION

1. If we were to accept George's explanation of the cause of homicide what steps could the community take to reduce its incidence?

2. How important would you say the threat of the death penalty was in influencing George's behavior either before or after the homicide?

3. If you were in George's shoes what defense would you make to the charge of second-degree murder?

4. What are the arguments pro and con for paroling those convicted of homicide sooner than is usually done?

5. How would a conflict and consensus perspective interpret this series of events and what further information would each seek?

6. Earlier Ball-Rokeach suggested that violence might be more plausibly linked to factors like access to weapons, alcohol, population density, or level of intergroup conflict. What other factors suggested by George's case might be significant or worth further exploration?

SUMMARY

The earlier questions related to whether crime was something really "out there" or whether it was simply a label affixed by official agencies quite independently of what the labeled one had done, can be raised about violent personal crime. The answer must be that it is both an interaction between behavior and status. Not only is there greater community consensus about the seriousness of violent personal crime, but there is also less ambiguity about whether it really took place. The killing of one human being by another is objectively observable and all would agree that it is a violation. The role of the criminal justice system is more reactive than proactive in this kind of situation. The initiative official agencies exercise is considerably less than in the case of public drunkenness. There is still considerable discretion that can be utilized but more so by the prosecutor and judge than by the police. The prosecutor may decide to go for first-degree murder if he feels he can prove his case or he may reduce the charge to second-degree murder or manslaughter. In short, the joint production of the status "murderer" is usually the result of objectively observable behavior on the one hand and strong official reaction on the other.

The situation of assault is similar to that of homicide, though its visibility is considerably less. Official reaction cannot be mobilized unless the crime is known. Once a complaint has been made and the machinery set in motion, then the imposition of the status "assaultist" is the result of the violent behavior of the one so charged and the official reaction to it.

The situation is much more ambiguous and complex in forcible rape. But here, as with homicide and assault, once it is reported and established to have taken place, then the production of the status "rapist" is similar to that of the other two—in short, it is a joint production. The situation is basically similar in property crime, the topic of Chapter 10.

10

conventional and professional crime

Conventional professional crime refers basically to crimes against property. There is widespread consensus that this kind of criminality is serious. It is similar to violent personal crime in the sense that it is not "created" by control agencies. The behavior to which the enforcement apparatus reacts may be generated by larger structural causes but is most certainly not produced by police activity. Hence it is difficult to take the position that the imposition of the status "robber" or "burglar" occurs only because of who the offender is, independent of what he has actually done.

There is an abundant literature that attests to the fact that patterns of larceny, burglary, and robbery function as direct behavior systems. They are sufficiently well organized that they can be pursued as a way of life. There are other behavior systems also that violate the law of theft—taking and carrying away goods from the possession of another without the owner's consent, such as confidence games, pickpocketing, shoplifting, forgery, and counterfeiting. But rather than deal with each of these patterns in detail this chapter will focus on the conventional crimes of theft: burglary, larceny, and robbery, with specific attention to the latter.

These offenses have been regarded as crimes for centuries but the punishment accorded offenders has fluctuated widely from medieval amputation of the right hand or execution, to placing the thief under community surveillance as is done in some socialist societies. Prisons in the United States are primarily used to punish these garden variety offenders. The persons who are convicted of these crimes are relatively unskilled, poorly paid for their work, and engaged in violative behavior on a part-time basis. The offenses are uncomplicated and usually committed alone or with one other person. Robbery of a liquor store or a gas station is an illustration.

There is some discussion among criminologists about whether robbery should be classified as a violent crime or a property crime. Robbery is officially defined as stealing or taking anything of value from the care, custody, or control of a person by force or violence or by threat, such as strong-arm robbery, stickups, armed robbery, assault to rob, and at attempt to rob.[1] The presence of or the threat of violence leads some to classify robbery as a personal crime. However, enforcers classify robbery as a property crime. Conklin's study of robbery led him to the conclusion that the average robber is a violent criminal since he has committed more violent crimes than property ones. "The robbery offender should be seen as one who often employs criminal violence in a nonutilitarian manner."[2]

By looking at robbery as a property crime, however, we can note that it is rational and calculative; it requires some decisions relating to a need for money that can't be satisfied legitimately, selection of the target based on the amount of money available and the risk of arrest, and how the robbery should be carried out. The rational-calculative component in robbery is a sufficient justification for interpreting it basically as a property crime though its potential for violence would also justify its being classified as a personal crime. This is because robbery is in fact both a property and a personal crime.

The element of actual violence in the commission of a robbery is relatively rare. The use of a weapon seems to reduce the incidence of violence. Feeney and Weir found that 66 percent of the victims of an unarmed robbery were injured compared to 17 percent who were victims of armed robbery.[3] Conklin also found that the less dangerous the weapon the more likely there was to be some injury.[4] Robbers who are likely to assault their victims look much like Wolfgang's subcultural assaultists: they are young, black, and usually perform the robbery on a street. The robbers were relatively inexperienced and little planning was involved in their crimes. The robber who is likely to use a gun is less disadvantaged than his unarmed counterpart and is generally older. Conklin suggests that the weapon serves some instrumental functions: it creates a buffer zone between the offender and victim; it intimidates the victim, making him more likely to cooperate; it shows that the robber means business; and it insures his escape.

---

[1] Federal Bureau of Investigation, *Uniform Crime Reports* (1974), pp. 15, 55.
[2] John E. Conklin, *Robbery and the Criminal Justice System* (Philadelphia: Lippincott, 1972), p. 105.
[3] Floyd Feeney and Adrianne Weir, "The Prevention and Control of Robbery," *Criminology*, 13 (May 1975), 102–5.
[4] Conklin, *Robbery*, p. 116.

EXTENT OF CONVENTIONAL
AND PROFESSIONAL CRIME

Data from the Uniform Crime Reports indicate that of conventional crimes known to the police, larceny-theft is most frequent, burglary is second, auto theft third, and robbery fifth.[5] Larceny-theft is the unlawful taking or stealing of property without force, violence, or fraud. It includes shoplifting, pickpocketing, purse snatching, theft from autos, thefts of auto parts and accessories, bicycle thefts, etc. It does not include embezzlement, "con" games, forgery, worthless checks, or auto theft (see Table 10-1).

The President's Commission estimated the economic cost of conventional crime in terms of losses to individuals.[6] Burglary was first, malicious mischief second, larceny third, auto theft fourth, and robbery fifth. The commission was careful to note, however, that these estimates must be put into perspective. When compared to the economic losses from such white-collar crime as consumer fraud, price fixing, and tax evasion, the conventional street crimes fade into insignificance. White-collar crimes are many times greater than all street crimes combined (see Table 10-2).

A comparison of officially recorded rates for conventional crimes with the National Opinion Research Center survey suggests that all but auto theft are underreported.[7] The robbery rate per 100,000 of the population

TABLE 10-1 Frequency of Major Crimes (1975)

	Number	*Rate per 100,000 inhabitants*
Larceny-Theft	5,997,700	2,804.8
Burglary	3,252,100	1,525.9
Auto theft	1,000,500	469.4
Aggravated assault	484,710	227.4
Robbery	464,970	218.2
Forcible rape	56,090	26.3
Murder	20,510	9.6

Source: *Uniform Crime Reports* (1976), p. 1.

[5] Federal Bureau of Investigation, *Uniform Crime Reports* (1976), p. 11.
[6] President's Commission on Law Enforcement and the Administration of Justice, *Task Force Report, Crime and Its Impact* (Washington, D.C.: Government Printing Office, 1967), pp. 44–49.
[7] Phillip H. Ennis, The President's Commission on Law Enforcement and the Administration of Justice, *Criminal Victimization in the United States: A Report of a National Survey:* Field Surveys II (Washington, D.C.: Government Printing Office, 1967).

TABLE 10-2   The Economic Cost of Crime (1965)

White-collar crime	Annual economic cost in millions of dollars
Embezzlement	200
Fraud	1,350
Tax fraud	100
Forgery	80
Total	1,730
Conventional crime	
Robbery	27
Burglary	251
Auto theft	140
Larceny ($50 and over)	190
Total	608

Source: President's Commission on Law Enforcement and the Administration of Justice, *Task Force Report, Crime and Its Impact* (Washington, D.C.: Government Printing Office, 1967), pp. 44–49.

is half again larger than that officially reported, burglary is three times greater, and larceny is a little over twice as great.

It is difficult to estimate the extent of professional crime. What differentiates this pattern is its degree of organization and possibilities for lifelong employment. Legal codes do not distinguish this kind of offense from other crimes. Crimes such as confidence games are usually prosecuted under fraud statutes. Recently there has been a movement to regulate professionally executed crimes more closely. It is a federal crime if a confidence man induces his victim to cross a state line, and the U.S. Postal Service can have confidence men prosecuted for using the mail to defraud.

The Uniform Crime Reports of the FBI includes a section dealing with less serious crime than the part one offenses of murder, forcible rape, aggravated assault, and so on. Of the 22 offenses listed in their part two crimes, only three—fraud; buying, receiving, or possessing stolen property; and forgery and counterfeiting—have any relation to professional crime. The FBI figures report only the *arrests* for part two offenses, not

TABLE 10-3   Total Arrests for Fraud, Forgery-Counterfeiting, and Offenses Involving Stolen Property (1975)

Crime	Total arrests
Fraud	171,300
Forgery and Counterfeiting	67,100
Stolen Property	122,000

crimes known to the police. Despite the fact that fraud is widespread among the middle class it usually is not reflected in police statistics (see Table 10-3).

The total number of individuals arrested for part one offenses in 1975 was 2,298,900; those arrested for the above crimes numbered 360,400.[8]

Robbery

The Uniform Crime Reports for 1973 provides us with an overview of reported robberies. They reveal that it is characteristically a large city crime (occurring eight times more often there than in rural areas). About 50 percent of the robberies were committed on the street and 50 percent in commercial establishments. The street robberies tended to be unarmed (strong arm) and the commercial ones armed. Robbery offenders who were arrested tended to be young; over three-fourths of them were under 25 years of age. Unlike homicide, aggravated assault, and rape, robbery tends to be interracial—young black males victimizing older white males whom they do not know. Unlike homicide, also, the extent of victim precipitation tends to be low (8 percent for robbery compared to 22 percent for homicide). There seems to be a trend for armed robbery to increase faster than strong-armed robbery (the overall percentage increase for robbery from 1968 to 1973 was 46 percent). Proportionally more robberies are reported to the police than burglaries but there is a reason to believe that the official figures underestimate the extent of professional robbery. Only 27 percent of reported robberies resulted in arrest. It seems safe to conclude that those arrested are the less sophisticated.

The most salient characteristics of those convicted of *conventional* offenses is their low economic status. Typically they come from urban lower-class areas where patterns of adult criminality are highly visible and attractive. Family backgrounds generally reveal a pattern found in lower-class neighborhoods—some instability due to the employment status of the father, occasionally a female head of household—but the family background does not differentiate between those who gravitate to law-abiding patterns versus those who do not.

The President's Commission summarized the kind of neighborhoods conventional criminals are likely to come from:

> Study after study in city after city in all regions of the country have traced the variations in the rates for these crimes. The results with monotonous regularity, show that the offenses, the victims, and the

[8] *Uniform Crime Reports* (1976), p. 179.

offenders are found most frequently in the poorest and most deteriorated and socially disorganized areas of cities.[9]

The *professional* criminal is classified separately from the conventional criminal because of the degree of skill involved and the more elaborate career. Professional crime is best illustrated by thefts of large sums of money through the use of skillful, nonviolent methods. There are a number of patterns that have been professionalized: shoplifting, pickpocketing, sneak thieving, working confidence games, robbery, burglary, forgery, and extortion. These crimes are all violations of the law of theft but not all are specifically recognized in the criminal law. Violations are usually prosecuted under the traditional laws that regulate property.

Professional theft recruits its members from all levels of society. Its members are not typically lower class. The most that can be said of them is that they are most susceptible to those values in American society that put a premium on getting something for nothing—sharp business practices and unethical conduct of various sorts. Since professional criminals are skilled in avoiding detection or incarceration the data on their social characteristics are meager. Nothing is distinctive about family background that would differentiate a budding professional criminal from his law-abiding counterpart.

GROUP SUPPORT FOR CONVENTIONAL AND PROFESSIONAL CRIME

The neighborhood from which conventional criminals come provides a certain amount of support, for whatever reason, for stealing. Most adult conventional criminals exhibit juvenile backgrounds of predatory gang behavior. As adults they accumulate extensive records and institutional commitments. Gibbons suggests that because of the low degree of skill involved in the criminal activity the risks of apprehension, conviction, and incarceration are high.[10] Because of the extensive amount of time spent in prison conventional offenders are likely to have a criminal self-concept. The conventional criminal seems to withdraw from his crime career by early middle age either because of the increasing risk or amount of energy required or the development of family commitments.

For professional crime to exist, a complex pattern of relationships has

[9] President's Commission on Law Enforcement and the Administration of Justice, *The Challenge of Crime in a Free Society* (Washington, D.C.: Government Printing Office, 1967).

[10] Don C. Gibbons, *Society, Crime and Criminal Careers*, 3rd ed. (Englewood Cliffs, N.J.: Prentice-Hall, 1977), p. 295.

to be worked out between offenders and key sectors of conventional society like policemen, tipsters, cab drivers, and lawyers. This suggests that there is a correspondence between professional criminal behavior and legitimate behavior, if only the agreement on the importance of skill and steady employment. Professionals enter their criminal careers later than their conventional crime counterparts, and come from occupational backgrounds that are marginal to both conventional society and a criminal underworld (salesmen, hotel clerks, bellboys).[11]

The career, compared to other kinds of criminal careers, is unusually long, possibly because few are ever arrested or serve time in prison. The skills required for professional theft usually involve some kind of behavior system and contact with peers who provide tutelage. The professional thief regards himself as just that, though he may have other names for it. He makes a sharp distinction between himself and part-time or amateur criminals.

The high status of professional criminals is indicated by the special treatment they receive from police and court officials. They are usually able to make arrangements with public officials that enable them to avoid conviction. Hence legal processing tends to be absent or relatively lenient. Social reactions to professional crime tend to be apathetic because of its low visibility. This is in sharp contrast to the reaction to conventional crime where societal and legal reactions are harsh and penalties severe.

ISSUES IN THE STUDY OF PROPERTY CRIME

There are no clear-cut issues in the literature of conventional and professional crime analogous to the death penalty argument in violent personal crime. The issues tend to be somewhat technical, like how best to classify the various kinds of property offenses. Substantive issues are related to how best reduce the incidence of property crime (better security measures versus the elimination of the criminogenic milieu), or how best resocialize offenders. Both conflict and consensus theorists would agree that one overriding issue is the lack of uniformity in laws relating to theft and their implementation. The conflict perspective would see the situation as an inherent feature of any system of inequality; the consensus explanation would interpret the problem as one of "culture lag" destined to disappear once community sentiment crystallized more fully on the seriousness of theft by middle-class offenders.

[11] Edwin H. Sutherland, *The Professional Thief* (Chicago: University of Chicago Press, 1937).

EXPLANATIONS OF CONVENTIONAL
AND PROFESSIONAL CRIME

The urban neighborhoods from which conventional criminals come are disorganized slums where legal as well as illegal opportunities are in short supply. The opportunity structure approach elaborated by Cloward and Ohlin seems to explain this pattern most adequately. Adult conventional criminals repeat the patterns of delinquency begun in adolescence. The adolescent pattern is one of delinquent theft. Boys characteristically engage in property theft as well as vandalism. The illegal activity takes place with one or two other persons—sometimes with a sibling, sometimes with a whole group of boys. The peers of the budding conventional criminal at this age are all delinquent. The self-concept of the adolescent is a delinquent one. He sees himself as skillful in delinquent activity, as cool, as self-reliant, and as an operator. The attitudes he picks up toward authority evidence a great deal of hostility. There is also a negative attitude toward conventional work. It is viewed as dull, boring, and low paying. The career of the adolescent involves increasing entanglement with the law in more serious crimes of theft. The extent to which an adult career develops from it is dependent on the extent to which there is contact with adult carriers of criminal norms. Irwin has characterized these habitual thieves as "state raised youth" with long criminal records.[12] The classic study of a state-raised youth is Shaw's *Jackroller*, which portrays a young man who tried to make his living by stealing from drunks.[13] As an adolescent he was in and out of reform school and graduated eventually to adult prison.

The explanations developed to account for *professional* crime are less comprehensive than opportunity theory. The basic explanation is Sutherland's differential association. Sutherland in his interpretation of the document written by Chick Conwell, a professional thief, has summarized its characteristics.[14] Professional theft requires a skill or complex of techniques for committing the crime; it has high status in the world of crime, a common set of shared values, beliefs, and attitudes, association with other professional criminals to the exclusion of the law abiding, and an organization which provides information and assistance for carrying out criminal activities. The adult interested in a career in professional

---

[12] John Irwin, *The Felon* (Englewood Cliffs, N.J.: Prentice-Hall, 1967).
[13] Clifford Shaw, *The Jackroller: A Delinquent Boy's Own Story* (Chicago: University of Chicago Press, 1930).
[14] Sutherland, *The Professional Thief.*

theft must first internalize its norms. Since the professional as far as we can determine is not distinguished by social class or neighborhood of origin, it is unclear from differential association theory where the criminal norms come from. Taft has attempted to identify criminogenic features of American society such as acceptance of quasi-criminal exploitation and the individualist ethos that play a role in professional crime.[15] He suggests that the professional thief's view of the world and philosophy are very similar to the laissez-faire businessman's. Yet, not all who share these values go on to become professional thieves. A budding professional must be recognized by other thieves as talented. Without this recognition and selection for further tutelage no career is possible.

Another explanation invoked for the conventional criminal is the societal reaction or labeling theory.[16] By virtue of living in a particular neighborhood with a low degree of privacy and a great amount of police surveillance, adolescents are much more likely to come to police attention. Relatively minor infractions are dealt with harshly. The impact of official agency reaction is to push the youngster further into delinquent activity. At some point the boy is incarcerated and this begins a long period of movement in and out of correctional facilities on into adulthood. More imaginative programs of diversion earlier in his career, it is suggested, would contain behavior problems at the local level and not create a large group of offenders who would later fill our prisons.

Einstadter in his study of career armed-robbers found Becker's model of sequential involvement relevant: his respondents recounted that they were in a situation where the bonds tying them to the larger community were weakened, thus freeing them to consider a variety of options.[17] Neutralization of societal demands plus the need for money led to experimentation with various illegal alternatives; and the process not only effectively closed off any conventional options but built up a commitment to the robbery partnership. Einstadter's approach could be characterized as an interactionist one, hence his concern with social psychological processes. But he also describes various robbery styles: the ambush, the selective raid, and the planned operation. The styles are differentiated on the basis of the amount of planning involved. The *ambush* involves the least amount of planning and is characterized by surprise. The target is random. This is characteristically the pattern preferred by the nonprofessional. Professionals are loath to engage in ambushes and only do so in emergency situations. The *selective raid* is not impulsive or random but is

[15] Donald R. Taft and Ralph W. England, Jr., *Criminology,* 4th ed. (New York: Macmillan, 1964).

[16] Irwin's "State Raised Youth" and Shaw's *Jackroller* seem best explained by the labeling perspective.

[17] Werner Einstadter, "The Social Organization of Armed Robbery," *Social Problems,* 17 (Summer 1969), 64–82.

designed to get enough capital to set up the *planned operation* that the professional desires. Einstadter also notes that there is a well-developed ideology that has been built up to justify robbery. The ideology has its roots in Restoration England and the frontier of the United States.

A more systematic kind of robber typology is proposed by Conklin, who bases his classification on motivation, nature of techniques used, and the degree of commitment to the career.[18] He came up with the professional robber, the opportunist robber, the addict robber, and the alcoholic robber. His analysis is basically compatible with Einstadter's, where the crucial distinction is between professional and nonprofessional. But Conklin is also interested in accounting for the tremendous increase in robbery rates in Boston and other large cities between 1960 and 1969. He rejects a number of explanations as inadequate: that the rise in rates is actually due to better reporting, to changes in the administration of criminal justice, changing age distribution, increased opportunities for crime, increased drug use, or increasing level of societal violence. He relates increasing robbery rates to the *improved* social conditions of the 1960s. He suggests that as black Americans increasingly improve their social conditions they are more likely to commit robbery (the proportion of black robbers increased from 56 percent in 1960 to 80 percent in 1969). His explanation for the phenomenon is *relative deprivation*. Absolute improvement in life situation led to increased expectations of equality with whites that were not realized. One consequence, among others, is increased robbery. His argument seems plausible and addresses the phenomenon of robbery as one aspect of abundance that has been previously left unexamined. His scheme is similar to the relative frustration and lack of external restraint explanations of personal violence discussed in the last chapter.

MIKE: A ROBBER

The excerpted life history that follows is drawn from a lengthy interview covering three major periods in Mike's life. The first part included family background and biographical data related to growing up. The second described his entry into armed robbery and the sequence of events leading to his apprehension. The third covered conviction and prison experience. Only excerpts from the second part of the life history are included here.

Mike was the only child of middle-class parents raised in a middle-

[18] John E. Conklin, *Robbery and the Criminal Justice System* (Philadelphia: Lippincott, 1972).

sized coastal city. The account of his growing up revealed nothing unusual for a boy of his class and social setting. He reported no experience of deprivation, either financial or psychological. He did well in school in those subjects that demanded precise thinking and was early drawn to mathematics. He did poorly in those subjects that didn't interest him; hence his high school record was spotty. He lived a law-abiding life while growing up, had a handful of friends but no delinquent peers. He could not recall any delinquent episodes, even relatively minor ones like cheating in school. He enlisted in the army after completing high school and served part of his duty in the Far East. While in the army he was aware of black market operations but reported that he did not participate in them nor had he any interest in them. He was discharged after three years in the armed forces and returned to live with his family for a period of several months until the money he had accumulated in service ran out.

QUESTION: Can you tell me a little bit about this period?

MIKE: I found myself rather desperately in need of a job so I went out and got some sort of job that didn't suit me and I didn't stay at it very long. I don't recall the exact sequence of these jobs. I know that I took a job with Standard Oil Stations and they sent me to a training station and I enjoyed this very much. They showed films on how batteries were made and tires, and so it was an educational experience and as is usual when learning how something is done, I liked it but as soon as I got out into a regular station and was dealing with customers and was hot and dirty for eight hours, I became quite disgusted and eventually just walked off this job. I had several such jobs, until finally the following summer I worked as a substitute bellhop at a hotel, and again I didn't like this any better than the others but at least there was a termination date to sort of stick until I reached it and that wasn't too far away, so I did. That brought me up very close to the start of the fall school season when I decided that I would go to junior college. I worked everything out and the government was going to reimburse me for the amount of $130 a month which I was sure I could live on and so everything looked like it was going to be fine. So, I quit, except that as it turned out it took some time for the government to process my request for this money and while I was going to receive it as of the first day of school, it was going to be about ninety days before I was actually getting it and I suddenly found myself in a position without any money and I was just quite discouraged about many things and it happened at this time that I would still once in a while in the evening go back to this hotel and watch the magazine stand—a young couple owned it and they would like to go out occasionally—and from the time I was working as a bellhop, I had come to know them pretty well—I would go in and watch it for a couple hours and do my homework and sell an occasional magazine and a candy bar—and while doing this I got to talking with a new bellhop and we became pretty good friends. It's always been the case that people sort of talk freely to me, so very shortly he mentioned that he had a criminal background and that he was currently an escapee from prison and that he hadn't done anything in two years and had married a woman who had a couple children and subsequently they had had another child, so there were three children and he had taken this job in desperation. He was having trouble feeding himself, this woman, and the three children and the job wasn't paying enough to do so—and so we used to stand around by the magazine stand there and gripe about our financial difficulties. And somehow or other the idea came up to do something active about it—and that resulted in the series of robberies that I mentioned earlier. So that takes me from the time I got out of the service until the time of the crime.

QUESTION: About the criminal activity itself, then—would you tell me in detail how you went about it?

MIKE: Once we decided to embark upon criminal acts my partner suggested a burglary—apparently he felt most at home doing burglaries—and so we set out to do a burglary and I felt very uneasy, particularly while we were in the house. We went through one house, we didn't get anything of any great value—and the whole time we were there I felt so thoroughly uneasy that I knew that I couldn't do that anymore. The one burglary we committed, people actually entered the house while we were there. So it developed that he had a book of payroll checks that had come out of a burglary somebody else had committed. He had access to these and so we set out passing checks and I wasn't very good at this. I felt ah much the same that I felt when I tried various sales jobs. I can't work as a salesman. This effort to go in and persuade somebody to buy something is so emotionally irritating that I simply can't do it, at least I'm not effective at it. I felt the same thing in trying to pass checks. I noticed at the time the similarity in the two—but again I found this emotionally disturbing and so we purchased pistols and initiated a series of armed robberies and in this I felt much easier.

QUESTION: How about the payroll checks?

MIKE: The checks—yes—we passed a number of them and ah made quite a bit of money. Interestingly enough I passed one where the fellow had been hit with a phony payroll check just a week previously and I walked up to him with my cart of goods and asked if he could cash my payroll check and he said he couldn't because of what had happened and explained it and so I listened to the explanation of this with my mouth hanging open. I said, "Well, gee, in that circumstance I could certainly understand it. Would you mind putting the basket of stuff behind the counter and then tomorrow I could cash the check and stop by at noon and not have to pick out everything again." This plea for saving my later time and effort touched him so that he cashed the check and I felt pretty terrible afterwards—but, ah—

QUESTION: Were these checks cashed in grocery stores—generally?

MIKE: Supermarkets—and later when we perpetrated armed robberies, for the most part these too were in supermarkets.

QUESTION: What was the thinking behind that—that a great deal of cash usually is in supermarkets?

MIKE: There's usually quite a bit of money. There is usually quite a bit of disorganized activity to cover your particular activity. There is very little danger of ah being shot in the store. Many stores will have a lookout arrangement and an armed person at the lookout arrangement from, say, a walled mezzanine or something. In a liquor store or something of this nature a robber is very apt to be shot from concealment. There are enough people moving about in a supermarket that this is not very apt to happen. Your safest bet is probably a supermarket. To indicate the degree to which a supermarket is safe I took one not too far from here on a Saturday night at about 7:30. The supermarket was around the corner from the police station. I took it alone, had my car out in front, no driver in the car, no one with me in the store and I took all the front money, that is, the money in the registers and left town with no difficulty.

QUESTION: What time of the day is best?

MIKE: We didn't ever develop any real pattern relative to time. We took one early in the morning when they were unloading supply trucks in the back, shortly after the time that we felt the safe would be open on its time lock. We've taken others in the late evening. Really there was, so far as we determined by operating it, no reason for taking it at one time of the day rather than at another—

QUESTION: Just as long as there were other people in the store?

MIKE: Yes, we preferred to take action either when there were other people in the store, which would be during operating hours or before they would have occasion to expect anyone to be able to enter and set up a defense. We took the one supermarket early in the morning when they were unloading trucks. We felt that it was improbable that anybody would be around inside at all. And therefore if there were a mezzanine with a firing position, it would not be manned. We were literally there when there were only two or three people in the store with the employees grouped at this back door unlocking the boxes, and unloading trucks. For the most part in establishing this sort of thing, it's just a case of being aware of the physical setup of the place you're going to take and using common sense.

QUESTION: What was the usual reaction of the cashier when you took a place?

MIKE: Most people are fairly cooperative. We used a service revolver, which is quite impressive to look at. You can look down the bore from several feet away and see the bullet. And it was rarely necessary to draw the gun. We would, simply by opening our coat—oh, we'd usually wear suits—by opening our coat we'd show that we were armed. We would inform the individual that we were professional thieves and to the extent that it could be avoided no one was going to be hurt and that there was little chance of anyone getting hurt by accident and that as long as they cooperated with us they were quite safe. I can recall no incidents where anybody became panicky. In one instance, a clerk happened to have a can of vegetables or fruit or something in his hand and raised his hand as if he might have considered throwing this but by cocking the hammer of the revolver, which makes a thunderous clunk, I was able to halt his action. At no time were we ever required to fire a round. At no time did we encounter any police officers while in the near vicinity of the place being robbed. This was partly due to the fact that we made it a point to become aware of the patrols in the area. All in all, the thing operated fairly smoothly, fairly safely, simply by being thoroughly aware of the situation before initiating it.

QUESTION: Would you concentrate on particular neighborhoods or towns?

MIKE: No, we operated throughout the central and southern [part of this state].

QUESTION: You stayed away from the area in which your family lived?

MIKE: No, we didn't. We pulled several jobs in this area. We weren't thinking in terms—incidentally I read the first chapter of that book of yours, *The Professional Thief,* while I was in the office and I found it amusing. There may have been people in the twenties that operated like that, I don't know. This business of having a place where you live and operate out of certainly didn't occur to us. We weren't thinking in terms of preserving any sort of past. If you had a past to preserve—say you owned property in an area, you might want to avoid that area—but we certainly found no reason to avoid this area.

QUESTION: And no fear that you would be identified?

MIKE: No. I should mention, however, we took some precautions not to be identified. While in a store we used whistle signals rather than voices. We used various forms of disguise that were of a positive rather than a negative nature. That is, rather than hiding features which a sharp person can spot, say you wear a silk stocking or something—an intelligent person will notice bone structure. We gave them features to identify, thus causing our actual figures to be lost by being on the periphery of interest. My disguise was usually serious burn scars on the face, which I did with greasepaint and colodion and we used costume effectively. When I took that supermarket alone, for instance, I went in dressed completely in black, black trousers and a black shirt to give the people something outstanding to notice, when some thirty minutes later I drove through the roadblock at the outside of town, stopping and chatting with the officer at the roadblock, I put on a white blazer. So by this sort of diversionary tactic we were able to pretty well preclude our being identified.

QUESTION: Were there any reactions from other customers, or the other clerks while you were taking a particular cashier?

MIKE: No, usually people didn't realize what was going on. And when leaving a cashier and going on to the next we would inform them that an outcry made before we had effectively left the area could possibly result in shooting and could possibly result in somebody's death and that the amount of money involved obviously wasn't worth it. When this reasoning is pointed out to them, they were usually in complete agreement. We made it a point not to take money that belonged to anybody. We would never have considered robbing a customer, or, say, taking the clerk's personal money, or holding up a place where the owners were themselves the workers on the spot.

QUESTION: What was the sensation actually when you were taking a place?

MIKE: Beforehand I would feel myself quite nervous, a feeling akin to stage fright and a good deal more intense, probably because I was aware that there was danger involved. However, while actually in the store I felt very little of anything. I was doing a job. I was, for the most part, executing a pretty mechanical process that had been thought out in advance and I was too busy being aware of what was going on around me and of watching everything and of communicating to the clerk and preventing panic, which was really our worst danger. If a clerk should panic and either faint away or run screaming or something, this can precipitate a situation that might be difficult to handle and with the complexity of the things that I had to keep in my awareness and under my control I didn't have time really to feel anything.

QUESTION: How about the sensation after it was all over?

MIKE: Afterwards there would be some reaction. There would be a strong feeling of relief, sometimes a bit of shaking, suppressed reaction coming to the surface. It was never anything terribly strong, probably because for a long while afterwards, that is, until we were quite far away from the scene of the crime geographically, there would be occasion for attention of selection of routes. We usually had alternate routes of travel and we would switch in the middle of routes to other routes and so on. There would be a great deal of attention to the traffic pattern to see if any vehicle stayed with us for an undue length of time and take evasive action if this did occur, so after we were outside of any real danger there was still a period of concentration that would tend to dissipate any reaction. By the time the thing was totally over much of the aftereffect would have already extended itself in this sort of dribbling through the second phase of concentration.

QUESTION: How long would the whole thing last—the initial take —plus the time getting away?

MIKE: Probably never more than a half an hour.

QUESTION: Was there any exhilaration or satisfaction, or depression or anything like that after you were completely free?

MIKE: No, some sense of a job adequately done. Certainly no pride in it as a job, no terrible amount of guilt. We rationalized away what guilt we might have felt by a number of devices—we pointed out to ourselves that the people losing the money would get it back from the insurance company and the insurance company would get value received in front-page advertising. We reminded ourselves that we were actually putting up a lot more in the way of stake than a businessman would. Where he only risks his money, we were risking our lives. We felt really that we were doing the only job that was left to us in the community. The jobs that we'd been able to command in terms of past training and experience were simply not adequate to support ourselves. Consequently, we pretty much approached this activity as a job. We certainly didn't do it for kicks. My partner had ah been in and out of prisons. He knew how unthrilling this whole sort of thing can be. And I didn't find anything particularly thrilling about pointing a gun at anybody. I didn't like it in the service and I didn't like it when I was doing it as a criminal. But I really felt that insofar as I could put my intelligence to work, this was the only thing left to do.

QUESTION: Now there's a certain amount of craft or talent in the sort of thing you described—in taking the supermarkets. I wonder how did you pick this up? Was this something you did research on yourself or was it communicated by your partner?

MIKE: It would actually be a mixture. He had some suggestions based both on direct and indirect past experience. I don't believe he'd ever robbed a supermarket before. He had perpetrated other types of robbery and he knew people who had robbed supermarkets, so some of his suggestions came from direct and indirect past experience, some from his common sense. I contributed from research, and common sense.

QUESTION: About how much money did you take in any one supermarket?

MIKE: About the most we ever got was a couple thousand dollars. Usually we just took the front money. We made no attempt to get at the safe in the back.

QUESTION: How many supermarkets would that mean you'd rob in a month?

MIKE: Well, we did more than we had to to make wages. The whole span of our criminal activities was only a couple months, and altogether there were around 20 robberies. We did quite a bit more than we had to.

QUESTION: How much would you average per month?

MIKE: Oh, gosh, it would be hard to say. We spent it as fast as we got it, for instance, almost literally throwing it away, giving it away. But I would say that average wages at this sort of thing as we were planning to operate when we were well equipped and slowed down a bit, we planned on making about $5000 a month. Course then we wouldn't have to work all year.

QUESTION: You mean you had planned it so far ahead there would be a period of activity followed by leisure?

MIKE: Period of inactivity—

QUESTION: How did this change your style of living—besides the things you've just mentioned—

MIKE: Well, it actually changed it for the worse in terms of my values. As I say I had been going to junior college. I had hoped that this was a way to pick up ah money without expending much time. I had thought that I would continue with my studies and move to a slightly more comfortable quarters and perhaps put some money away for future studies and not stay at this business too long. I found that it was a full-time occupation, that it involved obligations to the people you worked with, which meant giving up on—according to your schedule—things that didn't fit too well. You'd sort of be leaving somebody with something half done, and just generally the commitments were the same that they would be for any profession. So it caused me to give up the plans I'd had before and enter a nomadic sort of life and I didn't care for it too much. My plans then shifted to—well, I'll do this until I have enough money so I can be independent for a number of years and then I will rearrange my life and decide at that time what my future plans are going to be. I sort of postponed planning.

QUESTION: Now you mentioned earlier that you added several other people to your group, friends of your partner. Would you tell me a little about that?

MIKE: Yes, we ran into them where my original partner lived and we had been spending some time down there. He apparently had done time with them and had a fairly high opinion of their potential value. And I thought, well, with four of us, I can start running out squad-training techniques. Some of those I learned in the military and that possibly we could start doing some fairly large things. Because I had been thinking in terms of much larger jobs is probably one of the reasons I did as much time as I did on the first offense. [He was sentenced to five years.] On one job I approached the thing as I would a military problem, I ran general intelligence rather than just the sort of thing that usually in the criminal profession is called casing. My partner had made it a point to become acquainted with and questioned fairly thoroughly, if indirectly, a fellow that worked in the office there [a sports lodge where large sums of money were kept during several weeks of the year]. He was the assistant to the accountant and so we actually knew much of the scheduling of this money and the operation of the lodge and we were going to make our approach by water. And with four of us operating as a commando unit it would have gone quite smoothly. I had introduced such things as the disguise that didn't bear the earmarks of camouflage, whistles, and so forth. But probably armed robbery as an approach to crime is outdated. I think it's a crime that belonged to the twenties and thirties. It's not appropriate now.

QUESTION: What kind would be appropriate?

MIKE: I haven't given a lot of thought to that since I don't intend to go on with a criminal career. But I have a feeling that as our culture becomes more and more dependent upon the movement of information that effective approaches to crime in the future will have to do with the subverting, changing, and cornering of information.

QUESTION: Now in this partnership—when the four of you got together—were you the informal leader or—?

MIKE: Yes, and this is interesting because the other three, of course, had extensive professional criminal pasts, and I didn't seek leadership particularly. Unofficially it was purely a committee action. We would get together and exchange ideas, and officially and unofficially they seemed to just accept my leadership and more and more I would map things out.

QUESTION: You brought to bear your own planning and intellectual resources and so on, what did some of the others bring to it?

MIKE: Primarily past experience. My first partner, I'd say, contributed intellectually, too. He was a fairly brilliant fellow. While in prison he taught himself mechanical engineering, a couple languages, and things of this nature—I would say that he contributed quite adequately at an intellectual level. The other two, primarily for the very short period that they were with us, really just contributed bodies. In other words, I told one of them: "Be at this point and point your gun at these people," and they'd do it.

QUESTION: Did any of your activity involve what is popularly known as the underworld? You indicated there were no fences or anything like that, how about your associates?

MIKE: No, this is another thing I noticed in that book that you had [*The Professional Thief*]—there are people watching other people's operations and asking what town they're out of and this sort of thing. If, in meeting people, I met people that were criminals I didn't know about it. If I had some feeling that their activities were probably illegal—and I would judge by the same clues that, say, a police officer would judge in observing some people—I might actually see somebody committing a crime. If so, I would avoid any contact with those people. After meeting people I would judge by their spending habits, or by other aspects of their behavior that they were involved in criminal activity, in which case I would immediately start extending the distance between us—acquaintanceship dissolved, avoid them—this sort of thing. I think anybody involved in criminal activity that was doing so for monetary rather than for social reasons, and by social reasons I mean he's a member of a gang and is expected to do this or hangs around a pool hall where he's not one of the guys unless he does this—I'd say any criminal that is operating primarily for money would avoid any contact with other criminals simply because it extends his vulnerability. If they're apprehended and you're one of their associates you are very apt to be investigated, and if you're being investigated for something you didn't do it can very easily bring to light something that you have done. So I would say that no professional criminal would knowingly maintain an association with another professional criminal unless they're functioning together. This is, of course, just my guess but it's so solidly supported by reasons for behaving in this way that I'm sure that it's a universal attitude without having actually compared notes with anybody about it.

DISCUSSION

Because of the limited amount of information on professional criminals we don't get any sense of how atypical Mike is. Irwin has noted that the professional thief has good character, rightness, coolness in the face of difficulties, unobtrusiveness, and skill.[19] These characteristics fit our armed robber. But the generalizations that relate to length of career and relatively mild societal reaction upon apprehension do not apply in this instance. Mike's career was relatively brief and his sentence, even though a first offender, quite severe. Mike's partner seemed to be more of a conventional criminal with a history of incarceration as were the other two later partners.

Mike's explanation of how he got into armed robbery suggests a variation of the opportunity structure approach. But it is important to note that the opportunities available become important for Mike only as an adult not as a juvenile. Mike had economic problems generated by the larger community which did not provide employment commensurate with his ability. It channeled him into a marginal low-paying job where he learned what illegal options were open to him. It seems clear in the interview that the decision to experiment with illegal activity was perceived as the only way out. Mike said, "We felt that we were doing the only job left to us in the community—the jobs that we'd been able to command in terms of past training and experience were simply not adequate to support ourselves." From his account, legal means to solve his financial problems were not simply less effective but, under the circumstances, *would not work*. At the same time that he was exercising illegal options Mike was trying to generate a long-range plan—a college educa-

[19] Irwin, *The Felon*.

tion—that would enable him to adopt a legal option. His commitment to robbery was a provisional, temporary thing. At most, he saw it as a career escalator to more conventional endeavors.

It is also worth noting that professional crime like armed robbery adapts to societal changes. Changes in technology or the banking system make some kinds of theft obsolete and increase the risks associated with it. Mike thought that Sutherland's discussion of robbery as linked to a mob was quaint and outdated. By implication he suggests that Sutherland's depiction was historically specific and determined by the character of organized criminal activity related to Prohibition. There was differential association in Mike's career, however. Certain skills must be brought to the commission of a robbery but there was no structure that selected out the more promising thieves and introduced them to further training. The situation of unemployment plus contact with a partner who communicated a set of attitudes as well as some specific plans for getting money was more decisive in Mike's case than was the selection and tutelage by professional thieves. The skills brought to armed robbery, according to Mike, were provided by noncriminal learning structures. His military experience lent itself to the kind of planning required in robbing supermarkets. But the element of improvisation was critical.

The style of career robbery was one that favored the planned operation rather than the ambush which required little or no planning. It was done with one or several partners. Occasionally there were rehearsals so as to hold risks to a minimum. The rationale for robbery that comes through the interview was not picked up from other professional criminals but seems to have been based on attitudes fairly pervasive in the larger society. Thus sites were chosen because they were part of a larger enterprise. Small neighborhood grocery stores were not considered, partly because the potential take was small but also because the individual employee was likely to be the owner. In the larger supermarkets the encounters with store personnel were impersonal and the attitude conveyed was that no one loses since there is always the theft insurance. Mike and his partners did not rob the patrons of the store. Mike's self-conception was that he was a "criminal" though this may have developed during his period of incarceration. He expressed irritation in the interview at the deception required in being a salesman and passing bad checks. He did not feel that robbery involved the same kind of stealth and deception: it was a direct, visible, nondisguised demand. There was no subterfuge involved and, by implication, Mike seemed to see a certain honesty in the directness and candor of the encounter.

Sutherland's mob operated with several rules of thumb: a "no rat rule," expenses shared in common (including court costs), honesty among members, and membership support including "putting in the fix" in case of the arrest of one of the members.[20] The partnership that is more characteristic of present-day robbery shows less organization; there is little emphasis on the importance of not informing on the others or trying to fix cases. Einstadter has noted that the old rules and the old style are obsolete because of the decline of the political machine and the difficulty in fixing cases.[21] The newer style requires a small group with a loose type of specialization which is flexible and adaptable according to circumstances. It is basically a temporary partnership of entrepreneurs united for a specific purpose.

Neither the opportunity structure approach nor differential association point to the process of decision making that leads to illegal behavior. Behavior, whether legal or illegal is seldom simply determined. Mike reported that theft remained the one avenue open to him since all others were closed. Yet, in a part of the interview not quoted here, he stated that on retrospection he would have decided not to initiate his brief criminal career. Though estranged from his family and unable to ask for their assistance he stated that an older couple from whom he rented a room was prepared to help tide him over until his veteran's benefits arrived. Mike's discussion of how he became involved—"somehow or other the idea came up to do something about it (financial need) and resulted in the series of robberies I mentioned earlier"—suggests how commitment to it was built up. Once he engaged in the actual planning of a house burglary he felt obligated to his partner. His commitment became deeper after the first episode. He felt unable to back out and, more significantly from a career perspective, alternative action—like continuing with his education—was effectively excluded.

Mike's life history seems to bear on three different explanations: opportunity structures, differential association, and labeling. He was unemployed or marginally employed during this period. He felt himself to be in a state of "drift," uncommitted to any particular set of goals, people, or work plans. It was his economic situation combined with his lack of conventional commitments that made him vulnerable and open to theft as a realistic option. It was at this point that contact with someone who defined law violation favorably provided a loose learning structure. But even at this point criminal activity did not automatically follow. It grew in a tentative groping, advancing, backing off, and sounding out way. Labeling theory has generally emphasized the sense in which social or official reaction amplify deviance and this certainly did not operate in Mike's case. But Becker has described in more detail from an interactionist perspective the steps leading to an initially deviant act that highlights

[20] Sutherland, *The Professional Thief,* pp. 35ff.
[21] Einstadter, "The Social Organization of Armed Robbery."

its self-conscious character. A key turning point for Mike, and experienced by him as disruptive, was his military discharge and the problems of reentry to conventional society. This was the beginning of the chain of events that eventuated in armed robbery. Particularly adverse situations like the one described in the interview are sufficient to make one pause and take stock. Thus began a process of reassessment and reevaluation. At some point, especially when considering illegal activity, the question arose, "What have I to lose?" and the response was simply, "Nothing." If the problem is a shared one, as it was in this instance, the doubts about risks are resolved and motives to rob are built into final form.

QUESTIONS FOR FURTHER DISCUSSION

1. Mike mentioned lack of employment opportunities as one of the structural causes of his own illegal activity. What other structural characteristics did he point to, either implicitly or explicitly?

2. To what extent could Mike's brief robbery pattern be characterized as a "career"?

3. In what other legal occupations would you speculate that the same kind of ideology articulated by Mike is characteristic?

4. If a community policy to reduce the incidence of robbery were to be developed, what sort of strategies would be suggested by Mike's case?

5. How would a conflict and consensus perspective interpret Mike's story and what further information would each need?

6. Mike's comments on his uneasiness in committing burglaries and lack of sales ability suggest that certain kinds of persons are drawn to robbery. What hypotheses would you suggest relating to personality traits or specific skills required?

SUMMARY

If violent personal crime and property crimes are distinguished by their lack of ambiguity the same cannot be said for political crime, the subject of Chapter 11. It is the most ill-defined of all the crimes and there is a substantial body of criminological opinion that would exclude it entirely from any discussion of criminality. The main objection is that some of what is called political crime is not prohibited under the criminal code, thus to classify it as crime requires some broader notions of social harm. The inclusion here is related to the value orientation of the author as well as the fact that the topic most succinctly touches on the complex and conflicted interaction between definers and defined, and on the importance of organization, resources, and power in the criminalization process.

political
criminal
behavior

Our discussion of the emergence of criminal law suggested that all crime is political in that the laws against it protect the interests and rights of the law-making power. Schafer puts it this way:

> . . . it may be argued that all crimes are political crimes inasmuch as all prohibitions with penal sanctions represent the defense of a given value system or morality, in which the prevailing social power believes.[1]

Also, it is the organized power of the state which defines crime and imprisons offenders. Common-sense distinctions, however, have separated the conventional criminal and the political criminal. The former commits the usual garden variety kinds of offenses, and the latter is unjustly imprisoned for his political beliefs. Criminologists until quite recently have accepted this distinction.

Most conventional criminology texts, if they deal with the notion of political crime at all, give it a very narrow definition. It usually refers to treason; sometimes it includes sedition, sabotage, and the violation of military draft regulations. But the broader concept of political crime is practically unrecognized publicly and legally, especially in the Anglo-American tradition. There is a widely shared belief that obedience to the

[1] Stephen Schafer, "Concept of Political Criminal," *Journal of Criminal Law, Criminology and Police Science*, 62 (September 1971), 380–87.

law is an absolute. The stability of the system is seen to depend on operating within the legal rules of the game without which anarchy would prevail. Ingraham and Tokoro suggest that legitimating the notion of political crime by giving it legal definition would encourage more of it.[2] The majority of political offenses are dealt with nonpolitically under the present set of arrangements. Persons are arrested for disorderly conduct, breach of the peace, parading without a permit, trespassing, or loitering. The beginnings of public recognition of political crime in the U.S. occurred in the 1960s with the passage and strengthening of conspiracy and antiriot laws. These laws provided the state with the resources to move effectively and swiftly against dissenters. The conspiracy laws require only that the government show that defendants communicated in some way regarding a demonstration or draft resistance, not that they necessarily committed overt criminal acts. Antiriot laws make it a felony to travel in interstate commerce with the intent to incite or participate in a riot. A riot is defined as any assemblage of three or more persons in which at least one person threatens injury to another person or property, or actually does injure another person or property. From the point of view of federal prosecutors the success of these laws is minimal. Conspiracy is hard to prove to a jury's satisfaction and the laws have not resulted in any major convictions. Yet as Clinard and Quinney point out, conspiracy and antiriot laws are an effective form of political harassment whereby those who threaten the system can be detained for long periods of time at great personal expense.[3] Paul Goodman has more forcefully argued that the real purpose of the Chicago conspiracy trial and the various Panther trials was to tie up the political activity of the defendants.[4]

We also include under the category political crime offenses committed by governments or their agents against citizens, such as violations of constitutional guarantees and civil rights legislation. Violations of international law as in war crimes are also classified here.

Political crime at first glance seems to include a wide variety of offenses that do not logically hang together. One of our criteria for classification is that the type of crime should correspond to an identifiable behavior system "out there," or to a particular social world with meanings of its own. Political crime has less of an organized behavior system because the persons involved in it are usually not completely immersed in this social

[2] Barton L. Ingraham and Kazuhiko Tokoro, "Political Crime in the United States and Japan: A Comparative Study," *Issues in Criminology* 4 (Spring 1969), pp. 145–70.
[3] Marshall B. Clinard and Richard Quinney, *Criminal Behavior Systems: A Typology*, 2nd ed. (New York: Holt, Rinehart & Winston, 1973), pp. 156–57.
[4] Paul Goodman, "The Disrupted Trials: A Question of Allegiance," *The Village Voice* (March 9, 1970), pp. 5, 9.

world nor do they define themselves in terms of it. Their offenses constitute only one aspect of their lives and behavior; their identities are not
constructed around it as they are for some categories of professional
crime. Yet on the American domestic scene both those resisting what they
define as unjust laws and those government agents justifying their activities in terms of "national security" are symbiotically linked to each other.
In that sense they are operating in a common social world whose meanings both groups understand. They do not, however, operate with a
common set of codes or traditions, nor are they bound by common sets of
social relationships. It may be that political resistance constitutes more of
a group way of life than does crime committed by government agents,
with the exception of police criminality, which is more patterned. Government crime is closer to an aggregation of individual acts sharing the
same general motivational scheme.

The concept of political crime and the political criminal generally
challenges the traditional stereotype of the criminal. Overwhelmingly,
officially recorded crime is economic—committed for material gain. The
political criminal's actions, whether carried out by government agent or
dissenter, is not. The law is violated so that some other end might be
achieved. For dissenting groups the aim is to change the political system
or a government policy; for high status government or military officials it
is to protect national security or enhance one's career; for police reacting
to public disorder the aim is the reduction of unpredictability in their
work setting. The political criminal emerges as a person operating in a
particular problematic setting which poses problems for him, defines the
options available to him, and creates constraints which influence his decision. His behavior is very much a matter of choice within this context.
This can be illustrated by the activities of dissenting groups like the East
Coast Conspiracy (the conspiracy to kidnap presidential assistant, Henry
Kissinger) Catonsville Nine, and the Black Panthers. The choice as they
saw it was whether or not to resign themselves to a set of social arrangements that permitted an unpopular war to continue, or a pervasive pattern of discrimination against blacks to go unchallenged. The decision on
what to do about it was partly determined by the strength of their convictions, their moral outrage, and the effectiveness of the illegal option.
Persons engaged in demonstrations, protests, marches, or mass picketing
characteristically do not view their behavior as illegal, nor does the American criminal law define it as such. Only to the extent that these activities
are perceived by those who participate in them as ineffective will other
illegal options be considered. The one selected very much depends on
how effective it is likely to be. Raids on draft boards or destruction of
selective service files were chosen by war resisters to dramatize their opposition to the war and try to make the point that government leaders

were engaging in inlawful or morally wrong behavior. Hence great emphasis is placed on publicity for the cause to win over the general public. If the participants are arrested and tried, the trial is viewed as an opportunity to discredit the system of government policies that are being attacked, and to raise the consciousness of judge, jury, and general public.[5] In the trial of the Catonsville Nine the participants were reminded again and again that the activity of destroying files, pieces of paper, was much less serious than killing human beings. The character of their violation was partly shaped by ethical convocations, by its ability to elicit sympathy, and by comprehension, as well as the element of risk involved. The government contended in the trial of those engaged in the East Coast Conspiracy that they were planning more serious acts of sabotage (like blowing up electrical conduits and steam pipes in Washington, D.C.) because the draft board raids were not effective. Whether the conspirators were effective or not (the defendants were acquitted of the conspiracy charges) they did experience a deep sense of powerlessness to change government policy and a deepened sense of the official insensitivity to their demands.

It is possible to develop a typology of dissent based on the seriousness of the challenge posed to official authority. We start with a group seeking redress of grievances through peaceful means and end with attempts to overthrow the government. Dissent and official action operate together to create the final stage of the process in a series of actions and reactions (see Table 11-1).

The extent to which dissent is amplified depends on the "sophistication" of control responses. Usually the resources of modern states are sufficient to crush dissent but it may not always be desirable to do so since the government's legitimacy (the extent to which it has "won the hearts and minds" of its subjects) may be called into question by a wider

TABLE 11-1   Cycle of Dissent

Dissenters' Actions-Reactions	*Official Authority, Actions-Reactions*
1. Mass actions such as demonstrations, protests, picketing, etc.	1. Significant concessions to quell dissent or infiltration, arrests for disturbing the peace and rioting.
2. Nonviolent disruption such as draft board raids, publication of classified documents, etc.	2. Prosecution, imprisonment.
3. Violent disruption such as rioting, kidnapping, bombing, assassination.	3. Prosecution, suppression.
4. Terrorism, guerrilla activity.	4. Counterinsurgency.

[5] David Sternberg, "The New Radical Criminal Trials: A Step Towards a Class-for-Itself in the American Proletariat?" *Science and Society*, 37 (Fall 1972), 274–301.

circle of citizens for acting too harshly. Note also that the flexibility of the official response is greatest at the earlier stages when it can make concessions that will, in effect, nip dissent in the bud. The strategies available at the later stages are considerably narrowed.

Typically dissent is discouraged officially through the use of "show trials." The trials are primarily used for educational purposes. As Blumberg has observed:

> The arrest and trial of a person or group of persons is used as a warning to others not to engage in similar behavior involving political opposition. . . . Under the guise of prosecuting an individual or group of individuals, for some substantive crime, the regime uses the criminal trial as a platform from which to discredit and stigmatize the holders of opposing political views and thereby to label them and their views as socially opprobrious. . . . The trial is an attempt to manage in theatrical fashion the public abasement of the defendant and/or his ideas. The primary objective being to anathematize his political position, rather than to simply convict him of a crime.[6]

The increased level of dissent in the United States during the late 1960s and early 1970s led to new protest strategies designed to question the legitimacy of the trial itself. Sternberg has identified the essential features of the new strategy: the defendants were not docile or respectful of the court's authority, they tried to restructure the proceedings so that judge, prosecutors, and some witnesses were defined as those who should really be on trial, and the role of spectators was much more vocal.[7] The strategy was developed to educate a wider public to dissent and frustrate the proselytizing efforts of the state. There was some expectation that this innovation would lead to more fundamental and far-reaching changes in the criminal justice system but this has not occurred.

EXTENT OF POLITICAL CRIME

There are no reliable statistics on the extent of political crime. The Uniform Crime Reports of the FBI do not list it separately from conventional offenses. Conspiracy is included under Part II offenses under the category "all other offenses." Our definition of political crime includes all those arrested for conspiracy, antiriot and related offenses, violation of

---

[6] Abraham S. Blumberg, "Crime and the Social Order," in Abraham S. Blumberg (ed.), *Current Perspectives in Criminal Behavior* (New York: Knopf, 1974), p. 25.

[7] Sternberg, "New Radical Criminal Trials."

draft laws, desertion, and violations of civil rights (specifically, government agents).

Conspiracy

Despite the widespread publicity given the conspiracy trials in the late 1960s and early '70s only a relatively small number of persons have been arrested and tried under the conspiracy laws. Overwhelmingly they were war resisters or part of the black liberation movement.

Antiriot and Related Offenses

A series of riots in urban ghettoes beginning in 1965 has been cited by many social scientists and government officials as instances of guerrilla warfare in the cities. From August 1965 to July 1967 at least 9,500 persons were arrested for alleged offenses related to these riots.

Violation of Draft Laws and Desertion

Department of Defense and Justice Department figures disclosed that 206,775 men were "referred to United States attorneys as draft delinquents" between 1963 and 1973. It is not clear from their figures how many were actually arrested but roughly 10 percent (19,000) were prosecuted and of that number a little less than half (9,167) were convicted.[8] Official figures on desertion are less precise. The estimates prepared as background information for the presidential amnesty or clemency program in 1974 put the figure of deserters who were fugitives at 12,550. Other estimates range higher.

Crime by Agents of Government

The most sensational and widely discussed political crimes by officials were those linked to the "Watergate" affair. The original seven men who were arrested and brought to trial were charged with conspiracy to use illegal means (including wiretapping) to monitor conversations, steal documents, and intercept telephone conversations, and with illegal entry to steal. By mid-1974 the number of persons indicted in crimes connected

[8] *New York Times*, September 17, 1974, p. 24.

with the Nixon administration's war against its political enemies had expanded enormously.

Much more serious than these violations, however, were the allegations made against the U.S. government relative to the war in Indochina. The principles of Nuremberg (formulated by a UN-directed international law commission with U.S. support in 1950) set strict guidelines for proper treatment of civilian populations in occupied countries during wartime. The United States and its agents have been accused of the murder of civilian populations in Indochina, the ill-treatment and deportation of civilian populations, and the wanton destruction of cities there. Attempts to document these charges have been made by the Russell International War Crimes Tribunal and an American group, the Committee of Concerned Asian Scholars.[9] The most thoroughly reported and publicly acknowledged murders of the civilian population occurred at Mylai in March 1968 when 500 unarmed Vietnamese civilians met their deaths. Estimates of the Russell Tribunal are that the war has generated over three million refugees. They also accuse the United States and its agents of destroying hundreds of villages, poisoning fields and jungles by defoliants, and disregarding the internationally recognized limitations on bombing both in North and South Vietnam. The documentation has been meager because of the difficulty in getting information. Yet, if the war crimes trials of World War II are any precedent, more substantial and well-documented charges can be expected in the future.

Finally, police activities that violate citizens' rights can also be included under political crime. These violations have been discussed more fully in Chapter 6. Attention has been drawn in recent years to the illegal use of police violence in civil rights demonstrations, racial disturbances, political demonstrations, and campus unrest. The 1967 President's Commission on Law Enforcement and the Administration of Justice reported that police brutality was widespread in metropolitan police departments.[10] Estimates are difficult to come by, however, and arrests are infrequently made since this would require police cooperation.

The usual characteristics of age, sex, race or ethnicity, and social class do not differentiate political offenders as a whole from the general population. They include a broad spectrum of people—old and young, black and white, high and low economic status. The crucial factors in the career of the political offender are not personal and social characteristics per se, as Clinard and Quinney point out, but the values of the offender and the

---

[9] Committee of Concerned Asian Scholars, *The Indochina Story* (New York: Pantheon Books, 1970); Proceedings of the Russell International War Crimes Tribunal, *Against the Crime of Silence* (Flanders, N.J.: O'Hare Books, 1968).
[10] President's Commission on Law Enforcement and the Administration of Justice, *Task Force Report: The Police* (Washington, D.C.: Government Printing Office, 1967), pp. 178–93.

value systems to which he is actively responding.[11] The expansion of the U.S. government's power since the beginning of the Vietnam war has generated broad resistance to its excesses. The resisters do not represent any one particular segment of the society. Those involved in crimes by the government are more homogeneous in terms of race, sex, age, and social status. They are overwhelmingly older white males of high social status.

GROUP SUPPORT FOR POLITICAL CRIME

In America's large, heterogeneous, conflicted society there is considerable support for political crime. It seems to be most strong among the police where the values supporting illegal use of force against certain citizens receives sturdy informal occupational support. It is less strong among war resisters, but if their offenses are religiously inspired there may be considerable tenacious group support. Public reaction to crime by government agents seems relatively mild, in some cases conflicted. This usually doesn't mean there is group support for it but rather that there is a general unwillingness to believe that it can happen. The support the government agent gets for his violations comes mainly from his fellow workers who share his concern about what constitutes danger to the "national interest."

Legal processing of political offenders is mixed depending on whether crimes are by the government or crimes against it. Crimes by government officials are usually dealt with leniently.

> What happens in terms of legal processing when governmental crimes are detected? The results are usually predictable: the charges are dropped, the defendants are cleared, or, at most an official may be dismissed from his former responsibilities.[12]

The offender whose crime is against the government is dealt with much more harshly. Lemert observed that during World War II the average sentence for conscientious objectors was much more stringent than for many other convicted criminals.[13] Nearly 90 percent of the convicted conscientious objectors were sentenced to prison, with over 30 percent receiving a four- to five-year term. For the entire period only a little over 4 percent of the cases were granted probation.

---

[11] Clinard and Quinney, *Criminal Behavior Systems*, p. 160.
[12] Ibid., p. 180.
[13] Edwin M. Lemert, *Social Pathology* (New York: McGraw-Hill, 1971), pp. 203–4.

EXPLANATIONS OF POLITICAL CRIME

A close look at the behavior labeled "political crime" suggests that the decision to follow an illegal course is very much like one to follow a legal one. What is distinctive about the decision to commit a political crime is that it is well thought out, not impulsive, and the individual's moral convictions play a central role. The political criminal reveals man's activity as highly self-conscious, not unwitting. It suggests that even under circumstances where choices are severely restricted, human beings still make choices. The discussion of political crime has underscored criminology's links with other social sciences. The dynamics involved in deciding on an illegal option are similar to those involved in a legal option. We can expect that further study of political crime may decisively affect the way criminology conceives of the criminal.

Because the political criminal is so different from the conventional one Schafer has suggested using the term "convictional criminal."[14] This underlines the convictions he has relating to some kind of altruistic-communal end. He does not operate in terms of any egoistic motivation but nonpersonally in the light of larger ends. His law violation is designed to legitimate certain social ideas he holds, and is "instrumental" to his ideology. Schafer goes on to say that the convictional criminal is less concerned with the actual mechanics of the crime than is the conventional criminal and feels at peace when it is over, not agitated. The convictional offender is also distinguished from other offenders by lack of concern with secrecy—quite the opposite. Elliot has provided us with the following characterization:

> Although some political offenders are persons without integrity who have yielded to the extensive bribes paid either by foreign powers or by local groups, the vast majority are conscientious adherents to a political philosophy which threatens the existence of the government they are opposing. Political offenders represent a paradox for they are criminals who carry on their illegal activities in pursuit of their ideals. They are not imbued with sordid schemes for extracting vast sums of money from unsuspecting victims, nor are they motivated by basic desires to kill or destroy, although these crimes may be necessary in the pursuit of their ideals. They are generally idealists devoted to a cause.[15]

[14] Schafer, "The Concept of Political Criminal."
[15] Mabel A. Elliot, *Crime in Modern Society* (New York: Harper & Row), p. 180.

However, the "convictional criminal" constitutes only one of the sub-types within the category of political crime. The explanations for his be-havior are more likely to come from the study of social movements; the explanations for crimes by governmental agents are more likely to come from studies of organizational compliance.

Social Movements and the Convictional Criminal

Social movements—like the Black Panthers, Brown Berets, and the various peace groups—are characterized as "value-oriented movements" by sociologists. As Smelser has pointed out certain conditions must be present for a social movement of this sort to develop.[16] Among the most important is the unavailability of legitimate means to modify social policy in a desired direction. Legitimate alternative means for reconstituting the social structure are perceived as unavailable. The aggrieved population ranks low in wealth, power, prestige, or access to the means of com-munication. Their experience may be one of material deprivation or the deprivation of participation. The disaffection springs from a sense of powerlessness in the face of inflexible political structures. The deprivation is usually relative, not absolute:

> Such deprivations are relative to expectations. By an absolute meas-
> ure, groups which are drawn into value-oriented movements may be
> improving . . . improvement on absolute groups [may] involve
> deprivation on relative grounds; for the same group, with their new
> gains in one sphere (e.g. economic, cultural) is often held back in
> another (e.g., political).[17]

The absence of effective channels of reform combined with the blockage of protest contributes to the spread of value-oriented beliefs among aggrieved groups. The possibilities for disseminating the beliefs of the movements must also be present for the movement to take hold and grow.

The strain that preceded the value-oriented movements of the 1960s was caused by the black struggle for equal rights and the disruption of the Vietnam war. Established expectations about work and adult careers were shattered for draft-eligible young men. For minorities and working-class youth their sense of injustice was aggravated because of the in-equality of the draft laws; for middle-class youth a profound sense of uncertainty made them likely candidates for movements challenging the government's position. The potential candidates for dissent were younger people who were in a state of "drift," past adolescence yet not integrated

---

[16] Neil Smelser, *Theory of Collective Behavior* (New York: Free Press, 1963).
[17] Ibid., p. 340.

into the adult world, but more specifically rebellious youth rather than studious, athletic, or scrupulous young people.[18] The social movements that issued from this set of conditions developed a distinctive perspective and ideology that provided justifications for social change, weapons for attack and defense, and a deep conviction about the legitimacy of the cause as well as an optimistic outlook in the possibilities of success. Value-oriented movements inculcate a strong sense of solidarity among their participants. A movement is capable of evoking a powerful commitment among its membership. It is this dedication and selflessness that can transform the individual participant into a political offender.

Organizational Compliance and Political Crime

The criminality of government agents against their own citizens or those of other nations (war crimes) is best interpreted from an organizational perspective. Etzioni has distinguished three basic kinds of organizations that elicit different kinds of responses on the part of its members.[19] *Coercive organizations,* like prisons, characteristically generate alienative orientations among their membership; *utilitarian organizations,* like businesses, generate a calculative orientation; and *normative organizations,* like churches, universities, or nations, generate a moralistic orientation. The motivation of those who are morally oriented to the state is related to the manipulation of social and prestige symbols. In short, their rewards are symbolic rather than material. Characteristically governmental criminals are not motivated by personal gain. The organizational elites in governmental structures share the same kind of commitment to the organization as their dissenting counterparts do to their social movements. The nation takes precedence over all other affiliations and any act that can be justified in terms of the "national interest" is acceptable. In this sense crime by governmental agents is much like corporate crime discussed in Chapter 12.

The gap in explanations of political crime relates to the specification of the mechanisms leading from strong organizational or movement commitments to political violations. It seems quite clear that the dedication to national security among high officials of the Nixon administration did not automatically lead all of them to criminal activity; nor did the dedication of dissenters lead all of them to challenge governmental authority by breaking the law.

[18] David Matza, "Position and Behavior Patterns of Youth," in Robert E. L. Faris (ed.), *Handbook of Modern Sociology* (Chicago: Rand McNally, 1964).
[19] Amitai Etzioni, *A Comparative Analysis of Complex Organizations* (New York: Free Press, 1961).

Existing Law versus Higher Duty

The major issue in the literature on political crime is how "obedience to a higher authority" is to be defined when there are many divergent and conflicting concepts of morality. The Nuremberg trials attempted to establish the principle that individuals had higher duties than simple obedience to the laws of their respective states. It was the violation of these higher commands that led to the conviction of German and Japanese nationals. Some attempt was made to give substance to this principle in the Universal Declaration of Human Rights and the Covenant on Civil and Political Rights sponsored by the United Nations. Yet, as Friedmann has noted in the present stage of international law,

> . . . no sovereign state, including those that sat in judgment at Nuremberg and Tokyo, will accept the commands of a higher law as superior to those of the national legal order.[20]

Those who commit war crimes may violate "the conscience of humanity" but they are usually not violating the laws of their respective countries; nor is there any effective machinery established for prosecuting them. At present the only method for addressing war crimes is through international tribunals such as the United Nations Commission on Human Rights, the International Red Cross, the International Commission of Jurists, and Amnesty International. Typically they publicize violations and hope to curb them by embarrassing representatives of the nations involved.

Crimes by governmental agents against nationals are violations of national legal codes as well as violations of trust. They are justified in terms of the higher goals of national security. The public reactions to the violations of Nixon administration officials revealed deep divisions about what constitutes national security or the national interest. What did seem to crystallize as a widespread sentiment was that however lofty one's goal of the pursuit of national security it should not involve illegal acts. If it does the violator should be punished since "no one is above the law."

The "higher authority" appealed to by those who engage in civil disobedience has sometimes been a higher morality that transcends legal codes. But more recently the argument has been the legality of specific laws that have been challenged. Thus those who refused to be drafted argued that the Vietnam war was unconstitutional (since no war was declared) or that it violated international law. The major issue that the

---

[20] Wolfgang Friedmann, *Law in a Changing Society,* 2nd ed. (New York: Columbia University Press, 1972), p. 41.

limited and specialized type of resistance known as civil disobedience has raised is how much of it can be tolerated without leading to revolution. Friedmann points out that the resistance may start out as limited but end up threatening the entire legal order.[21] In that case the interest in maintaining the fabric of society should outweigh the right of the individual protesters. Others have stressed the positive role that civil disobedience has played in promoting or accelerating overdue legal change. Some of these issues are touched upon in the following interview.

TOM: A DISSENTER

Tom is a 21-year-old male who with three others entered a selective service office in a suburb of a large metropolis in 1971 and destroyed draft records. The interview was conducted six months after the violation while the trial was going on. The symbolic action taken against the government was based on a highly developed and articulate religious point of view which justified the activity.

QUESTION: What were the circumstances of going into the selective service center?

TOM: Myself and three other friends of mine, Jerry, Cathy, and Linda, decided, after many years of working in many other areas and many other avenues of protest to the war in Indochina, decided that we had to make a more definite commitment, so to speak, a more definite witness to that type of sentiment. We thought that we had to, in a sense, place our bodies where our mouths or minds had been for a long time. So we decided the best way we could attempt to do that and at the same time continue to do what we'd been trying to do for such a long time through high school and college—that is, trying to change people's minds, trying to change their heads—was to involve ourselves in an action of sorts, open ourselves up to as much communication with other people as possible. So we decided to go to the local selective service office one day and pour some blood over some 1A and high priority draft records, which we did do on that afternoon.

QUESTION: Why did you select that suburban selective service office?

TOM: There were about three or four reasons why we did it.

21 Ibid., p. 39.

The first one and perhaps the main one was that it was very accessible. We were a relatively small group because of the style which we were attempting, we wanted to have as much control over the situation in the office as we could. And we thought that the [local] office would be the most ideal, or most successful office to do that. And that turned out to be the case. Secondly, all of us come from predominantly middle-class, and even some cases, upper-middle-class backgrounds. And we saw [this suburb] as being very much the same type of community that all of us had come from. I, myself, was born and raised in this type of community. And so, [this suburb] to me was a very similar type of community. At the same time it was also a microcosm of a larger city around it that all of us had been working on in the most recent—in the past couple of years. We all—Jerry, Cathy and Linda—had graduated from [a nearby Catholic University] last year. And I presently have about a semester to finish. We're all living in the city in communities with other people. And therefore we wanted to address ourselves to a community which was very much a microcosm of the larger city which we were part of. [This suburb] while it has the image of being a very middle-class white community does have a very substantial black population, has a ghetto area, has a poorer population, has its problems with integrated schooling, with equal employment, etc. In relation to the draft itself, we found there, as you find in just about any community, or any area of the country that has a draft board, the poor, the black, the minority groups tend to go first, when it comes to being drafted, being conscripted into the army.

QUESTION: Did you come around prior to going in there on that afternoon and look over the place?

TOM: Yes, we did.

QUESTION: What did you find when you looked the place over? How did you know where the files were?

TOM: The files were very plainly marked. Our intention was to involve ourselves in what many people would classify as a symbolic action. So what we were mainly attempting to do other than, say, trash the whole place, destroy all the files, would be just get those files of men who were most susceptible to the draft, namely the 1A's, the high priorities, for instance, students who were just graduating who would be losing their deferment.

QUESTION: The file cabinets were clearly marked?

TOM: Yes, marked "1A," "High Priority," and in addition to that the drawers were also marked with red labels: "higher priority—remove first." There were only four drawers like that.

QUESTION: Those were the drawers you took out and poured blood on?

TOM: Correct.

QUESTION: What was the blood? Was it human blood?

TOM: The blood was beef blood which we obtained through a government permit from the U.S. Department of Agriculture for educational purposes.

QUESTION: How seriously were the draft files damaged?

TOM: Well, as we've been saying all summer and as we found out from the supervisor of the draft board as she testified in court this afternoon, the files were damaged to the extent that some were completely obliterated, some were completely stuck together so that when they were separated they would rip, and others were partially damaged so that not all the information could be read.

QUESTION: Would you describe the actual situation of entering the draft board and what happened?

TOM: We approached the office at approximately 4:20 in the afternoon, near closing time. We started by talking to the only clerk left in the office that afternoon. We originally started talking to her about the fact that we were nonviolent people concerned about American participation in Indochina—that we'd been concerned about this for some time. And we particularly wanted to ask the clerk whether she'd ever considered the role she was playing in allowing this war to continue, in allowing the manpower to be processed, to be gotten hold of, processed, and sent off to fight this war. At which point the clerk in the office asked us to come back the next day and talk to her supervisor. We then insisted that we really wanted to talk to her because we thought it was important for her to attempt to ask these questions of herself as well, not to just go to her supervisor. We then continued to talk to her about the possibilities of setting up a peace library starting with some of the books that we had brought along with us for registrants to have some type of alternative type of reading to go over before they registered for the draft. She again asked that we come back the next day and talk to her supervisor. We then noticed that there was a—what we found out later—was a registrant in the office at the time. So we asked her if we could talk with him in the office. And she said "Sure, as soon as I finish filling out his form." And we pointed out to her that it was very important for us to talk to him before he filled out any forms. At which point she kind of stepped back and the four of us walked into the office. We then explained that we were there for yet another reason and told her not to panic, to call the police if she thought that was necessary to do, that we would remain and wait around for arrest, that our main purpose for being there that day was to destroy by blood draft files that in our minds were holding men either with the threat of death themselves or at least the possibility that they would be trained to kill other people. So pretty simply that's what took place.

QUESTION: What happened then? Did she step aside?

TOM: She had already stepped aside. By this time we were already in the office and we proceeded to one of the four drawers that were marked and proceeded to pour blood, beef blood, over the files.

QUESTION: What did you carry the blood in?

TOM: We carried them in four containers, lotion bottles, and . . .

QUESTION: So you squirted it on the files then?

TOM: Kind of poured, squirted, they were half-gallon things. As the blood was being poured we discovered that, lo and behold, the drawers leaked. So we then proceeded to pull some of the files out to mop up the floor. The government today [at the trial] was talking about how we threw files on the floor, but we were actually attempting to help clean up by mopping up the blood that had gotten on the floor. At this point the clerk was becoming somewhat frantic so we again assured her that we were not going to harm her in any way, that she should not panic, that she should call the police if that's what she felt she had to do, that the only thing we would be doing was pouring blood over 1A records, and that we wouldn't be doing anything else to her office. She finally got ahold of the police, a sergeant came up after we had been there for a couple of minutes and informed us that we were under arrest for criminal trespass. At which point we asked him if we could hold an impromptu prayer service. He said we could do anything we wanted to for the next five minutes but destroy more files. We then proceeded to have an impromptu prayer service during which we asked people to recollect on the deaths that had been caused in Indochina, the civilian refugees that were there, the plight that the war had brought on many Americans here as well. We read a passage from the Bible and ended with the Lord's Prayer.

QUESTION: How many people were in the office at the time?

TOM: By this time there were the two reporters, which I neglected to tell you before, the two reporters that we brought along with us, the clerk, her boyfriend who had been waiting downstairs whom she had gone and gotten and brought upstairs, the registrant, and I would guess about five, six, or seven police officers. Quite a large group.

QUESTION: Who were the reporters that you brought along?

TOM: The reporters were a reporter from [a metropolitan newspaper] who was the first government witness today and a photographer from [the university Tom was attending].

QUESTION: The total amount of time you were there was from 4:20 to what time?

TOM: I recall being in the local police station, which is about a three-minute drive away, around a quarter or ten to five. So I would imagine we were in the office no more than fifteen minutes.

QUESTION: What were your own psychological feelings during this particular period?

TOM: A great amount of relief that the thing had finally taken place.

QUESTION: How about while it was happening?

TOM: The same thing. Personally a lot of natural tension and nervousness had left me. But more importantly I really felt a genuine sense of joy and hope that perhaps this time—as this had been a similar action of many others in the past—something was going to happen that would change people's heads, that perhaps other people, especially family and friends who we were particularly addressing ourselves to, that they could somehow look into their own consciences and decide what type of action or new commitment they, themselves, should take on.

QUESTION: What were you charged with when you were brought to the police station?

TOM: We were originally charged with state charges on criminal trespass and malicious destruction of property. We were then handed over to the FBI and spent a few interesting hours down at the FBI headquarters at the federal building downtown that same night. The FBI had quite a bit of trouble trying to fingerprint us and do things like that because these were top field agents—they weren't the regular staff, who had gone home for the day by this time. So we had quite a lot of fun showing them how to fingerprint us. We were then brought to the [city] police department lockup where we spent the night. By this time Linda and Cathy had been separated from Jerry and me.

QUESTION: And at that point you were charged under federal statutes?

TOM: No, at that time we were not. We were being held by the Federal Bureau of Investigation until a complaint would be issued against us the following morning. The following morning we were then transported from [the city jail] back to the federal court lockup. Around 10:00 A.M. we were brought into one of the commissioner's hearing rooms at which point the charges against us at that time were read to us and bond was set for $160,000 for the four of us—that being the security bond for the full amount. As we walked back to the lockup expecting a few days' rest in the county jail because we didn't see where $160,000 was going to come from, we had a lawyer approach us who offered to help us who is now Linda's attorney. He immediately set up an emergency bond hearing. The judge, after a short hearing, lowered our bonds to $5,000 apiece. We were then freed and ever since then have been attempting in whatever ways possible to communicate to whatever group is willing to hear us, to whatever individuals are willing to hear us trying to explain why we did what we did.

QUESTION: What were the specific charges that were brought against you?

TOM: Later the following month we were charged with four counts of a federal indictment, namely, destruction of government property, mutilation of selective service records, interference with the selective service system, and conspiracy to do so.

QUESTION: Do you know what the maximum penalty under these four statutes is?

TOM: Yes, the maximum penalty is 23 years and/or $30,000 fine.

QUESTION: O.K. Let's back up a little bit. You said you were feeling a little bit tense or anxious before the whole thing. Could you reconstruct that day for me?

TOM: As much as I'm able to do at this point, yes. The trial's still going on, there will probably be appeals after it. I'm sort of hesitant to go through everything and at the same time I have to honestly admit that a lot of it is pretty hazy because of the psychological shape we were in at that time. Jerry and Linda, Cathy and I met the night before and made final arrangements. We then contacted the two reporters the following morning, the morning of the action. We met them around 4:00 in the afternoon and drove to a side street near the selective service office. We then walked to the selective service office. I guess I should add that up until then I had been around [the university] at class. Had to put up a good front. And then we met. The group at that time was six with the two reporters met at a nearby intersection and just walked up the street to the draft board. I suppose the frame of mind we were all in changed almost from minute to minute. People ask me, "How long did you plan for this thing?" As far as specific planning for the particular action, again I can honestly say I really don't know how long it was. I do know that in a more general sense it's probably been something that I've been preparing for for some years, it being, at least in my own mind, a logical progression of the other activities I've been involved in in the past.

QUESTION: Were the four of you friends for some time?

TOM: Yes. Jerry was originally two years ahead of me in high school. When I graduated I went on to [a nearby Catholic seminary] and again met Jerry and probably got to know him a lot better there. It was the first time I started getting involved in various peace activities on campus. Our attempt was to awaken the seminary community to recognize or have a more conscious knowledge of just what was going on in Indochina, how all of us were part of what was continuing in Indochina. I have to admit that our efforts probably did not meet with that much success. We found a mainly apathetic campus and I know for myself that's one reason I left seminary in my sophomore year. [After transferring to a local Catholic university] I met Linda and Cathy, Linda particularly in an educational psychology class.

QUESTION: This was about two years ago?

TOM: Correct. We got to know each other through that class. We worked on a couple of class projects together. Jerry had taken some work the semester before so we found ourselves going to him from time to time for advice since it was the same professor teaching the course. At that same time all four of us with a large group of people were involved with a campus group known as CWN, "community without a name" which was an offshoot of a group that I had personally worked in two years before, its main slant was attempting to work for academic reform. It was that particular group which had scheduled to have a mass rally on Wednesday, May 6, which later turned out to be the first day of the student strike. It was more or less that same group of people who worked in CWN who got together after Cambodia was invaded and decided that something had to be done at [the university], it being a commuter school, a conservative Catholic school, we felt that something had to be attempted. Jerry, Cathy, Linda, and I plus others found ourselves on a student strike committee conducting nonviolent activities on campus. We succeeded in getting the student body as a whole to vote for a strike, which they did for about a week's period of time. We succeeded in getting the faculty to go on strike because we felt the particular issue of the invasion of Cambodia, and perhaps more important in the minds of many students on campus, the fact that Kent State had happened and Jackson State, the war had really come home, in a sense. People saw that they, too, could very easily be a victim of this type of mentality that we, ourselves, were talking about for such a long time. Actually during the strike particularly the people on the strike committee found themselves becoming closer and closer because of the long hours and all that. We found ourselves asking whether we should attempt to continue this type of being together on a more permanent basis. It was at that time that we decided to form what I guess some people could call a community or commune. We felt it necessary for ourselves and for other people as well to attempt to seek out alternatives for the society, particularly for the city and felt it necessary to live together on a day-to-day basis in order to try to figure out nonviolent alternatives on a day-to-day basis, very simply dealing with human beings on a one-to-one level.

QUESTION: Does this community have a name?

TOM: Yes. The committee eventually grew to a group of about ten people and they called themselves the *Union Community.* At the end of that particular summer I, myself, left for Europe on a study-travel program through the university so I was removed from the community, the [university] scene and the States for a period of about half a year. This, too, had an effect on why I ended up at the draft board. I had a bit of correspondence with the people at the community, but not all that much, I was pretty much on my own and spent quite a bit of time in Italy, where I lived, but also in Germany, and particularly, too, some time spent on a kibbutz in Israel. And I was able to meet quite a few different people with whom I still correspond in various parts of Europe and I guess quite often found myself, not being put on the defensive so much, considering the fact that I was an American because people saw that I wasn't a cut and dried American tourist, but being confronted very often with questions like: "What are you people still doing in Vietnam?" "Why don't you ever get out?" "What about violence in America? That's all we ever hear about." And this continual questioning of the European as a whole continued to come at me at various places that I spent time. I came back from Europe in January of 1971, this year, and found myself coming back to an atmosphere, an environment that was totally different from that which I had left six months before. The summer of 1970 people had just been through a student strike, there had been a lot of emotional outpouring, a lot of commitment. People had started working on campaigns of peace candidates, etc., the results were a different type and different forms of political activity going on. When I came back in January I found people really trying to—they had become, not apathetic but at least in my own terminology they had become apolitical. What I mean by that is that they more or less knew what was going on, they had a pretty good idea. They also had some idea how one usually goes about getting those things changed or accomplished within our society. But they had become apolitical because the politics of trying to attempt that change, as far as the accepted patterns of change, they had become turned off to—the power plays, the politicking, whatever, had really turned a lot of people off and they didn't want to deal with it anymore. This type of feeling was something that didn't just hit me when I came back but took two or three months to jell. And once I realized that, I again, even more so, felt I somehow had to first of all do something, as I said before, that would put my own body where my mouth had been for a long time and also perhaps to attempt to do something to get people out of this apolitical euphoria that they were in. I don't want to sound like I'm putting myself on a pedestal or anything. What I was merely attempting to do was, as I saw things, inasmuch as I could talk with friends of mine and with family, I wanted to try to affect that same circle of friends and family in a way that I felt would perhaps spark them up, awaken them.

QUESTION: As long as you mention your family, would you tell me a little about your personal background? What kind of family did you come from?

TOM: O.K. I myself am the oldest of five children. I've always considered myself fortunate in having a very close relationship with both my mom and my dad. My dad would go downtown to work in the morning and I would go to school. We would go together and found ourselves involved in many different sorts of conversations when I was in high school. Previous to that I picked up a lot of why I am in the position I am today through my parents. They've been involved in various religious social action groups for some time. I suppose initially that had the very definite effect on why I found myself in seminary, but more importantly had a very definite effect on the type of reading that I picked up on in high school and college—the lectures we would go to, the type of people who would be over at our house. It was always a kind of committed Christian Catholic action, social action type of environment that existed in the house. The whole family has always been really able to pull together whenever there were problems. We've always had a pretty open relationship. After the action took place, which I find now was a real blow to my parents, my mother in particular, we've still been able to continue to talk as human beings to each other, to work things out.

QUESTION: A blow to them, you mean they thought it was too extreme?

TOM: Yes, as much as I attempted to explain to them that I'm here today because of the way they raised me and I am truly indebted to them for that, as much as I would try to bring across that feeling of my own, my mom would say, "We never told you to break the law." They didn't see the difference, or the progression, or the possibilities of progression from my dad bringing me downtown in 1965 to hear Martin Luther King talk and then marching with him to City Hall to post demands up on the door. They didn't see the progression from that kind of activity to walking into the draft board and listing the same type of protest by pouring blood over pieces of paper. That particular understanding still eludes them today as far as I'm able to tell. I can understand very much that there is a greater fear and greater concern for my own personal safety and well-being. They are both very upset with the real possibility that I'll be spending a few years in prison, very concerned about the effect it's going to have on the future—jobs and things like that. These are the concerns affecting them very much now. But I still go back to the idea that we still have been able to pull together and the one common thing that we still share is our love for each other.

QUESTION: They really don't take issue with the idea that sometimes the demands of conscience and the demands of the state might be at odds with one another?

TOM: I think perhaps the best way to put that right now would be that particular concept isn't so real for them right now, being involved in that kind of thing, that they are really parents who have to . . . my mother, in particular, at least up until the past couple of weeks previous to the trial, has really been reluctant to get involved in any sort of discussion. We did talk a couple of days after the action and I tried to explain why I had done it, but I found out that in a couple of conversations I had with them in the previous week when I had opened up the possibility that I might be going to jail, they never really picked up on it. They never thought that I would consider the possibility. When the possibility became a reality it became something very hard for them to cope with. I'm confident that especially as we go over these things in the trial that they will, perhaps, see more of why I was there and how they really did play a role in it. [Later in the interview Tom reported that his brothers and sisters felt quite differently than his parents. A sister, one year younger and a brother two years younger, through discussions with him had come to share his convictions about nonviolence and the futility and immorality of the war. Another brother in high school set up an underground newspaper with a strong pacifist orientation.]

QUESTION: How would you account for the fact that although a number of people might have felt the same way, might have diagnosed the situation much as you did at the time, yet would not go on to make this kind of statement? How would you account for that?

TOM: I think that many people have. In the various speaking engagements and whatever, one argument that is put forth is "Why did you do that? It's been tried before, you know. The war is winding down, why bother trying to attack the war? The troops are coming home." Those would be two arguments that people would have thrown. As far as the first one goes, why did you try that again, it's been tried before. My own feeling was that, first of all, it's very consistent with my own progression of thought, very consistent with the type of activities and the type of tactics I had used in the past. Secondly, that while it had been tried before as long ago as 1967, I saw 1971 as being a new time, a new place. I saw [this metropolitan area] as a new kind of people and a new place. I also saw an American public that, as long ago as last January, said that 73 percent of them were against the war and as short ago as last week, according to another poll, some 60 percent of that number were against it because they thought the war was immoral. Now it seemed to me that, at least in my own mind, or the way that I consider my own thoughts or ideas is that I *had* to do something. My feeling was that I wasn't going to try to encourage other people to do the same thing. You could judge our acts and I think that you, yourself, if you look into your own conscience would find a way that best suits you.

QUESTION: During all of this discussion from January to April were you reading anything collectively that influenced you in the actions you took?

TOM: As far as reading goes I was still in school at that time, my extra reading was down very much. I cut down on stuff that I really wanted to read. I know one thing we shared in common on a particular night was the tape that Daniel Berrigan had made about two or three years ago . . . two years ago, I guess. [Fr. Daniel Berrigan and eight of his associates were convicted of destroying draft board files in April 1969 and sentenced to serve three years. He refused to surrender to federal authorities, went underground and communicated by letter, article, and tapes with his sympathizers until apprehended by the FBI four months later.] I never really considered myself a Dan Berrigan follower or a member of the Catholic left or anything like that. Those type of labels really turn me off because I really think they stereotype individuals and whatever that group may be too much. I have to admit that I really never read that much of the Berrigan writings. I have read quite a few other things, though, and I know one book that we, as a group had read, perhaps not during that particular time but at least some time over the past couple of years, was *The Nonviolent Cross* by Jim Douglas. That particular book laid down a pretty strong case that related very much to the philosophy and style of life that we were attempting to deal with ourselves and approach as a group. That particular group did not delve that much into the type of action that we took on, ourselves, but certainly pointed the way.

QUESTION: Was your action modeled after the Berrigan one at Catonsville?

TOM: Yes, but I see many different aspects between our group and our style and the Baltimore or the Catonsville action.

QUESTION: Have you been in touch with either of the Berrigans?

TOM: Jerry met Daniel Berrigan about three years ago before he was involved in Catonsville and spent a good part of that summer with Daniel Berrigan going over various aspects of how a Christian should respond first of all to the Church's silence on this particular issue, which we felt was a very pressing issue, and more importantly how an individual has a responsibility to respond and what way should he? So he had that contact.

QUESTION: Is he still in correspondence with either Daniel or Phillip Berrigan?

TOM: At this point, not really. We have been in correspondence with both of them on a couple of occasions as our trial has been coming up. At one point we considered bringing them in as witnesses. But finally decided not to. They've had contact with us since the action and sent us letters of support, as have many other people who have been working on the east coast.

QUESTION: Have all four of you read *The Trial of the Catonsville Nine?*

TOM: Yes, we have. We were also involved in a production of it. I wasn't, I was in Europe, but they were involved in a production of it in the fall of 1970. [In response to a question toward the end of the interview on who influenced him he named several priests and people involved in social action or peace organizations. When asked how much support he got from the faculty at his university he said, "Very little." Only one faculty member, he thought, supported his views, none of the others either encouraged or inspired him in his convictions.]

QUESTION: I can't ask you what the outcome of the trial would be but what would a guilty verdict mean for you?

TOM: I will not attempt to guess what the verdict would be but I'll attempt to explain what a verdict might mean. If you talk about victory after a courtroom trial, what constitutes a victory? In this particular case a conviction would not necessarily mean defeat, nor would an acquittal mean victory. What I mean by that is simply that if we were acquitted on the basis that the jury thought we were really nice kids that got mixed up and off on the wrong track for a minute, but we're such nice kids we won't do it again, and they would acquit us for that reason, it would be a defeat because they would have missed the purpose of our bothering to go to the selective service system, to wait around to be arrested, to come to the courtroom, to try to explain to them that the war is still continuing, that the war is a symbol of the deeper problems that are in society. Vietnam is a mirror of American society. And if the jury does not see this in our presentation there and testimony and they acquit us for some other reason, I would see this not being a victory. On the other hand, if it becomes apparent that we have pretty well said all that we have to say, that we have been allowed to bring the testimony to light and still have a conviction, I would not necessarily see that as a defeat on the basis that we did have our day in court, that we did talk to a jury that represents, so to speak, the conscience of

QUESTION:

the community. Hopefully that would mean that we are one step closer to one of these things doing something, the courts really taking the war on as an issue. In the discussion of this particular kind of action, you must have discussed the possibility that conviction could occur and the likelihood of a jail sentence. Had you somehow brought yourself to accept this fact and how long did you think the time would be?

TOM:

Well, that was very definitely something that each of us had to cope with ourselves. It was something we discussed often in the larger group but I think each of us, even now, approach it in very different ways. Speaking for myself, I've accepted the real probability that I would be in prison for a few years. The time I would be working for appeals would approach four or five. But that again is hard to say because there are so many variables involved. My own view of prison is that, as many of us saw with Attica, prison in our society has really not been dealt with by the great majority of Americans. My own feeling is that if more "good American kids" were put in jail there might be more concern for what our prisons are doing to the impoverished, to the person who usually ends up there. More importantly for myself I see prison as another environment that, while it will be binding and I will not be as free, is another very valuable area in which I could work, also time for reflection, reading, things like that.

DISCUSSION

There are several explanatory schemes relating to criminal behavior that seem inappropriate to explain Tom's behavior. Least adequate is labeling theory. This type of political crime is not impulsive but well thought out and highly self-conscious. Tom noted that much thought, discussion, prior political activity, and reading went into his attack on the local draft board. He said at one point that the symbolic action was something that he had been preparing for for years, that it was a logical progression of everything that had gone on in his social-political activities prior to it. Too, the reactions of control agencies in this case did not seem to be causal in further political deviation. The classical path traced by the deviant in labeling literature is initial deviation, a penalty associated with it, further primary deviation, followed by stronger penalties, and rejections, further deviation, community stigmatization, and ultimate acceptance of deviant social status by the original actor. This does not seem to fit our illustration of political crime. Tom's identity is shaped not by control agencies but by his and his associates' convictions about nonviolence and the character of the Indochina war. The original causes of his deviation do not recede, as predicted in labeling theory, and give way to the disapproving and degradational reactions of society. This is not to trivialize the reactions of official agencies, since their response can severely restrict one's life chances, but to point out the subsidary role they play in formation of one's identity as a "political criminal."

The ecological explanation is also irrelevant in Tom's case. His behavior was not the result of his spatial location in the society. The middle-income areas in which he grew up were not distinguished by the patterns of dissent to which Tom was exposed. The incredulity of his parents in response to the symbolic action suggests that what he did could not be explained as an automatic and culturally enjoined expression of the values they all shared. Though Tom saw a certain extension of his parents' views in what he did, they were not prepared to go along with him. According to his account his mother stated, "We never told you to break the law." They endorsed demonstrations, protests, and picketing but had not come to any consideration of alternatives if these actions were ineffective. The neighborhoods in which Tom was raised could not be characterized as disorganized nor were social control institutions weak. Quite the opposite—they were older, assimilated communities strongly identified with the larger society's control apparatus. The resources were available to guide children into law-abiding adult lives and satisfying business or professional careers. The areas did not constitute enclaves of any kind of counterculture. Young people growing up in this kind of setting were not trapped by their environment, as Shaw's delinquents seemed to be, nor drawn to a robust tradition of political crime.

The differential association explanation seems, on the face of it, to make more sense. But it was not unwitting contact with definitions favorable to law violations that led to the destruction of draft board files. Rather it was a responsiveness to religious values which recognized the possibilities of resistance to the state. These values, perhaps not as strongly supported by Tom's parents, were nevertheless present. Yet these values did not automatically lead to political violations—otherwise all or most of those exposed to them would react in the same way. Sensitivity to dissenting values needed to be supplemented and reinforced by others who shared them and could work out specific ways of expressing them. In Tom's case the values he held led to choices about the social relationships he selected. His political activities in high school, seminary, and college led him to identify those audiences and groups to which he wished to respond. The theory of differential association is helpful as a general principle but does not specify the precise mechanisms that lead to political violations. If the theory of differential association means that persons are saturated with particular meanings in their social environment and absorb them almost unconsciously, then it is not appropriate to our political criminal. There is a question also on how appropriate the differential association explanation is to other kinds of criminal behavior. Matza, criticizing Sutherland's theory, noted that he underestimated the symbolic availability of various ways of life everywhere and that men move intentionally in search of meaning.[22] They are not locked into structural niches that restrict their awareness of alternatives. Glaser's introduction of the term "differential identification" was designed to capture this aspect of violative behavior, namely that people pursue criminal behavior (or we would say any kind of purposeful behavior) to the extent that they identify with real or imaginary persons from whose perspective their behavior seems acceptable or desirable.[23]

Opportunity theory also seems inappropriate to explain Tom's behavior. It would have to be reformulated to address this kind of violation and even then would not be particularly illuminating. Opportunity theory, as formulated by Merton, Cloward, and Ohlin, is best suited to explain economic offenses. Those persons who accept the success goals extolled by the larger society, but are unable for structural reasons to realize them, are pressured to achieve them in illicit ways. An analogous situation for the kind of political violation under discussion would be the shared value of nonviolence and the limited opportunities for expressing it. We have seen that this value was not celebrated virtually above all others in Tom's milieu nor were opportunities for realizing it restricted so that illegal alternatives were the only ones available. When Tom and his friends invaded the draft board he was operating with a student deferment which prevented his conscription into a war he thought immoral. Even after graduation the options of conscientious objection and alternative service were available as legal possibilities. A more convincing case might be made for Durkheim's anomie approach. Tom was at a particular point in the life cycle where his links with the larger society were not yet formed. He was in transition from the status of student to one of adult citizen yet had not made any conventional commitments that would have made his political violation more costly. If we conceive of his situation as one of "drift," then we might be able to say that he was able to respond positively to one of the subterranean traditions—that of radical nonvio-

[22] David Matza, *Becoming Deviant* (Englewood Cliffs., N.J.: Prentice-Hall, 1969).
[23] Daniel Glaser, "Criminality Theory and Behavioral Image," *American Journal of Sociology,* 61 (March 1956), 433–44.

lence—that is present in the larger society and has always exerted a fascination for idealistic younger people. Thus the injunction not to break the law is neutralized by an appeal to higher loyalties which enabled Tom to destroy government property without guilt. He acted instead with a strong sense of the rightness of his behavior.

One part of an explanation of this political violation must take into account the stage of the life cycle at which it occurs. We can hypothesize that it is more likely to occur at those points where the bonds to the larger society are weakened, or for some dramatic reason called into question. Becker's discussion of *commitment,* a term used frequently by Tom in the interview, seems most appropriate for explaining his political violation.[24] The first step seems to be a critical turning point experienced as peculiarly anomic, having the effect of tearing one loose from former commitments. Strauss has pointed out that turning points brought on by incidents of one kind or another are a common human experience.[25] They tend to bring on surprise, shock, chagrin, anxiety, tension, self-questioning. Some disruptions demanding social realignments are built into our culture like graduation, certification, marriage, death of a loved one, retirement, and the like; others may be caused by experiences of betrayal, shame, humiliation, and indignation. These experiences by themseves are not causal, but are links in a chain that leads to violation. For Tom, the turning point seemed to be his return from the European travel-study program. His previous political activity was exhilarating and suggested that larger social structures, like universities and possibly the state, could be changed. But the excitement of the post-Cambodian period had given way to apathy. Tom felt that only something that went beyond the previous actions would awaken people to what the possibilities were, and would also relieve his own despair: "I *had* to do something." It was at this point that he turned to strategies previously not considered. These strategies were symbolically available. Tom reports that he and his associates were reading of the Berrigans, were in contact with them, and while he was in Europe his associates staged a production of *The Trial of the Catonsville Nine.* In the interaction with others sharing his disillusionment, any doubts as to risk were dissolved and the motive to destroy draft board records was built into final form. Out of this discussion and the give-and-take interaction came the development of commitment to a particular group of people and a particular set of values. Becker has suggested that commitment refers to making a side bet whereby the committed person acts in such a way as to involve other

[24] Howard S. Becker, "Notes on the Concept of Commitment," *American Journal of Sociology,* 64 (July 1960), 32–40.
[25] Anselm L. Strauss, *Mirrors and Masks: The Search for Identity* (New York: Free Press, 1959), pp. 93ff.

interests, originally extraneous to the action, to insure his consistency. In short, he stakes something of value to him on being consistent, so that the consequences of inconsistency will be expensive. It is difficult to tell from the interview with Tom whether or in what way the mechanism of side bet applies. He does not talk about the doubts that may have occurred along the way as risks and costs were weighed or about obligations he felt to his parents that gave him the feeling he couldn't back out. In Becker's terminology, however, staking one's reputation as loyal, courageous, and trustworthy would constitute a side bet and could provide consistency to the behavior of the person who participates in a political violation. Or perhaps more importantly in political violations such as Tom's, the consistency is a byproduct of the strength of one's convictions and the moral outrage provoked by the war.

QUESTIONS FOR FURTHER DISCUSSION

1. What are the pros and cons for engaging in this kind of highly publicized violation if your aims were similar to Tom's?

2. What influence would you say that the possible penalties for destruction of selective service records had on Tom and his group of dissidents?

3. If a community policy to reduce the incidence of political crime were to be developed what sorts of strategies would be suggested by Tom's case?

4. To what extent could Tom's involvement in this action be considered a "career?"

5. How would a conflict and consensus perspective interpret this account and what further information would each need?

6. One suggested hypothesis was that political crime like Tom's was due less to background factors than to "drift," i.e., his in-between status—not an adolescent, yet not considered fully an adult because of his student status. What other hypotheses might be suggested to explain Tom's behavior?

SUMMARY

As with personal and property crime political criminality is both a status and a behavior. The label "political criminal" is one that decisively affects the life chances of the offender, follows him into the correctional facility if he is sent there, and is part of his self-conception. Excluding the crimes committed by government agents the self-conception "political criminal" is self-imposed; it is not the end result of official processing. Crimes of dissent, unlike any other violations, self-consciously challenge existing social arrangements and for those who are not terrorists or guerrillas the aim is to be caught and tried. This kind of political crime is an instance of where the reported cases match the actual violations. In short, there is no hidden political crime of this variety. The initiative springs almost entirely from the offender, and the control agencies are sometimes put in the position of reluctantly trying them. One of the prosecutors in the Spock case reported that they were compelled to move ahead because the defendants supplied films of their violation. Thus if we were to classify crimes in terms of the initiative exercised by offenders it would be greatest in dissenting political crime, least in public order crimes. But violations related to political dissent are most likely to be prosecuted. This is in marked contrast to corporate crime, which is the subject of Chapter 12.

corporate crime

The study of corporate crime has thrust social scientists and criminologists into the heart of ideological and power conflicts in American society. It is for this reason that traditional criminology has tended to deemphasize it. It is considered to be a politically charged area of inquiry and the debates about corporate crime often tell us more about the author's political convictions than they do about the phenomenon of corporate crime. But examination of corporate crime challenges simple explanations of criminality that look to poverty as causal; it tells us a great deal about the distribution of power in our society and how it is exercised. Yet few pieces of original research have been published in this area during the past 20 years or more. Geis has observed that there has been perhaps one original investigation annually plus an occasional reiteration or reinterpretation of previous work and theory.[1]

A first step in sorting out what has been done is to define precisely what is meant by corporate crime. It refers to criminal acts of corporations and individuals acting in their corporate capacity. This excludes crimes like embezzlement which may benefit the corporate executive at the expense of his company. It also excludes those kinds of crimes committed by corporate executives that have nothing to do with the corpora-

---

[1] Gilbert Geis, "Avocational Crime," in Daniel Glaser (ed.), *Handbook of Criminology* (Chicago: Rand McNally, 1974), ch. 8.

tion, such as the conventional crimes or those that high-status people are most prone to commit, like overstating business expenses on income tax forms. It refers specifically to *illegal acquisitive behavior engaged in for the immediate purpose of increasing corporate (as distinguished from personal) wealth.* The behavior includes restraint of trade, false advertising, sale of fraudulent securities, misuse of trademarks, manufacture of unsafe foods and drugs, and pollution of the environment. All these business activities were made illegal during the past 100 years although their roots in English common law go much further back. The legislation grew out of industrialization, replacement of the entrepreneur by the corporation, and the development of large-scale trade unions. The regulation was occasioned by the growing consciousness of the need to preserve the vital assets of a community and to protect the health, safety, and economic welfare of its citizens.

Traditional laws against property offenses protected the individual from the acquisitive behavior of others. But the emphasis in the more recent legislation is not the protection of individual property rights, but the protection of social order against an individual or a group that is in a position to endanger it. The state enters the picture to protect the community as a whole from powerful industrial and commercial interests. The modern state is increasingly responsible for the maintenance of health and safety standards as well as trade and commerce. This accounts for the emergence of legislation relating to safety appliances, sanitary standards in factories and mines, and minimum quality of foodstuffs, drugs, and medical preparations sold to the public.

For those industrial nations concerned about protecting competition in the furtherance of a liberal economic philosophy the state's role is also to prohibit monopolies. The underlying notion is that all citizens should be given an opportunity to trade freely and that the pursuit of each trader to realize his own economic advantage would work out to the common good. But the danger is always that more powerful traders might corner the market and stifle competition. Outside the communist orbit every industrially advanced country has some legal remedies against the monopolization of an industry by one enterprise so that a competitive economy may be maintained. But even in the Soviet Union, where all industrial production of any significance is owned by the state, competition is encouraged among the various industrial units. For the efficient execution of state planning a large measure of personal responsibility and initiative on the part of managers is required; hence since 1936 Soviet enterprises have been put on the basis of "business accountability"—they are responsible for their own debts out of their assets. Managers and other personnel also receive bonuses based on the enterprise's profit. One of the major concerns of antitrust legislation—monopolization and restraint of trade—would not be relevant in a socialist society, but unfair methods of competition would.

The purpose of the recent protective legislation is to compel business to apply stricter standards of inquiry and control to transactions which may endanger public security. The trend is to impose strict liability for violations since the primary purpose is regulation, not the establishment of guilt. What seems to be emerging in the face of the state's reluctance to bear the cost of limitless trials is a kind of "negligence without fault" as in traffic regulations. But this touches on an area of corporate crime about which there is much dispute: the kind of formal social condemnation considered appropriate to prevent outlawed conduct, and the kinds of sanctions that might best insure this end. Another question that has been raised by students of corporate crime is: whose interest is served by proscribing certain kinds of corporate misbehavior? If we answer this question we can more easily address the other two. A recapitulation of the history of national regulation provides some clues and leads to the major issue that has divided criminologists in the corporate crime field: is antitrust an economic bill of rights or more simply a guarantee of free competition?

HISTORY OF NATIONAL REGULATION

The incursion of the national government into the regulation of business and industry to prevent monopolization took place earlier in the United States than in other industrialized nations. The open character of the country and the possibilities of expansion made it an ideal setting for the development of "high Capitalism" in Max Weber's phrase. A laissez-faire economy had greater possibilities of realization in a land with tremendous natural resources, a small but growing population, expanding markets, and the like. The possibilities of cornering a market in this fluid situation was less likely. But as the frontiers began to close, the need for regulation became more apparent. The central economic development after the Civil War was the growth of the railroad. It led to a centralized, unified, and more industrialized nation. It was the activities of the railroads in the South and West that led to the development of a grass-roots antimonopoly movement. The practice of using public officials to achieve personal gain was widespread as were pooling arrangements to prevent competition, stock-watering, and exorbitant railroad rates. Reaction to these activities was expressed in the Granger Movement that culminated in the passage of the Granger laws—state acts regulating railroads and sometimes grain elevator and warehouse practices. The agrarian discontent at the end of the nineteenth century generated a movement that led to national legislation to curb corporate abuses.

> From the outset, the alliances plunged into politics with a vehemence that startled and frightened the business interests, capturing state after state in the South and West and sending eloquent spokesmen to state legislatures and to Washington.[2]

The grievances were not only against the railroads but also against eastern credit institutions which were suspected of trying to check the independent economic development of the South and West. Discontent was strong too against "monopolistic" price policies of producers of agricultural machinery and other goods needed in rural areas, and against manufacturer's agents all of whom were regarded as conspiring against the farmer. By 1890 at least 14 states had written antitrust provisions into their constitutions while 13 others had adopted antitrust laws. The farmers were joined by other groups: those concerned about exploitation of national resources by corporations for profit, labor, which found bargaining with large corporations a distinct disadvantage, and small businessmen concerned about being driven out of business by the larger corporations. This coalition, in support of federal regulation, worked toward the passage of the Interstate Commerce Act in 1887. The act recognized that the regulation of railroad rates was beyond the competence of individual states and decreed that rates should be fair and just; it outlawed discriminatory practices and established the Interstate Commerce Commission. The act signaled a shift away from a laissez-faire attitude that had long prevailed among lawmakers, to a recognition that:

> a free market of traders is like a field of runners who start together but do not finish together. The field of initially equal free traders soon thins out. Resources, ability, ruthlessness, or luck, favor some competitors to surpass others. In that advantageous position, they can accumulate economic power that can enable them to establish a complete monopoly which extinguishes competition.[3]

The object of agitation was extended from monopolistic practices among railroads to industrial combinations generally, which were attacked in the Sherman Antitrust Act of 1890. The widespread resentment against the "trusts" stimulated a rich literature critical of bigness and monopoly, as well as a set of legislative proposals sharpening common law doctrines opposed to restraint of trade. The Populist movement provided a critique

[2] Arthur S. Link, *American Epoch: A History of the United States since the 1890's* (New York: Knopf, 1955), p. 8.
[3] Wolfgang Friedmann, *Law in a Changing Society*, 2nd ed. (New York: Columbia University Press, 1972), p. 293.

of big business and generated a number of other sociological and criminological critiques. The most famous sociologist was E. A. Ross, who wrote extensively on social control, law, and economic institutions.[4]

Thorelli's detailed account of the passage of the Sherman Antitrust Act states that the rationale underlying it was the common-law proscription against monopolies and in favor of competition.[5] No one in the Congress undertook a penetrating analysis of the economic theory behind it; the belief among legislators was that they were clarifying the common-law doctrine of restraint of trade to make it applicable to a modern industrial society. Though their analysis may have been absent, according to Thorelli their intuitions were sound. Basically there were three aspects of the old English common law concerning restrictions of trade: it was a violation to corner local markets by interfering with the distributive processes, especially with regard to the necessities of life; grants of monopoly could be made in recognition of innovations in trade or manufacture in the public interest—forerunner of the modern patent system; and contracts in restraint of trade are acceptable if those agreements are not injurious to the public interest, that is, if they are "reasonable." It was the first aspect of the English common law that was incorporated into the Sherman Act and eventually molded by the courts into a useful antimonopoly instrument. The law as it was finally passed was intended to be a federal codification of the common law and the laws of the various states. Its aims were modest but it did break new ground in sharpening the sanctions against outlawed behavior. Earlier the cases at common law were private suits between parties to restrictive agreements. The Sherman Act publicly condemned monopolization, restraint of trade, unfair methods of competition, and substantial lessening of competition. Violations were criminal offenses—misdemeanors punishable by a fine not to exceed $5,000, by imprisonment up to one year, or both. Any person injured by another's antitrust violation could recover triple damages—three times the actual amount of damage suffered.

Friedmann characterized the American antitrust legislation as a "revolutionary departure" from established concepts of the criminal law because it utilized criminal sanctions to discourage economic offenses which were formerly controlled by civil remedies.[6] The law that was finally passed was relatively brief. It stated some fairly broad principles and left it to the courts to give concrete meaning to terms like "restraint

---

[4] Edwin A. Ross, *Social Control* (New York: Macmillan, 1901); *Sin and Society* (Boston: Houghton Mifflin, 1907).

[5] Hans B. Thorelli, *The Federal Antitrust Policy: Origination of an American Tradition* (Baltimore: Johns Hopkins Press, 1954).

[6] Friedmann, *Law in a Changing Society*, ch. 6.

of trade" and "substantial lessening of competition." The character of the proscribed conduct was left ambiguous. Thus one of the requirements of the criminal law discussed earlier—specificity—is missing. The problem of defining the proscribed behavior with specificity so that fair notice would be given was not addressed in the original legislation. Congress chose instead to opt for a statement of principles rather than a lengthy list of forbidden behaviors. Certainly if the latter course were followed, the law would have been quickly outdated because of changing circumstances. But the vague formulation has left a legacy of confusion and divided scholars generally in terms of the general question: Is antitrust an economic bill of rights or more simply a sure guarantee of free competition?

ECONOMIC BILL OF RIGHTS OR FREE COMPETITION GUARANTEE?

Those who see the original antitrust legislation and later additions to it as an economic bill of rights focus on the consumer as the ultimate beneficiary. In this view the implied goal of antitrust is the maximization of consumer welfare so that the economic system might deliver a diversity of quality goods at lower prices. The enforcement of the law should be such that industry is structured to be competitive, not monopolistic, because this serves consumers best. The opposite view contends that if Congress intended to create a specific type of economic structure it would have chosen to enact competition rather than legislate against monopolies. It would have developed some positive prescriptions and regulations designed to move us toward this economic order. The Sherman Act should be viewed simply as an attempt to protect small business so that its survival is insured.

A closer look at the discussion before the Sherman Act was passed suggests that Congress saw the ultimate beneficiary as the consumer but the immediate beneficiaries were small business proprietors and tradesmen. No one felt any need during the original discussions to elaborate any conception of a just economic order. Free competition was a self-evident good:

> The government's natural role in the system of free enterprise was that of a patrolman policing the highways of commerce. It is the duty of the modern patrolman to keep the road open for all and everyone and to prevent highway robbery, speeding, the running of red lights and other violations that will endanger and hence, in

the end, slow down the overall movement of traffic. Translated into the terms of commerce this means that occupations were kept open to all who wished to try their luck, that the individual was to be protected in his "common right" to choose his calling and that hindrances to equal opportunity were to be eliminated.[7]

Conclusions on the intent of the legislation are difficult to come by when we realize that it was a symbolic attempt to dampen the discontent caused by economic dislocations. Hofstadter reports that most of the astute politicians of the day saw the Sherman Act as "a gesture, a ceremonial concession to an overwhelming public demand for some kind of reassuring action against the trusts."[8] His interpretation seems plausible since it was not used at all to check business consolidations for the first 12 years following its passage. Quite the contrary: the greatest merger movement in American history occurred from 1898 to 1902. This fact plus the dismal history of enforcement attempts against monopoly suggests that either the law was not meant to be enforced or that those who were its target managed to shape enforcement for their own ends.

Max Weber in a discussion of the significance and limits of legal coercion in economic life comments generally on the law's lack of success.[9] Unless there are strong interest groups committed to enforcement it will not be carried out forcefully enough. And if the penalties are relatively slight, as they are in American antitrust legislation, the inclination to forego economic opportunity disappears. The possible profits of an illegal action so outweigh the possible penalties that widespread noncompliance is inevitable. The resources of violators to resist the implementation of the law are also very great. Potential violators are quite knowledgeable in the ways of circumventing the law and disguising any violations. The end result, according to Weber, is that the intended meaning of the law is turned into its very opposite.

The situation is more complex, however, than a conflict between the public interest and the trusts as some historians have argued. Gabriel Kolko's thorough study of the political and economic history of America from 1900 to 1916 takes issue with the more conventional historical interpretations.[10] The situation as he describes it in rich detail shows big business *leading* the struggle for federal regulation of the economy. They led the fight because their own voluntary attempts to attain stability and control through mergers failed:

[7] Thorelli, *Federal Antitrust Policy*, p. 226.
[8] Richard Hofstadter, *The Age of Reform: From Bryan to FDR* (New York: Knopf, 1955).
[9] Max Rheinstein (ed.), *Max Weber on Law in Economy and Society* (New York: Simon & Schuster, 1954), pp. 37–38.
[10] Gabriel Kolko, *The Triumph of Conservatism: A Reinterpretation of American History 1900–1966* (New York: Free Press, 1963).

> Ironically, contrary to the consensus of historians it was not the existence of monopoly that caused the federal government to intervene in the economy, but lack of it.[11]

He provides case studies on all the key industries or "trusts" of the period (iron-steel, oil, automobile, agricultural machinery, telephone, and copper) showing that shifting markets and resources, loss of relative power by dominant companies, and the failure of merger movements to attain stability and control led businessmen to seek federal assistance. Not only were measures to regulate supported by all the key business leaders of the period but first proposed by them. Kolko argues that the antitrust legislation did not represent the triumph of small business over the trusts but the victory of big business in achieving the rationalization of the economy that only the federal government could provide. Their motivations were not primarily acquisitive. They did not want complete control over their industries, only a dominant position. As Kolko points out they preferred holding on to what they had rather than risking what they already possessed through encouragement of cutthroat competition. Economic losses were a very real prospect in unregulated capitalism but so too was political destruction:

> There were disturbing groupings ever since the end of the Civil War: agrarian discontent, violence and strikes, a Populist movement, the rise of a Socialist party that seemed, for a time, to have an unlimited growth potential. Above all, there was a labor movement seriously divided as to its proper course, and threatening to follow in the seemingly radical footsteps of European labor.[12]

The move for federal regulation through antitrust was also a way of undercutting state antitrust legislation, which was haphazard—or worse, more responsive to radical local constituencies. The motivations of business leaders which led to the drive for federal regulation in the 1890s are also the ones that explain corporate misbehavior today: the avoidance of uncertainty, formalization and predictability of outcome, minimization of risk.

Kolko's argument also extends to the passage of pure food and drug regulation. The standard interpretation is that the public became alarmed when Upton Sinclair provided a vivid account of the unsanitary conditions that prevailed in the Chicago stockyards around the turn of the century. This led to demands that the old motto "let the buyer beware" be replaced by "let the seller beware," that producers should be held responsible for the quality of food and drugs. The Pure Food and Drug Act of 1906 was the result. The legislation recognized that the dangers of

[11] Ibid., p. 5.
[12] Ibid., p. 285.

adulterated goods was no longer the responsibility of the individual consumer but that of the manufacturer and distributor. Kolko does not deny
the widespread popular concern about food and drug purity—certainly
burgeoning state legislation was a testimony to that. But he does contend
that it was not decisive in the final legislation. The major meatpackers
led the fight for federal regulation in an attempt to rule out what they
thought was unfair competition and to stabilize their own market positions.

Most of the regulatory agencies created to monitor business activities
in this country do not operate with any criminal sanction. They can refer
flagrant violations of cease and desist orders to the criminal courts but
this is an option rarely exercised. The bulk of the enforcement involves
administrative remedies. But the antitrust legislation is unique in this
respect. Though it can be enforced administratively it has clear-cut
criminal sanctions and these sanctions have been regularly invoked.
Under the Sherman Act and its various amendments the Justice Department is given the discretion in enforcing the law to utilize the procedures
of criminal court prosecution or to seek an injunction using several different methods: the violation can be prosecuted through the criminal court
as a misdemeanor; the U.S. Attorney General can petition for an injunction to cease and desist—a violation of the injunction is punishable as
contempt of court; and those who are injured by the violations are
authorized to sue for damages in the civil court with a mandatory provision that the damages awarded be three times the damages suffered. The
violations can be processed through a criminal or civil court.

Posner's 1960 study of cases brought by the Antitrust Division of the
Justice Department between 1890 and 1969 showed that almost half of
1,551 cases tried were criminal cases.[13] Fifty-seven percent of the 694
criminal cases were settled by the acceptance of a *nolo contendere* (no
contest) plea, 21 percent by a guilty plea or conviction, and 22 percent by
acquittals and dismissals. *Nolo contendere* pleas are popular because
judges usually treat such pleas leniently, even though admissions of guilt,
and the plea is not considered prima facie evidence of guilt in later
damage suits. By selecting a no-contest plea the defendant admits without trial that he committed the alleged offense. In the past decade the
percentage of convictions via *nolo contendere* has increased to 79 percent. The Justice Department's record in criminal antitrust convictions,
however, has not been spectacular: from 1890 to 1969 there were a total
of 153 convictions, or about 2.5 convictions per year.

The widespread dissatisfaction with the inability of the Sherman Act to

[13] Richard Posner, quoted in Mark J. Green et al., *The Closed Enterprise
System* (New York: Grossman, 1972).

halt mergers led to the passage of the Clayton Act in 1914. Stock acquisitions were prohibited under this act where the effect was "to substantially lessen competition." Also prohibited were certain interlocking directorates, price discrimination, and sales on conditions that the buyer cease dealing with the seller's competitors. The Clayton Act also exempted farmer and labor organizations from the reach of antitrust legislation but was unable to prevent mergers. Corporations continued to expand. The Clayton Act was amended in 1950 to prevent further mergers. That legislation, the Celler-Kefauver Act, prohibited corporations from acquiring the stock of any part of the assets of another corporation engaged also in commerce where the effects of such acquisition "may be to substantially lessen competition." The hope was that the "may be" language would prevent upcoming mergers. Thus suits could be filed against asset acquisitions whose dangers were potential rather than actual. The language of the act assumed some kind of economic expertise on the part of the government that could provide an intelligence function in enforcement. However, even with the 1950 act's conception of potential dangers to the economic order that could be nipped in the bud by an alert antitrust staff, the mergers continued. The fact that big business has become bigger, more powerful, and more monopolistic in the face of antitrust laws compels one to conclude, says John Galbraith, that the laws are absolutely indispensable to the traditional imagery of the private corporation.[14]

A further complication for the student of corporate crime was the 1914 legislation that set up the Federal Trade Commission to regulate mergers, root out unfair trade practices, uncover price discrimination, and study industrial trends. When moving against a corporation the FTC can ask it to stop violating the law (cease and desist). Violations are usually penalized by a straight fine or a consent decree—a voluntary settlement negotiated between the defendant and the government. If the decree is subsequently violated then the sanctions are severe. The FTC can recommend to the Justice Department that civil fines be levied against those who violate cease and desist orders (limited to $5,000 per day) but this sanction is rarely used. The legal foundations of the FTC are somewhat ambiguous and its enforcement powers are in doubt. The present situation is one where two agencies—the Justice Department and the FTC—now enforce the same laws. They have overlapping responsibilities and in practice there is a considerable amount of unproductive interagency rivalry. Some students of crime suggest that the decisions of civil courts and administrative agencies like FTC are often arrived at by procedures

14 John K. Galbraith, "On the Economic Image of Corporate Enterprise," in Ralph Nader and Mark J. Green (eds.), *Corporate Power in America* (New York: Grossman, 1973), p. 5.

that have less regard for due process than do criminal proceedings, so that the violations alleged are not really crimes. In short, there is some question whether the behavior would have been declared criminal if dealt with in a criminal court.[15] In this view only corporate violations dealt with through criminal proceedings should be part of the criminologist's consideration. Sutherland's position was that violations processed in agencies other than the criminal court were the legitimate concern of criminologists. He contended that violations of regulations were punishable by law and met the two fundamental criteria of crimes in Western society: (1) a legal description of the behavior as socially harmful, and (2) a legal provision of penalties for its violation. The dual enforcement of laws against economic crimes is somewhat confusing. It may be helpful to keep in mind that the Justice Department can invoke criminal penalties while the Federal Trade Commission is limited to civil remedies.

The law establishing the Federal Trade Commission to address unfair methods of competition seems in conception to lean toward an economic bill of rights interpretation of antitrust regulation. There was no statement of an economic structure that the legislation sought to create but it did suggest an industry-wide approach with the selection of cases of innovative impact emphasizing structure rather than misconduct. The dream of this legislation was not realized. Though businessmen were not as active in lobbying for a commission or in setting it up as they were with the earlier antitrust legislation, they seemed to know what they wanted from such a commission. The Federal Trade Commission seemed to be a more acceptable alternative to regulation by business groups than proposals for the federal chartering of corporations which had widespread support at the time.[16] The commission absorbed and reflected the predominant values of the business community. It never moved in the direction of becoming a trustbusting instrument. In the late 1920s the commission chairman urged the commission to bring major companies together to talk about the voluntary establishment of antitrust standards under FTC guidance, as any business advisory group would do. The sessions ironically degenerated into price-fixing sessions. As one businessman put it:

> When two businessmen get together, whether it is a chain institute meeting or a bible class meeting, if they happen to belong to the same industry, just as soon as the prayers have been said, they start

[15] Robert S. Caldwell, "A Reexamination of the Concept of White Collar Crime," *Federal Probation*, 22 (March 1958), 30–36.
[16] Mark J. Green et al., *The Closed Enterprise System* (New York: Grossman, 1972), ch. 10.

talking about the conditions in the industry, and it is bound definitely to gravitate, that talk, to the price structure in the industry. What else is there to talk about?[17]

The 1972 Ralph Nader study group report on antitrust enforcement documents the FTC's lack of activity in broadly attacking anticompetitive conduct even though the courts have recognized that this is part of their mandate.[18] The commission has chosen rather to expend most of its resources in protecting small businesses. Small businessmen managed to get the Clayton Act amended in 1936 making discriminations in prices and other practices unlawful so as to protect individual competitors at all levels. The 1936 amendments (the Robinson-Patman Act) were not consumer oriented. The act's proponents were retail druggists, retail grocers, and the National Farmers' Union. The implementation of the act by the FTC tends to protect inefficient firms, the rationale being that small firms are worth preserving for their social values regardless of efficiency.

In sum the original question relating to the major aims of antitrust legislation is not easily answered. The law and its implementation seem quite clearly to be the result of interest group pressure under the slogan of free competition. Yet recently consumer interest groups have pressed for broader interpretation of antitrust laws that would draw out their potential as an economic bill of rights for consumers.

HOW BEST CONTROL CORPORATE CRIME?

From the beginning of antitrust legislation there was a difference of opinion on how best to control corporate criminality. That difference of opinion has persisted to this day. One interpretation favored by owners of small businesses and agrarian groups held that the consolidation of corporations into giant enterprises was illegal. The size of the corporation made it automatically suspect. As the corporation grew, so the argument went, it would inevitably suppress competition in its own favor because big business by its very nature was incapable of acting honorably. The second view held that regulation, not trustbusting, should be the goal of federal legislation. This was the view favored by big business and its allies. Giant business corporations, so the theory runs, are normal and inevitable. In the last analysis they benefit society because they operate more efficiently than smaller enterprises. But there are immoral busi-

[17] Quoted in ibid., p. 149.
[18] Ibid.

nesses that unreasonably restrain trade. They require censure and minor business adjustments that would make violations less likely—but criminal sanctions are too extreme. Criminologists are divided on this question: some favor regulation only, others favor criminalization.

Arguments in Favor of Regulation

Herbert Packer, the distinguished criminal law scholar, has made the most telling argument for not using criminal sanctions. He holds that criminal sanctions are unproductive (relative to the expenditure of time and resources to process them through the criminal justice system) and that they divert attention from more appropriate community responses:

> There is also the possibility exemplified in the enforcement of the antitrust laws, that extensive criminal prosecution simply diverts attention and resources away from the more fundamental task of assuring a competitive structure for industry. In this instance, as in others, the criminal sanction may be not only ineffective but diversionary. Its ready availability makes us less astute than we otherwise might be to devise sanctions that are better adapted to the exigencies of economic regulation than those to be found in the powerful, but limited and crude, repertory of the criminal sanction.[19]

Others have emphasized the cultural resistance to criminal sanctions rather than their inefficiency. In the late 1950s, Newman found respondents generally reluctant to recommend the kind of harsh sanctions for business violators that they would for robbery or burglary.[20] A study conducted in 1966 by Rooney and Gibbons paralleled the earlier findings.[21] Newman felt that the effects of corporate violations and other white-collar crimes were diffuse so that community resentment was not mobilized. Thus the deterrent effect of the victim's wrath does not operate:

> The violence, the directness of murder, engenders social solidarity against the criminal, particularly as long as the press reports every detail. But what of the formation of an illicit monopoly with complex interlocking corporate structures? Even granting a crime has

[19] Herbert L. Packer, *The Limits of the Criminal Sanction* (Stanford, Calif.: Stanford University Press, 1968), p. 362.
[20] Donald J. Newman, "Public Attitudes Toward a Form of White Collar Crime," *Social Problems*, 4 (January 1957), 228–32.
[21] Elizabeth A. Rooney and Don C. Gibbons, "Social Reactions to 'Crimes Without Victims,'" *Social Problems*, 13 (Spring 1966), 400–10; see also Don C. Gibbons, "Crime and Punishment: A Study in Social Attitudes," *Social Forces*, 47 (June 1969), 391–97.

been committed, who is the criminal; who, the victim? Obviously public resentment of such offenses must take a different form than in conventional criminal cases. . . .[22]

Kadish takes the position that the criminal sanction has not worked in the area of corporate crime for reasons other than those Sutherland suggest—i.e., that powerful business interests don't want the law enforced.[23] The law has failed to operate, according to Kadish, because the behavior to be regulated is not regarded as morally reprehensible. He concludes that it is unwise to criminalize morally neutral conduct since it leads to the dilution of culpability in the service of regulation. The difficulties of tracing individual criminal responsibility—because the policy initiators are usually different from the policy implementers—have led to suggestions that negligence omission charges be made the basis of high managerial agent accountability. This is what is meant by dilution of culpability. It is not concerned with individual guilt. Kadish thinks that dilution in this area would undermine criminal responsibility in other areas.

The issue turns on the question of whether the criminal law is to reflect and implement consensus or anticipate it. Those who favor regulation point to the fact that there is no consensus regarding antitrust violations, hence their proscription should not be part of the criminal law. The critics of criminal sanction point out that the economic policy that antitrust was supposed to realize is unclear, "constituting largely a vague aspiration for a proper balance among competing economic goals." This has led to judgments of illegality based on evaluative judgments rather than factual determinations. In short, the antitrust legislation is bad law. Suggestions for the reform of legislation dealing with corporate malfeasance have been administrative remedies. Administrative codes can be enforced without conferring the status of criminal on anyone. The administrative agency conceivably could issue legislative regulations that would eliminate the present problem of just what is proscribed. The agency could also conceivably issue declaratory orders in which they render an advisory judgment on the legality of a contemplated course of action. The power to regulate under an administrative agency would consist of authorizing activities through its licensing procedures.

[22] Donald J. Newman, "White Collar Crime," *Law and Contemporary Problems,* 23 (Autumn 1958), 735–53, 745.
[23] Sanford H. Kadish, "Some Observations on the Use of Criminal Sanctions in the Enforcement of Economic Legislation," *University of Chicago Law Review,* 30 (Spring 1963), 423–49.

Arguments in Favor of Criminalization

The supporters of criminal sanctions make their case partly on common-law grounds. The laws against false advertising are related to common-law fraud; infringement of patents and copyrights laws is related to larceny. The National Labor Relations Law is an attempt to prevent coercion related to the common-law prohibition of restrictions on freedom in the form of assaults, false imprisonment, and extortion. The antitrust laws, as noted earlier, also had their basis in the common law. Generally those who argue for continuing to use the criminal sanction for corporate violations also suggest decriminalizing victimless crime and reducing the harshness of sentences in traditional crimes. This seems somewhat contradictory at first glance but is based on the conviction that citizens require protection against arbitrary actions by the state on the one hand and unregulated corporations on the other. This leads to recommendations that the state's authority be diminished in dealing with traditional victimless crime but strengthened in responding to corporate crime (which at present is massively underpunished). The fact that corporate crime, especially highly publicized misconduct, goes unpunished weakens the moral climate of the community and provides examples of wrong-doing for citizens generally. The problem of cultural resistance to criminal sanctions is recognized here. But public opinion also turns out to be more stringent than judicial reaction to corporate crime. In the Newman study mentioned above a sample of citizens was asked to select appropriate punishments to be meted out in cases of product misbranding and food adulteration.[24] Their penalties were more stringent than those actually invoked in cases studied. A surprisingly high proportion (80 percent) felt that the penalties should have been more severe. In short, the social condemnation that actually exists was not reflected in the implementation of the law. In 1969 the Louis Harris Poll reported that a manufacturer of an unsafe auto was regarded by respondents as worse than a mugger—68 percent to 22 percent—and a businessman who illegally fixed prices was considered worse than a burglar—54 percent to 28 percent.[25] Ball and Friedman take issue with Kadish on the futility of invoking criminal sanctions when there is little community support for it.[26] They observe that it is not necessary that those regulated be en-

[24] Newman, "White Collar Crime."
[25] "Changing Morality: The Two Americas," *Time*, June 6, 1969, p. 26.
[26] Harry V. Ball and Lawrence Friedman, "The Use of Criminal Sanctions in the Enforcement of Economic Legislation: A Sociological View," *Stanford Law Review*, 17 (January 1965), 197–223.

thusiastic about the law to insure their compliance. All that is required is that they be aware of the legislation. Lack of support doesn't necessarily lead to defiance.

Dershowitz argues that criminal sanctions can be very effective against corporate criminals.[27] His hypothesis is that the rate of acquisitive corporate crime will vary directly with the expectation of net gain to the corporation, and will vary inversely with the certainty and severity of the impact with which the criminal sanction personally falls on those who formulate corporate policy. His observation is confirmed by the director of the fraud division of the Justice Department:

> No one in direct contact with the living reality of business conduct in the United States is unaware of the effect of the imprisonment of seven high officials in the Electrical Machinery Industry in 1960 had on the conspiratorial price fixing in many areas of our economy; similar sentences in a few cases each decade would almost completely cleanse our economy of the cancer of collusive price fixing and the mere prospect of such sentences is itself the strongest available deterrent to such activities.[28]

Apparently the self-image of convicted corporate criminals is deeply affected. The conviction is unexpected, uncommon, awkward, inconvenient, and humiliating. The two major profit diminishing sanctions imposed in the present antitrust laws are criminal sanctions and the private treble-damage suit. The fine, notes Dershowitz, is ineffective because exceedingly low penalties are permitted by statute; the original Sherman Act provided for a maximum fine of $5,000, which was raised to $50,000 in 1955. The average fine is about $13,000, so that as presently administered, it constitutes little more than a "reasonable license fee." The treble-damage suit has possibilities but in the overwhelming number of cases where the government has convinced a court of violation, the convicted company paid nothing to private claimants in the form of damages or settlements. Dershowitz suggests that the treble-damage suit could operate more effectively as a deterrent if *nolo contendere* pleas were eliminated. If not eliminated they should be prima facie evidence of legal liability in later private actions. Criminal fines would be more effective by being raised. The corporation now retains the lion's share of illegal profits after a fine. The government should be enabled to recover from the convicted corporation all illegal profits much as it recovers stolen goods. Dershowitz would also increase the responsibility of policy makers to

[27] Alan M. Dershowitz, "Increasing Community Control over Corporate Crime: A Problem in the Law of Sanctions," *Yale Law Journal*, 71 (September 1961), 289–306.
[28] Gordon B. Spivak, "Antitrust Enforcement in the United States: A Primer," *Connecticut Bar Journal*, 37 (September 1963), 382.

exercise reasonable care in preventing acquisitive corporate crime. Failure to do so would be a misdemeanor. The corporate agent would be held liable if he has specific knowledge of a violation occurring and if he willfully defaults either to report or end it.

The strongest advocates of use of criminal sanctions in corporate offenses are consumer groups like Ralph Nader's Center for the Study of Responsive Law. Most of the recent investigations of corporate misconduct are not coming from criminologists but from consumer advocates. They have suggested that social science research in this area needs to be supplemented by economic and legal expertise. They have provided examples of how research can be conducted using a variety of techniques for data gathering, of how the legal process can be used to gain access to relevant materials, and of how to use publicity to get information or insure compliance with the law. Nader's "Raiders" have demonstrated that data can be gathered on government and business processes in the absence of high-level cooperation. The lack of cooperation by corporate offenders in detailing their illegalities and the absence of trial information because of the *nolo contendere* pleas has stymied criminologists. The Center for the Study of Responsive Law has made a number of recommendations for reform over and above those already noted. Some of them are:

1. Mandatory prison terms of four months for the first offense and one year for the second of any individuals found guilty or who plead guilty to an offense.

2. Any management member who obtains a criminal record relating to his corporate duties should be deprived of his position and be disqualified from exercising similar functions in other organizations for a period not exceeding five years.

3. Federal legislation should preempt state law to forbid indemnification of punitive fines for antitrust violations.

4. To address the reluctance of the media to publicize corporate criminality the Nader group recommends that corporations be compelled to advertise the fact of their criminal convictions. This would serve two purposes: it would educate the public to the phenomenon of breach of consumer trust and would suggest to corporate executives that violations in this area are similar to a labor leader appropriating funds from members. Both the Nader group and some criminologists have addressed themselves to the problem of community education on the dangers of corporate crime. Geis has pointed up the problem succinctly:

Corporate offenses . . . do not have biblical proscription—they lack, as an early writer noted, the "brimstone smell." But the havoc such offenses produce, the malevolence with which they are undertaken, and the disdain with which they are continued, are all antithetical to principles we as citizens are expected to observe. It is a long step, assuredly, and sometimes an uncertain one, from lip service to cries of outrage; but at least principled antagonism is latent, needing only to be improved in decibels and fidelity. It should not prove impossible to convince citizens of the extreme danger entailed by such violations of our social compact.[29]

The public trial of corporate criminals would be educational in itself. It would dramatize societal condemnation of the behavior and possibly induce a sense of guilt in those who might be potential violators.

5. Apart from compelling divestiture of companies to prevent monopolization, corporations would be required to sell off divisions that have been thrice convicted of antitrust violations within six years.

6. Whenever a trade association has been a vehicle for a conspiracy it should be abolished and its members barred for ten years from belonging to any other trade group whose membership is primarily intra-industry.

SUMMARY

We have stated the arguments on regulation versus criminalization somewhat sharply so as to point to the issues involved. Some criminologists take the position that criminal sanction may not be the wisest response to economic crimes but that it can insure the functioning of other less drastic sanctions like monetary settlements, private actions, injunctions, inspections, licensing, required reporting, and the like. The criminal sanction should be used only as a last resort and should be used selectively and discriminatingly when other sanctions fail. This view has the advantage of recognizing that corporate criminality is sufficiently heinous and that it should be forcefully condemned under the criminal code, while at the same time recognizing the limited and crude character of the criminal sanction pointed out by Packer. Also there seems to be some agreement by all students of corporate crime that price fixing constitutes a flagrant and clear-cut violation so that affirmative governmental measures to ferret out price fixers would probably have widespread support. It has been suggested that the antitrust division of the Justice Depart-

[29] Gilbert Geis, "Deterring Corporate Crime," in Nader and Green (eds.), *Corporate Power in America*, p. 189.

ment conduct systematic studies to get at price-fixing patterns. Some of the disagreements in the area of corporate criminality would be resolved with further information. For instance the argument about bigness and efficiency most certainly could be resolved. Friedmann, summarizing the position of economists, states:

> Economists have long debated the relative efficiency of bigness. Again this question cannot be answered absolutely, as the capital and technological requirements greatly differ from one industry to another. . . . Yet the general consensus seems to be that there are limits to the efficiency of bigness, and that beyond a certain point both the bureaucracy of the giant enterprise—which does not differ greatly whether it is publicly or privately owned—and the lack of spur from competitors have a negative effect.[30]

The weapon of divestiture has been the favored one proposed by consumer groups who believe that enforced competition is the instrument for shaping economic activity. Divestiture would substitute free enterprise for the twin beasts of monopoly and cartel. More detailed case studies of how enforced competition would maximize consumer welfare are needed. More serious discussion is also required on a desirable public policy on oligopoly. Antitrust laws have been unable to prevent oligopoly—the domination of a certain industry by a few leading corporations (no one of which has a complete monopoly) that tend to adopt parallel policies with regard to price, labor practices, and general policies. These parallel policies under present legislation are permitted so long as the actions of the corporations do not amount to technical conspiracy or combination.

EXTENT AND COST OF CORPORATE CRIME

The President's Commission on Law Enforcement and the Administration of Justice concluded that what they called white-collar crime, which includes corporate crime as used here, is pervasive in our society.[31] Although there are no "hard" statistics, Sutherland (investigating 70 of the largest American corporations) found that during a 45-year period the courts and regulatory commissions—under antitrust, false advertising, patent, copyright, and labor laws—had rendered 980 adverse decisions of which 779 indicated that crime had been committed.[32] He concluded

[30] Friedmann, *Law in a Changing Society*, pp. 309–10.
[31] President's Commission on Law Enforcement and the Administration of Justice, *Task Force Report: Crime and Its Impact—An Assessment* (Washington, D.C.: Government Printing Office, 1967), p. 102.
[32] Edwin H. Sutherland, *White Collar Crime* (New York: Holt, Rinehart & Winston, 1949).

that 60 percent of the 70 corporations he studied in depth were "habitual criminals"—having four or more convictions against them. Slightly over 97 percent of the corporations were recidivists with at least two convictions.

Clinard's study of black market violations in the United States during World War II showed that about 1 of every 15 business firms in the United States had received penalties for serious violations—roughly some 200,000 firms.[33] But the official figures did not reveal the extent of violations according to Clinard. One out of five business concerns was subjected to some kind of action by the Office of Price Administration. Hartung's study of the wholesale meat industry in Detroit paralleled Clinard's findings.[34] These violations of wartime regulations, he noted, also had a ripple effect throughout the manufacturing, wholesaling, and retailing stages. Illegal higher prices were passed on to the successive stages, thus inflating enormously the price the consumer ultimately paid.

The famous electrical conspiracy case revealed that electrical equipment manufacturers fixed prices among themselves for at least 20 years before the Justice Department brought suit against them.[35] The conspiracy involved 29 companies controlling over 95 percent of the industry. It is impossible to estimate the amount of price fixing that actually goes on. A sizeable proportion of the business community, however, believes it to be quite common. A 1970 survey of the presidents of the thousand largest manufacturing corporations asked whether many engaged in price fixing.[36] Of the top 500, 47 percent reported that such was the case; the report in the second 500 companies who felt this to be the case was 70 percent. Green states that the actual number of cases prosecuted each year is small, averaging 25 a year from 1960–64, and 11 a year from 1965–70, but the total number of industries involved in criminal antitrust acts in the past 30 years is very large:

> Nearly every conceivable industry has been affected, from milk and bread to heavy electrical equipment, from lobster fishing, shrimping and the cranberry and chrysanthemum industries to steel sheets and plumbing fixtures.[37]

The President's Commission was also concerned about the cost of corporate offenses. They argued that the loss to the public caused by a

[33] Marshall B. Clinard, *The Black Market: A Study of White Collar Crime* (New York: Holt, Rinehart & Winston, 1949).

[34] Frank E. Hartung, "White Collar Crime: Its Significance for Theory and Practice," *Federal Probation*, 17 (June 1953), 31–36.

[35] See Gilbert Geis, "The Heavy Electrical Equipment Antitrust Cases of 1961," in Marshall B. Clinard and Richard Quinney (eds.), *Criminal Behavior Systems* (New York: Holt, Rinehart & Winston, 1967).

[36] The study was conducted by the Ralph Nader Study Group and is summarized in Mark J. Green et al., *The Closed Enterprise System* (New York: Grossman, 1972), p. 150.

[37] Green et al., *The Closed Enterprise System*, p. 150.

single conspiracy in restraint of trade may be untold millions in extra cost by the buying public. They estimated that the annual cost to the public of securities frauds was in the $500 million to the billion dollar range. They also estimated that nearly $500 million each year is spent on worthless or misrepresented drugs and therapeutic devices. The financial burden of what they call white-collar crime is greater than that of robbery, larceny, and burglary. Green concluded that the electrical conspiracy alone robbed the public of more than all other robberies and thefts in 1961 combined.[38]

But apart from the financial cost the President's Commission was concerned about the social and psychological impact of this kind of criminality. They argued that it does serious damage to our social and economic institutions and undermines the legitimacy of our social system. The cynicism bred by highly publicized crimes of the powerful may actually generate further criminality among the powerless. Thio has maintained that the deviance of the powerful and of the powerless are directly related.[39] The widely reported crimes of corporate executives has a trickle effect on the behavior of the less advantaged. It convinces them that no one is honest, especially those in positions of power. The corporate criminal thus contributes to, or is one of the causes of the criminality of the lowest stratum. The cost is also high in terms of health and safety. Each year 200,000 to 500,000 workers are needlessly exposed to toxic agents such as radioactive materials and poisonous chemicals because of corporate failure to obey safety laws. Many of the 2.5 million temporary disabilities and 250,000 permanent disabilities are the result of executive acts that represent culpable failure to adhere to the law.[40]

EXPLANATIONS OF CORPORATE CRIME

The attempt to come to a scientific understanding of corporate criminality began in the United States with Sutherland's initial paper on the problem before the American Sociological Society in 1939.[41] He stated elsewhere that he was concerned with business malfeasance for some time and actually began collecting materials on it during the 1920s. His paper was largely a recital of decisions rendered against leading corporations for restraint of trade, infringement of patents, misrepresentation in

---

[38] Ibid.
[39] Alex Thio, "Class Bias in the Sociology of Deviance," *American Sociologist,* 8 (February 1973), 1–12.
[40] *New York Times,* December 27, 1971.
[41] Edwin H. Sutherland, "White Collar Criminality," *American Sociological Review,* 5 (February 1940), 1–12.

advertising, and similar violations. His argument assumed that the distinction between criminal and civil cases based on whether the injury involved was individual or public was not particularly helpful. He was convinced that the distinction between tort and crime worked to the advantage of the high-status offender. He disclaimed any attempt at muckraking by suggesting criminology be broadened to include more than the traditional kinds of crime. Yet Sutherland was following in the footsteps of his predecessor Ross who wrote about "criminaloids" of the upper world. Sutherland came from the same social stratum as Ross and shared the same resentments.

Geis goes further in suggesting that Sutherland in his work on corporate crime was basically a reformer though he tried to mask it by maintaining a "scientific" objective stand.[42] He was much more the old-time prophet squarely within the populist tradition thundering against all criminality no matter what the social position of the criminal, rather than the value-free scientist. Yet there was much that was viable in Sutherland's position. His hypothesis to explain the crimes of corporate executives was differential association: the frequency, intensity, and duration of exposure to law-violating definitions lead to crime. He did not see this as a mechanical process—there was considerable opportunity for variation, improvisation, and invention. His hypothesis on the importance of intimate personal relations as an initiating factor in crime can be tested against some evidence that is available. Sutherland also tried to account for the differential implementation of the law in corporate offenses. It was, he said, the result of a combination of fear and admiration of businessmen, and the cultural homogeneity of legislators, judges, and administrators. Another important element in differential implementation was the relationship between the law and the mores in corporate crime—the public feels no strong resentment against it. He also noted that the mass media treat corporate offenders more gingerly. It is possible to check out these hypotheses by looking at the electrical industry price-fixing case brought by the Justice Department in 1960. It was the largest criminal antitrust prosecution in the history of the United States.

Twenty-nine corporations and 45 executives received criminal court imposed sanctions for conspiracy to rig bids on heavy electrical equipment, divide up markets, and participate in other price-fixing schemes. The conspiracy seemed to have begun sometime in the mid-1940s when various electrical manufacturers met at the annual meeting of the National Electrical Manufacturers' Association.[43] Regular meetings of industry people were held during the war years and a frequent topic of

[42] Geis, "Avocational Crime."
[43] Richard A. Smith, "The Incredible Electrical Conspiracy," *Fortune*, 63 (April 1961), 132–80.

discussion was how they could best persuade Washington to jack up price ceilings. But the meetings continued after the Office of Price Administration was abolished and the discussion gradually turned to price fixing. By the 1950s there were some 19 smaller cartels fixing prices and allocating markets. Nearly every firm in the industry participated at one time or another with General Electric and Westinghouse being the most prominent. The conspirators went to elaborate lengths to conceal their activities and they all knew they were involved in law violations. This gives the lie to the contention of some critics of antitrust legislation that the law is so complex that innocent businessmen are very likely to be indicted for doing something which is standard operating procedure in their industry. The result of the price-fixing sessions was grossly inflated prices. The Antitrust Division of the Justice Department felt compelled to move against the conspirators after the Tennessee Valley Authority complained of suspiciously identical bids from electrical manufacturers and Senator Kefauver threatened to initiate an investigation of the entire electrical industry. The end result of the case was that all the corporate defendants who were indicted pleaded guilty. Of the 20 total indictments involving multiple defendants, 7 pleaded guilty and the remaining 20 pleaded no contest. The court levied fines totaling almost $2 billion and also handed out 30-day jail sentences to 7 executives—4 vice-presidents, 2 division managers, and 1 sales manager—and suspended jail terms for 23 other defendants placed on probation.

Smith's account of the electrical conspiracy case indicates that many of Sutherland's ideas about the behavior of corporate executives receive substantiation in this case. There was a stress on learning and associational patterns as important elements in the genesis of the violations. Trade associations and conventions were the sites of corporate criminal conspiracies. But some involved in the conspiracy expressed strong repugnance at the idea; others were convinced that it was necessary to avoid needless corporate risks; and others drifted into it without thinking much about it. Too, there were segments of the management group that did not engage in price-fixing discussions. As Geis has pointed out, the discussions did not occur in divisions that were not prone to erratic price swings, the threat of cutthroat competition, and low prices. He concludes:

> It was, therefore, not only personal associations which were important in determining participation in the price-fixing schemes, but also the economic structure against which such participation occurred.[44]

[44] Gilbert Gies, "Toward a Delineation of White Collar Offenses," *Sociological Inquiry*, 32 (Spring 1962), 160–71.

Sutherland's hypothesis about the temerity of enforcement agencies to move against corporate offenders was not borne out in this case. The interests of legislators, judges, and administrators were not identical, though they were a culturally homogenous group. Sutherland further hypothesized that the mass media would soft-pedal corporate crime. And so they did in the electrical conspiracy case.[45] There was little pretrial publicity, no names mentioned, and generally muted coverage in the press. It may be for this reason that the mores and the law relating to corporate crime are disparate. As Sutherland sardonically put it:

> Public opinion in regard to pickpockets would not be well organized if most of the information came to the public directly from the pickpockets themselves.[46]

Smith summarized the combination of factors that were present before the corporate electrical executives could participate in violations:

1. They had to perceive that there would be gains accruing from their behavior. These might be personal or professional or both. It could be corporate advancement that brought prestige and power, or it might more simply be vocational, in terms of a more secure method of carrying out tasks. The aspiration-opportunity disjunction advanced to explain low-status crime actually may be more relevant to the crimes of the powerful. The victim of the American dream as it turns out may not be the lower-class person but his upper-class counterpart. He is not disadvantaged nor does he lack objective opportunity. But upper-class persons do experience sociopsychologically induced obstacles to achievement or "subjective deprivation." There is some evidence to indicate that high-status people perceive their deprivation as unrealistically high. Those people with whom they compare themselves are perceived as more successful. We can hypothesize that subjective deprivation is positively related to the violations of the powerful but more adequate controls, like suggested reforms of the laws relating to economic crimes, would reduce them.

2. Offenders were able to neutralize or rationalize their behavior in accord with their image of themselves as decent, law-abiding, respectable persons. Even after their conviction they did not think of themselves as criminals but only as violators who had been convicted under the anti-trust laws.

3. The ebb and flow of price fixing indicates the relation between extrinsic conditions and illegal acts. When the market behaved in a satisfactory manner or when enforcement seemed threatening, the conspiracies

---

45 "Notes and Comments, Corporate Crime," *Yale Law Journal*, 71 (December 1961), 288–89.
46 Edwin H. Sutherland, "Is 'White Collar Crime' Crime?" *American Sociological Review*, 10 (April 1945), 132–39.

stopped. When market conditions deteriorated while corporate pressures for achieving attractive profit and loss statements remained constant and the enforcement activity remained weak, the price-fixing agreements flourished.

The corporate violations all took place in a context where success, greater profits, and maintaining the stability of the market were highly valued. Merton has been the most recent sociologist to remind us that this emphasis on acquisition without an equivalent sensitivity to the means utilized contributes to deviance. Tawey thought that this emphasis actually contributed to industrialism's triumph in the West:

> The secret of industrialism's triumph is obvious. . . . It concentrates attention upon the right of those who possess or can acquire power to make the fullest use of it for their own self-advancement. By fixing men's minds, not upon the discharge of social obligations, which restrict their energy . . . but upon the exercise of the right to pursue their own self interest, it offers unlimited scope for the acquisition of riches, and therefore gives free play to one of the most powerful of human instincts. To the strong it promises unfettered freedom for the exercise of their strength; to the weak the hope that they too one day may be strong. Before the eyes of both it suspends a golden prize, which not all can attain, but for which each may strive, the enchanting vision of infinite expansion.[47]

Though these overall widely shared values help account for the malfeasance of corporate executives they do not account for the internal variation in rates. This is better explained by market conditions that encourage violations. The conditions might be characterized as criminogenic. Leonard and Weber's study of criminogenic market forces in the auto industry suggested that the concentrated market power of auto manufacturers coerce violations on the part of the auto dealers.[48] McCaghy comes to the conclusion that the pressure situation is greater when there is monopolization by one or a few companies.[49] Lane, in a study of 25 New England industrial shoe firms, concluded that marginal and declining firms are more likely to violate the law than prosperous firms.[50] But interestingly the proportion of firms violating labor relations laws varied by the number of shoe firms in the community. Where a

---

[47] R. H. Tawney, *The Acquisitive Society* (New York: Harcourt Brace Jovanovich, 1920), pp. 30–31.

[48] William N. Leonard and Marvin S. Weber, "Automaker and Dealer: A Study of Criminogenic Market Forces," *Law and Society Review*, 4 (February 1970), 408–10.

[49] Charles H. McCaghy, *Deviant Behavior: Crime Conflict and Interest Groups* (New York: Macmillan, 1976), p. 210.

[50] Robert A. Lane, "Why Businessmen Violate the Law," *Journal of Criminal Law, Criminology and Police Science*, 44 (August 1953), 151–65.

community was dominated by a handful of firms the proportion of those violating was very high and declined as the number of shoe firms increased, thus suggesting that monopolization, not competition, encouraged violations. But even in a rapidly deteriorating market situation not all those who were pressured to violate did so. The last variable suggested is the one on subjective deprivation. The explanation then combines values, structural conditions, and persons experiencing high levels of subjective deprivation. The combination of all three leads to corporate violations.

The major focus of the chapter up to this point has been on antitrust violations as the major type of corporate crime. But as pointed out earlier it includes all corporate conduct that endangers the public interest in the health and safety field as well as the economic area. All laws in these areas are designed to control the conduct of business organizations and regulate the kind of activity permitted for the purposes of increasing corporate wealth. Some of the most detailed reports are available on price fixing but there has been a series of less publicized reports on corporate crimes related to health and safety that underline the similarity between these offenses and antitrust violations. The following interview concerns one such offense.

BENTON HARLOW: DISTRIBUTOR OF UNSAFE DRUGS

The following is a shortened version of an interview conducted with a former executive of a drug company in the Midwest, a subsidiary of a national parent corporation. He and several of his colleagues, were convicted of lying to the Food and Drug Administration about animal studies testing the effects of an antichloesterol drug developed by the company, and of fraud in responding to reports that the drug caused cataracts in the eyes of rats. The grand jury that indicted these three officers also returned a twelve-count indictment against the company and its parent organization. The subsidiary pleaded no contest to six counts and the senior corporation to two. The subsidiary was fined $60,000 and the parent enterprise $20,000. All three corporate officers indicted also pleaded guilty to six counts. At the time of the interview Mr. Harlow was in his early 60s and living in retirement. He was sentenced to six months probation and retired several years after his conviction because he felt his own opportunities to move ahead had vanished. The city within which he was born and worked was dominated by his drug firm and a large soap manufacturer. The executives of both companies were charter members of the city's business elite. Harlow was educated at a church-related liberal arts college and went on to get a master's degree in business administration. His first position after leaving school was in sales at a competing drug firm. He was recruited for his next company, the one from which he retired, seven years later.

QUESTION: Let's start by your telling me some of the circumstances surrounding the controversial drug HE/14.

HARLOW: Well, in the early 1950s there was a tremendous push to develop a drug that would be effective in treating heart disease. The public was clamoring for something especially since they were convinced that cholesterol was the culprit. So we began experimenting with a variety of compounds to reduce the body's cholesterol levels. That's how we developed HE/14. It was developed here in our own laboratories. It's one of a number of compounds that fall under the generic name of triparanol.

QUESTION: What is the usual procedure when a drug like that has been developed? How do you find out if it's effective or not?

HARLOW: We began a series of tests on rats, monkeys, and dogs and sent the results of those tests to the Food and Drug Administration. The tests showed that HE/14 reduced the cholesterol or inhibited its functions in lower animals. In our application to market the drug we had to show that it was safe for laboratory animals and had no serious side effects when taken with humans. They changed those regulations a few years later so that now you have to demonstrate a drug's effectiveness as well.

QUESTION: Was there considerable enthusiasm in the company for the new drug?

HARLOW: Oh, definitely. We thought we really had something. As you may know the drug industry is tremendously competitive and even if your market position is strong you can't stand still for long. We were hoping that HE/14 would be a shot in the arm for us, reinforce our position in the industry and bring in more money to finance our plans for expansion. We thought this would be the drug that would help us break into the big time.

QUESTION: Was there any concern within the company that the drug's introduction should be delayed until further tests were made to see if there were any negative side effects?

HARLOW: Well, this is something that was stressed by the government prosecutor but all I can say is that we thought we were operating in an unknown area where the risks were high and we knew our competitors were also working on the same kind of thing. It just would have been foolhardy to delay until further tests were made. When do you stop making tests? You can always be criticized for not going further no matter how much testing you do. We had faith in what we were doing and we thought we could save many lives with HE/14.

QUESTION: As I recall the FDA did not approve your application immediately but asked for further test data. Can you tell me a little more about that?

HARLOW: That's the role FDA is supposed to play. They move cautiously and some of their scientists are very suspicious of the drug industry. Our own scientists feel that the FDA group is basically obstructionist. They seem to get some secret pleasure out of blocking potentially useful drugs. The pharmacologists there are not very well respected in the industry.

QUESTION: Why is that?

HARLOW: They aren't very competent. If they were, they'd be working somewhere else. Also they seem very responsive to political pressure. That's what we thought was happening with the delay on our initial application. So we mounted a promotional campaign to persuade them. We asked physicians to try the drug on their private patients and report their results to us. I wasn't connected with that operation so I don't know how successful it was. But in 1960 the FDA approved our application with the condition that we list some side effects.

QUESTION: What were the side effects?

HARLOW: They had received scattered reports on vomiting, nausea, and dermatitis. So we put that on the label as possible side effects and started selling it.

QUESTION: Let's back up a little to the test results you sent in originally. Were there any problems with those?

HARLOW: The government made much of the fact that they were supposed to have been falsified. They relied mainly on a former disgruntled employee who claimed that what she recorded in her own laboratory book was left out in the original application. As a result of her complaint the FDA sent a team to look at our records and interview lab employees. The government claimed that the lab director instructed his assistants to revise their data. I think they put the wrong construction of this whole series of early tests. I'm not a pharmacologist but I do know that you have to rework laboratory data and summarize it concisely so it's understandable to a lay audience. All drug laboratories do this, it's called "smoothing out the data." It isn't falsification.

QUESTION: Was the drug called off the market after the FDA team looked at your laboratories and records?

HARLOW: No, not then, but there was a campaign developing against HE/14 which wasn't quite as disinterested as the FDA made it out to be. For instance our major competitor was encouraged to test our version of triparanol with its own anticholesterol drug which they were preparing to market.

QUESTION: What did they find?

HARLOW: Just what you'd expect—that HE/14 had negative side effects that their own compound didn't.

QUESTION: Did they list any side effects that you hadn't included on your label?

HARLOW: Yes, they said their animals developed cataracts and started losing their hair.

QUESTION: What was the reaction within your company to this report?

HARLOW: Some of us were beginning to have questions about the side effects. But we couldn't be sure it was related to HE/14 or something else. You can never know with absolute certainty. So we felt we had to go ahead and defend our product.

QUESTION: Was there ever any discussion about the ethics of the situation?

HARLOW: If you mean did we think we were unethical, absolutely not. The government accused us of being criminals. That upset me very much. I have always thought of myself as a law-abiding person. If it turned out that the negative side effects were due to something other than HE/14, then we would have been applauded for having stood up to the FDA. It's happened in other instances. I have a history of heart disease and I was taking HE/14 myself right up till the time it was withdrawn. I know several other executives here were also. That doesn't sound very criminal to me.

QUESTION: In your internal company discussions were there any suggestions that the drug should be withdrawn for safety reasons?

HARLOW: I don't recall that there were. If anyone felt that way privately it was not expressed. Our initial decision to go with HE/14 and all the investment of time, effort and money we put into it—well, we just couldn't back down. Even after it was withdrawn we still had a $2 million inventory of HE/14. How were we supposed to absorb that loss?

QUESTION: I take it you think the action of the Justice Department in proceeding against you was unfair?

HARLOW: Yes, I do—terribly unfair. If they're saying what we did was wrong, then I don't know what they're suggesting. What would you have done in a similar situation? If you don't have firms competing with each other to develop new miracle drugs, then you've got stagnation. Maybe that's what the FDA wants—complete control over developing and testing new drugs and selling them. That would mean the end of the drug industry.

QUESTION: What was the reaction within the company to your conviction?

HARLOW: If was expected and they knew someone had to take responsibility. If I refused then my case as well as a score of others would have gone to trial, which could have been disastrous both for me personally and the company. The judge in his remarks on sentencing held the company responsible. He said it was a failure of executive, managerial, and supervisional control. But the amount the company was fined was ridiculous.

QUESTION: So the reaction of your colleagues was that you sacrificed yourself for the organization?

HARLOW: Yes, but it wasn't that strong and it didn't last very long. I was given a substantial raise the following year but from then on my responsibilities were gradually shifted to others. I saw what was happening and requested retirement. They were quite generous— I'm on full salary now until I'm 65 and then will start drawing my retirement benefits.

DISCUSSION

There was an uncanny similarity between Mr. Harlow's background and those of the convicted electrical industry conspirators. He was somewhat older at the time of his conviction but he was making well over $100,000 a year. He graduated from a prestigious liberal arts college and received a master's degree from a nationally recognized school of business administration. He was married, the father of two grown children, and had been an officer in the U. S Army during World War II. He was active on a variety of boards and committees in his home community, including the YMCA, Chamber of Commerce, United Community Fund, and, ironically, Big Brothers. He was quite active in local fund-raising activities for the Presbyterian Church. He had no previous arrests.

The differential association explanation seems compatible with Harlow's account. He did not report any extensive discussion of the position the company was to take. Everybody seemed to agree on the course of action that should be followed. Harlow expressed some surprise that what he considered acceptable practice was viewed by the Justice Department as illegal. It was perhaps this unanimity among the executives about the appropriateness of their action that accounts for Harlow's surprise at the Justice Department's reaction. No one involved expressed any strong repugnance or even opposition to selling the unsafe drug. Rather they all seemed to drift into the activity without thinking a great deal about it. If anyone was opposed to the company's position, they didn't make their opposition known. Harlow saw the activity as necessary, though risky, and basic to his company's survival. He believed the activity was generated by the intense competition among drug firms. One conclusion that is implied in this account is that cutthroat competition does not insure product safety, at least in areas where the danger of the product is not immediately apparent.

The gradual building of commitment to marketing the drug was not recounted in much detail but it seems clear that there were a number of "side bets" to use Becker's terms that gave consistency to the plan of action that finally emerged. Harlow spoke of the investment of time, effort, and money put into it that precluded any backing out. An appellate court judge ruling on a later damages claim against the company also commented on this process: "some weight must be given to the human tendency to follow a course of conduct once decided upon even when considerations have appeared that would have led to a different decision at the outset, a tendency particularly strong when large investments of both effort and money have been made; the very fact of the initial decision importantly affects subsequent ones."

Harlow did not think of himself as a criminal. At most he would argue that what he did was technically illegal. In this his attitude paralleled those of the electrical conspirators. One General Electric vice-president stated before going to jail:

All of you know that next Monday, in Philadelphia, I will start serving a thirty-day jail term, along with six other *businessmen* for conduct which has been *interpreted* as being in conflict with *complex* antitrust laws.[51]

Even though his sentence of six months' probation was minimal it had a pronounced psychological impact on Harlow. The possibilities of a jail sentence seemed quite frightening, underlining the sensitivity of corporate offenders like Harlow to status deprivation and censure. The fact that violations carry criminal penalties addresses head on the tendency of corporate offenders to rationalize them. In this they are much like the shoplifters Cameron studied:

> Again and again store people explain to pilferers that they are under arrest as thieves, that they will, in the normal course of events, be taken in a police van to jail, held in jail until bond is raised, and tried in court before a judge and sentenced. Interrogation procedures at the store are directed specifically and consciously toward breaking down any illusion that the shoplifter may possess that his behavior is merely regarded as "naughty" or "bad." . . . It becomes increasingly clear to the pilferer that he is considered a thief and is in imminent danger of being hauled into court and publicly exhibited as such. This realization is often accompanied by dramatic changes in attitudes and by severe emotional disturbance.[52]

Harlow's justifications fit in with his self-image as a law-abiding person but these were shaken by his conviction. He saw nothing wrong with his identification with the company and its concern with healing the sick, its zeal for producing efficient effective drugs at low cost. The extent of his confidence is revealed by the fact that he took HE/14 for his own heart condition right up until it was removed from the market, though he had more reasons to question it than the hapless salesmen who distributed it.

The seriousness of the violations was never recognized by the company itself. Their philosophy was that the violations were part and parcel of the hazards inherent in discovering and marketing new drugs. A number of civil damage suits were brought against the company even though criminal trial records were not available as evidence. The reports on the effect of the drug were frightening: cataracts, loss of hair, painful dryness of the skin, and other complications. The impact of the fine on the company was trifling. One year after the fine, the company increased its profits by more than 10 percent—more than enough to cover the $60,000 fine imposed, the maximum limit possible under the law. Harlow thought that the fine was ridiculous and that its deterrent effect was nil. Pre-

---

[51] *New York Times,* February 11, 1961 (emphasis added).
[52] Mary O. Cameron, *The Booster and the Snitch, Department Store Shoplifting* (New York: Free Press, 1964), pp. 160–62.

sumably a larger fine or perhaps the requirement that all illegal profits from the sale of HE/14 be disgorged would bring home the lesson more forcefully. The one option the court had to deal more severely with the company was to reject their pleas of *nolo contendere*. This the judge chose not to do, thus making damages of claims against the company more difficult to sustain. Sutherland's original notions about corporate crime are substantiated in this case: the courts dealt sympathetically with all the violators and the news media covered the case briefly under "business news." The company had no training program to alert its executives to the legal hazards of what they were doing. Perhaps if that were a condition of the company's "probation," future violations would be less likely.

The company's response to Harlow's conviction also reveals their attitude toward the violations. He was given a substantial raise following the conviction and encouraged to resign before 65. Some of the electrical conspirators were fired by their companies, others were rewarded. There seemed to be some recognition that Harlow had performed a service for the company, but also some embarrassment at keeping him around any longer than necessary.

Harlow's comments on the way new drugs are marketed and his negative views of FDA attempts to regulate it suggest that the industry itself is criminogenic. There are few built-in safeguards to insure that the health and safety of potential consumers would be protected. The violations that occurred in the drug industry—as well as those in the electrical industry, milk and bread industry, plumbing, and other major industries —took place in a context where success, greater profits, and enlarging the company's market took precedence over all other values.

QUESTIONS FOR FURTHER DISCUSSION

1. What steps would you recommend that the company take to reduce the likelihood of further violations?

2. Harlow's report indicates that the industry itself is criminogenic. What public policy would you advocate that would make it less so?

3. How would a conflict and consensus perspective interpret this account and what further information would each need?

4. Harlow's illegal activity is difficult to conceptualize in career terms; what are the pros and cons for dealing with this kind of illegality as a "criminal behavior system?"

5. If you were the sentencing judge what conditions would you require Harlow to fulfill during his probation to remind him and
   others of the seriousness of his offense?

6. Harlow's account suggests that early decisions relating to distribution of the drug contributed to a kind of momentum which
   none of those responsible could resist, yet other research suggests that those with "less subjective deprivation" are less
   easily pressured. What further hypotheses do you think worth
   exploring in this area?

Corporate offenders would forcefully oppose classifying their behavior
in the same category with organized crime. But the similarities between
the two kinds of behavior are striking. The major difference for our
purposes is that the criminality of corporate offenders is less of a joint
production of violator and control agency than it is in organized crime.
Organized crime is discussed more fully in Chapter 13.

13

organized crime

All criminal activity that is not spontaneous and impulsive is organized, but organization varies considerably. The organization will be minimal if the activity is relatively simple and the number of persons required to carry it out is small. Street-corner boys engaged in an act of vandalism do not require extensive division of labor. But if the criminal activity is, for example, smuggling, a more complex kind of organization is required. For criminologists the term "organized crime" refers to a specific phenomenon related to the provision of illegal gambling services, usurious loans, narcotics, and prostitution. It is basically the organized vices. The organization may be local or national. It is variously called the "Syndicate," the "Mob," the "Combination," the "Mafia," or more recently the "Cosa Nostra."

Cressey has contended that organized crime is distinguished by its size, a chain of command resembling that of an army, extensive planning, the threat or use of force, interlocking leadership at the top, and relative immunity to prosecution at the higher levels. The character of organized crime is difficult to capture because, though it is a behavior system, it is technically not illegal. As Cressey has put it:

> The fact is that organized crime, as such, is not now against the law. It is not against the criminal law for an individual or group of individuals rationally to plan, establish, develop, and administer

an organization designed for the perpetration of crime. Neither is it against the law for a person to participate in such an organization. What is against the law is bet-taking, usury, smuggling and selling narcotics and untaxed liquor, extortion, murder, and conspiracy to commit these and other specific crimes.[1]

The complex known as organized crime most clearly lends itself to a career analysis, more so than any of the other patterns discussed. It exists within an organizational context, much like any legitimate business. It provides a variety of services that are not available through conventional channels; it needs legal services, financial assistance, credit, enforcement of contract, and places to conduct its affairs. The kinds of jobs available within this system relate to the overall management of the enterprise, the staff services required to conduct its affairs, an enforcement staff, and roles that involve the implementation of decisions made at the upper levels. The exact description of the organization has been the subject of scholarly dispute but at the least it involves an executive with his assistants, a buffer group of middle-management stratum, and a larger group of lower-level workers. There is also a large number of what could be called "part-time employees" who work at the fringes of the organization. It is the purpose of this chapter to describe this organization, to account for its emergence and persistence, and to look at some proposals for its control.

EARLY HISTORY

Some of the more popular accounts of organized crime stress its sinister character and depict it as a foreign cancer that has invaded an otherwise healthy society. These accounts stress the recent appearance of organized crime on the American scene and the central role played by Sicilians in *importing* this phenomenon. Serious criminological thought challenges these observations, and suggests instead that organized crime's vitality and scope is interrelated with basic cultural values, legal philosophies, law enforcement practices, and major social institutions in America. A broader historical perspective suggests that organized criminal activity is not a recent phenomenon, that it is not the peculiar contribution of any one ethnic group, and that it only appears under certain social conditions.

The first scholarly attempt to understand the social roots of organized

[1] Donald R. Cressey, *Theft of the Nation: The Structure and Operations of Organized Crime in America* (New York: Harper & Row, 1969), p. 299.

crime was Landesco's study of adult criminal groupings in Chicago in 1929.[2] His investigation was conducted during a period when the manpower of organized crime was at an all-time peak (because of Prohibition) and when the dominance of Sicilians and Italians was strongest. Yet he rejected the notion that organized criminal activity originated with Prohibition. He showed that there was a continuity of leadership and methods from the gamblers and vice lords of the early twentieth century and the bootleggers of the 1920s. He also rejected the view that organized crime was rooted in immigrant traits brought from the Old World. He anticipated the position of later sociologists who emphasized ethnic succession in organized crime—Italian dominance in early organized criminal activity was related more to the timing of their entry to urban America than to any criminal propensities.

He was the first serious student of organized urban crime to describe its linkages to conventional society and its impact on law enforcement. Organized crime, he observed, could not function without a stable and mutually cooperative arrangement with law enforcement. The existence and necessity of such an arrangement was clearly demonstrated in his chapter on the "beer wars" of the 1920s. That conflict riveted national attention on the warring gangs in Chicago. Warfare erupted, he showed, because the coalition between organized bootlegging and the political structure of the city disintegrated. It was this warfare that perfected the role of "executioner"—those who elicited compliance through violence.

Landesco also described the entrance of gangster elements into business and industry, noting that it occurred in situations of cutthroat competition among small businesses. If agreements to control competition are illegal, yet desirable because of high labor costs, small profit margins, and a high rate of failures, the stage is set for the entrance of the gunmen. Competition is thus eliminated by agreements on prices and wages and enforced by hired gunmen who operate as an internal police force.

Landesco's most enduring contribution, however, is his description of the neighborhood roots of organized crime. It was a ladder of social mobility for talented neighborhood youngsters whose opportunities for getting ahead were restricted. Its tolerance at the local level was related to values endorsing family solidarity, patriotism, and

> an unconditional mutual aid without hesitant criticism or question, against any danger whether it be constituted authority or from rival gang interests. As for the law, it is believed to be often an ally of the exploiter or a tool of the enemy gang. The "racketeer" is the example of success under grim conditions.[3]

[2] John Landesco, *Organized Crime in Chicago* (Chicago: University of Chicago Press, 1929).
[3] Ibid., p. 178.

He described in rich detail the kinds of specialties required to run a gambling establishment. It required "ropers"—who solicited or directed patrons to the establishment; "friskers"—who stood at the door and searched patrons for weapons; "stickmen"—who drew in the dice with a curved stick instead of the hand in order to have the dice in full view of all players before they were handed to the thrower; a "banker"—who took in and paid out money; "shills"—who played with the house's money but appeared to be patrons in order to keep the game going and excitement high. Though some of these activities were not very complicated, Landesco observed that they did involve a certain apprenticeship, a knowledge of customer psychology, and, for talented young ethnics, an attractive alternative to unemployment or dull low-paying jobs. Organized crime is the neighborhood gang grown up and professionalized.

The complexity of the activities involved in organized criminal activity and the code of secrecy that has shrouded its operations since the 1920s have discouraged most social scientists from duplicating Landesco's efforts. Access to reliable informants is difficult and the risks are high. The studies done since 1929 rely less on insider accounts and more on secondary sources, economic analyses, and interviews with law enforcement officials. Occasionally revelations about the structure of organized criminal activity and some insight into its operation have been provided by investigative journalists. Meyer Berger, using trial testimony of indicted murderers in Brooklyn, drew a picture of an organization called the "Combination," which was formed after the repeal of Prohibition for the purpose of applying profits of the 1920s to the development of new enterprises.[4] Berger asserted that it was a national association growing out of the *Unione Siciliane* controlled by Lucky Luciano.

Murder was one part of the Combination's business—though it was restricted to business needs. The need to remove disloyal or untrustworthy people or those who threatened the organization generated the role of "executioner." Berger described the skills necessary to fill this position and the apprenticeship involved. The recruits came from neighborhoods where assaultive crime rates were high. Troop chiefs in the Combination looked for those neophytes who had tried their hand at various stick-up jobs and had a reputation for their fighting ability and general bullying. They were taken on as apprentices and given various low-level tasks: stealing cars to transport corpses after a hit, stealing license plates to make identification of stolen cars more difficult, and convoy duty while disposing of bodies. The training consisted of learning how to beat someone severely without killing them and how to conduct one's self in a police lineup. Apprentices who demonstrated skill and

[4] Meyer Berger, "Murder, Inc.," *Life* (September 30, 1940), pp. 86–88, 92–96.

loyalty during this period were made junior partners to hit men and finally became executioners themselves. Not everyone, however, made it. Some were too undisciplined to follow orders, others were unable to give up their extracurricular activities. The chief characteristic of those who didn't make it was a lack of dependability that threatened the organization. Berger also noted that the Combination operated much like a corporation. It paid pensions to widows of deceased workers and had a variety of fringe benefits. It also had its own internal judicial system to regulate the conduct of its members. The judicial system was somewhat analogous to its upperworld counterpart. Every offender had a right to a hearing and to counsel. If the offender had high status he could appeal a local court's verdict to the national tribunal.

The Kefauver Committee

Berger's provocative description of a Combination with nationwide connections was not explored further until 1950 when a Senate committee under the chairmanship of Estes Kefauver began exploring the influence of organized criminality in interstate commerce. Kefauver's book, based on the testimony given before his committee, concluded that:

> A nationwide crime syndicate does exist in the United States of America, despite the protestations of a strangely assorted company of criminals, self-serving politicians, plain blind fools, and others who may be honestly misguided, that there is no such combine. . . . Behind the local mobs which make up the national crime syndicate is a shadowy, international criminal organization known as the Mafia, so fantastic that most Americans find it hard to believe it really exists.[5]

The Kefauver committee description of the organization was developed in the course of their inquiry into gambling and racketeering in a number of American cities. First-hand testimony about the outline of such an organization and its activities, however, was conspicuous by its absence until the late 1950s. The Kefauver committee gave widespread currency to the term "Mafia" or "Black Hand" which referred to an international criminal organization that had originated in Sicily and was still headquartered there. Kefauver's conclusions were based largely on the testimony of Harry Anslinger, Commissioner of the Federal Bureau of Narcotics at the time. Anslinger contended that the organization was made up of "families" (knit together by real and fictitious kinship ties) who gave allegiance to a grand council which governed them, and to a code of secrecy which called for death to informers.

[5] Estes Kefauver, *Crime in America* (New York: Doubleday, 1951), p. 12.

The Origins of the Mafia

The term "Mafia" first came to public attention in 1890 when the murder of the New Orleans police superintendent was attributed to 19
Sicilians who allegedly controlled the waterfront. They were arrested,
found "not guilty," and 11 of the 19 were lynched by an infuriated mob
who stormed the prison. The events created a national crisis with the
Italian government and marked a turning point in reporting Italian-Amer-
ican crime. All crime in Italian colonies thereafter was ascribed to the
Mafia.

Historically the Mafia was a preindustrial peasant institution which
grew out of a Sicilian situation of oppression and resentment. It placed
emphasis on cohesion among friends in the defense against common
enemies. It cultivated distrust of formal law and authority and encouraged secrecy. According to Inciardi about the only contribution that
the Mafia made to organized crime in America was in its ideals of lawlessness.[6] But even here it coincided with the American heritage of
frontier justice with its contempt for law. Inciardi asserts emphatically
that the Old World Mafia, as an organization and society of criminal
expertise, never existed in the United States. What did exist in Italian
colonies were extortion attempts through letters containing threats by one
immigrant against another. These offenses, internal to Italian colonies,
were characterized as "Black Hand" activities but had no Sicilian roots.
They were not organized into a criminal structure, nor were there any
organizational ties among individual Black Hand operators.

The Testimony of Joseph Valachi

In 1957 the U.S. Senate authorized an investigation by the McClellan
Committee of practices in American labor-management relations. The
committee's work lasted three years, involved over 1500 witnesses, and
produced 46,510 pages of testimony. *The Enemy Within*, a progress report of the committee, was a thorough and richly detailed account of
corruption and racketeering.[7] One of the most interesting contributions
of that committee for students of organized crime was the testimony of
Joseph Valachi in 1963–64. He was a 60-year-old man with a long criminal
record. He was serving a life sentence for murder and a 20-year sentence

---

[6] James A. Inciardi, *Careers in Crime* (Chicago: Rand McNally, 1975), p. 113.
[7] Robert F. Kennedy, *The Enemy Within* (New York: Harper & Row, 1960).

for a narcotics offense when he voluntarily agreed to provide an insider's account of organized crime. He was convinced his former associates were trying to kill him in prison and in 1962 had murdered a fellow inmate because he believed him to be the executioner. His testimony was in retaliation for the activities of his former associates against him. Valachi reported that the structure to which he belonged was called "Cosa Nostra" ("Our Thing").[8]

He described the organization of the Vito Genovese family in New York City as consisting of a boss, underboss, lieutenants, and soldiers. He also asserted that a commission composed of bosses of all the families (he identified five in New York) directed the operations of most organized criminal activity in the city. The commission had executive, legislative, and judicial functions.

One part of his testimony described the dispute-settling procedure that existed within the family of which he was a part. He discussed his initiation into the Cosa Nostra and the code to which new members are pledged. The code, in brief, was similar if not identical to the inmate code described in Chapter 9. It enjoined members to be loyal, to be a member of the team, to be honorable, to show courage in the face of adversity, and to be sharp. Cressey has noted that roles generated within the prison context, partly as a result of shared values which inmates import and partly in response to imprisonment, also correspond to fairly enduring roles in organized criminal activity. This similarity may be partly due to the values brought into the prison by those involved in organized crime. It is more likely, however, a common response to strong official governments—confederation government on the one hand, prisoner government on the other—which are limited in their means for achieving control.

The principal roles found in prison—"gorilla," "merchant," and "real man"—are also found in organized crime, according to Cressey.[9] Gorillas, those who coerce goods from other prisoners by threat of force, are analogous to "executioners" in organized crime. "Merchants," "peddlers," or "con politicians" do favors for fellow prisoners in exchange for payments. They are analogous to loan sharks on the outside—called variously "shylock," "shy," or "shell." Cressey observes that the "buffer" who shields the boss from police, prosecuting attorneys, and lower level employees is basically a peddler role. He also trades favors for payment, most often within the family—reassigning lower level personnel for a consideration,

---

[8] Government Operations Committee, *Organized Crime and Illicit Traffic in Narcotics*, Hearings before the Permanent Senate Subcommittee on Investigations, 88th Congress, 1st and 2nd sessions (Superintendent of Documents, Government Printing Office, 1963 and 1964).

[9] Cressey, *Theft of the Nation*, pp. 162–220.

providing access to the boss, and so on. The "right guy" or "real man" corresponds to the boss or underboss role outside prison. The right guy is perceived as acting to defend, maintain, and advance inmate interests rather than his own. The code, according to Cressey, is designed to protect the personal power of the boss by keeping underlings in line, and to discourage any challenges to his authority. The members of the organization are socialized into the conviction that the boss is operating in the best interests of all its members. When this conviction is undermined, then the structure of organized criminality is open to change.

This was the situation in 1930–31 when, by all reports, the present organization came into existence. At that time disagreements developed on the importance of older values related to loyalty and secrecy in the face of the changing market for illicit goods and services. Tyler reports that in 1929 a number of Sicilians engaged in organized criminality representing the "new breed" met in Atlantic City, New Jersey, and made four major resolutions:

1. A national trust with a well-defined hierarchy and jurisdiction should be set up;

2. A system of internal government and justice with its own brand of due process should be established;

3. A ministry of external affairs should be set up to relate to other powers both legal and illegal;

4. A scholarship fund should be set up to sponsor young sophisticates for the future.[10]

The resolutions seem quite innocuous and look much like decisions that would be made by a legitimate corporation. This move to "trustify" the gangs was an attempt to adapt to the American situation. The younger faction saw illegal profits to be made not from industrial racketeering (as they had been prior to 1920), nor from illegal alcohol, but from gambling. That required the rationalization of their efforts and the move away from clan organization. Anderson has observed that the Sicilian-based Mafia earlier had done the same kind of thing in response to changing circumstances.[11] The practice of artificially extending kinship ties was an attempt to overcome the drawbacks of family organization with the variability of interest, talent, and temperament of its members. But a further subordination of family ties to bureaucratic needs was required to take

---

[10] Gus Tyler, "The Crime Corporation," in Abraham S. Blumberg (ed.), *Current Perspectives on Criminal Behavior* (New York: Knopf, 1974), p. 198.
[11] Robert T. Anderson, "From Mafia to Cosa Nostra," *American Journal of Sociology*, 71 (November 1965), 302–16.

into account the shift from production to consumption occurring in the larger society.

> In the America of the last fifty years the main drift of society has been toward the rationalization of industry, the domestication of the crude self-made captain of industry into the respectable man of manners, and the emergence of a mass consumption economy. The most significant transformation in the field of "institutional-ized" crime was the increasing relative importance of gambling as against other kinds of illegal activity. And, as a multi-billion-dollar business gambling underwent a transition parallel to the changes in American enterprise as a whole. This parallel was exemplified in many ways; in gambling's industrial organization (e.g. the growth of a complex technology such as the national racing wire service and the minimization of risks by such techniques as lay-off betting); in its respectability, as was evidenced in the opening of smart and popular gambling casinos in resort towns and in "satellite" adjuncts to metropolitan areas; in its functional role in a mass-consumption economy (for sheer volume of money changing hands, nothing has ever surpassed this feverish activity of fifty million American adults); in the social acceptance of the gamblers in the important status world of sport and entertainment, i.e. "cafe society."[12]

The new breed in 1930 was essentially a force against the older and more violent-prone forms of illegality. The call was for a move away from a system based on rank and seniority in a family to one based on posses-sion of technical knowledge. Ideally the organization should purchase expertise in business administration, accounting, marketing, merchandis-ing, and law. If that shift was too dramatic and incompatible with a code of secrecy and honor, at least the various families should be sending their sons to universities to develop these skills.

Dissension within the Ranks

The major obstacle to the development of a more rational bureaucracy in 1930 was the old guard. Their resistance to change was revealed in what has been characterized as "The Castelammarese War," a 14-month struggle between Italian and Sicilian gangs in New York City. The older faction favored regional groupings and were distrustful of combinations. The young Turks favored centralization. Though the struggle occurred in New York City, its impact was nationwide. The outcome was a victory for

[12] Daniel Bell, "Crime as an American Way of Life," *Antioch Review*, 13 (June 1953), 131–54, 134.

the younger group and the development of an organization based on Caesar's command:

> After Masseria's funeral (he represented the old guard faction) Maranzano (one of the Young Turks) presided at a meeting attended by 500 people in a hired hall in the Bronx and explained that the days of shooting were over and that a period of harmony was about to begin. He then presented them with his plan of reorganization, one loosely based on Caesar's military command—the individual gangs each would be commanded by a *capo* or boss, under whom would be a *sottocapo*, underboss, and beneath the underboss would be a *caporegimi*, lieutenants who would supervise the squads of soldiers. Each unit would be known as a family and would operate within prescribed territorial areas. Over all the family bosses would be a *capo di tutti capi*, a boss of all bosses and it was this title that Maranzano bequeathed to himself.[13]

The organization that followed the 1931 war soon abolished the position of boss of bosses and relied more on rational economics than fear. This has deemphasized the role of the executioner. Cooperation, alliances, and joint investments replaced violence as a way of reducing competition. Cressey has reported that the reorganization did not remove the enforcer role but tended to de-emphasize the use of violence and coercion. As in legitimate business organization there is greater use of utilitarian power or monetary rewards. Bonuses and fines rather than threats are used as incentives. If an organization member has too many fines and reprimands it works against job advancement. The de-emphasis of violence has gone hand in hand with the increasing attention being paid to the skills of the money mover. This latter development, according to Cressey, has occurred because of the growth of investment in licit business.

The Castelammarese War followed the pattern of earlier dissensions within the Sicilian Mafia. The dissension occurs, according to Hobsbawm, between the ins and outs in a setting in which rewards are limited and unemployment high.[14] Sooner or later the young toughs who can't solve the problems of life by working (since there is no work) must solve it by crime. But the older rackets are under control and those responsible for them are reluctant to make way for younger men. Characteristically rival gangs are organized, warfare erupts, and each struggles to vanquish the other. Finally old and young combine after a redistribution of the spoils.

13 Gay Talese, *Honor Thy Father* (New York: World, 1971), p. 200.
14 E. J. Hobsbawm, *Primitive Rebels: Studies in Archaic Forms of Social Movement in the 19th and 20th Centuries* (New York: Norton, 1959), p. 46.

Relationship of the Police to Organized Crime

Valachi also testified that the Cosa Nostra had political interests related to its survival. He basically reiterated the observations made by Landesco 30 years earlier: organized crime needs the collusion of political and law enforcement leadership to exist. Where there is community ambivalence about gambling, prostitution, and sex laws the police, as noted earlier, develop a tolerant policy toward the vices. Inevitably in this situation a mutually advantageous arrangement is worked out between organized criminality and law enforcement. The symbiotic relationship between organized crime and the police was discussed in Chapter 7 as one of the problems police face. But the linkages between the suppliers of vice and local communities involve more than relationships with the police.

Gardiner, in his detailed study of a Wisconsin community of 75,000 ("Wincanton"), documented the intertwining of officialdom and organized crime.[15] The history of gambling and criminal syndicates in that community paralleled the history in other cities of the United States. Other research on municipal government conducted by political scientists suggests that the patterns he described are fairly widespread. Interestingly the syndicate organization in Wincanton preceded Prohibition. Gardiner traced the organization back to the early 1900s when it first appeared as private police or strikebreakers hired to block unionization attempts in local corporations. But it was Prohibition that provided the impetus for more recent expansion into gambling, prostitution, and drug distribution. The organization that Gardiner described seemed to have considerable local autonomy but was related to a large out-of-state syndicate from which it purchased technical and enforcement services. This combination of outside resources and control of local police activity through "payoffs" eliminated any competition and assured high profits. From the police side it insured community peace by, in effect, supporting one group in obtaining a local monopoly, thus minimizing the kind of violence and organizational strain that results from ruthless, open competition in providing illegal services. Gardiner suggests that the price for the tolerance of the vices, and the elimination of cutthroat competition, may be too high since it involves the loss of police integrity and public contempt for the law.

The Valachi testimony was greeted by a considerable amount of skepticism by some sociologists and criminologists. They questioned how

[15] John A. Gardiner, *The Politics of Corruption: Organized Crime in an American City* (New York: Russell Sage Foundation, 1970).

much a soldier in a "family" could know about the activities and structure of the larger organization. If Valachi had been a lieutenant or buffer (in the ranks of middle management) then his opportunities to observe the work of the "family" would have been much greater and his accounts greeted with less suspicion. What is fundamentally rejected is the notion of a "conspiracy" implied in Valachi's testimony and other official documents. As the sociologist Daniel Bell put it when discussing Kefauver's conclusions:

> Unfortunately for a good story—and the existence of the Mafia would be a whale of a story—neither the Senate Crime Committee in its testimony, nor Kefauver in his book presented any real evidence that the Mafia exists as a functioning organization. One finds public officials asserting before the Kefauver committee their belief in the Mafia; the Narcotics Bureau thinks that a world wide dope ring allegedly run by Luciano is part of the Mafia: but the only other "evidence" presented . . . is that certain crimes bear "the earmarks of the Mafia."[16]

Morris and Hawkins, in a critical analysis of the Valachi testimony, note that it is uncorroborated, it is contradicted in part by other witnesses, it contained internal inconsistencies (despite a code of "one for all and all for one," Valachi reported that the organization did not offer him any immunity from prosecution), and much of it was the loosest kind of hearsay.[17] Moreover Morris and Hawkins contend that the Valachi testimony produced nothing in the way of tangible results: two-and-one-half years after Valachi's testimony, J. Edgar Hoover reported that only one conviction resulted from the information provided by Valachi.

If allowances are made for the time lapse from the date Valachi was initiated into the secret society until his testimony in 1963 and his low-level position in the organization, we can discriminate between the part of his testimony that seems plausible because it has been corroborated and that which has not been corroborated. No one disputes that he was part of the Genovese family—it was organized in the fashion he described, it was linked to other units in New York City and New Jersey, and it was mainly Italian. *New York Times* correspondent Gay Talese, in his biography of Bill Bonnano, reported that Bonnano did not take issue with Valachi's testimony that Bonnano was his sponsor or Godfather in 1931.

> Valachi had given special prominence to Bonnano during the televised hearings in 1963, claiming that it was Bonnano who initiated him into the Mafia, pricking fingers and exchanging blood to symbolize their unity. This ceremony had supposedly occurred decades

[16] Bell, "Crime as an American Way of Life," p. 143.
[17] Norval Morris and Gordon Hawkins, *The Honest Politician's Guide to Crime Control* (Chicago: University of Chicago Press, 1970), pp. 202–36.

ago, and Bonnano since then had been no more aware of Valachi than an army general would be of a private; but Valachi's revelations about the secret society and Bonnano's link to the traitor were embarrassing to Bonnano.[18]

Infiltration of Business

The main focus of the McClellan Committee, however, was corruption in labor management relations or racketeering. Their 1960 report revealed many conflicts of interest, breaches of faith, bribery, extortion, theft, and violence in labor practices. It was organized crime's penetration of labor-management relations—the use of underworld methods to control a business or some area of business enterprise—that interested them. The pattern begins with petty preying on small businesses. The small businessman has to take out "insurance" to prevent "accidents." There follows an attempt to control trade through shipping, mainly trucks—fruits, vegetables, garbage, linen supplies, food for restaurants and hotels, and newspapers are all sensitive to interruption in the system of truck transport. The committee's concern about the vulnerability of transportation networks accounted for their interest in the Teamsters Union. The committee spent two-thirds of its energies investigating the Teamsters and the union's link with organized crime leaders.[19]

The committee feared that the control of transportation combined with terrorization of small entrepreneurs could lead to underworld domination not only in a given firm but also in trade as a whole through trade associations. Tyler states:

> Hence what started as undirected preying on individual businessmen turned into well organized capture, control and managements of trade associations.[20]

Penetration of legitimate business may proceed directly with acceptance of a business interest in payment for an owner's debt or various kinds of extortion. But Tyler notes that as sophistication has grown so have the methods of organized criminality. It can persuade legitimate businessmen with the services it can offer including capital, labor, raw materials outlets, transportation, an edge against competition, legal defense, and immunity from law enforcement. Control of legitimate businesses is a move toward respectability and corporate ownership. The excess of funds from illegal enterprises is transferred to legal enterprises. Tyler observes

[18] Talese, *Honor Thy Father*, p. 103.
[19] John Hutchinson, *The Imperfect Union: A History of Corruption in American Trade Unions* (New York: Dutton, 1970), ch. 18.
[20] Tyler, "The Crime Corporation," p. 200.

that the legitimate enterprise operates as a "front" that allows the rich criminal to make his settlement with the tax collector. The kinds of businesses acquired are usually trucking companies, casinos, nightclubs, hotels, and land investment companies.

Despite the emphasis on gambling, organized crime has also been involved, though less heavily, in providing other illegal services, like prostitution, and other illegal goods, like narcotics. It has consistently been involved in organized theft, excluding pickpocketing, holdups, or burglary. The thievery is specialized such as that in the trade of stolen automobiles. More recently organized criminals have moved into the business of stealing, forging, using, and selling credit cards.

The information yielded by the two senate committees and a presidential crime commission has encouraged further explorations of organized criminality. Yet the efforts are meager in comparison with that expended on what has been referred to as "street crime." The material on organized crime has raised several major questions: how organized crime has raised several major questions: how organized it really is, the significance of Italian prominence and its future viability.

HOW ORGANIZED IS ORGANIZED CRIME?

One of the major issues that has been debated since the reports of the Kefauver and McClellan committees is how tightly controlled the whole apparatus is. Supporters of the view that it is highly organized make much of the meeting that occurred in Apalachin, New York, in 1957. Some 58 or more persons from all over the United States converged on the residence of Joseph Barbera, a wealthy beverage distributor. They all had large sums of money on their persons, had extensive criminal records, and were of Italian extraction. The exact purpose of their meeting was never made clear. The federal government brought charges against the participants for conspiring to obstruct justice by lying about the purpose of their meeting but the convictions were later overturned by an appellate court. It was the government's contention that the purpose of meeting was to discuss policy matters. In short, it was a meeting of the National Commission of the Mafia to discuss problems they were having.

Donald Cressey in a paper prepared for the President's Commission on Law Enforcement and the Administration of Justice in 1967 described a structure that was highly organized.[21] His information was based on

[21] Donald R. Cressey, "The Functions and Structures of Criminal Syndicates," in President's Commission on Law Enforcement and the Administration of Justice, *Task Force Report: Organized Crime* (Washington, D.C.: Government Printing Office, 1967), pp. 25–60.

"police reports, informants, wiretaps, and electronic bugs." He stated that the core consisted of 24 families operating as a cartel in large cities across the United States. Their activity involved collusive price fixing and their monopoly was maintained by reliance on criminal violence. Each family had a membership that ranged from 20 to 700, with a total membership of 5,000. The top position of each family was filled by an executive who provided organizational leadership for the purpose of maximizing profits. Under him was an "underboss" who would be equivalent to a vice president in a conventional business organization. The underboss directed the line organization, but the staff organization was directed by a counselor who advised the boss and was usually an elder member of the family. Beneath him were lieutenants who were analogous to plant supervisors or sales managers in a business organization. At the bottom were the soldiers who carried on the organization's daily activities—running loan-shark operations, lotteries, bookmaking operations, smuggling, and so on. The organization as Cressey described it was overwhelmingly Sicilian-Italian. But the soldiers had a working relationship with employees and commission agents, many of whom were not of Italian descent. They were the bet takers, truck drivers, and employees in legitimate businesses that were controlled by Cosa Nostra (see Figure 13-1). The soldiers sometimes functioned as enforcers (who kept recalcitrant members of the organization in line) or corrupters (who established relationships with public officials and other powerful people whose assistance was needed). They were necessary to negotiate payoffs.

The 1967 President's Commission reported that organized crime was indeed highly organized. Though its numbers were small it was nationwide and controlled by a ruling body known as the "Commission." Family members looked to the Commission as the ultimate authority on organizational and jurisdictional disputes. Reportedly they controlled most of the illicit gambling and loan sharking in the nation and were heavily involved in labor racketeering and narcotics trafficking. Moreover the organization had a virtual monopoly over many licit enterprises such as juke boxes and cigarette vending machines. Though there were other racket groups of diverse ethnic backgrounds, the 24 families controlled all of them.

Linked to the issue of extent of organization are estimates on the size of the enterprise. Tyler noted that the 1933 estimate was $13 billion a year;[22] the 1950 Kefauver hearings estimated $22 billion a year.[23] In 1958, 88 billion a year Petersen estimated that the size was increasing four times faster than the

---

[22] Tyler, "The Crime Corporation," p. 194.
[23] U.S. Congress, Senate, Special Committee to Investigate Organized Crime in Interstate Commerce, *Third Interim Report* (May 1, 1951).

duplicate

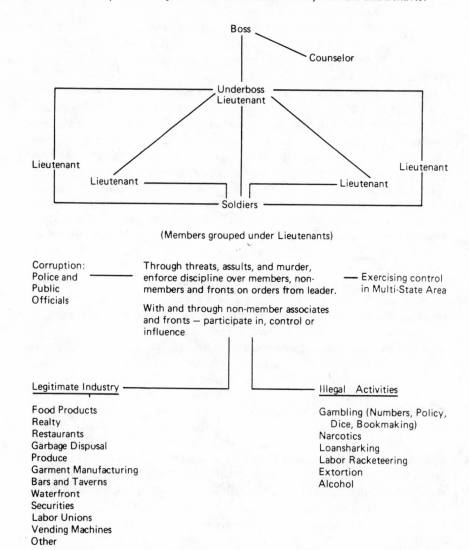

Figure 13-1 An organized crime family

Adapted from the President's Commission on Law Enforcement and the Administration of Criminal Justice, *The Challenge of Crime in a Free Society* (Washington, D.C.: Government Printing Office, 1967), p. 194.

population.[24] In 1968, the Research Institute of America estimated the income at about $40 billion a year or about 5 percent of the Gross National Product.[25] Woetzel estimates that the total take of the operation of organized crime was 10 percent of the Gross National Product or $80 billion in 1967.[26]

The opposite position on extent of organization is the "independent collectivities" view. This position does not argue that the profits are small—they may be quite large—but the organizations are autonomous and not directed by a national commission. The most influential spokesman for this view is former Attorney General Ramsey Clark, who was in office when the President's Commission on organized crime published its results. He noted that whole nations and entire states and regions of the country are free from organized crime. He observed that even the national crime commission could discover evidence of organized crime in only 25 of the 71 cities surveyed. He thinks the estimates of syndicate earnings also to be wildly improbable. His conclusion:

> As with all crime, we over simplify our definition of organized crime. There is far more to it than La Cosa Nostra. Our society is much too complex to expect only a single syndicate or type of illegal activity. There is no one massive organization that manages all or even most planned and continuous criminal conduct throughout the country. There are hundreds of small operations that engage in organized criminal activity—car theft rings, groups of burglars, safecrackers working together, gangs of armed robbers, combinations that occasionally smuggle and distribute marijuana and dangerous drugs—scattered throughout the nation.[27]

Morris and Hawkins, after a careful examination of the President's Commission view, also concluded that the existence of a monolithic nationwide syndicate is a myth. The myth expresses, enhances, and codifies beliefs about legitimacy, and safeguards morality. It provides a simplistic explanation of a fairly complex phenomenon and a focus for hostility. Talese's report of Bill Bonnano's reflections say substantially the same thing. He observes that the Mafia would not be receiving elaborate news coverage

> . . . were it not for the mythology factor, the George Raft reality, the fact that the Mafia in the sixties, like Communism in the fifties

[24] Virgil Peterson, "Fighting Nationally Organized Crime," *Vital Speeches* (October 15, 1958), p. 150.
[25] Research Institute of America, *Protecting Your Business Against Organized Crime* (April 15, 1968), pp. 4–5.
[26] Robert K. Woetzel, "An Overview of Organized Crime: Mores versus Morality," *The Annals*, 347 (May 1963), 1–11.
[27] Ramsey Clark, *Crime in America* (New York: Pocket Books, 1970), pp. 57–58.

had become part of a national illusory complex shaped by curved mirrors that gave an enlarged and distorted view of everything it reflected, a view that was widely believed because it filled some strange need among average American citizens for grotesque portraits of murderous villains who bore absolutely no resemblance to themselves.[28]

THE SIGNIFICANCE OF ITALIAN-SICILIAN DOMINANCE

The same observers who argue for the existence of a national commission of organized crime also contend that it is made up almost exclusively of Italians. The novelist Mario Puzo, who provided a fictional account of an organized crime family that seemed loosely based on the career of Vito Genovese, concluded reluctantly that you have to be Italian to achieve eminence in organized crime.[29] He does not dispute the fact that there are occasional staff workers and part-time employees who are non-Italian, but overwhelmingly the organization is Italian. The explanation for Italian prominence—which no one denies—is the issue that divides students of organized crime. Cressey takes the position that the criminalistic traditions of the southern Italians, especially Sicilians, provided a broader supporting set of values and techniques that made them more proficient than any likely competitors on the American scene.

Bell takes the position that Italian-Sicilian prominence is related to the timing of their entry to the American scene.[30] Their dominance is declining as the patterns of organized criminality change and Italians become assimilated. Their involvement for a period constituted for them "a queer ladder of social mobility." Even at the peak of their involvement in organized crime Italians constituted only 31 percent of the leadership group. Ogburn and Tibbits noted that of 108 kingpins of organized crime in Chicago in 1930, 29 percent came from Irish backgrounds and 20 percent were Jewish.[31]

Haller has explored more systematically ethnic specialization in organized crime.[32] He concluded that the Irish in Chicago who arrived be-

---

28 Talese, *Honor Thy Father*, p. 356.

29 Quoted in Nicholas Gage, *The Mafia Is Not an Equal Opportunity Employer* (New York: McGraw-Hill, 1971), p. 39.

30 Bell, "Crime as an American Way of Life."

31 William F. Ogburn and Clark Tibbitts, "A Memorandum on the Nativity of Certain Criminal Classes Engaged in Organized Crime and of Certain Related Criminal and Non-criminal Groups in Chicago," unpublished (July 30, 1930) in The Charles E. Merriam Papers, University of Chicago, p. 9.

32 Mark H. Haller, "Organized Crime in Urban Society: Chicago in the Twentieth Century," *Journal of Social History*, 5 (Winter 1971–72), 210–34.

fore the Italians specialized in gambling and were the major group at the turn of the century in policy games. They forged the coalition of criminals, politicians, and compliant policemen that the Torrio-Capone organization later inherited. The Irish also specialized in labor racketeering which developed from their importance as leaders of organized labor in general. Organized crime knit together the worlds of crime, politics, labor leadership, politically related businessmen, sports figures, and the night life of the city. It is important, according to Haller, to note that these worlds were all tied together and men in them moved easily from one to the other or held positions in two or more simultaneously. The worlds were joined not only by organized crime as a source of money and manpower but by interlocking careers and a common social life and shared values. The values related to the importance of deals, friendships, and mutual favors and the belief that all institutions, excluding the family and the church, were basically rackets. These values were not ethnically derived but flowed from a pattern of group adjustment to the American urban scene. The Irish-politics-gambling complex remained intact until World War I. By 1920 the developing black ghetto allowed black politicians to build independent gambling and political organizations. Jewish gamblers became increasingly important in the 1920s. The gambling picture in the 1920s was a complex mixture of Irish, Black, Jewish, and Italian entrepreneurs. By World War I the Italians had moved into important positions in the vice districts. But just as the Irish blocked Italians in politics so they also blocked Italians in gambling, which was perceived to be more respectable and profitable than prostitution.

Prohibition opened up a whole new set of opportunities for illegality, and each ethnic group struggled to monopolize a piece of the action. For the Italians bootlegging was the only major field of organized crime that was not dominated by the Irish. It was not foreordained that the Italians would succeed. Haller observes that the situation in Chicago during the early 1920s was chaotic and only gradually fell to the Italians. Nelli, another historian, has suggested that the adjustment of Italians in Chicago contrasted sharply with their experience in Boston and for that matter in other cities.[33] Where the situation facilitated assimilation, mobility was achieved through legitimate channels. Nelli observes that opportunities for assimilation gradually closed in the three decades following 1870 as earlier arrivals, especially the Irish, sought to erect barriers to prevent later ethnics from challenging their position. This situation might have been eased somewhat if the earlier, more successful Italian settlers had functioned as patrons for the newer southern Italian immigrants instead

[33] Humbert S. Nelli, *Italians in Chicago, 1880–1930: A Study in Ethnic Mobility* (New York: Oxford University Press, 1970), ch. 5.

of rejecting them. The process of political evolution that would have made the Italian presence felt and mobility easier was thus delayed. Italian dominance, according to Nelli, has lasted so long because no new ethnic mass has appeared to force them out. All those who espouse the ethnic succession argument, however, contend that new leadership is emerging.

Ianni, an anthropologist, studied black and Hispanic organized crime in New York City and New Jersey.[34] He concludes that succession is occurring and would be moving faster if blacks had an organizing principle equivalent to the Italian extended family. He described the powerful bonds that are forged in childhood gangs and through prison experience. These experiences generated a sense of intense loyalty that facilitated criminal organization but only of the most limited sort. In discussing the lack of any inherent organizational pattern in black organized crime Ianni says:

> We found that while there are characteristic patterns of organization within the various networks we observed, there is no overall pattern that ties the networks together. These patterns of behavioral organization grow out of the kinds of natural social relationships that link crime activists to each other in networks. Thus, we found that childhood gangs are an important recruitment device for organized crime networks; youngsters who grow up together on the street in such gangs do continue to operate as a group as they grow into adulthood. As they grow older, these youngsters acquire a street reputation for competence in crime and silence in the face of police investigation and are recruited—sometimes as a gang—into organized crime by older crime activists. A second pattern or organization grows out of prison experience; men who have been together in prison continue their association after release. Finally, there are a number of similar patterns that center around an entrepreneurial form of organization, a group of men and women working together for mutual profit in some criminal operation just as they might in a legitimate small business. There are . . . also some other important organizing principles; kinship, for example, seems to be important among Hispanic networks but much less so among blacks. Among blacks, however, the presence of women even in positions of some authority is as distinctive and important a feature of black criminal organization today as we have seen it to be historically.[35]

What Ianni's data suggest is not the absence of an Italian kinship pattern among blacks, but a kinship pattern organized around women

---

[34] Frances A. J. Ianni, *Black Mafia: Ethnic Succession in Organized Crime* (New York: Simon & Schuster, 1974).
[35] Ibid., pp. 121–22.

rather than men. It may be this situation that has inhibited black succession in organized crime—one of the last bastions of sexism. Ianni's emphasis on the strength of the Italian family in achieving ascendance in organized criminality puts him, unwittingly perhaps, on the side of those who interpret organized crime as a Sicilian importation. The question his inquiry leaves unanswered is how both the Irish and the Jewish involvement in organized criminality was possible in the absence of any extended kinship pattern. The significance of Sicilian traditions is called into question when we see groups without those traditions responding to the demands for illegal goods and services in the same way. Thus the Chinese in San Francisco and New York developed a pattern of organized crime that controlled gambling, opium dens, and prostitution. The gangs were called "tongs" and had an administrative hierarchy, professional warriors, and assassins who acted as guards, collectors, enforcers, executioners, and infantry men—in short, their organization bore an uncanny similarity to the later Cosa Nostra.

THE FUTURE OF ORGANIZED CRIME

The last major issue upon which opinion is divided relates to organized crime's future. Those like Daniel Bell, who see it as a path to economic and social betterment for new groups coming into the cities, expect that it will be around for a long time, though its pattern will change. It will no longer focus on gambling and prostitution as these activities become generally accepted or legalized. Criminality will consist of decentralized, small entrepreneurial activity. The other element forcing change is the decline of the political machine:

> With the rationalization and absorption of some illicit activities into the structure of the economy, the passing of an older generation that had established a hegemony over crime, the general rise of minority groups to social position, and the breakup of the urban boss system the pattern of crime we have discussed is passing as well. Crime, of course, remains as long as passion and the desire for gain remain. But big, organized city crime, as we have known it for the past seventy-five years, was based on more than these universal motives. It was based on certain characteristics of the American economy, American ethnic groups, and American politics. The changes in all these areas means that it too, in the form we have known it, is at an end.[36]

[36] Bell, "Crime as an American Way of Life," p. 154.

A further implication from Bell's analysis is that since the myth of the Mafia speaks to deep-seated tendencies within American society to look for conspiracies, the myth is likely to endure. It functions to maintain social solidarity by establishing the boundaries of acceptable behavior. In short, we may need the Mafia myth to "concentrate upright consciences."

McCall's study of the relationship between "hoodoo" and the numbers racket in several black communities suggests that developing a functional alternative to illicit betting might be very difficult.[37] Gambling is intertwined with religious and magical beliefs that abound in low-income black areas. There are special rituals that have evolved to divine the specific three-digit number that wins for the day. "Dream books" also are very popular. They list thousands of objects, events, or themes each with a three-digit number. In the face of failure to win, hoodoo provides abundant explanations for why one has lost. McCall concludes that the two games—numbers and hoodoo—in their intersection seem to have an integrative function for the black community, furnishing much of the content of casual conversation, imparting a temporal structure to the day, and offering a sense of participation in a community-wide institution.

Some observers have taken the position that this local pattern would remain essentially untouched by the legalization of gambling. But Ianni contends that the numbers game is one of the few community institutions which has some local control and this would be undercut through legalization. Some of his respondents in Harlem and in Paterson, New Jersey, saw legalization as an attempted "white takeover." If this is true the future likelihood is that both legal and illegal gambling will coexist in the ghetto. The numbers would still be linked to prostitution, loan sharking, and the sale of stolen goods and drugs. The real expansion that Ianni predicts for black organized crime is in the field of narcotics. Whites are wary of this activity but there is a growing market for illegal drugs. The situation is equivalent to the Italian predicament at the beginning of Prohibition. Ianni suggests that we can anticipate that black underworld activity will soon "take off" into self-sustained growth through illegal drug trafficking.

Others, generally economists, policy scientists, and legal scholars, are more optimistic about societal efforts to eliminate or control organized crime. The suggestions for controlling organized criminality have implicit assumptions about organized crime causation, and generally propose liberal reformist solutions. Academic specialists usually propose legalization of illegal services as a way of containing organized crime. Packer, a legal scholar much concerned with the overreach of the criminal law, has

[37] George McCall, "Symbiosis: The Case of Hoodoo and the Numbers Racket," in Howard S. Becker (ed.), *The Other Side: Perspectives on Deviance* (New York: Free Press, 1964).

suggested what might happen if all controls were taken off the sale of narcotics (a strategy he sees as politically unlikely):

> The economic effect of such a change is clearly predictable if economics has anything to teach us at all. With the disappearance of controls the price of narcotics would plummet, and the financial ruin of the present illegal suppliers would quickly follow.[38]

Schelling, an economist, suggests by implication that the dominant approach through indictment and conviction under the criminal law be replaced by attempts to regulate by accommodation and the restructuring of markets—as is done in the policing of public utilities.[39]

The President's Commission proposed that steps be taken to deal more effectively with this kind of crime. There are technical problems about obtaining proof because of the secrecy and complexity of the operations, witness fear of reprisal, inadequacy of state and local law enforcement resources to deal with organized crime, lack of coordination among local police, and lack of strategic intelligence to forecast the nature and future of organized crime. An attempt to address these technical problems was embodied in the Organized Crime Control Act which was passed by the Congress in 1970.[40] The act contained provisions in the area of expanded grand jury powers, use of electronic surveillance, and self-incrimination. Opponents of the act, though generally conceding its sophistication in getting at organized criminal activity, have questioned strengthening the inquisitorial powers of grand juries, increasing penalties for habitual offenders, and reducing a witness's protection against self-incrimination.

The philosophy underlying the new legal weapons developed to combat organized crime assumes that more vigorous law enforcement is the answer. Thus syndicate members' reluctance to cooperate by taking refuge in the Fifth Amendment would be addressed by granting immunity from criminal prosecution to witnesses willing to violate their oath of secrecy. The refusal to talk could lead to imprisonment for contempt of court. The new act forbids the defense from securing copies of wiretap evidence against the defendant if it was gathered more than five years before the crime for which the accused is being tried. The new act also provides for the use of civil suits against organized crime activists. In civil court the jury does not have to be convinced of guilt "beyond a reasonable doubt" which should make convictions easier. Verdicts against

---

[38] Herbert L. Packer, *The Limits of the Criminal Sanction* (Stanford, Calif.: Stanford University Press, 1966), p. 280.

[39] Thomas C. Schelling, "Economic and Criminal Enterprise," *The Public Interest* (Spring 1967), pp. 61–78.

[40] "Organized Crime Control," Hearings Before the Subcommittee on Criminal Laws and Procedures of the Committee on the Judiciary, United States Senate, 91st Congress (Washington D.C.: Government Printing Office, 1970).

a syndicate member could result in court injunctions against his activity and the forced breakup of the operation, including confiscation of any property involved. The penalties have also been increased under the new law—from 5 years in prison for persons who operate illegal gambling enterprises, if the business involves five persons or more or takes in $2,000 per day, to 30 years for those considered to be "dangerous special offenders." Finally long-term federal grand juries could be set up under the new law with the task of investigating organized crime and corruption. They would have power to issue critical reports asking for the removal of state and local public officials suspected of malfeasance, and to petition the Attorney General to replace prosecutors found lacking in investigating enthusiasm.

EXPLANATIONS OF ORGANIZED CRIME

The most common explanation of organized crime is the opportunity theory. Organized crime is located in areas of segregated vice that exist because of the larger community's tacit acceptance. The pattern is sustained by collusion with legitimate institutions and the local criminal organization is sufficiently strong to provide stability. The organized slum is not the setting for violent gangs or individual predators. Boys and girls growing up in this neighborhood are drawn to careers within the illegal organization. The developing interest of economists in this pattern has supplemented and extended this opportunity structure approach. Schelling has observed that there are specific market characteristics that determine whether or not criminal activity becomes organized.[41] Organization is invited only under certain conditions: *3 are listed here*

1. The provision of specific goods and services is deemed illegal. The enforcement of the law is sufficiently stringent to discourage those who are unwilling to pursue a criminal career. In effect the law "protects" the illegal industry. The laws against gambling, as an illustration, represent a kind of subsidy to organized crime.

> The successful conduct of a gambling operation requires a high degree of organization, whether it is a casino where the customer plays games of chance at varying odds or a bookmaking service that takes bets on a wide variety of sports events. Particularly in the latter, there has to be a continuous flow of both information and money through the organization. Then, too, there must be a system of insurance against severe losses, through "layoff" betting

[41] Schelling, "Economics and Criminal Enterprise."

and other devices. To these complexities, which would exist even if gambling were legal, are added the intricate organizational devices required to insulate the enterprise from detection and to ensure that if a breach of security occurs at one level it will not compromise the higher levels. Thus, for example, the use of telephonic and other communications systems permit the efficient functioning of a compartmentalized structure in which the man who takes the bet may not know the identity of the person at the next echelon to whom he turns in the bets. In short, the illegal business demands a high degree of organization. . . .[42]

Packer goes on to say that the combination of illegality and need for organization produces a "crime tariff," the law saying in effect that it will protect those who are willing to commit crime from the competition of those who are unwilling to do so.

2. A high overhead cost or some other element of technology that makes small-scale operation more costly than large-scale.

3. The prospect of increasing the prices of illegal services if the market is cornered.

4. The larger the firm, and the larger its share of the whole market, the more will formerly "external costs," like violence, become costs internal to the firm. With organization there is an incentive to take these costs (always there but previously disregarded) into account. In the case of violence a large organization can afford to impose discipline thus holding down violence.

5. Anything that requires a long investment in cultivating a consumer interest, a labor market, an ancillary institution, or relations with law enforcement can only be done by a large firm that can monopolize most of the market and get satisfactory return on its investment.

6. The attraction of power that organization brings. Large firms can provide a governmental structure to the underworld. Since they are a kind of "corporate state" they can give themselves the franchise for various "state sponsored monopolies."

To date no conflict explanation of organized crime has been worked out but the main outlines can be suggested. Hobsbawm's study of Sicilian Mafias characterized them as essentially conservative movements.[43] They represented a parallel system of government in the hands of a local businessmen's class. His Mafias were rural in character and incidental to the rise of rural capitalism, hence there is some question about how relevant generalizations about them would apply to urban organized crime. But there are some similarities. A conflict explanation would look to the system of inequality as ultimately causal. It creates and maintains

[42] Packer, *The Limits of the Criminal Sanction,* p. 350.
[43] Hobsbawm, *Primitive Rebels.*

an unequal distribution of power, wealth, and authority. The organized slum, which is the seedbed for organized crime, is viewed as a creation of powerful interests concerned about maintaining their position rather than something that has developed unwittingly. The incoming population has a substantial number of persons who accept the acquisitive ideology and organize themselves to climb out of the situation in which they find themselves. There is some evidence that leaders of organized crime are strongly committed to "free enterprise." Like their Sicilian counterparts studied by Hobsbawm they have a vested interest in private property as pirates have a vested interest in legitimate commerce, both being parasitic upon it. This fact precludes the developments of any political consciousness or leadership among the oppressed groups where organized crime flourishes. It is likely that the lack of forceful and determined official efforts to confront organized criminality—since its parallel government does represent a challenge to official legitimacy—is related to organized crime's ability to suppress demands for more sweeping social changes. From the perspective of the slum dweller the ability of crime activists to buy respectability means he can also.

Investigations that would assist us in resolving some of the issues raised by organized crime or suggest more detailed and adequate explanations are scarce. Hardly anything is known about specific mobility patterns within the organization itself. Cressey has observed that mobility varies by type of position held.[44] Those who are recruited as money movers (collectors of street-level bets) rather than "executioners" are more likely to move up. The career line of the moneymaker is much clearer than that of the disciplinarian. The following interview was conducted with a man who began his career as a street runner and then moved up in the organization. It reveals something of the character of the occupation, the amount of money to be made, motivations of participants, and factors leading to retirement. It also says something about the extent of organization, ethnic succession and likely future patterns.

FRANK: A NUMBERS CONTROLLER

QUESTION: Maybe we could begin by your telling me a little about your background.

FRANK: Well, what do you want to know? I was born in Brooklyn. There were five kids in the family—I was the oldest. My old man worked on the docks but he was killed in an accident when I was 12 and we moved to New Jersey.

[44] Cressey, *Theft of the Nation,* pp. 243–44.

QUESTION: And about that time you became aware of the numbers setup in your neighborhood?

FRANK: No, I knew about it in Brooklyn but the guys who were into it were all Italian so that left me out. They had it sewed up and you couldn't be part of the organization unless you were Italian. In New Jersey the setup was different. The neighborhood I lived in was Italian, Irish, and Slovak but the colored were moving in.

QUESTION: What is your own ethnic background?

FRANK: I'm Greek but we never lived in a Greek neighborhood. I remember we all used to go to the Greek church before my father died but not after we moved to New Jersey. Things were rough, my mom had a rough time just keeping the family together. She worked as a waitress and all I can remember about her now is that she always seemed tired and crabby. She was always hollering at us, especially me, about how hard boys were to handle.

QUESTION: Were you hard to handle?

FRANK: Yeah, I was nicknamed "Crazy Frankie" because I'd fight at the drop of a hat. I guess I had a pretty bad temper and I didn't like the kids at school calling me "The Turk." I was so good with my fists that I was thinking about becoming a prizefighter but nothing ever came of it.

QUESTION: What sort of contact did you have with the police during this high school period?

FRANK: I got arrested a couple of times for battery and they put me on probation. Once my mom turned me in to the Juvenile Court because she couldn't control me. I was picked up for breaking into a gas station with three other guys. I was the only one they caught, the other three got away. They didn't send me away but kept me for a couple of weeks in detention so I'd squeal on the rest of 'em. It was soon after that I was approached by the banker.

QUESTION: The banker?

FRANK: Yeah, that's what he was called but he wasn't that high up in the organization. He was the controller. This guy owned a tavern and had about six runners working for him. His business was expanding because more colored were moving in and he needed new runners.

QUESTION: Do you have any idea of why he picked you out?

FRANK: Yes, he told me. He said it was my muscle and the fact that I could keep my mouth shut. I had a route—three factories I picked up every day. I'd make the rounds before the morning shift started and turn the money and the slips over to the controller. The next day I'd be back to pick up some more.

QUESTION: Would you also pay off the people who won that day?

FRANK: No, that was the controller's job. If a guy won he'd go right to the tavern and collect.

QUESTION: How is the winning number selected?

FRANK: Well, it has to be something that can't be rigged. Like in New York City the number is the last three digits of the total parimutual handle of the 3rd, 5th, and 7th races of a given track. In our areas it was the last three digits of the total amount bet at a nearby track. The number appears every day in the paper. It's pretty simple—just pick a number from 1 to 999. The chances of winning are 1 in 999; the payoff at the time was $730 on the dollar. That leaves $269 to be split up among the runners, the controllers, and the bankers.

QUESTION: What keeps people coming back again and again when their chances of winning are so slim?

FRANK: Most of my customers were colored and they just couldn't save any money. They'd play a few bucks on the numbers every day of every week. If you do it all your life you're bound to hit a few times. Then you pay off some bills, buy some furniture, or just go on a binge. The people needed it—it was like a safety valve.

QUESTION: Now you said there were other runners working for the controller. Were any of them black?

FRANK: No, they weren't then but now they're all black in that neighborhood. Three of the runners were Italian, the rest were Irish, and I was Greek.

QUESTION: How about the controller?

FRANK: He was Italian and the banker behind him was Italian. It was just like in Brooklyn but you didn't have to be Italian at the bottom.

QUESTION: From my observation in other cities blacks have generally controlled the numbers business in their own neighborhoods. Why was this different in New Jersey?

FRANK: Maybe it wasn't but this neighborhood wasn't all colored. It is now—it's locally controlled. That don't mean that the banker is colored but everybody else is.

QUESTION: Are you saying that the gambling is still controlled by the Italians?

FRANK: Yes, at the top but things are changing. Maybe it isn't controlled like it was right after World War II. The guy who runs things now has connections with a

Cuban group that supplies him with drugs but it's strictly a business arrangement—he doesn't work for them. I guess you could say that the organization is a little simpler now—not so many levels.

QUESTION: But isn't some kind of organization necessary to handle a situation when the bank gets hit pretty hard?

FRANK: Yeah, that's the job of the banker—he's the one that handles layoffs. In the old days he was the boss, now he's more like an insurance agent who gets his cut.

QUESTION: Now you say that you started out as a runner sometime during high school—what happened next?

FRANK: I dropped out of high school when I was 16, which is about the time I started working for the organization. . . .

QUESTION: Did the organization have a name?

FRANK: It was called the "Combination." I know the newspapers call it the Mafia or Cosa Nostra but for us it was the "Combination," I never heard the other two names used. Anyway I worked with them for five years as a runner. I think I could have moved up quicker if I was a little older when I started. The controller got badly beat up, almost killed, and he was laid up for a while. He asked me to run the tavern and keep the runners in line. I guess the whole thing must have shook him up pretty bad because after a few months he offered to sell the tavern to me as well as his numbers operation.

QUESTION: How much was he asking?

FRANK: I know this doesn't sound like much but only $10,000. He thought the situation was getting out of hand, too much violence in the neighborhood and pretty soon the colored would take over his operation. So he got out while the getting was good.

QUESTION: Didn't he have to check with anyone else in the organization?

FRANK: I guess he did but they thought things were falling apart too and maybe I could pull it together. By that time the neighborhood was almost all colored so you couldn't have white runners anymore. I took on four new runners who seemed like they had a lot of street sense and kept the whole thing moving. Funny thing—I was the only controller in the city then who wasn't Italian.

QUESTION: Was there any local resentment because you were white?

FRANK: No, because all the runners were colored so the bread was being passed around. The money I made on the numbers I put back in the tavern. I opened up a back room where customers could shoot craps without being bothered. I opened up a few rooms upstairs where some hookers I hired could take the customers. The girls were better than what you'd find on the street—very high class.

QUESTION: What was the arrangement you had with them?

FRANK: I charged them $5 for every time they used the room. They could keep whatever the customer paid them over and above that. On a weekend the rooms would be used about 10 times a night—average. So I made only about $150 on the weekend night. It wasn't big money, only a service to the customers. All the money is in gambling—running a whorehouse is too much of a hassle.

QUESTION: Did you get anything else besides gambling and prostitution?

FRANK: You gotta keep the money circulating. If I was doing $15,000 a day business, which wasn't unusual, I was putting a lot of it back on the streets. I was loaning it out. I loan some guy $50 on Sunday and he'd pay me back $60 on Monday. I know that sounds pretty high but you gotta figure that these guys don't have no collateral. They sure as hell couldn't get it from a bank.

QUESTION: How about narcotics?

FRANK: No, I stayed away from that. All the people who were bringing it in were pretty wild—hard to work with. You couldn't be sure of what you were buying from them and there were always complaints about being ripped off. These Puerto Ricans and Cubans in New York City that supplied the stuff—junk—they were nuts. I think all of them were on the stuff.

QUESTION: Does that mean that there wasn't any junk in your neighborhood?

FRANK: Hell, no—there was plenty of it. One of my runners got into it and was setting up his own little organization. Things got pretty bad—the local colored people didn't like drugs, didn't want their kids taking it. And they thought I was bringing it in. My runners started getting roughed up and twice they tried to blow up my tavern. I decided I had enough—after all I'm a married man with kids and I didn't want my kids to be orphans, so I pulled out.

QUESTION: Pulled out—what does that mean?

FRANK: All the discipline was gone, my banker couldn't protect me—the organization couldn't protect me. It was falling apart. I used some of the money I laid aside to move out of numbers and into the restaurant business —now I'm an upright citizen in [this city].

QUESTION: Was this always your plan—to make enough money so you could go legitimate?

FRANK: It wasn't at first but I started thinking about it as I went along. Anyone who doesn't is crazy. I figured I couldn't go any higher in New Jersey. They let me become a controller but I was still an outsider and I wasn't going any higher.

QUESTION: Have you ever been arrested or spent any time in jail as an adult?

FRANK: No, never. I'm a good citizen; I am now and I was when I was into the numbers. We were just giving people what they want. We weren't out to harm anybody. I've never even had a traffic violation in 30 years —parking tickets, yes, but no moving violations.

QUESTION: You say you weren't out to harm anyone yet there have been reports of people getting roughed up, or sometimes killed. Is that part of what the Combination did?

FRANK: If they did, I didn't see much of it. If a guy was supposed to pay off a debt by a certain date he was expected to pay off. If he didn't or couldn't then something could usually be worked out. About the most you have to do is make a few threatening phone calls if he looks like he's trying to welsh on you. But it wasn't like in the movies where you bring in a hit man to enforce the contract. I never ran into what they call a "hit man." They might exist now but I think they went out with the old Anastasia family.

QUESTION: From what you said earlier it sounded like you were part of a family yourself in New Jersey. Is that right?

FRANK: Right. And we knew there were other families operating in northern New Jersey, but it was divided up by territory.

QUESTION: Can you say anything about how tightly organized the Combination was? It sounds like the families all operated under some kind of direction, either regionally or maybe nationally.

FRANK: I doubt very much that there was any national direction, or a national organization but I wasn't up high enough to tell. There was a commission in northern New Jersey but I can't say how much authority it had. I don't know how far they could go in enforcing decisions they made. They didn't have an army and each of the families was independent. It was like a bunch of businessmen getting together to work things out and not get in each other's way.

QUESTION: You mean more like a trade association than a ruling commission?

FRANK: Exactly.

QUESTION: You're aware that gambling is becoming legalized in parts of the United States. How do you think this will affect the future of the numbers game?

FRANK: I don't think it will make much difference. It just means that you're getting a new group of bettors. From what I can tell, my old customers are still playing the numbers and buying lottery tickets besides. Things might change if you didn't have to pay taxes on what you win in the lottery. It's one of the few loopholes that the workingman has (i.e., avoiding taxes on numbers earnings).

DISCUSSION

The major question about this interview is its validity. If we conclude that the account is too distorted, then it can tell us little about organized crime. We can expect that Frank's story would be told in such a way that it would evoke sympathy. His account suggests that illegal betting is really not very criminal and those who make their living from it, at least at the upper levels, turn out to be quite conventional. He reported that he saw himself as an upright citizen and that he was concerned about his family and respectability. He confessed to knowing little about enforcement and seemed reluctant to talk about the violence linked to his illicit enterprise. This suggests that his description might be somewhat sanitized for popular consumption. Some parts of the interview raise the question of its general plausibility—his report of the amount of money paid for the neighborhood numbers game seems remarkably low; his prostitution sideline seemed financially unrewarding in relation to the amount of money that could be made; and his recounting of the ease with which he took over the numbers game and retired from it strains belief.

The interview is silent on several important areas: the kind of activities that his organization cultivated other than illegal gambling, the relationship he had with law enforcement agencies that permitted him to operate without interference, and information on the higher levels of the Combination. This silence may have been related to his lack of information, his reluctance to talk about it, or the interviewer's unwillingness to question him in those areas. But if this were the only document we had concerning organized crime we would know nothing about his organization's penetration of legitimate industry or what other kinds of illegality were common. We get only the barest indication of the kind of careers possible within the organization, the actual amount of money involved (especially in loan sharking) and what happened to it.

But the interview does speak to the three major issues raised earlier and can be utilized to evaluate explanations of organized criminality.

On the issue of how organized this kind of criminality is Frank's response seems to support the independent collectivities view. He professed to have no knowledge of a national organization, and the regional one he described seemed ineffective. The picture that comes through the interview is that the organization does not have the authority it once had. The command structure seems loose and its ability to enforce discipline weak. Frank's account of the organization said nothing about any dispute-settling functions that it might have. The situation he described in his local neighborhood was one of disorganization as the older pattern began to change. Frank doubted that there was any national organization or direction. He characterized the various families in northern New Jersey as "a bunch of businessmen getting together to work things out and not get in each other's way." When the interviewer asked if the various families were more like a trade association than a ruling commission he replied "exactly."

Frank did not dispute the fact that organized crime in his area was controlled by Italians. But he saw that control shifting. His description of how his numbers business changed character as the composition of the neighborhood changed shows the process of ethnic succession at work. The new pattern was increasingly controlled by blacks and its relationship to other organized groups seems to have been more of a business than a clan arrangement. Frank did not report that any of the black operators who succeeded him managed to advance very far in the combination. Others, however, have reported that this is increasingly occurring. Salerno and Tomkins in 1969 reported:

> In recent years, . . . a few Negroes have risen to what might be called the "junior partner" level of the Confederation in such cities as Detroit, Buffalo, and Chicago. It is these rising executives of organized crime who are pushing harder for ghetto crime to become black, so they can control it and be equal in status to their white bosses.[45]

They go on to report that increasingly black and Puerto Rican gangs are joining in alliances and "banking" their own operations as they challenge

[45] Ralph Salerno and John S. Tompkins, *The Crime Confederation* (New York: Doubleday, 1969), p. 378.

the dominant Italian-Jewish criminal power structure in New York City. Black succession seems to be related to their ability to control importation and distribution of narcotics. Frank's account stressed the unstable drug trafficking situation and the amount of violence associated with it. The situation now is chaotic but to the extent it becomes better organized we can expect that the organization will be able to impose discipline and hold down the level of violence.

As for the future of organized crime Frank thinks the prospects are good even if gambling, the mainstay of organized criminality for the past 45 years or more, is legalized. His remarks about narcotics suggest that this will be the next area of expansion since public opinion is not likely to permit official regulation and control as with alcohol. The kind of emerging organization he describes seems simpler, possibly more decentralized, somewhat like the "networks" discussed by Ianni. Frank is skeptical about efforts to suppress or control the vices. Whether his skepticism is justified remains to be seen. Tyler, a long time student of organized crime, would disagree.[46] He suggests that more sophisticated law enforcement can be effective, that organized crime's influence will never be more than local, and that its capacity for generating internal dissension (jurisdictional and generational) will aid control efforts.

Frank's discussion of organized crime tended to confirm explanations that account for it rather than challenge them. The locale of organized criminality is the stable slum areas of large cities with a history of heterogeneous in-migration. Since legitimate opportunities are either scarce or completely closed off, the path upward for ambitious youth is through illicit channels. Frank's story confirmed Cressey's observations of how neighborhood youth are selected to become part of the organization.[47] The neighborhood with its complex street life is the stage upon which young men prove their abilities. Older Combination members look for "stand up" guys who will serve the enterprise well. Ianni has also noted that youth groupings and the relationships established there form a powerful bond that sustains later criminal activity.[48] Beyond this confirmation of opportunity theory the interview does not go. Frank does not give us enough detail about the market or its economics to add any further insights. Neither does the interview speak to the larger structural questions raised by conflict theorists. There is a question whether any single case study or career could speak to larger structural issues. The participant's own story is by its very nature milieu-oriented and unless Frank was also a sophisticated analyst as well as an organized crime activist, we should not expect more.

[46] Tyler, "The Crime Corporation," p. 208.
[47] Cressey, *Theft of the Nation.*
[48] Ianni, *Black Mafia,* pp. 121–22.

QUESTIONS FOR FURTHER DISCUSSION

1. Frank talked about his activity as a kind of "career escalator" to a more conventional and safer kind of occupation, much as our armed robber did earlier. In what other ways are these two accounts similar?

2. How valid do you think Frank's analysis of the effect of legalized gambling is?

3. There was a specific ideology or set of justifications that supported Frank's occupation of numbers controller. To what extent do you think this ideology is characteristic of other analogous but legitimate occupations?

4. How would a conflict theorist explain the attempts to outlaw certain kinds of behavior despite the fact that the proscription results in subsidizing organized crime?

5. What policies to control organized crime are suggested either implicitly or explicitly in this interview?

6. If narcotics is the next area of expansion according to Frank, what other areas would you hypothesize as similarly "organizable" in the future?

The relationship of the larger institutions of our society as well as our law enforcement apparatus to organized crime is more clear-cut than their relationship with either corporate criminality or political crime. Corporate crime is generated by acquisitive values and concerns about organizational maintenance and security, but organized crime requires the same set of values combined with the more active collusion of law enforcement to exist at all. Public order crime, the subject of our next chapter, shares some of the characteristics of organized crime in that it is generated by societal values, control agencies, and the participants themselves.

14

public order crime

Public order crimes include prostitution, homosexuality, drunkenness, use of illegal drugs, gambling, traffic offenses, disorderly conduct, vagrancy, and exhibitionism. This chapter will concentrate on the three most salient patterns—public drunkenness, illegal drug use, and prostitution—since the issues related to them are common to all public order crimes. Glaser has classified these violations as "illegal performance" and "illegal consumption" offenses.[1] Illegal performance laws proscribe drunkenness, disorderly conduct, indecent exposure, and the like as unlawful only if done in public. They usually don't involve any clear-cut injury to others. The laws were enacted at the initiative of influential groups offended by the behavior of those less influential. Glaser hypothesizes that restrictions on illegal performances seem to decrease as the society becomes more complex and heterogeneous.[2] Thus restrictions are least in port cities with high rates of in- and out-migration of diverse groups.

Definitions of what constitutes illegal consumption seem to vary widely. When a type of consumption disturbs a sufficiently influential public, then there is an effort to use the criminal law to suppress it. When the costs of suppression become too high, then it is replaced by regulation.

[1] Daniel Glaser, *Adult Crime and Social Policy* (Englewood Cliffs, N.J.: Prentice-Hall, 1972), pp. 27–66.
[2] Daniel Glaser, "Criminology and Public Policy," *The American Sociologist*, 6 (June 1971), 30–37.

If we take an interest-group approach to public order crime we can see that those most active in prohibiting behavior defined as against morality and public order have been linked to religious and kinship structures. Thus legislation prohibiting public drunkenness was inspired by religious groups deeply disturbed by those who openly violated injunctions relating to moral strength and personal discipline. Puritan concerns about exuberant behavior on the Sabbath resulted in Sunday laws designed to regulate behavior on that day. Laws regulating sexual conduct were designed to protect a particular kind of family system. Quinney suggests that the range of sexual conduct that is covered by law is so extensive in the United States that it makes potential criminals of most of the adolescent and adult population.[3]

Prostitution is usually defined as sexual intercourse characterized by barter, promiscuity, and emotional indifference. It is considered a profession if it's done full time, if one makes one's living from it, and if the self-conception is one of a prostitute. There are problems with the definition since sometimes goods are exchanged (not money) and sometimes intercourse does not take place as in the case of beating a masochistic customer for money. Gebhard provides the most comprehensive definition:

> A prostitute is an individual who will engage in sexual activity with strangers or other persons with whom the individual has no affectional relationship in exchange for money or other valuable materials that are given at or near the time of the act.[4]

EARLY HISTORY

Social reactions to mind-altering substances seem to have little to do with their harmful effects on the body. Thus there is an abundance of evidence that both alcohol and tobacco are dangerous, yet the public perception of them is benign. At the opposite end of the continuum is heroin, which is relatively harmless—prolonged use does not damage organs, tissues, or cells of the human body as does alcohol. But heroin is addictive, so this might provide the clue to social reaction. However, alcohol and tobacco use are also addictive, so classification of drugs by their addictive potential would not tell us much about public reaction. Some observers are impressed by the variety of public responses to drugs

---

[3] Richard Quinney, *The Social Reality of Crime* (Boston: Little, Brown, 1970), p. 86.
[4] Paul H. Gebhard, "Definitions," in Donald S. Marshall and Robert C. Suggs (eds.), *Human Sexual Behavior* (New York: Basic Books, 1971), p. 258.

depending on time and place. Thus opium was once considered a cure-all but now is strongly condemned. The reaction to cigarette smoking has also fluctuated widely; in some cultures the punishment for smoking was death.

A comparative survey of different cultures and different historical epochs can lead to the conclusion that social reaction to drugs is almost patternless. But a closer examination of the historical materials reveals a very distinct pattern. In the United States the first laws against opium use were city ordinances passed in San Francisco in 1875. Hill has argued that the legislation was directed against Chinese laborers imported to work on railroad construction crews.[5] Rising unemployment among white workers generated strong antagonism against Chinese laborers who were willing to work long hours for low wages. The threat the Chinese posed was the reason behind campaigns to eliminate Chinese opium dens. A pamphlet circulated by the American Federation of Labor put their position succinctly:

> What other crimes were committed in those dark, fetid places [opium dens] when these little innocent victims of Chinamen's wiles were under the influence of the drug, are almost too horrible to imagine. . . . There are hundreds, aye, thousands, of our American girls and boys who have acquired this deathly habit and are doomed, hopelessly doomed, beyond the shadow of redemption.[6]

The antiopium laws, according to Helmer, provided a legal basis for arbitrary raids and searches of Chinese premises.[7] The anti-Chinese drive culminated in a Congressional law in 1909 prohibiting the importation or smoking of opium. Several years later in 1914 the Harrison Narcotics Act was passed outlawing the sale or possession of opium and its derivatives. This legislation was directed at "the dangerous classes" whose potential for disruption seemed to call for control measures. Coincidental with the federal antinarcotics legislation was the active promotion of what Lindesmith has called "the dope fiend mythology."[8]

The laws specified what was prohibited and, by implication, what was enjoined. The law-abiding American was proabstinence. He was opposed to all mind-altering substances and in favor of "temperance." The temperance movement banning the sale and use of alcohol were led by the same antidrug forces in each of the states where they triumphed. The

---

[5] Herbert Hill, "Anti-Oriental Agitation and the Rise of Working-Class Racism," *Society,* 10 (January–February 1973), 43–48, 50–54.
[6] Quoted in ibid., p. 52.
[7] John Helmer, *Drugs and Minority Oppression* (New York: Knopf, 1972).
[8] Alfred Lindesmith, " 'Dope Fiend' Mythology," *Journal of Criminal Law, Criminology and Police Science,* 31 (1940), 199–208.

end result of their efforts was the national prohibition amendment enacted in 1919.

Gusfield's account of the abstinence movement shows that it was directed against the recent immigrants from southern and eastern Europe who were increasingly becoming part of a growing urban lower-class stratum.[9] They represented a "contaminating" influence that could be curbed by the prohibition legislation as well as a vigorous movement to restrict immigration and a eugenics movement to prevent the unfit from reproducing. The three movements—abstinence, immigration restriction, and eugenics—were all part of the same general nativist reactions to the potential threat the newcomers posed.

But the success of antidrug legislation was in marked contrast to the failure of the anti-alcohol legislation. Attempts to implement the prohibition legislation were undercut in urban areas where drinking values prevailed. But it was not only the immigrants who found the goal of total abstinence incomprehensible. An emerging and influential group of urban professionals whose values condoned moderate drinking was in favor of the abolition of Prohibition. The only remnant of the "noble experiment" that remains today are the laws against public drunkenness, another instance of class legislation.

The Marijuana Tax Act passed in 1937 to make the sale and possession of marijuana illegal was also directed at a particular population of users—Mexican migrant workers. Musto has presented a convincing body of evidence to demonstrate that the marijuana legislation was basically a political move designed, in conjunction with other legislative measures, to reinforce a system of subordination.[10] In short, the experiments to regulate or control drug use cannot be understood apart from a history of race and class relations in the United States.

Winick and Kinsie have suggested that the existence of and/or acceptance of prostitution is related to social structure.[11] Societies that accept nonmarital sex relationships and endorse the discussion of sex have practically no prostitution. Systems that provide for no discussion of sex but accept nonmarital sex for men have a high incidence of prostitution, some tolerance of it, and usually formal segregation of the activity. Thus prostitution was widespread during the Middle Ages. It was regarded as a necessary evil by religious authorities and functional to the family

---

[9] Joseph R. Gusfield, *Symbolic Crusade* (Urbana: University of Illinois Press, 1963).

[10] David F. Musto, *The American Disease: Origins of Narcotic Control* (New Haven, Conn.: Yale University Press, 1973).

[11] Charles Winick and Paul M. Kinsie, *The Lively Commerce: Prostitution in the United States* (Chicago: Quadrangle Books, 1971).

system. Davis has pointed out that prostitution is necessary as long as there is a relatively constant demand by males for impersonal and impartial sex that wives and lovers do not meet.[12] Attempts to repress prostitution have been followed most vigorously in Protestant countries with toleration and segregation being more common in Catholic countries. Lemert has pointed out that apart from formal variations, the vicissitudes of local policing and administration of the laws account for even greater variation in tolerance for prostitution.[13] Some of the variables he discusses are:

1. The number and visibility of prostitutes—the more visible the activity becomes the greater citizen outrage.

2. The dimensions of the venereal disease problem—increased incidence of venereal disease is characteristically attributed to prostitutes so a public health rationale is invoked for eliminating it.

3. The sex ratios of the population—the larger the proportion of men to women, the greater the tolerance for prostitution.

4. The relationship of prostitution to the institutionalized power struggles being waged in the community.

EXTENT AND COST OF PUBLIC ORDER CRIME

The estimates on the extent of illegal *drug use* in the United States suggest that about 30 percent of the adult population smoke marijuana, about 5 percent use LSD, and only 1 percent shoot heroin.[14] There seem to be several different patterns of use organized around the drug of preference. We can distinguish at least two: the opiate pattern and the psychedelic pattern. Both are linked to marijuana, though the meanings of marijuana differ in each pattern. The "junkie" and the "acid head" do not associate with one another in spite of the fact that both use illegal

[12] Kingsley Davis, "Sexual Behavior," in Robert K. Merton and Robert A. Nisbet (eds.), *Contemporary Social Problems*, 2nd ed. (New York: Harcourt Brace Jovanovich, 1966).
[13] Edwin Lemert, *Social Pathology* (New York: McGraw-Hill, 1951).
[14] These estimates are drawn from several surveys. National Commission on Marihuana and Drug Abuse, *Drug Use in America* (Washington, D.C.: Government Printing Office, 1973), pp. 65–71; and John A. O'Donnell et al., *Young Men and Drugs: A National Survey* (Rockville, Md.: National Institute of Drug Abuse, 1976).

drugs and both use marijuana; their patterns of life are distinct, their values often incompatible, their friendship networks disjunctive.

The Heroin Pattern

Illicit use of narcotics is characteristic of the young male slum dweller; blacks seem to represent about half of all addicts known to police, and Mexicans and Puerto Ricans almost another quarter. Use of heroin is rarely found on the college campus or among middle-class college-educated individuals with the exception of the physician addict described by Winick.[15] Heroin is the drug of choice of the street addict. The addict must resort to illegal activity to buy heroin. A tremendous amount of burglary and larceny has been ascribed to heroin addicts.

The Psychedelic Pattern

Illegal use of LSD-type drugs is more characteristic of middle-class college-educated young people. The social class and educational background of the typical user is not only higher than that for the heroin pattern but is higher than for the population at large. The pattern of usage also differs from the heroin pattern. The use of psychedelics is almost never as much as daily for any period longer than a week or two. Only a small proportion of those who have used LSD-type drugs continue to do so after more than several times. Aside from drug use the user is rarely criminal; it is unnecessary for him to commit money-making crimes since he does not typically take his drug of choice more than a few times. Finally there is a higher degree of proselytizing fervor among psychedelicists, who usually feel that the "whole world should be turned on," while the average junkie wishes to obtain his drugs and be left alone.

The characteristics that all illegal drug users share despite class differences is that they tend to be concentrated in large urban areas; they are mainly male; come from families where parents used legal drugs to alleviate tension, deal with insomnia, and the like. They are more likely to be estranged from religion and have unconventional outlooks. Contrary to beliefs about how people initially become users, they were intro-

---

[15] Charles Winick, "Physician Narcotic Addicts," *Social Problems*, 9 (Fall, 1961), 174–86.

duced to drug use by friends and they find it relatively easy to obtain drugs.

Alcohol

The extent of alcohol use is much higher than illegal drug use. A study done in the early 1970s showed that 68 percent of American adults drank alcohol.[16] One-half of those who drank did so infrequently. Another half drank in moderate or heavy amounts. There are about 10 million alcoholics in the population. The World Health Organization defined an alcoholic as one whose repeated use of alcoholic beverages interferes with his interpersonal relations or his social or economic functioning.[17]

The counterpart to the National Commission for Marijuana and Drug Abuse is the National Institute on Alcohol Abuse and Alcoholism. Its 1973 national survey found the highest rates of alcohol-related problems to be among young, male, urban dwellers; persons who are separated, single, or divorced; persons with no religious affiliation; persons who are beer drinkers (in contrast to wine and hard liquor); and among blacks and Irish-Americans. Proportionally more of the higher socioeconomic strata are drinkers but there are more problem drinkers at the lower levels. However there is some suspicion that there is no real difference in the alcoholism rates but that the higher status people are more adept at hiding their problem drinking.

The National Institute on Alcohol Abuse and Alcoholism has also come up with some rather startling figures on the cost of alcoholism: in 1971, the cost of lost productivity was conservatively estimated at $9.35 billion; the cost of alcohol-related medical problems at about the same; the cost of alcohol-involved auto accidents at $6.44 billion (half of each year's auto deaths and injuries can be traced to excessive drinking); and the cost to the criminal justice system for alcohol-related offenses at $.5 billion.[18] Alcohol use is directly or indirectly involved in a large number of offenses. Those directly related are public drunkenness, driving under the influence of alcohol, disorderly conduct, vagrancy, and the violation of liquor laws. Alcohol is associated with 64 percent of all murders, 41 percent of all assaults, 34 percent of all forcible rapes, and 29 percent of all other crimes.

[16] Second Special Report to the U.S. Congress on Alcohol and Health (Rockville, Md.: National Institute on Alcohol Abuse and Alcoholism, 1974).

[17] Quoted by Don Cahalan, *Problem Drinkers* (San Francisco: Jossey-Bass, 1970), p. 3.

[18] Second Special Report, p. 42.

Estimates on the extent of prostitution in the United States can be made according to the number of prostitution arrests. This is an unreliable index because the prostitute may be charged with vagrancy, disorderly conduct, or prostitution. Many prostitutes are never arrested. Winick and Kinsie, using law enforcement data in the late 1960s, reported that there were 95,550 arrests for violation of prostitution or related laws.[19] This they conclude is a very conservative approximation of the number of full-time prostitutes; and it doesn't include any women who work as part-time prostitutes. They estimate that the average full-time prostitute works six days a week and has three clients daily so that some 286,650 men daily use such services. They speculated that an average fee per contract was $10 so that all full-time prostitutes earn about $894 million a year. The average prostitute grossed about $9,300 per year and, of that, netted from $5,000 to $6,000. Winick and Kinsie report that the extent of prostitution seems to be fairly stable so that the proportion of men from each socioeconomic group who visit prostitutes is about the same as it was in the 1930s. The one major change they note is the shift from a brothel pattern to individual entrepreneurship.

GROUP SUPPORT FOR PUBLIC ORDER CRIME

The rationales to justify drug use, alcohol use, and prostitution are sufficiently well developed to suggest that there is widespread support for these offenses. Society generally condones the use of alcohol, tobacco, sedatives, tranquilizers, and stimulants. These legal drugs are used for recreation, to relieve tension, to help one sleep, and so on. Their use provides a broader supportive context for the use of illegal drugs like marijuana, heroin, LSD, and cocaine. The values generally approve the use of legal drugs in *moderation*. Excessive use leads to loss of self-control, which is discouraged. The campaign that the Federal Bureau of Narcotics mounted in the early 1930s to promote antimarijuana legislation underlined values related to work and ambition: ecstasy should not be sought for its own sake and self-control should never be relinquished.

[19] Winick and Kinsie, *The Lively Commerce.*

Blum characterized these values as "Appolianian" and they are widely shared in the larger society.[20]

But since the 1930s support has been growing for a competing set of values that enjoins the search for ecstasy and is not at all fearful of the loss of self-control. Blum characterized this value set as "Dionysian." These values are more likely to be characteristic of those under 30. This development has spurred the use of illegal drugs among middle-class youth. The move to soften the penalties associated with illegal drug use is testimony to the large number of conventional youth who have become illegal drug users. The group support for illegal drug use stresses the pleasurable mind-expanding character of the drug experience. To the extent there is a drug-using subculture, it rejects the negative definitions offered by the larger society which stresses unpleasant and horrifying effects like "going crazy," "flipping out," or having a psychotic experience.

The two kinds of alcoholism—that of the middle classes and that of the skid row alcoholic—differ in their amount of group support. The middle-class alcoholic is not part of a counterculture though he or she may subscribe to values that implicitly support the heavy use of alcohol. But there is an extensive body of literature that depicts the middle-class problem drinker as an isolate. He spends a considerable amount of effort in concealing the problem from family, friends, and work associates. To the extent the problem is addressed, agencies other than those of the criminal justice system come into play. Quite simply alcoholism among the middle class is not considered a crime, but rather a "disease"; an influential medically related movement has sprung up to press for public acceptance of the disease interpretation. It espouses various kinds of "treatment" involving individual or group therapy and sometimes "aversion therapy." The movement represents a clearly defined set of interests that can be most fruitfully analyzed in terms of a conflict perspective. But its significance at this point is in terms of the impact it has on group support for excessive use of alcohol. It has provided the problem drinker with an interpretation of his behavior and various strategies for coping with the social and physical consequences of drinking. The fundamental aim of the alcohol treatment movement is abstinence or moderation yet its effect has been to provide favorable group support for heavy drinking.

The situation is dramatically different for the skid row alcoholic. His drinking is defined as a crime, not a disease, and he does not have the

[20] Richard H. Blum, "Drugs, Dangerous Behavior and Social Policy," in President's Commission on Law Enforcement and the Administration of Justice, *Task Force Report, Narcotics and Drug Abuse* (Washington, D.C.: Government Printing Office, 1967), p. 68.

resources or the wherewithal to avail himself of other kinds of treatment. The initiative exercised by the criminal justice apparatus in relation to public drunkenness offenses has contributed to the creation of a sturdy subculture of drunkenness symbiotically linked to enforcement strategies. Despite recommendation by the 1967 President's Commission that public drunkenness be decriminalized, it still accounts for 30 to 40 percent of total arrests made each year.

The group support that exists for prostitution depends on the kind of pattern that exists. There are three basic patterns: the streetwalker, the employee of an organized house, and the high-class independent.[21] The extent of group support is least for the streetwalker since it is the least-organized pattern. In terms of status the streetwalker is the lowest, though this group outnumbers all the rest put together. Relationships among streetwalkers are highly competitive. The prostitute's locale is on the streets or in bars and hotel lobbies. Typically the streetwalker is not a full-time prostitute. Since she is the most highly visible of prostitutes she is most often arrested.

The most spectacular organized houses were called "parlor houses" and set up lavishly in disorganized areas. The parlor house was usually run by a female entrepreneur or by organized crime. Though the parlor house has disappeared its successor today is the massage parlor which flourishes in the same marginal areas of large cities. Relations between the girls are highly competitive but extent of group support is greater than that experienced by the streetwalker. Status is determined by the number of customers one has and the amount of money earned.

The high-class independent or "call girl" pattern has recently become more common. Visibility is low and the prostitute is adapted to the mobility of the urban area. It allows for greater individualization of operation and more part-time participants. This pattern is most often linked to conventions and the entertainment of out-of-town businessmen. The skills required in prostitution are relatively simple but do require some training. Characteristically the call girl is trained or "turned out" by another call girl. The relationship with other call girls is more mutually supportive than competitive, and a distinctive ideology is part of it. The ideology includes the notion that prostitution performs a necessary, important service for society, and that prostitutes are morally superior to conventional people. Some call girls carry on by tacit understandings with landlords and proprietors, setting themselves up in hotels or apartments and occasionally using go-betweens like bellhops and taxi drivers to get customers.

[21] Lemert, *Social Pathology*, pp. 247–52.

SOCIAL REACTION AND LEGAL PROCESSING

Public reaction to alcoholism, illegal drug use, and prostitution is much less severe than reactions to personal and property crimes. A movement to decriminalize these offenses as well as other "victimless" crimes has been gaining momentum. This is reflected in the softening of penalties for illegal drug use, the gradual use of detoxification centers rather than jail for public drunks, and the removal from the criminal code of proscriptions against sexual activity between consenting adults. Criminal law reformers have been leaders in the movement to decriminalize these offenses and have argued effectively against using the criminal law in this area as wasteful, irrational, and morally suspect. Those who are convicted under these laws, as were others discussed so far, tend to be lower-status offenders. The most flagrant failure to enforce the laws proscribing prostitution relate to the handling of the prostitute's patrons. Characteristically prostitutes are arrested but their customers are not, though both have broken the law. Feminist groups have urged that laws against prostitution be abolished or at least be enforced evenhandedly.

CONTROL OF PUBLIC ORDER CRIMINALITY

The major question here is how violations can be handled with minimum cost to the taxpayer, minimum damage to the offender, minimum strain to the police, and without creating anxiety among the public which expresses itself by pressuring for inappropriate laws. When a community or society concludes that a particular kind of behavior is problematic it has a number of options available to discourage the behavior. It might decide on the basis of some kind of cost-effectiveness analysis that the behavior is not worth discouraging. It may decide that an educational policy makes the most sense. It may decide that treatment programs for violators would be most effective. Or it may decide that a set of regulations to control the behavior, whether part of the criminal code or not, would be the best way to address the problem. Though these policies are sometimes mixed in actual practice, they do represent distinct logical and historical possibilities.

Do Nothing

The cost of enforcing the law is too high. Kadish has put the case well in discussing prostitution:

> . . . diversion of police resources; encouragement of illegal means of police control (which, in the case of prostitution, take the form of knowingly unlawful harassment arrests to remove suspected prostitutes from the streets; and various entrapment devices, usually the only means of obtaining convictions); degradation of the image of law enforcement; discriminatory enforcement against the poor; and official corruption.[22]

A thorough examination of the costs and benefits relating to imposing sanctions may lead to the conclusion that it is better to do nothing because the offensiveness of the conduct relative to other values is not that great. Packer uses as an illustration a law to suppress fornication between unmarried adults.[23] To prevent it would take enormous enforcement resources. In lieu of full enforcement, lawmakers may decide that a few exemplary prosecutions might deter fornication. But this would involve arbitrary decisions on whom to detect, apprehend, and prosecute. The lawmaker under these circumstances might conclude that suppressing fornication was not that high on his list of social objectives. Other proponents of decriminalizing public order offenses point to the role proscription plays in driving those who engage in violations to associate with those engaged in other criminal activities, thus contributing to the growth of an extensive criminal subculture subversive of social order generally. Basically, however, the argument is made on the basis of resource allocation: we can't do everything we wish to do because of limited resources. Therefore we might be better off doing nothing. The conditions favorable to this strategy is a general consensus that the behavior is not particularly harmful.

Lemert, in discussing alcohol control strategies, pointed out that in some societies there is a belief that it reduces stress and strengthens group bonds.[24] The fellowship which results from ingestion, apart from

---

[22] Sanford H. Kadish, "The Crisis of Overcriminalization," in Richard D. Knudten (ed.), *Crime, Criminology and Contemporary Society* (Homewood, Ill.: Dorsey Press, 1970), p. 8.

[23] Herbert L. Packer, *The Limits of the Criminal Sanction* (Stanford, Calif.: Stanford University Press, 1968), pp. 151–52.

[24] Edwin M. Lemert, *Human Deviance, Social Problems and Social Control* (Englewood Cliffs, N.J.: Prentice-Hall, 1967), pp. 78–84.

any negative outcomes, is sufficiently valued that no steps are taken to interfere with the individual's consumption. In some cases drunkenness may assume an institutionalized form which is a kind of control. In some societies, however, there is a minimum of any kind of institutional control. The response seems to be that whatever the cost it can be absorbed or written off. This was the situation in the United States for some kind of mind-altering substances prior to federal legislation. There were no federal controls over narcotics prior to 1915 and none over marijuana before 1937. Over-the-counter sales of marijuana were common.

The Education Model

The strategy of this model is to reduce the costs of violation by a system of indoctrination or information about the consequences of the behavior, thus leading to a decline in violations. Some evidence suggests that controlled presentation of information can lead to changes in attitudes.[25] The findings from studies of attitude change are not conclusive, however. In some cases specific attitudes were changed in the desired direction, leading to behavioral change; in some instances nothing happened; and in some instances there was a "boomerang effect" where attitudes were changed in the opposite direction. It is not clear at this point whether information exposure works to change specific values and attitudes or whether people with particular values put themselves in the way of certain information they feel they need.

In the United States the education model is best illustrated by the sex, drug, and alcohol educational programs in the public schools. In the absence of specific guidelines, educators operate with a public health rationale. The major difficulty with this model is that formal educational agencies charged with the training task are not as influential as peer group or family in shaping attitudes. As Lemert has noted in discussing alcohol education problems:

> . . . educators are faced with discontinuity between the learning process in the schools and what goes on in primary groups outside. Examples set by parents at home or pressures to conform in friendship groups easily cancel out the abstinence or moderation precepts of the school.[26]

[25] See Richard Blum and Mary L. Funkhouser-Balbaky, "Mind-Altering Drugs and Dangerous Behavior: Dangerous Drugs," in President's Commission, *Task Force Report, Narcotics and Drug Abuse.*
[26] Lemert, *Human Deviance*, p. 80.

The Medical-Motivational Model

In its most comprehensive form this view sees the users and suppliers of illegal services as sick and in need of treatment. There has been growing support for the transfer of social control from law enforcement to the medical profession. The widespread acceptance of this approach in the press and a wide variety of publics has paralleled the growth of the mental health movement in the United States. Spokespersons for this view assume that a major advance has been made if a violator is classified as a patient rather than a criminal. The more ominous features of medical intervention in the lives of those who do not view themselves as sick has been little explored to date.

A general acceptance of this approach would require a major commitment of scarce resources to basically untested treatment strategies. The major treatment strategy implied is some kind of hospitalization or outpatient therapy as in alcohol or drug treatment programs. The same rationale has been extended to the treatment of prostitutes, though no one to date has suggested that those who use the services of prostitutes are also sick. The problem is that those who are defined as ill by virtue of their behavior will not voluntarily seek assistance. To address this problem for illegal drug users the practice of "civil commitment" has been developed. The term "civil" is a misnomer, however, since no effective way has been worked out to encourage drug users who are not facing criminal prosecution to commit themselves for treatment. The civil commitment strategy, initially hailed as a major humanitarian advance, is now being seriously questioned as ineffective and insufficiently concerned with due process consideration. Despite its sophisticated terminology it turns out in practice, because of the use of the indeterminate sentence of the commitment, to be less responsible than the correctional view in terms of the constraints of the law. A more modest version of the medical approach in the area of illegal drugs is one that proposes that the medical profession be authorized to prescribe them.

The Abstinence Model

This strategy assumes that the costs of violation can be reduced by a system of laws and coercive controls making it illegal to manufacture or provide illegal services or to consume them. This is sometimes called the "prohibition model" and it has been tried with alcohol in a variety of situations. The failures of alcohol prohibition have been well documented. The main reason for its failure was the high cost of enforcing the law. The resources it would have taken to suppress alcohol use in the face of widespread alcohol consumption were more than the nation was prepared to expend at the time. A second factor in the failure of alcohol prohibition was the ambivalence of key supporters of prohibition, especially as the enforcement apparatus touched upon their own moderate drinking habits or those of their friends or their children. Glaser notes that an important factor in repeal of the prohibition amendment was "shock at the power of corruption and predation that accrued to the bootleggers."[27] The conviction among those who worked for the repeal of the prohibition amendment was that because of the widespread and serious violation of the law, law enforcement was impeded by overloading, and disrespect for law in general was generated.

The limited evidence available from historical and comparative sources suggests that prohibition is likely to work only under certain conditions: if there is widespread support for suppression; if a large number of power elites either see positive value gains in prohibition laws (e.g., the conviction that the costs of use are too high) or see them as a means of protection against threatened value losses, thus making it easier for them to pay the high costs of prohibition enforcement willingly; or if there is a replacement of the values related to the behavior or substitution of new means for achieving the old values. Lemert suggests that such conditions are difficult to approximate in the modern world.

> A precondition [of prohibition] would be relatively complete geographic isolation, similar to that found on islands, where behavior deviations have a high visibility. A social structure in which power is concentrated and little affected by public opinion or is upheld by supernatural sanctions perhaps would make for successful prohibition.[28]

Alcohol Control Model

This model has emerged from the attempts to control the intake of liquor. The notion is that the costs of intoxication can be reduced by legal regulation of the kind of substances consumed, its cost, its methods of distribution, the time and place where use occurs, and its availability to consumers according to age, sex, or other characteristics. Use of the mood-altering substance is defined as a privilege which can be withdrawn by regulatory agencies if abused.

This model has developed out of utilitarian concerns rather than moral

---

[27] Glaser, "Criminology and Public Policy," p. 32.
[28] Lemert, *Human Deviance*, pp. 79–80.

ones. Pressure was exerted by particular groups of alcohol users to assure that the quality of liquor sold met a certain standard. Also, financially hard pressed governing bodies needed a source of revenue. The control can be exercised through various kinds of distributor licensing systems or a state monopoly.

This strategy has also been used effectively to regulate prostitution in other countries. There has been some recognition of the limitations of the criminal law in this area. The United States is the only country today in which the prostitute is punished, although in many other countries she is arrested for street solicitation. Our national experience with alcohol control suggested that this kind of regulation is workable and the revenue aspects of it make it especially appealing to lawmakers. The regulations have significantly altered the forms and patterns of American drinking. Public opinion seems to be favorable to, or at least not strongly resentful of, the regulatory agencies. Distributors and retailers can be hurt economically and made more receptive to the regulations by suspension or revocation of licenses. The main problem with this suggestion is that illegal drugs and prostitution are not viewed as an alcohol equivalent by a majority of people, especially those over 30. To control prostitution and illegal drug use in terms of this model today would require a preliminary educational campaign coordinated at the highest national levels with the cooperation of health, welfare, and law enforcement elites to define the behavior as less serious. At the present time the possible supporters for this kind of educational campaign would be academic researchers, criminal law reformers, some medical personnel, and tax officials.

Summary

A careful assessment of different control strategies in the light of the inadequacies of public order legislation suggests that some improvements can be made. Some controls should be rejected as inappropriate: a do-nothing policy, a medical approach that involves compulsory civil commitment, and a prohibition approach.

A do-nothing policy seems ill-suited to the demands of a technological age. Citizens have come to expect the state to perform a public health role. Government intervention, other than through the use of criminal sanctions, seems to be required as long as there is some potential for harm. Government intervention could at least guarantee the purity or safety of the product or service. The reasons for rejecting the medical model is that its effectiveness depends on two conditions which do not now exist: we do not have adequate measures of therapy and those afflicted usually do not think of themselves as needing a cure. The abstinence approach is rejected because of the financial and social costs it entails. A rational and humane policy would substitute administrative sanctions for criminal ones and supplement the new policy with sophisticated and comprehensive educational programs on drug use and sex.

EXPLANATIONS OF PUBLIC ORDER CRIME

Anomie theory has supplied the most influential explanation of illegal drug use. The drug user is a person from a lower-class background who does not have access to either conventional or illicit avenues of advancement. Because of this, anomie theorists have characterized the drug user—and they are mainly talking about the heroin user—as a "double failure" who is unable to take advantage of legal or illegal opportunities either because they are unavailable or because he is unwilling to do so. In the face of this blockage the user "retreats" into drug use. Cloward and Ohlin maintain that the user is willing to use illicit means and that they are unavailable to him.

Lindesmith has developed another explanation for opiate addiction, sometimes called "the symbolic interactionist" explanation. He argued that it was not the effect of opiates on the body that led to addiction but only the user's realization that withdrawal distress can be alleviated by the drug:

> The power of the opiate habit is derived basically from effects which follow when the drug is removed rather than upon any positive effects which its presence in the body produces. Addiction occurs only when opiates are used to alleviate withdrawal distress, after this distress had been properly understood or interpreted, that is to say, after it has been represented to the individual in terms of the linguistic symbols and cultural patterns which have grown up around the opiate habit. If the individual fails to conceive of his distress as withdrawal distress brought about by the absence of opiates, he does not become addicted, but, if he does, addiction is quickly and permanently established through further use of the drug.[29]

The two theories, anomie and symbolic interaction, are designed to explain different phenomena. Cloward and Ohlin provide a plausible explanation of the pressures operative in specific parts of the social structure that generate illegal drug use. Lindesmith focuses on the process of becoming addicted. How a person becomes committed to drug use, or for

[29] Alfred R. Lindesmith, *Addiction and Opiates* (Chicago: Aldine, 1968), p. 191.

that matter any kind of behavior pattern, has been the concern of the labelists or interactionists who look at the drug's effects on users. A drug's effects are partially determined by the context within which it is ingested and the meanings associated with its use. Becker has identified the various stages in becoming a marijuana user that can be generalized to other kinds of drugs.[30] The neophyte first learns the techniques for getting high, he then learns to recognize the drug's effects, and lastly he learns to enjoy them. The process occurs in a supportive atmosphere where friends act as tutors.

Because anomie theory has been so influential it has been criticized much more thoroughly than social process explanations. The main criticism is that the image of the addict as a failure is invalid. This does not take into account those who have managed to combine heroin use with occupational success: namely the physician addict. Second, the effort to make a great deal of money illegally so that drugs can be purchased involves an extraordinary amount of "hustle," energy, and initiative not at all characteristic of a "retreatist." To date there has been no systematic critique of social process explanations because of the limited amount of research done from this perspective. But we can expect that challenges would be made on how generalizable a theory of stages is from one drug to another. It seems most appropriate when discussing relatively mild kinds of mind-altering substances where the effects on the body are somewhat ambiguous. Where the physical and chemical impact of a drug are overpowering and unambiguous, then the cultural context is less important.

The explanations of alcoholism are somewhat analogous to the theories of illegal drug use. Bales originally suggested an explanation of why some groups produce a higher rate of alcoholism than others.[31] He concluded that when a culture (1) produces acute inner tensions in its participants, while at the same time (2) approving of drinking as a means of relieving tensions, and (3) no substitute means for relieving tension are encouraged, alcoholism rates will be high. Thrice has tried to account for the internal group variation in rates and concludes that it requires (1) a vulnerable personality, (2) group encouragement of drinking as "manly" behavior, leading to (3) loss of control, group exclusion, and (4) the search for other uncontrolled drinkers.

The equivalent to the social process explanation of illegal drug use is Jellinek's discussion of the phases of alcoholism.[32] At the *introductory*

[30] Howard S. Becker, "Becoming a Marijuana User," *American Journal of Sociology*, 59 (November 1953), 235–42.
[31] Robert F. Bales, "Cultural Differences in Rates of Alcoholism," *Quarterly Journal of Studies on Alcohol*, 6 (March 1946), 480–99.
[32] E. M. Jellinek "The Phases of Alcohol Addiction," *Quarterly Journal of Studies on Alcohol*, 13 (1952), 673–84.

stage the potential alcoholic is merely a social drinker who finds release of his tensions in drinking. Increased tolerance leads to heavier drinking and additional tensions as a consequence. The potential alcoholic moves to the *early stage* when he begins to experience blackouts or memory losses as to what happened during drinking bouts. At this stage he begins to drink alone and drink in the mornings. The *middle stage* is reached when the candidate loses control over his drinking; when he takes one drink he is unable to stop until the supply runs out. At this point his eating patterns are affected and the person may suffer problems related to nutrition. *The final stage* is reached when the individual goes on binges, becomes completely dependent upon alcohol, and suffers from delirium tremens.

As with theories of illegal drug use no overall evaluation can be proposed at this juncture. Both the explanation of group rates and the description of becoming an alcoholic are partial theories with limited applicability. One major gap is an explanation of skid row alcoholism that extends, modifies, or challenges Bales's scheme. An integrated theory would tie together the explanations for alcoholism among different social strata and synthesize what is known about legal as well as illegal drug use.

Sociologists have noted that alcoholism and drunkenness are not the same thing. Reckless concludes:

> One can become drunk without being an alcoholic, but one can also become drunk and be a chronic alcoholic. . . . The alcoholic, however, is an uncontrolled drinker who has developed a dependence on alcohol and usually consumes large amounts daily. . . . More and more the accepted criterion of alcoholism is uncontrolled drinking. . . . A man may be a heavy drinker for twenty years without becoming an alcoholic.[33]

The person most likely to be arrested for public drunkenness may not be an alcoholic. What might be considered excessive and daily use of alcohol on skid row does not coincide with alcoholism. Hence theories of alcoholism may not shed much light on the crime of public drunkenness. Wallace reports that heavy drinking on skid row is the product of group norms rather than the result of individual addictive craving for alcohol.[34] The alcoholic actually turns out to be somewhat of an outsider in skid row culture, mainly because of his higher social status. The explanation of how a person becomes a likely candidate for processing as a skid row drunk mainly relies on notions of drift. The person may suffer a quick

[33] Walter C. Reckless, *The Crime Problem* (New York: Appleton-Century-Crofts, 1967), p. 186.
[34] Samuel Wallace, *Skid Row as a Way of Life* (Totowa, N.J.: Bedminister Press, 1965).

descent due to economic reversals or a more gradual one related to the conditions of migratory labor. Or a person may end up in skid row because of loss of or lack of primary contacts. The attraction to the skid row pattern is the social affiliation it provides. The most plausible explanation for the skid row drunk is the labeling one. Spradley's study depicted the criminal justice apparatus as a trap for any unfortunate enough to become enmeshed in it on a drunkenness charge.[35] Once labeled a drunk the individual is stripped of his previous identity and in jail learns the survival skills and life style of a tramp. His criminal record effectively insures that he will be unable to return to a noncriminal identity.

There are two major explanations of prostitution. One tries to answer the question of why prostitution exists; the other addresses the question of why some females become prostitutes. Kingsley Davis first put forward the notion that prostitution is an inevitable outcome of the institutional control of sexual expression.[36] Societies attempt to control the sexual impulse in the interest of social order, procreation, and socialization. Institutional control combined with the unequal scale of attractiveness and social inequality between classes and between male and female create the conditions for the emergence of prostitution. The moral order also defines certain kinds of sexual activity as illicit; a man interested in engaging in this deviant activity cannot do so with his present sexual partner. Society's attempt to tie sexual expression to the durable relationship of marriage and the rearing of children condemns to sexual inactivity those who because of age, physical appearance, or economic situation are unable or unwilling to fulfill these social requirements. Thus a demand is created for sexual services outside the marriage relationship. It also appeals to those who, though married, crave sexual variety. While limiting sexual expression to marriage our culture normally disposes women to use sex for many purposes outside the marriage relationship.

There are many accounts of why some females become prostitutes. Kingsley Davis raised the question why more women don't become prostitutes in light of its economic benefits. He concluded that the social stigma attached to the occupation deters most. Benjamin and Masters begin with a set of predisposing factors like parental promiscuity, traumatic childhood, and the like.[37] This is followed by factors that "pull" the woman to prostitution—larger earnings, easier and more adventurous life, etc. Lemert notes that women in certain occupations are

[35] James P. Spradley, *You Owe Yourself a Drunk* (Boston: Little, Brown, 1970).

[36] Kingsley Davis, "The Sociology of Prostitution," *American Sociological Review*, 2 (October 1937), 744–55.

[37] Harry Benjamin and R. E. L. Masters, *Prostitution and Morality* (New York: Julian Press, 1964).

more likely to be attracted to prostitution—there is an occupational affinity to it.[38] These occupations are waiting on tables, domestic service, show girls, manicurists, masseuses, and models. They are occupational analogues of prostitution because they involve dependency upon masculine largesse in the form of tips. From a situation of quasi-prostitution it is a short step to actual prostitution. The last stage in becoming a prostitute for Benjamin and Masters is the precipitating one—for example, economic pressures, persuasion by an intimate, or response to an unhappy love affair. After becoming a prostitute other skills must be learned. Hirschi summarizes these skills: learning to find customers, "selling" them, providing a suitable place in which to carry on their business, pleasing the customer, collecting money, protecting oneself from disease, pregnancy, and physical injury, and avoiding the police.[39]

The extent to which these explanations fit in individual cases is questionable. The following interview is illustrative. Donna's cooperation was secured through an attorney who previously represented her on a prostitution charge.

DONNA: A CALL GIRL

QUESTION: Why don't you tell me a little about yourself? What's your background, family, and what not?

DONNA: Oh, I have a wonderful family. I have a number of half brothers and sisters, stepbrothers and sisters. You're trying to get my pattern; that's what you're trying to do. Don't they all say that we go into this for a reason? There's got to be something in her background that drove her into this sort of degrading life. Like I said, I was born in [this city], my parents split up when I was one-and-a-half. I was from a broken home, and like they say, that's always at the bottom of everything. I lived with different relatives and things, till I was about 10 and my father remarried. When he remarried he married a woman who was pretty mixed up, of course he didn't realize it at the time. Most of her problem was based around me, which is making things look bad for me already. But she hated me, she was jealous of me, because she thought my father was in love with me—not like a daughter—but in love with me. That wasn't true, I had a wonderful father. We put up with that hassle for quite awhile.

[38] Lemert, *Social Pathology*, pp. 242–43.
[39] Travis Hirschi, "The Professional Prostitute," *Berkeley Journal of Sociology*, 7 (Spring 1962), 33–45.

He was with her for 10 years and he had twins by her and they finally got a divorce after I left home. My real mother had an alcohol problem so I was awarded to my father when they got divorced. So I was more or less raised by my father, until my trouble began. I had to leave because my stepmother disliked me and all that kind of stuff. I lived with a woman psychologist for awhile in high school until things calmed down at home. Isn't that sort of irrelevant to why I'm in the business? It isn't, but it is, I think; I feel I would be in this business even if I lived a completely normal life with two parents that stayed together and maybe two brothers and sisters, and were fairly wealthy.

QUESTION: Why are you in the business?

DONNA: Why am I in the business? Because I went through, after I got out of high school, several jobs. I worked in a department store, I sold insurance, and I wasn't satisfied with anything. I'm creative, at least I've always felt that I was creative. I would have like to have gone into sociology because I studied psychology when I was 15. Like I said I read every book that the psychologist I lived with had read herself. She was studying for her doctor's degree. So I already had some kind of a background. I'm not satisfied with working at somebody else's work. That's why I never liked typing—typing what somebody else thinks. So being dissatisfied I looked for something I would be satisfied with, where I could live well and be happy. So I was working as a cocktail waitress— which I tried for a month, which I swore I would never do—but I did and I was very dissatisfied with that. The person I was working for told me he knew a girl over in [another city] that was "working" and he called her up and she said she needed somebody. So I went over and talked to her. I liked her and packed up my bags and moved in. And she taught me, you know, "turned me out" in other words. She turned me out in three weeks. And a few months after we went down [south] together. She met a pimp down there that she liked very well and she gave me her book [from the previous city]. So I came back up here and went to work. I worked with her for awhile. And then I came here. And then I got busted.

QUESTION: When was that, a year ago?

DONNA: Yes, about that. It was really quite comical, because I knew—you have a feeling about those things. But I just hadn't been in the business long enough where I would have listened to my warning, you know. I knew I was getting warned I smelled a rat. But I had taken a couple of weeks off and went up to Reno with a jockey, who was a very good friend of mine and we had been palling around up there. And it was about two days before Christmas. I didn't have any money and a bull called me on the phone and wanted to come over. I told him it would be $50 and he said he'd be over in half an hour. He came over and got undressed, down to his shorts, and he goes barging out on my front porch. Really the whole thing was so funny because he was running around on my front porch in his underwear and this other guy comes in like Hopalong Cassidy with his pistol (laughter). They were very nice, very very nice as a matter of fact. They offered to take me out for a hamburger but I figured we might as well get this over with. We talked for a few hours. Naturally they wanted to know who I'd been working with and if I knew any pimps and if I knew who was pushing narcotics in their area, and all this kind of stuff. But I didn't anyway. So that didn't accomplish too much and the next day I bailed out.

QUESTION: Did you have to go to court?

DONNA: I bailed out before I went to court. Eventually I went to court but it was a couple of months later, though. They gave me a fine, I pleaded guilty.

QUESTION: They just fine you and that's it?

DONNA: Yes, they fined me $75. That's what they do. It's like having to pay a tax or something.

QUESTION: How about the attorney's fee? How much did that cost?

DONNA: About $300. That's a bad thing about us girls. It's kind of ridiculous to throw a girl in jail because in the first place if she had any thoughts of quitting whatsoever, which I did at the time, I was thinking about getting a square job because my family was around here and I went over to see them all the time. Not for my own sake, but for their sake I was afraid of any kind of publicity at all would hurt them. Because my friends all knew anyway. Naturally, if you throw somebody in jail, not only does she have the cost of bailing out and the cost of the attorney, the girl doesn't have any choice but to go back to work, now does she? No choice whatsoever if she's going to beat it at all. It's either that or go to jail. Go back to work and make the money or go back to jail.

QUESTION: Is that part of what you were saying when I first came in? That it's society that causes this?

DONNA: No, I wasn't saying that society pushes a girl into it. I'm saying that a girl goes into it, for probably reasons similar to mine. She wants money real bad, she's had dreams of living in an expensive house and thinks that that's the way to do it. Or she's lazy, like I am. I don't like to work for somebody else, you know. It's that simple. In all these books that you read, you read the girl is a heroin addict and she's driven to prostitution to support her habit. What I'm saying is the girl is perfectly normal until she got into prostitution and to escape society pounding on her all the time and watching all these hypocritical things like Sally Stanford being worshipped. They're pushing her losing faith in people in general. Unless you keep steady rein on your own mind and you have a strong character anyway it's almost impossible not to lose faith in people.

QUESTION: You said you know a lot of other girls, do you keep track of each other?

DONNA: Well, most of the girls stick close together, because, like I said, that's their protection. They like to be among friends, in other words. I don't, I don't socialize with them, that's what I'll say. I know them just because I have to hear about them because people are always talking about them—the people that come to see me are talking about them. They tell me where they are or if a girl needs someone to work for her, somebody maybe to give her a name she'll call me— this sort of thing.

QUESTION: Why would they need you to work for them?

DONNA: Because they've got so much—they can't handle it.

QUESTION: Would that mean you worked in a brothel? Are brothels still around?

DONNA: Yes, there are, but there's no need to go into that because they're becoming extinct. That's because whores or joint broads are becoming extinct. When they turn out now they turn out like I turned out. They turn out to make money and keep their self-respect. Some of these girls are really not degenerates but they have lost complete faith in people. All of them are on some kind of pills, alcohol.

QUESTION: Is pimping dying out too?

DONNA: No, it's around. I don't have a pimp. I don't care for them too much. But I know quite a few of them, they're charming people.

QUESTION: What's the purpose of a pimp if you can get your own customers?

DONNA: It's paying someone to love you. You see a pimp is a professional liar. He's a con-artist. His whole life is lying to prostitutes and this is what makes him valuable. The better liar you are, the more girls you have, the more money you'll make.

QUESTION: In what ways does the pimp lie?

DONNA: The girl is the only one in his life. Look, everybody needs somebody including prostitutes. And they prefer not to have anyone square because squares don't understand. Pimps understand prostitutes, they know their needs and you pay them to love you. A girl who is working all day long, she comes home, she doesn't want to cook dinner. I'm a little bit different because I like to lead a normal life. But a pimp will get up in the morning, cook your breakfast and serve it to you, and when you come home from work he'll baby you and listen to you holler and rant and rave because there are a lot of things to rant and rave about. And he listens to all of this and it bounces right off him. And then he tells you you're beautiful, the most wonderful girl in the world and this sort of thing which everybody likes to hear. But they do it to a degree that they can make you believe it even if you know it's a lie; and have five or six other girls and still make you think you're the main old lady. The way it is [in this city] is that pimps mainly work with joint broads. They'll get a broad and stick her in a joint and she'd be there for three weeks—you have to stay in a joint for three weeks or you can't work—and he'll get another old lady and put her in another joint. So whenever they get their "flowers" [your period]—that's when you come home. You come home for a week and then go back. This way they can fit in three or four girls and they've got all the time for the girl that's home and the other three are out working. Now if he's a good pimp, he'll save all the money and invest it, so if they break up she'll take her half and he keeps his half. Mostly the girls don't get anything if they break up. But pimps are very colorful people, very interesting. But unless you need one emotionally it doesn't make any sense. It's too easy to make money on your own and joints are terrible. I worked in a joint, not too far from here. This is very interesting, you might want to know about it. I only stayed one day, but long enough to know what it was like. It was an Oriental place, and it was $15. They lock you up underground for three weeks! But at 6 o'clock you go to work and a bus starts bringing in these carloads of Chinamen. And there are about six girls and we stand up in cocktail dresses. It was ridiculous—you had to wear funny little cloth slippers with a fancy cocktail dress. So they come in and start picking girls and all of a sudden you're going about 60 miles an hour running back and forth because there were so many of them. But it was an experience—I'm glad I went. It made me appreciate what I have. If a girl stayed for three weeks, though, she was bound to come out with some money. A lot of girls would prefer a joint to something like this because this has such a high overhead. You want clothes the minute you get depressed, a woman wants to buy clothes, so you spend all of your money as fast as you make it un-less you really have some principles. Most of the girls never save anything. They can make $100,000 in six months and never have anything to show for it. When you're in a joint, you can't get out in the streets and spend it, so when you come out you have about $5,000 or $6,000.

QUESTION: How about streetwalkers compared to call girls?

DONNA: Streetwalkers are different. They're maybe an alco-holic that needs a drink, a mother whose kids need something to eat. And they're mostly black. There are a few black call girls around. I know one [nearby] but she goes for much less—about half of what a white call girl goes for.

QUESTION: How would you define a prostitute?

DONNA: Anyone, let's put it that way, anyone who sells her body, which we don't believe we're doing.

QUESTION: What do you believe you're doing?

DONNA: Renting it (laughter). We're supplying a demand. If there's a demand for prostitutes someone's going to do it. There's no sense trying to stop it. Arresting a girl just makes things worse; it makes the girl harder than she was before. A prostitute sees people at their worst, just how bad people really are including cops and so-called public representatives, businessmen. Society says we're bad, yet they can't live without us. Society also says that a businessman who is trying to please customers has to entertain his clients with us. It's so hypocritical that you can't figure it out. It makes you lose your faith in people.

QUESTION: Have you had any desire to work anywhere else than here?

DONNA: Financially, it's not a matter of desire. You work where your book is. I have a book here with quite a few names in it and I'd be foolish to move. It'd take me 10 years to get up to where I am now if I went somewhere else.

QUESTION: I'm a little confused on just what a book is. Do you call up people whose names are in it?

DONNA: The woman that turned me out gave me her book. When I set up here I started calling people that were in my book. "I'm a friend of so-and-so and she told me to give you a call when I'm in town. Would you like to see me?" And they'd say, "Yes, I'd like to see you but I can't see you today, I'll call you tomorrow you give me your phone number." And if they don't want to see you at all then you just cross their name off. Or they may refer some of their friends to you.

QUESTION: You said earlier that you were busiest in the daytime. Why is that?

DONNA: I lead a very normal life. I get up in the morning around seven o'clock and I take my husband to work. He works at a square job. Then I come over here, get cleaned up for the day and take a shower. Then I work til about 6 o'clock. Then I go home, fix dinner, and sit and watch TV just like everyone else. Really, it's quite boring, no one would ever believe it.

QUESTION: You very rarely work nights?

DONNA: Yes, if someone makes that arrangement beforehand I'll work in the evening. Like someone will call up and say, "I'm having a party tomorrow night, can you come?" And I'll say, "Yes." But I don't sit around here all night waiting for people to call. I feel like I'm living a very normal life which is probably pretty hard for someone to understand unless they're leading it. I don't associate with rounders. All my friends are squares. A lot of them don't even know what I do. I go home for Christmas. I visit my folks once a week, just like everyone else.

QUESTION: Do you have any children?

DONNA: No. If I had children I wouldn't work. This isn't the kind of atmosphere you bring a child up in. Adults can't even understand it (laughter).

QUESTION: Does your husband ever have any reaction to your work?

DONNA: No. We discuss what needs to be discussed. No sense

in coming home and talking about it every night. After awhile you run out of things to talk about, just like anything else. He works—we talk about his work. There are no problems. We're saving our money, just as if I were working in an office. We're saving to do something with it, open up a gin mill, or something, go into business for ourselves. I save half of everything I make. Most of what I spend goes into overhead—that's pretty high—having an extra apartment, doctor's expenses, and things like that.

QUESTION: Do you have any observations to make about your tricks?

DONNA: They're normal, they're just like you, my father, my uncle, my brothers. They're just like anyone else. Naturally there are some you don't like, some you do, same as everybody else. But I've got another little thing, I don't see anyone I don't like because self-preservation is the main thing over money or anything else. You have to keep your own self-respect so I don't handle any kinds of freaks or I won't take anyone who's been drinking if I can tell they've been drinking. If they're doing something I don't like I kick them out, just like you would if you were running a bar and they were causing trouble.

QUESTION: You don't have any trouble getting rid of them?

DONNA: No, you just tell them in a very subtle way you don't want to see them anymore. If they call up I'll just tell them I'm busy.

QUESTION: What do you mean by freaks?

DONNA: You know, masochists and sadists and things like that. You get a call for them once in awhile. And when you do they just bug you to death but there's nothing you can do about it except to say you're busy or that you know of a girl around who takes care of that sort of thing. If I got stuck with one it would be pretty upsetting. Not only upsetting but degrading. I couldn't have much respect for a man crawling around with a dog collar around his neck. Very distasteful to me.

QUESTION: Have you noticed any changes in what tricks ask of prostitutes since you've been in the business?

DONNA: No, naturally if they can get away with it they'll get as much as they can. But you have to be strict, just like running a bar—you charge so much for a drink and that's it. If somebody gets drunk you don't give them anymore to drink or you kick them out. It's a business, a simple business. It's complicated mentally because there are other things to worry about, like cops trying to get an appointment or putting a spotter on your house. If they find out where you are you know you have to move. You can't have any irate customers. It's just like running a very small business. Most of my customers are friends. They come, have a drink, and we talk, get to know each other. If it's true that deep down most men hate prostitutes I don't see it. I don't find very much disrespect. Because I don't act disrespectfully—I don't give them an opening. Sometimes they just want to come over and talk, to tell you things they can't tell anyone else. Most of these people can't tell their wives or their friends what's on their minds, without being laughed at or ridiculed. But they know they can tell me. So really more than their sexual needs are being satisfied, their ego is built up because they have somebody to listen to them.

QUESTION: With this kind of "counseling" that you do you must spend quite a bit of time with each customer. Is that right?

DONNA: Not really, it doesn't take that long to talk. Twenty minutes maybe. Just being here relaxes them.

QUESTION: You mentioned earlier that you were just going to be in for two more years. Do you look forward to retirement?

DONNA: I look forward to it in a sense but not like retirement where you worry about what you're going to do when it's over. I know there'll be a very strong temptation to stay in it longer. But I usually stick pretty close to what I decide and I decided when I went in at 21 I would move out on my 25th birthday. And I'll do it. If you're just looking to make a certain amount of money, and you make about $3,000 a month it shouldn't take your whole life. Otherwise you end up as a 40-year-old streetwalker. That's what's pitiful.

QUESTION: You mentioned awhile back about society's hypocrisy. Could you say any more about that?

DONNA: They say that having sexual relations for money is bad but it's all right for a girl to go out and give it away. That to me is the same thing as what I'm doing, for dinner or the price of a motel. I think I have the same morals as everyone else, maybe even better. There are a lot of things I would never do, like I'd never steal. I wouldn't go out and sell myself for a drink. I don't see why people call us a problem—they're more of a problem than we are because they're trying to kid themselves.

QUESTION: If you had to move from here what sort of things would you take into consideration in getting another place?

DONNA: A good area with lots of apartments, big apartments. I don't mean number of rooms but that take up a block or more. You can't have neighbors seeing anyone going in or out. As you could see when you came in here no one knows where you're going as you come in. You can't have neighbors complaining. I think the police know where a lot of the girls are operating out of but don't do anything about it because there are no complaints. The only time they bother is around election time. You don't think they just find the girls at election time, do you? They save 'em up for a general cleanup.

DISCUSSION

The initial question we can raise concerns the plausibility of Donna's story. There are no glaring inconsistencies or contradictions. She seems to know mostly about the call girl pattern, although she had brief experience in a "joint" and knew several pimps. If questions can be raised about her story they would probably be addressed to the ease with which she reports moving in and out of various patterns. The risks involved in moving into a joint for a short period of time apparently were not great. For her it does not signal any kind of downward mobility.

Donna's reasons for becoming a prostitute seem mainly economic. Her job as a cocktail waitress provided opportunities to see what was involved. She seemed to view her waitress job as closely linked to the world of the prostitute. This realization made her more open to the suggestion that she try it out. The decision was highly rational and calculative. Donna's skills and educational background did not prepare her for anything but low-level jobs. A short career in prostitution might ensure mobility not otherwise possible. (". . . a girl goes into it for . . . reasons similar to mine. She wants money real bad, she's had dreams of living in an expensive house and thinks that's the way to do it.") She seemed very clear about the length of time her career would last and what she and her husband would do with the money. She was aware of the hazards involved in prostitution—cynicism, depression, loss of self-esteem, dependence on drugs—but was convinced she was strong enough to withstand them. She saw herself as a strong person, able to cope with the stigma "with society pounding on her all the time."

Though Donna's family background was troubled she thought it had no bearing on her decision to become a prostitute. Donna believed that the woman who decides on prostitution is normal, not neurotic. She believes that if prostitutes are neurotics it was a condition that developed after they entered the profession not before it; neurosis did not account for the decision to begin.

Another questionable area was Donna's relationship to the conventional world. She stated that she didn't associate with "rounders," that all of her friends were square, and that she led a very "normal" life: "Really it's quite boring, no one would ever believe it." Jackman, O'Toole, and Geis have distinguished three different kinds of prostitutes based on self-image:[40] the *dual-world* prostitute who works full time but who lives in the conventional world and does not associate with other prostitutes or criminals; the *criminal-world* prostitute who identifies with those on the fringe of the criminal world; and the *alienated* prostitute, belonging to neither the dual nor criminal world. They note that the dual-world prostitute (which Donna professes to be) is aware of the ideology but personally rejects it. They contend it is only lower-status prostitutes who endorse the ideology. This did not seem to be true of Donna. She seemed to be a forceful advocate of the ideology: condemning society's hypocrisy, claiming that society needed prostitution ("society says we're bad yet they can't live without us"), and professing a superior morality which eschews dishonesty ("I think I have the same morals as anyone else, maybe even better. There are a lot of things I would never do, I'd never steal. I wouldn't go out and sell myself for a drink").

The dual-world prostitute according to Jackman et al. does not have the self-concept of a prostitute and feels less compelled to justify her work. Donna did have the self-concept of a prostitute, a strong sense of solidarity with colleagues, and a strong need to justify prostitution. There is no indication of the hostility or competitiveness that Bryan observed among his call girls.[41] The woman who turned Donna out gave her the book she was using, she did not sell it to her. This seems unusual since it was built up over a period of years. Its importance is hinted at in Donna's response to a question about shifting her base of operations: "I have a book here with quite a few names in it and I'd be foolish to move. It'd take me ten years to get where I am now if I went somewhere else." The book includes a description of the customer who might phone so that he can be identified. If the prostitute has any reason to be suspicious of a call she may ask the caller where he works, his height, weight, and suit

[40] Norman F. Jackman, Richard O'Toole, and Gilbert Geis, "The Self Image of the Prostitute," *Sociological Quarterly,* 4 (April 1963), 150–61.
[41] James H. Bryan, "Occupational Ideologies and Individual Attitudes of Call Girls," *Social Problems,* 13 (Spring 1966), 441–50; and James H. Bryan, "Apprenticeships in Prostitution," *Social Problems,* 12 (Winter 1965), 287–97.

size, something police trying to entrap her are not likely to know. The informal rule is that a new customer is never admitted without checking with the person who referred him. Donna's unpleasant experience with the police occurred precisely because she ignored this rule. The arrest and conviction experience may have led to what seems to be a preoccupation with avoiding the police. The dual-world prostitute is less likely to be concerned about police because of her protected situation.

Donna is somewhat different from Bryan's call girls in the length of her apprenticeship. She reports it lasted just under one month. Bryan's girls reported that it lasted from two to eight months which seems inordinately long considering the low-level skills that are transmitted. The turning out process teaches the prostitute how to develop a clientele, how to manage it, how to collect money, and how to protect herself. It seems specific sexual techniques are not taught. Donna's apprenticeship may have been so brief because there was a sizable and lucrative clientele already in existence. For Bryan's call girls the length of training served the purpose of building up a clientele.

Donna's brief discussion of her husband's reaction to her work suggests that the dual-world adaptation is considerably more complicated than Jackman and his colleagues suggest. Donna's husband worked in construction as a taper (one who paints and smooths dry walls) and their friendship circle was largely drawn from his skilled blue-collar co-workers. The problem of what Becker calls "information control"—how to control potentially discrediting information about one's self—must have been considerable for Donna and her husband.[42] The area was not probed because of its sensitive character and Donna's reluctance to talk about it further.

In summary, the interview basically confirms the explanations of Hirschi, Benjamin and Masters, and Jackman et al. except in minor details. The interview suggests that the patterns discussed earlier are not nearly as clear-cut as the literature suggests and that there may be much more movement between them. Donna basically agreed that there was a trend toward more individual entrepreneurs in prostitution.

QUESTIONS FOR FURTHER DISCUSSION

1. Does Donna seem to have been "pushed" into prostitution because of emotional problems generated by her family back-

---

[42] Howard S. Becker, *Outsiders: Studies in the Sociology of Deviance* (New York: Free Press, 1963), pp. 66–72.

ground, "pulled" into it by the promise of independence and higher earnings, or a combination of both?

2. What conclusion would a conflict theorist draw from Donna's attitudes toward men in general or more specifically toward her customers?

3. If you were asked to come up with a legitimate vocational rehabilitation plan to capitalize on Donna's interests and talents what would it be and why?

4. What reaction do you think Donna would have to Davis's generalization that prostitution is functional to the marriage relationship?

5. If a community policy were to be developed to deter prostitution what strategies would be suggested, either implicitly or explicitly in Donna's account?

6. Lemert has suggested that some occupations are quasi-prostitutional in that they implicitly encourage careers in prostitution. What other research questions are suggested by Donna along the same lines that might be explored further?

SUMMARY

Critics of the criminal law's overreach have most often focused on public order criminality, sometimes called "crimes without victims." The basic argument is that persons have a right to "abuse" their minds, bodies, or morals as long as they desire if in doing so no one else is injured. The Wolfenden Report, discussing homosexuality and prostitution, put the matter succinctly:

> Unless a deliberate attempt is to be made by society, acting through the agency of the law, to equate the sphere of crime with that of sin, there must remain a realm of private morality and immorality which is, in brief and crude terms, not the law's business.[43]

It seems clear that public drunkenness and other kinds of illegal performance or consumption are not regarded by the public at large as crimes. Both public and legal evaluation are concerned mainly with the time and place of occurrence.

One particular feature of the laws against public order crime that is objectionable is the enormous discretion it provides police in implementa-

[43] Committee on Homosexual Offenses and Prostitution, *The Wolfenden Report* (New York: Lancer Books, 1964).

tion. Enforcement tactics designed to reduce the incidence of violation are aimed at making life difficult for violators—harassing them—not at prosecution and conviction. Typically police use the technique of "raids" which eventuate in mass arrests and total failure to prosecute. In some jurisdictions it is called "sweeping the streets." It is temporarily effective but the major objection to it is that it constitutes punishment without determination of guilt. The success of reformers in removing some status crimes, like addiction and vagrancy, from the criminal code has given momentum to the drive to decriminalize all crimes without victims. If the present trend continues we can expect the criminal sanction gradually to be replaced by other kinds of regulation for public order violations.

The demand to restrict the scope of state intervention through the criminal law does not, however, extend to occupational criminality, the subject of Chapter 15, where recommendations for change propose expanding the state's role. Initiative is greatest in public order criminality, least in occupational misconduct.

occupational crime

This category of crime involves violations committed in the course of one's occupational activity, including offenses of employees against employers. Attention of criminologists was directed to occupational crime by Edwin Sutherland, who was concerned about persons of high social status who violated legal codes in the course of the occupational activity. But it soon became clear that persons in every social stratum are engaged in some violative behavior as part of their occupation or profession. Quinney has suggested that all violations that occur in the course of any occupational activity be included, whatever the social status of the offenders.[1]

The kind of violations that come under the category occupational crime are usually civil or administrative violations, not criminal. Sutherland, early in his discussion of white-collar crime, proposed that criminologists not restrict themselves only to offenses against the criminal law but include civil offenses as well. Sutherland argued that acts which were defined as legally injurious that involved some kind of sanction, whether or not they were part of the criminal law, should be defined as criminal. He also maintained that what he called white-collar criminality, but we call occupational criminality ". . . is found in every occupation as can be discovered readily in casual conversation with a representative of an

[1] Richard Quinney, "The Study of White Collar Crime Toward a Reorientation in Theory and Research," *Journal of Criminal Law, Criminology and Police Science,* 55 (June 1964), 208–14.

occupation by asking him what crooked practices are found in his occupation."[2] The violations relate to illegal rebates; infringements of
patents, trademarks, and copyrights; misrepresentation; financial manipu-
lations; and embezzlement.

One influential bibliography of this kind of criminality includes embezzlement, pilferage, and black marketeering as well as a variety of
illegal practices of professions and businesses. The professions referenced
were mainly medicine and law where more has been written. The literature on occupational crime is meager, however, for two major reasons:
there is still some question among criminologists about whether it should
be studied as part of criminality, and it is difficult to gather data. There is
some reason to think that the amount of occupational crime that comes to
official attention relative to the amount actually going on is much greater
than for conventional criminality. Also to understand the context of occupational violations requires a detailed knowledge of the occupational
structure within which they occur. The serious study of occupational
crime would require a broader background than is usual for criminologists in the study of occupations and professions.

Occupational literature is extensive but would require some reanalysis
of the data with an eye to making some generalizations about situations
of law violations and the characteristics of those people who commit them.
The difficulties in initiating further studies of occupational crime should
not be underestimated. Polsky's study of the pool hustler took a look at
an illegal occupation using questions sociologists of professions ask about
work situations, careers within them, and problems of the external world;
it noted that even among pool hustlers there were practices considered
seriously wrong, perhaps immoral. One of them was the activity of
"dumping," which involves deliberate loss of a pool game to the player
who has more bet on it. The practice was so sensitive a topic that hustlers
rarely talked about it among themselves and never with outsiders. Polsky
in an aside makes the point that all professions have secrets that the
investigator must strive to penetrate if he is really to understand it. Some
are "open secrets" that only novices and outsiders don't know about,
some are "strategic secrets" that professionals often talk about among
themselves, and some are "dark secrets" that professionals not only keep
from outsiders but seldom talk about with each other.[3] One example of a
dark secret from the profession of banking might be embezzlement (discussed below); from the academic profession it might be plagiarism,
which offends professional codes but may also violate copyright laws.

The first major study of occupational criminality following Sutherland's

[2] Edwin H. Sutherland, "White Collar Criminality," *American Sociological Review*, 5 (February 1940), 1–12.
[3] Ned Polsky, "The Hustler," *Social Problems*, 12 (Summer 1964), 3–15.

new line of inquiry was conducted by Clinard on World War II black market operators.[4] The violations he looked at were those against rationing and economic control regulations. He concludes that violations were widespread because there was a generally hostile attitude toward regulations; this provided a justification for ignoring them, and the risks of getting caught or being dealt with harshly were minimal. By implication, the ideology of business, which did not value self-control or societal controls, provided the rationale for violation.

Hartung's study concerned violations of wartime regulations in the meat industry in Detroit.[5] His conclusion generally paralleled that of Clinard's though Hartung emphasized the lenient penalties as more of a cause for pervasive violation. A variety of studies has focused on consumer fraud by businessmen in the United States.[6] These have not usually been conducted by criminologists, so little attention is paid to the criminogenic character of the situation within which violations occur.

Clinard and Quinney point out that the legal regulation of occupations has had a long and varied history beginning with the licensure practices among the medieval guilds.[7] The regulations were designed to protect the community from harmful practices as well as the protection of economic interests of guild members. In the United States occupational associations have long regulated the activities of their membership. They have been mainly responsible for the laws that regulate the occupations. The history of these laws seems best analyzed from a conflict perspective. As each occupation felt its interests to be threatened by a competing group it worked to get favorable legislation passed that would assure its continued well being—all accomplished with the professional goal of maintaining high standards of service for the public good.

The few existing studies throw little light on the characteristics of the people who violate, or on which occupations have higher violation rates. Underlying many of the investigations is the assumption that businessmen are more likely to be violators than are professionals with the exception of lawyers. Sutherland suggested that criminality could be fruitfully studied among businessmen and doctors but perhaps best among law-

---

[4] Marshall Clinard, *The Black Market: A Study of White Collar Crime* (New York: Holt, Rinehart & Winston, 1952).

[5] Frank E. Hartung, "White Collar Crime: Its Significance for Theory and Practice," *Federal Probation*, 17 (June 1953), 31–36.

[6] See William N. Leonard and Marvin G. Weber, "Automakers and Dealers: A Study of Criminogenic Market Forces," *Law and Society Review*, 4 (February 1970), 407–24; David Caplovitz, *The Poor Pay More* (New York: Free Press, 1963); Howard R. and Martha E. Lewis, *The Medical Offenders* (New York: Simon & Schuster, 1970).

[7] Marshall B. Clinard and Richard Quinney, *Criminal Behavior Systems*, 2nd ed. (New York: Holt, Rinehart & Winston, 1973), pp. 189–90.

yers. "The inventive geniuses for the lower class criminals are generally professional criminals, while the inventive geniuses for many kinds of white collar crime are generally lawyers."[8]

For Sutherland the motivation to violate seems to be ubiquitous and the only reason more of it doesn't go on among professionals is that the opportunity doesn't present itself. You can expect to find it where powerful professional men come in contact with persons who are weak. Sutherland notes that "In this respect it is similar to stealing candy from a baby."[9] He thought the occupational crime of high-status people could be reduced basically to two categories—misrepresentation of asset values (like fraud or swindling), and duplicity in the manipulation of power. The latter focuses on the person who holds two antagonistic positions within an occupational structure which involves something like a conflict of interest. One of the trusts involved in the two roles is sacrificed to the other. This suggests that violations are likely to be higher among those suffering some kind of role strain where two sets of conflicting expectations are made on the same person.

Quinney followed up this lead in his study of prescription violations among pharmacists.[10] Pharmacy has characteristics of both a profession and a business. Thus strain is built into the occupation. He found that violators were more likely to have a business orientation and nonviolators a professional one. The professional orientation de-emphasizes the merchandising aspects of pharmacy and possibilities of monetary gain. Those who have a professional orientation are inhibited from violations that are at odds with the profession's ethics. This suggests that a well-developed profession with highly developed codes of desirable practice and powerful sanctions against those who violate them would tend to have fewer violations than those occupations with less organization.

Embezzlement is included here under occupational crime but it differs somewhat from other occupational violations. In this instance the victim is the employer and his position can't accurately be characterized in the same way as other victims of occupational crime. Employer organizations are not weak or defenseless. Sutherland reminds us that the laws against embezzlement were formulated long before the laws protecting investors and customers. Embezzlers violate positions of trust by stealing from their employer. They differ from pilferers in the amount stolen. The crime is generally hidden through the alteration of business records. More so

---

[8] Karl Schuessler, *Edwin H. Sutherland on Analyzing Crime* (Chicago: University of Chicago Press, 1973), p. 60.

[9] Ibid., p. 57.

[10] Richard Quinney, "Occupational Structure and Criminal Behavior: Prescription Violations by Retail Pharmacists," *Social Problems*, 11 (Fall 1963), 179–85.

than the pilferer, the embezzler's activity is lone wolf; neither fellow employees, employer, nor intimates of the embezzler know of this activity. The activity seems to be developed to deal with what Cressey calls a "nonsharable problem," i.e., some unconventional or discrediting situation.[11] The decision to embezzle funds is an attempt to maintain a standard of living for which legitimate income is insufficient, sometimes arising out of an emergency situation which highlights the fact. The embezzler finds himself in a situation which he cannot discuss with others; he can secure funds without detection; and he convinces himself that he is merely "borrowing" it. Hence his self-conception is noncriminal.

Cressey found that persons involved in criminal violation of financial trust developed a justification for their behavior in advance of the activity. The economic status of Cressey's embezzlers was high; they were all white and all male, but they did not seem to share any other social characteristics. It is tempting to speculate on the kind of personality that would be predisposed to embezzle since it seems certain that many who are in a position to violate a trust do not do so. This may be due to the fact that they have an abundance of "definitions unfavorable to law violation" sustained by family and friends and do not see the opportunity available to them as a crime-committing situation. Or it may be due to the size of the organization—the larger the work organization, the more impersonal and the less identification with the organization. Or perhaps the cohesiveness of the work group may be decisive, e.g., strong informal bonds among employees may facilitate or inhibit occupational crime.

Some of the literature on occupational crime has suggested that it is the marginal professional who engages in criminal activity. Reichstein's study of solicitation of cases by lawyers ("ambulance chasing") in personal injury situations noted that despite the fact that the activity was prohibited by the bar association and by legal codes, a number of lawyers were found to be involved.[12] Those who did came from small firms or operated independently and served a low-status clientele. They and their colleagues tended to view the practice tolerantly. Ladinsky, in a study of Detroit lawyers, showed that it was those barred from entry into high-prestige law schools and later into high-status firms that were required to do the "dirty work," some of it illegal.[13] An analogous situation is that of the doctor who performs illegal abortions. Generally doctors are sym-

---

[11] Donald R. Cressey, *Other People's Money* (New York: Free Press, 1953).
[12] Kenneth J. Reichstein, "Ambulance Chasing: A Case Study of Deviation and Control Within the Legal Profession," *Social Problems,* 13 (Summer 1965), 3–17.
[13] Jack Ladinsky, "Careers of Lawyers, Law Practice and Legal Institutions," *American Sociological Review,* 28 (February 1963), 47–54.

pathetic to the practice but because the risks are high refrain from doing it. Instead they sometimes refer the patient who requests it to a doctor who will perform abortions. Schur states that the abortionist doctors are marginal in one way or another.[14] Some have lost their licenses, some are foreign trained and not admitted to practice in the U.S., some are unable to build up a lucrative practice.

GROUP SUPPORT FOR OCCUPATIONAL CRIME

Group support varies by the kind of violation and the specific occupation within which it occurs. The violations by Clinard's wartime black marketeers, which can be classified under corporate or occupational crime, seemed to have considerable group support among their colleagues. The instances of cheating among Polsky's hustlers could lead to violent reprisals but there was a recognition that it occurred with some frequency. Pilfering from an employer, however, might have more substantial group support as revealed by statements that "the company owes it to me" or "they can afford it."

Horning observes that sometimes the norms relating to occupational violation might be quite specific.[15] In his study of blue-collar theft he reports that the work group provides two main guidelines for the person who pilfers: it should be confined to property that has no value or uncertain ownership, and it should be limited to that needed for personal use. Those who followed these guidelines were not defined as thieves nor did they experience guilt over their actions. The embezzler does not get the kind of explicit support of his work group that Hartung's pilferer does, though there may be some fellow employees who secretly sympathize with him. Yet the embezzler does not create the rationales supporting his action from thin air. As Cressey has pointed out his verbalizations exist as group definitions which make the behavior appropriate under certain circumstances.

There are any number of popular ideologies that sanction crime in our culture: "Honesty is the best policy, but business is business"; . . . "all people steal when they get in a tight spot." Once these

[14] Edwin M. Schur, *Crimes Without Victims* (Englewood Cliffs, N.J.: Prentice-Hall, 1965), pp. 25–26.
[15] Donald N. M. Horning, "Blue-Collar Theft, Conceptions of Property, Attitudes Toward Pilfering and Work Group Norms in a Modern Industrial Plant," in Erwin O. Smigel and H. Laurence Ross (eds.), *Crimes Against Bureaucracy* (New York: Van Nostrand Reinhold, 1970), pp. 46–64.

verbalizations have been assimilated and internalized by individuals they take a form such as "I'm only going to use the money temporarily, so I am borrowing, not stealing," or "I have tried to live an honest life but I've had nothing but troubles, so to hell with it."[16]

The criminologist Taft also has maintained that the wider society gives support to various kinds of criminal activity.[17] The belief that poverty or lack of wealth is an indicator of moral failure means that the importance of succeeding economically may also serve as a motive. This, combined with the widespread belief that everyone has a racket, provides a supportive framework for criminal activity. These are values which lend support to stealing but don't constitute positive injunctions to steal. Usually they are offset by other values that contradict them. The end result is that the conflict, confusion, contradiction, and ambiguity of moral priorities give rise to the possibilities that individuals will be afforded considerable flexibility and freedom in choosing which priorities to choose in dealing with a concrete problem.

It seems clear from the foregoing that though there may be a loosely structured behavior system that provides group support for occupational crime, it is not accurate to talk about it as career crime. Though a professional may have had a history of violation it does not constitute a career the way the term is ordinarily used. The norms and activities associated with it are usually not complex, nor do they become systematically incorporated into the individual's life plan. There is no conception of the self as criminal, no progression in criminal activity, nor any general identification with crime.

SOCIAL REACTION AND LEGAL PROCESSING

Public reaction to occupational crime seems generally apathetic. Violations sometimes are highly complicated and technical, hence difficult to understand, or are diffused over a long period of time. Statutes and enforcement agencies tend to be lenient. In the case of embezzlement, where the criminal law can be invoked, Hall estimates that only one percent of trust violations are dealt with as criminal actions. Partly this is related to the status of the offender, partly to the employer's fear of adverse publicity. Restitution is more important to the employer than prosecution.

[16] Donald R. Cressey, "The Respectable Criminal," Transaction 3 (March–April 1965), 14.
[17] Donald R. Taft, *Criminology*, 2nd ed. (New York: Macmillan, 1950), p. 298.

EXPLANATIONS OF OCCUPATIONAL CRIME

No specific explanations have been advanced for occupational crime. The underlying assumption in discussions of occupational crime is that it needs no sophisticated explanation. There are cultural values that justify stealing or cheating, and if the opportunity is provided many will do it. Little attention is paid either to the mechanisms by which values are translated into behavior or the specific situations which draw forth criminal responses. There are two major suggestive lines of inquiry that are relevant to occupational crime following the research already conducted. One relates to the study of occupations and values, the other to studies of employee morale.

Values of Various Occupational Groups

A study conducted by Rosenberg published in 1957 demonstrated that specific occupational aspirations of college students correlated with their values along three dimensions: self-expression, orientation toward people, and extrinsic reward.[18] Persons valuing self-expression gravitated toward occupations that would permit its realization like architecture, journalism, drama, and art. Persons who ranked orientation toward people highly were drawn to occupations like medicine, social work, teaching. Persons who valued extrinsic rewards planned to enter real estate, finance, sales promotion, hotel management, and law—occupations that stress the extrinsic rewards of money, status, and security. Rosenberg found that people concerned with monetary success were more likely than others to feel that "institutionally dubious means are necessary to get ahead." He pointed out that his data clearly suggested that those who value monetary success feel that an essential means for achieving it is the control and manipulation of others for one's own ends. Persons with little "faith in people" were also found to place a high value on monetary success.

Following Rosenberg's lead, Schwendinger conducted a study of delinquency in Los Angeles. He found that his "insider" group—those with delinquent values—was more likely to come from households where

[18] Morris Rosenberg, "Factors Influencing Change of Occupational Choice," in Paul F. Lazarsfeld and Morris Rosenberg (eds.), *The Language of Social Research* (New York: Free Press, 1965), pp. 250–59.

the father was in a money-oriented occupation.[19] He showed that those holding these values came from all social strata (not just the lower) and were also engaged in a higher proportion of delinquent activity. The values they shared all related to a success-dominated point of view. The values of property and money were not viewed, however, in the same context as they were among adults. Instead of land, stocks and bonds, factories, money, or even family status, it was expressed in invidious-competitive evaluation of clothing, grooming, ownership of the latest transistor radios, customized cars, and a host of other such "sacred" objects. Schwendinger tried to show that the process of value transmission is not a simple one but required age segregation whereby children are set apart in school. The junior and senior high school become the stage upon which the success-dominated outlooks are expressed and incorporated. The end result of adolescent socialization, a process carried out by peers rather than adults, is the emergence of a utilitarian, nonmoralistic set of values, an "instrumental" view of life which sees the world divided into the givers and the takers. Schwendinger contends that these values predispose youth to delinquent behavior and are opposed to the nonutilitarian values developed by nondelinquent youth. The primary goal of the youth who reflect the adult emphasis on success is to make a reputation on the basis of the commodities one has or can command. One side effect, Schwendinger notes, of the emphasis on reputation based on commodities is to develop a strictly utilitarian and nonmoral attitude toward others which means that they can be likely victims. They can be conned out of their money, or have their person attacked or their possessions taken or destroyed with the only consideration being a tactical one—are we likely to get caught? Schwendinger's research represents an advance over previous conceptualizations by specifying the mechanisms whereby exploitative values in the larger society are transmitted to adolescents and describing the social structure which supports them in junior and senior high school. Schwendinger did not carry his research into adulthood but his conclusions suggest that those most delinquent would gravitate toward occupations where their values could best be realized. His focus turns our attention away from occupational criminality that is a result of low status or marginality to that which is an expression of some core values in the larger society and committed by high-status people.

[19] Herman Schwendinger, *The Instrumental Theory of Delinquency: A Tentative Formulation,* unpublished Ph.D. Dissertation, University of California, Los Angeles, 1963.

Employee Morale

Some exploratory research conducted by social psychologist Zeitlin proposes looking at employee theft like petty larceny as functional for employee morale.[20] In his two-year study of theft by clothing store employees Zeitlin reports that in retail establishments internal theft averaged out to an unevenly distributed five to eight percent of the typical employee's salary. He summarized the available evidence on employee theft generally and concluded that "well over 75 percent of all employees participate to some extent in merchandise shrinkage. . . ." One crucial ingredient of the theft pattern, according to Zeitlin, is that management expected it and permitted a controlled amount of theft in lieu of reorganizing jobs and raising wages. A level of employee theft was tolerated because it was good for employee morale. The motivations of employees he interviewed were not mainly economic but related to "job enrichment." It was a way of coping with boring and low-paying jobs. The theft provided just the right amount of excitement that made the job tolerable. Employees reported a strong sense of satisfaction in getting away with it and felt no guilt connected to it. Some indicated that they felt theft was an unstated condition of their employment.

STAN: A PILFERER

The following interview was conducted with a young man who reported to the author that he engaged in extensive petty thefts of produce while an employee of a supermarket. The behavior is relatively insignificant both in terms of the amount taken and Stan's investment in the activity yet provides us with an opportunity to see how some explanations of this kind of crime fit.

QUESTION: Would you tell me a little about what kind of illicit activity is part of your occupation?

STAN: The major part of my crime . . . has been chances that I've taken in relation to my occupaiton. It's been kind of on and off with me for years. I just find opportunities, things to do, and I take advantage of the

[20] Lawrence R. Zeitlin, "A Little Larceny Can Do a Lot for Employee Morale," *Psychology Today*, 5 (June 1971), 22–26.

situation, so to speak. When I was younger, I was not totally a member of a gang but I was incorporated with a group of kids who were a member of a gang. We used to jackroll people. We had a couple of people pick out a target and then one of them—a very strong person we had had in our group—we'd pick on drunks preferably as they came out of taverns on Friday nights and he'd hold the guy as he went around the alley, most likely to relieve himself and another person such as I who was smaller would go through his pockets and take what he had and this bigger person would throw him down and we'd run like hell so the cops wouldn't catch us.

QUESTION: And you did it primarily for gain?

STAN: Well, we had a group and we liked to play ball and stuff and softballs were expensive. I grew up in a poor neighborhood and it's not that really I couldn't afford one but it's just something we did, something that didn't cost anybody anything. Money that we'd save we'd have for cokes or root beer after the game.

QUESTION: Was there a lot of this going on in the neighborhood?

STAN: Yes, this was a high crime rate type of neighborhood, lots of gangs and . . .

QUESTION: Was it mostly petty theft?

STAN: Yes, mostly petty stuff, if you could steal small stuff— lots of corner grocery stores we had there, you could get away with stuff like that.

QUESTION: How old were you at this time?

STAN: I started when I was about 8 years old and I stayed with that particular group until I was about 14, until I went to high school.

QUESTION: Going to high school took you out of that circle of friends?

STAN: Right, because, you see, when I left that particular group I was a freshman in high school and from that time I didn't have much time to affiliate with them. I'd see them on weekends or on a few nights during the week when I didn't have homework. Basically my parents always liked me to do well in my studies so I had to perform and that meant that I did homework.

QUESTION: Did any of the other guys in this jackrolling operation go into more advanced kinds of crime?

STAN: The last I remember two of them had joined the armed forces as an alternative to prison sentences, one of them was in for attempted murder—the big strong man—it was also with a drunk in front of a tavern, and the one other person I know is up for rape.

QUESTION: What would you say intervened to save you—just going away to school outside the neighborhood?

STAN: Right, I went away to a school outside the neighborhood, and after I turned 15 I started working and that left me less time to hang around with the fellas.

QUESTION: What kind of family situation would you characterize yours as?

STAN: Well, my family was kind of unique really in the neighborhood because I didn't know of too many people who had—who were middle-class living in a, like, lower-class neighborhood. I don't know too many other kids who had the opportunities to go to a school such as I did—a private school, who could afford to pay tuition. A lot of them went to the neighborhood high school. That's probably where the biggest split was—I hung around with people who I knew from high school and they did likewise. Nobody ever turned out to be against one another, we just went different ways. We saw each other on occasion.

QUESTION: What was it your father did?

STAN: My father was . . . worked for a factory. He was an expediter. After computer cards were punched out he would go out and look for certain products in shelf stock and things like that. Later on he was promoted up to the office. In fact, I'm not sure what he's doing right now.

QUESTION: But it's some kind of administrative thing?

STAN: Right, it's almost white-collar. It's blue-collar work but he goes to work in a suit and tie so I guess that makes him white-collar.

QUESTION: How about your mother, was she working?

STAN: Yes, she was. She worked during the evening and left my dad to take care of us. She worked for an automobile agency, bookkeeping in general. She handled accounts payable and receivable, things like that.

QUESTION: Would you say your family was a religious family?

STAN: Definitely. My mother, every Sunday morning would say, "Come, get up, it's time to go to church." I was even an altar boy—how's that?

QUESTION: How many brothers and sisters?

STAN: I have two brothers and one sister. One older brother and a younger brother and sister. I'm the second one.

QUESTION: In this particular jackrolling thing were you following in the pattern of your older brother?

STAN: No, my older brother is rather quiet, he didn't do too many activities like that as far as I know. In fact to this day he's lots straighter than I am.

QUESTION: Were your parents aware that any of this was going on at the time?

STAN: No, we kept it just far enough outside the neighborhood so that none of the boys' parents caught wind of it. In fact people used to compliment, "What a nice person—he does this and he does that and I never see him in any trouble. He doesn't hang around with any bad people." I used to get comments like that about me all the time. So I figured—what they don't know won't hurt them.

QUESTION: O.K. These are recollections about early delinquent activities. What's the next big event or series of episodes?

STAN: The next biggest thing is probably after I changed jobs, I went to work for a supermarket chain, a large one, when I turned 17. Before I was working for the same automobile agency that my mother worked for. I still hung onto that part-time after I started working for the supermarket. That's basically where I learned most of my habits and tricks and stuff. I was just a stock boy in the store and . . . well, really any basic personnel in a supermarket are not really honest. As far as stealing or not paying for purchases and things like that go, everybody does it. I'm definitely sure everybody does it because I've seen enough of it in the time I've put in. I know people do things like that.

QUESTION: How many years experience would you say you had now in supermarket work?

STAN: Almost five. The pattern hasn't changed in five years. Employees take what they can get away with.

QUESTION: When you say taking what they can get it means being aware of how you can pick up merchandise and take it home without being detected?

STAN: Right, little odds and ends, mostly.

QUESTION: It's not stealing money?

STAN: No, money is worked on a different basis. Money has to be accounted for and there are register tapes that have to be checked out at the end of the day. Your total in the bank has got to match the total on the register slip. Otherwise there's trouble.

QUESTION: It's very hard to do anything in that line?

STAN: To dip into the till—it's very hard to do.

QUESTION: Tell me about how you got into your first "ripping off" of the supermarket.

STAN: Well, when I was working for this chain I transferred out west [in the same city] because my family had moved. While I was working out there I was placed in a position of authority. I was a part-time employee but I had enough trust working that people trusted me and placed me in this position—I was handling a $50,000 to $60,000 store at night. I was doing it three nights a week at first and then I went to doing it five nights a week.

QUESTION: Were you the store manager?

STAN: No, I wasn't. I was just classified as part-time help but I did get a raise up to full-time pay. I think the maximum amount of pay . . .

QUESTION: You were like the assistant manager?

STAN: Almost. I didn't have the title except I ran the store at night. I really didn't have any title, though—anything I could show for it. It started out as really a favor and probably a challenge and I saw that I could do it and it was no problem, I just continued doing it.

QUESTION: Can you describe the circumstances of the first episode where you took some stuff, or was it so minor that you can't even recall?

STAN: The first episode took place about three summers ago. I was smoking at the time, as most of my friends were, and it wasn't too much of a problem to take a few cartons of cigarettes. Whatever I needed and whatever my friends needed, there wasn't any problem. And then in the wintertime it made it all the more easier because people wore heavier coats. The cigarettes were always kept in a room which I had access to and nobody would question me going in there, so I could get them and put them on the side to pick up later and walk out with them.

QUESTION: You could pick them up later because you were walking out alone?

STAN: Right, I had the keys to the store so I was the last one out the door. Usually there was maybe one other kid with me and I'd finish up the office work, whatever I had to do, and then say, "I'll see you, goodnight." And the kid would walk out the door because he'd be all done ahead of me and I'd shut off a few lights and leave.

QUESTION: Just a few cartons of cigarettes, how much would that run, would you say?

STAN: I'd say between $12 and $15 each time, about once every two weeks on the average.

QUESTION: Did you have any problems, yourself, in terms of your own principles related to property or anything like that?

STAN: No, not really, I figured like most all other employees they were a big chain, they could afford it.

QUESTION: And they weren't paying you enough besides, was that part of it?

STAN: No, not at first. That came later on. I should relate a couple of other times where my friends and I decided that we were going to have a feast, so to speak. What we did—I had ready access to food, and all, so I could get steaks and things that weren't that bulky, take them, put them in a cardboard box, and put them out back. When I went to close the back door I would pick them up.

QUESTION: About how much would that be worth?

STAN: I'd say about $20 to $25.

QUESTION: And that would have occurred how often?

STAN: About once a month at the most, sometimes less than that. Maybe once every two or three months. It all depended on when everyone was going to get together. When we got together we ate well.

QUESTION: Would you describe the circumstances surrounding the last one that led to your discovery?

STAN: We had a new employee in the store. He was working about a year when I was there and it turned out that his father was vice president of this division and while he was vice president his son was getting all sorts of special favors. And sooner or later the son worked himself up into a position that he could keep his eye on the store. At first, I'd say I was like third man on the totem pole. Now he had worked his way up into a position like mine. And really he was surpassing me, not because of his own talents. I didn't think he was any better than I was, except that his father had clout and everybody always listened to him because his dad was vice president. What really got me aggravated was the time that he took off work, on vacation and I got stuck closing up the store six nights a week, plus I worked Sunday—I worked 14 days straight, except for Sundays on overtime. I had to split my days in shifts to get two four-hour nights in there because they wouldn't pay me for an entire 56-hour week, 48 was maximum it could go. So I had to split my shifts to cover up for this person and I didn't get so much as a "thank you." It was accepted.

QUESTION: So this was a period of gradually building resentment?

STAN: Right, it was more or less resentment of him and the rest of the upper echelon in the company . . .

QUESTION: Because they weren't appreciating your talents or weren't recognizing what you were doing?

STAN: They recognized it and knew they could always depend on it. But I'd say they had been taking advantage of me, because they could depend on me and because they allowed someone to get away with all this just because his dad was a vice president.

QUESTION: Then there was a strong feeling of being unjustly treated on your part?

STAN: Right, I thought they were taking advantage of me.

QUESTION: O.K. What happened then?

STAN: During this period of resentment we had a couple of parties and I was . . . I always used to take orange juice to them. It was expensive, about 90 cents a half gallon, and we'd go through about four or five gallons of it. I was able to get an entire case of it, put it out back. Well one to two cases is between six and twelve bottles of orange juice. It was never missed because I'd be working the dairy department on a particular day, on a Saturday; that's when I always picked it up and I could take it out or during my lunch hour just walk it out the back door and put it in my car which was along the side. Nobody ever noticed. That's the way I got away with the minor ones. Finally after the whole vacation thing had blown over—it was the assistant's turn or the manager's turn to go on vacation. When somebody hadn't gone on vacation who was up above us we would split the weeks. That meant that during a certain amount of time, let's say four weeks, he got assistant manager's pay which is about $40 higher than what we'd normally get and during the other two weeks I got the assistant manager's pay, which was really nice because if you got a chance to work Sunday, you were making $275 for that one week, which wasn't bad at all. This time when the assistant and the manager went on vacation the vice president's son got it every time. This really blew my cool completely. I just didn't understand why and when I asked I didn't get any decent answers, so my natural attitude was "to hell with you people, I've had it with you right up to here." During the last episode, I was going on vacation myself. It was towards the end of September. I was taking three weeks and going away. One week would have been spent at a summer home and I was going with four of my friends who had known about my pilfering activities. So, through no suggestion of theirs, I decided I was going to get the food for the entire week, which amounted to a decent amount of dollars worth of groceries. Well, that Friday night I knew I only had three other people in the store besides myself, my younger brother being one of them, a couple of checkers, and a couple of other help. What I had done was to situate the people farthest away from my activity. I had them on the other side of the store at all times while I was on this side of the store. When they were in the front I was in the back. That made it a lot easier for me to get ahold of all of these items. I had taken vegetables, meat produce, dairy products, everything, you know, a complete week. In fact we planned out a meal chart for the entire week and I went by and selected all the things we would possibly need for five guys. And that's what I took. I gathered it all together . . .

QUESTION: How much was it all worth?

STAN: It's a little hard to judge but I'd say it must have been about $100. It had to be. At that time I had gathered it all together in boxes and made a phone call to a friend of mine who was supposed to pick it up back of the store. What happened was that he got there late, about 8:30—the store was closing at 9; 8:30 on Friday nights we got busy so I had all the people up in front while I was carrying on this activity in the back. It turned out that one of the boys had gone out for carts. When you go out for carts you're supposed to check all around the lot and that included behind the store. He just happened to see me and this other person putting boxes in the back seat of the car. He made no mention of this to me. In fact I had seen him back around the corner, when I glanced around the corner, with the carts. But I figured he wouldn't say anything, rather if he would say anything, I had a perfect excuse for it anyway. So at that time it didn't bother me in the least. In fact I even celebrated the fact that we had food for the entire week at no cost to us. I had these expensive items put in boxes, I put them in the back seat of the car and my buddy left. I went back in and finished up my nightly routine. I closed up and went home. The next day I had to stop in to return the keys to the store because I was going to be gone for three weeks and the manager came up to me and said, "Hey, Stan, I've got something to say to you." I said, "What would you like to know?" He said, "Someone said that you have been taking groceries." I said, "Come on now, who'd say anything like that?" So he went in back and showed me the clerk that said I was taking groceries out the back door. And I said to him, "Well, the logical thing for you to do instead of looking back at me from about 150–160 feet away was to walk on up to me and find out if I really did have anything in the boxes." At which point he was stumped because he couldn't say for sure whether I had or hadn't. The manager didn't know because he wasn't there. The whole thing was supposed to end in a lie detector test for me which I didn't have to take because it's in my contract. Since I didn't have to take it they had to prove that I'd taken the food. So it turns out—I never took the lie detector test. I went down there and I had to see my supervisor. So I cancelled one of my weeks' vacation going to the lake, the cottage. At that time I went down to see him and talked to him. They couldn't prove that anything was missing. The meat department didn't know anything was missing. Nobody in the store could put their hands on anything missing. And besides that fact I had just picked up three weeks worth of vacation pay plus my regular weekly salary. I had about $600 on me so I told him, "With all this money I could buy anything I wanted in the store, what do I have to take the stuff out back?" I told him this friend of mine who had come around back just wanted to pick up these boxes, you know, because he was moving. And they couldn't prove anything so it ended up where I left the store and I signed away on a separation notice that I'm quitting and going to school. They said that was all right with them, but in the little spot on the bottom, they didn't make any recommendations for rehiring. So they got away with pretty much even though they didn't know if I had taken anything or not and I'd say I got away with it. On the separation notice there were no bad remarks about my character. In fact I've got a copy of it so that when I went for future employment I had this right away as a reference, rather than have anyone call around and check up on my background, because sometimes you can get things out in telephone calls. So that's the way the thing ended, I got away with, like, an "honorable discharge" and no one was the wiser.

QUESTION: How long were you unemployed then?

STAN: I was unemployed for those three weeks I was on vacation and then I decided it was time to get a job so I went looking for another job part-time. I couldn't find anything that paid nearly what I was making so I decided to go back to the grocery chain business, another chain, different store. And I was hired immediately. I gave them my separation notice and filled out this application and I was hired right on the spot. So I got another job, and the funny thing is I'm nearing another position of authority. I think within about another month I'll have the keys to this store, too. Whether I'll continue that [pilfering] I don't know.

QUESTION: Well, now what you engaged in seems relatively minor and I gather you think it's relatively minor too, having been in a position to observe other people in the same setting. Is it your feeling that you have no more larceny in your heart than anyone else who lives in our society.

STAN: No, I don't think I'm very larcenous. My outlook is I'll try anything once, and if I get away with it, I'll do it again. That's basically what happened. I did it till I got caught. Now I don't think I'll go so far. You've been burned once by fire, why put your hand over the stove?

QUESTION: And so the first experience was one of risking a lot for relatively minor kinds of payoff, is that right?

STAN: I risked a lot and received little in return. But the last few were more of a personal vendetta so I gained personal satisfaction as well as material gain.

QUESTION: Would you say the only reason that you would not take things if you were in a position of trust would be if opportunity wasn't available or that the risks of getting caught would be fairly high?

STAN: This second chain, I think their security system is a little better, the risks are a little higher with this chain.

QUESTION: But, if you convinced yourself that the risks were not high and the opportunity was available, then you could see yourself doing the same thing again?

STAN: I imagine so. I'm not that moral.

QUESTION: In other words, you don't view it as a moral problem?

STAN: No, not really.

QUESTION: It's mostly because the outfit itself is impersonal, bureaucratic, or whatever, has no soul so to speak?

STAN: Very select people in the very select places and they really don't care about you so that's where you get your feeling that you don't care about them. You don't particularly feel that you're robbing from anyone. You're robbing from a thing, a corporation, an inanimate thing. It's just there. I guess that's why you do it. At least that's why I did it because it was there, the opportunity, and everything looked fine. I'd still be working at that store today and I'd probably still be pulling those little thefts if I hadn't got caught.

DISCUSSION

Stan's description of the neighborhood from which he came suggests that it closely corresponded to Spergel's area where a delinquent theft pattern prevailed.[21] The extent to which an adult career develops within it is related to the availability of illegal opportunities. Stan somewhat dramatically reports that his former associates all went on to adult criminal careers, but he was isolated from carriers of adult criminal norms by his high school experience. His neighborhood was a slightly higher income area than the one Shaw's *Jackroller* came from some 40 years earlier.[22] Yet his family situation was tightly knit and he felt he was carefully supervised. Even in Shaw's neighborhood presumably there were pockets of resistance to the predominant values which tolerated or encouraged illegal behavior. Stan's family was upwardly mobile and unusually hard working. Both mother and father worked and the children were encouraged to take part-time jobs after school. Whatever delinquent values may have been operative in Stan's local community, his exposure to them was minimal. His time was almost completely taken up with schooling and working outside the area in which he resided. A territorial explanation of his later pilfering does not seem convincing. Only if Stan's social space included other than his neighborhood would the ecological perspective be relevant. If territory can be interpreted to include different settings, like work and school, then an argument can be made that the values operative there were absorbed by him.

It's not necessary to go back to Stan's neighborhood for an explanation of his pilfering. A much more immediate cause is the work group. Stan reports that his experience in supermarkets convinced him that employees "are not really honest. As far as stealing or not paying for purchases . . . everybody does it." Stan implied that there were norms relating to pilfering and everyone seemed to understand that it went on, though he did

---

[21] Irving Spergel, *Racketville, Slumtown, Haulberg: An Exploratory Study of Delinquent Subcultures* (Chicago: University of Chicago Press, 1964).
[22] Clifford R. Shaw, *The Jackroller* (Chicago: University of Chicago Press, 1930).

not report that the employees explicitly discussed it among themselves. The norms may have been as specific as those reported by Horning on blue-collar theft. The fact that he was accused by a fellow employee of stealing might indicate that pilfering should be limited to what one can personally use. The number of boxes Stan was loading into his friend's car suggests that he may have been violating work-group standards on how much stealing can be done legitimately.

The differential association explanation applies in Stan's case as in most other instances of lawbreaking. His activity was not impulsive or pathological. He reported that he learned most of his "tricks" related to stealing at work, though there was some improvisation. His was normal and expected behavior under the circumstances. The rationales Stan used to justify his behavior reveal their group character. He states, "I figured . . . they were a big chain, they could afford it." And later: "You don't particularly feel that you're robbing from anyone. You're robbing from a thing, a corporation, an inanimate thing."

Opportunity theory does not seem appropriate to explain Stan's behavior. He seemed committed to success goals but there is nothing in the interview to suggest that he had any serious questions about realizing them for himself. He did not see himself as lacking the institutional means to realize the cultural goal of economic success. But he expressed strong resentment over the way privilege undermined the meritocratic system. His attempts to live by the value system he had been taught were frustrated when he witnessed a co-worker succeeding even though he lacked the valued qualities and experience. This generated demoralization, resentment, and a sense of injustice. It was not that he was so situated that he couldn't win in the success game, it was that others did not play by the rules and were able to outdistance him. His response to the contradiction between the experience of inequality and the rhetoric of equality in his work setting was to increase his pilfering as his way of getting back at the company. He reports that his last few predations were motivated by a "personal vendetta" and his success gave him a great deal of personal satisfaction. But even at that the sense of injustice accounted for only a fraction of his occupational crime. Earlier he reported that he did not feel unjustly treated by the company at first, quite the opposite. They trusted him enough to put him in a position of authority and though not given any official title he seemed to have enjoyed the status. Yet even at this juncture he was involved in petty thievery from the company.

Even if we expand opportunity theory to include a variety of role strains, not just those related to economic ones, it does not help us under-

stand Stan's behavior. He did not experience any role strain where conflicting demands were placed on him that were resolved by thievery. He
was not in an analogous position to Quinney's pharmacists, caught between two separate definitions of what the job consisted of and a series of
reference groups that created conflicting expectations. His behavior, at
least in the early stages, seems mainly expressive, done because of the
excitement it generated. The material gain was minimal and the sense of
injustice that developed later was absent.

Labeling theory offers little insight into Stan's behavior. His petty
thievery persisted for a long period of time and when it was finally
discovered Stan stopped doing it. His reasoning seemed quite calculating
—when the activity became too costly it was no longer worth it. The
official reaction by management personnel did not dramatically affix the
label of thief on him, nor increase his illegal activity as a result of being
stigmatized. Management seemed to be aware that a certain amount of
pilfering as well as theft by customers goes on and their only concern
seemed related to keeping it within bounds. They were not interested in
prosecuting Stan or sharply restricting any future employment opportunities that might be available to him. Stan does not emerge as a passive
actor in his encounter with official authority. He demonstrated a sophisticated sense of what would be required in the way of proof in a court of
law and negotiated his way out of a potentially hazardous situation. In
the classic labeling approach the actor becomes progressively involved in
his deviance because of the reaction of labelers and is willy-nilly thrust
into interaction with others involved in the same kind of deviance. As a
kind of self-protection the actor develops a deviant identity that enables
him to cope with the stigmatizing impact of official reaction. Clearly this
does not happen to Stan and it is difficult to imagine that it would
happen to anyone else engaged in the same kind of activity. "Pilferer" is
not a master status in our society and no role engulfment occurs once an
individual has been so named.

There is little in the interview that would test the relevancy of the
conflict perspective. Stan seems to feel in a conflicted reactionship with
company officials and is aware that he does not share any basic interests
with them. A Marxist interpretation of Stan's activity would focus on his
pilfering as expression of a false and prepolitical form of individualistic
consciousness. Stan seemed to be aware that the officials of the company
and the people who worked in it lived in different worlds, hence there was
no guilt attached to his stealing. He might have said: "Those are their
rules, not mine." But he was not sufficiently insulated from contact with
the upper echelons (he expected to end up there some day himself) to

develop any kind of political consciousness with his fellow employees. A Marxist would see Stan's behavior as a primitive political act and an expression of his alienated situation. If there were no conflict of interests between those who dominate and those who are subject to them there would be no theft. A fully human being would not, in this perspective, steal from himself. There is nothing in the interview that points to the overall social context of inequalities of power, wealth, and authority in an advanced industrial society like the U.S. Rather what Stan's story points up is the necessity of elucidating the mediatory effect of subjective features of life like "job satisfaction" and "monotony of existence." This elucidation would perhaps rescue us from interpreting a relatively minor kind of activity like pilfering as "just for kicks" or as simply a boost for employee morale or "job enrichment." Rather it could be interpreted as a creative way of coping with low-paying and boring jobs so that one's work life can be made more tolerable.

QUESTIONS FOR FURTHER DISCUSSION

1. Stan's activity and the justifications for it seem very much part of a group pattern, yet there were employees who had the opportunity to pilfer and did not. What hypotheses would you propose to account for the nonpilferers?

2. If a conflict interpretation would view Stan's behavior as an instance of prepolitical consciousness how would a consensus perspective interpret it?

3. To what extent would Stan be a likely candidate for a career as a professional thief?

4. If you were interested in reducing the incidence of employee theft what strategies would be suggested by Stan's interview?

5. What are the arguments pro and con for reacting to employee theft informally (as it was done in Stan's case) rather than formally?

6. What other options were open to Stan, by his own account, either to add excitement to his work or to address personal grievances other than pilfering?

Probably the most significant fact about occupational crime is that it is based on the fairly widespread sentiment that it is usually not very serious and that little needs to be done about it at a policy level. The situation is somewhat chaotic—there is a wide variety of codes relating to desirable occupational and professional behavior with a variety of sanctions that can be invoked when there are violations. The sanctions vary in their scope, punitive character, and effectiveness. The extent to which occupational and professional violations become crimes depends on the impact the group has on the public at large. Thus there is more concern over the misdeeds of doctors and policemen than there is over florists. But to return to an earlier theme, the concerns about violation are not automatically translated into law but require some interest-group initiative and the mobilization of influential opinion. If the profession to be regulated is a powerful one—as the medical profession is—its resistance can frustrate any regulatory attempts. The major policy question that a study of occupational criminality raises is: how is public accountability best achieved? The implications of this and other questions of concern to criminologists is the subject of the final chapter.

16

conclusion

This final chapter summarizes briefly some of the major themes developed earlier, attempts to place these themes in a broader comparative framework, and suggests a modest research agenda for criminologists. The central contention of this book is that a comprehensive theory of crime and criminality can account for why particular groups become candidates for official processing (the imposition of criminal status) and also why they behave as they do. The emergence of critical criminology recently has challenged the focus on behavior patterns of the criminally defined because of its narrow control orientation.

The argument made by traditional criminology is that once we know what causes individuals to commit crimes, we are in a better position to prevent criminality and rehabilitate offenders. But the social science promise on that score has not materialized. Hence personnel in the criminal justice system are willing to abandon the search for causes at this point because it is difficult to justify in terms of its social utility. Morris contends that basically etiological research has been unproductive.[1] He suggests substituting applied technologies drawn from other disciplines, like decision theory, cybernetics, and operations research. These techniques are becoming increasingly popular among practitioners because

[1] Norvall Morris and Gordon Hawkins, *The Hones Politician's Guide to Crime Control* (Chicago: University of Chicago Press, 1970), pp. 236–62.

of their immediate applicability to crime control. Whatever suspicions academic criminologists may have about the implications of this new development, the fact is that it has relieved them from coming up with immediate solutions to "the crime problem"—immediate solutions framed in terms of what criminal justice practitioners think best. The gradual separation of criminologists from official control perspectives shows promise for the development of criminology as an independent scientific discipline rather than an applied specialty. One immediate impact of this shift has been a revival of interest among younger criminologists in crime causation which includes the study of behavior patterns.

THE POSSIBILITIES OF A SYNTHESIS

Recent developments in the study of crime have paid much more attention to the study of lawmaking than lawbreaking. But modern criminology includes the study of both as well as the reactions to violations. A newer perspective emphasizes the correspondence between crime control generally and other kinds of control systems. One justification for organizing the text around conflict and consensus interpretations of crime is that it highlights these connections. The advantage of presenting criminology in terms of the conflict-consensus debate is that a wide array of investigations and positions can be summarized in an understandable and interesting way. A possible disadvantage of such an approach, however, is that the student of crime might try forcing contributions into one or another category when they simply do not fit. Although this may provide some satisfaction that the field has been mastered it does not lead to further knowledge. There are some areas of criminology where the questions about conflict and consensus assumptions are not particularly illuminating.

Some of the behavior patterns discussed in Part Three are illustrative. Traffic violations would be one such instance. Fort, a psychiatrist, has pointed out in his discussion of drug use that there are ways to measure the damage a drug can do independent of its political dimensions.[2] Thus we might all agree that the use of a drug that inflicts brain and other organic damage, or generates violence, accidents, and eventually death is undesirable. The proposition that traffic should be regulated in some rational way and violators evenhandedly sanctioned is not particularly controversial. Thus trying to draw out the unstated conflict or consensus

2 Joel Fort, *The Pleasure Seekers* (Indianapolis: Bobbs-Merrill, 1969), pp. 98–99.

assumptions of traffic law studies may not help us understand this behavior pattern very well. Movement toward an integrated theory would begin by specifying the areas that conflict and consensus perspectives are most useful.

CRIME AND SOCIAL REACTION

The organization of the section on behavior patterns was partly based on public perception of the seriousness of the crime insofar as that could be determined by amount of resources committed to prevent it and the fear it generated. This is best suggested by Table 16-1.

TABLE 16-1   Public Perception of Crime

Crime	Degree of Visibility	Intensity of Reaction	Kind of Social Response
Homicide	High	High	Fear, strong disapproval, long imprisonment, desire for revenge.
Property crimes			Arrest, jail, institutionalization.
Political dissent			Strong disapproval, dissenters are threats, should be imprisoned.
Public order crime			Arrest, jail, fines, "treatment."
Organized crime			Media concern but public toleration.
Corporate crime			Indifference, fines, injunctions.
Occupational crime			Apathy, lack of technical understanding.
	Low	Low	

Adapted from Marshall B. Clinnard and Richard Quinney (eds.), *Criminal Behavior Systems: A Typology* (New York: Holt, Rinehart & Winston, 1973), pp. 18–20.

This summary is primarily based on American materials and because of the lack of comparative data we cannot generalize. We might hypothesize that the social reactions to these crimes would be roughly similar in nations with similar economies and probably less applicable in underdeveloped countries.

But the fear of crime is a worldwide phenomenon that transcends differing social systems. It is a cause of deep concern in developing and developed countries as well as in socialist and capitalist nations. A recent United Nations report states that all nations are experiencing a significant and worrisome increase in serious crime, that is, the garden variety kind of personal and property assault.[3] The United Nations report assumes that there has been a real increase in serious crime that is not explained by better reporting systems or more efficient police work. Whether or not there has been a real increase is debatable but certainly there is no argument that there has been a worldwide increase in officially reported crimes related to personal and property assault. The explanation favored by the United Nations for the increase is the breakdown of informal controls and their replacement by more formal sanctioning institutions. Its explanation is almost identical to that proposed by the ecologists discussed in Chapter 3. The breakdown has been occasioned by economic development, urbanization, and expanding industrialization. The fact that the social control of crime has been taken over principally by the criminal justice system has diminished the influence of other control agencies like the school, the local community, and the family in the United Nations' view. It has also overburdened official agencies, led to long delays in the processing of cases, and seriously undermined public confidence in the criminal justice system.

The lack of attention in the United Nations report to any other theory of crime and delinquency seems to be an implied judgment on their relevance and overall explanatory power. Thus the views of Merton, Cloward, and Ohlin, so persuasive to American students of crime, seem appropriate only in an American setting. The discussion of property crime in Chapter 10 suggests further that anomie theory applies to adult property offenders but then only under specified conditions. It may be that opportunity theory is applicable in limited historical, structural, and cultural situations—those in which economic success is an overriding preoccupation to the exclusion of other values and opportunities for realizing it are limited. If this is true then we should be urged to develop explanations that have more general utility.

[3] Fifth United Nations Congress on the Prevention of Crime and the Treatment of Offenders, *Criminal Legislation, Judicial Procedures and Other Forms of Social Control in the Prevention of Crime* (Toronto, Canada: United Nations, 1975).

INCREASING ISOLATION OF CRIME
CONTROL ORGANIZATIONS

The fact that criminal justice agencies like the police and courts tend to replace other more informal groupings is an unintended consequence of industrialization and urbanization in the United Nations' view. They assume, contrary to what has been proposed here earlier, that the emergence of the criminal law is for the most part a crystallization of the general will. The discussion of the criminal law in Chapter 2 takes the position that its emergence is best understood from an interest-group perspective, but that after the criminal law has been codified it can function to symbolize a community's consensus. An interest-group approach on lawmaking underlines its influence in shaping the structure of a society. We have examined evidence that the criminal law and its accompanying legal institutions can partially determine the nature of the economy, how open a society will be, the opportunities for mobility, and finally the distribution of privilege and power.

The account of the police courts and corrections in Chapters 6, 7, and 8 suggests that the gradual disappearance of informal groups to handle "troublesome" people is not as unwitting as it might seem. The centralizing and coordinating thrust of all attempts at crime control seems inevitably to enfeeble local nonstate efforts. Criticism of these monopolizing tendencies has created a more hospitable climate in international forums for the encouragement of nonstate civic associations as a remedy. The United Nations has recommended more systematic and widespread diversion programs to address the undue burden problem and to encourage more community participation in the system. It argues that the lack of such participation at the present time contributes to massive domestic instability.

No matter what the political system or the stage of industrialization, the United Nations is convinced that all nations would benefit by increased community participation whether by use of neighborhood courts, use of laymen as judges, or public participation in trials and sentencing. It warns that the destruction of informal controls bodes ill for any nation, and points to situations where the traditional forms of control function simultaneously with the criminal justice system or are incorporated into them. The United Nations' views are that custom and the criminal law can mutually support one another. The focus on the relationship between the criminal law and custom points to another area that has high priority in any new criminology. Comparative research into nonstate dispute settlement mechanisms and evaluations of existing citizen courts would be a start. At present the burden of inquiry into the relationship of law and custom has been carried mainly by anthropologists not criminologists.

UNINTENDED CONSEQUENCES OF CRIME CONTROL

The United Nations' discussion of the negative effects of crime control could have been written by any of the labelists discussed in Chapter 5. The studies of hidden criminality, the United Nations argues, challenges traditional explanations of criminality. Hence persons who commit crimes should not be designated "pathological" and any strategy based on this assumption is bound to fail. Drawing on studies of control agencies, it points out the negative side effects of control attempts. It seems clear in the United Nations' view that the criminal justice system adds to social injustices that already exist and has criminogenic effects because of public reaction to the stigma "criminal." The UN report observes that in developed countries the question of who controls the criminal justice system is not as simple as it would seem. It sees a series of subsystems knit together by no common purpose or coordinated plan. The net result is that community needs for safety are not met. They could be met by better coordination, more training, higher salaries for practitioners, more emphasis on feedback between various components of the system, and utilization of systems analysis and cost benefit studies. The report does not address the question of the point of these reforms if the criminal justice actually reinforces existing system inequalities or further aggravates them. Under those circumstances, as noted earlier, efficiency is at odds with justice and the rights of those processed by the control agencies are better protected if the system is bumbling and inefficient.

DECRIMINALIZATION AND DEPENALIZATION

The United Nations is keenly aware of the burden put on the crime control system and argues for decriminalization and depenalization of victimless crimes. If the behavior is sufficiently undesirable (as in traffic violations, slander, nonpayment of child support) it suggests that it be handled by administrative or civil agencies. In this respect its diagnosis parallels that of Packer, who has argued forcefully for narrowing the scope of the criminal law.[4] This assumes that the criminal law is designed to keep the crime rate as low as possible, that the law should not over-burden the criminal justice system, that only those forms of behavior that might successfully be handled by the system be criminalized, and that socially unacceptable forms of deviant behavior be addressed by refer-ring those who express them to other agencies. The criteria they suggest to realize these objectives are:

1. The type of behavior to be criminalized is contrary to widely held social norms that are deemed to be legitimate by the authorities;

2. It can reasonably be expected that the criminal justice system would be capable of handling the conduct in question at an acceptable social and economic cost;

3. No other administrative or social policies that could achieve acceptable results with less interference in the lives of citizens are available;

4. It is improbable that unintended but predictable side effects of the proposed legislation would outweigh expected gains.[5]

The report comes out forcefully for more detailed guidelines for police and other enforcement agencies that would limit their discretion and build in more powerful organizational incentives for diversion.

THE NEED FOR MORE KNOWLEDGE OF CONFLICT GROUPS AND CRIMINALIZATION

Since the United Nations' concerns relate to the stability of its member states, they are less than enthusiastic about addressing the questions conflict criminologists raise. But any criminology research agenda that aspires to be comprehensive must explore the relationship between con-flict and criminalization, whatever the implications for social order. When we raise questions about the variability in public reaction to crime, the concerns of conflict criminologists about the operation of interest groups takes on significance. Conflict criminologists suggest that it is not only the dimension of public fear that should be taken into account, but the size and economic resources of the violators. The larger the violating group

[4] Herbert L. Packer, *The Limits of the Criminal Sanction* (Stanford, Calif.: Stanford University Press, 1968.
[5] Fifth United Nations Congress, *Criminal Legislation,* p. 21.

TABLE 16-2   Conflict Situations
Dimension of the Character and Relations of Parties in Conflict

Resulting popular definition of the conflict situation	Size and organization of party feared	Economic and political power of party feared relative to party fearing	Degree to which the well-organized opposing large minority or majority feels fearful or threatened
Deviance ("crime," etc.)	Individual or small, loosely organized groups	Almost none	Very high
Civil uprising or disorder	Small, loosely organized minority	Relatively low	Very high
Social movement	Sizable, organized minority	Relatively low	Mild
Civil war	Large, well-organized minority	Relatively high or almost equal	Very high
Mainstream party politics in the United States	Large, organized minority	About equal	Mild

John Lofland, *Deviance and Identity* (Englewood Cliffs, N.J.: Prentice-Hall, 1969), p. 15.

and the greater its economic resources, the more likely it is that the problem would not be handled through the criminal justice system. If we look at the question in terms of two parties in conflict then possible relationships can be specified (see Table 16-2).

Lofland's conceptualization of conflict relationships suggests several research areas for criminologists. One focuses on the size and level of threat posed by various problem populations. He indicates that some kind of processing other than the criminal one becomes necessary the larger the group becomes. His example of party politics where the groups in contention are roughly equal implies that no processing at all occurs. But if the level of threat is high and the group is growing, some response other than toleration would seem likely. In that case we could expect a broadening of the reaction system and an increasing centralization and coordination of control activities.

An alternative type of processing at an early stage may define problem groups as "sick" and in need of treatment but this strategy may be self-defeating if the group is too large. Where problem management is highly centralized, as it is in most advanced industrial nations, then threats to the social order may be addressed by vigorous efforts to incorporate troublesome groups into "prosocial" roles in the economy, as in public works projects. Generalizations in this area would be aided by further historical and comparative studies of the varieties of criminal law and how that law changes.

The organizational cases and individual histories presented earlier give some idea of how far we are from any systematic knowledge about individual and organization behavior patterns in criminality. Any theory that is developed needs more individual and organizational cases around which explanations can be built. The criminal justice agency case studies underline the necessity of drawing in organizational theory to account for the operation of criminal justice systems. The individual cases suggest that deviance within organizational settings is one fruitful area to explore further. This would help address more adequately the causes of corporate and occupational crime. The study of social movements would add to the study of organized crime, political crime, and public order crime. The study of cultural themes related to violence would aid in explanations of homicide, forcible rape, and aggravated assault. When all of these areas are synthesized with the study of adult socialization (which suggests the conditions under which persons opt for illegal rather than legal alternatives) the next steps that criminology must take as an emerging scientific discipline will become clearer.

index